DEVON AND CORNWALL RECORD SOCIETY

New Series, Vol. 39

General Editor: Mrs Margery Rowe BA, DAA

Tawstocke
1640

Disbursed by mee Richard Ellard
for the houshold Expence and other
disfrayments of the Right hono.ble Henry
Earle of Bath: from and after the 19.th
daye of October 1640: untill:—

Satturdaye the
34.th of October
1640

| | £ | s | d | ob |
|---|---|---|---|---|
| Imp.s said unto Hugh Coombe the Bayliffe devon his bill | 02 | 02 | 10 | 00 |
| Itm whyd Willm Lumson the Cutler devon his Bill | 00 | 15 | 06 | 00 |
| Itm payd the Carventer for worke done at Ilfardcombe by his Bill | 03 | 06 | 08 | 00 |
| Itm w.th the Smith for Iron worke at Ilfardcombe by his bill | 01 | 13 | 11 | 00 |
| Itm w.th Willm Ghmiter of Tawstocke for syx hundred of newland fish | 03 | 11 | 08 | 00 |
| Itm said the glasier he devon his Bill | 00 | 03 | 00 | 00 |
| Itm wayd Williams the Plumber he by Bill | 09 | 00 | 00 | 00 |
| Itm wayd Rich: Huxtable the Smyth | 06 | 00 | 00 | 00 |
| Itm p.d Willm Ellod in p.te of his wages | 06 | 00 | 00 | 00 |
| Itm more to hym for his Jorney to Bowd | 00 | 02 | 06 | 00 |
| Itm w.th Phillis yoland the Miller for halfe a yeares wages dued at Mihas last | 01 | 10 | 00 | 00 |
| Itm wayd Tho: Meare for making John Burk west rot e and for Ribbon to bynd it | 00 | 03 | 06 | 00 |
| Itm wayd for three young steares | 09 | 06 | 08 | 00 |
| Itm wayd Mr George Baker of Barry.le in p.te of his Promise | 20 | 00 | 00 | 00 |
| Itm p.d for Mr Wright liberty in u.son unto Mr Richard Horwood of Barry.le | 01 | 08 | 00 | 00 |

68—09—03

| | £ | s | d | ob |
|---|---|---|---|---|
| the totall summe of this weekes chardge ended the 31 of October 1640 | 68 | 09 | 03 | 00 |

*Frontispiece:* Tawstock Household Account, 31 October, 1640.

DEVON AND CORNWALL RECORD SOCIETY

# DEVON HOUSEHOLD ACCOUNTS, 1627–59:

## PART TWO

## HENRY, FIFTH EARL OF BATH, AND RACHEL, COUNTESS OF BATH, OF TAWSTOCK AND LONDON, 1637–1655

Edited with an Introduction by

## TODD GRAY

BA, PhD, FRHistS

1996

ISBN 0 901853 39 9

*Typeset for the Society by*
Colin Bakké Typesetting, Exeter
*and printed and bound for the Society by*
Short Run Press Ltd, Exeter
United Kingdom

For Sandie, Josh and Eric

# CONTENTS

*Page*

Frontispiece (Tawstock Household Account, 31 October 1640) . . ii
List of Maps, Genealogical Tables and Illustrations . . . . . . . . ix


INTRODUCTION . . . . . . . . . . . . . . . . . xi
    The accounts . . . . . . . . . . . . . . . . . . . xi
    Household accounts . . . . . . . . . . . . . . . . xvii
    Henry, fifth earl of Bath . . . . . . . . . . . . . . xix
    Rachel, countess of Bath . . . . . . . . . . . . . . xxii
    Revenue and the estate . . . . . . . . . . . . . . xxv
    Tawstock . . . . . . . . . . . . . . . . . . . . xxvii
    Lincoln's Inn Fields . . . . . . . . . . . . . . . xxviii
    Household administration . . . . . . . . . . . . . xxx
    Diet: provisioning and consumption . . . . . . . . xxxiii
    Household items . . . . . . . . . . . . . . . . xxxvii
    Private and public occasions . . . . . . . . . . . . xl
    Transportation . . . . . . . . . . . . . . . . . xlii
    Medical care . . . . . . . . . . . . . . . . . . xliii
    Clothing . . . . . . . . . . . . . . . . . . . xlv
    Gardening . . . . . . . . . . . . . . . . . . . xlv
    The Civil War and the Commonwealth . . . . . . . . xlvii
    Editorial Conventions . . . . . . . . . . . . . . . li
    Acknowledgements . . . . . . . . . . . . . . . . lii


THE ACCOUNTS
    Tawstock Household . . . . . . . . . . . . . . . 1
        Expenses, 19 September 1637 to 5 November 1639 . . . . . . 1
        Expenses, 19 October 1640 to 19 October 1644 . . . . . . 5
        Receipts, 30 October 1641 to October 1642 & expenses,
           21 January 1646 to 20 December 1646 . . . . . . . . 43
        Expenses, 19 October 1644 to 25 October 1645 . . . . . . 53
        Expenses, 31 October 1646 to 30 October 1647 . . . . . . 64
        Expenses, 10 April to 27 October 1649 . . . . . . . . . 75
        Expenses, 2 November 1650 to 25 October 1651 & receipts,
           28 October 1650 to 20 October 1651 . . . . . . . . . 83
        Expenses & receipts, 4 November 1654 to 28 October 1655 . 100

London Household . . . . . . . . . . . . . . . . . . . 113
   Expenses, 25 May 1642 to 23 March 1647 . . . . . . . . . 113
   Expenses, 26 March 1647 to 4 July 1649 . . . . . . . . . 131
   Expenses, 9 July 1649 to 29 July 1652 . . . . . . . . . . 148
General account and memoranda book of Rachel, countess of
Bath, 1639 to 1654 . . . . . . . . . . . . . . . . . . 169

APPENDICES
 1 Estimate by Richard Pollard of the weekly expenses for a
   noble household of eighty persons, n.d. . . . . . . . . . . . 297
 2 List of Tawstock servants, *c.*1645 . . . . . . . . . . . . 297
 3 Estimate of Tawstock room sizes for curtains, n.d. . . . . . 298
 4 Linen inventory, 1648 . . . . . . . . . . . . . . . . 299
 5 Linen inventory, 1652 . . . . . . . . . . . . . . . . 301
 6 List of coins, 1651 . . . . . . . . . . . . . . . . . 301
 7 List of disbursements, *c.*1646 . . . . . . . . . . . . . 303
 8 Sequestrators' inventory of Tawstock, 8 November 1648 . . . 304
 9 List of husbandry items at Tawstock, 20 January 1642 . . . . 305
10 List of stock at Tawstock, 5 November 1653 . . . . . . . . 306
11 List of medicine, 1639 . . . . . . . . . . . . . . . . 307
12 List of medicine for the countess, 1654 . . . . . . . . . . 308
13 List of mourners at the funeral of Henry, fifth earl of
   Bath, 21 September 1654 . . . . . . . . . . . . . . . . 309
14 Legacies to servants and others, *c.*1654 . . . . . . . . . 311
15 Inventory of Tawstock, *c.*1655 . . . . . . . . . . . . . 313

GLOSSARY . . . . . . . . . . . . . . . . . . . . . . 317

INDEX . . . . . . . . . . . . . . . . . . . . . . . . 321

The Devon and Cornwall Record Society . . . . . . . . . . . 339

# LIST OF MAPS, GENEALOGICAL TABLES
## AND ILLUSTRATIONS

## MAPS
*Page*

1. Devon . . . . . . . . . . . . . . . . . . . . . . . . . . . . . . . . . xv
2. North Devon . . . . . . . . . . . . . . . . . . . . . . . . . . . . xv
3. Estate of Henry, fifth earl of Bath . . . . . . . . . . . . . . xvi

## GENEALOGICAL TABLES

The Bourchier Family . . . . . . . . . . . . . . . . . . . . . . . . . liii
The Fane Family . . . . . . . . . . . . . . . . . . . . . . . . . . . . liv

## ILLUSTRATIONS
### Plates between pages xvi and xvii

1. Detail of oil painting of Tawstock, mid-eighteenth century.
2. Monument of Henry, fifth earl of Bath, 1654.
3. Monument of Rachel, countess of Bath, by Balthazar Burman, c.1680.
4. Map of manor of Harford with Newland (Landkey parish), c.1640.
5. Detail of Plate 4.
6. Painting of Lady Rachel by Sir Anthony van Dyck, c.1640.
7. Lady Rachel as Queen of Diamonds, early seventeenth century.
8. Map of Indicknowle (Berrynarbor parish), c.1640.
9. Detail of map of Marwood, c.1640.
10. Map of Worlington (Instow parish) and 'Stapparke' (Little Torrington parish), c.1640.
11. Map of manor of Nymet Tracey (Bow parish), c.1640.
12. Detail of Plate 11.
13. Detail of Plate 11.

# Introduction

## The accounts

The accounts published in this volume, from the papers of Henry Bourchier, fifth Earl of Bath, and Rachel, Countess of Bath, form the second volume of Devon household accounts for the first part of the seventeenth century. These Bourchier papers constitute, as far as is known, the only household accounts[1] for Tawstock which survived the great fire of 10 November 1787. There was a similar fire which consumed the London house in 1759 but it is unlikely that any Bourchier papers would still have been housed there at that late date. There are a number of additional and separate collections of documents concerning the earls of Bath. The Hengrave papers at Cambridge contain autograph letters of the Bourchier family.[2] There is a collection, including manorial accounts and rentals, at Bury St Edmunds mainly pertaining to John, second Earl of Bath, for the late fifteenth to the late sixteenth centuries. Some also relate to the first earl.[3] At Nottingham there are documents relating to William, third Earl of Bath, which form part of the estate and personal papers of his steward Thomas Hinson[4] and his family from 1580 to 1662. Neither are there any papers for the countess although there are several collections of Fane family papers, in Maidstone and Lincoln.[5] Finally, there are papers in Hertfordshire for the Granville family of Stowe, later earls of Bath, but which are not connected with the Bourchier family.[6]

---

1. For the later period there are accounts for the years 1784–1822, 1802–7 and 1833–46: North Devon Record Office, 1801M/1–67.
2. Cambridge University Library, Hengrave 88/1–3, the collection includes letter books of the Gage Family, sixteenth century onwards.
3. Suffolk Record Office, Bury St Edmunds branch, 412/58–60, 449/4/1–8 & 449/6/9–10, & 21 & HA 528.
4. Nottingham Record Office, DD.4P, 7/1–21, 37/4–38/18, 52/25–54 & 55/47–56. These are mainly leases relating to Tawstock, Holne, Rewe, Uffculme and Wantage with other related papers including the will of Thomas Hinson.
5. Kent Archives Office, U282 & U1794; Lincoln Record Office, Fane manuscripts. A further collection of the Fane family papers, of the Earls of Westmorland of Apethorpe, has not been examined: Northampton Record Office, W(A).
6. Hertfordshire Record Office, D/E Na/E4–17, A1 & A42–9. The papers relate to William Henry Granville, third Earl of Bath, of Stowe for 1701 to 1711 and are mainly estate accounts drawn up by Mme d'Auverquerque, the maternal grandmother and guardian of the Earl. The greater portion of the papers are in English with the remainder in Dutch or French.

The survival of all these papers is in stark contrast to the destruction of the main Bourchier family collection in 1787 and can be directly attributed to their being part of other collections located across the country. The existence of the estate, household and personal papers of the fifth earl is unexpected and fortunate but the reasons for this survival are equally intriguing. The three accounts edited last year in Part One exist because the papers were relocated after the marriage of the heir or his descendents: the families at Forde, Sydenham and Leyhill failed to produce male heirs and upon the daughters' marriages the houses no longer remained the family seat. At some point the papers were removed from their original location. The survival of the Bourchier papers is a more peculiar achievement. The documents cover the sixteen years of marriage of the earl and countess from 1639 to 1655. The documents were brought to Kent after the remarriage of the countess; in 1655, a year after her first husband's death, she married Lionel Cranfield, third Earl of Middlesex, and the papers were probably then or shortly afterwards put into his possession.[7] It may have been that the documents were normally housed in London rather than in Devon although there is conflicting evidence for this.[8] It is intriguing that Cranfield retained the collection after the failure of his marriage to Lady Bath. There may have been practical reasons for keeping the estate papers, particularly given that Cranfield has acquired a reputation for being financially immoderate if not grasping.[9] But it is fascinating that he, and generations of his descendants, held onto his wife's papers. It may be somewhat remarkable that Cranfield kept Lady Bath's personal account book and private correspondence but it seems extraordinary that he not only withheld but retained his former wife's love letters from her first husband.

The papers were inherited by Frances, daughter of the first earl of Westmorland, who married Richard Sackville, first earl of Dorset. The documents remained at Knole Park and now form part of the Sackville collection which was deposited at the Kent Archives Office in Maidstone in 1950. Their removal so far from Tawstock has ensured their safety but it has also effectively obscured them from the attention of historians.[10] This is despite the collection being catalogued by the

---

7. There is at least one letter dated 1656: Kent Archives Office, U269/C281.
8. It is clear from the accounts that some Tawstock documents were examined in London and then returned to Devon.
9. Charles G. Layley, *The Lords of Barnstaple* (Tawstock, 1983), 30.
10. The collection was catalogued as U269 and the subsequent Cranfield collection, which also has material relating to Lionel Cranfield, has been listed as U269/1. It has recently been re-listed but with the same prefix. The two collections are closely related but should be regarded as two distinct collections. Two historians have previously used these papers in relation to Henry Bourchier: Ian R. Palfrey, 'Devon and the Outbreak of the English Civil War, 1642–43', *Southern History*, 10 (1988), 29–46; Conrad Russell, *The Fall of the British Monarchies, 1637–1642* (Oxford, 1991).

Historical Manuscripts Commission and its report published in 1874.[11] Partly this lies with Tawstock being mistaken for the separate Devon parish of Tavistock[12] but more so because the catalogue fails to include any mention of the household papers. The cataloguer claimed that 'from the whole collection I have endeavoured to make notes of everything that could illustrate the history and political and social state of the kingdom'. The listing notes the Bourchiers' political correspondence. It may have been that the cataloguer was unaware of the household papers or considered that they lacked merit.

Later notes written on many of the papers shows that the collection was fairly extensively examined and sorted probably in the eighteenth century. This was most probably by Sir Nathaniel William Wraxall (1751–1831) who it is known examined the papers and considered writing a history of the earls of Dorset.[13] Many documents were endorsed with notes regarding their contents and comments on their worth. Several accounts were described as 'old accounts &c of no value' or 'of no interest whatsoever'. The merit of individual letters was determined by their degree of 'curiosity'. This has implications regarding the survival of the collection: because these specific papers were regarded as inferior, and yet still retained, it suggests that if there was any consolidation then the cull may have been limited. The collection includes only a few original bills and receipts. All such papers, of which of there were originally many hundreds, were probably either left at Tawstock or London, and subsequently destroyed, or were never sent on to London. Consequently, it would be reasonable to assume that the collection now available to the historian is comparatively similar in size to when originally acquired by the third earl of Middlesex.

There are three main sets of documents printed as the main text. The greater part of the volume comprises household receipts and expenses: there are eight accounts for Tawstock from 1637 to 1655 and three accounts for London from 1642 to 1652. In addition, there is the personal account book of Lady Bath for 1639 to 1654. All of the accounts, and much of the wider collection, are remarkably clean and relatively undamaged. Lady Bath's hand can easily be identified in her own account book but it is an assumption that the chief stewards wrote their own accounts. Descriptions of each of these twelve separate documents are given in the text preceding each one. The accounts begin shortly before the earl's marriage and end sixteen years later following Lady Bath's remarriage.

11. *Historical Manuscripts Commission, 4th Report, Part 1* (1874), 276–317.
12. This is not unusual, for another example see ACS Hall (ed.), *Guide to the Reports of the Royal Commission on Historical Manuscripts, 1911–1957: Part I, Index of Places* (1973), 460.
13. *Historical Manuscripts Commission, 4th report, Part 1*, 276.

The appendices contain lists of linen, coins, husbandry items, medicine, servants, disbursements in 1646 and of the mourners at the earl's funeral with a list of legacies. Other appendices are an estimate of costs for running a large household, curtain measurements for the principal rooms at Tawstock, the Sequestrators' inventory of Tawstock and a schedule of Tawstock's contents in about 1655.

There are also five estate or manorial maps which were drawn in about 1640. These are reproduced as Plates 4 to 5 and 8 to 13. The maps are all on vellum and some repairs were made to one map, possibly in the 1950s, with linen backing supplied. All are to some degree of irregular shape. Plate 4 is of the map of the manor of Harford with Newland in Landkey parish and measures 30½″ by 28″ with a 'neck'. Plate 5 is of a detail of the map. Plate 10 is of the map of Worlington in Instow and Stapparke in Little Torrington and measures 26″ by 30″. Plates 8–9 are of the map of Indicknowle in Berrynarbor, a tenement in Combe Martin and Marwood Barton. It measures 30″ by 28″. It also depicts Westcott Barton in Marwood parish. Plates 11–13 are two parts of the map of the Nymet Tracey manor in Bow parish. Plates 11–12 are of the first map which measures 22″ by 27″. The second map is reproduced as Plate 13 and includes West and East Hilldown. The map is now in two parts with the major portion measuring 29½″ by 28″ and a slip, which has become detached, which measures 27½″ by 5½″. There is no indication on any of these maps of the surveyor's identity although small payments were recorded in the accounts to one Thomas Berry for maps. There are other references to measuring and surveying land.[14]

Other material in the collection, including correspondence, estate papers,[15] audit books and miscellaneous political papers, is drawn upon for the purposes of the Introduction. Apart from the parish collection there does not seem to be any other collection of documents relevant to Tawstock.

The most apparent use of the papers is to further understanding in the complex machinations of household administration and life. Notwithstanding this more immediate interest it is self-evident that the accounts include incidental but detailed information on a wide range of other subjects. There is great potential in its contribution to the study of early seventeenth century English society. Finally, it should be

---

14. Kent Archives Office, P11/1–5. The addition to P11/4 was not previously catalogued and a reference number (P11/4/1) was introduced for the purposes of this book. F. Hull in *Catalogue of Estate Maps, 1590–1840* (Maidstone, 1973), p.241 attributes the maps to John Garfield in about 1675 but there does not appear to be any evidence to support this. The catalogue for the U269 collection suggests the maps were made in about 1640 and this date is more likely given that the general collection was acquired in about 1655. The repairs were made to map P11/3 reproduced as Plates 8–9.

15. The great number of surviving estate papers has precluded them from being included in this edition.

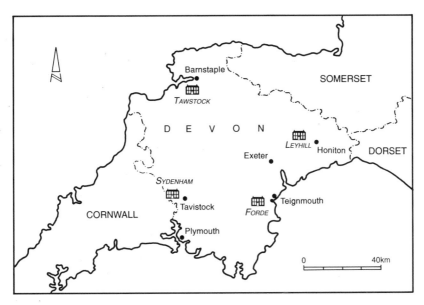

*Map 1.* Devon.

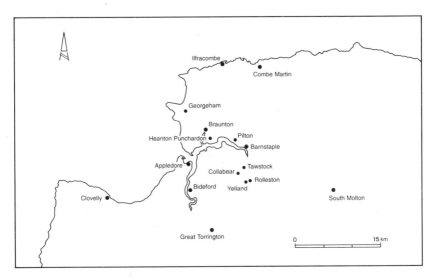

*Map 2.* North Devon.

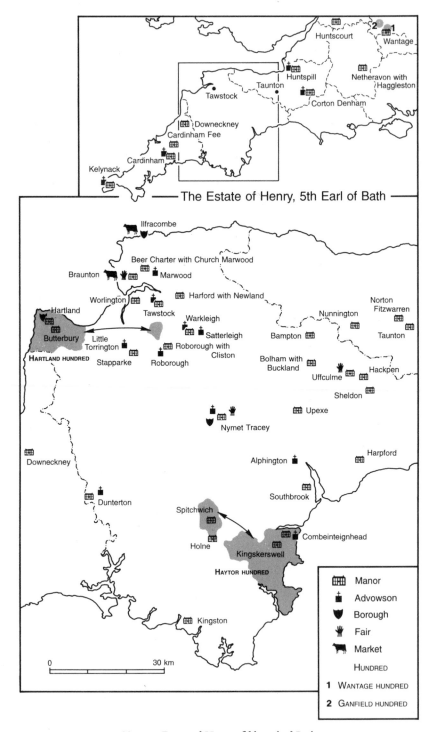

*Map 3.* Estate of Henry, fifth earl of Bath.

*Plate 1.* Detail of oil painting of Tawstock showing the sixteenth-century house with its extensive formal gardens and possible walled fruit trees, mid-eighteenth century (Gavin Graham Gallery).

*Plate 3.* Monument of Rachel, countess of Bath, by Balthazar Burman, c.1680, St Peter's Church, Tawstock. Burman copied a statue of the countess of Shrewsbury which had been made by his father Thomas.

*Plate 2.* Monument of Henry, fifth earl of Bath, 1654, St Peter's Church, Tawstock.

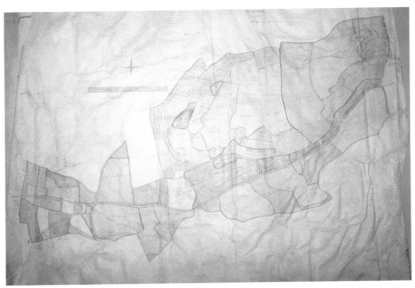

*Plate 4.* Map of Harford with Newland manor (Landkey parish), *c.*1640. The field boundaries closely match with those of the tithe map of 1846. On the bottom left is marked 'the way to Lankie church' and just above 'the way to Barnstaple'. There is 'a scale of 16 [perches] in an inch'. A compass point indicates north is oriented at the top. There are four small circles marked in pencil, possibly intended to indicate where to trim the map (Kent Archives Office, U269/P11/1).

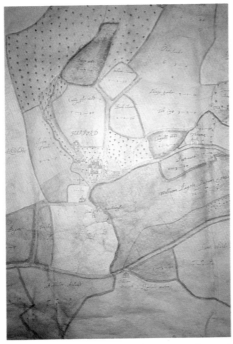

*Plate 5.* Detail of Harford hamlet, *c.*1640. Most of the field names are also on the tithe map of 1846: Bush Close, Pie (Pye) Park, Deepe (Deep) Meadow, Chapell (Chappel) Meadow and Canny (Canna) Park are all noted. The land use is also similar, notably the orchards planted around Harford; in 1846 one was a 'mazard garden'. Harford Wood is depicted at the top of the plate. A mill lies to the left of the house and a malthouse below.

*Plate 7.* 'Portrait' of Lady Rachel as the Queen of Diamonds placed upon one of her notebooks, early seventeenth century (Kent Archives Office, U269/F38/5).

*Plate 6.* Painting of the countess of Bath, by or in the style of Sir Anthony van Dyck, holding two white roses. This may be the portrait by van Dyck for which Lady Bath paid thirty pounds in 1641. There are several other paintings which have been attributed to van Dyck (Sotheby's 20/7/87, lot 5).

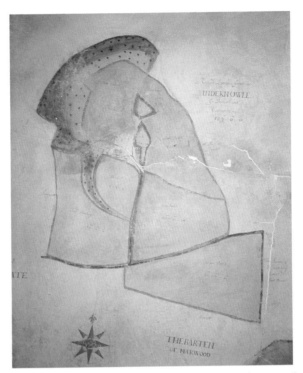

*Plate 8.* Detail of Indicknowle in Berrynarbor parish, *c.*1640. The scale is noted as 16 perches to an inch and a compass rose indicates north. Indicknowle Wood is depicted at the top (Kent Archives Office, U269/P11/3).

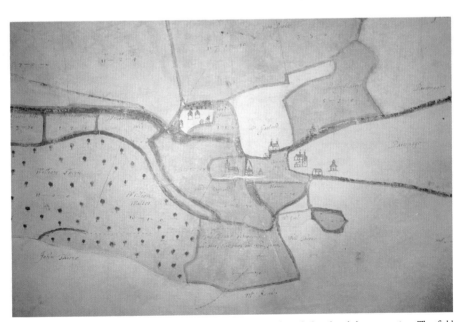

*Plate 9.* Detail of Marwood village showing St Michael's church and the church-house, *c.*1640. The field boundaries closely follow the tithe map of 1840. The field boundaries closely follow the tithe map of 1840. On the bottom left it is marked 'the way to Beercharter' and at the top left 'the way to Coombe'. The area to the bottom left of the church is Lee Wood.

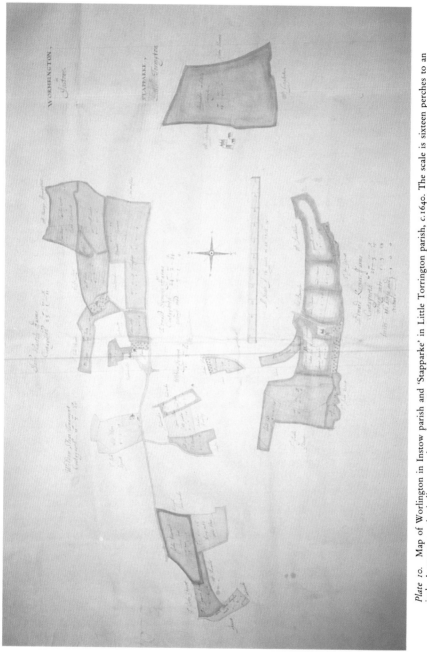

*Plate 10.* Map of Worlington in Instow parish and 'Stapparke' in Little Torrington parish, c.1640. The scale is sixteen perches to an inch. A compass point indicates north to the top. Stapparke has not been identified. The field boundaries for Worlington closely match those of the tithe map of 1841 (Kent Archives Office, U269/P11/2).

*Plate 12.* Detail of Nymet Tracey manor showing St Bartholomew's Church and Nymet Tracey hamlet, c.1640.

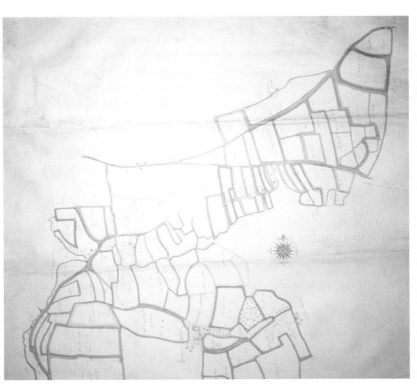

*Plate 11.* Map of Nymet Tracey manor in Bow parish, c.1640, with Bow hamlet on upper left-hand corner. North is oriented to the right and no scale is given (Kent Archives Office, U269/P11/5).

*Plate 13.* Second part of map of Nymet Tracey manor. The map is unfinished with several names in pencil and an un-completed table for representing land size, c.1640. The scale is 16 perches to an inch. Among the properties depicted are East and West Hilldown and 'Nimpe Wood' is noted as being to the left (Kent Archives Office, U269/P11/4).

remembered that Lady Bath had her papers compiled for her own purposes which were markedly different from the use made by them of the later historian.

## Household accounts

Household accounts are by definition concerned not with the general estate but primarily with the household's financial administration. There were several common forms in organisation but surviving accounts show how random this could be. Accounts were organised on a daily, weekly or in less structured intervals. Some accounts were made on a daily basis and then later divided into receipts and expenditure for auditing purposes. In practice, each household devised its own method of accounting. This is readily apparent from Devon's four early seventeenth-century accounts: whereas the Reynell account incorporates some details on estate management, the Wise account shows Sir Edward segregated his kitchen records from other accounts and the Willoughby papers indicate that the two generations developed markedly different accounting procedures, the Bourchier accounts for both Tawstock and London are remarkably consistent in form and content throughout their sixteen-year run. This could be attributed to a certain amount of continuity in the staff running the two households; the accounts remained concerned chiefly with the general household with some estate expenses.

Household accounts were made to account for expenditure and to show the level of spending. These were 'documents produced in the household, by household members, as records of its financial transactions'. Furthermore, they were 'the very lava disgorged from its tumultuous insides'.[16] The Bourchier accounts form a fairly long series with some gaps. Few other Devon household accounts of this period survive although coincidentally they exist for east, west and south Devon (map 1). There is little apparent reason for the patchiness of survival other than mere chance.[17]

In 1615 Gervase Markham wrote in *The English Housewife* of a clear division of household duties between the husband's responsibility for external affairs and his wife for all those indoors.[18] An ordinance for the household of the Hippisley family of Ston Easton in Somerset written

---

16. Kate Mertes, *The English Noble Household, 1250–1600* (1988), 76.
17. This contrasts with the abundance of accounts for the later Middle Ages for which it has been suggested there were other causes: Christopher Dyer, *Standards of living in the later Middle Ages* (Cambridge, 1989), 92–3. For a listing of early household accounts see Mertes, *The English Noble Household*, appendix; C.M. Woolgar, *Household Accounts from Medieval England* (British Academy, Records of Social and Economic History, new series, 1993, xviii), II, 691–726.
18. Michael R. Best (ed.), *The English Housewife* (Montreal, 1994), xxvii.

in about 1600 provides a further glimpse into the theory of household management. This sets out the intended administration by noting that:

> the disbursing of money by any office may be reduced to form one head of expenses which are one, usual ordinary and necessary [and] two, extraordinary—profit, pleasure, state.

It defined the first category as 'diet, apparel, fire, attendance, riding, maintenance of household stuff' while the second was 'extraordinary as projects in husbandry, building, making ponds, parks &c'. It specified that there should be 'general officers' who comprised a treasurer, clerk, bailiff, under-ploughman, shepherd, horseman and corn-keeper. The duties of the mistress and her officers were 'the taking and charge' of household goods and provision, swine and poultry, and apparel.[19] It was appropriate for the noble household at Tawstock to have a greater number of servants but the division in duties between husband and wife was not quite so separate. As will be discussed below, there may have been several reasons for this but the most likely cause was the Civil War.

Wages and food purchases formed the major part of expenditure. Lesser amounts were spent on clothing, household articles and a great range of other items. It is possible that the individual sums paid will, given their remoteness, be seen with modern eyes as quaint and charming while comparable accounts today would probably be viewed as tiresome and mundane. In fact, these are meticulous accounts drawn to monitor two substantial households and equivalent costs today would run into many tens of thousands of pounds.

An analysis of a collection of household accounts and papers of this size would, in a normal situation, be a daunting task: the amount of detailed information is quite extraordinary and it is not possible within this short introduction to examine every aspect of life. In effect this would amount to a social history of the fifth earl and his household. The intended purpose of this Introduction is to provide the necessary background of the collection and provide the overall framework needed to explain the accounts. There is an additional and overriding problem with this particular collection: the household was run during extremely turbulent years when on several occasions its members were forced to flee from advancing armies and when their homes were assaulted or occupied by both sides in the war. The highly politicized role of the earl created further complications. This was expressed in one letter Lord Bath wrote from Oxford to Lady Bath at Tawstock 'I pray you think of our winter quarter and of securing our principal goods in case any new troubles should arise in that country ... I have no desire to spend the

---

19. Somerset Record Office, DD HI 303.

winter in this place if I may be anywhere else with security'.[20] The difficulties of running a household, let alone monitoring expenditure, must have been extraordinary and should be continually borne in mind when assessing the accounts.

## *Henry, fifth Earl of Bath*

The Bourchier family had been connected with Tawstock since the beginning of the fifteenth century. Henry Bourchier was born in about 1587, probably in Ireland, to Sir George Bourchier, third son of John, second Earl of Bath, and Martha, daughter of William, Lord Howard of Effingham. Henry entered Trinity College Dublin as a Fellow Commoner in about 1597 and obtained his B.A. in 1605. He was knighted in 1621. In March 1637 he inherited his title from his cousin Edward who died without a male heir.[21] Not long afterwards, on 18 December 1638 at St Bartholomew the Great in London he married Rachel, daughter of Francis, first Earl of Westmorland.[22] It is difficult to assess Lord Bath's impact at Court where he was at least an occasional attender.[23] The earl became a member of the Privy Council in 1641 and three years later held the Privy Seal. Clarendon is noted for describing his 'sour-tempered unsocial behaviour'. He also wrote that he 'neither had or ever meant to do the King the least service' and that 'he had no excellent or graceful pronunciation'.[24] Historians have not viewed the earl as being an influential individual: his activities in the Civil War attract little attention on a national level but considerably more from those concerned specifically with Devon, particularly at the beginning of the war.[25] His accounts and letters indicate an enthusiastic interest in books but there are few other clues as to his personality and Clarendon's description is the closest to a character assessment. Consequently, subsequent accounts have largely but not exclusively followed Clarendon's opinion: he has been portrayed as 'a nobleman

---

20. Kent Archives Office, U269/C267/16.
21. The church bells at Hartland rang in 1630 for the birth of the 'young Earl of Bath' but he must have died an infant: *Historical Mss Commission Report, Appendix to the 5th report*, 146.
22. G.E. Cokayne, *The Complete Peerage* (1932), I, 19.
23. Kent Archives Office, U269/C267/6.
24. Edward Hyde Clarendon, *The History of the Rebellion and Civil Wars in England* (1815), II, 16 & I, 189.
25. Exceptions are Conrad Russell, *The Fall of the British Monarchies, 1637–1642* (Oxford, 1991) and Brian Manning, *Aristocrats, Plebians and Revolution in England, 1640–1660* (London and East Haven, 1996). All studies of Devon during the war give the earl considerable attention but even in neighbouring Cornwall, where he was particularly active in 1642, he is not discussed: Mary Coate, *Cornwall in the Great Civil War and Interregnum, 1642–1660* (Oxford, 1933) and more recently Anne Duffin, *Faction & Faith: Politics and Religion of the Cornish Gentry before the Civil War* (Exeter, 1996).

high in the councils of state, a great lover & supporter of the arts, and marked for his loyalty to Charles I', a 'great scholar', 'more a man of letters than a politician', and as 'a distinguished scholar, but a poor politician and certainly no soldier ... [and] a sour-tempered husband'.[26] Perhaps it should not be surprising that the accounts provide few insights into the earl's personality given that the countess had financial responsibility for the houses and consequently it is in regard to Lady Bath that the accounts are illuminating. His surviving correspondence, of a mainly political nature, reveals a great attachment and regard for his wife but little else.

There appears to have been great interest in north Devon with the prospect of a new earl. The town of Barnstaple welcomed Lord Bath's arrival into Devon in 1637 with 'a convenient dinner' as well as a present which cost £6 10s[27]. When the earl returned the following Spring he wrote to Lady Bath that 'we find a very empty House but a great expression of kind entertainment from the whole country'.[28] Relations with the local area soured considerably just a few years later at the start of the Civil War and appear to have remained unfriendly throughout the earl's life. The earl's death was recorded in the parish register for August 17 in 1654 with a note of the burial on the following day. The register also records the following month that 'the funeral rites of the right Hon. Henry Earl of Bath was solemnized the 21th day of this month 1654'.[29] Presumably the delay of five weeks allowed mourners sufficient time to travel to Devon. There were more than one hundred mourners but a list recorded only his wife's family, who would have journeyed considerable distances, some neighbours, his household and other servants (appendix 13). The funeral was not such an elaborate affair as that for the earl of Leicester in 1588.[30] Tawstock's account for the weeks following 11 November 1654 provides further details into the funeral arrangements: there was a payment of £126 to 'the servants in money given them by our most honourable and noble Lady as a remembrance of their honorable Lord and Master the Earl of Bath', a further order that 'her honour's poor old labouring men' be given £24, payment was made to a baker for his work before the funeral and the apothecary, presumably in relation to the earl's last days, was paid 'in full of his demands' more than twenty-two pounds.

---

26. Col. Harding, 'On Tawstock Church: Devon', *Exeter Diocesan Architectural Society*, 1858, V, 192–3; Lloyd, *Memories &c., of the Royalists*, 650; Richard W. Cotton, *Barnstaple and the Northern Part of Devonshire during the Great Civil War, 1642–1646* (1889), 59; Layley, *The Lords of Barnstaple*, 26.

27. Cotton, *Barnstaple*, 61.

28. Kent Archives Office, U269/C267/1.

29. Devon Record Office, Tawstock MF/PR3/31.

30. Simon Adams (ed.), *Household Accounts and Disbursement Books of Robert Dudley, earl of Leicester* (Camden Soc., 5th series, 6, 1996), 448–59.

Tawstock church is well-known for the superior and abundant memorials and the earl's monument stands prominently among them (Plate 2). It has received varying degrees of admiration: nearly one hundred years after its erection it was described as 'almost unequalled in singularity and absurdity',[31] just more than a century later W.G. Hoskins wrote that it was 'massive and ugly'[32] but more recently it was declared to be 'a splendid, relatively restrained free-standing monument of white and black marble'.[33]

## Rachel, countess of Bath

Rachel was the daughter of Francis, first Earl of Westmorland, and Mary Mildmay, daughter of Sir Anthony Mildmay of Apethorpe in Northamptonshire. She was born at Mereworth in Kent, baptised there on 28 January 1613 and had five sisters and seven brothers.[34] She married the earl at the age of 25 and there were no known children. She first came to Devon in July 1639 and the bells were rung to announce her arrival. Her husband wrote a few months earlier that 'your presence is much desired in Devonshire and many services presented by those that never saw you' and that there was 'a great desire of seeing you here'.[35] The Barnstaple borough records show that the Mayoress and the other townswomen rode out to meet her. The cost to the town in entertaining the earl and countess was ten pounds.[36] Her accounts show that she was continually visiting Tawstock from London. It is difficult to determine where they spent more time but their movements, to a great degree, were probably dictated by the fortunes of war rather than personal preference.

Throughout her accounts she consistently refers to her husband exclusively and rather stiffly as 'my Lord' but their correspondence suggests that they had an affectionate and close marriage: he refers to her as my 'dear wench', 'dear heart', 'dear girl', 'good girl', 'sweet girl' and 'sweetheart'. Many letters are caring and tender: in one letter he wrote 'according to promise I must again remember my wench whom I have not forgotten one hour together since I left her'. A few months after their marriage, and after a separation of only a few weeks, he wrote 'this is the third letter which I have writ to you since my coming

31. G.T. Harris, 'Some Memorials in Devon Churches', *DCNQ*, XIV, 90, citing J.H. Marland, *Remarks on English Churches, & on the Expediency of rendering sepulchal memorials subservient to pious & Christian uses* (1843).
32. W.G. Hoskins, *Devon* (Newton Abbot, 1954), 489.
33. Bridget Cherry and Nikolaus Pevsner, *Devon* (1989), 790.
34. John Bridges, *The History and Antiquities of Northamptonshire* (Oxford, 1791), II, 423, 425; Edward Hasted, *The History and Topographical Survey of the County of Kent* (1782), II.
35. Kent Archives Office, U269/C267/1–2.
36. Cotton, *Barnstaple*, 61.

hither and the 4th I hope will be myself' and at another time 'I much desire to be with my Dear Heart and think every day a year that I am from her'.[37] Their letters were often lighthearted: on one occasion he challenged her to guess the value of a ring of Oriental Amethyst he sent. She was requested to 'summon a Council of your Gossips ... and send me in your next letter your opinion what it is worth and then you shall know from me truly what it cost'.[38]

There is little indication in the accounts of her financial diligence but her own account book demonstrates a keen and active interest in the financial administration of the houses and estate. This may have been a necessity given that Lord Bath was actively engaged in the war and eventually imprisoned for nearly a year. In 1904 Lady Bath was described as the most famous of her sisters and 'a great lady' but also as 'a busybody, and all her cloud of kinsfolk held her in fear as their patroness and suzerain'.[39] This contrasts with more recent descriptions of her which have stressed her benevolence towards the clergy and their families.[40] This is largely due to the inscription on her memorial (Plate 3) which noted:

> in domestic, civil and religious affairs she had a genius exceeding that of a man, and such a motherly disposition that scarce a greater existed in the world. She was a humble and devoted daughter of the Church of England and in times of persecution a mother to distressed pastors, and in there parts, almost their only protectress. This alone was worthy of our tears ... and although she was childless yet she was parent to more than a thousand children, whom in a very genteel manner she brought up, gave them portions, consecrated and even ennobled. She still lives, and never will die, while any spark of gratitude remains in this country.[41]

It should be noted that her memorial was a gift of the Diocese of Bath and Wells. Lady Bath's account book provides further insights into her character. It supports the impression of a charitable nature with recurrent gifts to the poor as well as incidental notes such as the gift of cloth to make waistcoats for ten poor women.

There is also much evidence to support the claim regarding the clergy and children. William Bourchier, almost certainly a relative, came to

---

37. Kent Archives Office, U269/C267/6, 3–4.
38. Kent Archives Office, U269/C267/11.
39. Oswald Barron 'The Fanes', *Ancestor* (January 1905), XII, 9–10.
40. Charles G. Layley, *The Lords of Barnstaple* (Tawstock, 1983), 27–9 and *The Story of Tawstock Church* (Tawstock, 1981), 15, and most recently James Coulter, *Tawstock and the Lords of Barnstaple* (Bideford, 1996), 43.
41. A full transcription is in Layley, *The Lords of Barnstaple*, page 27. A lengthy description of the monuments to both the earl and countess will be found in A.W.B. Mesenger with John Benson, 'The Heraldry of Tawstock Church', *Devonshire Assoc. Transactions* (83, 1951), 135–9.

Tawstock in January 1639 and was later moved to Bow. He was seques-
tered after his move to Marwood[42] where the earl held the advowson.
Another minister, one Mr Wilde, came in 1646. There are a considerable
number of entries regarding children. In 1646 and 1647 there were quar-
terly payments for teaching individual children by one Ann Mullyns
and Mr Beckett. In 1654 Mullyns was paid three quarters' wages for
'teaching Ursula Hearder and another poor girl to read and work'. She
continued to teach and at one time had three girls. In 1652 Lady Bath
sent Jonathan Pikard to school at Barnstaple which had established
a grammar school by 1535 and produced two leading writers of the
English Reformation.[43] Three years later one Mr Humes was paid to
instruct Pikard who, in September 1645, Lady Bath had taken in as a
motherless infant. There were at least ten other children brought into
the household: three were eight years old, one not yet six and another
less than five. There was also a French boy and a ward. All these
children arrived at Tawstock after Lady Bath's marriage except for Ned
Lewin who came in May 1642 and whom she described as 'my boy'.
Lewin apparently came from Northamptonshire and was brought to
Lady Rachel when he was only three months old. In 1642 her house-
keeper noted that among the household were four members which Lady
Bath kept out of charity. Of them she wrote 'I need not name them I
presume your Honour knows who I mean'.[44]

Some of her interests are clearly seen in her accounts. Lady Bath
spent much time with her family: there are recurrent entries relating
to financial loans and travel to family christenings at Mereworth in
Kent, Bruern in Oxfordshire and Apethorpe in Northamptonshire. In
her own book she noted the deaths of 'my dear mother' and in much
greater length of William Bellamy 'the steward and faithful servant to
Sir Walter Mildmey, Sir Anthony Mildmey & Grace his wife, Francis
Earl of Westmorland & Mary his wife, & to Mildmey Earl of Westmorland, departed this life at Apethorpe in his sleep, having been a
servant there about 60 years'. She apparently had a great love for her
pet cat[45] and had a parrot. In one letter there is a reference to Lady
Bath working on the cloth hangings at Tawstock.[46] Her accounts also
show she had a great interest in games and gambling: she recorded her
losses which amounted to several pounds on individual occasions. This
interest may be demonstrated by her portrait as the Queen of Diamonds (Plate 7). She also played at loadum, dice, 'tablemen' (probably

---

42. Ian Gowers, 'Corrections and Additions to 'Walker Revised' as relevant to Devon
    entries', *Devon & Cornwall Notes & Queries*, Spring 1993, XXXVII, part III, 110.
43. Nicholas Orme, *Education in the West of England, 1066–1548* (Exeter, 1976),
    112–113.
44. Kent Archives Office, U269/C279.
45. Kent Archives Office, U269/C267/1.
46. Kent Archives Office, U269/C273.

backgammon) and she also owned 'a pair of ebony tables and men', bowls and troll madam. There was also an interest in music evidenced by miscellaneous payments such as in December 1640 of £1 2s 6d for 'music' and on 1 January 1644 five shillings to some musicians for their playing. Lady Bath was taught to play the viol by one Mr Coleman, as a child played in masques[47] and in her account book is a copy of 'Love's Diet' by John Donne. The interest in poetry may have been influenced by the writings of her elder brother Mildmay, second earl of Westmorland.[48] Her portrait was painted by Cornelius Johnson, Sir Anthony van Dyck (Plate 6) and possibly Richard Gibson.[49] Notwithstanding her depiction as the Queen of Diamonds, there are few references to Lady Bath's jewellry. In 1652 she commissioned a jeweller, one Mr Gumbleton, to make two pairs of lockets with a number of diamonds. There are other references to two pairs of pearl pendants and a screen fan.

On 1 May 1655, less than nine months after the death of her husband, she married Lionel, third Earl of Middlesex at St Bride's, London. She was aged 42 and her husband was some twelve years younger. The couple were already related by marriage: Cranfield's elder brother James, the previous Earl of Middlesex, married Anne, daughter of Edward, fourth Earl of Bath in 1646.[50] About ten weeks after the wedding there was a dramatic increase in spending for provisions at Tawstock: during the week of 21 July a calf's haunch, nine ducks, one hundred cod fish, fifteen geese and some 45 chickens were purchased. These items, together with a payment to the bell ringers, suggests that Lord and Lady Middlesex came to Tawstock for their first visit as husband and wife.[51] The marriage was not successful. Only two months after the wedding there was gossip was that 'there was like to have grown a little breach between the late married couple but was quickly peaced it seems he does not well brook some of her servants & perhaps begins to think the articles too much derogatory to the honour of a husband' and three years later it was reported that the earl had 'sold all her plate, most of the household stuff and all Lord Bath's library: all goes in play and rioting'. One report was slightly ambiguous: in 1658 it was recounted that 'Lady Middlesex is still in the West, & I hope will there continue: her Lord is wonderful brave in town & I hope will think no more of her'. She obtained a Royal warrant in 1660 to retain her title as Countess of Bath. It took precedence over the later

---

47. Kent Archives Office, U269/F38/3.
48. Alistair Fowler, *The Country House Poem: A Cabinet of Seventeenth-Century Estate Poems and Related Items* (Edinburgh, 1994), 208–58.
49. See Sotheby's sale catalogues for 15/7/53 lot 29, 20/3/78 lot 61 and 20/7/87 lot 5.
50. Anne, Countess of Middlesex, subsequently married Sir Chichester Wrey and became co-heir to Henry, fifth Earl of Bath. They inheirited Tawstock Court although never lived there due to the life interest of Lady Rachel.
51. The accounts show they were there by at least the end of September.

creation of the earldom of Middlesex and the earl was said to 'be very angry at her changing her title; he says it is an affront to him'. Six years after her marriage, on 13 June 1661, she was granted a separation on the grounds of desertion and cruelty.[52] Lady Bath died on 11 November 1680 at her house in the parish of St Giles-in-the-Fields, London and was buried at Tawstock on 20 January 1681.[53] Her monument (Plate 3) is a white marble copy made by Balthazar Burman of a sculpture of the Countess of Shrewsbury in St John's College, Cambridge made by his father Thomas in 1672.[54]

## Revenue and the estate

The estate extended over a considerable distance. Thirty-six manors were held in Devon, Cornwall, Somerset, Gloucestershire, Wiltshire and Berkshire (see map 3). Four Somerset manors (Huntspill, Norton Fitzwarren, Nunnington and Taunton) as well as four in Devon (Bampton and Bampton town, Uffculme and Hackpen) were set aside for the three daughters of Edward, fourth Earl of Bath and raised more than £337 in rent annually.[55] The rent of the remaining 28 manors was worth nearly £1000. Throughout the accounts are manorial receipts for rents, fines and other monies as well as payments for letters to the reeves. There was also the money raised from the boroughs of Nymet Tracey and Ilfracombe, an annual rent from Langford Barton in Ugborough, the fairs of Braunton, Nymet Tracey and Uffculme, and the markets of Braunton and Ilfracombe. The earl held Wantage and Gandfield hundreds in Berkshire, the fourth part of the borough and hundred of Hartland, the advowsons of Tawstock, Alphington, Combeinteignhead, Little Torrington, Marwood, Nymet Tracey, Roborough, Satterleigh, Warkleigh and the fourth part of Dunterton.[56] He also owned land in County Armagh: the earl claimed that his Irish estates generated the greatest part of his income.[57] Lady Bath noted the rentals on the Irish estate produced more than £2,609 for the years 1637 to 1641. Irish revenue was supplemented by agriculture: several thousand sheep were kept for both their meat and wool.

---

52. G.E.C., *The Complete Peerage* (1932), VIII, 691–2; *Historical Manuscripts Commission, Appendix to the 5th Report*, 183, 145–6. The Sutherland collection has since been deposited at the Staffordshire Record Office, D868, and the letters catalogued as 5/70a, 3/4a and 3/11b. I am grateful to Tim Groom for this information.
53. DRO, Tawstock MF/PR3/31. In contrast to her husband's notice her burial is noted simply as 'Rachel Countess of Bath'.
54. K.A. Esdaile, *The Eagle*, xlix, no. 215, July 1935.
55. Henry had to raise £12,000 for their inheritance: Kent Archives Office, U269/E311. A dispute with William Paget ran for over ten years regarding money for the three daughters: U269/C293. See also House of Lords Calendar for 5 August 1642: *Historical Manuscripts Commission, Appendix to the 5th Report*, 41.
56. Kent Archives Office, U269/T79/8.
57. Kent Archives Office, U269/O258.

The major source of income was derived from rents, heriots and fines. One of the first entries for Lord Bath's earliest Tawstock account concerns a meeting held with the tenants to discuss rents. The earl travelled to Tawstock in the spring of 1639 and he wrote to Lady Bath the following month of the difficulty in raising the inheritance money for the three daughters of the previous earl:

> I find the people of this country very crafty in taking all advantage for their profit and if they suspect that their landlord wants money they will make great use of it.[58]

Four years later, when there was an unwillingness to undertake leases during the war, the earl advised Lady Bath 'take heed of the crafty clowns of Devon & of your bargains with them'. The rent of one property in Hackpen in 1644 was to be increased on 'the conclusion of peace'.[59] On one occasion tenants refused to pay their leases: in 1651 the Sheriff was needed to force entry into two tenements in Tiverton and although a gun was fired no one was hurt.[60]

While the accounts show a sharp and careful interest taken in the tenants' financial dealings, the steward's letters also demonstrate an inquisitiveness, if not concern, in their private lives. In May 1642 Richard Pollard wrote to the earl:

> I have made bold to present your honour a few passages, and first concerning the said John Cunniber, a tenant of my Lords who (to cross my Lord in sitting a further estate in his tenement) about a quarter of a year since married a lusty young wife and this week his wife was delivered of a child as she was amilking of her ewes, but sayeth that the babe is not her husband's but hath named another man to be the father thereof, which hath almost broken the old man's heart but it is a just reward for him.[61]

In May 1648 Edward Wyot[62] wrote that a young woman of the parish travelled to St Erme in Cornwall to cure the ill health she suffered since her last childbirth. He wrote that she 'staying about six weeks grown worse and then desiring by litter to go home ... died ... leaving 11 young children'.[63]

Lady Bath considered Tawstock to be self-sufficient in wood, corn, hay, straw, hops, herbs and 'roots', apples, cider, milk and meat from cattle, sheep, pigs, deer, woodcock, pigeon, rabbit and salmon. The list of Tawstock's rooms such as the cheese chamber, brewhouse and still

---

58. Kent Archives Office, U269/C267/4.
59. Kent Archives Office, U269/C267/17.
60. Kent Archives Office, U269/C278.
61. Kent Archives Office, U269/C276.
62. The spelling Wyot has been taken from his memorial stone at Tawstock parish and for consistency used in preference to Wyatt or Wyat.
63. Kent Archives Office, U269/C278.

house confirms these activities. Revenue was raised in their sale as well as other items such as reed, hemp, hides, skins and willows which were locally known as welgars and sold by the parcel. Nearly 150 skins and hides were sold in 1642. The countess noted she had to buy fish, butter, cheese, vinegar, salt, wine, capers, coal and culm. The purchases of fresh fish are at odds with the considerable number caught and sold from the kiddle[64] and hatch in the river Taw just below the house: for example, over the course of a few months in 1642 sixty-two salmon were sold. Lady Bath also recorded that the other expenses were weekly rates, nursing charges and general wages.

Livestock, notably sheep and cattle, were purchased and sold at a number of local fairs. There were also Irish sheep but it is unclear whether these were an Irish breed or transported from Ireland. Curiously, the steward complained that they were 'rotten', that is that they were infected with sheep-rot: it was claimed that they 'will never be fat' and it was suggested that they be replaced by some 'country' sheep. From the accounts it is apparent that Tawstock had considerable agricultural activity. Appendices 8 & 10, of two lists of animals in 1648 and 1653, show a substantial number of animals particularly given they were recorded in November. The list of husbandry implements taken in 1642 further emphasizes the degree of agricultural activity. One notable undertaking was the growing of hops.

## *Tawstock*

Tawstock's prominent position overlooking the river Taw has made it a familiar landmark in north Devon (Plate 1). In the early seventeenth century Tristram Risdon wrote in his history of Devon 'this ancient court-like house and pleasant place is seated near a navigable river and an elegant town wanting none of those commodities set down by Cato as requisite in a well-accommodated commonwealth'.[65] Devon's other topographical writer, Thomas Westcote, whose family was a near-neighbour, considered it 'a pleasant and delicate seat'.[66] Both writers would have been familiar with John Hooker's slightly earlier and more expressive description of it as:

> This howse of Tawstoke is a verye famouse and an auncyent howse ... The house is a verye fayre house but lyeth in a valley & the waye declininge into it which is some blemishe of the beautie of

---

64. According to the glebe terrier of 1680 'in the river that runneth betwixt the marsh and the island there belongeth unto the parsonage a place to set a net called a kiddle to take fish in'. The island was a piece of ground of two acres, possibly a field, on the opposite side of the river: Devon Record Office, Tawstock glebe terriers, 1680. The accounts record the use of furze for making the kiddle.
65. Tristram Risdon, *The Chorographical Description or Survey of the County of Devon* (1811), 326.
66. Thomas Westcote, *A View of Devonshire in 1630* (Exeter, 1845), 292.

that house. It hath lyinge one the Southe syde a verye fayre parke
replenished with deer and other cattals. One the northe syde lyethe
the lardge and greate feildes which comonly are called the demeanse
or Barton of the house. At the lower end thereof standeth the
parishe church and not farre from it the parsons house, whereof the
Lorde the Erle of Bath is the sole lorde and patron & comonlye he
reserveth to himselffe the sheffe thereof for a reasonable rent. This
parsonedge for corne and this Barton for cattall and this parke for
deer, with other his good husbandrye, ar hable and be sufficient to
meantaine a very good house whiche the saide Erle dothe con-
tynewally keepe in most bountefull order, to his greate honor & to
the great good of the countri and to the Releefe of the Poore.[67]

Two surveys made in 1639–40 and another in 1655 noted as many as
63 rooms although this included several outbuildings. Among the
grandest in 1639 were the Great Chamber with its withdrawing room
and bed chamber but in 1655 the Blue Bed Chamber was noted as one
of the most prominent. The surveys also listed the furniture, linen and
pictures. Curtains were separately measured for the earl's bedchamber,
the higher drawing room, a room next to the dining room, the inner
and outer nurseries, the green bed chamber, the oak leaf chamber and a
chamber in the 'new building'. For these particular rooms it is possible
to compare the inventories with the measurements. For example, the
earl's own chamber had five pieces of Arras hangings with a sylvan
theme, a feather bed hung with green cloth and yellow lace, several
carpets (one red, another yellow and a third made of 'Turkey work'),
several silver items, two mirrors and numerous pieces of furniture. The
room appears to have been shaped like a gallery: it measured seventeen
yards in length and three in depth and had a fireplace and two
windows. The house was destroyed by the fire of 1787 and the only
surviving feature is the prominent gatehouse.

Although Tawstock was the larger household and a well-appointed
building the great distance from London denied it a fashionable use.
Devon's first visit by a monarch in many generations was that of
Charles I in 1625. Even then the king did not travel to north Devon.
The earl and countess, themselves strangers to the county, needed to be
in the capital to easily visit their circle of friends and, perhaps more
importantly, to have access to the Court.

## Lincoln's Inn Fields

It is unclear where the earl and countess initially resided in London
given that their letters were addressed to both Fetter Lane and
Aldersgate Street. They explored the possibilities of renting the earl of

---

67. British Library, Harl.5827, p.124d. I would like to thank Prof. Joyce Youings for
kindly providing me with this extract from her forthcoming edition of John Hooker's
'Corographical Description of Devon'.

Northumberland's house[68] before settling upon 53–4 Lincoln's Inn Fields. The house was built by David Murray in 1639 or 1640 and the accounts have regular payments to him beginning April 1641. The building, later converted into two dwellings, was demolished in 1912. Some early features were rescued.[69] Lord and Lady Bath resided in London when it was politically feasible and during the war considered other options for winter quarters such as Bristol and Exeter: on one occasion he wrote 'if there be a peace or cessation we may winter where we will'.[70] In November 1649 James, second Earl of Middlesex, leased the house, together with the stable and coach-house, for six months for the sum of fifty pounds. The agreement allowed Lord Bath access to a locked garret and William Lynn the use of one chamber and closet.[71] One near neighbour was the French Ambassador with whom they appeared to have friendly relations. The Portuguese Ambassador also lived nearby.[72]

The two houses were largely separate units but they were strongly linked: there was a constant exchange of letters and parcels and the sending of such items as linen and candles. The frequent pamphlets and diurnals would have been greatly welcomed by a news-hungry household in north Devon. When the earl sent Lady Bath copies of *Mercurius Aulicus*, the Royalist news-sheet, he wrote 'though it be stale here, yet it will be fresh for poor country folks' and on another occasion 'It will serve to inform poor Country Gossips how the business of the times go, that they may be by the fireside'.[73] Of course Tawstock also received news from the frequent letters from London. Pamphlets were also sent to Lord Bath when he was imprisoned at the Tower. The carriage of perishable items such as plants, turkey eggs and salmon pies is perhaps more surprising. There was also a continual movement of servants some of which can be explained by the necessities of war such as sending a butler, cook and groom to the earl at York in July 1642.[74] Appendix 4 notes the carriage of more than twenty boxes and trunks sent with a great number of the household from Tawstock to Lincoln's Inn Fields. With them went a hat-case, portmanteau, bundles of linen, animal skins and even a great cheese. The combined weight was more

---

68. Kent Archives Office, U269/C267/6. See also C293.
69. The parish was St Giles in the Fields. The building was occupied by the order of Franciscans in 1687 and a riot occurred the following year. A fire caused severe damage in 1759. Laurence Gomme & Philip Norman (eds), *Survey of London; Volume III (part 1) Lincoln's Inn Fields* (1912), 77–80.
70. Kent Archives Office, U269/C267/18–19.
71. Kent Archives Office, U269/E314/2.
72. Kent Archives Office, U269/C275. There was a riot at both Ambassadors' homes in 1641: Gomme & Norman, *Survey of London*, 13.
73. Kent Archives Office, U269/C267/14 & 19. See also no.17: '. . . sent the wench the *Mercury* to furnish her with knowledge stuff to entertain her gossips'.
74. Kent Archives Office, U269/C277.

than 2200 pounds. Clearly many luxury goods, such as Venetian glasses on one occasion, were purchased in London. Tawstock appears to have been furnished largely with items from London[75] and many purchases in the Lincoln's Inn Fields' accounts, such as the four new Spanish tables in 1640, may well have later been transported to Devon.

There were also expenses paid for travel to Charing Cross, Tottenham, Windsor, Westminster and Greenwich among many other places. But the accounts for Lincoln's Inn Fields were also greatly concerned with political affairs: there were continual payments which reflect the course of the war including sending servants on errands to Westminster, copies of Parliamentary bills, recurrent expenses regarding the earl's imprisonment in the Tower and reconciling life with the Commonwealth.

## Household administration

The papers reveal both the structure and composition of the households. Most of the senior officers can be identified although there was a considerable changeover in staff within both households. The central figure was the steward who was responsible for the running of the household. The first two stewards were William Weeks and Matthew Coyse. Richard Pollard was the longest serving steward, from 1640 through to 1651. It appears that the stewards resided at Tawstock, unlike Thomas Hinson, steward to the third earl, who lived at nearby Park Gate.[76] Bailiffs included Hugh Coombe and William Ellis at Tawstock and there was another for each manor. Thomas Wyot was the secretary at Tawstock and it was probably William Lynn who was employed as his London counterpart. The office of Thomas Pollard, brother of Richard, was not noted but he may have served as the London steward. Others include William Paget who was concerned with all the estates and Richard Atherton in Ireland. The auditors were Joseph Jackman and Hugh Prust.

The annual accounts merely suggest a cursory interest by Lady Bath and it is only in her own book that there is overwhelming evidence of a determined scrutiny of expenditure: her book was a series of meticulous records by which she could verify the accuracy of her stewards' accounts. Her correspondence with the housekeeper, recorded below, also suggests she was greatly concerned with prudent and cautious financial management. At least one servant understood that Lady Bath kept her own accounts: in the Tawstock account for March 1644 Richard Pollard finished a memorandum with a note to 'see my Lady's book'.

---

75. Kent Archives Office, U269/C277–8.
76. Thomas Hinson left the property to his son William. Martha, widow of William, later married Sir William Button. She died in 1658: Nottingham Record Office, DD.4P/ 37/4–18 & 52/28–30.

All the accounts were greatly concerned with the movement of money either through bills of exchange or in coinage: there were recurring notes as to the urgent need for funds.[77] There were also odd references to particular coins such as 'old gold of Edward 6 & Queen Eliz.', 'Eliz. crown', '2 piece of gold of Queen Marys'. Two additional lists were made of all the coins at Tawstock: this included coins minted from every reign from Henry VIII to Charles I and even one of Prince Charles. There were also French and Spanish coins with one noted as of 'Ferdinand and Isabella'.

A list made in about 1638, before the Earl's residence at Tawstock, shows there were 36 household servants: this includes the steward, an usher of the hall, two gentlewomen, chambermaid, three washmaids, dairymaid, butler, servant for the pantry, cook, undercook, cater, clerk of the kitchen, gardener, porter, coachman, postilion, two footmen, gentleman usher, gentleman of the horse, groom of the earl's chamber, three stable grooms, bailiff, brewer, baker, butcher's boy, scullery boy, a woman to make beds and two chamber grooms.[78] The earl and countess maintained a similar household in size although the underservants were not always clearly identified. Among Lady Bath's servants with descriptive names were Wilmot Toogood, a maid, and others who were more simply noted such as Irish Tom and Welsh Dick. There was also a servant defined as 'James the Blackamoore' but it is unclear whether this was actually his surname. The recurrent references to 'J.B.' may be to him. He may have been the first black servant in Devon.

Lady Bath kept notes on 105 members of her household: among the details she recorded was the date they first arrived at Tawstock and whether they received wages. Occasionally she also noted when their service ended: for example 'Hunnicot the porter, he died about 11 of the clock the 9th of February 1645 it being Shrove Monday' and of one woman she wrote 'she went to Hall to serve the Lord Chichester in 1642 and came to me again in the 17th of October 1646'. Lady Bath listed a fisherman, hop-man, firemaker, barber and fowler all of whom were not noted in 1638. The list of rooms at Tawstock made in 1640 shows there were rooms set aside for the curate, chaplain, gentleman sewer and for at least one musician. Lady Bath also recorded separate histories on 28 servants.

In addition to these household servants the accounts noted a considerable number of day labourers. The steward listed the workmen who were receiving daily wages as 'gardeners, fellers of wood, carpenters, masons & others' or merely as 'the workmen'. Others included joiners, chimney-sweepers, basket-makers, thatchers, wood-turners, masons, stone-carvers, millers, plumbers, barbers, bone-setters and hedge-makers or 'park hedgers'. A considerable amount of money was

---

77. For example: Kent Archives Office, U269/C275.
78. Kent Archives Office, U269/A527.

paid for cutting brush, faggots, hardwood and gorse. Many agricultural labourers were employed in clodding, mowing, weeding, loughing, gathering hops, sheep-sheering, hemp stripping, threshing, hay-making and cutting 'ferns' which presumably was bracken. In one case wages were paid for knitting fish-nets. There was also several instances of payments for land surveying. Smiths were employed in shoeing the horses and many others in the care of animals. There was also an armourer, huntsman and a clock or watch maker. There were recurrent payments for rowing or 'setting over' the earl and countess along the river Taw in their small boat. Some payments were for internal work such as the keeping of clocks, 'colouring' the withdrawing room and working on the planching there.

Although the household was primarily masculine in composition there was a considerable number of women. In 1638 at least eight of the 36 in the household were female but their actual number at other times is not possible to determine. Many women were employed on a casual basis in such labour as making hay, gathering and tying hops, washing, stripping hemp and weeding in the garden and fields. There are several instances of women being paid to clean the rooms and another for 'washing and cleaning the hangings and rugs'. In 1649 one woman tended a sick ox and in 1650 another spun 120 pounds of wool for 20 weeks. Midwives feature throughout the accounts, particularly in relation to rewards at christenings, but not in relation to any at Tawstock or Lincoln's Inn Fields. Nurses were employed to look after the children in the household. There were also the aforementioned recurrent payments to a woman for teaching several children to read. In many cases the women are referred to as being old, for example 'to the old hempstripper and her daughter'.

Lady Bath would have had several women as attendants such as her maid Rose Todd. At least five daughters of men of high social status were included within the household. Their age is uncertain and presumably were there as companions. One such individual was 'Ann Stevens [who] came 2 weeks before Michaelmas 1645 [and] was married to Sir Charles Boles of Louth in Lincolnshire the 23 of March after'.[79] One of the women was a relation: Rebecca, daughter of Sir Robert Lovett, was the sister of the previous earl's first wife. Others were Anne, daughter of Sir William 'Killygrey' and Elizabeth Fitzmaurice 'Lord Kerry's daughter'.

The household servants also included several members of the gentry. At the parish church at Tawstock is a memorial tablet to one of Lady Bath's attendants. It was erected:

> in memory of Sara, the wife of Richard Pollard, gent., educated in the French and English Courts and thought worthy to attend on the Right Honorable the Countess of Westmorland, and by her

---

79. Boles was a Royalist: Clive Holmes, *Seventeenth-Century Lincolnshire* (Lincoln, 1980), 175.

recommendation to wait on her most dear daughter, Lady Rachel, Countess of Bath. This Sara was daughter to Monsieur Voysin, a Syndique of Geneva, who most honorably lost his life in defence of that free city. Her grandfather was the learned Henricus Stephanus and Issac Causabon was her uncle. She died 30th of January 1652.

There are other memorials to the Tawstock household including one to Edward Wyot noted as a gentleman on his memorial and to Peter Bold originally of Upton in Chester who was the Gentleman of the Horse.[80] Lady Bath had a wall memorial erected to Bold in 1666 which claimed that he served Lord Bath for 33 years and was 'steady in his faith and loyalty, abhorred flattery & hypocrisy, loved his friends cordially and was of unwearied pains in any employment he took'.

Notwithstanding his higher status Richard Pollard was chastised for dining in the parlour. He explained to the earl that his:

> ambition was never so lofty but I could be contented with the poorest room in the house had it not been to give entertainment to those commands which came and so many as the pantry would not hold them. I pray God your honour receive no greater damage, I have given content to those captains which my Lord Roberts was pleased to place here for our safety.[81]

The accounts confirm the presence then at Tawstock of 'the two captains for preserving my Lord's house'.[82]

## Diet: provisioning and consumption

It is evident from the accounts that the diet was in keeping with those of other similar households. There was a great variety in meat including mutton, veal, beef, including barrels of Irish beef, venison, Spanish gammon and both salted and dry bacon. Other meat included rabbits, some of which came from Braunton Burrows, partridges, pheasants, ducks, capons, chickens, pullets, geese, turkeys, pigeons, snipes and on several occasions dozens of larks. Fish appears frequently including ling, salted salmon, lobsters and Appledore oysters. Some fish, as would be expected in Devon, was transported great distances including from Newfoundland, or 'Canada', and there were barrels of herring from Ireland. Eggs were a frequent purchase. There was also a great amount of Cheddar and other types of cheese. Butter was a frequent entry and was listed by the pot, gallon, tub or cask. Considerable amounts of

---

80. Lieut. Col. Harding, 'On Tawstock Church: Devon', *Exeter Diocesan Architectural Society* (1858), 193. Edward Wyot died 17 August 1656 aged 83. There is also a memorial to William Skippon, steward and treasurer to the third earl.
81. Kent Archives Office, U269/C276.
82. There was also the payment of ten shillings for 'their man for his pains'.

wine, including Malaga sack and claret, were imported but the household also produced its own ale and beer. The hop-yard was productive and home-grown barley must have lessened costs. Barm and malt, occasionally made from oats, were occasionally purchased.[83] Tawstock probably produced sufficient wheat, barley, oats, rye, peas, vetches and beans for most years. Many vegetables, such as carrots, parsnips, leaks, onions and cabbages, must have been grown. Other entries show the consumption of apples, plums, pears, cherries, strawberries, raspberries, grapes and figs. More unexpected items include jars of sallet oil, olives, sugar candy, eringo roots, syrup of gillyflowers and scurvy grass. In the store chamber in November 1653 were raisins, currants, prunes, nutmeg, cloves, mace, cinnamon, ginger, aniseed and sugar loaves. Many of these luxury items appear on an earlier list made in 1649. Many purchases were made in nearby markets or fairs such as at South Molton, Hartland, Torrington, Bideford, Barnstaple and even Bristol. Occasional payments were made to pedlars but the actual purchases cannot always be identified. One exception is the purchase by the countess of '8 horne flowers'.

There are kitchen accounts for Lincoln's Inn Fields for February 1642 to July 1646 with several notable gaps. One break was for the summer of 1642 when the earl and countess were agitating support for the King in Devon and begin again in October with the countess' return to help the earl then imprisoned in the Tower of London. The accounts continue until his release in August 1643 when Lord Bath again left London. The final accounts were for May to July in 1646 which coincide with the King's surrender. The kitchen accounts confirm the varied fare which would have been required of the earl and countess:[84] during the week of February 1642 there was beef, mutton, veal, lamb, tongues, neat's and calves' feet, sheep's trotters, pigs' pettitoes, capons, hens, chickens, woodcocks, snipes, teals, roasting pigs, green fish, ling, plaice, flounders, eels, lobsters, trout, carp, smelts, whiting, oysters, herring, butter, eggs, bacon, milk, oatmeal and bread. There was also three kinds of wine and a listing of 'herbs and roots, cabbages, alexanders and sallets'. Fruit included oranges, lemons and apples.[85] The household accounts supplement the kitchen records by showing purchases of such specialist items as kegs of sturgeon, conserve of rosemary flowers, pistachio comfits and nuts, quarts of olives, green ginger and sallet oil. There was also ambergis, cochineal, leaf gold presumably for Christmas and refined sugar and 3000 red roses for making conserve of red roses. Some of these items were also noted in general purchases from such individuals as the baker, butcher, poulterer, milk woman and herb woman.

---

83. Kent Archives Office, U269/E313.
84. Felicity Heal, *Hospitality in Early Modern England* (Oxford, 1990), chapter two.
85. Kent Archives Office, U269/A526.

Richard Pollard, as steward at Tawstock, estimated the costs of provisioning a noble household of 80 persons in meat, fish, dairy products,
bread, drink and stabling would run to between twenty and twenty-five
pounds weekly or up to £1,200 annually (appendix 11). This contrasts
with Lady Bath's own estimate made in 1641 that it cost £1000 to
maintain a household in London of between 30 and 40 members for
only 40 weeks. The London accounts are complicated by the inclusion
of money disbursed for general debts which are not easily separated
from household costs. The Tawstock annual disbursements, running
from October to October, were approximately as follows:

Tawstock Disbursements

| | |
|------|--------|
| 1641 | £1232 |
| 1642 | £1478 |
| 1643 | £1171 |
| 1644 | £1426 |
| 1645 | £1247 |
| 1647 | £891 |
| 1649 | £259 |
| 1651 | £1715 |
| 1655 | £1476 |

These disbursements included more than provisioning costs. Although
there are no kitchen accounts for Tawstock there were weekly lump-
sum payments to William Rumson, the cater, for those items which
needed to be purchased, and subsequently for the 'market bill'. Occasionally the letter 'h' was noted preceding provisioning purchases; this
may indicate housekeeping.[86] For the year from 31 October 1640 less
than £80 was given to Rumson but the actual provisioning bill was
higher: Rumson's payments do not include the costs of other victuals
purchased or of those produced on the estate. The table does demonstrate how the chaotic movement of the earl and countess affected
household costs and that comparisons between any two years are not
necessarily useful. These figures should be weighed against the effects of
the war, as for example, during the summer of 1642, when both the earl
and countess had fled Lincoln's Inn Fields, the household was reduced
to seven or eight members and put on board wages[87] as a cost-cutting
measure.[88]

The expense was obviously of tremendous concern to Lady Bath. On
21 April 1642 Richard Pollard wrote to her:

> ... Madam, I am sorry your honour should find fault with the
> expense in housekeeping here at Tawstock. I protest to God I
> know not how to make it less amongst so many company: our

---

86. Equally it may denote 'Hardwick'.
87. Board wages were paid when the household had moved locations.
88. Kent Archives Office, U269/C275.

bread is made of the coarsest corn and our beer very mean, and for
muttons we never kill above two in the week, which I hope your
honour will not think much; pigeons Mrs Hardwick hath sold
some and more shall be sold as they come fit, but for rabbits there
be very few, for I let them alone to increase, and there hath not
been one in the house since your honour went hence. I hope your
honour shall never find me guilty of any unnecessary expense in
anything. I beseech your honour not to condemn me, in anything
touching the horses, for as I hope to live, if my life had been
engaged for them I could not have done more to preserve them
then I always did and for the deer there died no more than usually
they do every winter ...[89]

The concern may have been caused by the loss of the Irish revenue or
the aforementioned uncertainties of war. At the same time Lady Bath
received a letter from Cordelia Hardwick who wrote:

I have conferred with him & some other good husbands in the
parish about keeping fewer husbandmen & they all tell me we have
brought them to as small a company as can be to do the business.
For the bread it is as brown as can be made of coarse wheat & we
eat all of it only we dress a quarter of a peck out of it for manchet
which serves our table & for white pots the wheat which we spend
is the out dressings of all. I am sure no baker would give above 5s
the bushel for it & this I do because I would make as much money
as I can and I protest I never took half that care to save for myself
when God took away my husband & all my means as I have done
since I heard of my Lord's great losses. I know there is not one loaf
of bread nor one jug of bear spent in waste throughout the week.
For our expense in vinegar I would it might a continued longer for
now our roots & herbs are gone which spent that & now we shall
spend more store of other things which will be more costly do
what I can. I verily believe there is never a farmer in the parish but
hath spent more meat in his house this Lent than we have done
now and hath lived so hardier in every respect for my part I must
needs confess I never kept so true a Lent without either fresh fish
or flesh, for to my remembrance there came not one bit in the
house. The truth is it was because of example to the rest & now I
have learned to eat washbrew & poor John if ever I be forced to
live hardly I must needs say for all that sit at our table they are
content also with any diet & I promise your honour I will study
still to do my best endeavour in all points of good housewifery. ...

Intriguingly, she had written the previous month that:

I hope your Ladyship will see by the bills that we keep as sparing a
house as we could if it was our own & as few servants excepting
those your Honour keeps of poor charity which is 4 & one
gardener.[90]

89. Kent Archives Office, U269/C276.
90. Kent Archives Office, U269/C279.

Perhaps she suspected some misgivings or unease regarding the household expenses. The financial worries continued. The following year, on 4 October 1643, the earl informed Lady Bath that revenue was inadequate due to the war: he wrote 'unless God send us peace ... we need live frugally'.[91]

There is little evidence for how meals were cooked. Fortunately Lady Bath's book of mainly medicinal remedies contains one recipe for making a marchpane tart. Marchpane, otherwise marzipan, was common from the later medieval period.[92] Her instructions were to:

> take a pound of almonds & beat them very well, then put into them a pound of fine searsed sugar, then stir it, then put the whites of 4 eggs & stir it sill in the mortar, then put into a silver dish & stir it round till it come to a paste then take it off from the fire & roll it out like a tart with little edges, then put it in the oven, temperately heat & before it is done take it out, do take the white of an egg & beat it with a little rose water & pour it thin upon it.[93]

Not surprisingly the accounts also show recurring purchases of 'pick toothes'.

## Household items

The three inventories provide a comprehensive listing of Tawstock's contents. Those of the kitchen are particularly vivid with the 'fifteen spits, two brass kettles, one large boiler, two pair of racks, one iron pot, one brass pot, four skillets, three frying pans, two dripping pans, two great iron bars and a great range of iron grates with other utensils'.

The accounts supplement the inventories by showing additional purchases. For example, wax candles feature regularly and there were entries for a great number of cooking items including commonplace ones such as trenchers and glasses as well as a paste board, pastry paper and oyster knives. Other items were referred to simply as cloam or as earthern pots. There were also two chamber pots and occasional husbandry purchases such as milking pails. Some purchases were listed made for building purposes such as the 22 dozen tiles intended for the dairy floor. Three hundred bricks were bought in 1644, an early use in Devon and presumably for chimneys. There were also a number of unusual items including matting for the earl's elaborate seat at Tawstock

91. Kent Archives Office, U269/C267/19.
92. C. Anne Wilson, *Food and drink in Britain* (1973), 336–7. See also Terence Scully, *The Art of Cookery in the Middle Ages* (Woodbridge, 1995).
93. Kent Archives Office, U269/F38/2. The recipe is not in Robert May's cookbook of 1660 or a household book of 1653: Alan Davidson, Marcus Bell and Tom Jaine (eds), *The Accomplisht Cook or the Art and Mystery of Cookery* (Blackawton, 1994); C. Anne Wilson (ed.), *A Book of Fruits and Flowers* (1984).

church and another 400 yards of matting 'for my Lady's closet'. Luxury purchases include silver items for the house and tobacco pipes for Lord Bath. One commonplace item which is unexpected to find listed was the purchase of 'a quire of paper for the stools'.

A detailed listing was made in 1639 of all the plate at Tawstock. This comprised more than 220 individuals items including at least four gold pieces. Lady Bath later amended the inventory to show which pieces were stolen during the war such as her silver toasting fork which she noted as being worth two pounds. She left the gold items with the Spanish Ambassador, presumably because she felt they were safer with him: if there was a robbery it was more likely Lady Bath would receive recompense.[94] An additional list shows there were 21 pieces of 'porcelain dishes of all sorts' and other porcelain was occasionally purchased.

There is extensive information on linen with detailed inventories made in May 1648 and again four years later of sheets, pillow cases, table cloths, napkins, towels, rubbers and dresser cloths. The principal purpose of the inventories was probably to determine the location of the dozens of articles. Many items were made in Ireland and some were bought in London and possibly Barnstaple. The lists also show considerable continual movement between Lincoln's Inn Fields and Tawstock. Lady Bath made similar notes, notably of which items were monogrammed.

Pamphlets and diurnals were regularly purchased as were books including law books, bibles, *The Faerie Queen*, *The Articles of the Church of England*, *Fleta*, *Commentary upon Magna Carta*[95] and several copies of Aesop's *Fables*. There was also a book of maps. There were several outlays to Cornelius Bee, a bookseller, and a price list of his for eighteen books.[96] Lord Bath also made two payments of ten pounds each for his books. The inventories of Tawstock list several maps, John Speed's *Scripture Genealogy*[97] and two globes.

The London accounts offer additional information. For example, they reveal that following the execution of Charles I the earl purchased a number of his books. There were also entries for having new clasps made. Other similar purchases include a book of the psalms by Dr King, a copy of the Act against delinquents, an untitled book by Bishop Davent,[98] William Camden's *Brittania*, 'History of Henry 8', 'History of the Civil Wars of France', 'Helmant Opusculum' and the works of John Taylor. Specialist items include Chinese porcelain such as

---

94. Three years later the house of the Portuguese Ambassador, a near neighbour of the Countess, was searched for goods belonging to an alleged Catholic and delinquent: Gomme & Norman, *Survey of London*, 13.
95. Kent Archives Office, U269/C275.
96. Kent Archives Office, U269/C293.
97. A copy of one of the editions of *The Genealogies recorded in the Sacred Scriptures*.
98. Possibly *St Paul's Epistle to the Colossians* (1631) by John Davenant, bishop of Salisbury 1621 to 1641.

the two 'beakers of china', two 'china band pots' and the two 'standers of China work'. Other luxury items include two red velvet night boxes, a silver clock and new crystal, two fine ivory combs, six dozen of sweet meat glasses, fruit dishes, an ebony perfumed box and four ounces of rose powder. There were also recurrent purchases of wash balls some of which were made with camphor. There were several entries for the purchase of spectacles, with their frames made of tortoise shell or silver, and one purchase of a tortoise shell spectacle case.

There were at least seven landscapes at Tawstock and there were many other references to works of art. A portrait of Lady Bath survives which has been attributed to Sir Anthony van Dyck or of his circle (Plate 6). In 1641 she paid him £30 for a portrait. This was in the year he returned to England and in which he died.[99] Lady Bath recorded that she gave an additional £10 for the frame. She also paid 'Lewie [?Levy] the painter' and one Mr Carwarthen[100] for copying pictures, possibly portraits. In 1640 the countess paid £12 to George Geldorp, a well-known portrait painter, for a copy of Lady Peterborough's portrait, although Lady Bath's brother considered Geldorp to be a poor artist,[101] and in 1649 the countess paid 'the picture drawer' fifty shillings for a copy of her mother's picture, presumably a portrait.

The principal sources of information on furniture are the three inventories of Tawstock. There was a substantial number of pieces. For example, in the Great Chamber were two dozen 'back' chairs with two 'great chairs of red wrought velvet' presumably for the earl and countess. In the chamber's withdrawing room were a further eight chairs and four stools all covered with red baize as well as a long cushion, couch, 'canopy of state' and Great Chair all of red velvet. The accounts include individual references such as the purchase of a great wicker chair and the payment 'to Seal the upholsterer for my own hangings and green cloth chairs and stools'. As well as furniture there are many references to coloured rugs and there were eleven Turkey-work carpets as well as a Persian carpet. In addition to the landscapes and Arras hangings at least one room had leather hangings.

An armourer was employed at Tawstock for cleaning the armour. Included within the countess' account book is a letter written in May 1639 from one Humphrey Peyton in Flanders to the earl regarding a consignment of arms. He mentions ten suits of armour as well as pistols and swords. This was probably the same armour noted in an inventory of June 1641 for Lincoln's Inn Fields and once again there was enough to suit ten men, with pieces noted for the head, breast, back, thighs and

---

99. *Dictionary of National Biography* (1992), III, 3054.
100. Possibly John Carwarden: *A Dictionary of British Miniature Painters* (1972), I, 197.
101. Fowler, *The Country House Poem*, 241, 242. This may have been a copy of a portrait of the countess by van Dyck now at Wilton House.

arms. There were also eleven pistols.[102] Interestingly, at the beginning
of the war it was suggested that the earl had a large cache of arms at
Tawstock.[103] The arms were surveyed again in February 1644; this
revealed muskets, coats of mail, swords, carbines, armour, pistols and
harquebuses. That year three cases of pistols and dragons were brought
from Oxford to Tawstock and in the accounts was the purchase of four
dozen arrows and a quiver.

## Private and public occasions

Many financial transactions in the accounts follow feast days of the year
such as Candlemas (2 February), Lady Day (25 March), Midsummer
(24 June), Lammas (1 August), Michaelmas (29 September) and Christmas. The accounts also recorded a multitude of social occasions and
events some of which were associated with these particular days. These
range from religious and seasonal occasions, such as Christmas, New
Year, Ash Wednesday, Lent and harvest celebrations, to the central
events of christenings, marriages and funerals which marked the pro-
gress of life. Everyday socialising in the form of visits to other homes
are seen in payments to their servants. This includes gifts at 'Mr Roll's
house', presumably Stevenstone near Great Torrington, 'amongst the
servants when my Lady dined there' and 'at Mr Mayors of Barnstaple
when my Lord and Lady dined there'. There was also largess noted
during the stay at Oxford. The aforementioned account of the earl's
funeral is the most detailed of all such references but there are some
others. There were entries regarding purchases of victuals for the
funeral meal, the ringing of knells and payments for making coffins and
the digging of graves. Baptisms were one of the most common references. Many entries were brief, for example a note of a payment of
one pound and ten shillings 'to the nurse & midwife at Henry Lynn's
christening'. In total there were seventeen baptisms where the earl and
countess spent more than fifty pounds in rewards to nurses and
midwives. Lady Bath's immediate family were involved on at least five
occasions and the earl was god-father to two children. Lady Bath acted
as god-mother on at least three occasions. Northampton, Westminster,
Mereworth and the Strand were the locations for some baptisms but
there were far fewer occasions in Devon: one was at Barnstaple and
another for the Giffard family of Brightley. They also travelled to
Cornwall for the baptism of the eldest son of Lord Mohun at Boconnoc
but their attendence was more likely coincidental given they were
escaping from the advancing Parliamentarian army. In one instance five
shillings were given as an act of charity to a midwife: the London
accounts noted it was to 'a poor Midwife came out of Ireland'. Finally,

---

102. There were further negotiations between them: Kent Archives Office, U269/C287.
103. Kent Archives Office, U269/C256/1.

Lady Bath gave fifteen shillings 'to the 3 children born at a birth'. It is not known whether she personally visited the triplets.

More descriptive information comes from Lady Bath's correspondence: in 1651 several letters were received from her sister Elizabeth in Oxfordshire regarding the baptism of her 'little cakebread'. The child was later named after the earl who acted as godfather.[104] The christening feast was probably representative of others Lady Bath attended. Her sister wrote that nearly all she invited had come:

> so that my dining room was filled from one end to the other all with the best sort of company ... the Ladies have since been a gossiping with me, with cakes of their own making where was much variety but all very good, so that twas hard to judge of the best housewife by her handiwork. I praise God I am very well yet & never had a more kindly nor better childbed than this.[105]

Scattered throughout all of the accounts are references to Christmas and New Year celebrations. Lady Bath's mother, the countess of Westmorland, vigorously celebrated the season and it appears this was continued at Tawstock.[106] In 1643 Pollard purchased at Bristol a great range of items for Christmas: this included barrels of wine, fruit (raisins, currants, prunes), spices (cinnamon, ginger, mace), olives, sugar, almonds, nuts, licorice, candy and syrup of mulberries. The London accounts show that boxes were given to servants and others at Christmas. There was a gift of £20 given to the King on 1 January 1640 and the following year the countess gave money to both the King's and Prince's drummers. In 1642 money was again given to the King's and Prince's drummers, the Queen's foot-men, another gift to the King and to the porters at Whitehall. Money was also disbursed in the presence chamber.

Tawstock was a centre of social activity. The bowling green was used in the summer months to entertain visitors and on at least one known occasion the parish was challenged to a game. There were recurrent entries for money spent to the earl and countess there playing bowls. The ladies also played troll madam outside presumably on the green. As mentioned earlier the countess regularly played cards, dice and tablemen. Lady Bath's interest in games may also have been responsible for the contents of the parlour. In it there was a billiard board with two sticks, three 'bowls', presumably balls, and a pin. There was also a pair of tables, probably used for the two chess boards with sets of men, and a 'goose board'. It may have been the same chessboard and set which was recorded in 1655 in her closet. At the time of the death of Lady Anne the parlour also contained goose and billiard boards. The London

104. Kent Archives Office, U269/C273.
105. Kent Archives Office, U269/C273.
106. Kent Archives Office, U269/C275.

accounts have several references to shuttle cocks, battledores with a box and a 'set of box table men for the hall'.

Hunting was another activity. Tawstock had a dog kennel by 1644 where Lord Bath kept some dogs, possibly including lurchers, for which presumably the purchase of 'dog meat' was intended. The estate acquired some hounds, notably 'old Caesar', from the Earl of Westmorland for hunting hares.[107] In 1639 the earl was given a hawk by Lord Chichester and twelve years later Lady Bath noted the payment for a 'male pillion [and] 2 lines & furniture for hunting'.

The accounts show a clear interest in music. When the earl and countess arrived in 1639 there were a number of musical instruments already at Tawstock including an organ and virginal, a chest of viols, a great double base viol, a violin and an Irish harp. These were all kept on the staircase and there was another organ in the Great Chamber. One bedroom was called 'The Musicians Room'. A new organ was acquired in 1641. Seven pounds were given 'to one Dallam an organist for work to be done', in the following year an organ, or part of one, was brought from Gloucester to Tawstock and an organist was employed to play it. There was a visit that Spring by Mr Lugg, the cathedral organist, of whom it was reported that he

> hath been here to try the goodness of the new organ and gives it a very good commendation to the sweetest that ever he played upon and that Mr Dolham hath well deserved 40s more according to the articles of agreement.

Lord Bath and the organist disputed the terms of the agreement but the full payment was eventually made.[108]

There were later purchases of a little pair of organs, viol, harpsicord, theorbo, wind instrument and a guitar. A bugle was acquired for the expressed purpose of sounding at the earl's arrival and departure at Tawstock. There were a few entries for payments to visiting musicians such as Sir Bevil Grenville's fiddlers and Prince Charles' musicians. Fiddlers played in August 1648, possibly at the end of the harvest. In 1640 it cost seven shillings and six pence for teaching a servant to play the fiddle, one pound was paid for a month's guitar lessons and another servant was taught by 'Moulins' over the course of ten weeks how to sing. Finally, in 1640 'Mr Hazard the dancer' was given four pounds, presumably for teaching dance.

## Transportation

On every page of the accounts there is the movement of goods, money and people by road or water. For the London accounts there were references to journeys by river to Westminster and by coach or sedan

---

107. Kent Archives Office, U269/C269.
108. Kent Archives Office, U269/C276.

throughout the city. A boat was maintained at Tawstock and the earl and countess travelled by river to such nearby places as Bishop's Tawton, Barnstaple, Appledore, Fremington and Heanton Punchardon. One of the most common references was the payment to carriers for packets, letters, parcels and other items for sending to Tawstock and other places. Roger Thorne was one commonly-used carrier and there was also a 'post boy'. The journey between north Devon and Lincoln's Inn Fields could be an elaborate affair: in 1648 twenty persons travelled with 18 horses, in the following year it was 23 servants and 21 horses and in 1651 20 horses with some 28 to 30 persons. Payments were frequent for 'horsemeat' and other stabling costs including at establishments such as the Bell at Barnstaple. In 1641 the 'Great Coach' was built by one Bowdler, or Bongler, for nearly £500. This included its construction, painting, furnishing such as the velvet, fringe, curtains and linings, and the liveries for the coachman, four footmen and a page. In addition, a new coach-house was built which cost more than £1000.

Horses were continually being purchased and some were acquired as heriots. Lady Bath compiled a list of nearly fifty horses which were kept at Lincoln's Inn Fields and Tawstock. Many were recorded by their particular attribute, such as their colour (a gray horse), but many were listed by name (Turk, Gundemoor, Loggerhead or Fiddle Faddle). She noted the horses' purchase price and which ones were lost during the war such as Pudding who was taken by the Barnstaple 'rebels'.[109]

## Medical care

Medicinal items such as diet drinks, cordial waters, 'new drugs for my Lord' and spirits of caraway and balm appear throughout the accounts. In her own book Lady Bath noted more than £110 was paid to some four apothecaries. Almost half that amount was spent in the London accounts and although there were few such entries for Tawstock the payments still amounted to more than twenty-seven pounds. Two London accounts were particularly detailed. In 1650 there were payments to an apothecary and physician following the five-week illness of Randall Payton, a young boy who was maintained by the countess. Earlier that year one Mrs Norton was ill for five months for which the London steward initially disbursed £39 13s 2½d. He also paid £11 to her physicians, £2 10s to her surgeons and £16 15s 6d to her apothecaries. There was also a horse-litter to carry her to Tawstock, which cost £15, and £6 8s 2d was given to the men who accompanied her.

Altogether in the accounts there were payments to more than a dozen apothecaries and there also recurrent entries for physicians, surgeons, druggists and bone-setters. A letter from Thomas Pollard to the

---

109. See also Kent Archives Office, U269/C277.

Countess in 1642 shows that he questioned several apothecaries regarding the cost of spirit of clary. Clary, *Salvia sclarea*, was introduced into England in the middle of the sixteenth century and among its medicinal uses was the treatment of the eyes and in women's ailments.[110] It was eventually suggested that the spirit was obtained from one Mrs Porter who could purchase it from a friend.[111]

Occasionally the accounts have references to the nature of the medical problem such as in 1648 for 'Doctor Chichester the 7th of December when he came to my Lord about his arm' or when servants were tended for having small pox. In 1640 Lady Bath was unwell on a return journey to Lincoln's Inn Fields: 'I began my journey on a Friday about the 20 of October & in a litter having had a dangerous sickness'. She also noted several visits to Bath. In 1649 the earl and countess spent a considerable amount of time there. There were payments recorded to the sergeant at one of the baths, an apothecary, one Doctor Brewer and to the pumper and his wife.

There are also two lengthy accounts of medicine for 1639 when the earl and countess were first married and again in 1654, a few months before Lord Bath's death (appendix 11 & 12). The earlier list is mainly of laxatives, clisters and fomentations supplied by Culpepper Clapham. Many items were written in Latin and one in Arabic. In contrast, the second list is more concerned with purging potions, compounds and emulsions but mostly 'aposeines'.

Several letters refer to the deaths of servants through disease, in one instance the coachman 'lay speechless all the last night & yet recovered & seemed pretty well & hearty till about 4 this afternoon since which time he is dead, tis much to be feared that it is the plague'.[112] After one servant 'had his time set beyond which he might not pass' the countess was consoled with 'I doubt not but his soul is in bliss and happiness, having made the last change of earth for heaven'.[113] There is also one reference to the death of a servant's 'little untimely born babe'.[114]

In addition to human medical care the accounts have recurring entries for the care of animals, some references to simply curing animals but more notably for dressing sheep and cows, bleeding and drenching of horses and curing farcy. Occasionally a particular animal is mentioned such as a payment in 1643 for 'the cutting of White Flank' or the following year when the black colt was castrated.

---

110. It was also called Clear Eye and Eyebright: Grieves, *A Modern Herbal; The Medicinal, Culinary, Cosmetic and Economic Properties, Cultivation and Folklore of Herbs, Grasses, Fungi, Shrubs and Trees with all their modern scientific uses* (1985), 203–5.
111. Kent Archives Office, U269/C275.
112. Kent Archives Office, U269/C273.
113. Kent Archives Office, U269/C276.
114. Kent Archives Office, U269/C278.

## Clothing

Articles of clothing appear frequently throughout the accounts. Among the entries are references to the spinning, making and mending of garments for servants including suits, cloaks and stockings. The colour and type of cloth was often mentioned including silk, kersey, mohair and linen. One of the most common entries was for children's apparel, particularly for their stockings and shoes. There were also many purchases of cloth for uncertain purposes as well as for lace, buttons, pins and other items of haberdashery. Occasionally the recipient was identified such as the silk and buttons paid for the footmen in February 1644. This was particularly noted in regards to the countess, for example there are payments for making handkerchiefs, silk mohair and in 1640 there was a sable fur purchased for her neck. Entire suits of clothes were noted for the earl and even several beaver pelts.

## Gardening

Plate 1 is a detail from an eighteenth-century oil painting of Tawstock which is the only known representation of the older house. This shows a large formal garden directly in front of the house some one hundred years or so after the death of the earl. In 1600 John Hooker made no mention of a garden there but only of the deer park and this creates some uncertainty regarding the development of the garden by the 1640s. It seems unlikely that Lord and Lady Bath would not have created or maintained a garden suitable for a noble house.

The accounts provide occasional details to show some garden activity. It is clear that several gardeners were employed and that the garden walks were fairly extensive given the number of boatloads of sand and gravel and that lime ashes were put down. There was also a bowling green where the earl and countess appear to have spent a considerable amount of time. A roller was purchased for keeping the grass in the green. In June 1650 the earl wrote to his wife that:

> there was a challenge at bowls made by the parish after they saw two of the best bowl[?er]s were gone; four of a side but it was entertained and played yesterday, though a wet day, and the parish shamefully beaten for they won but nine of the twenty-one ...[115]

Garden seeds were purchased, some of which were sent down from Lincoln's Inn Fields, and at least one box of 'flower plants'. Trees, presumably saplings or grafts, were also transported from London. Other known purchases were garden flower pots, garden baskets and a watering pot. In 1649 a gardener brought 'barberys' possibly plants or even fruit.

---

115. Kent Archives Office, U269/C276.

The accounts also show leather was purchased as tree supports. These were presumably fruit trees although they may have been ornamental. In 1644 a new orchard of more than two acres was planted in which there were 268 apple, pear, quince and damson trees 'set in perfect order'. In the following year 73 apricot, peach, cherry and nectarine trees were planted against the walls. The walls were slated and tiled. More than three pounds was paid for young trees in December 1645. Apple, cherry and pear trees were common throughout Devon but the others, particularly the apricot, nectarine and peach trees, may have been unusual although similar trees were planted by Sir Courtenay Pole at Shute in east Devon in the 1650s and 1660s. Unlike for the trees at Shute, where there were French Longstay apples, Katherine pears and May cherries, there is no information regarding the particular varieties. Many of the Shute trees were also planted against the walls.[116]

Two letters from Edward Wyot appear to demonstrate that the countess was interested in general agricultural matters and in these particular trees. He wrote on 21 April 1642 that:

> your businesses here in my opinion go well, your fair store of wheat in the ground looks very well which is now in weeding. Your pear trees, cherry trees, plum trees and many apple trees put forth their blossoms very well and kindly. And although the air here hath these last two months been somewhat cold, and tender, yet there falling competent showers of rain, hath done much good and you are like to have a fruitful year of all things. Corn in the market is a little value of its former price, but cattle and sheep are dear and consequently butchers' meat.

The following month he reported that:

> this year for corn and grass and garden herbs is very like to be fruitful, some pears and pretty store of apples are like to be, but few cherries or plums being much blasted with a dry easterly wind, but very lately we have had a good and kindly rain, corn and pulse with victuals in the market are at reasonable prices.[117]

Six years later it was related that there was a good crop of cherries, nectarines and peaches at Tawstock.[118]

A garden was kept at Lincoln's Inn Fields and the accounts show the purchase of a gardener's spade, roller, seeds and '4 dozen of roots of flowers'. A New Year's a gift of one pound was given to John Tradescant the younger, the celebrated Royal gardener. There was also a

---

116. Todd Gray, 'Their idols of worship: fruit trees and the walled garden in early modern Devon', Steven Pugsley (ed.), *Devon Gardens: an historical survey* (Stroud, 1994), 33–7.
117. Kent Archives Office, U269/C278–9.
118. Kent Archives Office, U269/C278.

payment of eleven shillings for 'drawing 5 garden plots by a gardener' but it is not clear whether this was intended for London or Tawstock.

An undated letter to Lady Bath from Dorothy Fane, her sister-in-law, demonstrates further interest in gardening. She informed the countess:

> about a fortnight since Mr Fane received a letter from your Ladyship wherein your ladyship desired to know when the *Mekas* were ripe which I could not possibly answer till I went to the Gentlewoman that gave me one of them the last year which I did as soon as she came home from London for there never was any of them in Kent nor England that I can hear of till she had some seeds given her by a [?]sraulter and I believe your Ladyship is now satisfied that it is nothing like a pompian nor any of that kind. The Gentlewoman tells me that when the stalk close to the *Meca* is so hard that the nail of ones thumb will not enter and that the *Meca* is of colour between a deep lemon and an orange then they are ripe and must be cut with so much stalk as one can hold them by and they must be set on a shelf either in the kitchen or else in some other room where there is fire kept but not too near the fire and they must be set one by one but not touch nor lie one above another ...[119]

The pompian was probably a pumpkin but the identity of the 'mekas' is not clear. It could be a member of the gourd or melon family.[120] Lady Bath may have had culinary or medicinal interests in the plant.

## The Civil War and the Commonwealth

It is not surprising that the war greatly disrupted Lord Bath's household administration given that he was Devon's leading Royalist. His wartime activities have been given considerable attention by historians interested in Devon[121] and the earl is principally remembered for his role at the beginning of the conflict.[122] One historian has even claimed that the earl had no subsequent role in Devon's affairs.[123] Lord Bath led

---

119. Kent Archives Office, U269/C273.
120. Curiously, the medieval name for a poppy was Mecos: Tony Hunt, *Plant Names of Medieval England* (Cambridge, 1989), 172.
121. See Richard W. Cotton, *Barnstaple and the northern part of Devonshire during the Great Civil War, 1642–1646* (1889); E.A. Andriette, *Devon and Exeter in the Civil War* (Newton Abbot, 1971); I.R. Palfrey, 'Devon and the Outbreak of the English Civil War, 1642–43', *Southern History*, 10 (1988), 29–46; Mark Stoyle, *Loyalty and Locality* (Exeter, 1994) and *From Deliverance to Destruction* (Exeter, 1996).
122. The earl's subsequent lack of influence is reflected by work on Devon in the middle of the war: Stephen K. Roberts, *Recovery and Restoration in an English County: Devon Local Adminstration, 1646–1670* (Exeter, 1985); John Wardman, *The Forgotten Battle; Torrington 1646* (Torrington, 1995).
123. Cotton, *Barnstaple*, 71.

the King's cause in August 1642 with his arrival in Devon with the Commission of Array, the means by which the Crown hoped to hold the militia. It was thought that he then had 'notable power and interest' in the county.[124] The earl attempted to rally the county with a visit to the Exeter Assizes from 9 to 12 August. Richard Pollard was sent ahead to make arrangements and presumably gather news. Lord Bath stayed at a house belonging to Joseph Hall, son of the former bishop, and was informed that there was a 'great expectation' of his visit.[125] He was met with politeness but also a marked lack of enthusiasm and on his departure the city was largely left to the Parliamentarians.[126] The lack of support was even more publicly expressed at the nearby market town of South Molton where he had a humiliating reception from the local inhabitants. It was reported that Lord Bath took shelter to escape a mob which gathered in protest at his visit. Among them was a butcher's wife who threw rams' horns and the crowd pelted the earl with stones as he left.[127] Lord Bath would have been wise to have consulted *A View of Devonshire in 1630* written by Thomas Westcote with whom the previous earl was on friendly terms. Westcote warned of the behaviour of the inhabitants of one of the earl's own manors near South Molton who could rise 'all up like a nest of wasps'. He cautioned 'it is folly for a wise man to anger a multitude causelessly'.[128]

Lord Bath's activities were cut short in Devon by his arrest at Tawstock less than two months after his arrival. He was immediately sent to London and imprisoned in the Tower. The earl solicited a number of individuals, including the King, for his release.[129] Lady Bath was also active and among others she wrote to the Queen to assure her of their loyalty. Their machinations to obtain his release must have made the gaolers suspicious: he was searched one morning in bed and Lady Bath's letters were confiscated. Lord Bath argued that a husband's correspondence with his wife was privileged.[130] He was freed the following August on the condition he travelled abroad and did not serve the Crown. Nevertheless, the earl wrote to the King two days afterwards[131] and proceeded to the court at Oxford. Only a few months later he was made Lord Privy Seal.[132] Irrespective of whether Clarendon was right regarding the earl's lack of enthusiasm for the Crown, it is clear what his perceived crimes were against Parliament. In December 1648 a

124. Clarendon, *History*, I, 528.
125. Kent Archives Office, U269/C276.
126. Stoyle, *Deliverance*, 59–61.
127. Cotton, *Barnstaple*, 66–9.
128. Thomas Westcote, *A View of Devonshire in 1630*, 291. The manor of Newland lies some eight miles on the main road from Barnstaple to Tiverton.
129. Kent Archives Office, U269/C294.
130. Kent Archives Office, U269/C294.
131. Kent Archives Office, U269/C294.
132. Kent Archives Office, U269/O261/3.

letter from the Standing Committee of Devon, which was responsible for the Articles of Delinquency, listed five principal charges: these were that he deserted the House of Lords and took up arms against Parliament, actively worked for the Commission of Array in Devon and Cornwall, lent money to the King, sat in the King's assembly at Oxford and was chosen Lord Privy Seal.[133]

Included within the accounts is the earl's notes of events at Oxford in 1644 and a list of the money owed by the Crown from 1639 to 1644. Perhaps the principal record is Lady Bath's account showing the movements from 1639 to 1644 of herself and her husband. The purpose is ambiguous; it may have been written for personal or political reasons. It does not appear to have been composed at one sitting. Among the events she noted was the earl's arrest at Tawstock at eleven o'clock at night by 'the rebels'.[134] She recorded his release from the Tower as 'we got from them the 4th of August & so came to Oxford'. Lady Bath also noted their travels in the summer of 1644 to the far west of Cornwall fleeing the advancing Parliamentarian army. The earl claimed he was slandered for his departure from Tawstock and petitioned the King for redress[135] but the reasons he gave, that he feared for his safety, differed from at least one other account: he also claimed he came to view his estates of which he had received 'an ill account'.[136]

The Civil War dominates the household papers with continual references to the course of the war. One of the first is the expenditure for the ill-fated meal at South Molton in September 1642 where he sent his cook to prepare a meal of venison.[137] There were many references to the consequences of local skirmishes: for example, there is an entry for 1649 'for going in the night to fetch my Lord's boat the soldiers carried away'. There are details on the provisioning for Prince Charles' visit to Tawstock in June 1645 in which a cook from Barnstaple was brought in, payments were made to the Prince's own cooks as well as to his musicians, and special provisions were purchased including lobsters, artichokes, raspberries and masards, the specialty fruit of North Devon. Tawstock was occupied by both sides and there was money spent on cleaning the house when the Parliamentarian soldiers left. Letters were received and sent to many correspondents regarding the course of the war: for example, the King's messenger arrived on 2 January 1644 at Tawstock with a letter. There were also many entries regarding the movement of the household servants during the war particularly for travelling expenses to Exeter, Cornwall, Oxford, London and York. When the servants evacuated Lincoln's Inn Fields in June 1642 they

---

133. Kent Archives Office, U269/O262.
134. Kent Archives Office, U269/C294. The earl wrote that it happened at 10 o'clock.
135. Kent Archives Office, U269/C280. A copy of his petition and the response of Charles I survives among several other papers.
136. Kent Archives Office, U269/C294.
137. Cotton, *Barnstaple*, 67.

took the plate and other valuables with them to Devon. It was suggested that they should travel lightly, with only the most valuable objects, in order to avoid suspicion.[138]

It would be logical to assume that the servants supported the earl and countess in the conflict but there is little evidence regarding their views: one exception is the case of Tom Bold, a servant of Lady Bath. He joined the Life Guards and the earl wrote that he 'much desired to see him in that habit'.[139] Anxiety was certainly expressed in a number of letters. In May 1642 Edward Wyot wrote 'we long to hear of good news from our King and Parliament fearing things there are not handled so successively as they ought to be' and also that month Richard Pollard wrote with political news and that 'our country is in great fears what will become of them, the times are so troublesome. God in his good time (I hope) will help all'.[140]

Following the war's end there were recurring payments for compounding within both the Lincoln's Inn Fields and Tawstock accounts. Appendix 8 comprises the Sequestrator's inventory of Tawstock in November 1648. Perhaps it is not surprising that there are few strong indications of personal loyalty: after all, the accounts moved between north Devon and London on several occasions and the houses were occupied by both sides. Nevertheless, there are some intriguing references: there is a payment for the 'K. of S[?cotland]. picture', another for a 'model of Prince Charles in gold' and in 1652 the countess brought 'the King of Spain's bible' from Lincoln's Inn Fields to Tawstock. Relations apparently were friendly with both the Spanish and French ambassadors. Evidence which was deemed to be incriminating should have been destroyed so the lack of it should not be unexpected.

In October 1643, several months following his release from the Tower, Lord Bath's disenchantment with his neighbours is evident by his comment to his wife 'remember me to as many in that country as you think worth the remembering'.[141] It seems unlikely that the earl and his neighbours, particularly at Barnstaple, managed to restore good relations by the time of his death in 1654, a few years after the king's execution. Perhaps this is not surprising given that Lord Bath was raised in Ireland and remained more familiar with London than he ever was with Devon. This appears to have been in great contrast with Lady Bath: notwithstanding her childhood in Northamptonshire and Kent, and obvious attachment to London, she seemingly regarded Tawstock as her home. She managed to survive through to the Restoration to live

---

138. Kent Archives Office, U269/C277–8.
139. Kent Archives Office, U269/C267/17.
140. Kent Archives Office, U269/C278 & C276. These comments were echoed by many of the correspondents: for example see U269/C278 in which William Lynn wrote on 4 June 1642 'I pray God send a good accord betwitx his Majesty and the Parliament that our fears may be removed'.
141. Kent Archives Office, U269/C267/14.

nearly thirty years after Lord Bath. Her retention of the title Countess of Bath and insistence on being buried in Tawstock indicates a strong affection and fondness for her 'very fair house' in north Devon. A Devon base far from the Court may have been inconvenient to Lord Bath but for his wife it may ultimately have proved her good fortune.

It is likely that Lady Bath and her household would have been astonished, if not amused or even indignant, to think that their accounts and personal papers would be printed and used by historians more than three hundreds years after their deaths. While the original purpose of the papers is remarkably different from the use made of them by historians, and the papers' very survival is a curious story, the accounts provide rare insights into Lady Bath's life and of many others in London and north Devon.

# EDITORIAL CONVENTIONS

Words which have evidently been omitted appear within square brackets. Uncertain transcriptions are preceded by a question mark enclosed within square brackets or a conjectural reading follows in italics within square brackets. Illegible words are indicated as such within square brackets. All Latin words appear italicized and translated into English with the exception of the medicinal items in Appendices 11 & 12. Modern spelling has normally been substituted except for the copy of John Donne's poem 'Love's Diet' and obsolete versions of words (or those which are unfamiliar or obscure) have been retained with a note in the glossary such as glister for clyster. Some punctuation has been modernized but capitals largely remain as in the text. Common abbreviations and contractions have normally been extended except ampersands and Christian names. The title Miss has been retained instead of Mistress which may have been originally intended. Christian names have normally been modernized except with the notable instance of 'Willy' where in some cases it uncertain whether it is an abbreviation or actual nickname. All surnames have been printed as in the original. Place names also appear as in the text with unusual spellings italicized and the modern form is noted within square brackets in the first instance. Also, ½ has been substituted for the Greek *ob* and the Latin *di*, ¼ for *q*(*uadrans*). The form of the numerals appear as in the original except that Arabic has been substituted for Roman. The form '&c' has been retained in preference to the modern use of 'etc.'. Page numbers were supplied to the original documents for the purpose of this edition in order to facilitate future identification of pages. The numbers are supplied within square brackets in the text. Distinct and separate sections, such as the weekly Tawstock accounts, have been presented in paragraphs rather than in singular lines. All marginalia precede two spaces before the closest line.

# ACKNOWLEDGEMENTS

During the course of the preparation of this volume a great many debts of various kinds were incurred. First of all, on behalf of the Society and myself I would like to thank the Centre for Kentish Studies, Gavin Graham Gallery, Sothebys and Revd John Carvosso for permission to print illustrations. The cover illustration ('A Bill of Fare'—Roxburghe Ballads I.18–19, STC 19270) appears by permission of the British Library. All documents are published with permission of the Centre for Kentish Studies on the understanding that copyright remains with the owner of the original records.

I would like to warmly thank Mrs Margery Rowe for first interesting me in household accounts and for her guidance as General Editor. Revd John Carvosso and James Coulter were particularly helpful with questions regarding Tawstock parish and Ian Ritchie of the National Portrait Gallery must be thanked for his assistance with locating portraits of the Bourchier family. I would also like to thank John Draisey and his staff in the Devon Record Office, Tim Wormleighton in the North Devon Record Office and the staff of the Kent Archives Office particularly Michael Carter. I am also grateful to Tim Groom of the Staffordshire Record Office for his help with Lady Rachel Newport's correspondence. As with Part One, I would like to thank Sue Roulliard for the care with which the maps and cover were accomplished and Colin Bakké for his meticulous work with typesetting.

# THE BOURCHIER FAMILY

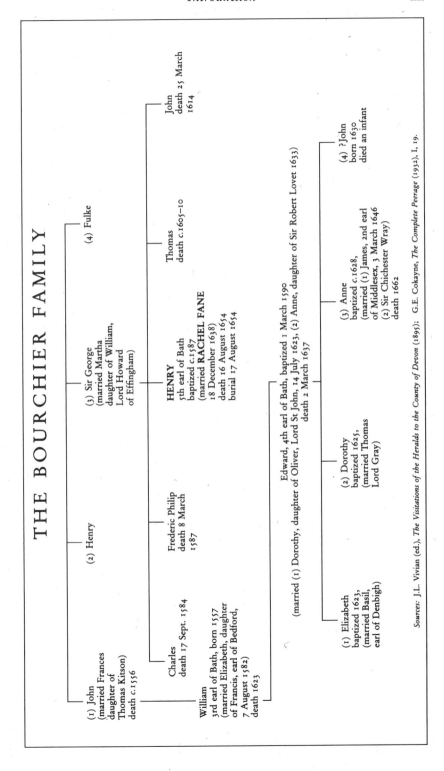

(1) John
(married Frances
daughter of
Thomas Kitson)
death c.1556

(2) Henry

(3) Sir George
(married Martha
daughter of William,
Lord Howard
of Effingham)

(4) Fulke

Charles
death 17 Sept. 1584

Frederic Philip
death 8 March
1587

John
death 25 March
1614

William
3rd earl of Bath, born 1557
(married Elizabeth, daughter
of Francis, earl of Bedford,
7 August 1582)
death 1623

**HENRY**
5th earl of Bath
baptized c.1587
(married **RACHEL FANE**
18 December 1638)
death 16 August 1654
burial 17 August 1654

Thomas
death c.1605–10

Edward, 4th earl of Bath, baptized 1 March 1590
death 2 March 1637

(married (1) Dorothy, daughter of Oliver, Lord St John, 14 July 1623; (2) Anne, daughter of Sir Robert Lovet 1633)

(1) Elizabeth
baptized 1623,
(married Basil,
earl of Denbigh)

(2) Dorothy
baptized 1625,
(married Thomas
Lord Gray)

(3) Anne
baptized c.1628,
(married (1) James, 2nd earl
of Middlesex, 3 March 1646
(2) Sir Chichester Wray)
death 1662

(4) ?John
born 1630
died an infant

*Sources*: J.L. Vivian (ed.), *The Visitations of the Heralds to the County of Devon* (1895); G.E. Cokayne, *The Complete Peerage* (1932), I, 19.

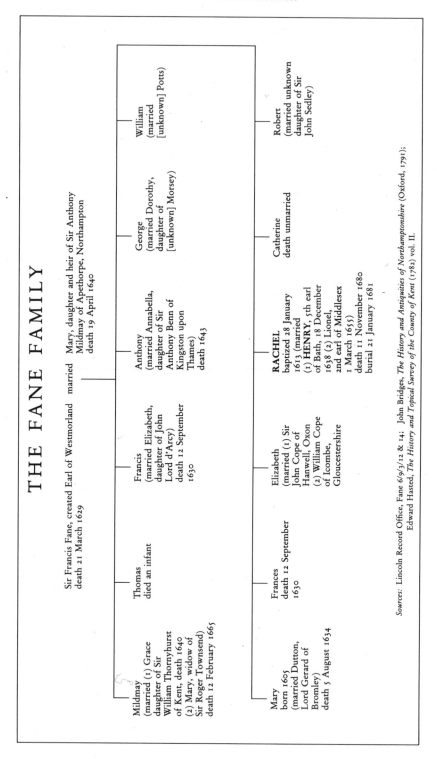

# THE FANE FAMILY

Sir Francis Fane, created Earl of Westmorland    married    Mary, daughter and heir of Sir Anthony
death 21 March 1629                          Mildmay of Apethorpe, Northampton
death 19 April 1640

Mildmay
(married (1) Grace
daughter of Sir
William Thornyhurst
of Kent, death 1640
(2) Mary, widow of
Sir Roger Townsend)
death 12 February 1665

Thomas
died an infant

Francis
(married Elizabeth,
daughter of John
Lord d'Arcy)
death 12 September
1650

Anthony
(married Annabella,
daughter of Sir
Anthony Benn of
Kingston upon
Thames)
death 1643

George
(married Dorothy,
daughter of
[unknown] Morsey)

William
(married
[unknown] Potts)

Mary
born 1605
(married Dutton,
Lord Gerard of
Bromley)
death 5 August 1634

Frances
death 12 September
1630

Elizabeth
(married (1) Sir
John Cope of
Hanwell, Oxon
(2) William Cope
of Icombe,
Gloucestershire

**RACHEL**
baptized 28 January
1613 (married
(1) **HENRY**, 5th earl
of Bath, 18 December
1638 (2) Lionel,
2nd earl of Middlesex
1 March 1655)
death 11 November 1680
burial 21 January 1681

Catherine
death unmarried

Robert
(married unknown
daughter of Sir
John Sedley)

*Sources:* Lincoln Record Office, Fane 6/9/3/12 & 14; John Bridges, *The History and Antiquities of Northamptonshire* (Oxford, 1791); Edward Hasted, *The History and Topical Survey of the County of Kent* (1782) vol. II.

# Tawstock Household Accounts

## Expenses, 1637–1639

### KENT ARCHIVES OFFICE, U269/A520/4

*The book measures 7¾″ by 11½″ with a paper cover. It is headed 'Disbursements' on the front and back covers. Also on the back, in a later hand, possibly eighteenth-century, is '1638 & 1639, old accounts &c of no value'.*

[p. 1] Tawstock House A book of disbursements for housekeeping & other provision for the service of the right honourable Henry earl of Bath begun the 9th of March 1638 by me Wil: Paget

b[ill]. *First* paid to the gardeners, fellers of wood, carpenters, masons & others as appears by several weekly bills from the 2nd of Febr. 1638 until the 23th of the same £06 5s 5d; b. Item for 14 muttons bought 12 8 6; Item to William Gibbons for 6 weeks' work in the hopyards 01 10 0; Item to Walter Vimbles for the like 01 7 0; Item for seacoal 1 weigh 01 10 0; Item for the bringing of a runlet of wine given by Mr Newton 00 2 0; b. Item for beer to Mr William Baker 06 18 0; Item for 46 pounds of tallow at 4½ per pound 00 17 3; b. Item for fresh cates 16 Mar. 02 12 10; The sum hitherto is £33 11s 0od ex.

b. Item paid to the workmen abovementioned from the 2nd of March until the 30th of the same as likewise appears by the weekly bills £07 0s 5d; b. Item for fresh cates &c 23 Mar. 03 14 10; Item for wheat, oats & other provision for the household & the stables 04 4 2; b. Item for nets, slips of thread &c for the fishing 03 1 4; Item for ½ of a kintal of Canada fish 00 8 6; Item for ¾ of *Newland* [Newfoundland] fish 00 11 0; b. Item for fresh cates 30 March 1639 01 17 11; b. Item to Huxtable the smith for shoeing the horses 00 19 9; b. Item to Hugh Coombe upon his bill 6 Apr. 1639 04 7 11; b. Item more to him 13 Apr. for the like 02 10 10; b. Item for fresh cates 5 Apr. 01 4 0; b. Item to John Willims the plumber for the quarter ending 25 Mar. 1639 01 13 4
The sum is £31 14 0d ex.

[p. 4] Item for oats & malt for the horses £00 14s 4d; Item for wine fetched at Mr Skitches 00 15 6; Item for 20 pound of sugar at 16d ½ per pound 01 7 6; Item for wick yarn 2 pound ½ 00 1 11; b. Item to Hugh Combe for the week ended the 20th of April 03 3 5; b. Item more to him upon his bill of the 27th of Apr. 11 15 5; b. Item paid the servants board wages for 3 weeks ended the said 27th of Apr. 07 4 0; b. Item more to Hugh Combe upon his bill for barley & oats bought 12 4 1; b. Item paid to him upon his bill for the week ended 4 May 09 0 11; b. Item upon his bill ended 11 May 04 1 4; b. Item paid the servants board wages for the

said 2 weeks 04 16 0; b. Item for necessaries bought for the dairy 00 16 8;
Item for cattle bought 4 May 26 17 4; b. Item in necessaries for the fishing
00 13 1; Item for carriage of sea coal and beer from *Barns'* 00 4 0
The sum hitherto is £83 15s 6d

b. Item paid to Hugh Combe his week bill ended the 18th of May 1639
£04 17s 0d; b. Item the servants diet the same week 02 8 0; b. Item for
20 sheep bought then 11 0 0; b. Item for 40 bushels of oats to make malt
04 0 0; b. Item paid to Hugh Combe upon his week bill ended the 25th of
May 03 14 9; b. Item to him upon his bill ended 2 *June* 06 2 4; b. Item
upon the like bill 9 *June* 06 17 9; b. Item upon the like bill 15 *June* 04 1 6;
b. Item upon the like bill 22 *June* 07 11 10; b. Item upon the like bill
29 *June* 03 4 2
Sum is £53 17s 4d

[p. 5]   b. Item paid the servants board wages for 6 weeks ended the 29th
of June £14 8s 0d; b. Item paid to Hugh Combe upon his week bill ended
the 2nd of July 01 8 0; b. Item to him upon his bill 9 July 00 12 5; b. Item
paid to the glasier upon his bill then 01 11 8; b. Item to Huxtable the
smith upon his bill for shoeing & iron work 02 9 4; b. Item to the
armourer for the quarter ended at Midsummer 1639 00 6 6; b. Item for
2 new kiddles, clothing & thread 00 18 7; b. Item more for oats bought
05 3 6; b. Item for oxen & sheep bought 39 1 8
Sum is £65 19s 8d ex.

b. Item paid to Humfry Gribble for 2 bedsteads, 2 field beds, bedcords
and staples £03 0s 0d; b. Item paid to the smith of Pilton upon his bill
00 14 6; b. Item paid to Huxtable the smith for shoeing &c from the 30th
of May until the 13th of July 00 17 4; b. Item to Mr William Verckill for
vessel timber 01 15 0; b. Item paid to Hugh Combe his week bill ended
the 6th of July 06 17 8; b. Item paid more unto him for wheat, beef and
other other [sic] necessaries bought 04 3 0; b. Item paid more to him upon
his week bill for the workmen 13 July 10 8 3; b. Item paid the servants
board wages for 2 weeks ended the 13th of July 04 16 0; b. Item paid to
the armourer for cleansing of andirons &c 00 5 6; Item paid for [blank]
weigh of sea coal brought in June 1639 07 14 0; Item paid to Mr Sparrow
of Tiverton which he disbursed to Loring the wagoner for goods brought
from London 13 8 6
sum 53 19 9 ex.

[p. 6]   Item paid more for bringing the said goods on horseback from
Tiverton £03 10s 0d; Mr Coys b[ill]. Item delivered to Mr Coys steward of
his Lordship's household 30 July 1639 £20 0 0; 13 1 0 Item paid to Chr:
Southwood for 20 wethers bought at *Bannton* & for sheering of them
13 1 0; Item paid to Goodman Loosemore for colouring the withdrawing
room 00 8 0; b. Item paid to Hugh Combe upon his week bill ended the
20th of July 1639 07 13 2; b. Item paid to the Cater for the same week
04 7 4; b. Item paid to Mr Holmes of *Exceter* for nails, bullion and
burnish 02 17 0; W. Item paid to Mr Philips for Mr Wright 06 0 0;
W. Item paid more to Mr Wright at Larkbeare 02 0 0; Item given to
Mr Hayne's messenger 5 Aug. 00 5 0; b. Item to Peter Flaye for the
pasturing of a horse and dressing of him 01 15 0; Item paid for a p[air] of

gold weights oo 5 6; Item paid to Loosemore for mending the wind instrument oo 15 o; b. Mr Coys. Item delivered to Mr Coys the 5th, 13th & 19th of August 1639 60 o o; Item for sending a packet to *Exceter* from *Barum* to the postmaster oo 2 6; Item for letters sent from the postmaster by Mr Roger Skinner at several times oo 3 6; Item delivered to John White of *Ilfarcombe* the 15th of September 1639 by my Lord's appointment 20 o o; b. Item paid to Humphrey Gribble for carpenters work as by his bill appears o2 8 o; Item paid to William Verman for 5 weigh & ½ of sea coal 2 October 1639 08 5 o; Mr Coy's. Item delivered to Mr Coys the 27th of August, the 9th, the 15th & 26th of September 1639 130 o o; bill. Item paid to Geo: Baker for a pluck cloth & pads for the Irish hobby & for inkle oo 5 5

*Sum page* £284 1s 5d ex.

[p. 7] Item delivered to Mr Coys the last of Octob. 1639 £80 os od; Item delivered to his Lordship at the audit 1639 150 o o; Item paid to Mr Rich: Ferris *last day of* Oct. 1639 102 o o; Item paid to Roger Thorne for carriages 79 6 8; ['£1018 12 o' erased] Item delivered to William Ramson the 5th of November 1639 by Mrs Hardwick's message ['411 6 8' erased] 24 o o

The sum of this book £435 6s 8d ex.

The sums of this book

| The sums as they stand in the copy | |
|---|---|
| £33 11s ood | £33 11 oo |
| 31 14 oo | 31 14 oo |
| 83 15 06 | 83 15 06 |
| 53 17 04 | 53 17 04 |
| 65 19 08 | 65 19 oo |
| 77 09 09 | 53 19 09 |
| 695 18 01 | 284 01 05 |
| | 435 06 08 |
| [total] £1042 05s 04d | [total] £1042 05s 04d ex. |

The total of the disbursements begun the 9th of March *as above* is £1042 5s 4d

The total in the other part of this book begun the 19th of Septemb. 1637 until this 5th of Novemb. 1639 is £1789 17s 6d

1042 5 4   1789 17 6   [total] 2832 2 10 ex.

Sum total of both disbursements is £2832 2s 10d ex.

Cast up and examined the 5th of November 1639 by us
[signed] Wil: Paget Hu: Prust Philip Elston

*[the following pages appear in the reverse]*

[p. 11] Disbursements for the right honorable Henry Earl of Bathe begun the 19th of September 1637

*First* delivered to his Lordship at his going to London in September aforesaid £30 os od; Item returned to his Lordship the same term 100 oo oo; Item for Mr Fane's pains & expenses in keeping courts at *Warkley* [Warkleigh] & Worlington oo 5 o; Item expended at Xmas sessions 1637 o1 6 o; Item given to Edward Garnesye for collecting the rents at

Harpford and Southbrook oo 2 6; Item expended at a meeting with the
Tawstock tenants about their rents oo 4 o; Item for a copy of the
Countess' declaration oo 1 o; Item delivered to Mrs Edward Wyott for
provision at *Exceter* in Lent 1637 20 o o; Item returned to his Lordship by
a bill of Mr Skinner's at Easter sessions 1638 160 o o; Item my expenses
then at *Exceter* were o1 5 o; Item at the courts kept at Nymet *Tracy*
[Tracey] *Bearchre* [Beer Charter] & *Ilfarcombe* [Ilfracombe] oo 7 o; Item
expended in going to the forest of Roche 5 days o1 15 o; Item at a meeting
at *Bydeford* [Bideford] about the Taw boat oo 1 1o; Item at the dispatch of
the second ejectment lease oo 1 4; Item delivered to his Lordship in
London in July 1638 60 o o; Item my expenses in going thither and during
my stay there o5 14 o; W. Item disbursed to Mr Wright in money &
workmen's wages o6 14 8; Item delivered to Sam Sterling 27 Aug. 1638
oo 5 o
[*page sum*] £388 2s 4d ex.

[**p. 10**]   Item delivered to his Lordship at Torrington 15 Sept. 1638
£o5 os od; Item delivered more to Sam: Sterling October 4 oo 2 o; Item
paid to Roger Thorne 11 October 1638 for carriages o4 o o; Item for stuff
to dress the Irish hobbies feet oo 3 o; Item for a bushel of oats & shoeing
of him oo 2 6; Item for shoeing Mr Wyott's mare oo 1 6; w. Item
delivered to Robert Randall for Mr Wright's helpers, & in money to
himself o9 4 6; w. Item expended in going to him & respecting his
imprisonment oo 7 8; w. Item paid to him upon a composition for work
done and to be done 12 o o; w. Item paid to Mr Barons for his diet
6 weeks o2 1o o; Item for diet & horsemeat during the audit at *Exceter*
from Tuesday till Saturday o5 2 o; Item returned then to his Lordship by a
bill of Mr Skinner's 40 o o; Item returned more by him about the same
time 60 o o; Item paid more to him for money furnished to his Lordship
by Mr Sowdon 40 o o; Item paid to Mr Tooker which was charged by a
bill of Mr Vaghan's 100 o o; Item expended at the commission concerning
the will and at Bow 9 Jan. 1638 o3 17 1; Item for Mr Bulworthies & pains
about Mr Wichehalse's examinations in the Star Chamber o1 14 7; Item
delivered to Robert Crosse at his going to his Lordship in London o2 o o;
Item paid to Mr Roger Skinner by his Lordship's appointment for the like
sum taken of Mr Bowdon 20 o o; *page sum* £306 4s 1od ex.

[**p. 9**]   Item returned to his Lordship in London by a bill of Mr Nottle's
charged upon Mr Dyman £100 os od; Item delivered to Mr Raph: Booth
the last of Jo: Vitrye's 2 payments 30 o o; Item delivered to him at
Modbury & *Vowelscombe* [Fowlescombe] o6 8 o; Item delivered to him
for the buying of Philip Thorne's gelding 10 o o; Item paid to the miller
for 11 weeks ended the 30th of March 1639 o3 6 o; Item delivered to
Mr Bold at *Exon* assizes o5 o o; w. Item delivered to Mr Wright when he
went to *Upex* [Up Exe] o5 o o; b. Item paid to Mr Tho: Vyner goldsmith
upon his bill 241 5 o; b. Item paid to Mr Stevens his disbursements for the
tenants at Tawstock that were distrained o2 16 1o; Item for my expenses at
Easter sessions 1639 and in my return by Bow o1 1o 7; Item expended in a
journey to Saltram & by the way oo 16 2; Item for bringing a heriot colt
from Uffculme oo 4 6; Item to Richard Williams for serving process at
Holne oo 5 o; Item returned to ['Mr' crossed through] his Lordship which

I received of Mr James Smyth at several times 400 0 0; Item ['rec' crossed through] paid to Mr Nathan Stephens for the like sum received of him by his Lordship in London 50 0 0; Item given to the ringers at Tawstock by my Lady's command at her first coming to Tawstock 00 10 0; Item paid to Mr Leuton's man for money bags 00 1 6; Item for letters brought out of Ireland to *Westmerland* house 00 2 0; Item paid to Dr Downe at Michaelmas 1639 100 0 00; Item to Mr Hugh Prust for searches in London in July 1639 00 15 6
*page sum* £958 1s 1d ex.

[**p. 8**]  Item delivered to his Lordship the 27th of October 1639 £100 0s 0d; Item paid to the *Exceter* carrier for a trunk brought from then weighing 320 pounds 00 13 4; Item delivered to Mr Slolye at several times 10 0 0; Item delivered to Mr Raph Boothe at *Bannton* Wellington & Bridgwater 11 0 0; Item paid then for Sir Edward Radwaye's expenses 01 18 4; Item disbursed in that journey upon several occasions 00 4 7; Item delivered Mr Raph Booth at Stow, *Croane* [Croan] & *Lanceston* [Launceston] 07 10 0; Dunterton. Item paid to Mr Dowrish & Bealbury for the tithe they disbursed for woods in *Dunterhow* [Dunterue] 06 3 0

| | | | | The sums as they stand in the copy | | |
|---|---|---|---|---|---|---|
| £137 | 9s | 3d | | | | |
| 958 | 1 | 1 | | 138 | 4 | 9 |
| 306 | 4 | 10 | | 797 | 11 | 7 |
| 388 | 2 | 4 | | 187 | 5 | 8 |
| the sums of this book hitherto £1789 17s 6d ex. | | | | 269 | 8 | 2 |
| | | | | 085 | 8 | 10 |
| | | | | 311 | 18 | 6 |
| | | | [total] | 1789 | 17 | 6 |

## Expenses, 1640–1644

KENT ARCHIVES OFFICE, U269/A525/5

*The book measures 7½" by 11¾". It is wrapped in vellum over a paper board. There are various scribblings on the front and back covers. The book is headed 'Disb. from Octo: 1640 & 1641, 1642, 1643 until 1644'. Even-numbered pages 2 to 100, 112 to 148, 156 to 170, 174 to 208 are blank as are pages 1, 103 to 110, 151–2 and 209.*

[inside page] Hugh Coombs wool weighing 89 lbs at 7d per lb, paid Hugh Coombs at Barnstaple fair £25.
£20 12 03 12 13 14 6  [total] 49 06 6
£77 04s 07d 72 13 01 47 02 10 45 14 09  [total] 242 15 03

[**p. 3**]  A note of such wages I have paid towards the mending of the weare at Conibers.

22th May 1642  Carpenters  *First* paid Charles Allen for 29 days at 10d per day £01 04s 02d; Item paid Abraham Shorne for five weeks 00 15 00; Item paid Lewis Beare for two weeks 00 06 00; Item paid Edward Brawne for two weeks 00 06 00; Item paid Mathew Jenkyn for 3 days drawing

stone oo o2 oo; Item paid Challacom's man for four weeks oo 12 oo;
12 *June* 1642   Item paid Edward Brawne for 15 days work at the hutch
oo o7 o6 oo; 21 *June*   Item paid Charles Allen for 19 days work & half
oo 16 oo oo; Item paid Abraham Sherne for 13 days at the hutch
oo o6 o6 oo; Item paid the stone drawer for 3 days work oo o2 oo oo; Item
paid Alexander Davy for 2 days at the hutch oo 10 oo oo

[p. 7]   *Tawstocke* 1640   Disbursed by me Richard Pollard for the
household expense and other defrayments of the Right Honourable Henry
Earl of Bath from and after the 19th day of October 1640 until:

**Saturday the 31th of October 1640**   *First* paid unto Hugh Coombe the
bailiff upon his bill £o2 o2s 1od oo½; Item paid William Runson the Cater
upon his bill oo 15 o6 oo; Item paid the Carpenter for work done at
*Ilfardcombe* [Ilfracombe] as by his bill o3 o6 o8 oo; Item paid the smith
for iron work at *Ilfardcombe* as by his bill o4 13 11 oo; Item paid William
Conniber of *Tawstocke* for six hundred of *Newland* [Newfoundland] fish
o3 11 o8 oo; Item paid the glasier as upon his bill oo o3 oo oo; Item paid
Williams the plumber as by bill o9 oo oo oo; Item paid Rich: Huxtable the
smith o6 oo oo oo; Item paid William Ellis in part of his wages
o6 oo oo oo; Item more to him for his journey to *Bowe* &c oo o2 o6 oo;
Item paid Phillip Yolland the miller for half a year's wages ended at
Michas. last o1 10 oo oo; Item paid Tho: Moore for making John Burk's
waistcoat and for ribbon to bind it oo o3 o6 oo; Item paid for three young
steers o9 o6 o8 oo; Item paid Mr George Baker of Barnstaple in part of his
account 20 oo oo oo; Item paid for Mr Wright's liberty in person unto Mr
Richard Horwood of Barnstaple o1 o8 oo oo
So the total sum of this week's charge ended the 31 of October 1640 is
£64 o4s o3d oo½   [page total] £68 o4s o3d

[p. 9]   *Tawstocke* Saturday the 7th of November 1640
*First* paid the bailiff upon his bill £o4 15s o7d oo½; Item paid the bailiff
more upon another bill o3 o6 o6 oo; Item paid Avise Starling for washing
of John Burk's lining [linen] oo o2 o6 oo; Item paid the Cater upon his bill
oo 11 o7 oo; Item for my expenses at *Biddeford* when I went to meet Mr
Prust to perfect my accounts oo o1 o6 oo; So the total sum of this week's
charge ended the 7th of 9ber 1640 is o5 17 o8 oo

**Saturday the 14th of November** *in the year* 1640
*First* paid Hugh Coombe the bailiff upon his bill for wages o2 oo 11 oo;
Item paid the Cater upon his bill oo o7 10 oo; Item paid the man that
brought the horses from London for money laid out more than received
oo o1 oo oo; [illegible crossed through] oo oo oo oo; Item paid for
22 dozen of tiles for the dairy floor at 2s per dozen o2 o4 oo oo; So the
total sum of this week's charge ended the 14th of 9ber is o4 13 o9 oo
Sum of this leaf is £10 11s 5d

[p. 11]   **Saturday the 21th of November** 1640
Item paid Hugh Coombe the bailiff upon his bill £o1 12s o5d oo½; no bill.
Item paid the Cater upon his bill oo o9 oo oo; no bill   Item paid John
Whiddon for shoeing of horses and other expenses oo o1 o6 oo; Coys
Item paid Lesland the fowler upon bill oo o4 o8 oo; Item spent at *Banton*
when my self and Hugh Combe was there oo o8 o8 oo; Coys   Item paid

the sadler of Pilton for webb for my Lady's cradle oo o5 oo oo
So the total of this week's charge ended the 21th of November is
£o3 o1s o3d oo

### Saturday the 28th of November 1640

Item paid Hugh Coombe the bailiff upon bill o2 12 o6 oo; Item paid the
Cater upon his bill oo o6 o6 oo; Item paid James Ricks for his pains in
packing up the goods when my Lord went to London, the 22th of
October 1640 oo o2 oo oo; Item paid Hugh Coombe upon another bill for
his expense at *Banton* oo o9 o4 oo So the total of this week's charge is
o2 10 o4
Sum of this leaf is £5 11s 7d

### [p. 13]  Saturday the 5th of December 1640

*First* paid the bailiff upon his bill for workmen wages o2 o3 11 o; Item
paid him upon another bill oo o4 o5; Item paid the Cater upon his bill
o2 o1 10; Item paid the Cater upon three several bills left to pay by
Mr Coyse 14 11 o4; Item paid Roger Thorne the carrier for carriage in
part 10 oo oo; Item paid John Williams the plumber for work done upon
the chancel o1 o5 o6; Item paid Mr Coyse for money laid out before the
audit last 10 oo oo
So the total of this week's charge is 40 o7 oo

### Saturday the 12th of December 1640

*First* paid Hugh Coombe upon his bill for wages and other things
o4 o7 o5; Item paid him for a bull bought o3 oo oo; Item paid him upon
his bill of charge at *Banton* the 12th of December oo o3 10; Item paid the
Cater upon his bill oo 13 o6; Item paid a messenger that brought a letter
from *Coombe* oo oo o6; Item spent at *Combe* [Ilfracombe] when I went to
buy fruit and other things for my Lord's use oo o1 oo; Item spent at
Torrington when I went to meet Mr Prust oo o1 oo
So the total of this week's charge is o8 o7 o3
Sum of this leaf is 48 14 o3

### [p. 15]  Saturday the 19th of December 1640

*First* paid to Hugh Coombe bailiff upon his bill for wages &c o1 18 o4;
Item paid the Cater upon his bill o1 oo o7; Item paid the glasier upon his
bill oo o5 oo; Item paid for Eringoes roots oo o2 oo; Item paid John White
of *Coombe* upon his bill for fruit o3 o7 o4; Item paid Huxtable the smith
upon his bill for one month o1 o4 o6
So the total of this week's charge is £o7 17s o9d

### Saturday the 26 of December 1640

Item paid the bailiff upon his bill o1 o9 o5; Item paid the Cater upon his
bill oo o8 o4; Item paid the armourer upon his bill oo o6 o6; Item paid
Gregory Hosgood for making the old wing's clothes as by bill oo o6 o6;
Item paid Bartholomew Skynner for hogsheads and pipes as by his bill
o3 12 oo
So the total of this week's charge is £o6 o2s o9d

### Saturday January the 2 1640

*First* paid Hugh Combe the bailiff upon his bill 11 13 o4; Item paid the
Cater upon his bill oo 11 o2; Item given to Mr Tomson a blindman of
Torrington oo o2 oo

So the total of this week's expense is £12 06s 06d
Sum of this leaf 26 07 00 ['one quarter ended' crossed through]

**[p. 17]   Saturday the 9th of January 1640**
*First* paid Hugh Coombe the bailiff upon his bill £01 17s 06d 00½; Item paid the Cater upon his bill 00 04 07 00
So the total of this week's expense is £02 02s 01d 00

**Saturday the 16th of January 1640**
*First* paid Hugh Coombe the bailiff upon his bill for wages £03 05s 04d 00½; Item paid him upon another bill 00 11 00 00; Item paid the Cater upon his bill 00 07 08 00; Item spent at *Banton* for myself and my horse two days 00 08 00 00; Item for shoeing my horse 00 00 06 00; Item paid Huxtable the smith upon his bill 01 04 06 00
So the total of this week's expense is £05 17s 00d

**Saturday the 23th of January 1640**
Item paid Hugh Coombe the bailiff upon his bill £02 00s 02d 00½; Item paid the Cater upon his bill 01 10 07 ½; Item paid John Willms the plumber upon his bill 02 02 05 00; Item paid Morkham the clockmaker 00 04 00 00; So the total of this week's expense is 05 17 02 ½

Sum of this leaf 13 16 05 ½   one quarter ended

**[p. 19]   Saturday the 30th of January 1640**
*First* paid Hugh Combe the bailiff upon his bill £02 07s 00d 00½; Item paid the Cater upon his bill 00 02 04 00; Item paid Thomas Yearder upon his bill for the curing the black horse 00 05 00 00; Item paid George Britton upon his bill for drenching horses 00 04 00 00; Item paid the sadler for mending saddles and other things as by his bill 00 06 00 00
So the total of this week's expense £03 04s 04d 00

**Saturday the 6th of February 1640**
Item paid Hugh Coombe the bailiff upon his bill £02 19s 10d 00; Item paid the Cater upon his bill 01 01 11 ½; Item paid for letters brought from Ireland for my Lord 00 01 00 00; Item paid for letter from London and sent from *Biddeford* by a messenger 00 01 00 00; Item paid the bailiff upon a bill for wages 00 06 08 00
Sum total of this week is 06 10 05 0 ½

**Saturday the 13th of February 1640**
Item paid Hugh Coombe the bailiff by bill 03 17 06 00; Item paid the Cater upon his bill 00 06 08 00; Item spent at *Biddeford* when I went to buy provision for the Lent 00 01 00 00; Item paid Mr Skitch upon a bill for wine for two communions 00 10 10 00
Sum total of this week's expense is £04 18s 00d 00
[page total] 14 12 09 ½

**[p. 21]   Saturday the 20th of Febr. 1640**
*First* paid Hugh Combe bailiff upon his bill £02 11s 02d 0; Item paid the Cater upon his bill 00 05 06 00; Item paid Cobley's wife her husband's quarter's wages by my Lady's command 00 10 00; Item paid James Nicks the carrier's man of Barnstaple for 3 quarters wages ended at Christmas last 01 01 00; Item paid the fuller for washing and dressing 13 pieces of hangings 00 03 06; Item paid for bringing two letters from Ireland for my

Lord oo o1 oo; Item paid the joiner for two frames for dials by bill
oo 13 oo; Item paid Mr Mason of Barnstaple for deal boards upon bill
o1 o2 o6; Item paid Mr Daw of Barnstaple for wine bought of Mr Coyce
and as by bill oo 16 oo; Item paid George Britton for drenching of horses
oo o8 oo; Item paid the glasier upon his bill oo 17 oo
So the total of this week's expense is £o8 o8s o8d

**Saturday the 27th of February 1640**
Item paid Hugh Coombe the bailiff upon his bill £o2 11s o6d; Item paid
the Cater upon his bill oo o6 o9; Item paid William Davy of Tawton for
carriage of 4 hogsheads of cider to Appledore oo o4 oo
So the total of this week's expense is £o2 o2s o3d   [page total] 1o 1o 11

**[p. 23]   Saturday the 6th of March 1640**
*First* paid Hugh Coombe the bailiff upon bill £o2 19s o5d oo; Item paid
the Cater upon his bill oo o6 o6 oo
So the total of this week's expense is o3 o5 11 oo

**Saturday the 13th of March 1640**
Item paid Hugh Coombe the bailiff o2 13 oo oo; Item paid the Cater upon
his bill o1 o4 o2 oo; Item paid [blank]——
So the total of this week's expense £o3 17s o2d –

**Saturday the 20th of March 1640**
Item paid the bailiff upon his bill o3 16 o1; Item paid the Cater upon his
bill o2 oo o8 oo; Item paid Tho: Moore for making the fiddlers coats in
part oo o8 oo; Item paid the smith upon two bills o2 o9 o6 oo; Item paid
for 200 of poor Johns to Downeman o1 o2 oo; Item paid John Parson for
coal as by bill o2 o3 oo; So the total of this week's expense is 1o 19 o3
[illegible crossed through, page total] 18 o2 o4

**[p. 25]   Saturday the 27th of March 1641**
Item paid Hugh Coombe the bailiff upon bill £o3 o4s o2d ½; Item paid
the Cater upon his bill oo 1o o8 oo; Item paid the armourer for his quarter
as by bill oo o6 o6; Item paid [blank]
So the total of this week's expense £o4 o2s o4d ½

**Saturday the 3d of April 1641**
*First* paid Hugh Coombe the bailiff upon his bill £o2 o9s o9d; Item paid
the Cater upon his bill oo o8 o7; Item paid James Nicks in part of the
carrier's bill o4 oo oo; Item paid John Parsons for bringing of coal, beef
and herrings oo o4 o6
So the total of this week's expense is £o7 o2s 1od

**Saturday the 10th of April 1641**
*First* paid Hugh Coombe the bailiff upon bill £o2 oos o5d; Item paid the
Cater upon his bill oo o8 oo; Item paid George Summers for a barrel of
herrings as by bill o1 oo oo
So the total of this week's expense is £o3 o8s o5d
[page total] £14 12s o7d ½

**[p. 27]   Saturday the 17th of April 1641**
*First* paid the bailiff upon his bill £o2 15s o2d; Item paid the Cater upon
his bill oo o4 o8; Item paid Mr Dodridge for one tearce of claret wine

bought by Mr Coyse as by his bill appeareth 02 10 00
So the total of this week's expense £05 09s 10d

**Saturday the 24th of April 1641**
Item paid Hugh Coombe the bailiff £02 05s 10d; Item paid William
Ramson the Cater upon bill 00 06 03; Item spent at Torrington fair when I
went to sell the fat oxen 00 01 00; Item paid for 2 oxen 10 03 04
So the total of this week's expense £11 16s 05d

second quarter

**Saturday the first of May 1641**
Item paid Hugh Coombe the bailiff upon his bill £00 12s 10d 00; Item
paid William Ramson the Cater upon bill [illegible crossed through]
00 05 09 00; Item paid for 2 barrels of Irish beef at 28s p[er] barrel
02 16 00 00
So the total of this week's expense is £03 14s 07d    [page total] £21 00s 10d

**[p. 29]   Saturday the 8th of May 1641**
*First* paid Hugh Coombe the bailiff upon bill £02 08s 06d; Item paid the
Cater upon his bill 00 12 00; Item paid Jo: Williams for his quarter's
wages and other things as by his bill 01 14 06; Item paid Mr Punchard for
5 yards of kersey for the old wingers clothes at 2s 6d per yard as by bill
00 12 06 00; Item paid Hugh Coombe for servants wages 03 06 03 00
Sum total of this week's expense is £08 13s 09d

**Saturday the 15th of May 1641**
*First* paid Hugh Coombe the bailiff upon his bill £02 19s 10d; Item paid the
Cater upon his bill 00 12 09; Item paid for a port scaffle [*skiff*] 00 02 06;
Item paid for two oars for my Lord's boat 00 02 00; Item paid for
bringing letters from *Exon* 00 00 06; Item paid for mending a curry comb
00 00 06; Item paid for 2 kine to the bailiff 08 10 00; Item paid Hugh
Coombe upon another bill 00 06 04
Sum total of this week's expense is £12 14s 05d

**Saturday the 22th of May 1641**
Item paid Hugh Coombe the bailiff upon bill £05 14s 04d; Item paid the
Cater upon his bill 00 16 06; Item paid Mrs Hardwick for earthen pots
00 01 06; Item paid James Nicks in full of the carriers bill 04 14 00; Item
paid Hugh Coombe upon a bill for drenching the labour horse 00 09 00
Sum total of this week's expense is £11 15s 04d    [page total] £33 03s 06d

**[p. 31]   Saturday the 29th of May 1641**
*First* paid Hugh Coombe bailiff upon his bill £03 07s 03d; Item paid the
Cater upon his bill 00 13 02; Item spent at *Coombe* [Ilfracombe] when I
went to enquire in what case the water bailiff [illegible crossed through]
left the office 00 01 00 00; Item paid John Parsons for bringing the new
boat from *Biddeford* 00 04 00 00
So the total of this week's expense is £04 05s 05d

**Saturday the 5th of June 1641**
*First* paid the bailiff upon his bill £06 02s 10d; Item paid the Cater upon
his bill 00 10 07; Item paid William Gibbons upon his bill 00 07 08; Item
paid for 10 bags of charcoal 00 07 06; Item paid Richard Huxtabell the
smith upon his bill 01 02 00
So the total of this week's expense is £08 10s 07d

**Saturday the 12th of June 1641**
Item paid Hugh Combe the bailiff upon his bill £02 14s 09d; Item paid the
Cater upon his bill oo 13 o8; Item paid Hugh Coombe for 2 steers as by
bill o7 o6 o8
So the total of this week's expense £10 15s o1d   [page total] £23 11s o1d

**[p. 33]   Saturday the 19th of June 1641**
Item paid Hugh Coombe the bailiff upon his bill £06 09s 1od; Item paid
the Cater upon his bill oo o7 o8
Sum of this week's expense is o6 17 o6

**Saturday the 26th of June 1641**
Item paid Hugh Coombe the bailiff upon his bills o3 16 oo; Item paid the
Cater upon his bill o1 oo o6 ½; Item paid to a man at *Banton* for curing
and dressing the sheep there o2 10 oo; Item paid Doctor Downe as by his
bill of receipt 50 oo oo; Item paid the Armourer for his quarter wages for
cleaning the armour oo o6 o6; Item paid the smith upon his bill oo 13 o6;
Item paid the smith upon another bill oo 17 o6
Sum of this week's expense is £59 o4s ood ½

**Saturday the 3rd of July 1641**
*First* paid the bailiff upon his bills o3 o6 10; Item paid the Cater upon his
bill oo 11 oo; Item paid the glasier for work done as by bill oo o9 oo; Item
paid the sadler upon bill oo o9 o6; Item paid Tho: Moor's man for three
day's work to mend things oo o1 oo
Sum total of this week's expense is £o4 17s o4d   [page total] £70 18s 1od

**[p. 35]   Saturday the 10th of July 1641**
Item paid Hugh Coombe upon his bills £o3 o4s ood oo; Item paid the
Cater upon his bill oo 15 10; Item paid Mr George Shurt of *Biddeford* for
one hundred and 3 quarters of sugar as by bill 11 12 11 oo
So the total of this week's expense £15 12s o9d

**Saturday the 17th of July 1641**
Item paid Hugh Coombe the bailiff upon bills £o4 19s o2d; Item paid the
Cater upon his bill oo 10 o5 oo; Item spent at *Banton* for myself and my
horse oo o7 o6 oo; Item paid Sebastian for 54 fathom of hages [*hedges*] at
7d per fathom o2 12 o4 oo; Item for one dozen of posnets oo o6 oo oo;
Item for nets for the kitchen oo o2 oo oo; Item spent at *Coombe*
oo oo o6 oo; ['Item paid Hugh Coombe the bailiff upon bill 3 3 oo oo'
crossed through]
So the total of this week's expense is £o7 17s 11d

**Saturday the 24th of July 1641**
Item paid Hugh Combe the bailiff upon bill o6 o8 o8 oo; Item paid the
Cater upon bill oo 17 o2 oo
So the total of this week's expense £o7 o5s 1od   [page total] £30 16s o6d
3rd quarter

**[p. 37]   Saturday the 31th of July 1641**
*First* paid Hugh Coombe the bailiff upon his bill £o5 19s ood; Item paid
the Cater upon his bill oo o3 o3 oo; Item paid Comer the fuller for
working of ten horse cloths and other things as by bill oo o4 oo oo; Item

paid Mr Baker of Barnstaple in full 03 07 00 00; Item paid Mr Nicholls of Torrington as by his bill 02 10 00 00
So the sum of this week's expense is £12 03s 3d

### Saturday the 7th of August 1641
Item paid Hugh Coombe the bailiff upon his bill £02 04s 09d; Item paid the Bailiff upon his bill for wage 05 14 07; Item paid the Cater upon his bill 00 11 10; Item paid Mr Booth for his journey to London with the horses 04 10 00; Item paid Mrs Hardwicke for 1 quarter of beef 01 06 00; Item paid Thomas Steeven for money disbursed at *Biddeford* when he went for culm 00 01 00; Item paid Hugh Coombe upon a bill of disbursements at *Banten* 14 02 08
So the sum of this week's expense is £28 10s 10d

### Saturday the 14th of August 1641
Item paid the bailiff upon his bill 03 03 01; Item paid the Cater upon his bill 01 07 00; Item paid John Williams the plumber upon his bill 01 16 04; Item paid Mr George Shurte of *Biddeford* for a quarter of a hundred of sugar at 13d per pound 01 10 4; Item more for the bag the sugar was in 00 01 00
Sum total of this week's expense is 07 17 9   [page total] £48 11s 10d

### [p. 39]   Saturday 21 of August 1641
Item paid Hugh Coombe the bailiff by bill £03 17s 04d; Item paid the Cater upon his bill 01 01 00; Item paid the smith upon two bills dated the third and 31th of July 01 18 06; Item given by Lord's command to a man that went to *Exon* with letters 00 03 06; Item given to Sir Lewis Pollard's man that brought letters from *Exon* and by my Lord's command 00 01 06; Item given to a man that did help home the coach 00 01 06; Item paid the fowler as by bill 00 03 06; Item given to the Sergeants of Barnstaple that presented the Mayor's gift 00 10 00; Item delivered my Lady in the bowling green 00 01 00
Sum total of this week's expense is £07 17s 10d

### Saturday 28th of August 1641
Item paid the Bailiff upon his bill £02 07s 00d; Item paid the Cater upon his bill 01 16 00; Item paid the fowler upon his bill 00 02 02; Item delivered my Lady in the bowling green 00 01 06; Item given to a messenger that brought letters from *Exon* 00 04 00; Item given to the six boatmen 00 06 00; Item given Mr Lam's man that brought partridges 00 02 06; Item paid Mr Wood for money laid out at Appledore 00 01 00; Item given to Mr Berrye's man 00 02 06
Sum total of this week's expense is 05 02 08   [page total] £13 00s 06d

### [p. 41]   Saturday the 4th of September 1641
Item paid the bailiff upon his bill £05 11s 00d; Item paid the Cater upon his bill 01 17 05; Item delivered my Lady for Mr Wright 00 10 00; Item paid the fowler upon his bill 00 02 11; Item paid him upon another bill 00 02 01; Item paid the glasier upon his bill 00 09 06; Item paid the post master's man 00 02 06; Item paid Mr Skitch for 2 wine pipes and for wine at several times 01 07 00; Item given to Mr Jaye's man by my Lady's command 00 02 00
Sum total of this week's expense is £10 02s 05d

**Saturday the 11th of September 1641**
Item paid the bailiff upon his bill £04 13s 06d; Item paid him for four
steers 16 19 00; Item paid the Cater upon his bill 02 05 09; Item paid the
joiner for mending my Lady's chair 00 03 00; Item given by Lord's
command to four Irish men 00 02 00; Item given my Lady in the bowling
green 00 00 06; Item paid Mr Wright by my Lady's command 01 00 00;
Item paid Bartholomew Skynner for hogsheads as by bill 03 05 00; Item
paid George Britton for dressing horses as by bill 00 09 00; Item paid the
fowler as by bill 00 04 00; Item given to Sir Lewis Pollard's man that
brought a stag and by my Lord's command 00 06 00; Item given for a
reward 00 02 00; Item paid Baker for 8 partridges 00 04 00
Sum total of this week's expense is £29 13s 09d   [page total] £39 16s 02d
1032 2 8½ Ex

**[p. 43]   Saturday the 18th of September 1641**
*First* paid the bailiff upon his bill £01 11s 04d; Item paid him upon another
bill 01 10 04; Item paid the Cater upon his bill 03 14 10; Item paid
Morkam for keeping the clocks 00 04 00; Item paid Moore the tailor by
bill 00 02 06; Item paid for a brass cock for the cellar 00 01 04; Item paid
for 3 dozen of larks 00 02 00; Item given to the harper by my Lady's
command 00 10 00; Item paid Baker for 16 partridges 00 08 00
Sum total of this week's expense is 08 14 04

**Saturday the 25th of September 1641**
*First* paid Hugh Coombe the bailiff upon bill £00 19s 01d; Item paid the
Cater upon his bill 02 08 10; Item paid a messenger that brought letters
from *Chimley* 00 01 06; Item paid for 4 dozen of larks 00 02 06; Item
given in reward to a man that brought grapes from Mr Sloweleyes
00 00 06; Item paid Moore for making Sam Starling's clothes as by his bill
00 05 00; Item paid the smith upon two bills of the 22th of August and
25th of September 01 09 06
Sum total of this week's expense £04 06s 11d   [page total] £13 01s 3d

**[p. 45]   Saturday the 2d of October 1641**
*First* paid Hugh Coombe the bailiff upon his bill £01 08s 08d; Item paid
the Cater upon his bill 02 04 03; Item paid the Carrier for a box delivered
at Molton 00 00 06; Item paid Thomas Steevens 00 00 06; Item paid
Thorne the carrier in part 10 00 00; Item paid the smith of Barnstaple for
hinges for the gallery door 00 06 00; Item delivered my Lord and Lady in
the green 00 03 00; Item spent at Torrington fair 00 04 00; Item paid the
fowler upon several bills 00 10 06; Item paid Mr Nicholls of Torrington in
full of his bill 00 15 00; Item paid for eight oxen at Torrington fair
44 03 04
So the total of this week's expense is £59 15s 09d

**Saturday the 9th of October 1641**
Item paid Hugh Combe the bailiff upon bills £01 06s 09d; Item paid him
upon another bill 00 15 00; Item paid the Cater upon his bill 02 12 08;
Item paid Mr Jammon for 6 hogsheads of sack in part as by bill 05 00 00;
Item paid William Meline 00 00 08; Item given at Mr Mayors of Barnstaple
when my Lord and Lady dined there 01 08 06; Item paid Parsons for two

weigh of coal as by bill 03 07 04; Item given to the Miller for the two first cocks at the rode 00 01 00
So the total of this week's expense £13 11s 11d [page total] 73 07 8 Ex

### [p. 47]   Saturday the 16th of October 1641
Item paid Hugh Coombe the bailiff upon bill £02 05s 04d; Item paid the Cater upon his bill 04 07 03 ½; Item paid the armourer for his quarter ended at Michaelmas last upon his bill 00 07 00; Item paid the postmaster's man by command 00 03 06; Item given to the poor people in the church by my Lord's command 00 10 00; Item paid at Barnstaple for one yoke of oxen for the plow 10 10 00; Item paid William Ellis upon his bill 00 12 00; Item paid the fowler for 15 partridges 00 07 06; Item paid John Gribble for going to *Chimly* with letters 00 02 00; Item paid James Nicks for 3 quarters wages ended at Michaelmas last 02 02 00; Item paid the hop gatherers upon bill 05 00 000; Item given to Sir John Chichester's man that brought quinches [*quinces*] to my Lady 00 01 06; Item given Mr Wyott's man that brought eight dozen of larks 00 01 00; Item given to Mr Henry Chichester's man that brought turkeys and cocks 00 02 00; Item paid Raph Booth for wax candles 00 01 06; Item delivered to my Lord in the green 00 01 06; Item paid the Smith upon his bill 01 09 03; Item paid Mr Gammon in full of his bill of eight pounds for a hogshead of sack 03 00 00; Item paid the bailiff upon another bill 00 16 10
So the total of this week's expense is £30 19s 02d ½
[page total] 30 19 02 ½

### [p. 49]   Saturday the 23th of October 1641
*First* paid Hugh Coombe the bailiff upon bill £01 19s 04d; Item paid the Cater upon bill 02 09 07; Item paid for 10 couple of rabbits 00 10 00; Item paid for 9 partridges 00 04 06; Item paid Mr Russell by my Lady's command 02 00 00; Item paid Mr Thomas Horwood upon a bill of Mr Yeos of *Bristoll* as appears 11 10 00; Item paid Mr Tonkins for strings 00 05 00; Item paid the plumber upon his bill and for his quarter ended at Michaelmas last 02 04 00; Item paid Huxtable the smith upon three bills due in Mr Coyse his time 03 11 04; Item paid him upon another bill 00 14 00; Item paid Mr Bold for the watchmaker 00 05 00; Item paid the servants for wages as appears by the particulars 58 10 00; So the total of this week's expense is £83 02s 11d

Sum of the last three pages is 13 01 03   73 7 8   30 19 2½
[total] 200 11 0 ½
Sum total till the 18th of September as appears in the pages til then 1032 2 8½ Sum total disbursed on this book from the 31 of October 1640 until the 25th of October 1641 is 1232 13 9

And His receipts in that time as appear on his books of receipts is 1177 8 4¾
So, remains due to Pollard this 25th of October 1641 55 5 4¼
To him for a year's wages then due 20 0 0
Whereof there was due from him upon a bill before this book began the sum of 4 11 4
So remains due to him the day above said 70 14 0½ ex.

**[p. 57]   Saturday the 6th of November 1641**
*First* paid Hugh Coombe the bailiff upon bill £oo 16s o1d; Item paid a woman that brought letters from *Ilfordcombe* for my Lord oo o1 oo; Item paid John Bennett for riding the Madd Robbyn o2 oo oo; Item paid a messenger that brought letters from Sir William Power to my Lord oo o1 oo; Item paid Gregory Hosegood upon bill oo 10 10; Item paid him upon another bill o1 o7 oo; Item paid Avis Starling for washing footmen's clothes as by bill oo 10 oo; Item paid George Britton as by his bill o2 oo oo; Item paid Mr Doctor Downe as by his acquittance 10 oo oo; Item given to Sir Lewis Pollard's keeper for his fee for a stag oo 10 oo; Item to Mr Hayne's man that brought the mare from *Hunspill* oo o4 oo
Sum total of this week's expense is 18 oo oo

**Saturday the 13th of November 1641**
Item paid Hugh Combe the bailiff upon his bill o1 15 o9; Item paid for eggs and pots for Seame oo o1 oo; Item paid John Gribble upon his bill for his work in the stable oo 12 o6; Item paid for 200 of poor Johns at 9s per hundred oo 18 oo; Item paid the Welsh dick for his wages as by bill oo 13 o6; Item paid for fresh fish oo oo o8; Item paid the bailiff upon his bill for wages o5 14 o7
Sum total of this week's expense is £o9 16s ood   [page total] £27 16s ood

**[p. 59]   Saturday the 20th of November 1641**
Item paid Hugh Combe the bailiff upon bill £oo o1s o8d; Item paid the market maid upon bill oo oo oo; Item paid for bringing the materials for the organ from *Gloster* [Gloucester] o1 12 oo; Item paid Rich: Maye for things bought at Barnstaple as by bill oo o3 o2; Item paid Mr John Thomas of *Biddeford* for things bought at *Bristoll* fair as by his bill 10 17 oo; Item paid the Welsh dick for his journey to London with the horse litter by his bill oo o5 o4; Item paid Mr Dolham the organ maker 33 oo oo
So the total of this week's expense is £46 19s o2d

**Saturday the 27th of November 1641**
*First* paid Hugh Coombe the bailiff upon his bill £o1 o9s 1od ½; paid Mr Isaac of *Biddeford* for 30 bushels of great culm o1 o2 oo; Item spent at *biddeford* when I bought fish oo o1 oo; Item paid Mr John Booth as by his acquittance o7 oo oo; Item paid for 12 lbs of week yarn oo o7 o3; Item paid Mr Fairechild in part for his steers 17 oo oo
So the total of this week's expense is £27 oos ood ½

**Saturday the 4th of December 1641**
*First* paid Hugh Coombe the bailiff upon bill oo 19 o5; Item paid the market bill oo 18 o5 oo; Item paid John Whiddon for his wages oo 12 o6 oo; Item paid him for money laid out in coming from London as by his bill appeareth oo o3 o8 oo; Item paid the bailiff upon his bill oo 12 o6
So the total of this week's expense is £o3 o6s o6d
[page total] £77 o5s o9d ½

**[p. 61]   Saturday the 11th of December 1641**
*First* paid Hugh Coombe the bailiff £oo 16s o9d; Item paid the Cater upon bill oo o6 o1 oo; Item paid Rich Maye upon a bill oo o4 11 oo; Item paid

for 18 bushels of culm oo 12 oo oo; Item paid Mr Punchard upon his bill
for Sam Starling's clothes o2 o7 o8 oo; Item paid for mending the
footmen's shoes as by bill oo o5 o4 o
Sum total for this week's expense £o4 12s o9d

### Saturday the 18th of December 1641

Item paid the bailiff upon his bill £oo 1os o6d; Item paid the market bill
oo o6 o7; Item paid the glasier upon his bill oo 18 oo; Item paid the smith
upon his bill o2 oo oo; Item paid for two keys oo o1 o6; Item paid for
2 jars of sallet oil oo o2 o6
Sum total of this week's expense is £o3 19s o1d

### Saturday the 24th [sic] of December 1641

*First* paid the bailiff upon his bill £o2 o7s o8d; Item paid the market bill
oo o8 oo; Item paid the armourer for Christmas quarter as by bill
oo o6 o6; Item paid the sadler upon his bill oo o7 o6; Item paid William
Meane for going to *Exon* with a letter to send by post oo o5 oo; Item paid
for a new key for the park oo o1 oo
Sum total of this week's expense is £o2 15s o8d   [page total] £11 o7s o6d

### [p. 63]   Saturday the first of January 1641 [1642]

*First* paid the bailiff upon his bill £oo 11s o9d; Item paid the market bill
oo o8 o1; Item paid Mr Dolham for what he disbursed for bringing the
residue of the things for the organ from *Gloster* o1 14 oo; Item paid the
carrier in part of his bill as by acquittance 1o oo oo; Item spent in my
journey to *Tottnes* as by bill o1 18 o6; Item more in that journey for
frosting my horses oo o2 oo; Item paid for sending a letter from *Exon* by
the post oo o1 oo
Sum total of this week's expense is £14 15s o4d

### Saturday the 8th of January 1641

*First* paid the bailiff upon his bill £oo 17s o9d; Item paid the market bill
oo o7 o1; Item paid for barm for the brewer oo o2 oo; Item paid the smith
upon his bill oo 14 oo; Item paid for bringing the things for the organ
from *Apledore* by boat oo o3 o6
Sum total of this week's expense £o2 o3s o4d   [page total] £16 18s o8d

### [p. 65]   Saturday the 15th of January 1641

*First* paid the bailiff upon his bills £oo oos ood [sic]; Item paid the market
bill oo o9 o4; Item paid Philip Morcombe upon his bill oo o4 oo oo; Item
paid John Willims upon his bill for Christmas quarter o1 19 oo; Item paid
for 6oo of poor Johns oo o1 oo
So the total of this week's expense £o2 13s o4d

### Saturday the 22th of January 1641

Item paid the bailiff upon his bill £o2 o1s o7d; Item paid the market bill
oo 1o o4; Item spent at Torrington when I went to meet Mr Prust oo o1 o6
So the total of this week's expense is £o2 13s o5d

### Saturday the 29th of January 1641

Item paid the bailiff upon his bill £o3 o2s o5d; Item paid the market bill
oo o6 1o; Item paid for sending letters by the post from Barnstaple to
London oo o1 oo; Item paid for one quarter's standing the Cater's horse at

*Barnestaple* oo oo o6; Item paid Mr Blanchard by my Lady's command
o2 oo oo
Sum total of this week's expense o5 10 o9   [page total] £10 17s o6d

**[p. 67]   Saturday the 5th of February 1641**
*First* paid the bailiff upon his bill £o1 19s o8 ½d; Item paid the market bill
oo o9 o3; Item paid James Nicks for his quarter's wages ended at
Christmas last oo o7 oo; Item paid for sending letter by the post oo oo o6
Sum total of this week's expense is o2 16 o5 ½

**Saturday the 12th of Feb. 1641**
*First* paid the bailiff upon his bill o1 10 o2; Item paid the market bill
oo 12 o3; Item paid Mr Page of Barn'ple for 10 bushels of salt as by bill
o1 o5 oo; Item paid Mr Roger Page for wine as by his bill o2 14 oo; Item
paid the smith upon his bill oo 11 o4; Item spent at Bow when I went to
talk with Mr Young oo o3 oo
Sum total of this week's expense is o6 15 o9

**Saturday the 19th of Feb. 1641**
Item paid the bailiff upon his bill £o1 18s o9d; Item paid the market bill
oo 16 10; Item paid for leather for to mend the pump in the brewhouse
oo o1 oo; Item paid for 2 bushels of salt oo o4 o8
Sum total of this week's expense is o3 oo o9   [page total] £12 12s 11d [sic]

**[p. 69]   Saturday the 26th of February 1641**
*First* paid the bailiff upon his bill £oo 14s o4d; Item paid the market bill
oo o9 o8; Item paid George Sweete for making of 2000 faggots and
7 dozen of hardwood oo 18 o8; ['Item Henry Davy for half a year's wages
ended the last of Feb. 1641 o1 10 oo' crossed through] Item paid the Welsh
dick for making browse faggots oo o7 o6; Item paid him for 7 weeks work
in the harvest last oo o7 oo; Item paid for sweeping four chimneys
oo oo o8
So the sum total of this week's expense o4 17 10

**Saturday the 5th of March 1641**
*First* paid the bailiff upon his bill £o1 o7s o2d; Item paid the market bill
oo 11 o1; Item paid for a new key for the buttery door oo o2 o4; Item paid
John Lerrawill for making of 1000 faggots at 7d per thousand oo o5 10;
Item paid him for 3 dozen of hardwood oo o3 oo; Item for a bundle of
spars oo oo o1
Sum total of this week's expense is £o2 o9s o6d   [page total] £o5 o7s o4d

**[p. 71]   Saturday the 12th of March 1641**
*First* paid the bailiff upon his bill £o2 16s o1d; Item paid the market bill
oo 10 o1; Item paid for a letter from my Lady p. pt oo oo o6; Item paid
for twenty bushels of salt o2 oo oo; Item paid for 12 bushels coal oo 10 oo
Sum total of this week's expense is £o5 16s o8d

**Saturday the 19th of March 1641**
*First* paid the bailiff upon his bill £o2 15s 11 ½d; Item paid the market bill
o1 o2 o6; Item paid George Britton for drenching and dressing of horses as
by bill oo o9 oo; Item paid the smith upon his bill o1 o9 o6; Item paid for
7 bushels of great culm at 10d per bushel oo o5 10; Item paid George

Sweete for making of 1000 of faggots at 7d per hundred 00 05 10; Item
more for 200 of hop-poles at 6d 00 01 00; Item more to him for 4 bundles
of spars 00 00 04; Item paid for a letter from London per post 00 01 00;
Item paid for bringing things from *Exon* 00 01 06; Item paid Doctor
Downe as by his acquittances 150 00 00; Item paid Mr Dolham in full
020 00 00
Sum total of this week's expense is £176 12s 05 ½d
[page total] £182 09s 01 ½d

### [p. 73]  Saturday the 26th of March 1642

*First* paid the bailiff upon his bill £00 17s 08d; Item paid the market bill
00 10 09; Item paid upon another bill for weaving 00 11 06; Item paid for
3 days work to John Midway for cleaving stakes 00 02 09; ['Item paid for
making of 11 dozen of hardwood at 16d per dozen 00 19 00; Item paid for
1 dozen and half of stakes 00 00 09' crossed through] Item paid for stuff to
make a drench for the horses by the groom 00 01 06; Item paid for 2 quire
of paper 00 00 08
Sum total of this week's expense is [illegible crossed through] £02 04s 10d

### Saturday the 2d of April 1642

Item paid the bailiff upon his bill £01 11s 00d; Item paid the market bill
00 10 06; Item paid upon another bill dated 31 *March* 02 17 11; Item paid
John Midday for cleaving of wood and stakes as by bill 02 02 02; Item
paid the servants' wages as by a bill of the particulars will appear 15 02 11;
Item paid Roger for Webb for girts 00 01 04; Item paid the armourer for
making clean the armour as by his bill 00 06 06; Item paid for nets for the
kiddle 00 15 06; Item paid Mr Walter Heard of Barnstaple for 1000 of
Poor Johns 05 00 00
Sum total of this week's expense is £28 07s 10d   [page total] £30 12s 08d

### [p. 75]  Saturday the 9th of April 1642

Item paid the bailiff upon his bill £00 04 10d; Item paid the market bill
00 07 11; Item paid Roger the groom for his journey to London with two
horses for my Lord 01 00 00; Item paid John Parsons for coal and other
things as by his bill appears 03 02 06; Item paid Roger Thorne the carrier
in part of his bill for carriage 05 00 00; Item paid George Sweete upon his
bill for making wood 00 17 08; Item paid William Meane for threshing of
66 bushels and 2 pecks of barley at 2d ½ per bushel 00 13 09
Sum total of this week's expense is £11 06s 08

### Saturday the 16th of April 1642

Item paid the bailiff upon his bill 00 03 06; Item paid the market bill
00 11 03; Item paid for 11 bushels of great culm 00 09 02; Item paid
Huxtable the smith in part of his bill left to pay by Mr Slowley 03 00 00;
Item paid him upon another bill 00 07 06; Item paid for my expenses at
Torrington fair 00 01 06; Item paid John Lerrawill for making of 1200 of
faggots 00 07 00; Item more for one dozen of hardwood and 3 seams
00 01 03; Item for 2 bundles of spars 00 00 02; Item paid Henry Davy for
7 weeks wages when I put him away 00 07 00
Sum total of this week's expense is 05 08 04

[page total] £16 15s 00d

**[p. 77]   Saturday the 23th of April 1642**
Item paid William Ellis the bailiff upon bill 01 05 06; Item paid John Williams for his Lady Day quarter as by bill 02 05 05; Item paid for 2 barrels of herrings 02 05 00; Item paid Mr Fairchild in full for six steers bought of him 13 00 00; Item paid Cobleye's wife in part of her husband's wages 00 10 00
Sum total of this week's expense is £19 05s 11d

**Saturday the last of April 1642**
Item paid William Ellis upon his bill £00 11s 11d; Item paid the market bill 00 05 10; Item paid the Welsh dick for his being in the stable 11 weeks 00 16 06; Item paid the green keeper for one year's wages 01 00 00; Item paid George Sweete upon his bill for making of wood 00 12 02
Sum total of this week's expense is £03 06s 05d

**Saturday the 7th of May 1642**
Item paid William Ellis upon his bill £06 05s 07d; Item paid William Meane for threshing of 80 bushels of barley at 2d ½ per bushel 00 16 08; Item paid for 6 pecks of beans 00 00 009
Sum total of this week's expense is 07 02 07   [page total] £29 14s 11d

**[p. 79]   Saturday the 14th of May 1642**
Item paid William Ellis upon his bill £00 19s 10d; Item paid the market bill 00 02 04; Item paid William Meane for his journey to London when he went with the horse litter 00 05 00
Sum total of this week's expense is 01 07 02

**Saturday the 21th of May 1642**
Item paid the bailiff upon his bill £00 07s 09d 0; Item paid the market bill 00 07 06 00; Lady Day   Item paid James Nicks for his quarter's fee for bringing letters 00 07 00 0; 26 May 1642   Item returned to my Lady by Mr Nottell of Barnstaple 80 00 00 00
So the sum of this week's expense is 81 02 03

**Saturday the 28th of May 1642**
Item paid the bailiff upon his bill £00 04s 02d; Item paid the market bill 00 04 04; Item paid Eliz. Sarle for half a year's wages due at our Lady Day last 01 10 00; Item paid for 2 quire of paper 00 00 09; Item paid Thomas Hearder for curing the bay nag as by bill 00 05 00; Item paid the smith upon his bill 01 01 00 ['Item paid John Midway for cleaving stakes and making of wood as by his bill 00 14 10' crossed through]
Sum total of this week's expense is 03 ... 03   [page total '£86 05s 06d' crossed through] £85 14s 08d

**[p. 81]   Saturday the 4th of June 1642**
Item paid the bailiff upon his bill £00 03s 06d; Item paid the market bill 00 06 04; Item paid Hugh Coombe upon bills due to him in Mr Coyse his time as by the bills appear 30 11 07; Item paid him more for wages due at our Lady Day last 04 17 08; Item paid for 3 scythes 00 07 09; Item paid for 6 whetstones 00 00 09; Item paid for 1 steer at Molton fair 03 16 08; Item paid for 2 oxen there 09 00 00; Item paid for my expenses there 00 01 06; Item paid for threshing of 86 bushels of wheat at 9d per bushel 03 04 06
Sum total of this week's expense is 52 10 03

**Saturday the 11th of June 1642**
Item paid the bailiff upon his bill £01 10s 07d; Item paid the market bill
00 05 00; Item paid John Midway for making of wood as by his bill
00 14 10; Item paid him more for making 3 dozen of wood 00 04 00; Item
paid Joseph Holland for threshing of twelve bushels of peas 00 03 00; Item
paid Zachary Cheevely for half a year's wages due at ['Mic' crossed
through] our Lady last 1642 01 00 00; Item paid for threshing of
66 bushels of wheat 02 09 4 ½
Sum total of this week's expense is 06 06 9 ½   [page total] £58 17s 00d ½

**[p. 83]   Saturday the 18th of June 1642**
*First* paid the bailiff upon his bill £01 03s 00d; Item paid the market bill
00 03 05; Item paid Thom: Moore for mending Ned Heale's clothes as by
bill 00 01 00; Item paid John Gribble for his charge in going to *Ilmester*
with two horses to send to London per carrier 00 06 06 0; Item more for
his wages 00 01 06; Item paid the armourer for making clean the armour as
by bill 00 06 06; Item Mr Humfry Tooker of *Exter* for grocery as by bill
02 07 00 0; Item paid Mrs Coop upon a bill 02 03 00 00
Sum total of this week's expense is 06 11 11

**Saturday the 25th of June 1642**
Item paid the bailiff upon his bill £01 04s 02d 00; Item paid the market bill
00 05 06; Item paid for threshing of 60 bushels of wheat 02 05 00; Item for
my expenses in my joureny at *Totnis* as per bill 01 10 02; Item paid the
basket maker for 17 days work 00 11 08; Item paid the carpenter for work
at the weir as by a bill 05 07 02; Item paid for 10 bushels of culm
00 08 06; Item returned to London by Mr Langwoorthy of *Exter* by bill
of exchange 100 00 00
Sum total of this week's expense is £111 12s 2d   [page total] £118 04s 01d

**[p. 85]   Saturday the 2nd of July 1642**
*First* paid the bailiff upon his bill 01 13 07; Item paid the market bill
00 13 08; Item paid four weigh and half of coal 06 19 06; Item paid for
bringing up of four weigh and half of coal 00 07 06; Item paid for one
steer 04 00 00; Item paid the servants that came down from London the
25th of June last for money laid out more than received 00 15 00; Item
paid the glasier upon his bill 00 15 00; Item paid the Smith upon his bill
01 06 09; Item paid Joseph Holland for threshing of 331 bushels of oats at
1d ½ per bushel 02 01 03 ½
Sum total of this week's expense 18 11 10 ½

**Saturday the 9th of July 1642**
Item paid the bailiff upon his bill £01 17s 02d; Item paid the market bill
01 02 08; Item paid Baldwyn Steevens upon his bill for barm 00 03 00;
Item paid for 3 dozen of trenchers 00 04 00; Item paid William Geare
upon his bill 00 04 10; Item paid upon another bill for jug trenchers and
glasses 00 12 08; Item paid for weeding of the garden 00 11 04
Sum total of this week's expense 04 14 08   [page total] £23 06s 06d ½

**[p. 87]   Saturday the 16th of July 1642**
*First* paid the bailiff upon his bill £02 06s 01d; Item paid the market bill
00 10 09; Item paid John Ramson upon his bill for making faggots
00 07 00; Item paid the smith upon his bill 00 14 04; Item paid for 100 lbs

of very fine loaf sugar at 16d per pound 06 13 04; Item paid Mr Walter
Tooker for one tearce of claret wine as by his bill appears 03 13 00
Sum total of this week's expense is 14 04 06

### Saturday the 23th of July 1642

Item paid the bailiff upon his bill £01 01s 09d; Item paid the market bill
00 10 06; Item paid for a pair of spurs for Tho: Bold 00 01 06; Item paid
for thongs and trussing straps for mending of pack saddles 00 01 06; Item
paid John Williams the plumber upon his bill for Midsummer quarter
01 14 04; Item paid Baldwyn Steevens for barm for 2 brewings 00 01 00;
Item paid him upon a bill for nets and other things belonging to the kiddle
last year 02 16 07; Item paid the weeders for weeding *peninles* banks walks
00 01 00; Item paid for letters per post 00 01 00
Sum total of this week's expense £06 09s 02d    [page total] £20 13s 08d

### [p. 89]   Saturday the 30th of July 1642

*First* paid the bailiff upon his bill £01 15s 05d 00; h. Item paid the market
bill 01 00 09; Item given to the ringers by command 00 05 00 00; Item
paid for two pair of pack girths 00 04 00 00; Item paid for two yards of
canvas 00 02 00 00; Item paid the smith upon his bill 00 16 00 00; Item
paid the glasier upon his bill 00 03 02 00; Item paid Amyas Lewes for one
yoke of steers 09 02 06; Item delivered my Lady in the green 00 01 00;
Item paid Tho: Moore upon bill 00 03 00
Sum total of this week's expense 13 12 10

### Saturday the 7th [sic] of ['July' crossed through] August 1642

*First* paid the bailiff upon his bill £01 16s 08d; h. Item paid the market bill
01 19 03; Item paid for 5 couple of rabbits 00 05 00 00; Item paid Roger
Thorne in part 10 00 00; Item given by command to Captain Pyne's
servant that brought a present 00 02 06; Item paid Morcombe for his half
year's fee due at Midsummer last for keeping of the two clocks 00 04 00;
Item delivered my Lady in two bags 100 00 00; Item given to Sir Hugh
Pollard's man for his fee 00 05 00
So the total of this week's expense is 114 12 05    [page total] £128 05s 03d

### [p. 91]   Saturday the 13th of August 1642

*First* paid the bailiff upon his bill £02 05s 08d; h. Item paid the market bill
02 03 04; Item paid for four couple of rabbits 00 03 08; Item paid the
woman that brought them 00 00 06; Item paid for 2 quire of paper
00 00 08; Item paid Johan Ellis upon a bill 02 12 00; Item paid as by a bill
for several things at Ex'id at the Assizes 15 18 07; Item paid Thomas
Moore upon his bill 00 03 00; Item paid Walter Heard upon his bill
00 04 04; h. Item paid for one barrel of butter 01 18 00
Sum total of this week's expense 25 09 09

### Saturday the 20th of August 1642

*First* paid the bailiff upon his bill 17 16 11; h. Item paid the market bill
02 07 04; Item paid four boats of gravel for the garden walks and the new
walk in park 00 16 00; Item paid for 10 dozen of trenchers 00 11 08; Item
given to him that brought them from *Baunton* 00 01 00; Item paid
Lesamoore for tuning the organ 01 10 00; Item paid Henry Hearder for

cutting and making of 6 acres of grass 01 04 00; Item delivered my Lady in two bags the fourth of August 1642 180 00 00
Sum total of this week's expense 204 06 11 £204 06s 11d

[page total] £229 16s 08d

## [p. 93]   Saturday the 27th of August 1642

*First* paid the bailiff upon his bill £02 02s 06d; Item paid the Cater upon his bill 01 08 10; Item paid Humfry Gribble upon his bill 00 12 10; Item paid Mrs Dawe in part for wine 10 00 00; Item paid Richard Downman upon his bill for cloth 02 11 8; Item paid Mr Lambe upon his bill 21 00 00; Item paid the fowler upon his bill 00 03 00; Item paid John Parsons for twice rowing my Lord by water 00 08 00; Item paid the fowler for rowing my Lord and Lady to Heanton 00 01 06
Sum total of this week's expense 38 08 04

## Saturday the 3rd of September 1642

Item paid the bailiff upon his bill £00 14s 06d; Item paid the Cater upon his bill 02 15 06; Item paid Will: Geare upon a bill for nails 00 04 01; Item paid the smith upon three bills 02 09 07; Item paid upon a bill for gloves for the workmen 00 04 06; Item paid Thomas Moore for work as by bill 00 18 00; Item sent my Lady by Sama' 00 10 00; Item paid Banton for mending the hangings 00 01 06; Item paid Mr Prust's man for money laid out in Cornwall as by bill 00 04 02; Item paid the fowler upon his bill 00 01 04; Item disbursed in my Lord's journey into *Corwall* as appears 025 02 06
Sum total of this week's expense is £33 05s 08d   [page total] £71 14s 00d

## [p. 95]   Saturday the 10th of September 1642

*First* paid the bailiff upon his bill £01 08s 09d; Item paid the Cater upon his bill 02 08 00; Item paid Baldwyn Steevens for barm 00 02 00; Item paid the Baker for barm 00 02 06; Item paid James Nicks for his quarter's fee due at Midsummer last 00 07 00; Item paid the smith upon his bill 00 08 04; Item given to the porter for helping to load the things that came from London 00 01 00; Item paid for making clean my Lord's sword 00 02 06; Item for making clean of Irish Tom's sword 00 02 00; Item spent at *Biddeford* 00 00 06; Item delivered my Lady in the green 00 02 00; Item given to Sir Hugh Pollard's man that brought a stag 00 10 00; Item spent at Molton 00 01 00
Sum total of this week's expense is 05 15 07   [page total] £5 15s 07d

## [p. 96]   Saturday the 17th of September 1642

*First* paid the bailiff upon his bill £05 11s 03d; Item paid the Cater upon his bill 02 11 09; Item paid Mrs Hardwick upon a bill 00 16 06; Item given to Sir Bevil Grenvill's fiddlers by command 00 05 00; Item paid for 7 couple of rabbits from *Branton Barrowes* 00 07 00; Item paid him that brought them 00 00 06; Item given to my Lord's musicians by command 00 05 00; Item paid for 3 partridges 00 00 06
Sum total of this week's expense is 09 17 06

## Saturday the 24th of September 1642

*First* paid the bailiff upon his bill 03 01 11; Item paid the Cater upon his bill 01 16 05; Item given to Mr Welshe's groom 00 01 00; Item paid

Gregory Hosegood upon his bill oo oo1 04; Item given to a poor Irishman by command oo o2 oo; Item spent in my journey to Mr Acklands oo o2 oo; Item spent at Molton when my Lord dined there as by bill oo 19 10; Item paid upon a bill for locks, rings &c oo o8 o6 So the total of this week's expense is £o6 18s ood [page total] £16 15s o6d

### [p. 99]   Saturday the first of October 1642

*First* paid the bailiff upon his bill £oo 13s o7d; Item paid the Cater upon his bill o1 63 o2; Item given my Lady to give away oo o2 oo; Item paid the hop-gatherers upon bill o4 o4 o4; Item delivered my Lady the morning her Ladyship went towards London last 40 oo oo; Item delivered Wilmot Toogood for her journey to London oo 12 oo; Item delivered Mrs Voysyn when she went for London o5 oo oo; Item [blank] Sum total of this week's expense is £51 15s o1d

### Saturday the 8th of October 1642

Item paid the bailiff upon his bill oo 11 09; Item paid the Cater upon his bill oo 14 o6; Item given to Mr Prust's man for bringing the gray mare from thence oo o1 o6; Item paid Philip Morcome for a new bell for the clock, for mending my Lady's watch and for his quartering due at Michaelmas last oo 10 oo; Item paid the Welsh dick for his expenses when he went to the Sheriff's oo o4 o6; Item paid ['him' crossed through] for a letter per post oo o1 oo; Item paid the smith upon four bills o1 18 o8; Item paid William Meane for fetching the boat oo oo o6; Item paid George Thorne for 2 day's work oo o1 oo Sum total of this week's expense is o4 o3 o5    [page total] £55 18s o6d

### [p. 101]   Saturday the 15th of October 1642

*First* paid the bailiff upon his bill £oo 09s 1od; Item paid the Cater upon his bill oo o3 o3; Item paid the Carpenter upon his bill o1 o5 o8; Item paid the Welsh dick for his journey into the South Hams oo o4 oo; Item paid the wheat threshers for threshing of 18 bushels of wheat oo 13 o6; Item paid for threshing of 160 bushels of oats o1 o6 o8; Item paid for wine and casks &c as by bill o1 17 oo Sum total of this week's expense is ['o5 o6 o5' crossed through] o5 19 11

### Saturday the 22th of October 1642

*First* paid the bailiff upon his bill oo o9 11; Item paid the Cater upon his bill oo 13 o5; Item paid Mr Bulworthy upon his bill oo 17 oo; Item paid Thomas Moore upon two bills o1 14 oo; Item paid Mr Howard for so much received by my brother in London for my Lo: use o2 10 oo; Item paid Mrs Coop upon bill for the coachman's suit o2 14 oo; Item paid Rowe the shoemaker upon his bill o1 o6 oo; Item paid Williams the plumber for Michaelmas quarter o1 19 o6; Item paid the Cutler for making clean my Lord's sword oo o2 o6; Item paid Avis Starling upon her bill oo o6 oo; Item paid Mrs Baker upon bills 14 17 o6; Item paid upon a bill for butter & feathers o5 18 11; Item paid Huxtable upon bills due in Mr Slowleye's time being gentleman of the horse o2 o9 oo; Item paid him upon another bill oo o8 o6; Item paid Baldwyn Steevens upon his bill for nets and thread for the fishing o1 o3 o3; Item paid James Nicks for Michaelmas quarter oo o7 oo; Item paid Will Rumson for 3 weeks wages

oo o3 oo; Item paid the servants wages due at Michaelmas last as by a bill of the particulars 53 13 04
So the total sum of this week's expense £91 12s 10d
[page total] £97 12s 09d

[p. 102]  The total of this year's disbursements from the Audit 1641 until the Audit 1642 is as by this book doth appear £1429 18s 02d
More delivered to my Lady's own hands in the audit week 1642 the sum of 830 00 00
More disbursed upon several bill as appears by the particulars being showed and allowed by my Lady the sum of 049 06 06
Sum total of my disbursements is 2309 04 08
Whereof received in the said year as by my own books receipts in particular doth appear £2210 04s 09 qr
So rest due to this account £98 19s 10d ½ qr
[signed] R. Bathe

**26 October 1643.**  The receipts & disbursements above mentioned have been cast up & examined & found to be true by us. [signed] Hu. Prust Joseph Jackman

[p. 111]  **Tawstock.**  Disbursed by me Richard Pollard for the household expense and other defrayments of the right honourable the earl of Bath from the 22th of October 1642 until &c.

**Saturday the 29th of October 1642**
*First* allowed myself that was due unto me upon my last account made the 20th of October last £99 00s 01d; Item paid the workmens bill oo o2 06; Item paid the market bill oo o2 11; Item paid Humfry Gribble upon bill oo o3 04; Item paid the smith upon his bill oo o5 oo; Item paid Will: Geare upon a bill oo o1 06; Item paid Roger Thorne in part of bill o5 oo oo; Item paid for 40 fat wethers 21 oo oo Memorandum there is six pounds more due on this leaf.
Sum total of this week's expense is [illegible crossed through] 125 15 04¼ [sic]

**Saturday the 5th of November 1642**
Item paid the workmen's bill oo o2 06; Item paid for letters per post oo o1 oo; Item paid for wine to Mr Stitch as by his bill o1 19 oo; Item paid Nell Hartnall for 12 days work oo o3 oo; Item paid for things for little Ned oo o8 o1 ½; Item delivered Mr Cobb oo 10 oo
Sum total of this week's expense o3 o3 o7 ½

**Saturday the 12th of November 1642**
Item paid the workmens bill £oo o4s o6d; Item paid the market bill oo 11 oo; Item paid Jo: Midway for 2 days work oo o1 10; Item paid for letters per post oo o1 oo
Sum total of this week's expense is £oo 18s o4d
[page total] £129 19s o3d ½

[p. 113]  **Saturday the 19th of November 1642**
*First* paid the workmen's bill £oo 10s ood; Item paid the market bill oo 11 oo; Item paid the smith upon his bill oo o9 10
Sum total of this week's expense is o1 10 10

**Saturday the 26th of November 1642**
Item paid the workmen's bill 01 02 00; Item paid the market bill 00 13 06;
Item paid the Carrier in part of his bill 05 00 00; Item paid Mr Mason for
a butt of rich *Malligoe* sack 17 00 00
Sum total of this week's expense is 23 15 06

**Saturday the 3rd of December 1642**
Item paid the workmen's bill 00 15 06; Item paid the market bill 00 16 00;
Item paid Ann Mullins upon her bill 00 07 03
Sum total of this week's expense is 01 18 09

**Saturday the tenth of December 1642**
Item paid the workmen's bill 00 08 00; Item paid the market bill 00 19 01;
Item paid for half a hundred of poor Johns 00 07 00
Sum total of this week's expense is 01 14 01   [page total] £28 19s 02d

**[p. 115]   Saturday the 17th of December 1642**
*First* paid the workmens bill £00 10s 09d; Item paid the market bill
00 14 08; Item paid for threshing of one hundred bushels of barley
01 05 00
Sum total of this week's expense is 02 10 05

**Saturday the 24th of December 1642**
Item paid the workmen's bill 00 17 06; Item paid the market bill 00 09 03;
Item paid upon a bill for things for the boys as appears 00 07 08; Item
given to Mr Rools his keep[er] for his pains in killing 2 brace of does
against Christmas 00 05 00
Sum total of this week's expense is 01 19 05

**Saturday the 31th of December 1642**
Item paid the Market bill £00 06s 00d; Item paid Thurstyn Heymer in part
of his ['part of' crossed through] wages 01 00 00
Sum total of this week's expense £01 06s 0d   [page total] £05 05s 10d

**[p. 117]   Saturday the 7th of January 1642**
Item paid the workmens bill of wages £00 10s 06d; Item paid the market
bill 00 08 00; Item paid Mr John Jerman for so much paid my Lady in
London 06 00 00
Sum total of this week's expense 06 18 06

**Saturday the 14th of January 1642**
Item paid the workmens bill of wages £01 14s 10d; Item paid the market
bill 00 06 01; Item paid Mr Page for 10 bushels of salt at 2s per bushel 01
08 04; Item paid Mrs Dawe in full of her bill for wine bought as appears
02 16 00
Sum total of this week's expense 06 05 03

**Saturday the 21th of January 1642**
Item paid the workmens bill of wages £00 15s 05d; Item paid the market
bill 00 05 01; Item paid John Willms for his quarter wages due at
Christmas last 01 13 04; Item paid for letters per post 00 01 00; Item paid
for mending a pair of billows [bellows] 00 01 04; Item paid the smith upon
his bill 01 11 06; Item paid Hugh Combe for his horse 12 days in harvest
00 04 00
Sum total of this week's expense is 04 11 08   [page total] £17 15s 05d

**[p. 119]   Saturday the 28th of January 1642**
Item paid the workmen wages upon bill £00 06s 03d; Item paid the market
bill 02 18 09; Item paid Edward Bauton for mending the boys clothes as
by bill 00 09 00; Item paid for 2 quires of paper 00 00 09; Item paid for
leather to nail up the trees 00 00 03
Sum total of this week is 03 15 00

**Saturday the 4th of February 1642**
Item paid the workmen wages upon bill £00 08s 01d; Item paid the market
bill 00 01 11; Item paid the Welsh dick for going to Mr Prust of an errand
00 01 00; Item paid for a collar of brawn 00 03 00; Item paid for letters
per post 00 00 06
Sum total of this week's expense is 00 14 06

**Saturday the 11th of Feb. 1642**
Item paid the workmens bill for wages £00 06s 08d; Item paid the market
bill 01 00 00; Item given to the old Tomson an Embroiderer 00 02 00;
Item paid Thorne the carrier in part of his bill for carriage 05 00 00
Sum total of this week's expense is 06 08 08   [page total] £10 18s 02d

**[p. 121]   Saturday the 18th of February 1642**
Item paid the workmens wages by bill £00 08s 04d; Item paid the market
bill 00 09 09; Item paid for 9 bushels of culm 00 07 06
Sum total of this week's expense is 01 05 07

**Saturday the 26th [sic] of February 1642**
Item paid the workmens wages upon bill 00 06 05; Item paid the market
bill 00 06 00; Item paid for 8 bushels of culm 00 06 08
Sum total of this week's expense is £00 19s 01d

**Saturday the 4th of March 1642**
Item paid the workmens bill of wages £00 15s 09d; Item paid the market
bill 00 07 09; Item paid the smith upon his bill 00 16 10; Item paid him
more upon bill 01 00 00; Item paid for threshing of 49 bushels of barley at
3d per bushel 00 12 03; Item paid Mr Cobb 02 00 00; Item paid
Mr Thurstin in part of his wages 00 10 00
Sum total of this week's expense is [illegible crossed through] 06 02 07
[page total] £08 07s 03d

**[p. 123]   Saturday the 11th of March 1642**
Item paid the workmens wages upon bill £01 07s 05d; Item paid the
market bill 00 16 11; Item paid for ringing John Payn's knell 00 06 00;
Item paid for fruit and wine for his funeral 00 06 00; Item paid for 2 quire
of paper 00 00 09
Sum total of this week's expense 02 07 01

**Saturday the 18th of March 1642**
Item paid the workmens bill of wages 01 00 06; Item paid the market bill
00 09 05; Item paid Symon Lake for half a years wages due at Candlemas
last 02 15 00; Item paid the widow Cuniber for six cheeses weighing
73 pound at 2d ½ 00 15 00; Item paid Edward Fairechild for five weeks
wages after his quarter was up 00 07 00; Item paid for threshing of
200 bushels of oats at 14s per hundred 01 08 00; Item paid Mr Howard for

so much rec. by Mr Lyn in London 03 00 00; Item paid for 10 bushels of lime at 7d ½ per bushel 00 06 03
Sum total of this week's expense is 09 01 02   [page total] £11 08s 02d

**[p. 125]   Saturday the 25th of March 1643**
Item paid the workmens wages upon bill £00 14s 11d; Item paid the Market bill 00 04 04; Item paid for bringing home a Mill stone 00 01 00; Item paid for seeds for the garden 00 07 06; Item paid the glasier upon his bill 00 15 06; Item paid my brother Thomas upon his bill 01 11 06
Sum total of this week's expense 03 14 09

**Saturday the first of April 1643**
Item paid the workmens bill for wages £00 18s 02d; Item paid the market bill 01 04 04; Item paid for 2 yards and half of stuff to make Ned Heale a suit at 2s 6d per yard 00 06 00; Item paid Joseph Ley for 2 fat oxen bought of him before my Lord went to London last 10 13 04; Item paid Nathaniel Merrick for one cask of butter weighing 88 lbs at 4d ½ per pound 01 13 00; Item paid for a new key for the great gate 00 02 ½; Item paid for a pair of shoes for Ned Heale 00 02 ½
Sum total of this week's expense 14 19 10   [page total] £18 14s 07d

**[p. 127]   Saturday the 8th of April 1643**
Item paid the workmens bill of wages £00 12s 06d; Item paid the market bill 01 05 02; Item paid James Nicks for one quarter's fee due at Christmas last 00 05 00; Item paid Ned Banton for making Ned Heal's clothes as by his bill of particulars 00 08 10; Item paid for a lock for the park gate 00 00 06; Item paid James Hartnoll for half a year's wages due at our Lady Day last 01 13 04; Item paid for brooms 00 01 01
Sum total of this week's expense 04 06 05

**Saturday the 15th of April 1643**
Item paid the workmens bill of wages £01 07s 11d; Item paid the market bill 00 13 08; Item paid for one weigh of coal 01 12 00; Item paid for bringing the coal from Pilton 00 02 06; Item paid for threshing of 50 bushels of barley 00 12 06; Item paid Baldwyn Steevens for barm 00 00 06; Item paid for threshing of 150 bushels of oats at 14s per hundred 01 01 00
Sum total of this week's expense is 05 10 01   [page total] £09 16s 06d

**[p. 129]   Saturday the 22th of April 1643**
Item paid the workmens bill of wages £01 16s 01d; Item paid the market bill 01 03 02; Item paid James Cocke upon his bill for work done 00 03 06; Item paid for making of 300 of faggots and 100 poles 00 02 06; Item paid for a mill-stone 03 00 00; Item paid Charles for one day's work at the mill 00 01 04
So the total of this week's expense 06 06 07

**Saturday the 29th of April 1643**
Item paid the workmens wages upon bill £00 14s 04d; Item paid the market bill 01 05 00; Item paid for mending the key of the buttery door 00 00 08; Item paid for dressing the boy's hat 00 00 04; Item paid for a hange [*hinge*] lock for a gate 00 01 04; Item paid John Willims for his quarter's wages due at our Lady Day last 01 13 04
Sum total of this week's expense is 03 15 00   [page total] £10 01s 07d

**[p. 131]   Saturday the 6th of May 1643**
*First* paid the workmens wages upon bill £oo o6s ood; Item paid the
market bill oo 15 11; Item paid for cutting of Whitflanke oo o2 o6; Item
paid the smith upon two bills oo 11 o3
Sum total of this week's expense is o1 15 o8

**Saturday the 13th of May 1643**
Item paid the workmens bill of wages £oo o8s o7d; Item paid the market
bill oo 18 o4; Item paid for mending of sieves oo o1 oo; Item paid Alice
Searle for her half years wages due at our Lady Day last o1 oo oo; Item
paid Bess Randle for the like o1 oo oo; Item paid Bess Searle for the like
o1 10 oo; Item delivered my brother when he rode for London with
Mr Howards o2 oo oo
Sum total of this week's expense is o6 17 11   [page total] £o8 13s o7d

**[p. 133]   Saturday the 20th of May 1643**
Item paid the bailiff for workmens wages £oo 11s o1d; Item paid the
market bill o1 o3 o6; Item paid for mending the boys shoes oo oo o8; Item
paid for 2 bushels of lime oo o1 o4; Item paid for pigs rings oo oo o8; Item
paid for mending my Lady's bit oo o3 oo; Item paid for mending a key
oo oo o6; Item given to the post boy oo oo o6
So the sum total of this week's expense is o2 o1 o3

**Saturday the 27th of May 1643**
Item paid the bailiff upon his bill of wages oo 13 o6; Item paid the market
bill o1 o2 o8; Item given to Mr Pagett's man for plowing oo o1 oo; Item
paid for threshing of 200 bushels of oats at 14s per hundred o1 o8 oo; Item
paid Banton upon his bill for mending the boys clothes oo o1 o6; Item
paid for 2 quire of paper oo oo o8
Sum total of this week's expense is o3 o7 o4   [page total] £o5 o8s o7d

**[p. 135]   Saturday the 3d of June *in the year* 1643**
Item paid the workmens wages upon bill £oo 15s ood; Item paid the
market bill oo 13 10; Item paid the smith upon his bill oo o7 o8; Item paid
Mr Wright for measuring of the marsh into acres oo o2 o6; Item paid for
making of two new keys for pistols oo o2 oo
Sum total of this week's expense is o2 o1 oo

**Saturday the 10th of June 1643**
Item paid the workmens wages upon bill £o1 o2s ood; Item paid the
market bill oo 16 10; Item paid for threshing of 87 bushels of barley at
3d per bushel o1 o1 o9
Sum total of this week's expense is o3 oo o7

**Saturday the 17th of June 1643**
Item paid the workmens wages upon bill £o1 o2s ood; Item paid the
market bill o1 oo o1; Item paid Thorne the carrier upon his bill o5 o1 oo;
Item paid for mending the boys shoes oo oo o8; Item [blank]
Sum total of this week's expense is £o7 oos [sic] o9d
[page total] £12 o2s o4d

**[p. 137]   Saturday the 24th of June 1643**
Item paid the workmens bill of wages £oo 19s 1od; Item paid the market

bill 01 06 04; Item given a messenger that came from the high sheriff
00 01 00
Sum total of this week's expense is 02 07 02

### Saturday the first of July 1643
Item paid the workmens wages upon bill £00 02s 09d; Item paid the
market bill 00 18 09; Item paid for threshing of 194 bushels of oats at
14s per hundred 01 07 02; Item paid for a man to carry reed to
Mr Wichalls 00 00 06
Sum total of this week's expense 02 09 02

### Saturday the eight of July 1643
Item paid the bailiff's bill of wages £00 06s 11d; Item paid the market bill
01 04 11; Item paid James Hartnoll for his quarter's wages due at
Midsummer last 00 16 08
Sum total of this week's expense is 02 08 06   [page total] £07 04s 10d

### [p. 139]   Saturday the 15th of July 1643
Item paid John Willm for his wages due at Midsumer last as by bill
01 13 08; Item paid Mr Cobbe 01 10 00; Item paid for ten fat wethers
05 10 00; Item paid workmens wages upon bill 00 02 00
Sum total of this week's expense is 08 13 08

### Saturday the 22th of July 1643
Item paid the market bill £00 19s 11d; Item paid Mr Skitch upon his bill
00 17 08; Item paid Tho: Moore for 4 day's work for making the boy's
clothes 00 02 08; Item paid Scott for putting Bridge meadow into acres
00 01 06
Sum total of this week's expense is 02 01 09

### Saturday the 29th of July 1643
Item paid upon market bill 00 09 04; Item paid the smith upon his bill
00 13 00; Item paid Eliz: Serle for one quarter and a month wages due at
Midsummer last 00 18 00; Item paid for washing the horse [illegible]
00 01 06; Item paid Roger Thorne in full of his account as appears
03 12 00
Sum total of this week's expense is 02 13 10   [page total] £13 11s 03d

### [p. 141]   Saturday the 5th of August 1643
Item paid the market bill £00 17s 04d; Item paid Symon Lake for half a
year's wages due at Lammas last 01 15 00; Item spent at Torrington being
sent for by Colonel Digby 00 02 00
Sum total of this week's expense is 02 14 04

### Saturday the 12th of August 1643
Item paid workmens wages as by bill 00 10 09; Item paid the market bill
00 11 06; Item paid the apothecary upon his bill 00 03 00; Item paid Jo:
Gribble for going to Tiverton 00 03 00
Sum total of this week's expense is 01 08 03

### Saturday the 19th of August 1643
Item paid the market bill 00 03 07; Item paid for my expenses at
Torrington being sent for by Col. Gifford 00 02 00
Sum total of this week's expenses 00 05 07

**Saturday the 26th of August 1643**
Item paid the market bill oo 16 06; Item paid Robert Wood in part of his wages 02 oo oo; Item paid Eliz: Randle for half a year's wages then due 01 oo oo
Sum total of this week's expense is 03 16 06   [page total] £08 04s 08d

**[p. 143]   Saturday the second of Sept. 1643**
Item paid the market bill £oo 16s o6d; Item paid the smith upon his bill oo 18 07; Item paid Mr Wood for his journey to Oxford 01 05 00; Item given to a messenger that brought a letter from my Lord oo 01 06
Sum total of this week's expense 03 01 07

**Saturday the 9th of September 1643**
Item paid the market bill £oo 14s 1od; Item paid the hop-pickers for the wages as by bill 05 01 02; Item given unto a messenger that brought a letter from Dulverton from my Lord oo 02 06; Item given to a Tinker for mending a kettle oo 01 06; Item paid Christopher Quick for going to Tiverton after Mr Woode oo 02 oo
Sum total of this week's expense 06 02 oo

**Saturday the 16th of Sept. 1643**
Item paid the workmens wages upon bill oo 12 05; Item paid the market bill 01 oo 11; Item paid Rich: May upon a bill oo 04 06; Item delivered Raph Booth for his journey to Oxford with seven horses 02 oo oo; Item paid Thurstin in part of his wages oo 10 00; Item given Col. Digbye's groom for procuring gray Lyn again oo 05 00; Item for my expenses in getting him oo 02 oo
Sum total is 04 14 10   [page total] £13 18s o5d

**[p. 145]   Saturday the 23th of September 1643**
Item paid the workmens bills oo 09 06; Item paid the market bill oo 19 03; Item paid the smith upon bill oo 10 06; Item paid Gregory Hosgood upon bill oo 01 06; Item paid for 2 quire of paper oo oo [08]; Item paid William Ramson for his expenses in going to Hartland for sheep oo 02 06
Sum total of this week's expense is £02 03s 11d

**Saturday the 30th of September 1643**
Item paid the workmen wages upon bill £oo 07s 07d; Item paid the market bill oo 04 10; Item paid for sweeping 10 chimneys oo 01 08; Item paid for 2 weigh of coal 03 oo oo; Item given to the ringers by command oo 05 00; Item delivered Mr Bolde 02 18 06; Item [blank]
Sum total of this week's expense is [illegible crossed through] 06 17 02
[page total] £09 01s 01d

**[p. 147]   Saturday the 7th of October 1643**
Item paid the workmens wages by bill £oo 09s 08d; Item paid the market bill 01 18 00; Item paid for tape for my Lady oo oo 10; Item paid for black bobbin for my Lady oo 01 00; Item paid for two pair of worsted stocking for the postillion and footman oo 09 00; Item delivered Mr Booth for his journey to Oxford 02 oo oo
Sum total of this week's expense is 03 18 06

**Saturday the 14th of October 1643**
Item paid the workmen's wages by bill oo 13 02; Item paid the Cater bill 01 16 09; Item given to the page by command oo oo 06; Item given to a

man that brought a letter from my Lo: oo o1 oo; Item given to Sir John
Chichester's groom oo o1 oo; Item given to my La: Pollard's man that
brought a letter from my Lord oo o1 oo; Item paid Mr Bold oo 12 oo;
Item given to Gribble for his journey to *Exter* by command oo o3 o6
Sum total of this week's expense is o3 o8 11   [page total] £o7 o7s o7d

**[p. 149]   Saturday the 21th day of October 1643**
Item paid the workmens wages £oo o8s o5d; Item paid the Caters bill
o2 o7 o6; Item paid for 2 pair of gloves for the page oo oo 1o; Item paid
the apothecary for things for the horses oo o2 o6; Item paid Rich: Lake
upon a bill o2 o7 o4; Item given the page by command oo o2 oo; Item paid
Jo: Terry for one fat cow o3 1o oo; Item paid him for lime oo 1o oo; Item
paid Mr Prust for 40 fat wethers 19 oo oo; Item delivered my Lady
oo o2 o6; Item paid John Willms for his quarter due at Michaelmas last
o1 15 o9; Item paid Mrs Hardwick upon bill o2 17 o6
Sum total of this week's expense is 32 o4 o4

**[p. 150]**   Sum total of my receipts from the Audit 1642 until the Audit
1643 as by a book of the particulars doth appear £1220 o6s o9d
Whereof disbursed for the said year as by this book doth appear
£369 12s o7½d
More disbursed as by a bill of particulars doth appear being showed and
allowed by my Lady the same 802 oo oo
Sum total of my disbursements 1171 12 o7½
So rest due in the accountant's hands £48 14s o2d
[signed] R. Bathe

**26 October 1643.**   The receipts & disbursements above mentioned have
been cast up, examined & found to be true by us. [signed] Hu. Prust
Joseph Jackman

**[p. 153]**   *Tawstocke* disbursed by me Richard Pollard for the household
expense and other defrayments of the right honourable Henry Earl of Bath
from the 21th of October 1643 until

**Saturday the 28th of October 1643**
Item paid the workmen wages as by bill £oo 16s o2d; Item paid the Cater's
bill o1 12 o9; Item paid Mrs Hardwick upon a bill o5 o8 o7; Item paid
Tho: Irish upon his bill oo o5 oo; Item given to Mr Chichester's man that
brought a present oo o2 oo; Item spent in our journey to Hartland
oo o6 o6; Item paid for a pair of slings for my La: oo o4 oo
Sum total of this week's expense is o8 15 oo

**Saturday the 4th of Novemb. 1643**
Item paid the workmens wages as by bill oo 14 o7; Item paid the
Cater upon his bill o2 11 o3; Item paid Huxtable the smith upon bills and
in full oo 17 oo; Item paid him upon another bill o1 1o o4; Item paid John
Hamblyn upon his bill o1 o3 oo; Item paid Lawrence Chamberlyn upon
his bill oo o8 oo; Item delivered Mr Wood to buy glasses and other things
oo 1o oo
Sum total of this week's expense is o6 14 o2   [page total] £15 o9s o2d

**[p. 154]**   ['Audit 1643. Paid to my Lady in great sums £590 oos ood ...'
crossed through]
Sum is 597 16 o8d

**[p. 155]　Saturday the 11th of November 1643**
Item paid the workmens wages upon bill oo o9 o6; Item paid the Cater
upon bill o4 oo o6; Item paid for 17 yards a half of hair cloth at 2s per
yard o1 15 oo; Item paid for thread oo oo o3; Item paid for 28 yards of
plutch at 9d per yard o1 o1 oo; Item paid for twine to sew it oo oo o6;
Item given the ringers by command oo o5 oo; Item paid Lawrence Berry
upon two bills oo o9 oo; Item spent in my journey to *Bristoll* as by bill
o1 15 o4; Item paid Banton upon his bill oo o1 1o; Item disbursed at
*Bristoll* for several commodities as by bill 45 o2 o1; Item paid Lawrence
Berry upon bill oo o1 o8
Sum total of this week's expense is 55 o1 o8

**Saturday the 18th of November 1643**
Item paid the workmens wages upon bill oo 15 o6; Item paid the Caters
bill o2 1o 1o½; Item paid for oat malt oo 18 oo; Item paid the servants
wages as by bill 84 o5 o1; Item paid for oat malt to Richard Stanbury
o1 o1 o4; ['Item paid for a pair of slings for my Lady oo o4 oo' crossed
through]; Item paid Roger Thorne in part of his bill o5 oo oo; Item paid
John Peane's father in full of his son's wages due when he died o2 oo oo;
Item paid for one fat cow o3 oo oo; Item paid for 3 bushels of peas
oo 12 oo
Sum total of this week's expense is 1oo o2 o9½
[page total] £155 o4s o5d½

**[p. 157]　Saturday the 25th of November 1643**
Item paid the workmens wages upon bill £o1 o3s o8d; Item paid the Cater
upon his bill o3 o8 o5; Item given to a poor man by command oo o1 oo;
Item paid the sadler upon his bill o3 13 oo; Item given to a poor Irish
woman by command oo o1 oo; Item given the fiddlers by command
oo o5 oo; Item given to a woman that brought a present oo o2 oo; Item
given my Lady Pollard's man that brought a present oo o3 oo; Item given
Mr Incledon's man oo o2 oo; Item paid for my Lady to Mr Avis Pollard
oo o6 oo; Item delivered my Lady to play oo o1 oo; Item given to a
woman that brought a present oo o2 oo
Sum total of this week's expense o9 o8 o1

**Saturday the 2nd of December 1643**
Item paid the workmen wages upon bill £oo o7s o9d; Item paid the Cater
upon his bill o2 19 o7; Item paid for black velvet for my Lady oo o6 oo;
Item paid Sir Raph Sydenham by command 4o oo oo; Item paid for
2oo nails and glue oo oo o8; Item paid for mending of two pair of pistols
oo o2 o6; Item given Mr Collamoor's woman that brought a present
oo o2 oo; Item paid for weaving of 18 yards of cloth oo o7 o6; Item for
spinning of 21 lbs of yarn oo 1o o6; Item paid the smith upon his bill
o1 o1 oo; Item paid for a pair of shoes for George oo o3 oo
Sum total of this week's expense is 46 oo o6　[page total] £55 o8s o7d

**[p. 159]　Saturday the 9th of December 1643**
Item paid the workmens wages by bill £oo 11s 1od; Item paid the Cater's
bill o1 16 1o; Item paid the masons for 8 days work oo o4 oo; Item paid
for making clean Tho: sword and for a new sheath oo o3 oo; Item paid for
fulling 13 yards of cloth oo o5 o6; paid for a book of gold oo o1 oo; paid

for a comb brush oo oo o6; paid my Lady for Mr Bulworthy 30 oo oo; paid Will Heard for 4 day's work oo o1 o4; paid two poor Irish soldiers oo o2 oo; paid a tinker for mending a kettle oo o2 o6; paid for 2 tons of vessels o1 oo oo; paid for thread and nets for the hutch oo o6 oo; paid for 2 snipes oo oo o3
Sum total of this week's expense 34 14 o9

### Saturday the 16th day of December 1643

Item paid the workmens wages upon bill oo 18 o; paid the Cater upon bill o1 o1 o1; Item given Mr Smith maids that brought a present oo o2 o6; paid Rose that she gave the carrier for letters oo oo o6; paid the smith upon his bill oo 17 oo; paid for making of 540 faggots oo o3 o6; paid for bringing two weigh of coal from Appledore oo o5 oo; paid for 2 men and horses to bring it home oo o2 oo; paid for threshing of 54 bushels of barley oo 13 o6; paid William Meane for 4 day's work oo o3 o4
Sum total of this week's expense is o4 o6 o5    [page total] £39 o1s o2d

### [p. 161]    Saturday the 23th of December 1643

Item paid the workmens wages upon bill £o1 o6s o5d; paid the Cater upon bill o3 o2 11; paid Tho: Lovering for 3 steers in p[ar]t 10 oo oo; Item given my Lord Chichester's man oo o5 oo; paid my brother upon a bill oo 10 o8; paid Thurstyn upon his bill oo 10 oo; given Mr Pollard's man that brought a present oo o2 o6; given Doctor Chichester's man that brought a present oo 12 oo; given Mr Snow's man that brought a present oo o2 oo; Item disbursed at *Exon* as by bills delivered my Lady 25 12 11
Sum total of this week's expense is 41 14 o5

### Saturday the 30th of December 1643

Item paid the Cater upon his bill £o2 17s 1od; Item given to the poor when my Lord did receive the sacrament oo 10 oo; Item delivered my Lady in gold 20 oo oo; paid John Midway for making of 11 dozen of wood at 11d per dozen oo 10 o1; paid for bringing the wine and other things from *Bristoll* oo 15 oo; paid for thread oo oo o6; paid the glasier upon bill oo 13 oo; Item delivered my Lady to play o1 oo oo; paid for one fat cow o3 o2 oo; paid the shoemaker upon bill o1 o5 oo
Sum total of this week's expense is 30 13 o5    [page total] £72 o7s 1od

### [p. 163]    Saturday the 6th of Jan. 1643

Item paid the Cater's bill £o3 11s ood; Item paid for making two shirts for old wing oo oo o8; given to Mr Berry's man that brought a present oo o2 o6; given to Mr Smiths servant that brought a gammon of Spanish bacon oo o1 o6; given to the old Tomson oo o2 oo; paid for 6 bushels of wheat o2 o2 oo; paid for a pair of spurs for Jo: Buck oo o1 oo
Sum total of this week's expense is o6 oo o8

### Saturday the 13th of Jan. 1643

Item paid the workmen wages upon bill oo o3 1o; Item paid the Cater upon bill oo 17 o4; Item paid the fiddlers by command o1 oo oo; Item paid for hooks and a saw for the garden oo o4 oo; Item paid Lawrence Berry upon his bill oo o4 oo; Item paid James Blackmoore for one quarter's wages due at Christmas last o1 oo oo; paid for 7 yards and half of cloth for John Buck's suit and for silk as by bill o2 o3 oo; Item given Baldwyn Steevens and Bess Randle by command oo o5 oo; Item paid Oxford carrier

oo o1 oo; given the page oo oo o6; Item paid Wilmot Toogood for her
quarter wages due at Christmas last oo 10 oo
Sum total of this week's expense is o6 o8 o8   [page total] £12 o9s o4d

**[p. 165]   Saturday the 21th of January 1643**
Item paid the workmens wages by bill £oo 19s o4d; Item paid the Cater
upon bill oo 11 o1; Item paid for boots and shoes and gloves for John
Burke oo 15 oo; paid Tho: Irish for money laid out oo o2 oo; paid for
mending of 3 pair of pistols and 3 carbines with fire locks oo o9 oo; paid
for 2 lbs of shot oo oo o6; paid Avis Starling for washing [?clothes] of
Jo: Burke and Tho: Irish oo o8 oo; paid for two weigh of coal o3 o4 oo;
paid James Whitfeild for 3 weeks work in the garden oo o3 oo
Sum total of this week's expense o6 11 11

**Saturday the 28th of January 1643**
Item paid the workmen wages upon bill oo oo9 o6; Item paid the Cater
upon bill o1 o2 o2; Item paid Banton upon his bill oo o4 oo; Item paid the
smith upon his bill o1 11 oo; Item delivered my Lady in Spanish money
o2 o3 o4; Item paid John Midway for making of four dozen of hardwood
oo o3 o8; Item spent at Bideford oo o1 o6; Item paid for threshing of four
score and eight bush: of oats at 2d p[er] bushel oo 14 o8; Item paid for one
fat ox bought of Mr Pagett o6 oo oo
Sum total of this week's expense is 12 o9 11   [page total] 19 o1 10

**[p. 167]   Saturday the third of February 1643**
Item paid the workmen wages by bill oo 11 oo; Item paid the Cater upon
bill o2 o2 oo; Item paid John Willm upon his bill for his quarter due at
Christmas o1 13 o4; Item given the fiddlers by command oo o5 oo; Item
given to a maid that brought a parrot to my Lady oo o1 oo; Item paid for
a fat steer bought of Mrs Hartly o4 12 oo; Item paid for 6 bushels of culm
oo o5 oo
Sum total of this week's expense is o9 o8 o4

**Saturday the 10th of February 1643**
Item paid the workmens wages by bill £oo 12s o2d; Item paid the Cater
upon his bill o1 o5 11; Item given to a poor Irish man by command
oo o2 o6; Item given to Mr Berrie's man that brought a lamb oo o2 oo;
Item paid for a yoke of oxen 10 oo oo; Item paid for making clean of guns
as by bill oo 11 oo
Sum total of this week's expense 12 14 o1

**Saturday the 17th of February 1643**
Item paid the workmen wages upon bill o1 o9 o5; Item paid the Cater
upon bill o1 o8 o2; Item paid Gregor Hosgood upon bill oo o2 oo; Item
paid Will Heare upon bill oo o2 oo; Item paid for a bit to ride a great
horse oo o3 oo; Item paid for silk and buttons for the footmen clothes
oo o4 oo; Item paid Thomas Berry for cloth for the boy oo o8 o9; Item
spent at *Barnestaple* when I went in with soldiers oo o3 oo
Sum is £o4 oos 4d   [page total] £26 o2s o9d

**[p. 169]   Saturday the 24th of Feb. 1643**
Item paid the workmens wages upon bill £oo o5s o6d; Item paid the Cater
upon his bill oo 16 o7; Item given a messenger that brought letters from
*Coome* oo oo o6; Item paid George Pitts for making of 500 faggots

oo o3 o9; Item paid him more for making of 100 hop poles and 6 bundles of spars oo o1 oo; Item paid George Balch for making of 500 of faggots oo o3 o9; Item paid him more for cutting out of 100 hop-poles and 3 bundles of spars oo oo o9; Item paid for one seam of hardwood oo oo o1; Item paid for threshing of one hundred and eleven bushels of barley o1 o7 o9; Item paid for theshing of 66 bushels of oats oo 11 oo; Item paid for 6 days work to men to fetch in the mowe oo o5 oo; Item given to a poor Irishman by command oo o2 o6
Sum total of this week's expense o3 18 o2

**Saturday the 3d of March 1643**
Item paid the workmens wages upon bill oo o5 o6; Item paid the Cater upon bill o2 13 o9; Item paid for 4 bushels of culm oo o4 oo; Item paid my lady in gold 14 13 oo; Item given to the carrier oo o1 o6; Item paid Rob: Wood oo oo o4; Item paid for 6 bushels of culm oo o6 oo; Item paid for shoeing of my horse oo oo o6; Item spent at Bow for Mr Wyout and myself oo 14 o8; ['Item paid the smith upon bill …' crossed through]
Sum total of this week's expense 18 19 o3    18 o9 o3
[page total] £22 17s o5d

**[p. 171]    Saturday the tenth of March 1643**
Item paid the workmens wages upon bill £oo o6s o9d; Item paid the Cater upon his bill oo 14 o1; Item paid my Lady of Preston's money 20 oo oo; Item given to a poor woman by command oo oo o6; Item given to widow Cuniber's servants oo o1 o6; Item paid Richard Stanbury for plowing the barley ground not accounted the last year oo 13 o4; Item given to Mr Roll's house amongst the servants when my Lady dined there oo 10 oo; Item paid William Balch for making of 500 faggots oo o3 o9; Item paid him for 150 hop poles oo oo o9; Item paid George Pitts for making of 800 faggots oo o6 oo; Item paid him more for 200 hop-poles oo o1 oo; Item paid him more for 7 seams of hardwood oo oo o7; Item paid more for 2 bundles of spars oo oo o2; South End Park. Item for making 20 yards of the park hedge o1 oo oo
Sum total of this week's expenses 23 18 o5

**Saturday the 17th of March 1643**
Item paid the workmens wages upon bill oo o7 o2; Item paid the Cater upon his bill o2 o2 o3; Item paid the smith upon his bill o1 o4 o8; Item paid my Lady of James Parrett's money 38 oo oo; Item paid John Hamblyn in part of his bill o3 oo oo; Item paid him upon another bill oo o3 oo; Item paid Mr Cobb for so much laid out for my Lady oo o2 oo; paid Edward Banton for one day and nights wages oo oo o6; paid Losamoore for mending a vial and my Lord's holsters oo o2 o6; paid John Midway for breaking of ten dozen of hardwood and 1 seam oo o9 o3; paid more for 14 dozen of blocks oo o7 oo; paid more for 11 dozen of pales oo o3 10
Sum total of this week's expense is 46 o2 o2    [page total] £70 oos o7d

**[p. 172]    Memorandum** that my accounts from the 28th of October 1643 unto the 23th of March were examined by my Lady and then I was indebted to my Lord as appears, the sum of nineteen pounds eleven shillings four pence. See my Lady's book.

**[p. 173]  Saturday the 23th of March 1643**
Item paid the workmen wages upon bill £oo 09s 11d; Item paid the Cater
upon his bill 05 09 08; Item paid the apothecary upon his [bill] oo 16 04;
Item paid for 2 ounces of silk at *Exter* oo 06 oo; Item spent at *Exter* upon
bill oo 07 02; Item paid the chimney sweep oo o1 oo; Item given to a man
that brought letters oo o1 oo; Item paid George Pitts for 400 faggots
making and for 100 hop poles and 6 seams of hardwood oo 04 09; Item
paid William Balch for making 400 faggots, 100 poles, 11 bundles of spars
and 14 seams of hardwood oo 04 09; Item paid my Lady of rent which
Edward Randle brought o8 oo oo; west end. Item paid the hedgers for
making of 49 yards of the Park Hedge by the bowling green o2 09 oo;
Item paid a messenger that brought letters from my Lord oo o1 oo; paid
for threshing of 64 bushels of barley oo 16 oo; Item spent at *Exon* and
*Banton* as by bill o1 19 oo; Item paid George ['Pitts' crossed through]
Balch for making of 300 faggots oo o2 03; Item paid him more for making
of 3 seams of hardwood and 3 bundles of spars oo oo 06; Item paid
George Pitts for making of 100 faggots 3 seams of hardwood and
3 bundles of spars oo o1 06; Item paid for a boat of sand for the garden
oo o2 06
Sum total of this week's expense 21 11 07
Ex.   [page total] £21 11s 07d

**[p. 175]  Saturday the 30th of March 1644**
Item paid the workmens bill £oo o2s o8d; Item paid the Cater upon his bill
03 18 oo; Item paid the shoemaker upon his bill o1 06 oo; Item given
Mr Carie's man by command oo o2 06; Item paid Charles Allen for
3 day's wages oo o1 06; Item paid Morcome for half a year's fee due at
Our Lady Day oo 04 oo; Item paid him more for line for the clock and
mending a key for my Lady oo o2 oo; Item given to Sir Jo: Chichester's
grooms oo o1 oo; Item paid for setting over the water at Cunibers
oo oo 06; Item paid for setting my Lady over from Tawton oo o1 oo; Item
paid the gold finders oo 06 o8; Item allowed myself for half a year's wages
due at our La: day 10 oo oo; Item given the boatmen oo o5 oo; Item paid
George Pitts for making of 500 faggots at 7d per hundred oo o2 11; Item
paid him more for making of 6 seams of hardwood and 4 bundles of spars
oo oo 10; Item paid Johan Ellis upon bill oo 11 03; Item paid William
Balch for making of 500 faggots oo o2 11; paid the smith upon two bills
o1 19 06; paid Richard Stanbury for hay at parsonage 04 oo oo
Sum total of this week's expense is 23 o8 03   [page total] £23 o8s 03d

**[p. 177]  Saturday the 6th of ['March' crossed through] April 1644**
Item paid the workmens wages upon bill oo 03 06; Item paid the Cater
upon bill 03 06 oo; Item paid for mending of 3 pistols oo o5 oo; Item paid
Mr Atkey for fat sheep in part by Mr Prust 09 18 oo; Item paid Mr Skitch
upon bill for wine 03 13 oo; Item paid Richard Lake for half a year's
wages due at our Lady Day last 03 10 oo; Item given a messenger that
brought letters from *Chimley* to my Lady oo o2 oo; Item paid Thurstyn in
full of his bill and for money laid out at *Yolston* [Youlston] oo o5 oo; Item
paid Tho: Lovering in full for three bullocks 03 10 oo; Item paid Will: Lee
for threshing of 19 bushels of oats at 2d per bushel oo 03 o2; Item paid
Mrs Coop in full upon bill oo 17 oo; Item paid John Hamlyn in full his

bill of four pounds oi oo oo; Item paid a messenger that brought letters
oo oi oo; Item paid for 200 of oysters oo o2 oo; Item paid my Lady in the
bowling green oo oo o6; Item paid Lawrence Chamberlyn for a cow
o3 o8 o4; Item paid him more upon his bill for wages oo o8 oo; Item paid
Zachary Chiveley for 1 truss of hay oo o8 oo; Item given to Mr Jo:
Down's maid oo o2 o6; Item paid for one weigh of coal oi 14 o6
Sum total of this week's expense 32 17 o6

**[p. 179]  Saturday the 13th of April 1644**
Item paid the workmen wages upon bill £oo o5s oid; Item paid the Cater
upon his bill o2 10 o7; Item paid for two quire of paper oo oo o8; Item
paid George Pitts for making of 300 faggots and 9 seams of hardwood
oo o2 o6; Item given the poor by command oo 10 oo; Item paid Coop for
making of 20 yards of the park hedge oi oi o8; paid Thomas Sum'er for
ten trusses of hay at 8s per truss o4 oo oo; Item paid for 4 bushels of great
culm oo o3 o4; Item paid for twine oo oo o6; Item paid for a lb of cork
oo oo o5; Item paid the saddler in part of his bill o5 oo oo; Item given to
John Marchant by command oo o5 oo; Item paid the Fremington hedgers
for 12 yards of hedge oo 12 oo; Item paid the Fremington hedgers for
making of 25 yards of the park hedge oi o5 oo; Item paid for a mill brass
for the mill oo 19 oo; Item paid the servants wages upon bill o9 o7 oi;
Item paid Zachary for half a truss of hay oo o4 oo; Item paid Baldwyn
Steevens for money disbursed when he went for the arms at *Biddeford*
oo o4 o6; Item paid Zachary for half a truss of hay oo o4 oo; Item paid
William Balch for making of 1400 faggots at 7d per hundred oo o8 o5;
Item paid him more for making of 7 seams of hardwood oo oo o7
So the total of this week's expense 27 o4 o4

**[p. 181]  Saturday the 20th of April 1644**
Item paid the workmens wages upon bill oo o4 o4; Item paid the Cater
upon his bill o3 o7 oi; Item paid George Pitts for making of 600 faggots
and 16 seams of hardwood and two bundles of spars oo o5 oo; Item paid
for making of 5 halters oo oo o6; Item paid for my Lady in the bowling
green oo o2 oo; Item given my Lady Sydenham's man oo o2 o6; Item given
my Lady in the green oo oi o6; Item paid Mr Bold oo o3 oo; Item
delivered my Lady oo oi oo; Item paid for one quarter of veal oo o3 o4;
Item paid for our horses at Barnstaple oo oo o4; Item paid William Lee for
threshing of 31 bushels of oats oo o5 o2; Item paid for my Lady in the
green oo oo o6; Item paid Lawrence ['Ch' crossed through] Berry upon bill
oo o4 oo; Item given Sir Jo: Chichester's groom oo oi o6; Item paid
Fremington hedgers for making of 30 yards of the park hedge oi 10 oo;
Item delivered my Lady in the green oo oo o6; Item paid Tho: Irish
oo o5 o6
Sum total of this week's expense is o8 19 o9

**[p. 183]  Saturday the 27th of April 1644**
Item paid the workmens wages upon bill £oo 14s o4d; Item paid the Cater
upon his bill oi o8 o6; Item paid George Pitts for making of 400 faggots at
7d per hundred oo o2 o4; Item paid him more for 9 seams of hardwood
oo oo o9; Item paid for tuning the organ oo o5 oo; Item paid for six fat
steers at Torr. fair 20 15 oo; Item paid Lawrence Chamberlyn in part for
one yoke of fat oxen o7 oo oo; Item paid for expenses here oo oi oo; Item

paid May upon his bill oo 03 09; Item paid for two calves 01 04 00; Item
paid Tho: Amsbey when he went away 01 00 00; Item paid for 6 bushels
of wheat 02 02 00; Item paid Coop for two boats of gravel oo 08 00; Item
paid the Fremington hedgers for making of 29 yards of the park hedge
01 09 00; Item paid for dishes and bowls oo 04 06; paid for turning 4 pair
of bowls oo 03 00; Item paid William Steevens for 4 truss of hay 01 00 00;
Item paid Coop: in full for making of 69 yards of the park hedge 01 14 09
Sum total of this week's expense is 39 15 11

[p. 185]   Saturday the 4th of May 1644
Item paid the workmens wages upon bill £oo 07s 11d; Item paid the Caters
bill 01 19 00; Item paid Wilmot for white wine and a glass oo 01 08; Item
given Jo: Parsons and his man for rowing my Lady to *Apledore* oo 03 06;
Item given two boatmen oo 02 00; Item given the trumpeter oo 02 06; Item
delivered my Lady at bowls oo 01 03; Item paid the smith upon bill
oo 08 06; Item given at Mr Roll's his servants oo 04 06; Item paid Robert
Wood oo 00 04; Item paid my Lady of William Watters heriot of
Marwood 05 00 00; Item paid for 10 bushels of coal oo 06 08; Item [paid]
Avis Starling for washing upon bill oo 08 00
Sum total of this week's expense is 09 05 10

Saturday the 11th of May 1644
Item paid the workmens wages upon bill £oo 12s 10d; Item paid the Cater
upon bill 01 06 10; Item paid for 6 bushels of coal oo 04 00; Item paid for
a boat of gravel oo 04 00; Item paid for 2 weigh and half of coal 04 00 00;
Item paid for threshing of 59 bushels of barley at 3d per bushel oo 14 09;
Item paid for threshing of 22 bushels of oats oo 03 08; Item paid George
Pitts for 630 faggots oo 04 00; Item paid for 13 seams of hardwood
oo 01 01; Item delivered my Lady at bowls oo 01 09; Item given a woman
oo 01 00; Item delivered my Lady oo 01 00; Item paid for hay 03 15 00;
Item given a messenger with letters oo 00 06
So the total of this week's expense is 11 10 05   [page total] £20 16s 03d

[p. 187]   Saturday the 18th of May 1644
Item paid the workmens wages upon bill 301 09s 06d; Item paid the Cater
upon bill 02 16 07; Item disbursed at *Exter* upon bill 17 07 11; Item
delivered my Lady to play at cards oo 01 06; Item paid John Williams
upon his bill for our Lady Day quarter 01 13 04; Item given Mr Harle's
man that brought a fat lamb oo 01 00; Item given Mr Berrie's man
oo 02 00; Item given Mr Welshe's groom oo 01 00; Item given the poor by
command oo 02 06
Sum total of this week's expense 23 15 04

Saturday the ['28' crossed through] 25th of May 1644
Item paid the workmen wages upon bill 01 ['16' crossed through]12 08;
Item paid the Cater upon his bill oo 19 06; Item spent at *Coombe* upon
bill 02 08 07; Item paid John Burke upon a bill oo 03 04; Item spent at
*Exter* upon bill 05 09 09; Item paid the smith upon bill oo 16 00; Item
paid Mr Tyson of *Bristoll* upon bill 04 19 00; Item paid Johan Ellis for
making of 12 handkerchiefs for my lady oo 02 00; Item paid Mary White
for lobsters &c oo 03 03; Item paid for making clean the meadows
oo 02 00
Sum total of this week's expense is 16 16 01   [page total] £40 11s 05d

**[p. 189]  Saturday the first of June 1644**
Item paid the workmens wages upon bill £00 13s 04d; Item paid the Cater
upon bill 01 03 05; paid for keeping of a stray mare at Norton Fitzwarren
02 00 00; Item given the Oxford carriers boy 00 02 00; Item paid
Mrs Hardwick upon bill 00 10 08; Item spent at Bow upon bill 00 06 02;
Item paid the widow White for lobsters and other things ['00 03 06'
crossed through] Item paid Rose for a pair of stockings 00 07 00; Item
given my Lady to play at cards 00 01 00; Item paid the glasier upon bill
00 08 04; Item paid Banton for 3 days wages 00 01 00; Item given a man
that brought a letter 00 01 00; paid for one weigh of coal 01 16 00; given
to a collection in the church 00 02 06; paid for 300 nails 00 03 06
Sum total of this week's expense is 06 14 11

**Saturday the 8th of June 1644**
Item paid the workmens wages upon bill £01 01s 08d; Item paid the Cater
upon bill 01 08 02; Item paid for bringing home a tearce of claret wine
from Barnstaple 00 02 00; Item paid Mr Atkey for thirty fat sheep
19 10 00; Item spent at *Biddeford* when I went to buy sugars 00 02 00;
Item given to a collection in the church 00 02 06; Item spent for my Lord
and Lady in the green 00 02 00; Item paid for cutting the black colt
00 02 06
Sum total of this week's expense 22 09 10   [page total] £29 04s 09d

**[p. 191]  Saturday the 15th of June 1644**
Item paid the workmens wages upon bill £00 04s 10d; Item paid the Cater
upon his bill 02 10 01; Item paid for Edward Lowens clothes by bill
00 17 00; Item paid John Parsons and his man 00 02 06; Item given the
trumpeter 00 02 06; Item given the two boatmen 00 02 00; Item paid for
two pecks of peas 00 04 00; Item paid Lawrence Chamberlyn in full for
two oxen 06 15 00; Item paid Tho: Irish for money laid out 00 01 00; Item
paid the Smith upon bill 02 19 06; Item paid for garden seeds upon bill
00 09 11
Sum total of this week's expense is 13 08 04

**Saturday the 23th of June 1644**
Item paid the workmens wages upon bill 01 00 08; Item paid the Cater
upon his bill 01 16 07; Item paid my brother upon bill 00 05 00; Item paid
for beans 00 00 06; Item given Sir Jo: Chichester's man that brought
strawberries 00 01 00
So the total of this week's expense is 03 03 09   [page total] £16 12s 01d

**[p. 193]  Saturday the 29th of June 1644**
Item paid the workmens wages £00 15s 08d; Item paid the Cater upon bill
01 19 00; Item paid the carrier in full of his bill 03 12 00; Item delivered
John Burke for my Lord 00 05 00; Item given to the poor of Barnstaple
00 10 00; paid for standing my Lord's horses in Barnstaple 00 02 00; Item
paid for 50 muskets 00 06 00; Item paid the Cater upon a bill for several
things 05 09 06; Item paid for scurvy grass and lobsters 00 03 00; Item
given a man that brought letters from Cornwall 00 02 06; Item given
Baldwyn Baten when he went with the carrier 00 05 00; Item paid
Mr Wyot when he went into Cornwall 01 00 00
Sum total of this week's expense is 14 09 08

## Saturday the 6th of July 1644

Item paid the Cater upon his bill [blank]; Item paid the workmen wages upon bill oo 16 08; Item given Mr Booth when he went into Cornwall oo 03 oo; Item given Thomas Ambsby for his journey into Cornwall oo 05 oo; Item given Tho: Irish for his journey oo 03 oo; Item given to soldiers oo 02 oo; Item paid for threshing of 36 bushels of barley at 3d per bushel oo 09 03; Item paid for mending my Lord's boat oo 03 oo; Item paid Tho: Steevens for his horse hire oo 06 oo

Sum total of this week's expense 02 06 11    [page total] £16 16s 07d

## [p. 195]   Saturday the 13th of July 1644

Item paid the workmens wages upon bill £o1 oos 1od; Item paid the Cater upon bill oo 16 10; Item paid for mending the boat as by bill from Jo: Parsons oo 15 oo; Item paid for cutting ferns in the park ten days oo 06 08; Item paid the miller upon a bill for mending the mill oo 06 01; Item paid Jo: Parsons for his pains oo 02 oo; Item paid for making of one acre of hay in Bridge meadow oo 03 oo; Item given the two captains for preserving my Lord's house 08 oo oo; Item given their man for his pains oo 10 oo; Item paid for making of 3 acres of hay in *Rolston* [Rolleston] Meadow oo 09 oo

Sum total of this week's expense is 12 09 05

## Saturday the 20th of July 1644

Item paid the workmens wages upon bill oo 18 02; Item paid the Cater upon his bill [blank]; Item paid John Whitfeild for making of one acre of hay in *Rolston* [Rolleston] Meadow oo 03 04; Item paid Robert Coop for one week cutting ferns in the park oo 04 oo; paid for 3 bushels of beans oo 03 oo; Item paid for paper oo oo 08; Item given three soldiers oo oo 06

Sum total of this week's expense is o1 09 08    [page total] £13 19s o1d

## [p. 197]   Saturday the 27th of July 1644

Item paid the workmens wages upon bill £oo 08s 07d; Item paid Jo: Warren a mason for two week's wages oo 06 oo; Item paid Johan Whitfeild for 6 weeks weeding the garden oo 04 06; Item paid Rebecca Cooner for 4 week's weeding the garden oo 02 08; Item paid for a pound of pepper oo 03 oo; Item paid for making of one acre of hay in *Rolston* [Rolleston] meadow oo 03 04; Item paid for a protection oo 02 06; Item paid for making of one acre of hay in Bridge meadow oo 03 04; Item paid for making of two acres of hay in Bridge meadow oo 06 06; paid for a horse one day oo oo 04

So the total of this week's expense 02 oo 09

## Saturday the 3rd of ['July' crossed through] August 1644

Item paid the workmens wages by bill £oo 06s ood; Item paid the Cater upon bill 02 oo 02; Item paid Simon Tassell for making of 4 acres of hay oo 14 oo; Item paid John Gribble for his journey into Cornwall oo 05 oo; Item paid for 2 dozen of spoons oo 02 oo; Item paid Tho: Hearder for dressing a lame cow oo o1 06

Sum total of this week's expense 02 08 07    [page total] £4 09s 4d

## [p. 199]   Saturday the 10th of August 1644

Item paid the workmens wages £oo 05s ood; Item paid the market bill oo 03 11; Item paid for making of one acre of hay in Bridge meadow

oo o3 oo; Item paid for cutting of thirteen pigs oo o1 o6
So the total of this week's expense is oo 13 o5

**Saturday the 17th of ['September' crossed through] August 1644**
Item paid the workmen wages upon bill £oo 13s o4d; Item paid the market
bill oo o7 o1; Item paid for eggs oo o1 o6; Item paid for eight bushels of
great culm oo 10 oo; Item paid for workmen for digging of it oo o1 oo
Sum total of this week's expense is o1 12 11

**Saturday the 24th of August 1644**
Item paid the workmen wages upon bill £oo o4s o2d; Item paid for 5 joints
of mutton oo o3 o6; Item given to Jo: Gribble for his charge being in
Barnstaple prison oo o5 oo
Sum total of this week's expense is oo 12 o8

**Saturday the last of August 1644**
Item paid the workmen wages upon bill oo o6 oo; Item paid for beef and
mutton oo o6 oo; Item given Mathew Desbury oo o1 oo
Sum total of this week's expense is oo 13 oo   [page total] £3 12s ood

**[p. 201]   Saturday the 7th of Sept. 1644**
Item paid the workmens wages upon [a bill] £oo o6s ood; Item paid the
market bill oo 10 o4; Item paid for 4 bushels of culm oo o5 oo
Sum total of this week's expense is o1 o1 o4

**Saturday the 14th of Sept. 1644**
Item paid the workmens wages upon bill £oo o3s 1od; Item paid the smith
upon his bill oo 14 oo; Item paid for 3 lbs of cherries to preserve oo o1 o6;
Item paid Katheren Richards for making of 3 acres of hay in Bridge
meadow oo 10 o6; Item paid more for making of 6 acres and 3 quarters of
hay in Stone close oo 16 o3
Sum total of this week's expense is o2 6 o2

**Saturday the 21th of Sept. 1644**
Item paid the workmens wages upon bill oo o6 o9; Item paid for six
pounds of pitch to mend the cider pound oo o1 oo; Item paid for eggs
oo oo 10
Sum total of this week's expense is oo o8 o7   [page total] £3 16s o1d

**[p. 203]   Saturday the 28th of Sept. 1644**
Item paid the workmen wages by bill oo 10 o3; Item paid the market bill
oo o9 oo; Item given a man that brought a present of grapes oo o1 oo; Item
paid for 8 bushels of lime oo o8 oo; Item paid for scurvy grass oo o2 o8;
Item paid the smith upon bill o 17 11
Sum of this week's expense o2 o7 10

**Saturday the 4th [sic] of October 1644**
Item paid the workmens wages oo 10 o3; Item paid the market bill
oo o3 10; Item paid for bringing of letters from *Exter* oo o2 oo; Item paid
for 2 lbs half of black wool oo o2 o3; Item paid Raph Both for money laid
out oo oo o6; Item paid for ribbon for my Lord's shoes oo o1 oo; Item
given to Mr Pagett's man that brought a present oo o2 oo; Item paid for
combing of 3 lbs of wool oo o1 o6
Sum is o1 o3 o4

**Saturday the 12th of Octob. 1644**
Item paid the workmens wages by bill 01 00 03; Item paid the Cater upon
bill 01 17 08; Item given my Lady in the green 00 00 06; Item paid for
3 bushels of wheat 00 18 06; Item paid the shoemaker upon bill 02 10 06;
Item paid for a boat of gravel 00 04 00
Sum total is 06 11 05 [page total] £10 02s 03d

**[p. 205] Saturday the 19th of October 1644**
Item paid the workmens wages 00 08 00; Item paid the Cater upon his bill
02 03 06; Item paid the smith upon his bill 00 19 08; Item paid Maye upon
his bill 00 02 07; Item delivered my brother when he road towards
*Bannton* 00 02 06; Item delivered Jo: Burke for my Lord 00 02 06; Item
given a woman that brought grapes and pears 00 02 00; Item paid for
300 of bricks 00 03 00; Item paid Mrs Hardwick 00 02 06; Item paid for
twenty fat sheep 10 00 00; Item paid for 2 gallons of butter 00 06 00; to
the cobbler for mending Ed: Foster's boots and shoes 00 02 00; Item paid
Tho: Amsby for his journey to Oxford by command 01 05 00
So the total of this week's expense is £16 11s 03d

**[p. 207] Audit 1643**
Paid my Lady in great sums £590 00s 00d. Allowed to Mr Prust for the
great land rate in Hartland due from my Lord 004 10 00. Allowed Edward
Randle for a heriot brought in 003 06 08.
Sum is £597 16s 08d.
Allowed to myself for half a year's wages due at Audit 1644 10 0 0.
Sum total of my receipts from the Audit 1643 until the Audit 1644 as by a
book of the particulars doth appear is £1435 00s 08d ⅓.
Sum total of my disbursements in the said year as by this book will appear
£1426 08s 02d.
So rest due in my hands £0008 12 06⅓
The receipts and disbursements above mentioned have been cast up and
examined and found to be true by [signed] R. Bathe.

*[The following two pages appear inverted]*
**[p. 211] 20 Feb. 1640.**
Rec. of Edward Randle of *Wartley* for one quarter's rent ended at
  Christmas last £10.
18 Feb. 1643 [illegible crossed through.]
7 *March* Rec. of Mr Pagett then £5.
14th of March 1640 Rec. of Robert Whitfeild for part of his tithe wheat at
  *Tawstocke* 20s.
25 *March* 1641 Rec. of Mr Pagett at *Exon* £2.
2 April 1641 Rec. of Mr Pagett £10.
16 April 1641 Rec. of Hugh Coombe 10s.
17 April 1641 Rec. of Hugh Coombe £3.
May 25th 1641 Rec. of Hugh Coombe 20s.
May 29 1641 Rec. of Mr John Slowley for 1 oxen £10 7s.
June 25 1641 Rec. of Mr Pagett then £5.
July 14 1641 Rec. of Mr Pagett £6.
July 23 1641 Rec. of M'chant & Warren for sheep £5.
30 July 1641 Rec. of Mr Pagett £10.

3 *August* 1641 Rec. of John Grant of Torrington for 733 lbs of fell wool at
7d per lb £21 7s 7d.
Rec. for 140 lbs of wool at 6d per lb being full of earth and scabs
£3 10s 00d.

[p. 210]   An account of money paid in great sums and since the
Audit 1640.
*First* paid my Lady £020 00s 00d. Item paid Mr Ferris to be returned to
London 100 00 00. Item paid my Lady 050 00 00. Item paid my Lady
100 00 00. Item paid my Lady 030 00 00. Item paid Mr Booth for my
Lord 020 00 00. Item paid Mr Ja: Gamon to be repaid in London
100 00 00. Item paid Doctor Downe as by his acquittance 100 00 00.
Sum is £520 0 0.

# Receipts, 1641–1642, and Expenses, 1646

KENT ARCHIVES OFFICE, U269/A525/1

*The book measures 5¾" by 7½". The paper cover has several misc. sums
and notes. The book is headed 'Receipts in the year 1641'. Even-
numbered pages 4 to 28 are blank. The book contains both estate and
household accounts.*

[p. 3]   Manor Debits received at the Audit 1641 by me Richard Pollard
*Upex* [Up Exe] *manor*   Rec. of Humfry Browne bailiff £010 08s 05d 00
*Nymett Tracy* [Nymet Tracey]   Rec. of John Mortimer bailiff
   013 14 02 00
*Ilfardcombe* [Ilfracombe] *borough*   Rec. of William Brutton bailiff
   016 04 06 00
Kingston   Rec. of Richard Harvy bailiff 034 07 06 ½
*Nymett* [Nymet] *borough*   Rec. of John Withebrooke bailiff [illegible
   crossed through] 006 16 05
Holne   Rec. of Edward Hanaford bailiff 018 18 01 ½
Sheldon   Rec. of John Mills bailiff 013 16 01 ½
Spitchwick   Rec. of William Hanaford bailiff 012 12 01 00
*Warkley* [Warkleigh] *and others*   Rec. of Edward Randell bailiff
   023 12 09 ½
*Combintynhead* [Combeinteignhead]   Rec. of Jasper Randell bailiff
   009 14 02
*Bollham* [Bolham]   Rec. of George Welshe bailiff 012 17 03 ½
*page sum* 173 01 07 ½

[p. 5]   Dunterton   Rec. of Arthur Cornish bailiff £003 10s 04d ¼
Tawstock   Rec. of Richard Berry bailiff 036 06 00
*Cardynham* [Cardinham] *with other*   Rec. of Mr Rascarrocke
   010 03 03 ½
Hartland manor   Rec. of John Vyne bailiff 039 16 05 ½
Hartland *borough*   Rec. of Hugh Prust 004 14 03 ½
Sum total of the debits is £267 12s 00d ¼

[p. 7]   Fines received by me Richard Pollard at the Audit 1641; Rec. of Mr Cox of Instow in full of his fine £030 00s 00d; Rec. of Richard Berry of Tawstock in part of his fine 040 00 00; Rec. of Thomas Sweete in part of his fine 005 00 00; Rec. of Richard Preston in part of his fine 007 05 00; Rec. of John Tozer in part of his fine 045 00 00; Rec. of Mr Lethbridge in part of his fine 078 00 00; Rec. of John Grone in full of his fine 010 00 00; Rec. of Thomas Hobson in part of his fine 050 00 00   [total] 265 05 00

[p. 9]   Rec. of John Johnson in part of his fine £080 00s 00d; Rec. of Henry Chollish of Sheldon in ['part' crossed through] full of his fine 005 00 00; Rec. of Nicholas Chollish in part of his fine 040 00 00; Rec. of Roger Bethem of *Nymett tracy* in part of his fine 140 00 00; Rec. of Wilmot Lethbridge in part of her fine 020 00 00; Rec. of William Ellis in full of his fine 035 00 00; Rec. of Dorothy Tinker in full of her fine 030 00 00; Rec. of Joseph Ley in full of his fine 060 00 00; Rec. of James Marchant in full of his fine 070 00 00
Sum is 480 00 00

[p. 11]   Rec. of Roger Whitfeilde in full of his fine £017 00s 00d; Rec. of Eleanor Wynn in full of her fine 003 00 00
Sum total of the fines received by me Richard Pollard for which I am accountable is £765 05s.
Item more received of your honour to pay Mr Dolham £23.

[p. 13]   Tawstock Received by me Richard Pollard for the household expense & other defrayments of the right honourable Henry Earl of Bath since the 30th of October *in the year* 1641 until

18 December 1641.   *First* received of Mrs Hardwick £30 00s 00d; Item rec. of Richard Berry reeve of Tawstock for a herriot due upon the death of John Whitfeilde 00 13 04 00; Rec. of my brother for pasturing of 4 yearlings the summer 01 16 00; Rec. of George Rowclife for pasturing of 3 yearlings 01 07 00; Rec. for pasturing of Doctor Down's gale 00 10 00; 6 Feb. 1641   Rec. for a heriot due upon the death of Mr Box 02 16 08; 17 Feb. 1641   Rec. of Austin Travis for two fat oxen 14 03 04; 15 *March* 1641   Rec. of Mrs Hardwick 30 00 00   [page total] 81 06 04

[p. 15]   18 *March* 1641   Rec. of Mr Pagett to pay Doctor Downe £150 00s 00d; 25 *March* 1642   Rec. of Mrs Hardwicke 010 00 00; Rec. of Andrew Martyn a butcher for 8 fat oxen 068 00 00; 19 Apr. 1642   Rec. of Mrs Hardwick 010 00 00; 16 May 1642   Rec. for twenty fat lambs 006 15 00; 17 May 1642   Rec. for twenty fat sheep 016 00 00; 19 May 1642   Rec. of Mr Pagett for my Lord's use 060 00 00; 20 May 1642 Rec. of Mr Wyott for my Lord's use to be returned to London by bill 020 00 00; Rec. of Hugh Coombe upon several bills 072 11 03; Rec. for black Wyott which William Ellis sold 003 05 00; 23 *June* 1642   Rec. of Mrs Hardwick 010 00 00   [total] £426 11s 03d

[p. 17]   24 *June* 1642   Rec. of Mr Forde at *Totnis* 265 00 00; Rec. of Mr Hearle being part of his fine 060 00 00; Rec. of John Johnson being part of his fine 050 00 00; 5 July 1642   Rec. of Mr Pagett the last of David Langdon's two payments 070 00 00; Rec. of William Ellis for reed and straw as by his bill 002 19 06; 20 July 1642   Rec. of Mr Wyott 022 00 00   [total] 469 19 6

15 *August* 1642   Rec. from my Lady by Mr Bold when my Lord went
into Cornwall 006 00 00; 27 *August* 1642   Rec. from my Lady by
Mrs Hardwick 028 00 00; 30 August 1642   Rec. from Mr Bold out of my
Lady's closet 021 00 00; 21 Sept. 1642   Rec. of Mrs Hardwick 020 00 00
[?total] 2031 7 5   [page total] 544 19 06

[**p. 19**]   29 7bris [September] 1642   Rec. from Mr Hearle for my Lord's
use £030 00s 00d; Rec. of John Gibbons ['in part' crossed through] for my
Lord's use 010 00 00; 7 8bris [October]   Rec. for one heifer and calf
003 15 00; 10 8bris 1642   Rec. for one steer 003 07 00; 14 8bris 1642
Rec. of Edward Randle for Midsummer quarter's rent due from the several
manors 010 00 00; Rec. of Richard Britton for grass sold 005 10 00 00
[total] £62 12s 00d

[**p. 21**]   Tawstock Received for hides and sheep skins since the 30th of
October *in the year* 1641

| | |
|---|---|
| 30 Octob. 1641 | Recd for 5 sheep skins £00 10s 00d |
| 6 Novemb. 1641 | Recd for 2 sheep skins 00 04 06 |
| 13 Novemb. 1641 | Recd for two hides & two skins 01 06 00 |
| 20 Novemb. | Rec. for two skins 00 04 04 |
| 27 Novemb. | Rec. for two hides and 2 skins 00 18 09 |
| 4 Decemb. 1641 | Rec. for two skins 00 04 06 |
| 11 Decemb. 1641 | Rec. for 3 sheep skins 00 07 00 |
| 18 Decemb. | Rec. for 3 sheep skins 00 07 00 |
| 25 Decemb. | Rec. for 2 hides and 3 skins 01 13 08 |
| 1 January 1641 | Rec. for 4 skins 00 09 04 |
| 8 Jan. 1641 | Recd for one hide and two skins 01 00 04 |
| 15 Jan. 1641 | Recd for 3 skins 00 07 00 |
| 22 Jan. 1641 | Rec. for 2 skins 00 04 08 |
| 29 Jan. 1641 | Recd for one skin 00 02 04 |
| 5 Feb. 1641 | Recd for one hide and three skins 01 01 06 |
| 12 Feb. 1641 | Recd for two skins 00 05 00 |
| 19 Feb. 1641 | Rec. for 1 hide and 2 skins 01 09 00 |
| 26 Feb. 1641 | Recd for 3 sheep skins 00 08 00 |
| 9 Apr. 1642 | Recd for 2 sheep skins 00 07 00 |

*sum page* £11 09 00d

[**p. 22**]

| | |
|---|---|
| 16 Apr. 1642 | Recd for one hide and 3 skins 01 09 00 |
| 23 Apr. 1642 | Recd for one sheep skin 00 04 00 |
| 31 Apr. 1642 | Recd for two sheep skins 00 08 00 |
| 20 May 1642 | Rec. for two skins 00 07 00 |
| 27 May 1642 | Recd for two sheep skins 00 07 00 |
| 3 *June* 1642 | Recd for one hide and one skin 00 19 10 |
| 10 *June* 1642 | Rec. for one sheep's skin 00 04 03 |
| 25 *June* 1642 | Rec. for one ['heifer' crossed through] hide and 2 skins 00 17 00 |
| 2 July 1642 | Rec. for one yearling's skin and 3 sheep's skins 00 09 00 |
| 9 July 1642 | Rec. for one hide of a heifer and two skins 00 12 09 |
| 16 July 1642 | Recd for two skins 00 01 10 |
| 23 July 1642 | Recd for one hide and 2 skins 00 10 06 |

| | |
|---|---|
| 27 July 1642 | Recd for one hide & 4 skins 01 05 04 |
| 6 August 1642 | Recd for 6 skins 00 05 06 |
| 13 Aug. 1642 | Recd for 1 hide and 4 skins 00 18 00 |
| 20 Aug. 1642 | Recd for one hide and 5 skins 00 18 00 |
| 27 Aug. 1642 | Rec. for one hide and 5 skins 01 01 10 |
| 3 Sept. 1642 | Recd for one hide and 6 skins 01 03 06 |
| 10 Sept. 1642 | Recd for one hide and six skins 01 02 00 |
| 17 Sept. 1642 | Rec. for one hide & nine skins 01 06 06 |
| 24 Sept. 1642 | Recd for 2 hides and ten skins 02 01 00 |

*Sum page* 16 11 11

[p. 23]

| | |
|---|---|
| 1 Oct. 1642 | Recd for 2 hides and 7 skins £01 15s 03d |
| 8 Octob. 1642 | Recd for 1 hide and 3 skins 00 16 06 |
| 15 Octob. 1642 | Recd for one hide and 2 skins 00 13 10 |
| 22 Octob. 1642 | Recd for 6 skins 00 07 00 |

Sum is £03 12s £03 12s 7d
Sum total recd for hides and sheeps skins is £31 14s 4d

[p. 25]  Received for salmons and peals taken and sold from the hatch and kiddle since the 9th of Apr. 1642 until the 15th of October following

| | |
|---|---|
| 9 Apr. 1642 | Recd for one salmon £00 04s 00d |
| 25 *June* | Recd for 2 salmons and one pug 00 08 00 |
| 3 July | Recd for one salmon 00 02 10 |
| 9 July | Recd for 7 salmons and 23 peals 01 05 08 |
| 16 July | Recd for 1 salmon & 11 peals 00 06 00 |
| 23 July | Recd for 4 salmon and 21 peals 00 14 08 |
| 3 Sept. | Recd for 9 salmons 00 17 00 |
| 15 Oct. | Recd for 37 salmons 03 00 06 |
| | Recd more for lampreys and peals from the kiddle 00 05 08 |

Sum total is £07 04s 04d

[p. 27]  Particular sums delivered my Lady *in the year* 1641

15 October 1641 delivered my Lady £100
18 October 1641 delivered my Lady £100
20 October 1641 delivered to my Lady £400
21 October 1641 delivered my Lady £100
23 October 1641 delivered to my Lady £30, delivered to my Lady £100
Sum is £830

[p. 29]  21 Jan. 1645  Item paid the bookbinder of Barnstaple 00 18 08; 23 Jan. 1645  Item paid John Williams for his quarter by bill 02 02 0; Item paid my brother for his journey 02 10 0; Item paid Bess Umbles for knitting 00 04 06; Item paid John Warren for eight days 00 08 00; Item paid Wilmot 00 10 00; 30 Jan.  Item paid William Ramson in part 05 00 00; Item paid John Burk for garters for my Lord 00 05 06; Item given to a woman for scurvy grass 00 01 00; Item paid Mary Horsom for 3 bushels of barley 0 13 00; Item paid for pins for my Lady 0 01 00; Item paid for pips and for tagging points for my Lord 0 01 00; Item paid Simon

Tolsell for making 600 and 60 faggots 0 03 06; More for making 4 dozen and half of hardwood 00 04 06; 2 Feb. Item paid John Underdon in full of all his wages 01 00 00; more spent at Hartford 00 00 06

[p. 30] Item paid George Rooke in part 01 10 00; Item paid for two hens 00 02 00; 5 Feb. Item paid the glasier 01 02 00; 7 Feb. Item paid William Ramson in full of his bill of 7 Feb. 00 13 09; Item paid Zachary for straw 0 05 0; Item paid for sprats 0 00 6; Item paid Eliz: Umbles for barm 0 01 0; Item paid quarter-master Braddon 0 11 0; Item paid Will Davy for 3 times carrying down wood to Barn. 0 02 06; 1 *March* Item paid William Richards for making 2100 faggots 00 10 00; Item paid him more for making 9 dozen of hardwood 00 06 00; Item paid him more for 6 days wages 0 02 00; 7 *March* Item paid Tho: Steevens in part for making wood 0 10 0; Item paid Jo: Hamlyn 1 11 00; Item paid Sander Davy for 5 days wages at plough 0 01 08; Item paid the spinster for spinning 0 06 00; Item paid William Ramson for twenty sheep 09 10 0

[p. 31] Item paid for one pound of pepper at Bideford £00 02s 08d; Item paid for pigs rings 00 01 06; Item paid for 3 quire of paper 00 01 00; to Ramson. Item paid for one veal and one pork 01 11 00; 13 *March* Item paid for one bushel of peas to sow 00 05 00; Item paid John Gibons in part for hay 01 00 00; Item paid for 3 chickens 00 01 06; 16 *March* Item [paid to] William Ramson in part of his bill 00 14 0; Item paid for mending sieves 0 01 00; Item paid William Ramson in part for fish 03 00 00; Item paid John Hamblyn for one bushel of apples 00 04 06; Item paid Simon Tolsell for making of 1200 faggots and eight dozen of hardwood 00 14 06; Item paid Tho: Steevens for making of 1900 faggots 0 09 06; Item more for 10 dozen of hardwood 0 07 06; 4 bundles of spars 0 00 04

[p. 32] paid Tho: Steevens for 26 days wages £00 06s 06d; Item paid William Vigires 00 08 00; Item paid George Rooke in full for 8 sheep at 8s 6d 00 18 00; 3 Apr. 1645. Item paid Charles in full of all his bills unto the 31th of Jan. 1645 09 08 09; Item paid Robt Norcott for 5 days wages 0 01 08; Item paid for mutton and lamb and veal in the market 02 4 4; Item paid William Ramson in part of his bills 15 0 0; 5 *April* 1646 Item paid the overseers of the poor of Tawstock for 13 months pay to the poor for Ammer's tenement at *Colliber* 00 05 05; ['Item lent Sir Allen Apsley servant for his journey to his Lady £1 10 0' crossed through]; 10 Apr. 1646 Item paid William Ramson in full of all bills and for 4 ewes and lambs 02 06 0; 2 bills due to him. Item paid Francis Martyn for two hogs 04 6 8

[p. 33] Item paid Richard Britton for 10 sheep £2 05s 0d; Item him more for 4 bushels of oats and 1 truss of hay 0 12 0; Item him more for other things 0 05 0; 9 Apr. 1646 Item paid for 3 quarters of veal and 2 quarters of lamb in the market 00 12 08; Item paid my Lady of part of our Lady Day's quarters rent due from Tawstock 06 00 00; Item paid Robyn for garden seeds upon bill 0 04 01; 13 April 1646 Item paid Will Ramson in full of all bills then due 10 00 00; Item paid Mr Nash for cheese as by bill 00 11 00; Item paid May for pips for my Lord 00 00 06; 15 Apr. 1646 Item paid Richard Britton upon his bill for several things 13 19 02; Item paid my Lady in part of our Lady Day quarter recd of Tawstock 04 16 00

**[p. 34]**   Item paid for 3 quarts of neats foot oil for the coach harness
oo o2 o6; 19 Apr. 1646   Item paid Mr Beckett for 3 quarters of a year's
teaching of Randle oo 15 oo; Item paid Will Coop for 6 bushels of barley
at 4s o1 o4 oo; Item paid for one quarter of beef [smudged] o1 6; Item
paid Thomas Sumner in full of his bill 30 14 10; Item paid for 4 weeks
wages to two weeders oo o4 oo; Item paid Tho: Steevens in full of his
wages oo o3 o6; Item paid Symon Lake for two fat oxen o8 13 o4; 20 Apr.
1646   Item paid my Lady in part of the rent for Tawstock o5 oo oo; Item
paid Mr Bassett in full for 45 bushels of wheat at 6s the bushel o2 10 o;
20 Apr. 1646   Item paid Mr Tooker of Barnstaple for wine as by bill
11 oo oo

**[p. 35]**   20 Apr. 1646   Item paid Richard Huxtable in full of 5 bills
£07 o3s 1od; Item paid Phill Eeles for 12 bushels of barley at 5s 4d
o3 o4 oo; 22 Apr. 1646   Item paid Robt Whitfild for 20 bushels of oats
o3 oo oo; Item paid Tho: Ambsby for barm for 14 weeks oo o7 oo; Item
paid John Gribble for going two journeys oo o2 oo; Item paid Tho: Sadler
in full of one bill o1 10 oo; Item paid him more for my saddle o o5 oo;
22 Apr. 1646   Item paid the carrier for things brought from London
oo o1 o6; Item paid Bess Umbles upon her bill oo 11 oo; Item paid John
Hamblyn upon a bill o 16 o6; Item given for handsel to the butcher
o o1 oo; Item paid Humfry Lake for 9 bushels of barley o1 19 oo; 24 Apr.
1646   Item paid Rumson in part of his bill o5 oo oo; Item paid for two
quires of paper oo o1 oo

**[p. 36]**   24 Apr. 1646   Item paid the masons in part of their wages for
20 days £o1 oos ood and then were 17 days to pay; 25 Apr. 1646   Item
paid John Underdon in full of all his wages o1 o1 oo; Item paid the paver
in full for his work done and for 8 days wages at 6d per day oo o7 oo;
Item sent to the market for beef o o6 oo; Item paid Baldwyn Steevens
upon his bills o4 19 oo; Item paid John Baller in part of his bill o1 oo oo;
25 Apr. 1646   Item paid William Meane in part of his wages o1 oo o;
More due to him oo o8 11; Item given a messenger that brought a letter
from *Exon* from Mr Fane oo o3 oo; Item paid John Terry for 8 bushels of
lime oo o6 oo; Item paid George Pitt in full of his wages oo o8 o6

**[p. 37]**   Item paid Tho: Ley for cheeses upon bill £o1 14s o4d; 30 Apr.
1646   Item paid William Ramson in full of all then due o2 o4 11; Item
paid for one peck of salt oo o1 oo; Item paid for one quire of paper for the
stools oo oo o6; 1 May 1646   Item paid Walt Vumbles in full of his wages
o1 o2 6; Item paid hop tiers for 13 days oo o5 5; Item paid Richard Rooke
in part of his wages oo 10 oo; for beef.   Item paid Rumson oo 13 oo; Item
paid for lock and key for the garden door oo o3 oo; Item paid Hearder for
dressing a sick cow o o2 oo; Item paid Joseph Delbridge in full o1 o5 oo;
7 May 1646   Item paid Willm Rumson in full of half a year's wages due at
our Lady Day last o2 10 oo; Item paid him in full of all bills o1 10 oo

**[p. 38]**   7 May 1646   Item paid Mr Cooper in part o3 oo o; Item paid
George Pitts in part oo o1 oo; Item paid for cheeses and canvas and thongs
for saddles oo 10 o5; Item paid for eggs o o7 oo; Item paid Simon Tolsell
for cutting and binding of 4500 furse faggots 1 o2 6; Item paid Humfry
Eure for one truss of hay oo o9 oo; Item paid for 500 faggots for the weir

01 05 00; 13 May   Item paid Mr William Beere by command from my
Lady 40 11 10; Item given William Rumson to pay furse carriers 00 05 00;
Item paid George Pitts for making of 700 faggots and 11 seams of
hardwood and nine bundles of spars 00 05 09; Item paid John Symons for
5 days wages 00 03 8; Whitsunday   Item paid due to the masons 01 00 6;
Item paid William Steevens in full of his wages 01 00 00

[p. 40]   22 May   paid the smith upon a bill 01 18 00; Item paid for fish at
market 00 02 00; Item paid the thatcher 7 days 00 03 06; Item paid
Richard Britton to buy a cow for Mr Bold 05 00 00; Item paid for two
weigh of coal and half 03 10 00; Item paid Rich: Stanbury for hay
01 10 00; Item paid him more for oats and straw 00 09 00; Item paid for
40 bushels of oats at 2s 4d the bushel 04 13 4; Item paid for blue starch
00 00 6; 29 May   Item paid George Pitts for making 800 faggots 00 04 8;
Item more for 150 hop poles 00 00 9; Item more for two dozen of
hardwood 00 02 00; Item paid for eggs 00 01 00; Item paid the
basket-maker for 8 days wages at 8d per day 00 05 04; Item paid for
1 truss of old straw 00 01 06; Item paid for bringing of coal 00 03 06

[p. 40]   7 *June* 1646   Item paid the nurse for 2 months nursing Jonathan
00 08 00; Item paid her more for a pair of shoes and curing the child's
tongue 00 01 10; Item paid the thatcher for 5 days 00 02 06; Item paid his
man 4 days 00 01 04; Item paid William Meane for making of 900 faggots
00 05 3; Item paid him more for 4 dozen of hardwood 00 04 00; Item paid
him more for 100 hop poles and 6 bundles of spars 00 01 00; Item paid
him more for 20 days wages 00 06 8; Item paid Mary Tolsell for 32 days
weeding 00 10 8; Item paid for cutting Randle hare [?hair] 00 00 06; Item
paid Pauline Meane for 25 days weeding at 5d per *day* 0 10 05; Item paid
the post for one letter 0 00 06; Item paid the masons in part of their wages
01 00 0

[p. 41]   13 *June*   Item paid William Rumson in full of his bill of 23 May
1646 £00 04s 3d; Item paid Lakes' man for 7 days wages 00 02 4; Item
paid Rich: Lake for 8 days horsehire to carry wood 00 04 0; Item paid
John Holgood for his horse 7 days 00 02 4; Item paid the boat man for
bringing oats from *Barnestaple* 00 02 00; Item paid for six bushels of lime
to Maynard of Barnstaple 00 06 00; Item paid for one dozen of spoons
00 02 04; Item paid for 3 bushels of wheat 01 04 00; Item paid for eggs
00 00 08; Item paid for an *Isops fables* 00 00 06; Item paid for [illegible]
for fowls 00 01 00; Item paid for 6 bushels of charcoal 00 07 00; Item paid
for George Pitts for making wood as by bill 00 12 08; Item paid Coop for
making one acre of hay 00 04 00; Item paid for making of 2 acres of hay
in the salt meadow 00 07 04

[p. 42]   30 *June*   Item given Sir Samuel Rolls his clerk for a pass
00 01 00; Item spent at *Bowe* with Mr Hyne for ourselves and horses
0 05 06; Item paid Bess Umbles for 6 days wages at hay 0 2 6; Item paid
Avis Starling and two women haymakers for 12 days wages 0 5 00; Item
paid Welsh Dick for going to Bow 0 2 6; 4 July 1646   Item paid for one
quarter of beef weighing 71 lbs at 2½d *the* pound 00 14 8; Item paid for
gelding of pigs 0 01 06; 7 July 1646   Item paid for one quarters schooling
of the young Reece to Ann Mullins 0 02 00; Item paid Avis Starling for

3 days making hay o o1 o6; Item paid for eggs o o1 oo; 9 July   Item paid
John Warren in full of his wages for 3 weeks and 5 days a piece o1 o3 oo;
Item paid Wil: Britton for an ox o5 13 o4

[p. 43]   Item paid him more in full for making the wall £o 15s ood;
10 July   Item paid for beef oo o7 o4; 12 July 1646   Item paid Richard
Rooke in full of half a years wages due at our Lady Day last oo 15 oo;
Item paid for 3 hens o o1 oo; 12 July   Item paid Walter Umbles in full of
his wage o 14 oo; Item paid the smith upon b[ill]. o1 o7 oo; 12 July   Item
paid the nurse for one month then due o o4 oo; 13 July   Item paid for
veal and mutton o o6 4; 17 July   Item paid for one quarter of beef o 12 6;
Item paid for mutton and veal o4 o; Item paid for 5oo furses for the weir
o o3 9; Item paid for cutting 5oo furse faggots o o2 o6; Item paid George
Skitch for 5 bushels of peas o 18 o4; Item spent at Bow for 3 men and
5 horses o 11 9

[p. 44]   25 July   Item paid for 3 sieves o o1 6; Item paid for one quarter
of mutton and one breast of veal o o3 o8; Item paid John Martyn the
miller for one year's wages due at our Lady Day last past o3 oo oo;
26 July   Item paid William Ramson upon a bill o3 12 8; Item paid
William Steevens in full of his wages oo 14 oo; Item paid for eggs o o 8;
1 August   Item paid John Marchant for 3 quarters of mutton 1 6 6; Item
paid William Lee for cutting and making the stone close hay being 7 acres
at 4s per acre o1 8 oo; Item paid Joseph Holland for making Knevett's
meadow oo 16 8; Item paid for one piece of beef oo o2 4; Item paid
Captain Pyne for 3o bushels of oats at 2s 8d o4 oo oo; Item paid for
cutting of 2o acres of wheat in part o4 15 oo

[p. 45]   7 *August*   Item paid John Hobbs in part for a barrel of soap
£o1 1os ood; Item paid John Baller o1 oo oo; Item paid Mr Pridis upon a
bill for fruit and spice oo 16 o4; Item spent at Torrington when I went to
pay Mr Lam oo o1 oo; Item paid for eggs oo o1 oo; Item delivered
Thurstyn for his journey to London oo 12 oo; 13 Aug.   Item paid for a
pair shoes for Randle oo o2 o6; Item paid Mr Lambe upon a bill from
London 5o oo oo; Item paid for two quarters of beef o2 o5 oo; Item given
the poor oo o5 6; 15 [August]   Item paid for 2 weigh of coal and half
o3 1o oo; Item paid for p[a]p[er] oo o1 4; Item given a messenger that
brought letters o o1 o6; Item paid William Meane for cutting and making
4 acres of hay in the stone close o 16 1o; 23 *August*   Item paid Walter
Umbles in full of his wages 9 weeks o o9 oo

[p. 46]   23 *August* 1646   paid for culm £oo 1os od; paid for one quarter
of beef oo 15 4; paid William Coop for 6 bushels of barley at 4s o1 o4 o;
paid Mr Notles man in full of one bill charged from London 1oo oo oo;
paid the clerk of the committee at *Exon* oo o2 6; given the door keeper
oo o1 oo; paid for a book of the highways in England oo o1 o6

[p. 47]   22 Aug.   paid William Rumson oo 12 oo; paid for a pair of shoes
oo o2 o6; 24 Aug.   paid John Underdon in full of all his wages due to him
o1 oo oo; 7 7bris [September]   paid John Randle for making a wharrow
for the pound oo o7 o; paid for a quarter of beef to Jo: Marchant oo 12 6;
1 8bris [October] 1646   paid for mutton oo o4 oo; 2 8bris 1646   paid

Mr Nottle's servants in part of a bill of exchange of £100 20 00 00; paid
John Underdon 05 0 0; paid Mr Coop 01 10; paid Anth: Ash for iron
work 00 04 6; paid Mr Nottle more in part of his bill 30 0 0; paid two
men for bringing colts from Hartland 0 05 0; 21 Octob. 1646 paid
Mr Downe in part 02 00 00; paid Mr Jackman 05 0 0

[p. 48] 13 8bris [October] paid for a fish 00 01 06; 15 8bris paid
Mr Bold upon a bill from my Lady 15 00 00; paid for 6 chickens 00 02 3;
paid Gribble for going to *Exon* with letters 00 05 00; paid a woman for
going to Torrington 0 01 0; 15 Oct. paid the carrier in part of his bill
04 0 0; paid for eggs 00 2 0; paid for brooms 00 2 6; paid [for] chickens
00 02 6; paid Besse Sarle for her journey 0 10 0; paid for 3 boats of sand
0 07 6; paid for bring[ing] up coal 0 03 4; 19 Octob. paid Ramson to buy
butter and cheese 01 10 00; paid Humfry Lake for 4500 furse faggots at
8d per hundred 01 10 00; Item given my Lord Chiches[ter's] man that
brought half a stag 0 06 0; 20 8bris paid Mr Horwood for 2 pieces of wet
stuff 01 10 00

[p. 49] 22 8bris [October] Item paid Mr Lambe in full of one bill of
exchange sent from my Lady in London £50 0 0; paid Richard Britton for
18 bushels of wheat at 9s per bushel 08 00 00; paid Mr Nottles man in full
of a bill of £100 charged from London 50 0 0; paid Richard Britton in full
for one ox 07 10 0; paid Mr Wood for his journey to London 00 12 00;
25 8br paid Lawrence Chamberlyn for work done by bill 0 10 00; paid
the hop-gatherer by bill 5 12 6; Item spent at *Ilfardcombe* 0 04 06;
27 Octob. 1646 Item paid John Williams the plumber in part of his bill
03 12 3; paid for one loin of veal 0 02 0; paid John Chilcott the beadle in
1643 for a ['dis'illegible crossed through] [?]pean upon Rich: Lake which
was forgiven him 0 06 00; paid Tho: Lovering for a horse 02 15 00

[p. 50] paid Gribble at his going to *Exon* with letters £0 04s 07d; paid the
chimney sweep 0 01 0; paid for eggs 0 02 0; paid Gregory Hosgood upon a
bill 00 05 2; paid for a rode cord 0 1 4; paid for ink and bottle 0 1 0; paid
for halters 0 1 0; paid Mr Bourcher for so much laid out at Bow for a
messenger 0 3 6; paid John Johnson for 6 fat sheep at 14s 04 05 0;
4 Novemb. 1646 paid Roger Thorn's man in part of a bill 03 10 0; paid
Lawrence Berry upon a bill for mending shoes 0 04 8; paid Simon Lake
for one year's wages due at Michas. last 03 15 0; 9 brs [November] 1646
paid the saddler in full of one bill 03 0 0; 3 Novemb. paid Mr Bold for
London journey 20 0 0

[p. 51] 7 9bris [November] 1646 Item paid John Terry in full for one
year's wages due at Michas. last £01 10s 0d; Item paid for a pair of cards
for wool 0 02 0; Item paid Ann Mullyns for one quarter teaching May
Reeve her boy due at Michas. 0 02 0; paid for one month's nursing
Jonathan due 18 Octob. 0 4 0; paid for a pair of shoes for him 0 1 0; paid
for a pair of shoes for Mary Reymor 0 2 4; 8 9bris 1646 Item given the
22 poor alms people 0 05 6; Item spent at *Exon* when my Lord went to
London 0 06 00; 9 9bris 1646 Item paid Mr Beckett for half a year's
teaching of Randle then due 00 10 00; paid for one quarter of mutton
00 02 4; paid for 2 hooks for cut down hops this year 0 02 4

**[p. 52]**   paid Mr Skitch for two cows bought of him £o6 6s 8d; given John Sumner for his pains at plow two days o 2 6; given his man o 1 o; 12 9bris   paid for eggs o 1 4; 13 Novemb. 1646   paid Mr George Shurte in part of his bill o9 o o; Item spent at *Apledore* when I went to buy fish o 2 6; Item paid for one bushel of salt o 4 4; 14 Novemb. 1646   Item paid John Swyne the shoemaker in part of my Lord's bill o1 o o; Item paid for beef & mutton at market oo o6 6; Item given Mr Pagott men for plowing o o3 o; 15 9bris   Item paid James Whitfeild for 8 weeks wages at work in the garden o 12 o; Item paid for mutton o o2 o; 20 Nov.   Item paid for a lock o o1 o4; Item paid for egg o o1 o

**[p. 53]**   paid Gregory Hosgood for Mr Wyott suit 2 o o; 21 Nov.   paid him more for making Thomas Cooman suit o 2 6; paid for beef & mutton o 12 o; 23 Nov. 1646   paid the nurse for one month then due for nursing Jonathan o o4 o; paid for soap for her o oo 4; paid John Gribble for going to Stow o o4 o; paid him more for going to journeys to *Exon* o o2 o; paid James Blackmore for 3 quarters wages due at Christmas next o3 o o; in park   paid John Midway for 7 days wages and half o o6 3; 26 Nov.   paid for mutton 4 jo. o o4 o; paid George Wheler upon a bill for fulling o 13 1o; paid for making clean 12 pair of pistols o o2 6; 26 Nov.   paid for eggs o o1 o; paid Robt Whitfeild in full of ['his' crossed through] one year of wages due at Michas. last o2 1o o; paid Rumson for market o1 1o

**[p. 54]**   27 Nov.   paid Ames for mutton oo o1 oo; 29 Nov.   given the poor people oo o5 6; paid Charles in full of all bills then due o2 18 6; paid for making panifer bed 68 yards at 4d per yard 1 2 8; 30 Nov. 1646   paid Mr John Lambe in part of one bill of one hundred pound 5o o o; paid him more for my self by bill o5 o o; 1 Dec.   paid for serge and bunting oo 5 o; paid for fish to Rumson oo 1o o; given John Hamlyn to buy Mrs Ashton and her 2 maids clothes o3 1o oo; 2 1obris paid for one quarter of mutton o o3 o; 3 1obris paid   Huxtable the smith in part of his bills o2 oo oo; paid for making of 460 faggots oo o2 8; paid for making 20 seams of hardwood o o1 8; Item given Doctor Copston oo 1o o

**[p. 55]**   11 xbris [December]   paid for one quarter of beef £o 16s [o]d; paid for mutton oo 11 6; paid for eggs o o1 6; paid for weaving 24 yards of cloth oo o6 o; paid the poor oo o5 6; paid Rumson to buy salt &c o2 1o o; paid Thurstyn upon bill o5 11 oo; 16 1obris   paid William Lee for making 770 faggots o o4 6; paid him more for 2 doz & 8 seams of hardwood o2 8; more for 5 bundles of crooks o 5; more for threshing ten bushels of peas o 2 6; 16   paid for eggs o o 1o; paid Rumson o 5 oo; 19.   paid Rumson for market o1 o o; given Doctor Coplestone o 5 o; 20   paid the nurse for one month and for soap o 4 6; paid John Whitefeild in full o o7 o

**[p. 56]**   27th January 1645
Rec. of John Coop in part of our Lady quarters rent now next ensuing £1 3s 4d; ['Rec. of Mathew Moore in part of the rent' illegible crossed through]; 8 Feb. 1645

Rec. of Mathew Moore in part of the rent £2 1os 8d
Rec. from Mathew Moore in part of Christmas quarter rent £2 1s
Rec. from Mr Bold for my Lady £9 1os o

Rec. from Mr Bold 10s; Rec. from my Lady 10s
15 *March* Rec. from Mathew Moore 11s 4d
Rec. from Mathew Moore £4

## Expenses, 1644–1645

KENT ARCHIVES OFFICE, U269/A525/6

*The book measures 11¾" by 7" and is wrapped in paper. The front cover is noted as the 'Earl of Bath's Book' in a later hand and is headed 'Disbursed from Octo. 1644 until 1645'. The back cover has some scribbling. The even-numbered pages are blank as are the last 20 pages.*

[p. 1]  Disbursed by me Rich: Pollard for the household expense and other defrayments of the right honourable Henry Earl of Bath from the 19th of October 1644 until 1645

### [p. 3]  Saturday the 26th of October 1644
*First* paid the workmens wages upon bill £00 14s 11d; Item paid the Cater upon bill 00 16 07; Item paid Will Geare for 5 lambs 01 00 00; Item paid for 100 lbs of butter by bill 01 13 04; Item paid Oxford carrier upon bill 00 17 00; Item paid the hop gatherers upon bill 05 08 01; Item paid Lawrence Chamberlyn upon bill 00 06 07
Sum total of this week is 10 16 09

### Saturday the second of November 1644
Item paid the workmen wages upon bill 00 13 02; Item paid the Cater upon bill 00 14 09; Item paid the Miller for eight bushels and half of wheat and for mending the mill 03 02 05; Item paid the workmen their wages due at Michas. last as by bill 09 05 10
Sum of this week is 13 16 02

### Saturday the 9th of Novemb. 1644
Item paid the workmens wages upon bill 00 15 00; Item paid the Cater upon bill 00 19 01; Item paid Mr George Shurte upon bill 13 08 00; Item paid Mr Isaac for oats 12 10 00; Item spent in my journey to *Exter* as by bill 01 15 05; Item paid Mr Bell of *Biddeford* for one hogshead of wine 08 16 00
Sum of this week is 38 03 6  [page total] £62 16s 03d

### [p. 5]  Saturday the 16th of Novemb.
Item paid the workmens wages upon bill £00 12s 00d; Item paid for spinning of worsted 00 01 06; Item paid for buttons and loop lace 00 01 04; Item paid Thomasin Lake for 4 truss of hay 01 00 00; Item spent at *Banton* as by bill 02 00 05; Item paid my Lady of money rec. at *Banton* 17 05 04
Sum total of this week is [illegible crossed through] 20 00 07

### Saturday the 23th of Novemb. 1644
Item paid the workmen wages upon bill 00 12 10; Item paid the Cater upon bill 01 14 09; Item paid Tho: Ambsby 00 04 00; Item paid Johan

Whitfeild the weeder for four weeks wages oo o3 oo; Item paid for two
boats of sand oo o5 oo; Item paid for bringing up of coal oo o5 oo; Item
paid for bringing wine from Bid. oo o2 o6; Item paid Avis Starling upon
bill oo 14 oo; Item given Edward Loven to buy tools oo o2 oo; Item given
my Lady Chichester's maid that brought brawn oo o2 o6; Item given to
the man oo o2 oo; Item paid for mending the great gun oo o1 o6; Item paid
for mending a lock oo oo o6; Item paid for half a pound of powder
oo oo o6; Item paid Mr Southcott for the tithe of Wonham o3 o6 o8
Sum total of this week is [illegible crossed through] o7 15 o9
[page total] £27 16s o4d

## [p. 7]  Saturday the 30th of Novemb. 1644

Item paid the workmens wages by bill £oo 12s ood; Item paid the Cater
upon bill oo 12 o6; Item paid Baldwyn Steevens for nets and other things
as by bill o1 13 oo; Item paid for eight bush. of culm oo o9 oo; Item given
Sir Raph Sydenham's servant oo o2 oo; Item paid for three weigh and
eighteen bushels of coal o6 15 oo; Item paid for 6 bushels and half of oats
oo 11 o7; Item paid for 4 bushels of oats oo o8 o8; Item paid for bullocks
and sheep at Barnstaple as by bill 17 19 oo
Sum total of this week is 29 o1 o9

## Saturday the 7th of Decemb. 1644

Item paid the workmens wages upon bill oo 19 o3; Item paid the Cater
upon bill oo 16 o6; Item paid Mr Bourgchier for so much given by
Command to Sir Jo: Ch: coachman oo o2 oo; Item paid for two bushels of
salt oo o8 oo; Item paid for 8 bushels of oats oo 12 o2; Item paid for
8 bushels of oats oo 13 o6; Item paid for one lamb oo o5 oo; Item given
Mr Lithbridg servant that brought a present oo o1 oo; Item given
Mrs Downe's servant oo o2 o6; Item paid for one pork oo 10 o6; Item paid
the smith upon two bills o2 o5 o6
Sum total of this week's expense o6 15 11   [page total] £35 17s o8d

## [p. 9]  Saturday the 14th of Decemb. 1644

Item paid the workmens wages upon bill £oo 16s ood; Item paid the Cater
upon his bill o3 o9 o9; Item paid for fruit and spices at Barnstaple
o3 oo o4; Item paid for one yard and 3 quarters of kersey oo 10 10; Item
paid for 6 lbs of shot oo o1 o6; Item paid for 4 glasses oo o3 o6; Item paid
for a quart of olives oo o1 o4; Item paid for bringing a firkin of soap from
*Exon* oo o2 o6
Sum total of this week's expense is o8 o5 o7

## Saturday the 21th of Decemb. 1644

Item paid the workmens wages upon bill £o1 o4s o9d; Item paid the Cater
upon his bill oo 14 oo; Item paid the tinker for mending the cutlass
oo o3 o6; Item paid Williams the plumber upon a bill oo 12 o6; Item paid
the smith upon his bill o1 o8 oo; Item paid for 6 lbs of sucket oo o8 oo;
Item spent at *Biddeford* oo oo o6; Item paid for oats upon a bill o3 12 oo
Sum total of this week's expense is o8 o3 o3   [page total] £16 o8s 1od

## [p. 11]  Saturday the 28th of Decemb. 1644

Item paid the workmens wages upon bill £oo o5s o1d; Item paid the Cater
upon his bill o3 o6 oo; Item paid James Towill for bringing trenchers
oo o2 oo; Item paid a messenger from John Mills oo o1 oo; Item paid my

brother for so much delivered my Lady at play oo oi oo; Item delivered
my Lady by George to play oo o3 oo; Item paid for two bedcords
oo o2 o6; Item paid John Underdon for wages by bill oi o3 oo
Sum total of this week's expense is o5 o3 o7

**Saturday the 4th of Jan. 1644**
paid the workmen wages upon bill oo o4 o4; paid the Cater upon bill
o3 o7 io; Item given to the sergeants of Barnstaple oo io oo; Item paid for
cocks and snipes oo oi o4; Item paid for 6 lbs of powder oo o8 oo; Item
paid Will: Booth upon bill for his journey to *Exter* oo o4 oo; Item paid
Mr Cobb for so much disbursed oo o7 oo; Item delivered my Lady to play
oo o2 oo; Item given a messenger oo oi oo; Item paid the glasier upon his
bills o3 i7 oo
Sum total of this week's expense is o9 o2 o6   [page total] £14 o6s oid

**[p. 13]   Saturday the 11th day of January 1644**
Item paid the workmens wages upon bill £oo o6s ood; Item paid the Cater
upon bill o2 oi ii; Item spent in my journey to *Exon* by bill oi o5 o6;
Item paid for one weigh of coal o2 o2 oo; Item paid for bringing it up
oo o2 o6; Item paid my Lady Sydenham for so much laid out for my Lady
o2 o7 o6; Item paid for 2 lbs of powder oo o2 o6; Item paid Rich Hamlyn
for the use of Doctor Downe in *Exon* io oo oo
Sum total of this week is 18 o7 ii

**Saturday the 18th of Jan. 1644**
Item paid the workmen wages upon bill £oo 18s o8d; Item paid the Cater
upon bill o3 i7 io; Item paid for one weigh of coal and for bringing it
home from *Apledore* [Appledore] o2 o4 o6; Item paid for 2 lbs of powder
oo o2 o6; Item paid my Lady in part of so much rec. at *Exon* 146 12 o6;
Item paid for four bushels and half of wheat as by bill ooi o5 ii; Item
paid Mr Bourcher for so much given my Lady oo oi oo; Item paid John
Williams the plumber for Christmas quarter wages by bill o2 o7 o5; Item
paid the hedgers for 2oty yards of hedge making in the park oi oo oo;
Item paid for a pair of gloves for Ned Foster oo oo io
So the total sum of this week is 158 ii o2   [page total] £176 19s oid

**[p. 15]   Saturday the 25th of Jan. 1644**
Item paid the workmen wages upon bill £oo 13s iod; Item paid the Cater
upon bill oi oi o7; Item paid my brother for so much laid out for my
Lady oo o6 oo; Item paid for 32 bushels of oats o2 13 o4; Item given
Mr Lee's servant oo o2 oo; Item given Mr Isaac's servant oo oo o6; Item
paid for two bushels of barley oo o6 o4; Item paid James Hartnoll for his
quarter wages due at Cristmas oo 16 o8; Item paid Mr Bold upon bill
oo 14 oo; Item paid for 26 bushels of oats at Barnstaple oi 16 o6; Item
paid the hedgers for making twelve yards of the park hedge oo 12 oo; Item
paid Mrs Lovett for so much delivered my Lady oo o6 oo6; Item paid for
things bought by bill o5 oo oo; Item paid Avis Starling upon bill oo o4 oo;
Item delivered my Lady at play oi io oo
So the total of this week's expense is 19 o2 o9

**[p. 17]   Saturday the first of February 1644**
Item paid the workmen wages upon bill £oo 15s od; Item paid the Cater
upon bill oi 19 2; Item paid John Harris for 9 bushels of barley at 3s 6d

per bushel 01 13 03; Item paid Morkham for Christmas quarter 00 02 00; Item paid my Lady 30 00 00; Item given Mr Berrie's servant 00 02 06; Item paid for 9 bushels of wheat by bill 02 12 08; Item paid Mr Cobb for so much laid out for my Lady 00 10 00; Item paid the park hedgers for 14 yards 00 14 00; Item paid my brother for so much delivered my Lady 00 02 00; Item paid Zachary for peas straw 00 09 06; Item paid for corn and other things bought at Bideford by Agnes 01 16 03; Item paid the smith upon bill 04 07 00

Sum total of this week's expense 45 03 04

### Saturday the 8th of Febr. 1644

paid the Cater upon bill £01 10 10d; Item paid the workmen wages upon bill 00 12 00; Item paid Mrs Downe in full of her bill for corn as by her acquittance 56 00 00; Item paid the hedgers for making 10 yards of the park hedge 00 10 00; Item paid Simon Tossell for making of 1000 faggots 00 05 10; Item paid him more for 2 dozen of hardwood 00 02 00; Item paid for a boat of sand for the garden 00 02 06

Sum is of this week 59 03 02    [page total] £104 06s 06d

### [p. 19]   Saturday the 15th of Febr. 1644

Item paid the workmens wages by bill £00 19s 01d; Item paid the Cater upon bill 02 16 03; Item paid Mr Page for salt by bill 01 19 00; Item paid for wine by bill 03 18 06; Item paid the smith upon bill 01 14 03; Item given a woman that brought letters 00 00 06; Item paid for four fat sheep 01 11 00; Item paid the hedgers for 12 yards of making the park hedge 00 12 00; Item paid Lawrence Chamberlyn for 13 days work 00 06 06; Item paid the glasier for work done as by bill 00 08 00

Sum total of this week is 14 05 01

### Saturday the 22th of Feb. 1644

Item paid the workmens wages by bill £01 07 04; Item paid the Caters bill 01 06 06; Item paid Mr Clapham as by his acquittance 04 05 00; Item paid for twenty bushels of oats at 1s 6d per bushel 01 10 00; Item paid for making of 1000 faggots to Welsh Dick 00 05 10; Item paid him more for 6 bundles of spars 00 00 06; Item paid Simon Tossell for making 1000 faggots 00 05 10; Item paid him more for making of 2 dozen of hardwood and 7 seams 00 02 07

Sum total of this week's expense is 09 03 07    [page total] £23 08s 08d

### [p. 21]   Saturday the first of March 1644

Item paid the workmens wages by bill £00 18s 01d; Item paid the Cater upon bill 02 13 03; Item paid for 16 bushels of oats at Torr. 01 04 07; Item paid Mr Smith for fish and for carriage 00 13 06; Item spent at Torrington 00 01 00; Item paid the hedgers for making of twenty yards of hedge 01 00 00; Item paid the Welsh Dick for making of 300 faggots and for 6 seams of wood 00 02 03; Item paid for lime upon bill 00 14 00; Item paid my lady to play 00 05 00

So the total of this weeks expense £07 11s 08d

### Saturday the 8th of March 1644

Item paid the workmens wages by bill £000 19s 04d; Item paid the Cater upon his bill 01 10 05; Item paid my Lady 106 00 00; Item paid Rich: Britton upon a bill for corn and other things 014 17 06; Item paid for

making of 50 yards of the park hedge 002 10 00; Item paid William
Richards for making 1120 faggots, 200 hop poles, 8 bundles of spars and
4 seams of wood 000 08 06; Item paid the smith upon two bills 001 15 06
Sum total of this weeks expense is [illegible crossed through] 128 01 03
[page total] £135 12s 11d

**[p. 23]   Saturday the 15th of March 1644**
Item paid the workmens wages by bill £01 07 04; Item paid the Cater
upon his bill 03 02 05; Item paid Mr Fairchild for 6 fat sheep 03 04 00;
Item given the plowmen 00 03 06; Item spent at Hartland 00 02 06; Item
paid the Welsh Dick for making 500 faggots, 200 poles and 6 bundles of
spars 00 04 06; Item paid upon my bill of disbursements at *Exon* 30 00 08
Sum total of this week's expense is £38 04s 11d

**Saturday the 22th of March 1644**
Item paid the workmens wages by bill 1 08 02; Item paid the Cater upon
his bill 4 18 07; Item paid the cobbler for 7 days wages for mending the
coach 0 07 00; Warren. Item paid the Masons in part for the new orchard
wall 2 10 00; Item paid for 7 yards and half of silk mohair by command
2 00 00; Item paid for making of 1350 faggots 0 07 10; Item paid him
more for 10 bundles of spars and 4 seams of wood 0 01 02; Item paid the
smith upon bill 1 05 00; Item paid for bringing home wine 0 03 00; Item
paid for a case of knives and other things as by bill to William Hamblyn
0 08 06; Item paid for carriage of things from *Exon* 0 02 06
Sum total is £13 11s 3d   [page total] £51 16s 02d

**[p. 25]   Saturday the 29th of March 1645**
Item paid the workmens wages upon bill £0 14s 01d; Item paid the Cater
upon bill 3 12 10; Item paid the bean setters for their wages 0 01 00; Item
given to Mr Welshe's groom 0 00 06; Item paid Rich: Britton in full of his
bill 0 03 10; Item paid for bringing letters 0 01 00; Item paid Welsh Dicke
for making 800 faggots, 300 hop poles, 6 bundles of spars and 12 seams of
wood 0 07 08; Item paid Simon Tossell for making of 850 faggots in the
park and 13 seams of hardwood 0 06 00; Item given to a collection for the
town of Axminster 0 02 06; Item paid for 15 bushels of culm 0 15 06; Item
paid for mending a key 0 00 08; Item paid for a paste board 00 00 04; Item
paid Will Richards for making faggots and hardwood 0 03 00; Item paid
for a pair of gloves for Forster 0 00 10
Sum total of this week's expense £06 09s 09d

**[p. 27]   Saturday the 5th of April 1645**
Item paid the workmens wages by bill £0 19s 05d; Item paid the Cater
upon bill 3 08 02; Jo. Hill Item paid the Cornish masons in part for the
new orchard wall 01 12 00; Item given Mr Chichester's man 00 01 00;
Item paid May upon bill 00 01 06; Item paid Mr Wyott upon bill
00 12 02; Item paid Warren the mason for part of the new wall 02 10 00;
Item paid for silk laces for my Lady 00 02 04; Item paid for my Lord at
bowls 00 01 00
Sum total of this week's expense is £09 07s 07d

**Saturday the 12th of Apr. 1645**
Item paid the workmens wages by bill 00 14 04; Item paid the Cater upon
bill 02 08 10; Item paid Maye upon bill 00 06 00; Item paid Avis Starling

for washing by bill oo o4 oo; Item spent at Bow and homeward for
Mr Bulworthy and myself oo 16 o2; Item paid Mrs Coop for serge and
other things for Forster and Randle as by bill o2 oo oo; Item paid
Mrs Baker for things bought of her as by bill oo o6 10; Item paid the bean
setters oo o1 o6
Sum total of this week's expense £o6 17s o8d    [page total] 16 o5 o3

**[p. 29]   Saturday the 19th of April 1645**
Item paid the workmens wages by bill £o1 o1s 4d; Item paid the Cater
upon bill o4 o2 4; Item delivered my Lady in money o5 oo oo; Item paid
John Williams for his quarter due at our Lady Day last o1 13 o4; Item
paid for bringing up two weigh and one quarter of coal oo o2 o6; Item
given Sir Jo: Chichester's man that brought rabbits oo o1 oo; Item paid the
weeders of the garden oo o3 o6; Item paid Cutter oo o1 o4; Item paid the
Welsh Dick for making 800 faggots, 200 hop poles 18 seams of hardwood
and one bundle of spars oo o4 o3; Item paid the Smith upon bill oo 10 oo
Sum total of this week's expense is £13 10s o7d

**Saturday the 26th of Apr. 1645**
Item paid the workmens wages upon bill o3 o2 o5; Item paid the Cater
upon bill o2 oo o4; Item paid William Coop for 11 bushels of barley at
3s 6d per bushel o1 o8 o6; Item paid for two oxen at Tor[rington] fair
o8 10 oo; Item paid for two oxen more then o7 oo oo; Item paid for
fustian for my Lady oo 16 o8; Item paid for my expenses at fair oo o1 oo;
Item paid servants wages upon bill 38 o6 o2; Item paid John Sumner for
42 lbs of tallow at 4d per lb oo 14 oo
Sum total of this week's expense is 61 19 o1    [page total] £75 o9s 8d

**[p. 31]   Saturday the 3d of May 1645**
Item paid the workmens wages upon bill £o1 17s o1d; Item paid the Cater
upon bill o4 16 o5; Item paid the pedler upon bill o1 oo oo; Item paid the
green keep for lurches oo oo o6; Item given Mr Slowley's boy oo o1 oo;
Item paid Connett Manning upon his bill o5 o3 oo; Item paid Zachary for
hay o1 o2 oo; Item paid Rich: Sumner for hay o1 o5 oo; Item paid George
Balch in full of his bill oo 12 oo; Item paid for a quart of oil oo o2 oo;
Item paid Warren the mason in part for the new wall o3 oo oo; Item given
to a man that brought 6 couple of rabbits oo o1 o6; Item paid Rich:
Britton in full of his bill which my Lady hath 12 o9 oo
Sum total of this week's expense is 37 o9 o6

**Saturday the 10th of May 1645**
Item paid the workmens wages upon bill o1 12 o6; Item paid the Cater
upon bill o4 o3 o8; Item paid Constable Ley for the great land rate by my
Lord's command o5 oo oo; Item given to poor Irish men and women by
command oo o5 oo; Item paid the barber oo o2 o6; Item paid John Burke
for ribbon for my Lord oo oo o6; Item paid Welsh Dick for making of
1200 faggots oo o7 oo; Item paid him more for making of 13 seams of
hardwood and 300 poles, 8 bundles of spars and 100 bundles o o3 o6
Sum total of this week's expense is £11 14s o8d    [page total] £49 o4s o2d

**[p. 33]   Saturday the 17th of May 1645**
Item paid the workmens wages upon bill £o1 10s 11d; Item paid the Cater
upon bill o3 o7 oo; Item given to the poor at Barnstaple oo o6 oo; Item

given to the guard of soldiers oo 03 oo; Item paid the furse-cutters in part
o1 05 oo; Item paid two women for two weeks tieing up hops at 5d per
day oo o5 oo; Item paid for two lurches for my Lord oo o1 oo; Item paid
for letters per post oo oo o6; Item paid for 94 bushels of oats at 1s 8d per
bushel from Jo: Ridler o7 16 o8; Item paid my Lady in the green oo oo o6
Sum total of this week's expense £14 15s o7d

### Saturday the 24th of May 1645

Item paid the workmen wages upon bill £o2 o1s ood; Item paid the Cater
upon his bill o4 11 o3; Item paid Mrs Coop in full of her bill oo o8 o4;
Item paid the boatmen for rowing my Lord to *Apledore* oo o5 oo; Item
paid the stone-carver for 3 days oo o2 oo; Item paid for 2 lbs of shot
oo oo o6; Item paid Barnard Jewell for 3 days pulling down the hedge at
task oo o3 oo; Item paid John Roll in part for the new wall o5 10 oo; Item
paid John Warren in part for the wall o3 oo oo; Item paid my brother
upon two bills oo 17 oo; Item paid Tho: Steevens for 3 days wages at task
oo o2 o6; Item paid Welsh Dick for making of 8oo faggots, 8 seams of
wood, 3 bundles of spars, 1oo binders and 5o hop poles oo o6 o1
Sum total of this week is 17 o6 o8   [page total] £32 o2s o3d

### [p. 35]   Saturday the 31th of May 1645

Item paid the workmens wages upon bill £o2 o2s o4d; Item paid the Cater
upon his bill o3 o9 3; Item paid Edward Randle upon his b[ill] of charge
o1 o5 9½; Item paid Nicholas Jerom for two days wages at task oo o1 o8;
Item paid for fringe for a bed upon bill oo 12 o7; Item paid John Hill and
his men for 6 days redding the foundation oo o6 oo; Item paid John
Cunniber for 15o faggots for the weir oo o6 oo; Item paid Simon Tossell
for cutting and binding 4ooo faggots o1 oo oo; Item paid Thurstin for so
much laid out at Barnstaple oo o1 oo
Sum total of this weeks expense is o8 o4 o7½

### Saturday the 7th of June 1645

Item paid the workmens wages by bill £o2 o4s 1od; Item paid the Cater
upon bill o4 12 o8; Item paid William Lee for burning of 6 acres of beat
o1 10 oo; Item paid for a lb of sugar candy oo o2 o6; Item paid for a lb of
brimstone oo o2 o6; Item paid Johan Ellis upon bill oo o7 oo; Item paid
my brother for so much disbursed oo o1 oo; Item paid for sedge oo o1 o6;
Item spent at *Exon* by bill 21 13 o4; Item paid my Lady of money received
from Mr Butler in *Exon* 10 oo oo; Item paid my Lady of money received
from Leonard Bond of Crediton 10 oo oo
Sum total of this week's expenses is 5o 15 o4   [page total] £58 19s 11½d

### [p. 37]   Saturday the 14th day of June 1645

Item paid the workmen wages by bill £o1 o3s o1d; Item paid the Cater
upon bill o5 14 10; Item paid my Lady in the green oo o1 oo; Item paid
for 3 dozen of buttons for Ned Forster oo o1 oo; Item paid Math: Jeakin
for 4 days work in the quarry oo o2 o8; Item paid John Chilcott for
farcins by b[ill] oo 14 oo; Item paid Simon Tossell for 8 days and half at
task oo o7 oo; Item paid Mrs Lovering for 16 bushels of oats o1 o6 o8;
Item paid the garden weeders for 7 weeks oo o7 oo; Item paid the smith
upon his bill o2 o9 o6; Item paid May for 4lbs of shot and seed oo o1 oo;
Item paid William Balch for 3 days wages and his wife for one day

oo 03 oo; Item paid Will Heard for making of 3 pair of linen stockings
oo 01 oo; Item paid Will Lee for 2 days wages and Nicholas Jerron for
2 days oo 03 04; Item paid four women for 8 days oo 03 04; Item paid my
Lady to play 01 oo oo; Item paid Welsh Dick for making of 1000 faggots,
80 hop poles, 50 binders, 4 bundles of spars and 12 seams of wood
oo 07 08
So the total of this week's expense is £14 06s 01d

### [p. 39]  Saturday the 21th of June 1645

Item paid the workmen wages by bill £01 11s 09d; Item paid the Cater
upon bill 07 12 10; Item paid for one weigh of coal 01 14 06; Item paid
Lawrence Chamberlyn upon his bill for wages oo 10 oo; Item paid the
glasier upon his bill oo 15 06; Item paid for cherries and artichokes and
raspberries when the Prince dined here oo 05 oo; Item paid for rabbits then
oo 10 oo; Item paid Mrs Baker upon bill oo 14 09; Item paid for fresh fish
oo 05 06; Item paid for masards oo 04 oo; Item given the Prince's cooks
02 10 oo; Item given the Prince's musicians 01 oo oo; Item given Robert
Cross oo 06 oo; Item given to Simon Collyns oo 02 06; Item given the
feather driver for his wages oo 06 08; Item paid for 3 lobsters oo 01 oo;
Item paid John Hill in part for the new wall 03 10 oo; Item given the
Barnstaple cook oo 10 oo; Item paid John Warren in part 02 oo oo; Item
paid him more for 6 days wages for mending healing oo 03 oo
So the total of this week is £24 13s 00d

### [p. 41]  Saturday the 28th of June 1645

Item paid the workmens wages £01 05s 09d; Item paid the Cater upon bill
04 10 06; Item paid my brother Tho: oo oo 06; Item paid William Meane
for 3 days work at task oo 02 06; Item paid Bernard Jewell the mason for
3 days wages to pull down the hedge oo 03 oo; Item paid for my Lord at
bowls oo oo 06; Item paid for bringing up coal oo 02 oo; Item paid
Baldwyn Steevens for nets 01 oo oo; Item [blank]
Sum total of this week's expense is £07 04s 09d

### Saturday the 5th of July 1645

Item paid the workmen wages by bill £01 12s 10d; Item paid the Cater
upon bill 04 13 07; Item paid James Hartnell for his quarter's wages due at
Midsummer last oo 16 08; Item paid Richard Britton for oats and beans
oo 16 05; Item paid for four weigh of coal 04 oo oo; Item paid the
constable Ley for the last payments of the said rate 05 oo oo; Item paid for
14 truss of straw oo 14 oo; Item paid Mr Smith for 100 bushels of barley at
3s 4d per bushel 16 13 04; Item paid for nine yards of dowlas for Randle's
shirts oo 11 03; Item paid for 16 bushels of charcoal oo 13 04; Item given
my Lady for my Lord Hopton's keep oo 05 oo
Sum total of this week's expense is £37 16s 05d    [page total] £45 9s 2d

### [p. 43]  Saturday the 12th of July 1645

Item paid the workmens wages by bill £02 11s 08d; Item paid the Cater
upon bill 04 01 09; Item paid Avis Starling for washing of Foster's clothes
oo 04 oo; Item paid John Warren for 13 days & half redding of the
foundation for the wall oo 13 06; Item paid for carriage of the beer and ale
to *Barstable* oo 02 oo; Item given Mr Roscarrock's boy oo 02 06; Item paid
Welsh Dick for making of 1000 faggots and six seams of hardwood

oo o6 o4; Item paid John Harris for 19 bushels of oats at 1s 9d per bushel
o1 13 o4; Item paid my brother for so much disbursed for my Lord's uses
oo oo o6; Item paid Agnes Bond for her quarter's wages oo 10 oo; Item
['paid' crossed through] given the poor at *Rowley* by command oo o1 o6;
Item paid John Terry for culm oo o6 oo; Item paid Mrs Hardwick upon
bill oo 15 oo; Item paid for making the maids clothes oo o2 o6; Item paid
Mr Prust's boy oo o1 o6; Item paid the barber for my Lord oo o2 o6; Item
paid the cobler for mending the coach harness oo o1 oo; Item given my
Lady at play oo 10 oo
So the sum of this week's expense is £12 11s 09d

### [p. 45]  Saturday the 19th of July 1645
Item paid the workmen wages by bill £01 15s o6d; Item paid the Cater
upon bill o3 oo o4; Item paid for a lock for the buttery hatch oo o1 o6;
Item paid the garden weeders for 6 weeks wages oo o6 oo; Item paid
Simon Tossell for 3 days making faggots in the park oo o2 o6; Item paid
the smith upon bill o1 o1 o8
Sum total of this week's expense is o6 o7 o6

### Saturday the 26th of July
Item paid the workmen wages upon bill £01 o8s o7d; Item paid the Cater
upon bill o2 16 oo; Item paid for measuring the beat in park oo o2 oo;
Item paid Elias Richard for 2 weeks wages oo o2 o6; Item paid for making
of 10 acres and half of hay in the barton o1 o6 o3; Item paid Tho: Steevens
for 4 days wages at task oo o3 o4
Sum total of this week's expense is £05 18s o8d

### Saturday the second of August 1645
Item paid the workmen wages by bill £01 17s o6d; Item paid the Cater
upon his bill o2 o1 o5; Item paid Anthony Ash for work done oo o3 o1;
Item paid Mr Booth for sugar candy and given to the poor oo o3 oo; Item
paid for claret wine oo o1 o8; Item given the poor by command oo 10 oo;
Item paid the Smith upon bill o1 10 oo
So the total of this week's expense is o6 o6 o8   [page total] £18 12s 1od

### [p. 47]  Saturday the 9th of August 1645
Item paid the workmens wages by bill £01 o7s 11d; Item paid the Cater
upon bill o2 o9 o9; Item paid the widow Symons for sugar as by the
acquittance appeareth o3 o4 o6; Item delivered my Lady at play oo o5 oo;
Item paid Mr Cobb for so much paid my Lady oo o1 oo; Item paid for
worsted for my Lord oo o2 oo; Item given my Lady to play oo o2 o6; Item
given to Sir Allen Apsley's clerk oo o2 o6   .
Sum total of this week's expense is o7 12 o2

### Saturday the 16th of August 1645
Item paid the workmens wages by bill £01 o1s o6d; Item paid the Cater by
bill o3 oo o1; Item paid for gelding and spaying of pigs oo o2 oo; Item paid
for culm oo 16 o6
Sum total of this week's expense is £5 oos o1d

### Saturday the 24th of August 1645
paid the workmen wages upon bill £01 o2s o2d; Item paid the Cater upon
his bill o1 19 o6; Item allowed to myself for eight lambs at 5s the piece

02 00 00; Item more allowed myself for eight ewes at 6s a piece 02 08 00;
Item paid at Barnstaple for 6 bushels of wheat at 6s per bushel 01 16 00;
Item paid the widow Peard for two fat steers 08 00 00; Item paid for
twenty bushels of oats 02 03 04
Sum total of this week's expense is £19 07s 00d    [page total] 31 19 3

### [p. 49]    Saturday the 30th [sic] of August 1645

Item paid the workmens wages upon bill £00 18s 11d; Item paid the Cater
upon bill 03 14 03; Item paid John Burke for dressing my Lord's hat
00 01 06; Item paid the tinker for mending the brass pots 00 05 00; Item
paid Mrs Hardwick 00 01 03; Item spent at *Ilfardcoombe* 00 01 06; Item
paid for cloth for Owen 00 12 00; Item paid for culm 00 07 00; Item paid
for fish and other things bought at market 00 09 00; Item paid the widow
Sumner for two pigs 01 03 [faded]; Item paid the garden weeders 00 04 00;
Item paid the smith upon two bills 02 00 10
Sum total is 10 01 03

### Saturday the 6th of September 1645

Item paid the workmens wages upon bill 01 01 05; Item paid the Cater's
bill 02 07 05; Item paid for cutting two acres of grass 00 02 06; Item given
for bringing plums 00 02 06; Item given my Lady to play 00 01 00; Item
given my Lord in the green 00 00 06; Item paid for one fat ox at
*Barnestaple* 04 12 00; Item paid for standing my horse 00 00 06; Item paid
for a basin for my Lord 00 03 00
Sum total of this week's expense is £08 10s 10d    [page total] £18 12s 1d

### [p. 51]    Saturday the 13th of Sept. 1645

Item paid the workmens wages upon bill £01 11s 08d; Item paid the Cater
upon bill 03 02 08; Item paid John Warren and his brother for 17 days
wages 00 08 06; Item paid for one fat cow bought at Frem[ington]
03 07 08; Item paid for 20 bushels of wheat at 5s 8d 05 13 04; Item paid
for 3 boats of gravel 00 12 00; Item paid for a butt of sack 24 00 00; Item
paid for a fallowing steer 00 04 00; Item paid Mr Major in full of his bill
01 11 04; Item paid for 12 sheep 03 18 00; Item paid Mrs Hardwick
00 05 00; Item paid for 6 lbs of shot 00 01 06
So the sum of this week is 44 15 08

### Saturday the 20th of Sept. 1645

Item paid the workmens wages by bill £01 12s 08d; Item paid the Cater
upon bill 02 16 10; Item paid for 2 lbs of plaster of *pallas* 00 00 06; Item
paid John Jonson for oats and barley per b[ill] 09 05 02; Item paid
Mr Weeks upon bill for Bradworth fair 23 18 03; Item paid Simon Tolsell
for casting sixty yards the bank in the park 01 00 00; Item paid William
Davy for two days going to boat 00 02 00; Item paid for casting ten acres
of beat 00 15 00; Item paid for garden seeds 00 01 02; Item paid Gregory
Hosgood for 6 days wages at 4d and his man 6 days 00 03 04; Item
delivered my brother when he went to Comb. 00 04 00
So the total of this week's expense 39 18 11    [page total] £84 14s 07d

### [p. 53]    Saturday the 28th of Septem. 1645

Item paid the workmen wages upon bill £01 15s 00d; Item paid the Cater
upon bill 02 16 08; Item paid Eliz: Randall for half a year's wages then
due 01 00 00; Item paid for standing my horse at Barnstaple and for my

expenses when I bought slates oo o1 oo; Item paid Wilmot for money laid
out oo o1 oo; Item paid Will Meane for so much laid out at *Apledore*
oo o1 o6; Item paid the hop gatherers by bill o3 o9 o7; Item paid for
bringing up one boat of stones from *Apledore* oo o5 oo; Item paid
Baldwyn Bater for his expenses about taking partridges oo o1 oo
So the sum of this week's expense o9 10 o9

### Saturday the 4th of October 1645

Item paid the workmen wages upon bill £o1 14s ood; Item paid the Cater's
bill o2 o6 10; Item paid Tho: Marchant for hay bought o2 oo oo; Item paid
for 9 bushels of oats oo 15 oo; Item paid Eliz: Umbles for knitting
stockings for Randall oo o1 oo; Item paid for 9600 Cornish slates at 5s the
thousand o2 o8 oo; Item paid Lawrence Chamberlyn upon bill oo o8 o8;
Item paid the smith upon two bills o2 13 o6; Item Humfry Lake for
2500 furse faggots at 6s 8d the thousand oo 16 o8; Item given his man and
for his horse oo o1 oo; Item paid Tho: Sumner for 5600 furse faggots at
6s 8d the thousand o1 17 o8; Item paid Richard Britton for 4 trusses of
wheat straw oo o6 oo
Sum of this week 15 18 o4   [page total] £23 o9s o1d

### [p. 55]   Saturday the 11th of October 1645

Item paid the workmens wages upon bill £o1 15 od; Item paid the Cater
upon bill o2 o5 o2; Item paid Richard Britton for 23 truss of barley straw
oo 16 oo; Item paid him more for a knife for buttry oo o1 oo; Item paid
Peter Sumner for 3 truss of hay at 4s 4d the truss oo 14 oo; Item paid for
4 weigh of coal o7 o4 oo; Item paid Morcombe for 3 quarters wages for
keeping the clocks oo o6 oo; Item paid for 20 bushels of seed wheat at
6s 5d the bushel o6 10 oo; Item paid Mr Shurte upon bill 11 oo oo; *not
sold* Item paid the glasier upon bill for work o1 12 o7; Item paid Arch:
Ackland for 20 bushels of barley at 3s 2d the bushel o3 o3 oo; Item paid
Simon Tossell for casting the fence in the park o1 10 oo
So the whole sum is ['37 11 o7' crossed through] 36 16 o9

### Saturday the 18th of October 1645

Item paid the workmens wages upon bill oo 18 o7; Item paid the Cater's
bill o2 17 o4; Item paid for two boats of gravel oo o8 oo; Item paid for
bringing of two boats of coal oo o6 oo; Item paid for 20 bushels of culm
o1 oo oo; Item paid the Cornish masons in full as by a bill will appear
o2 10 11; Item paid John Hearson for 15 bushels of lime at 8d per bushel
oo 10 oo; Item paid him more for bringing up of two boats of slates from
*Apledore* oo o9 oo; Item paid for 4 bushels of culm oo o4 oo; Item paid for
two days wages to a mason at the mill oo o1 10; Item given to the poor by
command oo 10 oo
*page sum* 10 o1 o8

### [p. 57]   Item paid Rumson upon his bill for corn o3 10 oo; Item paid for

1 bushel of seed wheat oo o6 o6; Item paid Rose for apples bought
oo o7 oo; Item spent at *Exon* as by bill o1 o5 o6; Item paid Mr Mason for
one barrel of sugar by bill o4 19 oo; Item paid Zachary Chidely for
6 bushels of wheat at 6s per bushel o1 16 oo; Item paid for 10 bushels of
culm oo 10 oo; Item Avis Starling for washing oo o4 oo; Item paid for
7 bushels of peas at 3s 2d o1 o1 o2; Item paid Eliz: Umbles for knitting

my Lord's socks oo o2 oo; Item paid for bringing of one boat of stone from *Apledore* oo o4 oo; Item paid [blank]
Sum total of this week's expense 24 o6 10

This book was seen, examined and allowed by me the 26th of October 1645
[signed] R: Bathe

The whole sum of the disbursements contained in this book amounts unto the sum of £1244 5s 8½d
Also due to me for one year's wages £20
Rec. in this year before going £1247 2s 3d
So remains due to this accountant £17 3s 5½d

**[p. 59]   Saturday the 25th of October 1645**
Item paid the workmen wages upon bill £01 07s 00d; Item paid the Cater upon bill 03 14 03; Item paid William Britton for two barrels of herrings o1 14 08; Item paid him more for 109 yards of matting and for bringing to Barnstaple oo o9 10; Item paid him more upon a bill oo o5 oo; Item paid Symon Lake for half a year's wages due at Michas. last o1 17 o6; Item paid John William upon bill for two quarters due at Michas last o4 12 oo; Item paid Mrs Hardwick upon bill o4 o2 07; Item given *Banton* messenger for two journeys oo o2 oo; Item paid for 650 furse faggots for the weir oo o5 o6; Item paid for 5 truss of straw oo o4 o6; Item paid Henry Sherland for 10 bushels of oats at 1s 1od the bushel oo 18 o4; Item paid Edward Randle upon a bill for sugar and soap o4 15 07; Item paid Mr Farchilde in part for corn as by his letter will appear o3 o2 o9; Item allowed to myself for my wages 17 o3 o5; Item paid my Lady at two several payments 40 oo oo
Sum total of this week 84 15 o1

# Expenses, 1646–1647

KENT ARCHIVES OFFICE, U269/A525/7

*The book measures 8″ by 12″ and is in a paper wrapper. The front cover is headed 'Disbursment from the 24th of October 1646 until &c 1647'. There are a few additional notes on the cover. Pages 1, 4, 6, 8, 10 and 36 are blank and the final twenty sheets were torn out.*

**[p. 2]**  Tawstock A book of the weekly disbursements for the household expense and other defrayments of the right Honourable Earl of Bath from the last day of October 1646 until
By me Rich: Pollard

**[p. 3]   Saturday the last of October 1646**
*First* allowed myself for one year's wages due at Michaelmas last £20 oos ood; Item paid the workmens wages by b[ill] o2 o7 o1; Item paid for a rode cord oo o1 o6; paid for a bottle of ink oo o1 oo; paid for 4 halters oo o1 oo; paid Mr Bourgchier for so much laid out by him for a

messenger oo o3 o6; paid John Johnson for 6 fat sheep at 14s the sheep
o4 o5 oo; paid Mrs Hardwicke upon a bill o1 o8 oo
Sum total is 27 o7 o1

### Saturday the 7th of Novemb. 1646

paid the workmen wages by bill £o1 o4s ood; paid Thorne the carrier in
part o3 10 10; paid Lawrence Berry upon his bill oo o4 o8; paid the saddler
in full of one bill o3 oo oo; paid wages as by bill 18 15 oo; paid Mr Bold
for my Lord's journey to London 20 oo oo; paid John Terry in full for
one year's wages due at Michas. 1646 o1 10 oo [?sic]; paid for a pair of
wool cards oo o2 oo; paid Ann Mullyns for one quarter teaching young
Reece oo o2 oo; paid the nurse for one month oo o4 oo; paid for a pair of
shoes for Jonathan oo o1 oo
Sum total is 48 12 o8   [page total] 75 19 9

### [p. 5]   Saturday the 14th of November 1646

Item paid the workmen wages upon bill £o1 1os o2d; paid for pair of shoes
for Mary oo o2 o4; Item given the poor oo o5 o6; Item spent at *Exon* when
my Lord went last to London oo o6 oo; paid Mr Beckett for half a year's
teaching Randle oo 10 oo; paid for a quarter of mutton oo o2 o4; paid for
two hooks to cut down the hops oo o2 o4; paid Mr John Skitch for two
cows o6 o6 o8; given John Sumner for his pains two days at plough and to
his man oo o3 oo; paid for eggs oo o1 o4; paid Mr Shurte in part of a bill
o9 oo oo; spent at *Apledore* when I went to buy fish oo o1 o4; paid for one
bushel of salt oo o4 o4
Sum total is 18 15 o4

### [p. 7]   Saturday the 21th of November 1646

Item paid the workmen wages by bill £oo 15s o8d oo; paid John Swyne in
part of his bill o2 oo oo; paid for beef & mutton at market oo o6 o6; Item
given Mr Pagett's men for plowing oo o2 oo; paid James Whitfeld for
8 weeks wages at 1s 6d per week oo 12 oo; paid for mutton oo o2 o4; paid
for a lock for the coach house oo o1 o4; paid for eggs oo o1 10
Sum total is o3 oo 10

### Saturday the 28th of November 1646

Item paid the workmens wages by bill £o1 oos o4d; paid Gregory
Hosgood upon his bill oo o2 o6; paid Rumson upon his bill oo o9 o8; paid
for beef & mutton oo 12 o6; paid the nurse for one month & for soap
oo o4 o4; paid John Gribble for going to Stow with a letter oo o4 oo; paid
James Blackmoore for 3 quarters wages due to him o3 oo oo; paid John
Midway for 7 days wages for mending the park pale oo o6 o3; paid for
4 joints of mutton oo o4 oo; paid the fuller upon bill oo 13 10; paid for
making clean 2 pair of pistols oo o2 o6; paid for eggs oo o1 oo
Sum total is o7 oo o7   [page total] £10 1s 5d

### [p. 9]   Saturday the 6th of Decemb. 1646

Item paid the workmen wages by bill £oo 15s o8d; Item paid Gregory
Hosgood for making old Mr Wyott's suit as by bill o2 oo o8; Item paid
Rumson upon a bill oo 17 o5; Item given to the poor oo 15 o6; Item paid
for one joint of mutton oo o1 oo; Item paid for making 68 yards of hedge
in *pannyuer* at 4d per yard o1 o2 o8; Item paid Mr John Lambe in full of
one bill of £100 taken up by Mr Lynn 100 oo oo; Item paid for serges &

bunters for the miller at the mill oo o5 oo; Item paid for 5 yards of kersey
for old Mrs Alston Cote o1 o9 o6; Item paid for 8 yards of serge at
4s 6d per yard for Mr Week's girls o1 16 oo; Item paid John Hamblyn
upon bill oo o6 o2; Item paid for one quarter of mutton oo o3 oo; Item
paid for eggs oo o2 oo; Item paid the smith upon 4 bills o4 o7 oo; Item
paid for making 460 faggots and 20 seams of hardwood oo o4 o4
Sum total is 113 15 ['15 11' crossed through] 11    [page total] £113 15 11

**[p. 11]    Saturday the 13th of December 1646**
Item paid the workmen wages by bill £o1 o3s o9d; Item paid for one
quarter of beef oo 16 1o; Item paid for mutton oo 11 o6; Item paid for
eggs oo o1 o6; Item paid for weaving 24 yards of white coarse cloth
oo o6 oo; Item paid the poor oo o5 o6; Item paid Thurstyn upon bill
o5 11 oo
Sum is o8 15 o3

**Saturday the 19th of December 1646**
Item paid the workmen wages by bill £oo 13s o9d; Item paid Rumson
upon a bill o3 1o o3; Item paid William Lee for making 770 faggots
oo o4 o6; Item paid him more for making 2 dozen and 8 seams of
hardwood & 5 bundles of crooks oo o3 o6; Item for threshing 1o bushels
of peas oo o2 o6; Item paid for eggs oo o1 oo; Item paid the nurse for one
month oo o5 o6; Item paid James Whitfeild for 5 weeks' wages oo o7 o6
Sum total is o5 o7 o6    [page total] £14 o2s 9d

**[p. 12]    Saturday the 26th of Decemb. 1646**
Item paid the workmens wages by bill £oo 1os o6d; Item paid Symon
Tossell for 11 days wages working in the park oo o7 o4; Item paid for
threshing 48 bushels of oats oo o8 oo; Item paid given the poor oo o5 o6;
Item John Medway for 8 days wages oo o6 o8; Item paid for mutton
oo o6 oo
Sum is o2 o4 oo

**Saturday the 2d of Jan. 1646**
Item paid the workmens wages by bill £oo o7s ood; Item paid upon a bill
for dying of cloth o3 oo oo; Item paid Rumson in full of two bills
oo 14 o6; Item paid Agnes Row for for [sic] barm for 12 weeks to bake
with oo o6 oo; Item paid for mutton oo o5 o6; Item paid for eggs oo o1 oo;
Item given the poor oo o5 o6; Item paid for a hat for Randle oo o6 oo;
Item paid Mr Weeks oo o1 oo; 3 quarters 26 lbs Item paid John Hobbs in
full for soap oo o7 oo
Sum total is o5 13 o6    [page total] 7 17 6

**[p. 12b]    rec. for peal & salmon 1647**

| | |
|---|---|
| Saturday the 5th of June 1647 | Item rec. for 2 peals 1s 6d |
| Saturday the 12th of June | Item rec. for 13 peals 4s 2d |
| Saturday the 19th of June | Item rec. for 13 peals 4s 2d |
| Saturday the 26th of June | Item rec. for 33 peals 1os 6d |
| | Item rec. for 1 pug 2s |
| Saturday the 3rd of July 1647 | Item rec. for 29 peals 12s 6d |
| | Item rec. for half a salmon 1s 4d |
| Saturday the 1oth of July | Item rec. for 3 peals 8d |
| | Item rec. for half a salmon 11d |

Saturday the 17th of July      Item rec. for 2 peals 10d
                                 Item rec. for half a salmon 1s
Saturday the 24th of July      Item rec. for 2 peals 6d
                                 Item rec. for 5 millets 1s
                                 Item rec. for 1 pug 1s 6d
Saturday the 21th of August 1647      Item rec. for 4 peals 1s
                                 Item rec. for 1 salmon 3s 6d
Saturday the 28th of August      Item rec. for 48 peals 7s 10d
Saturday the 11th of Septemb. 1647      Item rec. for 19 peals 4s
                                 Item rec. for 1 salmon 2s 6d
Saturday the 18th of Sept.      Item rec. for 6 peals 8d
                                 Item rec. for 2 salmons 6s 8d
Saturday the 25th of Sept.      Item rec. for 1 salmon 3s
Saturday the 2nd of October 1647      Item rec. for 4 salmons 8s 8d
Saturday the 9th of Octo.      Item rec. for 1 pug 1s 6d
4 1 10   0 13 2

**[12b dorse]**   **disbursements**
Saturday the 23th of October
Item rec. for 2 salmons 4s 2d    Sum total is £4 6s

Item paid for a new kiddle 6s; Item paid for 1 slip of thread 9d; Item paid more for 1 dozen of thread 8s; Item paid for knitting of 12 slips of thread 4s; Item paid for for a rope for the draught net 1s 4d; Item paid for 1 lb of cork 4d; Item paid for barm for the brewer 3s
Sum total is £1 3s 1d
Rec. 7 17 6   pd 2 8 9   due 5 8 9

**[p. 13]**   **Saturday the 9th of Jan. 1646**
Item paid the workmen wages by bill £00 10s 10d; Item paid for half a mutton 00 05 06; Item spent at Torrington 00 01 06; Item given to the poor 00 05 06; Item paid the boatmen for bringing corn from *Apledore* 00 05 06; Item paid Mr Weeks for his expenses 00 01 04; Item paid for making of 29 yards of hedge at 6d per yard 00 14 06; Item paid Tho: Hobson by bill 19 15 00
Sum total is 21 18 10

**Saturday the 16th of Jan. 1646**
Item paid the workmens wages by bill £00 14s 09d; Item paid for beef & mutton 00 17 06; Item paid for making 400 faggots & 2 dozen of hardwood 00 04 04; Item paid for threshing 9 bushels of oats 00 01 06; Item paid Rose for her journey to London 02 00 00; Item paid Ann Mullyn for Christmas quarter teaching the young Reece 00 02 00; Item paid for eggs 00 02 00; Item paid for two bushels of oats 00 05 04

Sum total is 04 07 05   [page total] 26 6 3

**[p. 14]**   **Saturday the 23th of Jan. 1646**
Item paid the workmens wages by bill £00 17s 04d; Item paid the nurse for one month 00 04 06; Item given the carrier for bringing the garden seeds & two black boxes 00 03 00; Item paid for 20 bushels of wheat 09 00 00; Item paid for 30 bushels of barley 09 00 00; Item for my expenses at *Coombe* [Ilfracombe] 00 03 06; Item for eggs 00 01 00; Item

paid for 39 lbs of cheese at 2½d oo o8 o2; Item paid for mutton oo o5 o6;
Item paid for 2 gallons & ½ of butter oo 12 o6; Item more paid for
2 gallons & ½ of butter oo 15 oo; Item paid for 2 lbs of soap oo o1 oo;
Item paid Mary Tolsell for 18 ['day' crossed through] weeks wages
oo o9 oo; Item paid [blank]
Sum total is 22 o6 oo

### [p. 15]   Saturday the 30th of Jan. 1646

Item paid the workmens wages by bill £oo 11s o7d; Item paid for beef &
mutton o1 o9 10; Item paid for eggs oo o1 oo; Item paid for making
500 faggots, 8 seams of hardwood & 60 poles oo o3 11; Item paid Simon
Tolsell for 9 days wages oo o7 o6; Item paid Jo: Whitfeild for 5 weeks
oo o7 o6; Item given to the poor oo o5 o6; Item paid the chimney sweeper
oo o1 o6; Item paid for two sieves oo o1 o4
Sum total is o3 o9 o8

### Saturday the 6th of Feb. 1646

Item paid the workmens wages by bill £oo 17s 11d; Item paid for beef
oo oo oo [sic] Item paid Rumson upon his bill o3 12 o8; Item given to the
poor oo o5 o6 Item paid for making 36 yards of hedge about Forberry at
6d per yard oo 18 oo; Item paid for threshing 51 bushels of oats oo o8 o6;
Item Will: Lee for 2 days wages oo o1 o6; Item paid for eggs oo o1 o6;
Item paid for carriage of hops to Barn. oo o1 oo; Item paid Mr Lambe
upon a bill 100 oo oo; Item spent at Torrington oo o1 o6
Sum total is 106 o8 o1   [page total] £109 17s 3d

### [p. 16]   Saturday the 13th of Feb. 1646

Item paid the workmen wages by bill £oo 18s 17d; Item paid at several
times for Baldwyn Bater during the time of his sickness and after as by bill
o2 o2 o4; Item paid for 10 lbs of candles oo o5 o8; Item paid for a pair of
wool cards oo o1 o6; Item paid for 3 lbs of pitch oo oo o6; Item paid for
one quart of mustard seed oo oo o6; Item paid for a comb brush for
Randle oo oo o3; Item paid for 2 quarters of mutton oo o7 oo; Item paid
for beef o1 13 oo; Item paid for lime as by bill oo 14 o8; Item paid for
eggs oo o1 oo; Item paid for thread & tape oo oo o6; Item paid for
threshing 51 bushels of oats oo o8 o6; Item paid the poor oo o5 o6
Sum total is o6 19 o6

### Saturday the 20th of Feb. 1646

Item paid the workmen wages by bill £oo 18s o8d; Item paid the nurse for
one month oo o4 o6; Item paid the poor oo o5 o6; Item paid for 3 boats of
sand oo 10 o6; Item paid John Midway for 10 days wages for making pales
for the park oo o8 oo; Item paid Mr Shurt in part o5 oo oo; Item paid
Roger Thorne in full of all o2 17 oo; Item paid for eggs oo o1 oo; Item
paid for one dozen of pewter spoons oo o2 o4; Item paid for beef
o1 12 oo; Item paid for mutton oo o7 oo
Sum total is 12 o6 o6   [page total] £19 6s od

### [p. 17]   Saturday the 27th 1646

Item paid the workmens wages by bill £o2 o2s o3d; Item paid for beef
o1 11 o3; Item paid for mutton oo o5 o4; Item paid for half a pound of
pepper oo o1 oo; Item paid for 41 lbs of butter o1 oo oo; Item for one
cheese oo o2 o9; Item for dishes of wood oo o1 10; Item for cloam

oo oo 03; Item paid for a pair of shoes for May oo 02 02; Item paid
Ja: Whitfeild for 5 weeks oo 07 oo; Item given the poor oo 05 06; Item
paid for two boats of sand oo o8 oo; Item paid for half hundred & 11 lbs
of soap and for cask & freight oo 19 06; Item paid for eggs oo o1 oo
Sum total is o6 07 oo

**Saturday the 6th of March 1646**
Item paid the workmen wages by bill £o1 o6s o4d; Item for weaving
18 yards of cloth oo 07 06; Item paid for 6 lbs of candles oo 03 06; Item
paid the poor oo 05 06; Item paid John Gribble for 10 days wages in the
garden oo 03 04; Item for eggs oo o1 06; Item to John Warren 4 days
oo 02 oo
Sum total is £o2 o9s o8d  [page total] £8 16s 8d

[p. 18]  **Saturday the 13th of March 1646**
Item paid the workmen wages by bill £o1 o1s o4d; Item paid the poor
oo 05 06; Item paid for eggs oo o1 06; Item paid for one barrel of beef and
one barrel of herrings 03 04 oo; Item paid for bringing the beef & herrings
from Barnstaple oo o1 06; Item paid The smith upon two bills o2 13 06;
Item paid Thomas Moore for 3 days wages for him & his man and for
thread to make Mary clothes oo 03 oo; Item paid for trouts oo o1 oo
Sum total is 07 16 04

**Saturday the 20th of March 1646**
Item paid the workmen wages by bill o1 o2 04; Item paid for 35 lbs of
butter oo 16 04; Item paid for eggs oo o2 oo; Item paid for starch oo oo 06;
Item for inkle for May oo oo o2; Item for 2 cheeses oo 05 oo; Item for
dowlas and canvas for Mary oo 15 o8; Item for dowlas for Jonathan's
shirts oo 03 o8; Item for mending the furnace by bill 04 oo oo; Item given
to the poor oo 05 06; Item paid for making 850 faggots, 27 seams of
hardwood & 9 bundles of spars oo 07 11
Sum total is 07 o9 o1  [page total] 15 5 5

[p. 19]  **Saturday the 27th of March 1646 1647**
Item paid the workmen wages by bill £oo 19s o1d; Item paid at market by
bill o1 18 04; Item paid the poor oo 05 06; Item paid Mr Lovering upon
his bill for oats 13 15 oo; Item paid for 7 couple of lug fish oo 10 06; Item
paid for 4 couple of poor Johns oo 03 04; Item paid for 2 joints of veal
oo 03 oo; due at our Lady Day 1647 Item paid Morcombe for one year's
fee for keeping the clocks oo o8 oo; Item given a messenger that brought
letters from Mr Prust oo o1 oo; Item paid for threshing of 97 bushels of
oats oo 11 o2; Item paid Will: Lee for 2 days oo o1 o8; Item paid
Mr Shapley by bill 21 oo oo; Item paid George Pitts for making
300 faggots, 3 bundles of spars & 6 seams of hardwood oo o2 06; Item
paid for six score and fourteen pounds of pork at 2d per pound o1 o2 04
Sum total is £41 o2s o5d
Thus far of my accounts are sent to my Lady 483 12 2

[p. 20]  **Saturday the 3th of April 1647**
Item paid the workmens wages by bill £o1 oos o5d; Item paid for cloam at
*Biddeford* oo o1 o9; Item paid for a boat to bring the corn oo 03 oo; Item
returned to London from *Exon* by Mr Buttler 100 oo oo; Item paid for
21 bushels of barley oo8 oo oo; Item spent at *Coombe* oo o1 oo; Item paid

Rich: Rooke for half a year's wages due at Michas. last 001 05 00; Item given the poor 000 05 06; Item paid for weaving of 15 yards of cloth at 5d per yard 000 06 03; Item paid George Pitts for making 700 faggots, 2 dozen of hardwood, 150 poles and six bundles of spars 000 06 04; Item paid Charles upon a bill for wages 000 16 10; Item paid the market bill 01 00 03

Sum is 113 06 04

### [p. 21]   Saturday the 10th of April 1647
Item paid the workmens wages by bill £01 07s 08d; Item paid upon a bill for butter 01 10 00; Item paid Mrs Weeks upon her bill for the boys clothes 00 12 00; Item paid Jonas Harris for two bushels of oats when my Lord was at home 00 05 04; Item paid James Whitfeild for 3 weeks 00 04 06; Item paid for eggs 00 01 00; Item given the poor 00 05 06; Item paid a woman for two weeks weeding in the garden 00 02 00; Item paid for one boat of sand 00 02 06; Item paid the nurse for one month 00 04 04; Item paid for glasses to put preserves in 00 06 00; paid for dressing the pied mare 00 01 06

Sum total is 05 02 04

### Saturday the 17th of April 1647
Item paid the workmens wages by bill £01 00s 11d; Item paid the market bill 01 03 03; Item paid for eggs 00 01 00; Item paid for gums and other things to make ink 00 01 06; Item given to the poor 00 05 06; Item paid for milk pans at Bideford 00 01 06; Item paid for making 800 faggots, 2 dozen and 8 seams of hardwood, 200 hop poles & 2 bundles of spars 00 08 06; Item paid Thurstyn for one year and quarters wages due to him and twenty shillings given by my Lady 06 00 00

Sum total is 09 02 02   [page total] £14 4s 6d   sent to London

### [p. 22]   Saturday the 24th of April 1647
paid the workmen wages by bill £00 13s 06d; paid the market bill 01 05 11; paid Mr Prust upon bill 00 19 06; paid George Pitts for making 600 faggots, 2 dozen of hardwood, 100 poles 00 06 06; paid for 4 dozen of brooms 00 03 04; paid for weaving of 14 yards of cloth at 4d per yard 00 04 08; paid Agnes Row for half a years wages due at our Lady Day 1647 01 00 00; paid her more for barm 00 02 00; paid the poor 00 05 06; paid for eggs 00 01 00; Item given in hansel for one ox 00 04 04; Item for Mrs Hardwick's charge when she went from hence to *Exon* with 2 horses 00 15 00

Sum is [illegible crossed through] 06 02 03

### [p. 23]   Saturday the first of May 1647
paid the workmens wages by bill £00 13s 03d; paid the market bill 01 09 00; paid Simon Tolsell for making 700 faggots, 4 dozen of hardwood and eight seams 00 08 09; paid him more for 3 days wages 00 02 06; paid the fuller upon bill 01 00 06; paid George Pitts for making of 750 faggots 00 04 04; paid him more for 3 dozen of hardwood & half and 200 poles & half & one bundle of spars 00 05 03; paid Elias Richards for 12 weeks 00 06 00; paid for eggs 00 01 00; paid the poor 00 05 06

Sum total is 04 16 01

**Saturday the 8th of May 1647**
paid the workmen wages by bill £oo 12s 1od; paid the market bill
o1 oo o4; paid Doctor Chichester by bill 30 oo oo; paid the nurse for one
month oo o4 oo; paid for two Aprons for Mary oo o2 o6; paid for
11 bushels of oats o1 15 oo; paid for one quarters teaching of young Reece
his book due at Lady Day oo o2 oo; paid the smith upon two bills
o2 o9 oo; paid the hop tiers for two weeks oo o5 oo; paid the poor
oo o5 o6
Sum total 36 16 o2   [page total] £41 12s 3d

**[p. 24]   Saturday the 15th of May 1647**
paid the workmen wages by bill £oo 14s o2d; paid the market bill
o1 12 10; paid the weeders of wheat by bill o3 o5 oo; pd for two weigh of
coal o3 oo oo; paid for cheeses to Dick Britton oo 12 oo; paid Elias
Richards for beating of one acre in the park oo 13 o4; paid the poor
oo o5 o6
Sum is 10 o2 10

**Saturday the 22th of May 1647**
paid the workmen wages by bill £o1 o3s o4d; paid the market bill
o1 o1 oo; paid the tailor for making Mary's clothes oo o1 oo; paid Simon
Tolsell for one week oo o5 oo; paid Mr Dennis of *Bristoll* in full of his bill
for things bought long since as will appear o3 o9 oo; paid for 6 bushels of
culm oo o6 oo; paid Charles for work done by bill oo 11 11; paid David
Basly for 2 days wages oo o2 40; paid Sander for one day oo o1 o2
Sum is o7 oo o9   [page total] £17 3s 7d

**[p. 25]   Saturday the 29th of May 1647**
paid the workmen wages by bill £oo o9s 1od; paid the market bill
o1 11 oo; paid the glasier by bill oo 16 o9; paid Mr Palmer of Barnstaple in
part of his bill from France 45 oo oo; paid for 2 bushels of oats oo o7 o8;
paid Joan Whitfeild for 4 weeks oo o4 oo; paid the nurse for one month
oo o4 oo
Sum is 48 13 o3

**Saturday the 5th of June 1647**
paid the workmen wages by bill oo 15 o2; paid the market bill oo 18 o3;
paid for cutting of calves & pigs oo o2 oo; paid for making of one acre of
hay in Knevett's meadow oo o4 oo
Sum total is o1 19 o5

**Saturday the 12th of June 1647**
paid the workmen wages by bill oo o9 o2; paid the market bills o1 10 o8;
paid Welsh Dick for making one acre of hay in Knevett's meadow
oo o4 oo; paid the weeders of oats by bill o2 o6 o3; paid for eggs oo oo o6
Sum is o4 10 o7   [page total] £55 3s 3d

**[p. 26]   Saturday the 19th of June 1647**
Item paid the workmen wages by bill £oo 11s o8d; paid the market bill
o1 13 o4; paid the making 4 acres of hay in the marsh oo 16 oo; paid for
letters per post oo o1 oo; paid for making of of [sic] one acres of hay in
Knevett's meadow and one in marsh oo o8 oo; paid Joseph Holland for

making two acres of hay in the marsh oo o8 oo; paid for bringing up the coal oo o2 o6; paid for thongs & a butter pat oo oo o6; paid for tar oo oo o6

Sum is o4 o1 o6

### Saturday the 26th of June 1647

paid the workmen wages by bill £oo 10s 11d; paid the market bill o1 14 o6; paid for making of two acres of hay in Knevett's meadow & one in the marsh oo 12 oo; paid William Coope for making one acre of hay in the marsh oo o4 oo; paid more for half an acre in the marsh oo o2 oo; paid Silly Balch for making two acres of hay in the marsh oo o8 oo

Sum total is o3 11 o5   [page total] £7 12s 11d

### [p. 27]   Saturday the 3d of July 1647

Item paid the workmens wages by bill £oo o8s o4d oo; Item paid the market bills o1 o5 o8; Item paid for eggs oo oo o6; Item paid the nurse for 1 month oo o4 10; Item paid Welsh Dicke for making one acre of hay in *Rolsten* [Rolleston] meadow oo o3 o4; Item paid Coop for the like oo o3 o4; paid Elias Richards for beating of one acre of beat in park oo 13 o4

Sum is o2 18 o6

### Saturday the 10th of July 1647

Item paid the workmen wages by bill £oo 11s o5d; Item paid the market bill oo 18 o6; Item paid William Ramson upon a bill for ropes & scythes &c o2 o1 o6; Item paid for one bushel of oats oo o4 o4; Item paid for making of 8 acres of hay in *Rolston* meadow at 3s 4d o1 o6 o8; Item paid Joseph Holland for making of one acre of hay in *Roston* meadow oo o3 o4; Item paid Giles Adams for making of one acre of hay in Bridge meadow oo o3 o4; Item paid for curing the pied mare of the farcin to a man of Barnstaple oo o3 oo

Sum is o5 12 o1   [page total] 8 10 7

### [p. 28]   Saturday the 17th of July 1647

paid the workmen wages by bill oo 10 o2; paid the market bill o1 o1 oo; paid Lawrence Berry upon bill oo o5 oo; paid for letters per post oo o1 oo; paid for making of two acres of hay in Bridge Meadow and one in *Roston* oo 10 oo; paid Joseph Holland for making of two acres of hay in Bridge Meadow oo o7 oo; paid for 2 lbs of fine sugar oo o4 oo; paid for garden weeders one month oo o4 oo

Sum is o3 o2 o2

### Saturday the 24th of July 1647

paid the workmen wages by bill oo 10 10; paid the market bill o1 14 o2; paid the poor oo o5 o6; paid for 3 bushels of rye oo 18 oo; paid for eggs oo o1 oo; paid for one bushel of oats oo 4 oo

Sum is o3 13 o6

### Saturday the last of July 1647

paid the workmen wages upon b[ill] oo 16 o8; paid the market bill o1 11 o2; paid the smith upon two bills o1 13 oo; paid the poor oo o5 o6; paid Will: Geare in part of his wages o1 oo oo

Sum total o5 o6 o4   [page total] £12 2s 1d

**[p. 29]   Saturday the 6th of August 1647**

Item paid the workmen wages £oo 16s 1od; paid the market bill o1 16 o9; paid the [sic] two bushels of rye oo 12 oo; paid for two bushels of oats oo o8 oo; paid for the poor oo o5 o6; paid to Eliz: Umbles 6 days wages oo o1 o6; paid Doll Cooman 6 days oo o1 o6; paid Avis Starling 6 days oo o1 o6; paid Pauline Meane 4 days oo o1 oo; paid Doll Starling 2 days oo oo o6; paid Thomasin Kneebone 2 days oo oo o6; paid for 2 bushels of rye oo 11 o4

Sum total o4 17 o5

**Saturday the 14th of August 1647**

paid the workmen wages oo 15 oo; paid the market bill o1 13 o5; paid John Williams the plumber in full of one bill 40s and for Christmas quarter 1 13 4   o3 13 o4; paid for 2 bushels of rye oo 11 oo

Sum is o6 12 o9   [page total] 11 1o 2

**[p. 30]   Saturday the 21th of August 1647**

Item paid the workmens wages by bill £oo 15s 4d; paid the market bill o1 19 o9; paid for 6 bushels of rye bought a month before o2 o2 oo; paid for 2 bushels of rye oo 1o oo; paid for 4 boats of sand oo 1o oo; paid for 19 bushels of culm oo 19 oo; paid the poor oo o5 o6

Sum total o7 o1 o7

**Saturday 28 of August 1647**

paid the workmen wages by bill £oo 12s 11d; paid the market bill o1 o3 1o; paid the nurse for one month oo o4 oo; paid the thatcher for four days and half wages oo o2 o3; paid for eggs oo oo o6

Sum is o2 o3 o6

**Saturday 4 7bris [September] 1647**

paid the workmen wages by bill £oo 13s o4d; paid the market bill o1 13 1o; paid for making Randles clothes oo o6 o4; paid the smith upon two bills o1 o1 oo; paid for serges and bunters oo o3 oo; paid for 4 boats of sand oo 1o oo

Sum is o4 o7 o6   [page total] 13 12 7

**[p. 31]   Saturday the 11th of Sept. 1647**

paid the workmens wages by bill £oo 14s o2d; paid the market bill oo 14 o3; paid Richard Rooke for half a year's wages due at our Lady Day last o1 o5 oo; paid for eggs oo o1 oo

Sum total is o2 14 o5

**Saturday 18 of Sept. 1647**

paid the workmen wages by bill £oo 12s o8d; paid the market bill o1 o4 oo; paid for 2 boats of sand oo o5 oo; paid the poor oo o5 o6

Sum is o2 o7 o2

**Saturday the 25th of Sept. 1647**

paid the workmen wages by bill £o1 oos o4d; paid the market bill o1 oo o8; paid for 3 weigh of coal o4 1o oo; paid for two bushels of oats oo o6 o6; paid the nurse for one month oo 14 oo; paid Raph Booth for his journey to London with 4 horses o2 1o oo; paid Mrs Hearle for 20 bushels of oat malt o4 1o oo

Sum is 14 1o o6   [page total] £19 12s 1d

**[p. 32]	Saturday the 2nd of October 1647**
paid the workmens wages by bill £01 01s 00d; paid the market bill
01 02 09; paid Ramson upon a bill 01 00 10; paid for paper 00 00 10; paid
for threshing of 12 bushels of barley at 3d per bushel 00 03 00; paid for
6 bushels of culm 00 06 00; paid John Terry for 200 bushels of lime
06 00 00
Sum is 09 14 05

**Saturday the 9th of October 1647**
paid the workmen wages by bill 01 19 05; paid the market bill 01 07 1;
paid for Dick Willes his suit 01 15 2; paid Charles upon two bill for wages
02 10 00; paid for eggs 00 00 06; paid for threshing 21 bushels of barley
00 05 03; paid Burrowe the ship-carpenter for one week 00 12 00; paid for
him more for 3 days 00 06 00
Sum is 08 15 05   [page total] 18 9 10

**[p. 33]	Saturday the 16th of October 1647**
Item paid the workmen wages by bill £02 03s 04d; Item paid the market
bill 01 13 11; Item paid the ship carpenter for 6 days 00 02 00; Item paid
for one quart of tar 00 00 06; Item paid David Basley for one week
00 09 00; Item paid for eggs 00 00 06; Item paid a boy to attend the
carpenter 00 01 06; Item paid the chimney sweeper 00 02 00
Sum is 04 12 09

**Saturday the 23th of October 1647**
paid the workmen wages by bill 01 17 16; paid the market bill 03 10 10;
paid the hop gatherers by bill 03 17 08; paid for eggs 00 00 06; paid the
ship carpenter for one week 00 10 00; paid David Basly for 5 days wages
00 07 06; paid Eliz: Brothers for one pot of butter cont. 20 lbs at 5d per
pound 00 08 04; paid her more for 54 lbs of cheeses at 2d per pound
00 09 06; paid for threshing of 11 bushels of oats 00 01 05; paid the nurse
for one month 00 04 00; paid for a pair of shoes for Jonathan 00 01 00;
paid Humfry Lake for 200 bushels of lime at £3 per hundred 06 00 00
Sum total is 17 08 03   [page total] £22 1s 1d

**[p. 34]	Saturday the 30th of October 1647**
Item paid the workmens wages by bill £1 7s 4d; Item paid the market bill
1 1 11; Item paid Agnes by bill 0 9 0; Item paid Mrs Baker by bill for
35 yards of packing canvas 1 12 0; Item paid her for twine 0 1 0; Item paid
Baldwyn Steevens upon a bill for charge in fishing nets &c 5 6 6; Item
paid for salt & eggs 0 1 0; Item paid Tho: Sumner for 4 bushels of wheat
bought in 1646 1 18 0; Item paid him more for 16 lbs of tallow at 6½d per
pound 0 8 8; Item paid the smith upon two bills 2 10 10; Item paid
Baldwyn Steevens upon a bill 2 8 9; Item paid the ship carpenter for
4 days wages 0 10 0; Item paid Basley for 5 days 0 7 6; Item allowed of
Mr Isacke in part for Randle's diet 3 13 4; Item paid the servants wages as
by bill 22 10 6; Item disbursed for our journey as by bill 02 14 6
Sum total is 47 00 10

**[p. 35]**
Sum total of my receipts from the audit 1646 until the audit 1647 is
£904 2s 2d

Sum total of my disbursements for the 30th of October 1646 unto the 30th
of October 1647 is in all £891 13s 10d
So rest due from me £12 8s 4d
[signed] Richard Pollard   The book is examined and allowed by me.

## *Expenses, 1649*

### KENT ARCHIVES OFFICE, U269/A525/8

*The book measures 6" by 14" and is headed 'Disbursements and Receipts
p me R:P: from the 19th of April 1649 until the 27th of Octo. 1649'. The
back is noted as 'Receipts 1649 R:P:'. There is also the note that 'The
gold was 11 12 0 of it to Jo: Taylor 0 11 0 the rest changed in to silver
with 12s profit 11 13 0'. The book has some damage by worms and even-
numbered pages 2 to 8, 12 to 24 are blank.*

[p. 1]   Disbursements for the weekly expenses at Tawstock for the Right
Honourable Henry Earl of Bath since the 10th of April 1649 until
27 October 1649.

**Saturday May 5th**
*First* paid the workmen wages by bill with the poor people and Jonathan's
[blank] for one month then due 1 7 10; Item paid the market bill 0 11 3;
Item paid for eggs 0 0 6; Item paid Will: Ramson & two more with him
when they went to Hartland with the young cattle and colts
0 10 [smudged]; Item paid Jonathan's nurse for 1 lb of soap 0 0 4; Item
spent in my journey from London 3 4 1; Item paid for mending a bit 0 1 0
Sum total of this week is 5 15 10

**Saturday May 12th**
*First* paid the workmen wages by bill and Will: Balch for threshing of
6 bushels & a peck of wheat & to the poor 1 12 8; Item paid the market
bill which must serve for near two weeks for beef and other provision as
doth appear 2 5 7; Item paid for eggs 0 0 6; Item paid for mending the key
of the garden door & the lock of a gun 0 2 0; Item paid for threshing of
23 bushels & two pecks of barley at 3d ½ p[er] bushel 0 4 10 ½
Sum total of this week is 4 5 7

**Saturday May 19th**
*First* paid the workmen wages by bill 1 2 10; Item paid the market bill for
several things 0 11 3; Item paid Welch Dick for cutting & binding
800 browse faggots at 8d p[er] 100 0 5 4; Item paid Henry Pickard for
making 1000 faggots at 7d p[er] 1000 0 5 10; Item paid Marchant for two
weeks weeding in the gardens 0 1 0; Item paid Eliza: Humbles for three
days tying hops 0 1 3
Sum total of this week 2 7 6   [page total] 12 8 11 ½

**[p. 3]   Saturday May 25th [sic]**
*First* paid the workmen wages by bill 1 8 5; Item paid the market bill
0 3 6; Item paid the poor people [blank]; Item paid for making 900 faggots
0 5 3; Item paid for two quarts of vinegar 0 0 7; Item paid for two pound

of shot o o 4; Item paid for eggs for two weeks o o 6; Item paid John
Terry in part of his bill for lime ashes for the walks 1 o o
Sum total is 2 18 7

### Saturday June 2nd

Item paid the workmen wages by bill 1 8 4; Item paid the market bill
o 3 4; Item paid for letters p[er] post o 1 o; Item paid the weeders of
wheat by bill o 15 5; Item paid the poor o 5 o; Item paid for eggs o o 6;
Item paid Will: Lee upon his bill for making of faggots & hardwood 1 9 8;
Item paid for the carriage of a black box o 2 o; Item paid for the carriage
of my box from London o 12 o; Item paid for a milking pail o 1 o; Item
paid for vinegar o o 3; Item paid the nurse one month for Jonathan o 6 o;
Item paid the bone-setter for dressing an ox that was lame o 2 o; Item paid
for signing for the sheep o 1 o
Sum total is 5 7 6

### Saturday June 9th

Item paid the workmen wages by bill 1 7 5; Item paid for two joints of
mutton o 2 6; Item paid Will: Balch for making 500 faggots at 7d p[er]
hundred o 3 o; Item paid him more for making 23 seams of hardwood
o 1 10; Item paid him more for 7 bundles of spars and 50 poles o o 10;
Item paid an old woman that weeds the garden for two weeks o 1 o; Item
paid Jo: Marchant for two weeks weeding in the garden o 1 o; Item given
a woman for dressing the sick ox o 2 6; Item paid Agnes for her bill at
*Biddiford* as appears o 6 1; Item paid for eggs o o 6; Item paid Welch Dick
for threshing of 20 bushels of barley at 2d ½ o 4 2; Item paid for a neck of
veal o 1 2
Sum total is 2 12 1   [page total] 10 18 2

### [p. 5]   Saturday June 16th

*First* paid the workmen wages by bill 1 1 6; Item paid for 2 joints of
mutton o 2 o; Item paid for 15 couple of poor Johns o 8 6; Item paid for a
peck of oatmeal o 3 4; Item paid for 4 lbs of soap o 1 2; Item paid for ale
to drench the ox o 1 o; Item paid for threshing of 22 bushels & one peck
of barley o 4 8; Item paid Will: Balch for making 800 faggots & 4 dozen
of hardwood o 8 8; Item paid a woman to weed the garden one week
o o 6; Item paid young Marchant for weeding one week in the garden
o o 6; Item paid the poor people o 5 o
Sum total is 2 16 10

### Saturday June 23th

Item paid the workmens wages by bill o 18 10; Item paid for mutton and
lamb o 3 8; Item paid for a peck of oatmeal o 3 4; Item paid for half a
peck of salt o o 9; Item paid for sugar & other things for Mary Reymor
o 1 o; Item paid to the poor people o 5 o; Item paid for two pounds of
shot o o 4; Item paid for a bill for weeding 2 o o; Item paid for a quarter
of veal o 2 8
Sum total is 3 15 7

### Saturday June 30th

Item paid the workmen wages by bill 1 3 6; Item paid the market bill
o 6 4; Item paid Jonathan's nurse for one month o 6 o; Item paid for

5 bushels of culm 0 5 0; Item paid Mary Rumson and others upon a bill for haymaking 1 2 2; Item paid for ringing Mary Reymor's knell 0 5 0; paid the poor people 0 5 0

Sum total is 3 13 0   [page total] 10 5 5

### [p. 7]   Saturday July 7th

*First* paid the workmen wages by bill 1 12 3; Item paid for beef, mutton & veal 0 5 0; Item paid for a quarter of lamb 0 1 2; Item paid for a peck of oatmeal 0 3 2; Item paid for Callis sand & chalk 0 0 6; Item paid for three boats of sand 0 9 6; Item given Will: Care for one day working in *Rolston* [Rolleston] meadow 0 0 6; Item given Mr Heartes man for the like 0 0 6; Item given John Lymbury for the like 0 0 6; Item given to the poor 0 5 0; Item given to Geo: Pitts for going in the night to fetch my Lord's boat the soldiers carried away 0 0 6; Item paid for 6 pieces of beef 0 7 6; Item paid for 8 bushels of charcoal 0 6 0

Sum total is 3 11 7

### Saturday July 14th

Item paid the workmen wages by bill 1 19 8; Item paid for 6 pieces of beef 0 9 9; Item paid for a quarter of veal & a neck of mutton 0 5 0; Item paid for twine to mend the matting in my Lord's seat in the church 0 0 2; Item given Peter Sumer's man one day mowing 0 0 6; Item paid Joseph Holland for making two acres of hay in *Rolsten* meadow 0 6 8; Item paid for one dozen of creasts 0 1 6; Item paid for 1000 of lath nails 0 1 6; Item paid for a quart of vinegar 0 0 4; Item paid the glasier upon two bills 2 10 0; Item paid John Gribble when he went to Huntspill 0 12 0; Item paid Marchant for two weeks weeding 0 1 0; Item paid 3 boats of gravel for walks 0 9 0; Item paid for two weigh of coal at 32s p[er] weigh 3 4 0; Item paid for half a peck of oatmeal 0 1 9; Item paid for 6 pound of soap 0 2 0; Item paid for starch 0 0 10; Item paid Welch Dicke to go to *Ufculme* with the venison 0 1 4; Item paid the poor 0 5 0

Sum total is 10 2 4   [page total] 13 13 11

### [p. 9]   Saturday the 21th of July 1649

*First* paid the workmen wages by bill 1 3 [smudged]; Item paid the Cater upon bill 2 9 9; Item paid him for 2 scythes and 6 hones 00 8 6; Item paid for 8 pieces of beef 00 16 10; Item paid for a shoulder of veal 00 01 00; Item paid for a shoulder of mutton 00 01 02; Item paid for a key for the gardener 00 00 06; Item paid for 4 pieces of beef 00 09 00; Item given Mrs Pagget's maid 00 01 00; Item paid for a q[uarte]r of veal 00 00 06; Item paid a woman for two weeks help to make clean the rooms 00 02 00; Item paid for eggs 00 00 02; Item paid Will: Meave for 11 days mowing 00 01 10; Item paid Hearder for 8 days 00 01 04; Item paid the poor 00 05 00; Item paid the haymaker's by bill 04 8 8; Item paid for 2 boats of sand 00 06 00

Sum total of this week's expense is 10 19 04

### Saturday the 28th of July 1649

Item paid the workmen by bill 00 14 03; Item paid the Cater upon his bill 01 09 01; Item paid Jonathan's nurse for one month 00 06 00; Item given Capt. Pyne's man 00 02 06; Item paid for bringing a hogshead of wine

from Barnstaple oo o1 o6; Item paid Lee for 18 days keeping and mowing the green oo 15 oo; Item paid Balch for making 600 faggots and 3 dozen and 9 seams of hardwood oo o7 o3; Item paid Peckard for making 150 faggots, 32 seams of hardwood, 21 bundles of spars and 300 poles oo o6 o9; Item paid him for making Mary Reymor's grave oo oo o6; Item paid for four boats of sand oo 12 oo; Item paid for making 6 acres of hay in barton meadow at 2s 6d p[er] acre oo 15 oo; Item paid for making of 7 acres of hay in Stone Close at 2s 6d p[er] oo 15 oo; Item paid the women for 7 days weeding the barley oo o3 oo
Sum total of this week's expense 16 10 4   [page total] 17 7 8

[p. 10 inverted]   ['15 July Received from John Scottt, reeve of the manor of *Tawstocke*, in part of Midd [Midsummer] quarters rent 3 oo oo. 21 July received from my Lady 5 14 oo. Received for one steer's hide oo 17 oo. Received for two sheep skins oo o2 o4. 26 July Rec. from my Lady o2 o5 oo' crossed through]

### [p. 11]   Saturday the 4th of August 1649
Item paid the workmen wages by bill £o1 o7s o1d; Item paid the cater's bill o2 o4 8; Item paid for brooms oo o2 o6; Item paid for a bar sieve oo oo 10; Item paid Mr Hobb's upon his bills more then he received in *Bristoll* oo o8 oo; Item paid Balch for making of 400 of faggots and 4 dozen of hardwood oo o6 o4; Item given a soldier that found the heriot oo o1 o6; Item paid Jo: Grible for 3 weeks oo o6 oo
Sum total of this week's expense is o4 16 11

### Saturday the 11th of August 1649
Item paid the workmen wages by bill o1 10 o5; Item paid the Cater's bill o2 o4 o3; Item paid for small nails oo oo o6; Item paid for 15 bushels of culm oo 15 oo; Item paid the carrier by bill oo 16 oo; Item paid Balch for making 200 faggots and 22 seams of hardwood oo o3 oo; Item paid for making the hay oo o1 o6; Item paid the tinker for mending the kettles and skillets oo o5 oo; Item paid for 400 yards of matting for my Lady's closet oo o5 oo; Item paid for twine to sew it oo o1 oo; Item paid for 600 nails for matting oo o2 oo; Item paid for 7 lbs of raisins *sun* oo o2 11; Item paid for 2 lbs of currants oo o1 o2; Item paid for a basket oo o1 oo; Item paid for two sieves oo oo o6; Item paid Tho: Ambsby for 10 weeks barm to bake oo o2 o6; Item paid him more for 4 weeks barm since my Lord came home oo o2 oo; Item paid him more upon a bill for bunters and serges oo 10 oo; Item paid for 3 boats of sand oo o9 oo
Sum total of this week's expenses o7 12 o9   [page total] 12 9 8

### [p. 13]   Saturday the 18th of August 1649
Item paid the workmen wages by bill o1 16 10; Item paid the Cater upon bill o1 15 o8; Item paid for two new oars for the boat oo o6 oo; Item paid John Parsons for for [sic] rowing my Lord to *Apledore* oo o2 oo; Item paid the three men went with him oo o3 o6; Item paid for 1 boat of sand oo o3 oo; Item Tho: Amsby for his expense at Torr[ington] oo oo o6; Item paid for glue and pilchards oo o1 oo; Item paid William Heard upon a bill oo o1 o6; Item paid the fuller for washing and cleansing the hangings and rugs oo o1 oo; Item paid for a quarter of veal oo o4 oo
Sum total of this week's bill o4 17 oo

**Saturday the 25th of August 1649**
Item paid the workmen wages by bill 01 19 06; Item paid the Cater upon
bill 01 16 03; Item paid for ten bushels of culm 00 10 00; Item given Sir
Ra: Sydenham's man that brought a box of plums 00 01 00; Item paid
Jonathan's nurse for one month 00 06 00; Item paid for making the new
hay 00 02 06; Item paid for cloth to make the footman bands 00 04 00
Sum total of this week's expenses 4 19 03

**Saturday the last of August [sic] 1649**
Item paid the workmen wages by bill 02 00 04; Item paid the Cater upon
bill 02 11 05; Item paid the glasier upon bill 00 16 00; Item paid the
Carrier for a box of flower plants 00 03 9; Item paid for 3 sieves for Agnes
00 01 5; Item paid her for expenses at Torrington 00 00 06; Item [paid]
Peter Hearder for 10 days mowing 00 01 08; Item paid his wife for
10 day's work 00 02 06; Item paid for a roller for the walks 00 18 00; Item
paid for bringing 2 boats of coal 00 06 00; Item [paid] Avis Starling for
10 days wages 00 02 06; Item paid Doll Cooman for 10 days wages
00 02 06; Item paid Mary Rumson for 10 days 00 02 06; Item paid El.
Herwill for 3 days 00 00 09
Sum total 7 18 10   [page total] 17 15 1

**[p. 15]   Saturday 8 Sept 1649**
Item paid the workmen wages by bill 1 17 10; Item paid the Cater upon
bill 00 10 00; Item given Mrs Stitches man for his help in harvest 00 00 06;
Item paid John Chamberlyn upon his bill 00 16 03; Item paid Tho: Berry
for 6 maps 00 03 06; Item paid the gold finders 00 07 00; Item paid for
12 garden pots 00 02 00; Item paid for her expenses and coverage 00 00 06;
Item paid for a new key and mending the lock in the back stair 00 02 00;
Item paid for sending letters p[er] post 00 01 00; Item paid the free mason
for cutting the roller in the green 00 04 00; Item given Mr Fleming's man
that brought two gammons of bacon 00 02 06
Sum total of this week is 4 15 07

**Saturday the 15th of Sept. 1649**
Item paid the workmen wages by bill 01 09 00; Item paid the Cater upon
bill [blank]; Item paid for a new key and mending the lock for the back
stairs in the drawing room below 00 02 00; Item paid Pauline Meave for
12 days wages in harvest at 3d p[er] *day* 00 03 00; Item paid her son for
13 days 00 02 03; Item paid Will: Meave for 10 days mowing in harvest
00 01 08; Item paid John Gribble for 5 weeks wages and then clear
00 10 00; Item paid him more for his expenses in the South Hams
00 01 04; Item paid Agnes for 10 chickens 00 03 04; Item paid upon a bill
for several things at *Barnestaple* fair 50 02 09
Sum total of this week is 52 15 04   [page total] 57 10 11

**[p. 17]   Saturday the 22th of September 1649**
Item paid the workmen wages by bill 01 14 8; Item paid the Cater by bills
[blank]; Item paid for two boats of sand 00 06 00; Item given my Lady for
Mrs Slowley's maid 00 01 00; Item paid May for 6 maps and for tobacco
pipes for my Lord 00 03 06; Item paid Agnes for expenses at Bidd.
00 00 07; Item given my Lord for a poor man 00 01 00; Item paid the

carrier's wife in part for carriage of 3 boxes oo 10 oo; Item paid the hop
gatherers by bill 02 04 02
Sum total of this week's expense is 05 oo 11

### Saturday the 29th of September 1649

Item paid the workmen wages by bill 01 13 01; Item paid the Cater upon
bill 01 19 09; Item paid for a pair of shoes for Kitt oo 03 oo
Sum total of this week is 03 15 10

### Saturday the 6th of October 1649

Item paid the workmen wages by bill 01 13 04; Item paid the Cater upon
bill 02 18 08; Item paid the glasier upon bill 01 08 08; bought last year.
Item paid for wine cask cont. two tons & half at 13s p[er] tons 01 12 06;
Item paid for 7 bushels of salt at 4s 8d the bushel 01 13 06; Item paid
Mrs Baker for fruit and spices by bill oo 16 06; Item spent in my journey
into the South Hams by bill 01 01 09
Sum total of this week is 11 04 03   [page total] 20 1 o

### [p. 19]   Saturday the 13th of October 1649

*First* the workmen wages by bill 01 15 07; Item paid the Cater by bill
02 08 11; Item paid Annis for her expenses at Tor oo oo 06; Item paid
Joan the garden weeder for two weeks oo 02 oo; Item paid Harry Peckard
for spading 4 acres of beat at 1s 8d p[er] acre oo 06 08; Item paid the men
that cut the trenches in the marsh 19 days oo 19 oo; Item paid Jo: Hobbs
by his bill 02 12 oo; Item paid Charles for Mary Raymor's coffin oo 05 6;
Item paid the painter at several times 02 05 [damaged by worms]
Sum total of this week's expenses is 10 15 02

### Saturday the 20th of October 1649

Item paid the workmen wages by bill 01 14 04; Item paid the Cater upon
bill 03 01 01; Item paid Morcombe for one year and half for keeping the
clocks due at Michas. last and then clear oo 12 oo; Item paid him more for
a bell for the parlour clock oo 07 oo; Item paid him more for brass for the
Eagles Jesse oo oo 06; Item paid Mr William Fane by command 05 oo oo;
Item spent in my journey to the South Hams the second time oo 10 oo;
Item paid for two hats one for the footman and the other for Watt
oo 10 oo; Item paid for a padlock for the bin in the stable oo oo 10; Item
paid for a pair of shoes for the footman oo 04 oo; Item paid for 21 days
work in the cutting the dike in the marsh 01 01 oo; Item paid my Lady in
part of the £37 10s received in the South Hams of Mr Hyne 20 oo oo; Item
paid Jonathan's nurse for two months and then clear oo 12 oo; Item paid
my Lady in gold from Barnstaple 25 oo oo
Sum total of this week's expense is 58 12 9   [page total] 69 7 11

### [p. 21]   Saturday the 27th of October 1649

Item paid the workmen wages by bill 02 oo 02; Item paid the Cater's bill
02 08 06; Item paid Rich: Britton upon bill 08 oo oo; Item paid John
Gribble for 6 weeks wages wanting four days oo 11 08; Item paid the
locksmith upon his bill 01 10 oo; Item paid Annis for her expenses at
*Biddeford* and for earthen pots oo 03 10; Item paid Lawrence Chamberlyn
upon his bill for wages oo 18 oo; Item paid for leather and thongs and
naples for young Croyde's shoes oo 01 oo; Item paid Simon Tolsell and his
fellows for 30 days work about the way in the park at 10d p[er] *day*

01 05 00; Item paid Wilmot for so much given Mr Wood for Doctor's maid 00 02 00; Item paid Rich: Maye upon bill 00 08 06

Sum total of this week's expense 17 08 08

Sum total of the disbursements in this book as by the particulars will appear is £259 09s 04d

Sum total of my receipts as by this book will appear is £268 10s 11d

So remains due from me to be accounted for £9 1s 7d

[signed] Richard Pollard

*Last of* October 1649

These general accounts of receipts and disbursements were examined and are thereupon allowed by me.

**[p. 28 The last three pages are reversed]**

Receipts since the 10th of April 1649 until [blank]

By me Rich: Pollard

Received of Mr Lynn for my journey £3 10s 06d

Received of William Coop for half a year's rent due at our Lady Day for Coop's Close 2 16 8

6 May Rec. of Mr Wyott for my Lord's use 1 0 0

Received of Mr Wyott for my Lord's use 00 10 00

16 May Rec. of Mr Wyott for my Lord's use 5 00 00

Rec. for 14 pair of pigeons 00 4 8

Recd of the saddle-tree maker for timber 01 04 00

Recd of the reeve in part of our Lady quarter 04 00 00

Rec. for 10 pair of pigeons 00 3 00

2 *June* Rec. of Mr Wyott for my Lord's use 5 00 00

Received for one steers hide 00 17 00

Recd for a calf 00 16 00

Recd for five fat lambs [at] 7s a piece 01 15 00

Recd for one oxe hide that died 00 18 00

22 *June* Rec. of Mr Wyott for my Lord's use 05 00 00

Recd for 2 couple of rabbits 00 2 00

Recd of Barnes part of £7 10s due for rinds sold by Mr Weekes 02 00 00

Recd for a calf 00 13 4

3 *July* Rec. of Mr Wyott for my Lord's use 02 00 00

Rec. of Johan Ellis for a tree 01 00 00

4 July Rec. of Mr Wyatt to buy coal 05 00 00

Recd for 3 nails sold Mr Welsh 00 01 6

Rec. for 4 peals sold 00 02 06

Recd for 3 peals 00 01 04

8 July Recd of John Scott reeve of Tawstock in part of midsummer quarter's rent 3 00 00 [total] 46 15 0

**[p. 26]**

15 July 1649 Received of John Scott reeve of *Tawstocke* in part of Midd. [Midsummer] quarter's rent 03 00 00

20 July Recd from my Lady 02 15 00

Rec. for one steer's hide 00 17 00

Rec. for 2 sheep skins 00 02 04

Recd from my Lady 05 14 00
29 July Recd of John Scott reeve of *Tawstocke* in part of midd. quarter's rent 14 00 00
Rec. for a heifer's hide 00 12 00
Recd for two sheep skins 00 02 04
3 August Rec. for 3 sheep skins 00 03 06
8 August Rec. of Nico: Prust in part of Midd. quarter rent of Hartland 10 00 00
Rec. for one heifer's hide 00 09 00
10 August Rec. for 3 sheeps skins 00 03 06
17 August Rec. for one hide 00 13 00
Rec. for two skins 00 02 00
24 Aug. Recd for one hide 00 16 00
Recd for 4 skins 00 04 06
25 Aug. Rec. of Agnes for one seam of apples 00 07 10
Rec. for 4 skins 00 04 06
31 Aug. Rec. of John Barnes in part for rinds 02 00 00
1 Sept. Rec. of Agnes for one seam of apples 00 05 6
4 Sept. Rec. of Agnes for one seam of apples 00 05 03
Recd of the gardener for carrots 00 05 11
8 Sept. Rec. of Mr Wyott for my Lord's use 08 00 00
Rec. from my Lady to pay for corn and other things 20 00 00
11 Sept. Rec. for one seam of apples 00 05 03
Recd for pears 00 01 08
13 Sept. Rec. of the gardener for carrots 0 05 00
Recd of my Lady for the carpet 25 00 00
16 Sept. Recd of Mr Wyott for my Lord's use 5 00 00
18 Sept. Recd of Agnes for apples sold at *Biddeford* 00 04 06
19 7ber Rec. of Mr Wyott for my Lord's use 01 00 00
3 October Rec. of Mr Tho: Hyne for my Lord's use 7 10 00
6 8ber [October] Rec. of Annis for one seam of apples 00 04 09
6 8ber Rec. of one steers hide 00 14 00
Rec. for 4 sheep skins 00 05 00
12 8ber Rec. for one hide 00 15 0
Rec. for 3 sheep skins 00 04 06   [total] 14 3 10

[p. 25]
19 8ber [October] Rec. for one cow hide 00 14 0
Rec. for 4 sheep skins 00 06 0
23 8ber Rec. for one seam of apples 00 06 01
26 8ber Rec. for one steer's hide 00 16 00
Rec. for 6 skins 00 10 00
['Recd of Mrs Baker of Barnstaple by bill of exchange from …' crossed through]
Rec. of Robt Thoring in full of his fine 20 00 00
Rec. of Emmanuel Lange of *Coombyntinhead* [Combeinteignhead] in full of his fine 26 00 00
Rec. of John Hanaford of *Exon* which he had from Mr Hyne 31 00 00
[total] 79 12 11

Sum total of my receipts £268 10s 11d   [signed] Richard Pollard

# Expenses, *1650–1651* and Receipts *1650–1651*

## KENT ARCHIVES OFFICE, U269/A525/9

*The book measures 7" by 12". There is no cover. Even-numbered pages 6
to 60 and 2, 61, 63, 65, 69, 71, 73 and 75 are blank.*

**[p. 1]   Saturday 2 November 1650**
Item paid my Lady of the debit money which Mr Cobb received at Audit
1650 £100 00s 00d; Item paid Mrs Downe by Mr Lovett 100 00 00; Item
paid the workmen wages by bill 002 05 08; Item paid the Cater by bill
002 13 11; Item paid Rich Britton for 17 pigs at 6s 005 02 0; Item paid for
four new hogsheads 001 04 00; Item paid for two wine pipes for cider
000 17 00; Item paid for Thurstin for his wages and other things by bill
010 17 10; Item paid Mrs Downe for a boar 001 06 08; Item paid upon a
bill for thread and nets and other things for the fishing 001 00 09; Item
paid for my expenses on Monday last when I went to speak with the
Commissioners at Torrington concerning the light horses 000 02 06; Item
paid for 4 swords and 3 belts 001 10 00; Item paid for a carbine 000 10 00;
Item paid for making clean 2 p[air] of pistols 000 02 06; Item paid for a
spanner for the pistols 000 00 06; Item for expenses at Barnstaple
000 01 00; Item paid the four riders 000 12 00; Item paid for standing of
our horses 000 00 09; Item paid for my expenses at Torrington 000 02 06;
Item paid the two boys that went with the horses 00 00 06; Item given the
musicians 00 04 00; Item paid Mr Britton in part of his bill 011 00 00;
Item paid the smith upon bill 003 09 0[obscured by ink]; Item paid the
plumber in full by bill 03 10 00
Sum total of this week's expense is 246 15s 07d

**[p. 3]   Saturday the 9th of November 1650**
Item paid the workmen wages by bill 01 08 09; Item paid the Cater by bill
00 15 09; Item paid for brooms 00 05 00; Item paid for a pair of wool
cards and spills 00 02 00; Item paid the Apothecary upon bill 04 12 00;
Item paid for [?]honey for my Lady 00 06 00; Item paid the sadler by bill
03 03 02; Item paid for 3 quarters washing the kitchen boy 00 09 00; Item
paid for rates for Heale's tenement 00 08 05; Item paid for 5 quarts of
tent. for com[union] 00 10 00; Item paid for two bed mats 00 02 00
Sum total of this week is 12 02 01

**Saturday 16 November 1650**
Item paid the workmen wages by bill 01 15 05; Item paid the Cater by bill
01 09 10; Item paid Mr Morkham for half a year's fee for keeping the
clock 00 04 00; Item spent at *Biddeford* 00 01 06; Item paid
Mr Coplestone for 20 sheep 10 10 00; Item paid Dorothy for two hogs
01 04 00; Item paid Balch for 1 bushel of wheat 00 10 06; Item paid Rich:
Hambling for one bushel of wheat 00 11 00; Item paid for excise for a butt
of sack 02 10 00; Item given a woman that brought a letter from
Mr Dennis 00 00 06; Item paid Thomas Penrose for his expenses at
*Biddeford* 00 01 00; Item paid the nurse for 1 month for the two boys and
for schooling 00 12 08
Sum total is 19 10 05   19 10 05   [page total] 31 12 6

**[p. 4]**
The nineteenth day of November 1650 was a butt of sack laid into the cellar, bought of Mr Dennys of *Biddeford* and cost £21 10s.

**[p. 5]  Saturday the 22th [sic] of November 1650**
Item paid the workmen wages by bill 02 06 5; Item paid the Cater by bill 02 10 4; Item paid for 3 bearing sieves 00 02 00; Item given Mrs Skitche's maid 00 01 00; Item paid Mrs Baker upon her bill and then clear of all demands 32 05 00; Item paid for bringing a butt of sack from *Biddeford* 00 06 06; Item paid for mending shoes by bill 00 04 00; Item paid Eliz: Searle for Ann Mullins 00 02 00; Item paid Maye for 2 bottles of vinegar 00 01 00; Item paid Joseph Ley for a bushel of peas bought before harvest 00 10 00; Item paid Mrs Nash for butter and cheese by bill 02 02 00

Sum total is 40 10 03

**Saturday 30 November 1650**
Item paid the workmen wages by bill 02 03 04; Item paid the Cater by bill 02 03 06; Item paid Romson in part of a bill for bullocks bought at Hartland 30 00 00; Item paid the five troopers that rode my Lord's horses two days at 2s per *day* 01 00 00; Item paid for two pair of holsters 00 12 00; Item paid for one pound of powder 00 01 06; Item paid Will Lee by bill 00 11 09; Item paid John Gribble for 8 weeks 00 16 00; Item paid two troops on Saturday 00 04 00; Item paid John Hobbs for bringing goods from *Bristoll* 00 02 06; Item paid the glasier upon his bill 01 14 00 [total] 39 08 07  [page total] £79 18s 10d

**[p. 7]  Saturday 6th December 1650**
Item paid the workmen wages by bill £01 08s 06d; Item paid the Cater by bill 01 15 08; Item paid John Hobbs for Mr Deane of *Bristoll* as by his acquittance 05 05 00; Item paid the feather driver for 4 days 00 03 04; Item paid for threshing of 5 bushels of wheat at 10d p[er] bushel 00 04 02; Item paid for threshing of 16 bushels of oats 00 04 00; Item paid Tho: Steevens for one day 00 00 10; Item paid for 4 lbs of butter 00 01 08; Item paid Peter Terry by bill 00 06 09; Item paid for standing my horse 00 00 06; Item paid Peter Summer in part of £22 due to him for 32 fat sheep 10 00 00

Sum total 19 10 05

**Saturday 14 December 1650**
Item paid the workmen wages by bill 01 12 08; Item paid the Cater by bill 04 12 00; Item paid the six troop[er]s for one week pay at 2s per *day* 04 04 00; Item paid the nurse for one month and for schooling 00 12 08; Item paid for 11 oranges 00 00 09; Item paid for caraway seed 00 00 09; Item paid for six pullets 00 04 00; Item paid for standing of my horse and shoeing 00 00 08; Item paid for brooms 00 01 00

Sum *total* 11 08 06   [page total] £30 18s 11d

**[p. 9]  Saturday 21th of December 1650**
Item paid the workmen wages by bill £02 00s 09d; paid the Cater's bill 01 06 11; paid Mr Wyatt as by a bill of the particulars 06 18 11; paid Will Lee for making six dozen of hardwood and 200 faggots 00 07 08; paid for 40 bushels of lime ashes 00 06 08; paid the lath maker for making 16000 of lath at 20[d] per 1000 01 02 06; paid for my dinner and horsemeat at

North Tawton and given at Nympton oo o5 o6; paid for a pint of sack
oo oo o6; paid Roger Wilkey and his man for 18 days sawing timber in the
park o1 o3 o9; Item spent at Barnstaple oo o1 o6; paid for a peck of peas
oo o2 o2; paid the 6 troopers for one day oo 12 oo; paid Ammis for seaves
oo oo o8; paid her expenses at *Biddeford* oo oo o5; paid for threshing of
10 bushels ½ of wheat oo o8 o9; paid for threshing 18 bushels of barley
oo o4 o6; paid for threshing 8 bushels of oats o1 oo o5; paid for two day's
wages for getting in the mow oo o1 o8
Sum total £16 o6s o6d

**[p. 11]   Saturday 28 December 1650**
Item paid the workmens wages by bill £oo 18s o2d; paid the Cater upon
his bill o2 18 o2; paid my Lady of Diggorie's money which was part of his
fine o5 oo oo; paid Rich Hearding for 6 week's pay for Heale's tenement
oo o3 oo; paid for a certificate oo o1 o6; paid Mr Cobb for sending letters
p[er] post oo o2 oo; Item given Mr Northcott's servant oo o1 o6; paid the
fuller for dressing cloth oo o8 oo; paid Jane Gloyne the carrier in full
o3 15 oo; given a boy that brought two capons oo o1 oo; paid Larimer for
100 of reed oo 16 oo; spent at Barnstaple oo o1 oo; Item paid the smith
upon bill o3 11 oo; paid for butter oo o1 o8; paid for a bed mat oo o1 o4
Sum total 17 19 4

**Saturday 4 Jan. 1650**
Item paid the workmen wages by bill o1 o1 o6; paid the Cater upon his
bill o5 14 o8; paid John Bragg in part for cattle and sheep 16 oo oo; paid
Mr Cobb for my Lady oo 10 oo; paid for mending a gimme[?r] oo o1 oo;
paid for two powder horns and mending the fowler's gun oo o2 6; paid
John Wood for 15 bushels of salt o3 oo oo; paid for cleaving six dozen of
hardwood oo o6 oo
Sum total 26 15 o8   [page total] £44 15s ood

**[p. 13]   Saturday 11 January 1650**
Item paid the workmen wages by bill o1 o9 o2; Item paid the Cater upon
his bill o1 10 o8; paid for deal boards oo o5 oo; paid for 4 lbs of shot
oo o1 oo; paid Mr Cobb for my Lady o8 oo oo; paid for 2 lbs of powder
oo o3 o4; paid for sending letters per post oo o1 oo; paid Simon Connell
for his pains oo o6 oo; paid George for maps oo o2 o6; paid Eliz: Searle
upon her bill oo o7 o8; paid the nurse for one month oo 12 o8; paid for
threshing of 8 bushels of wheat oo o6 o8; paid for threshing 8 bushels of
barley oo o2 oo; paid for threshing of 54 bushels of oats oo 13 o6; paid for
3 days wages for getting in the mowe at parsonage oo o2 o6
Sum total 20 o3 o4

**[p. 15]   Saturday 18 January 1650**
Item paid the workmen wages by bill £o2 o1s ood; paid the Cater upon his
bill o8 oo o1; paid Rich: Hambling for 3 bushels of wheat o1 13 oo; paid
for 4 quarts of sampire oo o2 o8; paid for 4 ounces of turnsole oo o2 oo;
paid for two brass sconces oo o9 oo; paid for a grater for the cook
oo o1 o8; paid for 3 bed-mats oo o4 oo; paid for a butt of *Malligoe* sack
19 oo oo; paid for putting of it in the boat oo o2 oo; paid for expenses at
*Biddeford* oo o1 oo; paid Mr Deane of *Bristoll* by bill o2 o6 oo; paid

Mr Vaughon of *Bristoll* 02 11 3; paid John Hobbs by bill for soap &c
01 17 00; paid for a jar of olives 00 01 04; paid Roger Wilby and his man
for 2 weeks 01 10 00
Sum total of this week's expense is 40 03 00

[p. 17]   **Saturday 25 Jann. 1650**
Item paid the workmen wages by bill £01 16s 05d; Item paid the Cater's
bill 08 04 08; Item given a boy that brought sprats 00 00 06; Item paid
Mr Skitch upon bill 01 16 06; Item paid her upon another bill 01 02 00;
Item paid for brooms 00 03 00; Item lent to Tooker the carrier 01 10 00;
Item paid for threshing of 28 bushels of wheat 01 03 09; Item paid for
threshing 11 bushels of oats 00 02 09; Item for threshing of 13 bushels of
barley ½ 00 03 04; Item paid for weaving 18 ['bushels' crossed through]
yards of cloth 00 06 00; Item paid Peter Simmner in full for 32 fat wethers
12 00 00; Item paid him more for hay bought by bill 03 00 00; Item paid
the servants wages due at the last audit as by a bill of particulars 46 13 04;
Item paid for making 60 faggots, 12 bundles of spars and six seams of
hardwood 00 06 06
Sum total of this week's expense is 78 15 07

[p. 19]   **Saturday *first* February 1650**
Item paid the workmen wages by bill £01 13s 00d; Item paid the Cater
upon his bill 05 10 07; Item paid for arrears of the rates in Tawstock
03 06 06; Item paid John Bragg of Hartland in part of his bill for sheep
and bullocks 20 00 00; Item paid for brooms 00 01 06; Item paid Robert
Coop for making 700 faggots, 12 bundles of spars, 1 dozen of poles and
3 seams of hardwood 00 07 10; Item paid for six yards of cloth for the
boys 01 00 00; Item paid for Mr Fane by command 02 00 00; Item paid
Thurstyn by bill 01 17 06; Item paid Roger Wilkey and his man for ten
days and half wages 01 06 03; Item paid Will Lee by bill 00 09 10; Item
paid Richard May by bill 00 03 00; Item paid John Gribble for 4 weeks
00 08 00; Item paid for 4 quarts of tent for the communion 00 08 00
Sum total of this week's expense is £38 12s 1d

[p. 21]   **Saturday 8 February 1650**
Item paid the workmen wages by bill £02 04s 09d; Item paid the Cater
upon his bill 05 04 01; Item paid for four bed mats 00 06 08; Item paid for
culm 00 01 06; Item paid the sadler by bill 02 02 00; Item paid Thomas
Ley for hay bought by bill 05 00 00; Item paid Simon Collins for his help
00 05 00; Item paid for a cream strainer 00 00 08; Item paid the poor by
command 00 10 00; Item paid the nurse for one month 00 12 08; Item paid
for making 600 faggots, 150 poles, 9 bundles of spars, 1 dozen of
hardwood 00 07 06; Item paid Welsh Dick for 600 faggots, 1 dozen of
hardwood and half, 7 bundles of spars and one hundred poles 00 08 07;
Item paid for threshing 15 bushels & half of wheat at 10d per bushel
00 12 11; Item for threshing of 68 bushels of oats 00 17 00
Sum total of this week's expense is 18 13 04

[p. 23]   **Saturday 15 February 1650**
Item paid the workmen wages by bill £02 12s 8d; Item paid the Cater
upon his bill 09 10 07; Item paid Huxtable the smith upon 3 bills 10 03 00;
Item paid for mending two bits 00 03 04; Item paid for eight gallons of oil

02 00 00; Item spent at Bideford 00 04 00; Item paid for bringing home a
butt of sack from *Biddeford* by water 00 05 00; Item paid Roger Wilkey
for two weeks wages 01 10 00; Item paid Robert Coop for making
500 faggots, one dozen of hardwood, 200 poles, 6 bundles of spars and
100 binders 00 06 02
Sum total of this week's expense is 26 14 09

**Saturday 22 February 1650**
Item paid the workmen wages by bill 02 02 11; Item paid the Cater upon
his bill 05 04 02; Item paid the six troopers for two weeks pay 08 08 00;
Item paid for a sword and belt 00 08 06; Item paid for a bushel of peas
00 08 00; Item paid the smith for work done at the hutch 00 18 11; Item
paid the carrier by bill 01 08 00; Item paid Dick Lake for 200 2 quarts of
sugar 10 00 00; Item paid the cobbler upon bill 00 09 00; Item paid Welsh
Dick for making 500 faggots, 100 poles, 8 seams of hardwood, 100 binders
and 6 bundles of spars 00 05 02; Item paid Robert Coop for making
400 faggots, 15 seams of hardwood, 100 poles, 100 binders and 6 bundles
of spars 00 04 08; Item paid the threshers for 11 bushels 3 pecks of wheat
and 28 bushels of oats 00 17 04; Item paid David Hill for 3 weeks pay
01 14 6
Sum total of this week's expense is 32 09 02   [page total] 59 3 11

**[p. 25]   Saturday *first* March 1650**
Item paid the workmen wages by bill £02 05s 08d; Item paid the Cater by
bill 04 04 02; Item paid Coop for making 400 faggots, 1 dozen of
hardwood, 100 poles, 50 binders and 6 bundles of spars 00 04 06; Item
paid Welsh Dick for making 500 faggots, 6 seams of wood, 6 bundles of
spars, 100 poles and 50 binders 00 04 08; Item paid the threshers for
71 bushels of oats 00 17 09; Item paid them more for 25 bushels of barley
00 06 03; Item paid Will Richards for 10 days wages 00 08 04; Item paid
him more for 10 dozen of hardwood 00 10 00; Item paid Peter Summner
for one month rates 03 11 04; Item paid for fowl 00 02 06; Item paid for a
hook for the gardener 00 01 06
Sum total is 12 16 08

**Saturday 8 *March* 1650**
Item paid the workmen wages by bill 01 17 00; Item paid the Cater upon
his bill 05 05 09; one week due from the Lieutenant. Item paid the
constables of Tawstock for two weeks pay for six troop[ers] 08 12 06;
Item paid for poor Johns 00 08 00; Item paid Ames for cloam and
expenses 00 02 00; Item paid Mrs Baker upon her bill and then clear of all
accounts 11 13 02; Item paid for mending my Lady's bit 00 02 06; Item
paid for sawing timber 01 00 00; Item paid the nurse for the two boys one
month 00 12 08; Item paid Welsh Dick for making wood 00 04 02; Item
paid Robert Coop for making wood 00 04 08
Sum total of this week is 30 02 05   [page total] £42 19s 1d

**[p. 27]   Saturday 15 *March* 1650**
Item paid the workmen wages by bill £01 19s 03d; Item paid the Cater
upon his bill 05 09 08; Item paid for 10 bushels of charcoal 00 07 06; Item
paid the chimney sweep 00 01 06; Item paid the fuller by bill 00 07 00;
Item paid for 400 of Appledore oysters 00 05 00; Item paid for a butt of

sack to Mr George Shurt of *Biddeford* in part 20 00 00; Item paid Ric: Lake in part for sugar 05 00 00; Item paid Jo: Kimpthorne for 10 sheep 04 06 08; Item paid Ann Tolsell for half year's wages 01 00 00; Item paid for 18 bushels of charcoal 00 13 06; Item paid John Hobby for bringing things from *Bristoll* and for two chamber pots 00 04 04; Item paid Robert Coop for making wood 00 03 09; Item paid Welsh Dick for making wood 00 05 03; Item paid for pap[er] 00 01 00; Item paid for sack bought at Barnstaple 00 16 10

Sum total of this week's expense is 41 01 03

### [p. 29]   Saturday 22 *March* 1650

Item paid the workmen wages by bill £02 08s 04d; Item paid the Cater upon bill 04 00 00; Item paid the locksmith upon his bill 00 18 00; Item paid Thurstyn upon his bill for his wages and other things 06 19 00; Item paid John Williams upon bill 04 03 00; Item paid John Austyn for a cow & calf 06 00 00; Item paid for cheesecloth for the dairy maid 00 02 00; Item paid the sawyers for sawing timber 01 00 00; Item paid the threshers for threshing of 9 bushels 1 peck of wheat 00 07 08 ½; Item paid for threshing of 65 bushels of barley 00 16 04 ½; Item paid for 94 bushels of oats 01 02 06; Item paid paid [sic] Welsh Dick for making 400 faggots, 6 bundles of spars, 100 binders, 6 seams of hardwood & 50 poles 00 03 10; Item paid Robert Coop for making 350 faggots, 6 bundles of spars, 8 seams of hardwood, 50 poles and 100 binders 00 04 00

Sum total of this week's bill is 28 04 09

The 26th of March 1651
Received then of my honourable Lady in full of all my accounts for what I have disbursed more than received as by this book doth appear the sum of £32 00s 10d   [signed] Richard Pollard

### [p. 31]   Saturday 29th of March 1651

Item paid the workmen wages by bill £03 02s 05d; Item paid the Cater upon his bill 07 13 02; Item paid the dairy maid for things bought 00 02 09; Item paid the carrier upon bill 02 02 00; Item paid for one weigh of coal and bringing it home 02 10 06; Item for fishing nets 00 19 00; Item paid for poor John by bill 00 09 07; Item paid Peter Sammely for one month rates 03 11 04; Item paid Rich Lake for a cow and calf 05 05 04; Item paid the gunsmith upon bill 00 10 00; Item paid for weaving 19 yards of cloth 00 08 00; Item given the post man by command 00 01 00; Item paid Jo: Gribble when he went with Mr Fane 00 01 00; Item paid Richard Rooke when he went to *Exon* 00 01 00; Item paid for sawing 2528 foot of board at 2s 2d per hundred 01 07 06; Item paid for threshing 5 bushels of wheat 00 04 02; Item paid Holland and his son for 1 day 00 01 08; Item paid for six seams of stones for the garden gutter 00 06 00; Item paid for five turkeys 00 08 00

Sum total of this week's expense 29 04 05

### Saturday 5 April 1651

Item paid the workmen wages by bill 01 10 08; Item paid the Cater upon bill 02 17 01; Item paid Mr Downe as by her acquittance 20 00 00; Item paid to the poor of Torrington per command 02 10 00; Item paid the nurse for one month 00 12 08; Item paid for culm 00 09 00; Item paid for

12 chickens oo o4 oo; Item paid Mr Forard by bill oo o8 oo; Item paid
Robert Coop for making eight hundred faggots, 400 poles & 2 dozen of
hard wood, 100 binders & six bundles of spars oo o9 o6; Item paid Welsh
Dicke for making 300 faggots, 8 seams of wood, 6 bundles of spars &
1000 poles oo o4 oo; Item paid the bean-setters two days oo o1 o4; Item
paid for powder oo oo 10
Sum *total* of this week is 29 o7 o1    [page total] £58 11s 6d

## [p. 33]   Saturday the 12th April 1651

Item paid the workmen wages by bill £o3 o8s o5d; Item paid the Cater
upon bill o7 o7 o5; Item paid for cloam at Budds oo o5 oo; Item paid for
bringing wine from *Bristoll* oo o3 oo; Item paid Mr Shile for 3 barrels of
herring o3 15 oo; Item paid the sawyers for ten days apiece o1 o5 oo; Item
paid for making two mats for beds oo o1 o6; Item paid for making three
hundred faggots & six seams of hard wood & six bundles of spars
oo o3 oo; Item paid for threshing of 18 bushels & 3 pecks of wheat
oo 15 o6; Item paid for threshing of 62 bushels of oats oo 15 o6; Item paid
the gold finders for cleaning the maids house oo o7 o6; Item paid for ten
chickens oo o3 oo
Sum total of this week is 18 o9 10

## Saturday the 19th of April 1651

Item paid the workmen wages by bill o3 18 oo; Item paid the Cater upon
his bill o5 10 oo; Item given Mr Chichester's servant oo o1 oo; Item given
Mr Norcott's servant oo o2 oo; Item paid Richard Rooke when he went to
*Baunton* oo o5 oo; Item paid for two pounds of shot oo oo o6; Item paid
for brooms oo o5 oo
Sum total of this week is 10 o1 o6

## Saturday the 27th of April 1651

Item paid the workmen wages o3 17 o5; Item paid the Cater upon his bill
o5 o5 [smudged]; Item paid the carrier by bill & then clear
o[smudged]5 oo; Item paid Richard Britton for ten sheep o5 10 oo; Item
paid the thresher 6 bushels & two pecks of wheat oo o5 o5; Item paid
them more for 26 bushels of oats oo o6 o6; Item paid Peter Sumner for
one months pay o3 11 o4; Item paid Mr Nicholls of Torrington for
5 yards of gold & silver lace oo o7 o6; Item spent at Torrington oo o2 oo;
Item paid for five bushels of lime at Taunton oo o3 o4
Sum *total* 21 13 10    [page total] 50 5 2

## [p. 35]   Saturday the 3 of May 1650

Item paid the workmen wages upon bill £o3 o9s ood; Item paid the Cater
upon bill o4 o6 o9; Item paid for my dinner & other expenses at *Torington*
two several days upon my Lord's occasions oo o7 oo; Item paid for a boat
of gravel for walks oo o5 oo; Item ['paid for' crossed through] spent at
[blank] on Friday last oo o1 oo; Item paid the nurse for one month
oo o1 oo; Item paid for making clean the meadows oo 12 o8; Item paid for
Sedge for to stuff the pack saddles oo o2 o6; Item paid for five weeks
lodging at Mill Lees for the two dikers o o1 oo; Item paid for watering pot
oo o2 o6; Item given Mr Norcott's servant oo o4 o6
Sum *total* o9 12 11

**Saturday 10th of May 1651**

Item paid the workmen's wages by bill 02 18 02; Item paid the Cater upon bill 05 07 08; Item paid Mr Squire in part of £27 12s for six steers 20 00 00; Item paid Mr Shurt of *Biddeford* in full for a butt of sack 06 00 00; Item paid Mr Tooker for excise as by his receipt 04 00 00; Item paid for two ['way' crossed through] weigh and an half of coal 06 00 00; Item paid Avis Starling & Silly Balsh for thirteen days clodding barley 00 05 06; Item paid Jo: Grible for ten weeks wages 01 00 00; Item paid the furs[e] cutters for cutting & binding 6000 *fur* [fir] faggots 01 15 02; Item paid Edw: Bainton for going to *Baunton* 00 02 00; Item paid for four milking pails 00 05 04; Item paid for 63 bushels of lime ashes 00 18 00; Item paid Will Booth for so much disbursed 00 03 00; Item paid for weaving of 18 yards of cloth 00 07 08; Item paid Richard Lake in full for one chest of sugar 02 13 04;

Sum *total* 51 15 10   [page total] 61 8 9

**[p. 37]   Saturday the 17th of May 1651**

Item paid the workmen wages by bill £05 05s 07d; Item paid the Cater upon bill 05 13 10; Item paid the saddler upon his bill 02 03 06; Item paid Mr Britten in part for 14 bushels of choice barley for seed 02 10 00; Item paid upon two bills for clodding barley 01 07 00; Item paid for thread & sugar candy 00 03 10; Item given the stone drawers 00 00 06; Item given my Lady for the mason 00 00 06; Item given the trooper to drink 00 05 00; Item lent to Tooker the carrier by my Lady's command 01 00 00; Item paid Mr Forard for so much disbursed 00 10 00; Item paid John Hobbs as by his bill 01 14 06

Sum *total* 20 13 09

**Saturday the 24th of May 1651**

Item paid the workmen wages by bill 03 02 11; Item paid the Cater by his bill 03 18 10; Item spent and disbursed in my journey to *Exon* as by a bill of the particulars appears 57 18 10; Item paid William Larrimer for two months pay at £3 11s 4d per [illegible crossed through] *month* 07 02 08; Item paid the two sawyers for nine days breaking timber in *Shorley* [Shorleigh] wood 01 02 06; Item paid for threshing of twenty-eight bushels of wheat at 10s per bushel 01 03 09; Item paid for twenty three bushels of [sic] & one half of barley at 3d per bushel 00 05 10; Item paid for 17 bushels of oats 00 04 03; Item paid the tinker for mending the furnace as by his bill 01 00 00

Sum *total* 75 19 07   [page total] £96 13s 4d

**[p. 39]   Saturday the 31th of May 1651**

Item paid the workmen wages by bill £04 11s 11d; Item paid the Cater upon bill 05 10 00; Item paid Robert Cooper for making 700 faggots and 17 seam of hardwood 00 05 06; Item paid for cutting turf for the buts 00 02 00; Item paid Mrs Dennis of *Biddeford* for a quarter of a hundred of fine sugar 02 05 00; Item paid the locksmith upon his bill in part 01 01 00; Item paid the weaver for weaving 19 yards of cloth 00 08 04; Item paid the plasterer for 17 days 00 11 06; Item paid his man for 6 days 00 03 00; Item given a messenger that brought a letter from Exford 00 04 00; Item paid John Hobbs for sugar 02 00 00; Item paid for sending letters per post 00 01 06; Item paid the nurse for one month 00 12 08; Item paid for

making 600 faggots and one dozen of hardwood 00 04 06; Item paid
Lawrence Berry upon bill 00 03 06; Item paid for weeding the wheat
00 07 06; Item paid Mrs Page of Barnstaple upon a bill for salt & peas
03 14 00; Item paid John Terry upon a bill for lime ashes for walks
02 10 00; Item given Sir John Chichester's servant 00 02 00; Item paid
Mrs Faine by my Lady's order when Mrs Trott went to London 05 00 00
Sum *total* 29 17 11

**[p. 41]  Saturday 6 *June* 1651**
Item paid the workmen wages by bill 03 19 07; Item paid the Cater upon
his bill 10 04 06; Item paid for culm at *Alscott* 00 05 00; Item paid Martha
Berney for half a year's washing 00 06 00; Item given Mr Larrence's
servant that brought a carpet from Hartland 00 05 00; Item paid
Mr Forrand 00 01 00; Item paid Mr Boole of *Biddeford* for wine by bill
03 02 00; Item paid Mr Harris of B[?ideford] for loaf sugar 01 07 00; Item
paid May for letters by bill 00 02 00; Item paid Thurston in part of his bill
01 01 00; Item given the doctor's maid that brought a present to my Lady
00 02 00; Item paid Mr Harris for 6 quarts of sack 00 08 00; Item paid the
threshers for twenty bushels of wheat 00 16 08; Item more for 44 bushels
of barley 00 11 00; Item more for 82 bushels of oats 01 00 06; Item paid
the glasier in full of two bills 03 04 00; Item paid for brooms 00 07 00;
Item paid Tho: Penrose & Welsh Dicke for going to & coming from
*Banton* 00 05 00
Sum *total* 27 07 03
Item paid upon a bill for servants wages due at our Lady Day last as by
the bill of particulars doth appear 47 01 08

**[p. 43]  Saturday 14 *June* 1651**
Item paid the workmen wages by bill £03 10s 00d; Item paid the Cater
upon his bill 07 10 10½; Item paid David Balsy for himself & his man for
4 days mending the boat 00 10 00; Item paid for [blank] for the boat
00 01 00; Item paid him for rowing my Lord to Fremington 00 01 06;
Item paid John Parsons for him & his son 00 03 06; Item paid Will Davy
for his pains 00 01 00; Item ['pd'] given Mr Norcott's man that brought
pheasants 00 02 06; Item paid Pawlyn Mayne for 18 days winnowing &
two days tying hops 00 05 06; Item paid the carrier in full 01 03 06; Item
paid the fuller by bill which my Lady hath 01 17 06; Item paid for two
quarts of stawberries 00 01 06; Item paid Robert Coop for making
400 faggots & eight seams of hardwood 00 03 00
Sum *total* 15 08 4½

**Saturday 21 *June* 1651**
Item paid the workmen wages by bill 03 04 07; Item paid the Cater upon
his bill 07 08 00; Item paid for Eringo roots for my Lord 00 03 04; Item
paid Mary Holman for malt by bill 06 08 10; Item paid for bringing up a
boat of coal 00 03 00; Item paid Humfry Lake for two acres of furse
02 13 04; Item given at Mr Norcotts when my Lord & Lady dined there
by command 00 12 00; Item spent at Torrington fair 00 01 06; Item paid
for threshing of twenty-six bushels and three pecks of wheat 01 02 03;
Item paid then more ['ther' crossed through] for threshing of 32 bushels of
oats 00 08 00
Sum *total* 22 04 10

**[p. 48]   Saturday the 28 of June 1651**
Item paid the workmen wages by bill £02 07s 06d; Item paid the Cater by
his bill 05 04 00; Item paid Thurstin Hamer for twenty sheep bought for
my Lord's use 12 15 00; Item paid for culm to dry malt 00 04 06; Item
paid Mr John Hearle ['by command 50 being part' crossed through] of
£100 due to Doctor Downe for tithe *in the year* 1650 and which my Lady
undertook to pay to Mr Hearle 50 00 00; Item paid for letters sent by the
post 00 01 00; Item paid Mr Wood for 6 quarts of tent for the last
communion 00 11 06; Item paid the nurse for one month 00 12 08
Sum *total* 71 16 02

**Saturday 5 July 1651**
Item paid the workmen wages by bill 03 00 00; Item paid the Cater by his
bill 08 03 07; Item paid the barley weeders by bill 00 10 02; Item paid the
hay-makers on the south marsh by bill 02 00 09; Item paid the goldfinders
00 07 00; Item given Mrs Pagget's servant 00 01 00; Item given Jo:
Underdon's boy that brought raspberries 00 00 06; Item given a distressed
Irish minister by command 00 05 00; Item paid the sawyers of timber for
three days 00 07 06; Item paid the threshers for 56 bushels of oats 00 14 00
Sum *total* 15 09 06   [page total] 87 5 8

**[p. 47]   Saturday 12 July 1651**
Item paid the workmen wages by bill £02 19s 08d; Item paid the Cater's
bill as appears 04 05 10; Item paid Mr Shurt of *Bidd.* by bill for fish &c
04 18 00; Item paid the cobbler for mending the coach harness 00 02 00;
Item paid Dick Rooke for so much money disbursed 00 01 00; Item paid
for carrying my Lord's halt[?er] to *Exon* & bringing again 00 03 00; Item
paid for letters from *Exon* 00 01 00; Item paid the threshers for 44 bushels
of oats 00 11 00; Item paid the 7 strange mowers for one day 00 03 06;
Item paid May upon a bill for glasses 00 04 02; Item paid Mr Palser for
excise for one quarter due at Midsummer last 03 05 00; Item paid for my
expenses then at B. 00 01 00; Item paid for making of 300 faggots
00 01 09; Item paid for bringing lead from B. 00 02 00; Item paid Hugh
Edwards of B[blank] for stuff to make two new millstones 15 13 00
Sum *total* 32 11 11

**Saturday 19 July 1651**
Item paid the workmen wages by bill 02 18 08; Item paid the Cater upon
his bill 05 06 02; Item paid William Larrimer for two months rates then
due 07 02 08; Item paid 7 strange men cutting grass in Bridge Meadow one
day 00 03 06; Item paid for cutting & making of 6 acres of hay in Coop's
Close at 4s 4d per acres 01 06 00; Item paid for cutting & making of six
acres of hay in the Barton meadow at 4s 6d per acre 01 07 00; Item paid
Thurston by bill 00 15 00; Item paid Mrs Baker in full of old accounts
00 06 06; Item paid the lock-maker upon his bill 00 13 06; Item paid Wm
['Hamden' crossed through] Hamblyn upon his bill 02 10 06
Sum *total* 25 09 06

[page total] 58 1 5

**[p. 49]   Saturday the 26th of July 1651**
Item paid the workmen wages by bill £02 17s 01d; Item paid the Cater
upon his bill 03 15 00; Item given a women from *Biddeford* 00 00 06; Item

paid for 7 bushels & an half of culm oo 14 oo; Item paid for brooms
oo o2 oo; Item paid Edw: Banton for 3 days at hay oo o2 o9; Item paid the
thresher for 57 bushels of oats oo 14 o4; Item paid them more for
15 bushels of wheat oo 12 o6; Item paid Tho: Stephens for 5 days wages
oo o4 o2; Item paid Roger Wilkey for 2 days wages oo o5 oo; Item paid
him more for sawing pales for the lodge in part o1 oo oo; Item paid Wm
Lorrimer for 2 months rate o7 o2 o8
Sum *total*

### Saturday 2 August 1651
Item paid the workmen wages by bill o2 11 o1; Item paid the Cater upon
bill o2 o8 o7; Item paid for cutting & making the grass in the Stone Close
at 4s 6d per acre o1 o9 o4
Sum *total* o6 o9 oo  [page total] 23 16 o

### [p. 51]  Saturday 9 August 1651
Item paid the Cater upon his bill £o2 o5s 1od; Item paid the workmen
wages upon bill o2 o1 o2; Item paid for cutting & making 5 acres ½ of hay
my close bewest of the Barton Meadow o1 o5 oo; Item paid John Grible
for ten week's wages o1 oo oo; Item paid James Croyder for half a year's
wages due at Midsummer last o1 oo oo; Item paid Mary Holman for mault
by bill o6 1o oo; Item paid the threshers for 12 bushels of wheat oo 1o oo;
Item paid for bringing home two boats of coal oo o6 oo; Item paid for
bringing home the goods from *Apledore* oo o4 oo; Item paid for 1o days
mowing to Peter Harder oo o1 o8; Item paid Wm Meane for 9 days
oo o1 o6; Item paid Kate Richards for 3 weeks weeding oo o2 o3; Item
paid upon a bill of disbursements for several things bought at *Bristoll* fair
44 11 oo; Item paid John Williams in part of his bill o3 oo oo; Item spent
at *Apledore* & given to the seamen oo o1 o6; Item spent at *Barstable* on
Friday last oo oo o6; Item paid the the haymakers for making hay this year
o4 o6 o3; Item paid Jo: Brogge of Hartland in part of his bill for bullocks
& sheep £33, whereof I received of my Lady this day £28 for him & £4 I
paid him formerly 33 oo oo
Sum *total* 1oo o6 o8

This week was brought in 4 weigh & ½ of coal for store which my Lady
paid for & was £1o 19s  £1o o9 oo

### [p. 53]  Saturday the 16th of August 1651
Item paid the workmen by bill o2 o1 o1; Item paid the Cater upon his bill
o2 15 o8; Item paid Richard Rook for his journey to *Banton* oo o6 o3;
Item paid Martha Berrye's daughter for 1o days making hay in the marsh
& meadows oo o3 o4; Item paid for cloam at *Bidd.* oo o2 oo; Item paid
Agnes for her expenses for herself & horse oo oo o4; Item paid Tho:
Suminer for 7 bushels of coarse corn at 3s 6d & for one bushel of peas
o1 12 o6; Item paid John Hobbs for freight upon bill oo 18 oo; Item given
the boatman for fetching the boat out of the water oo o1 o6; Item paid
Tho: Berry for mops oo 11 oo; Item paid for fourteen bushels of charcoal
oo 1o oo; Item for my expenses at *Barstable* oo o1 oo; Item paid J. Wilkey
for sawing pale for the lodge garden o1 1o oo; Item paid the threshers for
15 bushels of wheat & more for 3 bushels and half of wheat oo 15 o5
Sum *total* 11 o8 o1

### Saturday the 23rd of Aug. 1651

Item paid the workmen wages by bill 02 03 00; Item paid the Cater upon his bill 01 01 03; Item paid for pots for the gardener 00 02 04; Item paid for bringing home the brasses for millstones & for plaster of *Parris* 00 02 06; Item paid the smith in part of his bill 06 00 00; Item paid Roger Wilkey & his man for 3 days wages at 15 00 07 06
Sum *total* 09 16 07

### Saturday 30 August 1651

Item paid the workmen wages by bill 03 07 04; Item paid the Cater's bill 02 14 02; Item paid Ramson upon a bill for cutting wheat & making hay & for salt 04 01 04; Item allowed to the reeve of *Wolrington* for rates as by his bill appears 00 03 03
Sum *total* 10 06 01     [page total] 31 10 9

### [p. 55]   Saturday 6 Sept. 1651

Item paid the workmen wages by bill £03 13s 02d; Item paid the Cater upon his bill 00 18 01; Item paid Mr Rich Harris in part for sack 03 00 00; Item paid for cutting, binding and setting up of 24 acres of barley and oats at 2s 6d per acre 03 02 06; Item paid the nurse for one month 00 06 00; Item paid for threshing of 81 bushels of oats 01 00 03; Item spent in going twice to *Exon* 00 08 00; Item given Mr Roll's servant for the pass 00 02 00
Sum *total* 12 10 06

### Saturday 13 7bris [September] 1651

Item paid the workmen wages upon bill 03 12 04; Item paid the Cater upon his bill 02 17 08; Item paid Roger Wilkey for sawing timber 02 00 00; Item paid for mending the rode nets 00 03 06; Item paid for mending the coach harness 00 02 06; Item paid for two diurnals 00 01 00; Item paid for the hire of men & horses to bring home tithe as by a roll of particulars 02 18 00
Sum *total* 11 15 00

### Saturday 20 7bris 1651

Item paid the workmen wages by bill 03 04 10; Item paid the Cater upon bill 01 12 07; Item paid the corn carriers for men & horses by bill 02 14 00; Item paid the excise Com. for Michaelmas quarter 03 05 00; Item paid the nurse for one month 00 06 00; Item given Mrs Slowleye's boy that brought grapes 00 00 06
Sum *total* 11 02 11     [page total] £35 8s 5d

### [p. 57]   Saturday the 27 7bris 1651

Item paid the workmen wages by bill £02 11s 07d; Item paid the Cater's bill 01 10 08; Item paid Will: Larrimer for two months pay 07 02 08; Item paid the chimney sweeper 00 02 00; Item paid Roger Wilkey for sawing pale for the lodge 02 10 00; Item paid for a peck of white salt 00 01 00; Item paid for cloam and expenses 00 01 03; Item paid Baldwin Stephens upon a bill for nets 00 06 10; Item paid for sieves for Amis 00 03 04; Item paid her expenses 00 00 06
Sum *total* 14 09 10

### Saturday 4 8bris [October] 1651

Item paid the workmen wages by bill 02 01 09; Item paid the Cater upon his bill 01 02 07; Item paid Mr Pike upon his bill for wine 01 02 00; Item

given Rich: Rooke when he went to *Exon* oo o5 oo; Item spent at
Torrington fair oo o2 o6; Item paid John Bagge for ten fat steers 40 oo oo;
Item paid Rich: Huxtable the smith in full of all his bills to 9 Aug.
12 o1 oo; Item paid Lawrence Berry upon bill oo o5 oo; Item paid Baldwin
Stephens for nets o1 oo oo; Item paid for 1000 slates 04 o5 oo; Item given
the poor by command oo 10 oo; Item paid the thatcher for 21 days
oo 10 o6; Item spent at *Coombe* [Ilfracombe] oo o2 oo
Sum *total* 71 o7 o4
**Saturday 11 8bris 1651**
Item paid the workmen wages by bill o3 o6 o6; Item paid the Cater upon
bill o3 o1 o2; Item paid for 400 of poor Johns at 11s 6d per hundred
o2 o6 oo; Item spent at Appledore oo o1 oo; Item given Will Featherstone
& Penrose per command oo 10 oo; Item paid the hop-pickers by bill
o1 15 oo; Item paid Rich May for diurnals & letters oo o2 oo; Item paid
for culm oo o4 o6; Item spent at *Barstable* Friday last oo o1 oo
Sum *total* 11 10 11 [page total] 97 8 1
**[p. 59] Saturday the 18th of October 1651**
Item paid the workmen wages by bill £04 oos o7d; Item paid the Cater
upon his bill o2 18 o4; Item paid the drainers in the park for one week
oo 18 oo; Item Mr Boole of *Biddeford* for wine by bill o5 16 oo; Item paid
Roger Wilkey in full of a bill of sawing o2 o2 o4; Item paid for culm to
dry malt oo o4 o6; Item paid Tho: Ley for a parcel of old hay o1 13 o4;
Item paid for twelve bushels of barley malt o3 12 oo; Item the nurse for
one month for Balch oo o6 oo; Item paid for one month pay to Jonas
Harris o3 11 o4
Sum total of this week is 25 o2 o4
**Saturday 25 October 1651**
Item paid the workmen wages by bill £o2 o8s o8d; Item paid the Cater
upon bill o5 o6 o3; Item paid for 150 *Apledore* oysters oo o2 oo; Item paid
Rich May for 3 diurnals oo o1 oo; Item paid Morcombe for one year
keeping the clocks oo o8 oo; Item paid Will Lee upon a bill for making
wood oo o9 o4; Item paid Mary Holman upon a bill for malt o4 o8 oo;
Item paid Rich Britton in full for 14 bushels of barley for to sow at 8s per
bushel o3 o2 oo; Item paid Humfry Lake in full for lime and lime ashes as
by bill o2 o9 oo; Item paid Tho: Lovering for malt upon bill o9 16 o8;
Item delivered John Gribble for his journey to Huntspill oo 10 oo
Sum total of this week is 29 oo 11
So I have disbursed since the audit 1650 until the audit 1651 as by this
book of particulars doth appear the sum of £1715 2s 9d
Sum total of my receipts within the forementioned time as by my book
doth appear is £1622 10s 5d
So remains due to me £0092 12s 4d
The 27th of October 1651. This book was seen examined and allowed by
my Lady.
[signed] Richard Pollard

**[p. 76]** [*These last pages appear in reverse order*]
Receipts from the 28th of October 1650 until
*First* rest due from me upon my last accounts as by my books appears
£004 10s 02d.

Recd upon the debits due from several manors at the Audit 1650 as by a book of the particulars appears 246 01 06.

Recd from Richard Britton for the pasturing 3 oxen, 1 steer and 2 yearlings 003 04 8.

Recd more of him for 28 lbs of hops 001 08 0.

Recd of Thurstin for summering of Nich: Carder's, John Pope's, Gilbert Pridham's and Rich: Hall's bullocks upon Wonham as appears 012 00 00.

Recd of Mr Downe for summering 2 oxen 001 06 08.

Recd of Edward Striblings for summering bullocks 002 03 04.

Recd of Willm Lymbury for summering bullocks 001 16 08.

Recd of Thomas Langdon for summering his cattle 004 03 04.

1 November. Recd for one hide and 3 skins 001 02 00.

12 November. Recd from my Lady to pay wages &c 032 10 00.

8 November Recd for one hide and two skins 001 04 00.

16 November Recd from my Lady 012 10 00.

19 November Recd from my Lady to pay Mrs Baker's bill 032 05 00.

Recd of Philip Harris for summering two oxen upon Wonham 001 06 08.

Recd of Humfry Cure for summering his two bullocks upon Wonham 01 03 04.

15 9br 1650 Recd for one hide and two skins 001 02 00.

24 November Recd from my Lady to pay part of a bill for bullocks and sheep 030 00 00.

Recd of John Baker for summering cattle upon Wonham 005 00 00.

3 10br [December] Recd of David Hill by my Lady's order 020 00 00.

Sum is 415 17 04.

## [p. 74]

Recd of James Whitfeild for summering one yearling upon Wonham £00 06s 08d.

Recd of Rich Hearding for one year's rent due at Michaelmas last for Heale's tenement 00 17 04.

Recd more of him for his half pat of rates 00 04 04.

22 9brs [November] 1650 Recd for 3 sheep skins 00 07 06.

29 9brs Recd for one hide and 2 skins 01 03 00.

Recd of John Sumner for summering cattle 07 03 00.

13 December Recd of my Lady by Mr Cobb 07 00 00.

Recd of Amis for onions 00 09 00.

Recd of Hobson and Britton for their fine concerning Heale's tenement 09 08 08.

Recd more for rates 00 04 00.

Recd for two hides and six skins 02 08 00.

Recd of Digory Pounstock in part of his fine of £33 10 00 00.

Recd of Mr Elston for summering his cattle upon Wonham 04 13 00.

Recd of Willim Jose for summering cattle 02 10 00.

Recd of Digory Pounstock more in part of his fine 10 00 00.

Recd for 3 hides and 6 skins 02 18 00.

3 Jan. Recd for one hide and five skins 01 11 00.

17 Jan. Recd for my Lady by Mr Cobb 10 00 00.

Recd for two hides and 4 skins 02 12 00.

18 Jan. Recd from my Lady by Mr Cobb 10 00 00.
23 Jan. Recd from my Lady by Mr Cobb 20 00 00.
28 Jan. Recd from my Lady by Mr Cobb 20 00 00.
*Page sum* 123 13 6 [page total] £123 13s 6d

**[p. 72]**
24 Jan. Recd for one hide and 4 sheep skins £01 12s 00d.
31 Jan. Recd for one hide and 4 skins 01 02 00.
Recd for two bushels of beans 00 13 04.
30 Jan. Recd of Mrs Baker in part of a bill of exchange from Mr Hanaford
10 00 00.
7 Febr. Recd for one hide and five skins 01 17 08.
10 Febr. Recd from my Lady by Mr Cobb to pay the smith 10 00 00.
Recd from Lady Sydenham for trenchers 00 14 00.
14 Febr. Recd for one hide and two skins 00 18 00.
15 Febr. Recd from my Lady by Mr Cobb 10 00 00.
21 Febr. Recd from my Lady to pay Dick Lake in part for sugar 10 00 00.
Recd of Mr Wyatt of money which he recd of Mr Salisbury of Barnstaple
being part of £90 returned from *Exon* by John Hanaford 10 00 00.
Recd of Will Mullyns for reed 00 05 00.
21 Febr. Recd for 3 sheep skins 00 12 00.
28 Febr. Recd for 4 sheep skins 00 16 00.
2 *March* 1650 Recd of my Lady by Mr Cobb 10 00 00.
4 March this bill was £50. Recd from Mr Baker in full of bill of exchange
of money returned by Jo: Hanaford of *Exon* 20 00 00
Recd for one seam of apples 00 05 00.
8 *March* Recd for one hide and 3 sheep skins 01 04 00.
8 *March* Recd of Will Richards for wood sold in the park 01 10 00.
9 *March* Recd of Mr Cobb by my Lady's order 05 00 00.
14 *March* Recd of Mr Cobb by my Lady's order to pay Dick Lake for
sugar 05 00 00
*page sum* 101 09 00

**[p. 70]**
4 *March* 1650 Recd of Richard Britton for to pay Mr Shurt of *Bidd.* for a
butt of sack £20 00s 00d.
14 *March* Recd for 3 skins 00 13 00.
19 *March* Recd from my Lady by Mr Cobb 15 00 00.
22 *March* Recd from my Lady 05 00 00
[total] 40 13 0

The whole sum of my receipts from the 26th of October last to this 22th
of March is £681 02s 10d.
More received for tithe corn sold 105 00 00
*In total* £786 2s 10d.
Disbursed within the said time 818 03 08.
So remains due to me 32 00 10.
R[ichard]P[ollard]

The 26th of March 1651 Received then from my Honourable Lady in full
of what I have disbursed more than received as by this book doth appear
the sum of £32 00s 10d. [signed] Richard Pollard

[p. 68]

Received of Mr Cobb by my Lady's appointment the 13th day of March
1650 as by my Lady's book doth appear, but then forgotten to be set
down in my book £05 00s 00d.

28 *March* 1651 recd for one hide and a calf's skin & 2 sheep skins
01 12 00.

31 *March* recd from my Lady 05 00 00

4 Apr. recd for one hide and four skins 01 16 00

5 Apr. recd from my Lady to pay Mrs Downe 20 00 00

6 Apr. recd from my Lady to give to the poor of Torr 02 10 00

recd of Mr Cobb to pay Mr Skiles for herrings 03 15 00

recd for half a hundred of reed 00 10 00

9 Apr. recd of Mr Cobb to pay Rumson 06 00 00

11 Apr. recd for 4 sheep skins 00 16 00

12 Apr. recd from my Lady 10 00 00

18 Apr. recd for two hides and 5 skins 02 09 06

recd for 60 sheaves of reed 00 12 00

24 Apr. recd from my Lady to pay for sheep &c 10 00 00

25 Apr. recd for one hide and 4 skins 01 12 00

27 Apr. recd from my Lady to pay a month's pay 04 00 00

Sum is £75 12s 06d

[p. 67]   for hides and skins

30 May 1651 recd for one hide and 3 skins £01 13s 06d

6 *June* recd for one hide and 6 skins 01 18 00

13 *June* recd for one hide and 5 skins 01 12 00

20 *June* recd for one hide and 2 skins 01 03 00

27 *June* recd for one hide and 4 skins 01 09 00

4 July recd for one hide and 5 skins 01 08 04

11 July recd for one hide and 3 skins 01 03 06

18 July recd for one hide and 4 skins 01 04 00

25 July recd for one hide & 4 skins 01 05 00

1 *August* 1651 recd for one hide and 4 skins 01 05 00

9 *August* recd for one hide and 4 skins 01 05 06

16 *August* recd for one hide and 5 skins 00 17 10

23 Aug. recd for one hide and 3 skins 00 17 06

30 *August* recd for one hide and 6 skins 00 16 02

6 Sept. recd for one hide and 2 skins 00 14 00

13 Sept. recd for one hide and 6 skins 00 15 00

20 Sept. recd for one hide and 7 skins 01 00 00

27 Sept. recd for one hide and 2 skins 00 16 00

4 Octob. recd for one hide & 4 skins 00 19 00

11 Octob. recd for one hide and 4 skins 00 18 06

17 Octob. recd for one hide and 4 skins 01 00 00

24 Octob. recd for one hide and 4 skins 01 01 00

[total] 25 02 00

[p. 66]   2 May 1651 Recd of Mr Selden of Barnstaple money rec. in
*Cornub.* £02 02s 00d; 20 [sic] May recd for one hide and four skins
01 16 00; 9 May recd for one hide and 4 skins 01 13 00; 9 May 1651 recd

from my Lady by Mr Cobb 40 00 00; recd from my Lady to pay Myles
his wages due at our Lady Day 02 00 00

10 May recd of Mrs Baker of Barnstaple upon a bill of epc. for Mr John
Hanaford of *Exter* 50 00 00; recd of John Sallisbury of Barnstaple for so
much paid for him in *Exon* by Mr Hanaford 10 00 00; 16 May recd for
4 skins 00 13 00; 22 May recd of Robt Drake of *Upex* by my Lord's
command 60 00 00; recd then from John Hanaford for my Lord's use
13 00 00; 23 May recd for one hide and 3 sheep's skins 01 10 00; 25 May
recd of Mr Cob for my Lord's use 05 00 00; recd of Mr Jo. Seldon of
Barnstaple for so much received by him in Cornwall for my Lord
05 10 00; 28 May recd from my Lady by Mr Cobb 40 00 00; recd of
Mrs Baker of Barnstaple upon a bill of exchange from Jo. Hanaford of
Exon 06 10 00; 30 May recd of Damaris Joanes of Barnstaple upon bill of
exchange from John Hanaford of Exon 03 14 00
Sum is £243 08s 00d

[p. 64]   9 *June* 1651 Recd of Mary Frace of Barnstaple upon a bill of
exchange from Mr Hanaford of Exon £02 18s 00d; Recd of John Williams
of Barnstaple for so much to be paid him in Exon by Mr Hanaford
10 00 00; recd of Mr Cobb by my Lady's command 10 00 00; 22 June recd
of Mr Cobb 05 00 00; recd of Jo: Salisbury of Barnstaple upon bill of
exchange from Hanaford of Exon 25 00 00; 25 *June* recd of Mr Cobb to
pay Thurstyn for 20 sheep which he bought for my Lord's use for
Wonham 12 15 00; 25 *June* recd of Tho: Edmond's servant to Mr Elston
of Exon by Mr Hanaford's appointment 55 00 00; 4 July recd of Mr Tho:
Wyatt for my Lord's use 04 17 04; 11 July recd of Mr Cobb to pay Hugh
Edwards of Barnstaple for brasses and plaster for two millstones 15 00 00;
12 July recd of Mr Cobb for my Lord's use 05 00 00; recd of George
Balch reve of Tawstock in part of Midsummer quarter rent due to my
Lord 20 00 00; 19 July recd of Mr Cobb by my Lady's order 02 00 00;
1 Aug. recd of Mr Wyatt for my Lord's use 02 00 00; recd of William
Parker deputy reve of *Warington* for 3 quarter's rent due at Midsummer
last 01 13 00
Sum is £171 03s 04d

[p. 62]   3 August Recd of Mr Cobb for my Lord's use £10 00s 00d;
7 Aug. recd from my Lady to pay Bristol's bills 50 00 00; 12 Aug. recd
from my Lady to pay several bills 50 00 00; *same day* recd from my Lady
50 00 00; 12 Aug. recd for 13 lbs of old hops at Bidd. 00 17 06; recd for a
basket of apples 00 03 00; 15 Aug. recd of Mr Williams Nottle of
Barnstaple by bill of exchange from Jo: Hanaford of *Exon* 20 00 00;
19 Aug. recd for ten pounds of hops 00 14 00; recd for a seam of apples
00 05 00; recd for 21 lbs of old hops 01 08 00; recd then for two gallons of
kitchen stuff 00 06 00; recd of the gardener for carrots and cabbage
00 03 04; recd from my Lady by Mr Cobb 50 00 00; 23 Sept. recd for
28 lbs of old hops sold at Bidd. 01 15 07; recd for carrots sold then in the
market 00 02 00; 27 Sept. recd for 26 lbs of old hops at 1s 4d per lb
01 14 06; recd for 5 pots of kitchen stuff 00 06 10; 1 Ocotob. recd from
my Lady to Rich. Huxtable the smith 12 00 00; 5 Octob. recd from my
Lady to pay for slates &c 05 10 00; recd of George Balch in part of

michealmas quarter rent 07 00 00; 21 Octob. recd of Mr Lynn by my
Lady's command 10 00 00
Sum is 272 05 09

Recd for the tithe of Tawstock *in the year* 1651 00  £153 6s 7d
Sum total of my receipts is [illegible crossed through] £1622 10s 5d

# Expenses and Receipts, 1654–1655

## KENT ARCHIVES OFFICE, U269/A525/10

*The book measures 8" by 12¼" and is headed 'Disbursements'. The back
cover is headed 'Receipts' and there is no front cover. Even-numbered
pages 2 to 46 and odd-numbered pages 47 to 55 are blank. Some twenty
sheets were removed between pages 46 and 47.*

[p. 1]  Tawstock 1654 Disbursements for the household expense and other
defrayments of the right honourable the Lady Rachel Countess Dowager
of Bath from the Audit 1654 until

**Saturday 4th of November 1654**
Item paid the workmens wages by bill 000 18 04; Item paid the Cater
upon his bill 001 06 08; Item paid for five new bed mats 000 07 06; Item
paid Balch for to buy wood 000 02 06; Item paid for a pair of stockings
for Will: Booth 000 05 00; Item paid for two boats of gravel for walks
000 10 00; Item paid for a pair of stockings for the footman 000 05 00;
Item paid for pastry paper 000 01 00; Item given the doctor by command
for his directions concerning Tho: Hathor's leg 000 10 00; Item paid the
Apothecary in full of his demands 020 00 00; Item paid Mrs Baker in part
of her accounts 040 00 06; Item paid Mary Holman in full for 41 bushels
of oat malt at 2s 6d per bushel 005 02 06; Item paid for 10 bushels of culm
000 16 08; Item paid for threshing of 65 bushels of barley, oats, peas at
2d the bushel 000 10 10; Item paid for one day's wages winnowing
000 00 10; Item paid for John Males for five days in harvest 000 05 00;
Item paid John Terry upon two bills 000 15 09
*Sum total* 071 17 07   R.P.

**[p. 3]  Saturday 11th of Novemb. 1654**
Item paid the workmens wages by bill £001 05s 10d; Item paid the Cater
upon his bill 002 13 07; Item paid the servants wages due at the last audit
as by particulars 137 13 04; Item paid the servants in money given them by
our most honorable and noble Lady as a remembrance of their honorable
Lord and master the Earl of Bath 126 00 00; Item paid Jo: Williams upon
his bill 005 01 00; Item paid Bess Searle upon bill for May 000 14 00; Item
paid Ann Mullyns for 3 quarters teaching Ursula Hearder and another
poor girl to read and work 000 13 06; Item given the Irish messenger by
command 001 00 00; Item paid for Cobleye's coffin by command
000 06 06; Item paid for expenses at *Banton* 000 18 00; Item paid Balche's
nurse for one month 000 06 08
Sum is 276 12 05

**Saturday the 18th of November 1654**
Item paid the workmen wages by bill £000 19s 00d; Item paid the Cater
upon his bill 003 16 02; Item paid Mr Selden of Barnstaple in part
040 00 00; Item paid the glasier in full of his bill 004 02 00; Item paid
Huxtable the smith in part 010 00 00; Item paid for threshing 92 bushels
of barley and oats at 2d per bushel 000 15 00; Item paid Simon Collyns by
command 000 11 00; Item in money given by my honourable Lady to her
honour's poor old labouring men 024 00 00; Item paid for two steers and
one cow 014 02 06; Item paid Lewis Singe in part of his bills 010 00 00;
Item paid for letters by post 000 00 06
Sum is 108 06 02   [page total] £384 18s 7d

**[p. 5]   Saturday the 25th of Novemb. 1654**
Item paid the workmen wages by bill £001 08s 05d; Item paid the Cater
upon his bill 2 01 11; Item paid Mr Bowen in full of his bill for wine and
butter, as by Mr Gammon's receipt of Mr Bowen's order 023 03 04; Item
paid Mr Geaton the apothecary in full of his bill and of all demands
002 06 06; Item paid Mrs Downe upon her bill 001 13 00; Item given to
the baker for his help four days before the funeral 000 03 00; Item paid
John Hamblyon in part of his bills 010 00 00; Item paid Mr Delbridge in
part of his bill 040 00 00; Item paid for eight pound of currants 000 06 00;
Item paid Lawrence Chamberlyn upon bill 002 10 06; Item paid Mr Hill
upon his bill for wine and court dinners 010 11 00; Item paid for two beer
s[?t]aves for the malt house 000 02 06; Item paid Jo: Britton upon his bill
for wine 013 05 00
Sum total [illegible crossed through] 107 11 02

**[p. 7]   Saturday 2 December 1654**
Item paid the workmen wages by bill £01 02s 09d; Item paid the Cater
upon his bill 04 09 11; Item paid the worsted comber 00 05 05; Item paid
Rose the shoemaker by bill 01 19 00; Item paid the mason for wages
00 05 10; Item paid for culm 01 03 06; Item paid Wilkey and his man for
cleaving wood 00 04 00; Item paid the locksmith by bill 01 00 00
Sum is 10 10 05

**Saturday 9 December 1654**
Item paid the workmen wages by bill 01 08 03; Item paid the Cater upon
bill 04 13 06; Item paid for beer at *Chittenholt* [Chittlehamholt] 00 01 06;
Item paid for carriage of a black box to *Exon* 00 01 00; Item paid Paul
Budd for carrying down 12 hogsheads to Barnstaple and a hogshead of
wine 00 02 06; Item paid for sending letters to *Exon* 00 00 06; Item paid
Lee for making 1200 faggots, 21 bundles of spars and 600 hop poles &c
00 10 06; Item paid Balche's nurse for one month 00 06 0 8
Sum is 07 04 05   [page total] 17 14 10

**[p. 9]   Saturday the 16th of December 1654**
Item paid the workmen wages by bill 01 01 02; Item paid the Cater's bill
03 09 02; Item paid John Woode in full for 200 weight of sugar 06 13 04;
Item paid Mr Forrard for 8 gallons of Mallaga sack at 4s the gallon
01 12 00; Item paid Robert Coop for making 1200 browse faggots at
8d the hundred 00 08 00; Item paid for knitting fishing nets by bill
01 02 00; Item paid for landing and bringing home three barrels of

herrings oo o2 oo; Item paid Anthony Ashe the smith for iron work for
the hutch oo o4 oo; Item paid Will Richards for making 6oo faggots,
5o hop poles and 14 bundles of spars and 3 seams of hardwood oo o5 o6;
Item paid him for two days wages cleaving wood oo o1 o8
Sum is 14 18 10

**[p. 11]   Saturday 23 Decemb. 1654**
Item paid the workmen wages by bill £oo 19s o7d; Item paid the Cater
upon bill o7 o2 11; ['Item paid for bringing home 3 barrels of herrings
oo oo1 o6' crossed through] Item paid for threshing of 4o bushels of oats
at 2d the bushel o o6 o8; Item paid Will Balch to buy wood oo o2 o6; Item
paid for rabbits and veal and cocks oo o8 o6; Item paid Mr John Downe
for twelve bushels of salt at 6s the bushel o3 12 oo; Item paid the thatcher
for twelve days oo 10 oo; Item given the post man by command oo o2 o6;
Item paid for six oyster knives oo o3 oo; Item paid for pastry paper
oo o1 oo; Item paid Ann Mullyns by bill oo o9 10
Sum is 13 17 o6

**Saturday 30 December 1654**
Item paid Cater upon his bill o7 16 o4; Item paid John Terry upon bill
oo 14 oo; Item paid for a silver bowl o2 o8 oo; Item paid for the louth
[*lough*] of twelve hogsheads oo 12 oo; Item paid for garden flower pots
oo o4 oo; Item paid for spinning of 4 pound of worsted oo o6 oo; Item
paid John Britton for blooding and drenching 18 horses o1 oo oo
Sum is 13 oo o4   [page total] £26 17s 1od

**[p. 13]   Saturday 6 January 1654**
Item paid the workmen wages by bill £oo 15s o3d; Item paid the Cater's
bill o4 o3 3o; Item paid Mrs Baker in part of her bills 7o oo oo; Item paid
Mr Delbridge in part of his bill 4o oo oo; Item paid for 3 couple of rabbits
oo o5 oo; Item given a messenger that brought two cheeses from Mr Fane
o1 oo oo; Item paid John Hamblyn in full of his bills 24 o oo; Item paid
John Baller for fringe by bill o3 14 o6; Item given Mr Bold for my Lady
o1 oo oo; Item paid for mending the boys shoes oo o4 oo
Sum is 145 o2 oo

**Saturday 13 January 1654**
Item paid the workmen wages by bill o1 o3 o2; Item paid the Cater upon
his bill oo oo oo [sic]; Item paid Mr Wyatt for Mrs Fane o1 oo oo; Item
paid Balche's nurse for one month oo o6 o8; Item paid for knitting
Mr Harries stockings & gloves oo o2 oo; Item paid Mrs Delbrldge for
3 months for Jonathan o1 o4 oo; Item paid her more for mending his
clothes oo o3 oo; Item paid Bess Searle upon her bill for several things
o1 o8 o6; Item paid for letters per post oo o1 o6; Item paid Rose and the
rest for their journey o3 oo oo; Item paid the sadler by bill and then clear
o5 17 oo; Item paid for brooms for the house oo o2 oo; Item paid Lewis
Singe in part of his bill 15 oo oo
Sum is 29 o4 o8   [page total] £174 6s 8d

**[p. 13b]   Saturday 20 January 1654**
Item paid the workmen wages by bill £o1 o6s o6d; Item paid for beef
oo 11 oo; Item paid for a bushel of oatmeal oo o5 o; Item paid for a bunter
for the mill oo o1 o6; Item paid Thomas Amsby and Baldwyn for barm

oo 11 oo; Item paid Thurstyn in part of his wages o1 10 oo; Item paid
Mr Shiles for usquebaugh oo 10 o6; Item paid Charles upon bill for wages
o1 o6 o9; Item paid for standing letters per post oo o1 oo; Item paid for
carrying things to Appledore oo o2 oo; Item paid for 200 hop poles
oo 14 oo; Item paid Rich Maye for stockings by bill oo o4 o7
Sum is o7 2 o1

### Saturday 27th Jan. 1654
Item paid the workmens wages by bill o1 o9 o4; Item paid for beef and
mutton o1 oo o6; Item paid for eggs oo o4 oo; Item paid Agnes by
command o1 oo oo; Item paid for strainers and cheese cloths oo o4 oo;
Item paid for spinning 6 lbs of worsted oo o9 oo; Item paid for knitting
cuffs oo oo o6; Item paid 4 lbs of week yarn oo o3 oo; Item paid for 16 lbs
of candles o o7 o6; Item paid for salt oo o6 oo; Item paid for threshing
73 bushels of oats oo 12 oo; Item paid for an iron bought at Barnstaple and
left at the funeral oo 11 oo; Item paid Mrs Deane of *Bristoll* in full by
Mr Fleming o9 14 oo
Sum is 16 o1 10   [page total] £23 3s 11d

### [p. 15]   Saturday 4 Febr. 1654
Item paid the workmens wages by bill £o1 o1s o4d; Item paid for beef and
mutton o1 o3 o2; Item paid for eggs oo o1 o6; Item paid for white salt
oo o1 o8; Item paid for letter per post oo o1 oo; Item paid Balch's nurse
for one month oo o6 o8; Item paid for culm oo o8 oo; Item paid for cloam
and the maid's expenses oo o4 o6; Item paid for John Williams by bill
o2 o8 oo; Item paid for baize and tape for Kate oo o2 o6; Item paid for
four hats for the boys oo 10 oo; paid for a quarter teaching Ursula Hearder
oo o3 oo
Sum is o6 11 o4

### Saturday 10th of Febr.
Item paid the workmen wages by bill £o1 12s 11d; Item paid for beef and
mutton and veal o1 15 o6; Item paid for eggs oo o2 oo; Item paid for
mustard seed oo o2 o6; Item paid for a fork for the stable oo o1 o8; Item
paid for a shovel oo o1 o6; Item paid for a bushel of oatmeal oo o5 o4;
Item paid [for] 25 lbs of candles oo 11 o6; Item paid Will Lee for making
wood oo 16 o6
Sum is £o5 o9s o5s   [page total] £12 os 9d

### [p. 17]   Saturday 17 Febr. 1654
Item paid the workmens wages by bill £o1 11s 1od; Item paid for beef &
mutton o1 12 o8; Item paid for eggs oo o2 oo; Item paid for a bushel of
salt oo o6 oo; Item paid Ned & Steeven for *Banton* oo o5 o6; Item paid for
paper & ink oo o1 o6; Item paid for sending letters per post oo o2 oo; Item
paid Avis Goolcott for 9 weeks wages oo o6 o6; Item paid for a bushel of
peas to boil oo o5 oo
Sum is o4 13 oo

### Saturday 24th of Febr. 1654
Item paid the workmen wages by bill £o1 11s o5d; Item paid for beef &
mutton o1 o5 o6; Item paid for eggs oo o2 oo; Item paid Thomas Berry for

maps by bill oo o8 oo; Item a bill for John Glaston's diet at Bideford lying there for a wind oo 14 oo; Item paid Rumson upon a bill oo 18 o6
Sum is o4 19 o5

### Saturday 3 March 1654

Item paid the workmen wages by bill o1 10 o4; Item paid for mutton and veal oo o3 o4; Item paid for eggs oo o2 oo; Item paid for candles oo o4 oo; Item paid Balche's nurse one month oo o6 o8; Item paid for making 1500 browse faggots oo 10 oo; Item paid for expenses at measuring the wood at *Warkley* o o2 o6
Sum is o2 18 10   [page total] £12 11s 3d

### [p. 19]   Saturday 10 *March* 1654

Item paid the workmens wages by bill £o1 17s o4d; Item paid for mutton & veal oo o5 oo; Item paid for eggs and oatmeal oo o3 o2; Item paid for white salt oo o1 o4; Item paid for 4 lbs of candles oo o3 o6; Item paid for a shoulder of mutton oo o1 o2; Item paid Tho: Cooman for going to *Exon* oo o7 oo; Item paid for letter per post oo o1 oo
Sum is o2 19 o6

### Saturday 17 *March* 1654

Item paid the workmen wages by bill £o1 12s o4d; Item paid for beef and muttton & veal o1 15 o6; Item paid for eggs and candles oo o3 o4; Item paid for a peck of oatmeal oo o1 o4; Item paid letters per post oo o1 o2; Item paid for measuring *Warkley* wood oo o8 oo; Item paid Tho: Cooman for *Exon* journey oo o5 oo; Item paid the baker for bread and two days wages oo o3 oo; Item paid for letters per post oo o1 o3; Item paid for 30 bushels of oats to sow o2 o5 oo; Item paid the miller at Claper's mill oo o2 o6
Sum is o6 18 o5   [page total] £9 17s 11d

### [p. 19b]   Saturday 24 *March* 1655

Item paid the workmen wages by bill £o1 14s o4d; Item paid for beef & mutton & veal oo o8 oo; Item paid for eggs oo o2 oo; Item paid the old hemp stripper and her daughter 8 weeks wages o1 o2 o6; Item spent at Chillington oo oo o6; Item spent at Barnstaple in getting my Lady's horses again oo o5 o6; Item paid Mr Payton for his journey o3 oo oo
Sum is o6 12 10

### Saturday 31 *March* 1655

Item paid the workmen wages by bill o1 14 o8; Item paid for mutton & veal oo o7 o4; Item paid for eggs and white salt oo o3 o6; Item paid for 1 peck of oat meal oo o1 o2; Item paid for mending the boys shoes oo o3 oo; Item paid for letters per post oo o1 o3; Item paid Balche's nurse for one month oo o6 o8; Item paid Doctor Chichester by command o5 oo oo; Item paid Alice Delbridge for four months for Jonathan o1 12 oo
Sum is o9 o9 o7

### Saturday 7 Apr. 1655

Item paid the workmen wages by bill o1 16 o6; Item paid for mutton & veal oo o6 o6; Item paid for eggs and 6 lbs of candles oo o5 oo; Item paid for 6 chickens oo o2 oo; Item paid for culm oo 10 oo; Item paid for letters

per post oo oi oo; Item paid for half a weigh of coal oi oo oo; Item paid
for Christmas quarter for Balche's rent oo o4 oo; Item paid for a bill hook
oo oi o2
Sum is o4 o6 o2   [page total] £20 o8s 7d

**[p. 21]   Saturday 14 April 1655**
Item paid the workmen wages by bill £o2 oos ood; Item paid for veal and
mutton oo o5 o9; Item paid for eggs oo o2 oi; Item paid for making
1200 faggots, 600 poles and 8 bundles of spars oo 10 oo; Item paid for
making 1200 browse faggots oo o8 oo; Item paid for letters per post
oo o2 oo; Item paid for 3 barrels of Irish herrings o3 15 oo; Item paid
Magg Hearder for her help to winnow and all other works 10 weeks
oo o8 o8
Sum is o7 o9 11

**Saturday 21 Apr. 1655**
Item paid the workmen wages by bill oi o4 o7; Item paid for beef, mutton
& veal oi 11 o2; Item paid Joan Saunders for her half years wages and
3 weeks over oi o3 oo; Item paid for 5 bushels of oats oo o8 oo; Item paid
Leaydon a miller for 3 weeks wages at Clapper's mill oo 15 oo
Sum is o5 oi o9

**Saturday 28 Apr. 1655**
Item paid the workmen wages by bill oi o8 o9; Item paid for beef and
mutton and veal oi 12 o6; Item paid for two pair of shoes for the boys
oo o5 o6; Item paid for 6 lbs of suet oo o2 o6; Item paid for 2 pecks of
oatmeal oo o2 o6; Item paid for a bushel of white salt and a bushel of Bay
oo o7 o6; Item paid for eggs oo oo o4; Item paid for expenses at the fair
oo oi o6; Item paid the tinker by bill for mending the kettles and great
furnace oi o2 oo; Item paid for a milking pail oo oi o8
Sum is o5 o4 o9   [page total] £17 16s 5d

**[p. 23]   Saturday 5 May 1655**
Item paid the workmens wages by bill £oi oos o8d; Item paid for beef and
mutton oi o8 oo; Item paid for timber for your Honour's closet door
oo 10 oo; Item paid Balche's nurse for one month oo o6 o8; paid for dogs
meat oo o4 10; paid Huxtable in part of his bills o5 oo oo; paid for a
bushel of peas oo o5 oo; paid for brooms oo o3 oo; paid for veal oo oi o8;
paid for 3 bushels of oats oo o3 o9; paid for letters per post oo oi o3; paid
for making 1400 faggots and 400 poles oo o9 o6; Item spent at Barnstaple
oo oi oo
Sum is o9 14 o6

**Saturday 12 May 1655**
Item paid the workmen wages by bill £oi o5s o4d; Item paid Lee for
making wood oo o4 o6; Item paid for culm oo 12 oo; Item paper oo oi oo;
Item paid for eggs and candles oo oi o6; Item paid Ann Mullyns for one
quarter teaching three girls oo o8 oo; Item paid for a weigh of coal
oi 19 oo; Item paid for two bushels of oats oo o2 10
Sum is o4 14 o2   [page total] £14 8s 8d

**[p. 25]   Saturday 19 May 1655**
Item paid the workmen wages by bill £oo 19s o9d; Item paid for shoes for
Lymberry oo o2 oo; Item paid for stockings for him oo oi o5; Item paid

for gloves & shoes for Kate 00 01 08; Item returned to my Lady to
London 50 00 00; Item paid for 3 months pay 05 07 00; Item paid for
4 dozen of crests 00 06 00; b[ill] Item paid Edward Gribble for horse meat
01 08 00; Item paid Richard Cooper for weeding hops 00 07 06
Sum is 58 13 04

**Saturday 26th of May 1655**
Item paid the workmen wages by bill 01 05 06; Item paid for beef and veal
01 12 00; Item paid Rumson for expenses at fair 00 00 08; Item paid for
new laying of a axe 00 01 00; Item paid for a bushel of meal 00 05 00;
Item paid for 3 quarts of tar 00 01 06; Item paid 3 pounds of pitch
00 01 00; Item paid for vinegar 00 01 00; Item paid for a breast of veal and
mutton 00 02 06; Item paid for candles 00 10 00
Sum is 03 11 02

**Saturday 2 June 1655**
Item paid the workmen wages by bill 01 04 00; Item paid for beef and veal
01 10 00; Item paid for a scythe and two hones 00 03 04; Item paid for
cutting calves and pigs 00 02 00; Item paid Ramson for his expenses at
*Banton* for himself and two or three servants 00 16 06; Item paid for eggs
00 03 00
Sum is 03 18 10   [page total] £66 10s 4d

**[p. 27]   Saturday 9 *June* 1655**
Item paid the workmen wages by bill £00 16s 04d; Item paid for beef and
mutton and veal 01 08 06; Item paid for oats 00 02 00; Item paid for
stones for the drawing room 00 04 06; Item paid [for] half a dozen milk
pans 00 02 06; Item paid for crests for mending the garden wall 00 09 06;
Item paid for half a bushel of white salt 00 03 00; Item paid for ved grease
[*verdigris*] 00 00 06; Item paid for charcoal 00 01 05; Item paid for
expenses at market 00 00 03
Sum is 03 07 10

**Saturday 16 *June* 1655**
Item paid the workmen wages by bill 00 19 10; Item paid for beef and veal
01 13 06; Item paid for half a bushel of oatmeal 00 02 06; Item paid for
vinegar 00 01 00; Item paid for 4 lbs of chalk 00 00 04; Item paid for a
bushel of bay salt 00 06 03; Item paid for 8 chickens 00 02 06; Item paid
for 2 bushels of oats 00 03 06
Sum is 03 09 05

**Saturday 23 *June* 1655**
Item paid the workmen wages by bill 01 02 10; Item paid for beef and veal
01 14 00; Item paid for measuring the marsh 00 01 00; Item paid for eggs
00 02 00; Item paid for Hosgood's daughter for two weeks weeding
00 05 00; Item paid Avis Starling one week's weeding 00 02 06; Item paid
for expenses at Barnstaple 00 00 06; Item paid for 13 chickens 00 02 10;
Item paid for letters per post 00 00 10
Sum is 03 10 08   [page total] £16 7s 11d

**[p. 29]   Saturday 30th of June 1655**
Item paid the workmen wages by bill 01 11 00; Item paid for beef
01 08 00; Item paid for Balche's nurse for two months 00 13 04; Item paid
the weeders of corn by bill 01 05 10; Item paid for making a new

winnowing sheet oo oi o6; Item paid Ned Maye and Hearder for their
expenses at Plymouth for wine oi oi o6; Item paid letters per post
oo oi oo; Item paid for two weigh of coal o3 18 o6; Item paid Avis
Starling and Ann Hosgood for two weeks weeding oo o5 oo; Item paid for
mending the boiler & kettle oo o4 o6; Item paid the plasterer four days
oo o3 oo; Item paid the chimney sweep oo oi o6
Sum is 10 14 o8

### Saturday 7 July 1655
Item paid the workmen wages by bill £oi oos ood; Item paid for beef
oi o4 oo; Item paid the carpenters for two weeks about mending the boat
oi 11 oo; Item paid for brooms oo oi o6; Item paid Avis Gooscott for
o7 weeks oo o5 oo; Item paid for iron work for the boat oo 10 oo; Item
paid for eggs and candles oo o3 oo; Item paid upon a bill for pitch & for
the boat oo 18 o4; Item paid for letters per post oo oi oo
Sum is o5 13 10   [page total] £16 8s 6d

### [p. 31]   Saturday 14 July 1655
Item paid the workmen wages by bill £oi o4s o6d; Item paid for beef
oi o6 oo; Item paid for 16 chickens oo o3 oo; Item returned to London for
my Lady 50 oo oo; Item paid for letters per post oo oo o9; Item paid for
brooms oo oi oo; Item paid Charles upon bill for wages o3 o5 o7
Sum is 56 oo 10

### Saturday 21th of July 1655
Item paid the workmen wages by bill oi oi o6; Item paid the Cater upon
bill o3 18 10; Item paid for cutting four acres of grass oo o6 oo; Item given
the ringers by command oo 10 oo; Item paid for paper & ink oo oi oo;
Item paid for oatmeal 1 bushel oo o5 oo; Item paid for 12 lbs of Callis
sand oo oi o6; Item paid for 6 lbs of chalk oo oo 6; Item paid for a quarter
of a hundred of poor Johns oo o7 oo; Item paid for nine ducks oo o3 o6;
Item paid for 15 geese oo 15 o6; Item paid for 19 chickens oo o4 2; Item
paid for a calf's haunch oo oo 10; Item paid Balche's nurse for one month
oo o6 o8; Item paid Croyde's wife for chickens oo o2 o6; Item paid for
chickens oo o3 oo
Sum is o8 o6 o6   [page total] £64 7s 4d

### [p. 33]   Saturday 28 July 1655
Item paid the workmen wages by bills £oi o2s ood; Item paid the Cater by
bill o3 17 o9; Item paid for two couple of rabbits oo o2 oo; Item paid for
treacle oo oo o6; Item paid Myles by bill for going to *Bannton* oo o7 o6;
Item paid [for] charcoal 5 bushels oo o2 o6; Item paid for ten chickens
oo o2 o2; Item paid James Gloyne in part of his bill 10 oo oo; Item paid
Peter Rowe for horse meat by bill oi o2 oo
Sum is 16 16 o5

### Saturday 4 *August* 1655
Item paid the workmen wages by bill oi o4 oo; Item paid the Cater upon
bill o2 oi o2; Item paid Ann Mullyns for 9 days work oo oi o6; Item paid
for horsemeat at the Bell in Barnstaple o2 oo oo; Item paid for eggs
oo oo o6; Item paid for Avis Starling for 12 days wages oo o5 oo; Item
paid for brooms oo oi o6; Item paid for two young curlews oo oi oo
Sum is o5 14 o8

**Saturday 11 *August* 1655**

Item paid the workmen wages by bill 01 00 04; Item paid the Cater upon bill 03 08 02; Item paid Steeven for his wages by command 04 00 00; Item paid James Gloyne the carrier by bill 10 00 00; Item paid the locksmith upon bill 01 00 00; Item paid for two bushels and half of peas 00 12 06; Item paid for making two acres and half of hay 00 10 00
Sum is 20 11 00   [page total] £42 12s 1d

**[p. 35]   Saturday 18th of August 1655**

Item paid the workmen wages by bill £01 00s 02d; Item paid the Cater upon bill 02 15 11; Item paid for cutting 15 acres of grass in *Roston* [Rolleston] meadow at 1s 8d per acre 01 05 00; Item paid the rat-catcher for killing rats 01 00 00; Item paid for letting of Ned's blood 00 02 06; Item paid for a basket of pears 00 01 00; Item paid for fowl 00 05 00; Item paid Balche's nurse one month 00 06 08; Item paid Simon Tolsell for 3 weeks 00 12 06; Item paid for eggs 00 06 06
Sum is 07 09 03

**Saturday 25 *August* 1655**

Item paid the workmen wages by bill 01 10 00; Item paid the Cater by bill 01 17 03; Item paid Thomas Leg for two heifers bought the last year 07 05 00; Item paid for culm 00 05 00; Item paid for tobacco pipes for my Lord 00 01 00; Item paid for paper and ink 00 01 06; Item paid Ann Mullyns for one quarter teaching three girls 00 08 00; Item paid Cilly Balch for making hay 00 11 06; Item given Mr Giffery by command 00 10 00; Item paid for letters per post 00 00 09; Item paid Dobb by bill for bringing wine 00 14 06; Item paid for fowls 00 05 00; Item paid Alice Delbridge for five months for Jonathan 02 00 00
Sum is 15 09 06   [page total] £22 18s 9d

**[p. 37]   Saturday first of Septemb. 1655**

Item paid the workmen wages by bill 01 05 00; Item paid the Cater by bill 04 07 10; Item paid Mr Delbridge in part of £50 20 00 00; Item paid Simon Collyns for wages 00 04 06; Item paid John Hobbs for a hundred of soap 01 11 00; Item paid Pitt for so much given to the poor 00 01 00; Item paid for a pair of gloves 00 01 00
Sum is 27 04 04

**Saturday 8 Sept. 1655**

Item paid the workmen wages by bill 01 03 08; Item paid the Cater upon bill 01 11 06; Item paid for a bottle of tent 00 02 04; Item paid for a weigh of coal 02 00 00; Item paid for mending the billiard table 00 01 00; Item paid for mending the setting nets 00 01 06
Sum is 05 00 00

**Saturday the 15th**

Item paid the workmen wages by bill 01 06 04; Item paid the Cater by bill 05 01 10; Item paid Avis Gooscott for wages & haymaking 00 06 08; Item paid Balche's nurse for one month 00 06 08; Item paid for a pair of stockings for Nick 00 00 09; Item paid for bringing home a weigh of coal 00 03 06; Item paid Avis Starling for haymaking 00 06 00; Item paid Ned Lyddon upon bill 00 13 02
Sum total 08 06 11   [page total '£36 11s 3d' crossed through] £40 11s 3d

**[p. 39]   Saturday 22 Sept. 1655**
Item paid the workmen wages by bill £01 05s 08d; Item paid the Cater by bill 04 19 03; Item paid for cutting turfs for the butts 00 02 06; Item paid Penrose for expense at Bideford 00 00 06; Item paid for the excise for hops for my Lord 00 12 00; Item paid my Lady 10 00 00; Item paid Huxtable the smith 05 00 00; Item paid Mr Jeffery by command 00 10 00; Item paid for curing the roan nag of the farcin 00 05 00; Item paid for brooms 00 02 08; Item paid for twine to sew hop bags 00 01 00
Sum is 22 18 07

**Saturday the 29th of September 1655**
Item paid the workmens wages by bill 00 17 02; Item paid the Cater upon bill 04 01 07; Item paid for two capons 00 05 00; Item paid Jo: Williams in full of all accounts 09 01 06; Item paid Mr Bold by command 05 00 00; Item paid for knitting the fishing nets 0 09 02; Item paid Mr Humes the schoolmaster for two years teaching Jonathan due at All. next 02 00 00; Item paid him more for two year teaching him to write 00 16 00; Item paid for paper 00 01 00; Item paid the wood-cleaver for 5 days 00 06 08; Item paid Edith Gooscott for wages for her tending Ned and winnowing 00 05 00
Sum is 23 03 01   [page total] £46 1s 8d

**[p. 41]   Saturday 6 October 1655**
Item paid the workmens wages by bill 00 12 06; Item paid the Cater's bill 05 11 06; Item paid the apothecary for 13 ounces of the syrup of Gilleflowers 00 06 00; Item paid Mrs Baker of Barnstaple in part of her accounts 40 00 00; Item paid for figs and other things for my Lord's use 00 01 00; Item paid for letters per post and from *Exon* 00 01 06; Cloppery mills   Item paid Mr Hearder for the poor of *Moulton* the last year 00 10 00; Item paid for 3 months rates 05 07 00; Item paid for 150 foot of boards for the withdrawing room planching 01 00 00
Sum is 53 10 00

**Saturday 13 October 1655**
Item paid the workmen wages by bill 00 09 00; Item paid the Cater upon his bill 02 12 04; Item paid for twelve chickens 00 05 00; Item paid Mr Morcham for his fee 00 08 00; Item paid for mending my Lady's gold fork 00 02 06; Item paid for ten bushels of oats 00 18 04; Item paid for a letter per post 00 00 06
Sum is 04 15 08   [page total] £58 5s 8d

**[p. 43]   Saturday 20 Octob. 1655**
Item paid the workmen wages by bill £00 14s 00d; Item paid the Cater upon bill 03 08 05; Item delivered my Lady for my Lord 50 00 00; Item more delivered my Lady 10 00 00; Item paid Thom Cooman in part of his wages 00 10 00; Item paid Ramson for his expenses at *Banton* 00 05 06; Item paid the hop pickers by bill 04 02 06; Item paid Pauline Meane by bill 00 18 04; Item given more by command for &c [sic] 00 10 00; Item paid Balche's nurse for one month 00 06 08; Item paid Honor Croyde for hay-making &c 00 05 00; Item paid for binding young Balch apprentice 02 00 00; Item paid for ten bushels of oats 01 00 00; Item paid for fresh fish and oysters 00 04 02; Item paid for 9 chickens 00 03 00; Item paid for

veal and calf's feet oo o1 10; Item paid for ten bushels of oats oo 18 06;
Item paid Mr George Shurte in full of all o8 oo oo; Item paid for mending
the kettle oo o2 oo; Item paid for deal boards o1 16 oo
Sum is 85 o5 11

[p. 45]  **Saturday 28 October 1655**
Item paid the workmen wages by bill £oo o8 o4; Item paid the Cater upon
bill o6 o8 o5; Item paid for ten bushels of oats o1 o1 o8; Item paid for four
woodcocks oo o1 o8; Item paid for crying the goods oo oo o6; Item paid
for 4 bushels of oats oo o8 oo; Item paid for 14 bushels of oats o1 o8 oo;
Item paid for six halters oo o1 o6; Item paid Mr Lovett for so much
returned Mr Peyton by Doctor Wyld 12 o3 oo; Item paid Ramson for
expenses on the pig drivers oo o1 oo; Item paid more for deal boards
oo 10 oo; Item Mr Loosmore by command in part of £21 o5 oo oo; Item
paid Alice Wood for 120 lbs of sugar o6 oo oo; Item paid for brooms
oo o1 o6; Item paid Besse Terry for harvest work oo o3 ooo; Item paid for
12 chickens oo o3 oo; Item paid for cloth for a jelly bag oo o1 oo; Item
paid Mr Selden in full of all accounts 16 15 oo; Item paid him more for
Mr Pyke for wine 24 17 oo; Item paid for culm oo 17 oo; Item paid
Mr Delbridge in full of all accounts 31 15 oo; Item paid Mr Rowe in full
o1 18 oo; Item paid for matting and cord oo 14 oo; Item paid for mending
the highways oo 12 oo; Item paid Lawrence Berry by bill oo o4 oo; Item
paid the huntsman for his wages o1 o5 oo
Sum is 113 16 o7

Sum total of my disbursements in this book is £1476 9s od

*[The following pages are reversed and are preceded by a page of misc.
sums.]*

[p. 56]  Tawstock 1654 Received for all the household expense and other
defrayment of the right honorable the Countess Dowager of Bath, from
Audit 1654 until

per Rich Pollard

*First* remain due to my Lady upon my last year's account £o19 o1s o6d;
Recd from Mr Cobb by my Lady's command 266 oo oo; Recd from
Mrs Baker upon a bill of epc. by my Lady's command o59 o4 o2; Recd
from my Lady by Mr Cobb o12 11 o6; Novemb. 14   Recd from my Lady
by Mr Cobb o50 oo oo; Recd from my Lady to pay Mr Selden in part
o40 oo oo; Recd from my Lady to pay several bills 100 oo oo; Recd for
one seam of apples oo o5 o2; Recd for one seam of apples ooo o6 o3; Recd
for one seam of apples ooo o5 o9; Recd of Miles Kinge for half hundred of
new hops at £7 5s *for a hundred* oo3 12 o6; Recd of Mary White for 29 lbs
of new hops oo1 17 o6; Recd of Will Britton for half hundred of new hops
at £7 5s *for a hundred* oo3 12 o6; Recd from Mr Hyll for 34 lbs of the last
year's hops at 1s 6d per lb oo2 11 oo; Recd from Mr Cooke for three
hundred and ten pounds of new hops at £7 *for a hundred* o21 12 o6; Recd
of Joseph Ley for 8 lbs of new hops ooo 10 o8; Recd for one seam of
apples ooo o5 oo; Recd for a parcel of welgars oo1 19 oo; Recd of John
Gread of Barnstaple for 200 of hops at £7 per 100 o14 oo oo; Item Recd

for six hogsheads of cider at 12s the hogshead 003 12 00; 5 January 1654
Recd of Mr Wyatt by my Lady's order 110 00 00; Recd from my Lady to
pay Jo: Hamblyn 024 00 00   [total] £735 07 0d

[p. 54]   12 Jan.   Recd from Mr Wyatt £39 00s 00d; Recd for tithe corn as
by account 46 00 04; 27 Jan.   Recd for two bushels of wheat 00 08 00;
Recd for the rent of the little island belonging to the north marsh
01 10 00; Recd for one seam of apples 00 05 06; Recd for one seam of
apples 00 06 02; Recd for one seam of apples 00 06 04; Recd from
Mr John Gread of Barnstaple in full for 400 3qr 21 lbs of hops at £7
20 08 04; Recd for half a bushel of wheat 00 02 00; Recd for two seams of
apples 00 15 06; Recd for two seams of apples 00 13 00; Recd for two
bushels of wheat 00 08 00; 30 *March* 1655   Recd of Mr Wyatt for
Mr Peyton 03 00 00; Recd for two bushels of wheat 00 08 06; Recd for six
bushels of wheat 01 06 00; Recd for two pecks of wheat 00 02 02; Recd
for 8 hogsheads of old cider 04 16 00; 13 Apr.   Recd for one oxe
12 00 00; 26 Apr.   Recd for 10 fat lambs 04 00 00; 27 Apr.   Recd for
4 bushels of wheat 00 17 04; Recd for a cow and two calves 04 19 00;
28 Apr.   Recd for one fat oxe 11 00 00; 4 May   Recd for four bushels of
wheat 00 18 04; Recd for one cow & calf 04 04 00; Recd for 3 bushels of
wheat 00 13 09; 11 May 1655   Recd for 6 fat lambs 02 08 00; Recd for
two heifers and calves 07 14 04; Recd for four bushels of wheat 00 17 04;
14 May   Recd for twenty ewes & lambs sold 12 00 00; Recd for one
heifer and calf 03 14 06; Recd for one fat oxe 11 00 00; Recd for 3 young
pigs 00 16 06; Recd for 175 lbs of hemp at 4d & 3d per lb 02 05 00; Recd
for 26 bushels and half of wheat 05 15 02; Recd for 4 bushels of wheat
00 18 00; 26 *June*   Recd of Mr Wyatt 01 10 00

['£197 07s 6d' crossed through] sum is 198 7 6

[p. 52]   6 July   Recd for 6 bushels of wheat £01; 8 July   Recd from
Mr Wyott at several times 05 10 00; Recd of Thomas Hobson in part of
Midsummers quarters rent 09 00 00; Recd for 3 fat oxen sold 32 00 00;
Recd for 3 fat lambs sold 01 04 00; Recd for a parcel of welgars sold
04 00 00; Recd for 350 sheaves of reed 03 10 00; 20 July   Recd from
Mr Wyatt for my Lady's use 05 00 00; Recd from my Lady 25 00 00;
Recd for 3 acres of grass in the marsh 02 08 00; Rec for two acres of grass
there 01 12 00; 3 Aug.   Recd from my Lady by Mr Tho: Prust to pay
John Randle of Barnstaple 25 00 00; More Recd from my Lady by
Mr Cobb 05 00 00; Recd from my Lady to pay the carrier 10 [obscured by
ink]; Recd from my Lady by Mrs Rachel [obscured by ink]00; 9 Aug.
Recd from my Lady to pay Mr Delbridge in part of his bill of £50   £20 for
to pay Steeven his year's wages £4   24 00 00; 26 Aug.   Recd from
Mr Lynn by order 10 00 00; 30 Aug.   Recd from my Lady 25 00 00;
4 7brs [September]   Recd for one bushel of wheat 00 06 02; Recd for
14 lbs of new hops at Bideford 01 05 08; 11 Sept.   Recd for one bushel of
wheat at Bid. 00 06 04; 12 Sept.   Recd from my Lady to pay for coal
02 00 00; Recd for 6 bushels of wheat at 6s 4d per bushel 01 17 10; Recd
for two bushels of wheat at 6s 10d the bushel 00 13 08; Recd for two
bushels of wheat at 6s 9d *the* bushel 00 13 06; 17 Sept.   Recd for two
bushels of wheat 00 12 08; Recd for two oxen sold 11 18 00; Recd for one
seam of apples 00 02 06; 21 Sept.   Recd for four bushels of wheat

[at] 6s 10d 01 07 04; Recd for four bushels of wheat at 4s 9d 01 07 04; Recd for four bushels of wheat at 4s 10d 01 07 04; 27 Sept. Recd for one bushel of wheat o 06 10; Recd of Dick Britton for 3 cows 14 00 00; Recd from Joseph Ley for 5 calves 07 10 00
[page total] £230 15s 10d　　230 15 10

[p. 50]　28 Sept. Recd from Thomas Ley for four plow oxen sold to him £21 00s 00d; Recd for two bushels of wheat 00 14 08; Recd from Jo: Williams for 420 lbs of old pot mettle at 6d the pound 10 10 00; Recd from Mr Sanders in full of his fine 80 00 00; Recd from Richard Britton for two oxen 11 10 00; Recd from Mr Hearder and Digory Caule of Molton for twelve acres of wood 27 00 00; Recd of Daniel Hill for four bushels of wheat at 7s 4d the bushel 01 09 04; Recd of Mrs Wichalls for nine pounds of hops 00 19 06; ['Recd for two oxen 11 10 00' crossed through] Recd for nine pecks of apples 00 03 09; Recd for 42 lbs of coarse wool 01 05 10; Recd for two seams of apples 00 08 00; Recd from Mr Lovett for ['two' crossed through] one colt 05 02 06; Recd from Mr Lovett for the little wheat mowe 14 00 00; Recd from Mr Lovett for two pack saddles and 3 pair of pots and a pigs trow 01 08 06; Recd of Thomas Ley for old dung pots 00 05 00; Recd from Rich: Britton for the chestnut mare's colt 01 07 00; Recd for 13 great hogs and 4 little ones 12 07 00; Recd of Joseph Ley for two pack saddle trees 00 08 00; Recd of Davy Hill for six pounds of new hops 00 09 00; Recd for one sow pig 01 00 00; Recd for a saddle tree of Mr Nedd 00 05 00; 27 Octob. Recd from my Lady by Mr Cobb 35 00 00; Recd from my Lady by Mr Cobb 37 07 05; Recd from Mr Drake of Barnstaple for 300 3qrs of new hops at £8 per *hundred* 30 00 00
[page total] 312 02 00

[p. 48]　Recd for one pack saddle £00 06s 08d; Recd for the great bull and boar 05 10 00; Recd for one pack saddle 00 06 00; Recd for one pack saddle 00 04 06; Recd of Tho: Penrose for both herriots 02 15 00
[total] £9 2s 2d

Sum total of my receipts in this book is £1475 14s 6d
Recd for hides and sheeps skins since the audit 44 £17 6s 7d

# London Household Accounts

## Expenses, 1642–1647

### KENT ARCHIVES OFFICE, U269/A518/1

*The book measures 8" by 12" and has a paper cover marked 'A Book of all receipts and payments made by William Lynn for the right honorable the Earl of Bath since the 25th of May 1642'. There are a further five pages of estate fines which have not been edited.*

[p. 1]  May the 25th 1642.  Item paid the sub sheriff of Somerset his agent the fee for allowing my Lord's Creation money £0 16s 8d; for paper parchment and wax oo oo 8; May 26 to Mr Thomas Pollard to account for 5 oo o; To Sam: to buy him a pair of shoes and stockings o o7 6; to Mr Isbell and Mr Ursley at my Lord Brad: house 1 oo o; to the fishmonger from the 14th of May to the 28th 2 o3 6; to the poulterer for the same time by bill 1 o4 6; to the butter woman for the same time 1 o1 9; to the cook upon 3 little bills o 1o 9; to Ro: Wood upon 2 bills for wine 1 o1 o; to him for 6 lbs of candles o o2 1o; to him for washing 2 dozen of napkins o oo 7; to little Ned to bear his charges down to *Tawstocke* o o8 o; to Mrs Scott for 2 barrels of beer at my Lord Bruder o 12 o; to her which she paid for sweet oranges o o1 o; for water spent in the house o o1 3; to Teig in earnest for carrying the dung away o oo 6; my own journey down in Lent o o9 o; my journey to London this May o o7 6; to goodwife Hall for Ned Lewin &c 3 oo o; to goodwife Redhead o 1o o; to the farrier for dressing your Honour's mare o o9 6; to myself for a year ending last Easter 20 oo o; more to Mr Pollard to account for 5 oo o; my charges down at Whitsuntide o o4 o  [total] 44 12 6

my charges to London in June o o2 o; to Tho: Armsby in part of £2 1os for wages due at our Lady Day 2 oo o; for a horse to carry me down at Whitsuntide your Ladyship had mine o 12 o; to Ja: Br: for Midsummer 1642 2 oo o; for my board wages from the last of June to the 9th of July o 15 o; my charges down to *Glathorne* this July o o5 o; for horse hire to carry me down then o 1o o; for my mare's grass 8 nights in London o o4 8; my own charges into Devonshire in Octo. 1642 with Thom: Armsby & returning to London with James & Armsby as by bill 4 18 1o  [total] 11 8 o  [page total] 56 oo 6

[p. 2]  To the carrier for having them 2 hackney horses to London £0 o6s od; for your honour's watch mending & a new crystal o o8 o; to Ja: Br: which he spent before he left London 1 1o o; to your Ladyship in gold the 1oth of November 1642 4 1o o; to the farrier in part of his old bill of £6 4s 2d 2 oo o; to Mr Price the shoemaker in part of £7 11s on 3 bills 2 oo o; to my Lady Conyer's footman o o2 o; to my Lord Mayor's servant about the coach horses o o5 o; to the ostler for the horses at the taking them o oo 4; to the paver in further part of £25 9s 1od for paving the street being 556 yards 200 foot £18 1os paid before 4 oo o; for an order out of the Parliament about your Honour's coach horses going into the Tower o 14 6; Mr Barry and my dinner that day o o1 3; going to the Tower that day & once before by water o o1 o; for a letter sent to *Tawstocke* then by post o oo 6; to the glasier in full of £4 4s by bill for the new rooms 1 o4 o; 2 pint bottles 6d, aniseed water 1s 1½d o o1 7½; to my Lady Bradenell's housekeeper for washing of linen when your Honour was gone to *Yorke* o o8 7; 13 of Octo. to Mr Pollard to buy hay and straw against your Honours coming to London 3 oo o; to the poor with your Ladyship 2d, 3 books then 3d oo oo 5; to the carrier for my geldings going down o o3 o [page total] 20 16 2½ 20 16 2½

Sum total disbursed from the 25th of May 1642 until the 22th of No. following 76 16 8½

And rec. in the same time as appears at the other end of this book 70 oo o So rem. due to Will: Lynn on this account 6 16 8½

[p. 3] To Mr Browne for £200 for 6 months due the 23th of November 1642 £8 oos od; to Mr Linton the scrivenor o 1o o; my horse in London 4 nights before I went into Devon o o6 o; to a tailor for mending Jo: Burke's clothes &c o o4 2; for a proclamation from the Close Committee for your horses 1 oo o; for a pass for your servants to go into Devon o o5 o; for going by water then 3 times o o1 6; a letter by post from Mr Wyatt 5 Decem. o o1 o; to Mr Barry by bill 1 o7 o; to Tho: Armsby his wages in full for Michas. 1642 3 oo o; to your Honour to carry to the Tower 6 Decem. put into gold 1o oo o; to the paver in full of his bill for paving 2 19 o; to the farrier in further part of his old bill of £6 4s 2d 2 oo o; for an Ebony box 1 1o o; to Mr Keene the joiner in part of £9 9s 3d by bill 6 oo o; to the poor at the gate 3d, 2 books 4d o oo 7; to the ostler in Friday Street for your coach gelding o oo 6; for the dung carrying away o 12 o; for 5 pamphlets to the Tower o oo 5; for my dinner when I attended about the horses o o1 o; for a pass from my Lord Mayor for Mr Pollard o o1 o [total] 37 19 2

Sum total disbursed from the 22th of Novem. 1642 to the 28th of Decem. following £37 19s 2d

And due to Will: Lynn on the other side 6 16 8½ [total] 44 15 10½ Rec. in the same time as appears at the other end of this book 30 oo o so remains due to Will: Lynn on this account the sum of 14 15 10½

[p. 4] 1642 Novem. 1 To Mr Bourcher for Midsummer last £1o oos od; to Mr Thomas Pollard to pay a debt borrowed 1o oo o; to Anne Howard due at Midsummer last 4 oo o; to Edward Barry his ½ year's wages due at Michas. last 5 oo o; to Mrs Voyceine her year's wages due at Michas last 1o oo o; to Mrs Baldwin the like 1o oo o; to Roger his year's wages now due 4 oo o; to Mr Thomas Pollard to pay the butcher due last August 8 o9 6; to him that day upon his book for the house 5 1o 6; ['due £1o more to him' crossed through] to Robert Woode in full for wages then due £5 oo o; 1oo o o to Mr Murry his Michaelmas quarter rent 28 oo o; to the coachmaker in part of £27 os 3d due to him upon his bills till the 16th of

April 1642 10 00 0; to Mr Dunterfeild in part of £61 3s 6d due to him
9 10 0; to him in full of his old bills before the 1 of April 1642 20 10 0; to
Mr King in part of £100 18s 3d due to ['the' crossed through] him the 27th
of December 1641 20 00 0; for 7 yards of livery cloth by him at 12s
4 04 0; to Mr Tho: Pollard upon his book for the house 24 19 9½; to my
Lady for their honours' expenses at the Tower 10 16 2½; 100 0 0
Decem. 19 to your honour in gold 100 00 0; to Mr Barrow in part of
£33 4s 5d remaining due by bill 20 00 0; to Mr Pasmore in part of £66 due
by bill 20 00 0; to Mr Becke the brewer in part of £22 19s by bill 20 00 0;
to Mr Tho: Pollard for a year's wages due Michas. last 10 00 0; 24. to
him upon his book for the house 35 00 0; to the tower to pay the cook
and others there 20 00 0; 27. to Mr Pollard on his book for the house
10 00 0; to the Tower that day for Mr Sherbourne in full of £22 40s for
lodging there 11 10 0; To Mr Cowes my Lord's keeper then 5 00 0; to the
cook there then on his book 4 00 0; to the coachmaker in further part of
his said bill 10 00 0; to the mason in full of all his work by bill 5 15 0; for
11 pair of pistol cases by bill 3 06 0; to 13 prisons at Christmas by their
box carriers 1 12 0; to the farrier in full of his bill till Michaelmas last
2 4 0; to another farrier whilst the horses was in St Barthol: 0 10 0; to
Price the shoemaker in further part of his old bills 3 00 0; due to me upon
my account ending the 28th of December 1642 as appears on the other side
of this leaf 14 15 10½ [page total] 296 12 10½

[p. 5] Decem. 31 1642 To Will: Lynn upon Mr Pollard's book for the
house £3 07s 1½d
Sum total disbursed from the last day of October 1642 unto the last day of
December following out of the monies recd from Mr Rich: Polla: as
appears £500 00s 0d
Recd in the same time from Mr Richard Pollard and Mrs Hardwicke
as appears amongst the receipts at the other end of this book the sum
of 500 00 0
And so the accounts is [sic] even.

January 16th for a cornelian ring & crystal pendants for your Ladyship
£00 14s 0d; to Rose Todd in full of her wages 02 05 0; to the cook in full
of his wages due at Christmas 07 00 0; to him that he laid out coming
from Devonshire 00 19 6; to the cook in full of his book laid out at the
Tower from the 22th of December unto the 14th of January 08 08 0; to
Price the shoemaker in full till the 18th of Janu. 04 05 00; to the armourer
in full till Midsummer last 01 10 0; to the embroiderer in full for your
Honours furniture 01 15 0; 18th. to your honour in gold 100 00 0; to
your honour to use for expenses at the tower 20 00 0; to Mr Anderton the
tailor in full 01 08 0; to Darby the joiner in full of his bill 04 00 0; to
Keene the joiner in full for wainscoting your Honours house 03 09 0; to
the sadler in part of ['14' crossed through] £15 4s 10d by bill 05 00 0; to
the coachmaker in full til 16th of April 1642 07 00 0; to Mrs Tarry by bill
and for spirit of balm 01 08 6; to Mrs Voyceine then which she laid out
00 01 0; to your Honour then 02 00 0; to Mr Bold then which he laid out
00 10 0; to my Lord in silver by your Ladyship to the Tower 01 00 0; to
Goodwife Bradshaw by Jesep for last Mich. 01 00 0 [?total] 173 13 6; to
Mr Bracy the sempster in full by bill 00 19 0; 21th to Mrs Baldwin in full

of a debt under your Honours hands 46 09 0; to Mr Ager the body maker
in full of his bill 01 06 0; to Mr Prust which he spent lying at *Abington*
[Abingdon] one night oo 03 8; 24. to Mr Pasmore in part of £46 due on
his bill 10 oo 0; to Mr ['Cath' crossed through] Kinge in part of his whole
debt of £124 2s 1d due till the first of January 1642 10 oo 0; to Mr Tatt in
part of his bill of £50 7s 6d 10 oo 0; to Mr Clarke in part of his bill of
£26 12s 6d ending the 7th April 10 oo 0 [total] 88 17 8 [page
total] 262 11 2

[p. 6] 1642 To Lewie the painter in part of his bill of £15 5s od
£5 os od; to Will: Lynn for Michas. 1642 10 0 0; to Sanders the porter his
year's wages due last Midsummer 1 o 0; to the paver for paving the
gatehouse new and for mending the coach house yard by bill 2 9 0; to
your Ladyship to pay for pins &c 1 o 0; 31 Janu. to your Ladyship in
money 7 o 0; to Mrs Voyceine by your Ladyship's appointment 3 o 0;
1 Febru. to Mr Becke the brewer in full till last April 2 19 0; *at the same
time* to Mr Murry his quarter's rent for my Lord's buildings due at
Christmas last the great House £25 th'other 25 o 0; Janu. 28th to Will:
Lynn upon Mr Pollard's book for the house 15 15 3¾; Febru. 11 to my
Lady to the Tower which Mr Beaple paid 35 o 0; 11 to Will: Lynn upon
Mr Pollard's book for the house 15 15 3¾; to your Ladyship for the
Tower by Mr Prust 10 o 0; for a coat for Mr William Fane's first child
o 16 0; for petticoats and other appurtenances o 17 0; for 3 combs for your
Ladyship o 6 0; to Lewie the painter in further part of his bill 5 o 0; for an
order out of the house of Commons o 6 8; March 9th to your honour in
gold by Mr Hoare 40 o 0; to Mr Bradborne in full for gloves by bill 2 o 0;
10th to Will Lynn upon Mr Pollard's book due for the house 20 1 2¾;
for three new bits 8s; for lining 3s; for curbs 1s o 12 0; 17th Item paid
the last payment of the 4 Royal subsidies Mr Marrie paid which he must
allowish 25s 6 5 0; to Mrs Voyceine to give to Joyce o 10 0; [March] 29
1643 to Mrs Serborne ['for' crossed through] in full of £30 for 12 weeks
for my Lord's lodgings in the Tower at £2 10s the week ['th' crossed
through] £22 16s being paid out of the ['money' crossed through] £45
formerly d[elivere]d to my Lady for the Tower 7 4 0; £22 4s od the rest
of that £45 was disbursed by my Lady as followeth to my Lord 26 of Feb.
£1, to the cook the 4th of March £10, to Mr Jarvis £1, to the cook the 20th
of March £5, to my Lady 10s, to Mrs Sherborne's man and maid £1, for
coals for 12 weeks firing at 5s a week £3, for a barrel and half of beer 9s,
for water in that time 5s o o 0; 31th to your Ladyship to the Tower for
the cook 10 o 0; to your Ladyship to give away on Good Friday 2 o 0;
1 April to Mr Knight for a beaver for my Lord 2 10 0
[page total] 247 17 6

[p. 7] for a pair of roses and 3 yards of pink coloured ribbon for your
Ladyship bought at Mr Gumble-tons £oo 5s 6d; to your honour to the
Tower 7th of April 1643 10 o 0; to Mr Trassell in Paternoster Row for
blue stuff 3 7 6; to the sadler in part of £10 4s 1od by bill 5 o 0; to the
coachmaker in part of his bills since the 16 of April to the 25th of March
1643 amounting to the sum of £48 1s 4d 8 o 0; March 31th 1643 to Will:
Lynn upon Mr Pollard's book due for your house 21 18 3; to Clargis the

farrier in full of his bills till our Lady Day 1643 5 18 0; April the 13th
to Mr Murry his quarter's rent due at our Lady Day last for my Lord's
house & the addition to it 28 oo o; to Mr Dunterfield for 19 yards of silver
lace with 17 ounces at 5s 4 05 0; to him for 30 yards of black lace at
2s 8d a yard 4 oo o; to Mr Bradborne for 12 ounces quarter of gold &
silver lace at 5s 4d 3 04 0; to Mr Trussell for 2 yards ¼ more of the blue
stuff 1 04 6; 17th   to your Ladyship in money at your house in the fields
2 oo o; to Mr Trussell for more stuff bought there by bill 10 09 0; for a
hat for Tho: Bold & a silk & silver band o 15 0; for dressing my Lord's
hat & lining it o 03 0; to Mr Cowes sent by Tho: Irish to the Tower
5 oo o; to Mr Parr your Ladyship's tailor in part of £24 3s 10d due to him
before our Lady Day 1643 by bill 10 oo o; to Mr Bowrcher for Christmas
1642  10 oo o; to Mrs Voyceene for half a year due at our Lady Day 1643
5 oo o; to Mrs Baldwin the like 5 oo o; to Mr Lynn the like 10 oo o; to
Mr Barry the like 5 oo o; to Robert Wood the like 4 oo o; to Richard the
barber the like 2 oo o; to Keepe the Coachman the like 4 oo o; to Tho:
Arnisby the like 2 10 o; to James the Blackamoor the like 2 oo o; to Rose
Todd the like 1 10 o; to Wilmot Toogood the like 1 oo o; to Tho:
Whimper the cook for a quarter then due 4 oo o; for 6 ounces of lace for
your Ladyship's blue waistcoat at 5s 1 10 o; for a yard & half of fine bone
lace 2 10 o   [page total] 183 9 9

[p. 8]   1643 April 21   to your honour to the Tower £50 oos od; to
Mr Bold his half year's wages due last Lady Day 05 oo o; to the clerk of St
Gileses his wages at Easter oo 05 o; to J.B. for Christmas 1642  02 oo o;
for frieze for his suit oo 12 o; for making it up oo 06 5; to goodwife
Redhead o1 oo o; May the 5th   to Will: Lynn upon Mr Pollard's book
due for the house 46 11 3½   [total] 105 14 8½

Sum total disbursed from the last day of December 1642 until the 6th day
of May 1643 is £799 13s 1½d
And rec. in the same time as appears at the other end of this book
£797 15s 6½d
So rem. due to Will: Lynn this day £1 17s 7d

May the 20th   to Will: Lynn upon Mr Pollard's book due for your house
12 5 11½; 20   to Mr Thomas Pollard then to account for 10 oo o; 20   to
your honour to the Tower the same day 50 oo o; to the painter in full for
colouring the wainscot in the great chamber drawing room & the other
1 02 o; to the nurses & midwife at Henry Lynn's christening 1 10 o; to
Mr Evans the shoemaker in part of £4 os 6d per bill 2 oo o; going to the
Tower and thence to Westminster by water o 2 o; the £50 above charged
to my Lady to the Tower the 21th of April 1643 was disbursed there as
followeth to Mrs Ann Howard £4, to the cook on his book 22 April £6, to
him the 29 of April £10, to my Lady Westmorland's nurse & midwife £2,
to the cook 16th of May £5, to Mrs Sherborne for 8 weeks lodging in her
house in the Tower due the 9th of May but paid the 19th £10, to the cook
in full of his book to the 27th of May £9 os o½d & d[elivere]d then to
account for £3 19s 4½d oo oo o; to Sir Peter Temple's groom oo o2 o; to
his coachman oo o2 6; to your Honour the 7th of June oo 10 o; to

Mr Ridger the scrivenor his fee for the continuance of Mr Browne's 200
due 23th of May oo 10 o; to Mrs Dell's maid to go for my Lord Denby
oo o1 o; going by water about the horses oo o1 o; to my Lady Veare's
coachman at my Lord Westmoreland oo o1 o; for the dung carrying away
in March oo o7 o   [page total] 80 12 o½

[p. 9]   to Seaton for going to Staines about the horses which Sir Arthur
Hasebrigg took away from your Honour £o 5s od; to a man made an elegy
upon Mr Shaite's death o 2 6; to your Ladyship for 4 ounces of rose
powder o 2 o; your Honour going by water from the Tower to
Westminster o 1 o; my going from Westminster then by water o o 6; for
an order from the Lords about your Honour's keeping in your lodgings in
the Tower o 14 6; for going twice to Westminster by water about then &
your horses o 1 o; for an order of the 20th of June from the house of
Lords about your Honour's horses o 14 6; the £50 charged to my Lady to
the Tower the 20th of May was disbursed there as followeth to
Mr Browne 4th of June for £200 due the 23th of May £8, to your
Ladyship that day £2, to the cook the 3 of June £5, to Mr Pollard the 7th
of June for the house £10, the 11th of June to send Mr Bold £10, to the
cook the 20th of June £5, to Mrs Sherborne the 22th of June for a month
for her lodgings in her house in the Tower due the 6th of June £5, to
Mrs Jarvis for Midsummer quarter 10s, to my Lady's purse 2s, to the
book-binder for Camden 8s, to the cook the 29th of June £4 o o o; to the
door keep[er] of the Parliament House when Captain Pyle was warned to
appear before the Lords o 2 6; to the Lieutenant of the Tower's coachman
then o 5 o; to the Lady Crooke's coachman then o 5 o; paid for your
Honour's horsemeat and shoeing for 17 days that Captain Pyle had them
2 9 4; to your coachman and groom to drink there o 1 o; to a smith for
mending the lock & ironwork about the back gates that the soldiers broke
open o 5 o; to the carpenter for his work about them o 5 o; to the
churchwardens of St Gileses for their levy for my Lord's house for the
year 1642 ending last Easter o 10 o; to Mr Bourcher for books by bill
o 8 o; to Toby for a barge to *Greenewich* o 15 o; June 29th   to
Mr Pollard upon his book for the house 18 o o; to the cook to the Tower
that day 5 o o; for a paper of long pins o o 6; for a gray stone horse 8 o o;
for a pad and furniture 2 3 o   [page total] 40 10 4

[p. 10]   July the 6th 1643   2 letters sent by post one to Mr Hind the
other to *Tawstocke* £o 1s od; a pair of puff roses for your Ladyship o 3 o;
a worm for a pistol 3d, 2 bands Jack Burke 2s 9d o 3 o; for a male pillion
& straps & 2 old mail girths o 1 o; to bear Burke's charges o 10 o; for a
mail to carry clothes in o 8 o; for Burke's cloak altering by bill o 3 8; a
pair of boots for him 5s 6d, a pair of spurs 10d o 6 4; to the beadle of St
Gileses his midsummer quarter wages o 2 6; for going by water to the
Tower with Mrs Voyceine o 1 o; to Mr Bold £1, a rapier for him £1 8s, a
gauntlet for him 10s 2 18 o; to John Burke & Tho: Irish laundress for
Midsummer quarter o 10 o; for the dung carrying out 10th July o 4 o; to
Mr King for Mr Bold to buy cloth for his suit 6 o o; 14th   to the cook in
full of his book for expenses at the Tower 8 12 o; to him to account for
4 8 o; to a boy brought a key from Oxford o o 6; to Mr Ward which he

paid to an apothecary in *Fanchurch* street o 10 o; 15th to your Honour
to the Tower the 15th of July 40 o o; to Mr Coleman for Tho: Bold for
3 months now ended 3 o o; 17th to Mr Becke the brewer in part of
£23 11s due to him the 28th of May by bill appears 10 o o; to the
collectors of the poor of St Gileses for Midsummer quarter o 10 o; 2 letters
to Wantage & one from thence o o 6; a letter printed at Oxford 6d,
2 other books 4d o o 10; for 2 grosse & half of pick tooths o 2 o;
24th for an order of the house of Lords upon by Lord's petition for
liberty to go to the *Spawe* [Spa] o 14 6; for a scarf for Mr Bold 3 10 o;
25 to the water woman for helping Wilmot to wash o 5 o; 25 to
Mr Bowdler the coachmaker in further part of his bill of £48 1s 4d of
which there was £8 paid and now paid him 5 o o; *at the same time* to
Mr Pasmore in part of £30 due on his bill 5 o o; *at the same time* to
Mr Barrow in part of £13 4s 5d remaining due on a bill 5 o o; to the clerk
of St Martins in the fields on the fast day o 2 o; 27th to Mr Evans the
shoemaker in full on 2 bills 2 4 6; *at the same time* to Mrs Pecke due the
12th of July 12 o o; for 6 gallons of white muscadine & a runlet &c 1 14 o;
a quire of paper to the Tower 4d, to the poor 2d o o 6; my Lady's watch
mending o 1 o [page total] 114 7 4

[p. 11] for a picture 4d; a declaration 8d; my Lord's spectacles men. 4d
£0 1s 4d; by water to & from the Tower in 3 days 4 times o 4 o; gilt paper
for my Lord a quire by Tho: Irish o o 9; Augu. 3 for an order to release
my Lord out of the Tower o 14 6; to the clerk that writ it o 2 6; to Sir Jo:
Conyer's Lieutenant of the Tower which he claimed as his fee for my
Lord's commitment & for composition for furniture 100 o o; more to him
which he claimed as due to him for my Lord being freed from his diet for
41 weeks at £2 per week 82 o o; to his clerk o 10 o; to Mr Cowes then £15
being paid him before he being my Lord's keeper during his imprisonment
2 o o; to the Warders of the Tower 3 o o; to Mrs Sherborne for her
lodgings for a month and 2 nights ending the 4th of August when my
Lord came out 5 7 o; to Mr Tho: Pollard the 5th of August 20 o o; for
your Lordship's pass from the house of Lords for France o 14 6; to
Mr Browne the clerk of the Parliament for his fee upon my Lord's
enlargment 3 6 8; to Mr Throgmorton his fee for the same 1 o o; to his
clerk that drew the pass o 1 o; for my pass to go to Wantage o 1 o; spent
at *Maidonhead* supper &c on Monday o 3 o; for horsemeat there o 2 o; at
Dorchester dinner and horses o 4 o; at Oxford spent on Tuesday o 1 1; a
pass there to Wantage o o 6; at *Abington* Tuesday supper and Wednesday
dinner o 5 o; horses there then o 3 2; the ferry 10d, shoeing horses 1s 6d,
another pass 6d o 2 10; Tho: Armsbies diet from Wednesday till Monday
o 4 o; my diet there in that time o 6 6; horsemeat there for 2 horses in that
time o 16 o; spent coming to London o 2 6; for 2 horses hire for 8 days
1 12 o; a coach for Mrs Porter to Bishopsgate o 2 o; to Westminster by
water for my Lord's pass into France o o 6; for my Lord Mayor's pass
2s 6d, to Mr Phillips there 1s o 3 6; the £40 charged to my Lady to the
Tower the 15th of July was disbursed there as followeth to Mrs Sherborne
for a month £5, paid 20th July to Mr Cowes then £5, to the cook £10, to
Mr Barre £1, to my Lady £1, to Mr Lynn the rest being £18 which is
charged in this book as a receipt o o o [page total] 223 12 10

[p. 12]   Sum total disbursed from the 6th of May 1643 until the 6th of
August following is £459 2s 6½d
And rec. in the same time as appears at the other end of this book
£458 os od

So rem. due to Will Lynn upon this account as appears £1 2s 6½d;
the 17 of Augu. to your honour when you went from London
towards France 30 0 0; to Tho: Whimper the cook for his wages due
Midsummer quarter 4 0 0; to Keepe the coachman the like 2 0 0; to
Wilmot to give away 0 10 0; to Mr Bradbourne for gloves for your
Ladyship 2 15 0; 3 hoods for your Ladyship 0 12 0; 3 pair of gloves for
my Lord 0 11 0; 3 laces for your Ladyship 0 2 6; to Mr Bale for my
Lord's garters & roses 2 13 6; to Mr Coleman in full then for teaching
your Ladyship 1 00 0; to him then for viol strings 0 09 0; to Mr Phillips
when he went out of town with your Honours 0 10 0; to the poor at the
gate then 1 0 0; to the cook in full of his book at the Tower 0 5 0; paid
for a pair of shoes for your Ladyship 0 3 6; to the water woman for
helping to wash &c 0 5 0; to a porter to carry things by Mrs Porter's
directions 0 5 2; to a porter to carry linen & pewter 0 6 0; for 4 ounces of
powder for your Ladyship 0 2 0; to the coachman which carried you
which Mr Pollard paid short 0 2 6; to pay the week book in full ending
the day you went away 6 4 0; Augu. 25 to Mrs Bowdler in part of a
remains of £35 1s 4d of the bill delivered at the Annunciation 1643 3 0 0;
to Tho: Irish laundress for a quarter Jo: Burkes 3 weeks 0 5 0; to a man
brought a letter of the 2 of September 0 2 0; for carrying away the dung
the 2 of September 0 1 6; to Will: Decon brought letters 0 2 0; to
Mr Howard in part of ['we' crossed through] [blank] wages due to him
5 0 0; to Seaton to bear his charges to Wantage 0 12 0; to Mr Howard for
a month's board wages for the 17th of Augu. to the 14th of September
2 0 0 [page total] 66 1 8½

[p. 13]   to Tho: Armsby his diet for a week after your Honour went
£0 6s od; Augu. 24 to Tho: Armsby when he went to his wife 0 10 0; for
James his diet for 7 weeks from the 17th of Augu. to the 5 of October at
5s a week 1 15 0; drawing & making an affidavit about my Lady Eliz:
Cope's goods 0 3 6; to the beadles their Michas. quarteridge 0 2 0; to
Mr Cavell in part of his bill of 5 1 10 for my Lord's saddle 2 8 0; to
Mr Evans for 6 pair of shoes for my Lady 0 18 0; to him for one pair of
slippers for my Lord 0 6 0; to James to pay for his passage & bear his
charges to *Oxon* 0 10 0; to Mr Clargis the farrier in part of his bill of
£2 13s 9d 1 2 0; to J.B. for Midsummer last 2 0 0; to his Mother by
15 strike of molt & 4 strikes of barley 2s 6d 2 7 6; to Tho: Armsby in part
of his Michas. wages 2 0 0; Octo. 26 to Mrs Bowdler in part of 32 1 4
remaining of the coachmaker's bill delivered at the Annunciation 1643
5 0 0; 27 to Mrs Cavell in full of an old bill due to her husband 5 4 0; to
her more by bill for my Lord's saddle in full 2 13 0; 30 to Mrs Clargis in
full of all due to her to this day 1 11 0; to Mr Stirril the grocer in full
6 11 0; to Mr Cooke the apothecary in full 1 0 0; 31 to Mr Rosier the
grocer in full 4 18 0; *at the same time* to Mr Moore & Mrs Hix the
apothecary in full 2 19 0; *at the same time* to Mr Shelbury Sir Morris
Willyam's apothecary in full 3 10 0; to Tho: Whimper his wife his

quarter's wages for Michas. 4 0 0; to the collectors of the poor for Michas. quarter 0 10 0; to the paver for mending all the pavement from the Common shower to the gate 84 yards stones & gravel 3 14 0; to Mr Evans for 2 pair of boots & 2 pair of shoes my Lord 2 2 0; to Will Decon that carried some of them 1s, one brought a letter 6d 0 1 6; Novem. 30 to the scavengers for a year ending last Michas. 0 10 0; to Sergeant Rolls his fee about attending the Committee of Sequestration about the goods 1 0 0; for a coach to carry him 3 times 0 3 0; for an order to continue the goods unsold 4 weeks 0 3 0; to Tho: Armsby in full of his Michas. wages 0 10 0; for a copy of the order for my Lord's enlargement 0 3 0; to the clerk of the parish for Christmas 0 6 0; to the beadles for Christmas quarter 0 2 6 [page total] 60 19 6

[p. 14] Decem. 23 to Mr Browne for £200 due 23th of November £8 0s 0d; 26 to Mrs Ann Howard for £100 for a year 8 0 0; 27 to Mrs Bowdler in part of her bill of 27 1 4 2 0 0; to the collecters for the poor for Christmas quarter 0 10 0; to Mr Knight the hatter by bill 1 0 0; to Mr Howard's tailor which must be part of his wages 0 11 0; to Tho: Whimper's wife in part of Christmas quarter's wages 1 0 0; Janu. 6 to Mr Dunterfeild in part of £64 10s 9d due to him 10 0 0; 9 to Mr Hassett in part of his bills & his writs of £9 13s 7d 5 0 0; to the scavengers for Christmas quarter 0 2 6; Item paid for the purple coach beds & picture frame & other things which was part of the wardrobe 3 0 0; to Tho: Armsby more when he came to London when he should have gone with old Saunders but he did not come of 3 weeks after he was gone 0 12 6; for 2 pair of gloves for my Lady of Mr Bradborne 0 4 0; for 3 ounces of hair powder for her Honour 0 1 6; for 2 bunches of viol strings Mr Coleman 0 15 0; Item paid for certain lumber left in the house by inventory by the Sequestrators 4 10 0; to Joan Parker which my Lady Katherine Fane gave to your Ladyship at *Brewerne* [Bruern] 1 0 0; March 4 to Mr Murry his quarter's rent due last Midsummer for my Lord's house and the addition 28 0 0; 4 to Mr Bowdler in part of £25 1s 4d remaining of the coachmakers bills delivered at the Annunciation [16]43 6 0 0; to a porter brought things from Mrs Porter 0 4 0; 1644 April 6 to the collectors for the poor for our Lady Day quarter 0 10 0; to goodwife Readhead she lying very sick 0 5 0; to J.B. for Christmas ['quar' crossed through] last 2 0 0; to his mother for Michas last 1 0 0; to them since Christmas last 8 strikes of molt 1 0 0; to him 2 yards ¼ green cloth last May 1 1 4; to him 2 yards ½ of frieze last December 0 10 10; to him 3 quarters & ½ of French green cloth then 0 12 0 [page total] 87 9 8

[p. 15] to the beadles for our Lady Day quarter 1644 £0 2s 6d; to the scavengers for that quarter 0 2 6; to the beadles for Midsummer quarter 0 2 6; to the scavengers for Midsummer quarter 0 2 0; for repairing the house where it rained in 0 2 0; Augu. 8 to Mr Browne due the 23th of May 1644 8 0 0; 9 to the collectors for the poor for Midsummer quarter 0 10 0; 9 to Mrs Ann Howard due at Midsummer last 4 0 0; 10 to Mr Pecke for £150 which he lent my Lord of Westmorland which your Honours was willing to pay £4 being due about 6 Februa. last & £2 about 6 March 1643 6 0 0; 10 to Mrs Mary Baldwin due the 12th of Janu. 1643 12 0 0; 10 to Mrs Bowdler in part of £19 1s 4d remaining of the

coachmakers bills delivered at the Annunciation 1643  8 o o; for mending
the iron works of the cellar windows o 1 o; for the repairing three
windows by bill o 7 6; for repairing the water tubs o 1 2; Octo. 26  to the
beadles for Michas quarter 1644  o 2 6; to J.B. for Midsummer last 2 o o;
to his mother by 4 strike of barley o 8 o; to his mother for a year at
Michas last 1 o o; to Tho: Armsby when he came to London by my man
3 May o 2 6; to him by myself then at London o 5 o; to him by my man
to bear his charges to Taw. 20 May 1 o o; to his wife then by Joseph
1 10 o; to her by Joseph in August o 5 o; to the collecters for the poor due
last Michas o 10 o; to the scavengers for Michas quarter 1644  o 2 6; for
standing for a trunk of linen 15 months 1 o o; paid for the coach in part
which was taken at Bowdlers 20 o o; Novem. 27  to Tho: Whimper
['more' crossed through] in part of £3 due for wages 1 10 o;
Decem. 21  to Mrs Keepe in part of £2 due to her husband for wages
1 o o; Janu. 18  to Tho: Whimper more in part due to him o 10 o; to the
beadles for Christmas quarter 1644  o 2 o; to Mr Browne due the 23 of
November 8 o o; to Mrs Ann Howard due at Christmas last 4 o o; to Tho:
Whimper in full of £3 due to him 1 o o; 25.  to Keepe's wife in full of £2
due to her 1 o o; to the clerk for Christmas o 6 o; to the collecters for the
poor for Christmas quarter o 10 o; to J.B. for Christmas 1644  2 o o
[page total] 87 15 8

[p. 16]  by Mr Delbrige  2 pair of gloves 5s, 2 hoods a love & ducape 9s
£0 14s od; viol strings 8s 6d, 4 ounces of hair powder 2s o 10 6;
11 March 44  to J.B. in clothes this winter 1 o o; to his mother 12 strikes
of barley 1 10 o  [total] 3 14 6

Sum total disbursed from the 6 of August 1643 until 25 March 1645
306 1 o½
And rec. in the same time as appears at the other end of this book 305 o o
So remains due to Will Lynn upon this account 1 1 o½

27 March 1645  to Colonel Grantham  to Mr Manby that married
Mrs Mary Baldwin for a year ending the 12th of January last for £300
24 o o; to the beadles for our Lady Day quarter o 2 6; to the Collecters
for the poor the like o 10 o; 30  to Mrs Jarvis by direction o 5 o; to
goodwife Readhead o 5 o; for water 2s 8d, & the water woman to help to
wash the linen 2s 6d o 5 2; May 10  paid to the collecters for the first
payment of the monthly tax for Ireland which was taxed upon
Mr Murryes rent which he must allow in part of his rent 1 13 4; to
Mrs Jarvis o 5 o; 15  for mending the casements in the hall & your
Ladyship's chamber o 6 8; June 14  paid to Mr Dunterfeild in part of his
bill of £54 10s 9d 20 o o; 21  paid Mr Kinge in part of £151 os od the sum
of 20 o o; 21  to Mr Murry [blank] 50 o o; 23 to Mr Browne for £200 due
23th of May 8 o o; to him then in part of that 200 principal debt 100 o o;
26  to Mrs Jarvis more o 5 o; 28  to Mrs Bowdler in part of £11 1s 4d
remaining of the coachmakers bills delivered at the Annunciation 1643
6 o o; to the collecters for the poor for Midsummer quarter o 10 o; 28 to
the beadles the like o 2 6; 30  to Mr Linsey Mr Beck's partner in part of
£20 16s due for beer till 12th of August 1643 10 o o; 30  to the collecters
for the weekly tax for Sir Thomas Farefax the first payment it being for

the rent, Mr Murry must allow it out of his rent 2 1 8; to Mr Story in the old Exchange for lace for boot hose when my Lord was in the Tower 1 1 0  [page total] 246 13 10½

[p. 17]  July 3  to Mrs Ann Howard for £100 due at Midsummer 4 0 0; 4  to Mr Hasset & his wife in full by bills 7 0 0; 7  to Mr Cooper the hatter in full 8 15 0; for new covering a great trunk 0 6 0; to J.B. by a quarter of barley his mother £1 & for Midsummer £2  3 0 0; 21  to Mrs Jarvis 0 5 0; 16  to Mr Parr in part of his old bill of £14 3s 10d 10 0 0; Augu. 6 to Mr George Manby by Colonel Grantham for £300 due 12 July last 12 0 0; 28  to Mrs Jarvis at her extreme importunity 0 5 0; 29  to Mr Outen the bricklayer for rep[air]s by bill 1 12 0; Septem. 1 to the collectors for the weekly tax for Sir Thomas Faiorfax the second payment it being for the rent Mr Murry must allow it our of his rent 2 10 0; 17  more to Mr Bowdler in part of his bills 1 0 0; to J.B. to buy him clothes this winter 1 0 0; to his mother for this Michas 1 0 0; to Mrs Jarvis 0 5 0; to the beadles for Michas quarter 0 2 6  [total] 53 0 6

Sum total disbursed from the 25 March 1645 until the last of October following £299 14s 4½d
And rec. in the same time as appears 350 0 0

for a trunk of linen standing & portage 1 0 0; Novem. 27  to Keepe upon Mr Richard Pollard's letter 1 0 0; by Mr Forard  for a large sarsnet hood 4s, a crimson silk lace 3 yards long 6d, 3 ounces of powder 1s 6d 0 6 0; for emptying the little house to Teige 1 0 0; paid in full for the coach taken at Bowdlors 9 0 0; Decem. 17  to the collectors for the weekly tax for Sir Thomas Faiorfax the 3 payment it being for the rent Mr Murry must allow it out of his rent it being [a]ssessed at £100 per *year* for 2 months 6d per pound 2 10 0; to Mrs Jarvis 0 10 0; to the clerk at Christmas his due 0 6 0; to the beadles for Christmas quarter 0 2 6; to the collectors for the poor for 2 quarters 1 0 0  [page total] 16 14 6

[p. 18]  1645 January  21 to Mrs Jarvis £0 5s 0d; 17  to Mrs Ann Howard for 100 due at Christmas last 4 0 0; Febru.  laid out upon a bill sent by George Fraine 7 13 2; more sent by him to the same 0 10 0; for Tho: Armsbyes diet 3 weeks then 0 15 0; to J.B. for Christmas 2 0 0; to him in barley & for his mother 2 0 0; to him to furnish him to a service in clothes 2 0 0; March 17th 1645  to the collectors for 6 months tax for Ireland ending 1 Septem. 1645 for the rent on Mr Murry 1 0 10; 1646 26  to Mrs Jarvis 0 10 0; 31  to the Collectors for the poor for this quarter 0 10 0; to the beadle for this quarter 0 2 6; April 7th  spent that night at a town near *Bagshawe* [Bagshot]; Tuesday dinner 2s, spent at *Rumsie* [Romsey] that night 5s 0 7 0; Wednesday night at *Shasbury* [Shaftesbury] 0 5 0; spent Thursday noon 2s, at night at *Crookhorne* [Crewkerne] 5s 0 7 0; Friday noon at Tiverton & a crupper there 0 2 6; Friday night at *Chinmley* [Chulmleigh] 0 3 0; spent at *Harteland* [Hartland] 1s, shoeing at *Shasbury* [Shaftesbury] 8d 0 1 8; to Tho: Baughton went to Mr Lamb 0 0 6; for an order of the Lords for my Lord to come with the linen 0 14 6; going by water 6d, my horse setting up 3d 0 0 9; for an order of the Lords for the gentleman usher to bring my Lord to the house to put in bail 0 14 6; going by water 6d, 2 comb brushes 6d o 1 o; for 18 yards of coarse ribbon at 2½d o 3 9; April 30   to my Lady at Basingstoke Hodge's heriot 4 10 o, to my Lady then Bauche's heriot 1 10 o, to her Ladyship then which I rec. at *Netherhaven* 7 10 1; May 6   to Mr Pollard upon his book 14 o o; 8   to Mr King for cloth &c for my Lord's clothes 6 o o; for a glass, a screen and a basket by my Lady 3 o o   [page total] 61 2 9

[p. 19]   1646 May 11   to Mr Clarke in full of all due to him £16 oos ood; for half a pound of tobacco for my Lord oo o5 oo; to Mr Pollard upon his week's book 10 oo oo; to Mr Goldsmyth for 4 yards ¾ of flowered tabby o5 oo oo; for 3 papers of long pins oo o3 oo; for a book at Mr Bellamyes oo o1 oo; to Tho: Cannon for helping to furnish the house oo 10 oo; to the glasier by bill o3 o8 oo; to the smith by bill;   [total] 35 13 o

to J.B. for a cloak &c o2 oo oo; for 6 ells of ¾ lockram at 1s 4d for Mrs Killigrew oo o8 oo; 14   to my Lady in money 41 18 o6; *at the same time*   to Will: Lynn in part of £60 due to him 10 oo oo   [total] 89 19 o6

Sum total disbursed from the last of October 1645 until 13th May 1646 £167 16s o9d

And rec. in the same time as appears 167 16 o8½

June 1   to your Ladyship in money by Mr Bold £100 oos ood; to the parish clerk for Easter oo o6 oo; to the poor at St Gyles Church oo o1 oo; for searching for Mrs Pasmore's administration oo o2 oo; to Mr Grigg attorney for advising a course in it oo o5 oo; to the sergeants for arresting her oo 10 oo; for altering the action which the sergeants did mistake oo o4 oo; laid out by Mr Forard when he found the hangings &c oo o2 10; for one to help Cannon 4 days and two weeks 3 days in the stable oo o9 oo; for carrying part of the hired goods to Longlon oo o1 o2; for weeding the court oo o2 oo; to Henry Bradshaw for J.B. diet in part for a qu. o2 oo oo   [page total] 1 o4 o3 oo

[p. 20]   Mr Forard and my dinner at *Maidonhead* [Maidenhead] & horses £oo o2s ood; ferry there 2s, spent at *Redinge* [Reading] 7d oo oo o9; at *Pangborne* [Pangbourne] supper there &c oo o2 o4; horses there and shoeing oo o3 oo; Wantage dinner Tuesday & supper &c oo o6 o6; horses there 4s, shoeing *Reding* 2s, soldiers there 5s oo o1 o2 [sic]; at *Twiford* [Twyford] dinner and horses oo o2 o2; June 2   to Mr King in part of £131 os 2d due to him 10 oo oo; to Mr Webber in part of £6 9s od due of old to him o6 oo oo; to Mr Fox the wax chandler in full due to him o1 15 oo; to Mr Perry in part of £55 due to him £5 being paid more by my Lady to him 20 oo oo; to Mr Reade in part of £45 2s 9d due by bill 10 oo oo; to Mr Browne for £100 for a year due 23th of May o8 oo oo; to Mr Dunsterfeild in part of £34 10s 9d and my Lady paid him £10 more so paid by me 10 oo oo; to Mr Orlibeare in part of £59 os 8d 10 oo oo; 2   to Mr Pollard in full of his book ending 29 May o9 o9 o6; for a velvet bonnet for Mr Wm Fane's son oo o5 oo; for an ell of stuff for Mr Tarrye's child oo o6 oo; the declaration against Mrs Pasmore's 9 sheets oo o6 oo; for 4 ounces of hair powder for your Ladyship oo o2 oo; 4   for 2 letters sent to Wantage & one from thence this day oo oo o6; to Goodwife Redhead by Joseph since Michas oo 10 oo; 6   to your Ladyship by Mr Bold o1 oo oo; 8   to Mr Pollard in full upon his book till 6 June 10 o9 oo; to

Mr Goldsmyth for black satin 01 03 06; to Tho: Armsbye's wife by Joseph since Michas 00 05 00; to Mr Bold upon a bill given to your Ladyship 00 16 03; to Mr Fuller brought a present 00 05 00; 11 to the brewer in full of old until 31 Augu. 1643 10 16 00; for a pewter standidge [*standish*] for my Lord 00 06 04; for pens & ink 4d, a quire of paper 4d 00 00 08; for 2 sugar loaves with 10 lbs ¾ at 20d for conserves 00 17 11; for a dozen of black boxes for Mr Wyatt 00 05 00 [page total] 114 00 07

[p. 21] for sending a letter to Wantage 2d, one from Devon 2d £00 00s 04d; for a letter by the post of Holland from the La: Killigrew 00 00 06; June 16 for a letter by post from *Tawstocke* to the porter 00 00 02; to the collectors for the 6 & 8 months being the 4th payment for Sir Tho: Farfax seized on the rent 01 13 04; *at the same time* to Mr George Manby by Colonel Grantham for £300 due 12th of February last 12 00 00; for repairing the coach, half of it must be reckoned in the price of £25 03 07 00; 17 a letter from Mr Southby 00 00 02; to my Lady to give Mrs Potts 01 00 00; for weeding the court 00 01 04; to Richard Wills to buy sleas [*slays*] & combs &c 00 05 00; for mowing the garden 00 01 00; for a white sarsenet hood by Mrs Pollard 00 04 00; 19 to Mr Bold by your Honour's appointment 50 00 00; *at the same time* to Mr Cobb which he paid for hoods &c 00 16 00; for ingrossing Mr Murrie's lease for the houses 00 06 00; for a set of tablemen & dice 00 01 02; 22 to Mrs Jarvis 00 10 00; for subpoenas for 8 witnesses in the suit with Mrs Pasmore against the trial 00 04 00; *at the same time* to Mr Pollard upon his book ending 19th June 23 13 10½; to Goodwife Redhead for 3 quarters now ended 00 13 0; 23 to her which your Ladyship gave her 00 02 6; to a porter brought the harness & saddles 00 02 0; to one brought the subpoena from Guild Hall 00 00 6; a letter sent to Mr Pollard by post 00 00 06; to the 8 witnesses to appear in Pasmore's suit 00 08 00; for a letter sent to Mr Southby 00 00 02; 26 for a letter sent to Mr Michell 00 00 02; to Mr Carpenter attorney in the suit with Pasmore by bill 01 07 04; to Connon to serve the subpoenas & attend 2 days 00 04 00; *at the same time* for 3 ells of Holland at 14s & 29¼ at 7s 6d 13 01 00; for lace then £2, for a piece of work like a sampler 5s 2 15 00 [page total] 112 18 6½

[p. 22] spent in beer with all the witnesses £00 00s 05d; to the poor in the *Coven* garden 00 00 02; June 27 to the weights of St Giles 00 05 00; to J.B. to buy bands & gloves 00 04 00; to a man at my Lord Fitzwillyams 00 01 00; to Mr Pollard upon his book till 26 June 10 16 01½; July 1 to the collectors for a assessment to the house of correction 00 04 00; for a latitat to arrest Mrs Pasmore 00 04 01; for a warrant 4d, to the sergeants to arrest her 00 00 04; to the paver for repairing the street by bill 02 18 00; 3 for a gray coachhorse bought of one Mr Browne 14 10 00; 6 paid for household stuff by bill 41 11 00; to Colonel Grantham for Mr George Manby for £300 due instant 12 00 00; for bringing that household stuff home 00 01 08; ['for carrying 4 beds &c to *Barbycann* 00 01 06, for 3 rasers [razors] for my Lord by Jo: Burke 00 09 00' crossed through] for 2 pair of shoes for my Lady 00 07 00; 7 for a letter sent by post with several letters in it 00 01 02; for carrying 4 beds &c to *Barbycann* 00 01 06; for 3 rasers for my Lord by John Burke 00 09 00; 14 to

Mr Murry when he sealed the new lease of the house in the fields in part
of £301 2s 6d which is & will be due for rent for the same at Michas next
the sum of 100 00 00; *at the same time*  to Mr Dunsterfeild in full of all
due to him 21 19 00; to Mrs Bourcher she lying in of 2 boys 01 00 00; to
the beadles for their wages due at Midsummer quarter 00 02 06; to a
porter for carrying home a bed 00 00 04; 16  to Mr Pollard in full upon
his week book til 11th July 21 04 03; for a letter from Wantage & one
book & one from Sir F.F. 00 00 06; 17  to Mr Lambe the surgeon for
curing George 01 10 00; 20  to the collectors for the poor for Midsummer
quarter 00 10 00; to Tho: Comon for packing the bedding that was bought
& mending some of them at 2 days 00 03 00; 21  to Mr Kinge in part of
£121 0s 2d due per old bills 20 00 00; for half a pound of tobacco for my
Lord 00 04 06; paid James Fox his bill in full for keeping the old coach for
iron and woodwork 04 11 00  [page total] 254 19 6½

[p. 23]  July *at the same time* for ingrossing  a release for Sir Fras Cooke
of lands that was his in *Armah* in Ireland to my Lord £00 02s 04d;
22  going by water 6d, an order from the committee of Sequestration
00 05 06; to Mr Forward his charges to Mr Southby &c in part 00 05 05;
24  to Thurston to bear his charges to *Tawstocke* 00 15 00; to Mr Trussell
for tabby &c in full per bill 03 15 00; 25  to Mr Pollard in full upon his
week's book ending the 18th of July 09 18 00; to him then to account for
10 02 00; paid a bill by your Ladyship's appointment of 11 09 00; to your
Ladyship to lay out 06 11 06; for a ream of paper sent Mr Pollard
00 06 00; for 2 quire to write with all 00 00 10; to the scavengers for a
year ending Mich. next 00 10 00  [total] 44 00 07

Sum total disbursed from the 13th of May 1646 until 29th of July
following £630 2s 3d
And rec. in the same time as appears 634 19 6

So turn to the receipts

Augu. 4  for a letter from Mr Pollard by post £00 00s 02d; a letter sent
him by post 00 00 06; a letter from Merwood & one from Wantage
00 00 04; 7  to Mr Bold to pay the bill for the horses grass 07 10 00;
10  to Mr Pollard upon his week's book ending the 8th of August
22 11 11; for a quire of paper and ink 00 00 06; 12  2 ells ducape tafffeta
sarsenet 01 03 00; for ingrossing the deed for the lands in *Ardmagh*
[Armagh] 00 07 00; a letter from Merwood 4d, one to *Tawstocke* 4d
00 00 08; to Sir Henry Ley at play 00 06 00; paid Owins which he spent
coming up 00 06 04; 16  a packet of letters sent by post 00 01 00; to
Mr Bold upon a bill 01 05 00  [page total] 33 12 5

[p. 24]  1646 Augu. for a paving the coach yard your Honour's part
£00 10s 4d; to the poor from the balcony 00 00 4; for scouring 2 blankets
00 01 4; for a letter from *Merreworth* 00 00 4; 22  for glassing the sedan
00 01 0; to the 2 chair men that day 00 02 0; to the clerk at *Lincolnsin*
00 02 0; to the poor going thither 00 00 8; to the chair man that Sunday
00 02 0; 24  spent by the coachman & postilions at Greenwich &c
00 03 3; to the poor by the way 00 00 8; 25  to Mr Browne for £100 for
3 months 02 00 0; for a letter by post 2d, a packet sent by post 1s 00 01 2;
to Mary Thorpe for a hood 00 04 0; for tenter-hooks 3d, a folding

screen 12s oo 12 3; for 3 green velvet cushions by Mr Bold 02 o o; to the
porter brought them 6d, a letter [?from] Wantage 2d oo o 8; Septem. 3   a
letter to Wantage oo o 2; to your Honour in gold in 10s pieces 05 o o;
4   to Mr Pollard upon his week's book in full til 29 Au. 33 18 0; to your
Ladyship to play by Mrs Lovitt oo o6 o; to Mrs Pollard for pins and laces
oo 18 o; 4   to Mr Glover's man 2s, the chair men 2s oo o4 o; paid
Mr Bowdler's bill for the old coach 05 oo o; for 4 ounces of powder at 6d
for my Lady oo o2 o; 5   to the porters of *Lincolnsin* chapel oo o1 o; to
2 chair men that day oo o2 o; to the poor by the way oo oo 3; to the
painter for painting the rails in the balcony & the yard &c in part of 3 1 8
o2 oo o; to your Ladyship to give Mr Faringe oo o2 6; to Merwood carrier
for bringing pears &c & porter oo o1 8; paid for hiring of staff by bill
05 oo o; paid for 2 feather beds & bolsters, 1 green rug & 4 verders &
1 odd blanket per bill o7 oo o; a letter to Merwood 2d, a letter from
*wanting* 2d oo oo 4; a letter to *wantinge* oo oo 2   [page total] 65 18 1

[p. 25]   paid for a large carpet & a square one £o7 oos od; to Mr Trassell
for 11 yards fagerd satin for my Lady at 12s 9d cinnamon colour o7 oo o;
Septem. 10   to your Honour in money for bone lace 10 oo o; to *Oandle*
carrier for a buck & ½ a stag bringing o1 oo o; to Mr Fuller came with
it 5s, to the porter 2s oo o7 o; to the clerk of the Parliament his fees for
my Lord's restraint, recognizance & discharge o6 o5 6; 11   going by water
several times 1s 6d, my dinner 1s oo o2 6; to the officers that wait at the
house oo o4 o; for a stool covered with green cloth o1 o6 o; for the order
of the Committee of Sequestration oo o3 o; setting up my horse oo oo o1;
to Mr Osberstone's man brought peaches oo o1 o; to Mr Forward which
Mr Bold had for lace o2 o8 o; for 3 quire of paper oo o1 o   [total] 35 19 1

to Mr Coleman for Mr Cobb for 3 months o3 oo o   [total] 38 19 1

Sum total disbursed from the 29th of July 1646 unto the 14th of September
following £137 19s 7
And rec. in the same time as appears 151 7 3

So turn to the receipts

To Mr Pollard upon his week book to account for the sum of £13 7s 8d

[p. 26]   31th Octo.   to Mr Richard Pollard at *Tawstocke* as by his
acquittance appears £32 10s o1d; to Richard Wills a pair of shoes oo o3 o6;
to goodwife Tenby for wages oo 10 oo; to Thomas Cannon to buy some
malt oo o4 o2; Novem. 10   a letter came by post oo oo o6; to Mrs Jarvis
in full till Michas. last oo o5 oo; to her in part for Christmas quarter next
oo o5 oo; to Mr Robert Fane for books for my Lord oo o5 oo; 13   to
Mr Beare for his advice upon the declaration against Mrs Pasmore
oo 10 oo; for 6 turkey work back-stools o4 10 o6; paid for 24 yards of
green serge for screens at 3s 6d o4 o4 oo; 14   to Mr Bowdler the
coachmaker in full of all his bills until the 17th of August 1643 o7 10 oo;
to Mr Keene the joiner in part of £12 10s 11d by bill o8 oo oo; to the
painter in full for work by bills o1 10 oo; to the beadle for Michas quarter
oo o2 o6; to the paver for work in the kitchen yard oo o4 o6; to Mr Kinge
in further part of his bills 10 oo oo; 14   to Mr Pollard in full on his book
to this day 43 o9 o6; 17   to Mr Fitzwillyams the mason in part of

£11 16s 8½d for work done about the two pavements & in the cellar by
bill 06 00 00; for 18 gallons 3 quarts & a pint of Canary at 4s 8d with
3s 6d for the 2 runlets 04 11 00; for 6 tongues 12s, 2 hams weight 17 lbs
at 10d 01 05 06; to the porters that carried them 00 01 00; 17   to
Mr Barwood in further part of £20 for the organ, £5 paid by your
Ladyship 19th October 05 00 0; to Mrs Anne Howard due last
Midsummer for £100 04 00 00; to Mr Seale the upholsterer in full due to
him 10 00 00; for a quarter of pound of tobacco for my Lord 00 03 00; *at
the same time*   to Doctor Gifford's apothecary Mr Weely by bill 02 01 00;
20   for 1 lb of candied eringoes the best 00 05 00   [page total] 147 10 09

[p. 27]   for 12 pair of white & 11 pair of brown gloves Mrs Everatt
£0 19s 00d; to Cannon for work in the house by bill 00 18 00; in single
pence & two pences 01 00 00; No. 23   to Mr Pollard upon his book in
full till 21 Nov. 11 04 07; for a pair of black silk hose for my Lord
01 15 00; 24   for 2 letters came by post 00 01 06; for 1 packet sent by
post 00 01 00; to Mr Rydor the carpenter in part of £20 9s 6d due to him
upon 3 bills 10 00 00; 26   to my Lady in money 07 00 00; for 10 yards of
lace by Wilmot at 2s 01 00 00; 27   for thread and tape by her then
00 14 06; to Mr Jackson linen draper in part of £40 15s 3d by bill
30 00 00; to your Ladyship by Mr Pollard 02 00 00; to Mr Bassett
apothecary for Thurston 02 10 00; Decem. 1   for a packet by post & one
returned 00 01 10; to the surgeon that let your Ladyship's blood 00 10 00;
a letter from Wantage 00 00 02; paid for gravel by bill 01 05 00; for a
pound of Spanish tobacco my Lord 00 08 00; 7   for 2 yards broad cloth
to give Owen 01 01 00; for a letter by post 6d, to the porter 2d 00 00 08;
5   to the chair men for carrying your Ladyship to church twice 4s, to
2 pew keepers 2s by Mr Cobb 00 06 00; for half a pound damask powder
at 4d 00 02 08; for 4 ounces hair powder 00 01 10; 8   for a letter sent by
post 00 00 06; to the collectors for the poor for Michas quarter 00 10 00;
to the collectors for the houses which are visited 00 10 00; 14   to Mary
Thorpe in full upon a bill 01 17 00; *at the same time*   to Mr Pollard in
part of 36 0 11½ due on his book 18 03 00; to Wilmot to pay for thread
00 04 06; for 4 yards ¼ of lace by her at 1s 9d 00 07 05
[page total] 94 13 02

[p. 28]   to Mr Beare for his advise upon the entail about the Ladies
portions raising &c £01 00s 00d; to John Davis brought a doe from my
Lord Westmor' 00 05 00; to a porter that brought it 00 01 00; to a porter
for bringing the cypress chest, 2 velvet cushions & a square table 00 01 04;
for 18 yards green ribbon & 18 black at 2½d 00 07 06; paid 4 months tax
to Sir Thomas Faiorfax ending with March last set upon the rent which
Mr Murry must allow out of his rent 04 03 04; to Mrs Pollard her half
year's wages due last Mich. 05 00 00; to Mrs Lovet the like 05 00 00; to
Mr Thomas Pollard the like 05 00 00; to Robert Wood the like 04 00 00;
to William Booth the like 02 00 00; to George Chevely the like 01 00 00;
to Richard Willes the like 01 00 00; to Owins the like 01 00 00; to Thomas
Armsby the like 02 10 00; to Wilmot for a year then ending 02 00 00; to
Elizabeth Serle for a quarter due this Christmas 00 15 00; to Anne the like
00 10 00; to Whimper for a quarter & 5 weeks due Michas last 05 00 00;
to John Burke in full of 40s then due to him 00 12 00; to Will: Booth in

part of wages due to Mr Howard oo 10 oo; to Mr Bold which he laid out
in a journey o1 o4 oo; paid to Mr Pollard to pay for wood and coals in
part of [blank] £10 being paid before 10 oo oo; for an order of the Lord's
House for my Lord to have leave to stay in London oo 14 o6; paid for
4 half firkins of soap & 3 lbs & a box in which 12 lbs of it was sent to
wash a bed in Kent o1 16 o3; 19 [illegible crossed through] to Mr Pollard
in full of his week book to that day 32 o7 o9 [page total] 87 17 o8

[p. 29] 22 to Mrs Jarvis in full of her allowance to this day oo o5 oo; to
a man brought a post letter oo oo o2; 24 to Mr Cavill the sadler in full of
his bill o3 15 oo; to Gibons a smith in full of his bill o6 oo oo; to goodwife
Redhead for half a year now ended oo 10 oo; to goodwife Bradshaw for a
year ended at Michas o1 oo oo; to Mrs Devaux in part of £201 2s 6d due
to him by bond the last of November & paid of the day 100 oo oo; 25 to
the weights [waits] at Christmas oo 10 oo; to the collier's men's box
oo o2 o6; to the brewer's men's box oo o5 oo; to the farrier's men's box
oo o2 oo; to a porter brought 4 carpets from Mr Seale oo o1 oo; 26 to
your Ladyship at play oo oo o6; to the sexton at St Giles oo o5 oo; to the
clerk's boys' box that brings bills oo oo o6; to the porter at Sergeant's Inn
at a sermon oo o2 oo; to the poor there oo oo o6; 28 to the brewer in
part of his bill of £31 11 o 10 oo oo; to 13 prisons to their boxes o1 o6 oo;
to the chair men twice to church oo o4 oo; 28 to Mr Pollard upon his
week book in part of £11 2s 6d due to 26 instant 10 oo oo; to my Lord at
cards oo oo o6; for blankets &c for a child by bill o4 12 o6; to your
Ladyship at cards with Mr Bradnell oo o3 oo; a letter from *Exon* by post
with a bill of exchange oo oo o6; to the clerk of St Giles for Christmas
oo o6 oo; Jan. 2 to my Lady at cards oo o2 oo; to the chapel keep[er] at
Sergeant's Inn oo o2 oo; for a letter from Mr Walsh & one returned
oo oo o4 [page total] 139 16 oo

[p. 30] to Tho: Comon to buy several things by bill £o2 o8s ood; for a
cradle of joiners work second hand oo 18 oo; to a porter carried home the
4 carpets oo oo o8; for thread & lace & thread by Mr Pollard in December
oo 10 oo; Janu. 5 to my Lady at play at cards oo oo o6; to the beadle for
a quarter now ended oo o2 o6; for letters by the carrier oo oo o6; to a
gardener that nailed and pruned the trees oo o2 oo; to Mr Bayles in the
new exchange for gloves oo 18 oo; to Mr Bold for single money o1 oo oo;
11 to Mr Glover the lawyer o1 oo oo; for the order of the Committee of
Sequestrations oo o2 oo; to Will Decon by Mrs Clargis oo 10 oo; 2 pair of
spectacles & a case for my Lord oo o6 oo; a letter by post to Mr Hind
oo oo o6; 14 for a load of hay by Will Booth o1 17 oo; to Tho: Cannon
to buy buckram oo o6 oo; for a canopy frame oo o4 oo; for 1 lb of hair to
mend the sedan oo oo o6; 16 to my Lady at loadum oo oo o6; to
Mr Bowdler in part of £7 16s due to him o5 oo oo; for 18 yards orange
ribbon oo o3 o9; 19 to your Ladyship at play with Mr Bradnell oo o1 oo;
to Cannon to buy 4 cups for your rich bead oo o4 oo; 22 to Mr Glover
about the petition to the Lords o1 oo oo; to my Lady at loadum oo oo o6;
to my Lady at loadum oo oo o6; to my Lord at loadum oo o1 oo; 25 to
my Lady then on[?e] Elizabeth oo 11 oo; to the porter at Sergeants Inn last
Sunday oo o1 oo; for a letter from Wantage and answer oo oo o4
[page total] 17 o9 o9

[p. 31]   28   to my Lord & Lady at loadum £00 01s 00d; to the porter at
Sergeant's Inn by Mr Forard 00 01 00; to the wagoner in earnest for Rose
00 05 00; to Mr Forard in part for the velvet for the cradle 00 02 00; for
3 yards coarse cloth sent to *Tawstocke* to make cheese cloths 00 02 08;
paid for my Lord's garters & roses 00 18 00; Feb. 1   to the embroiderer
for setting the lace upon the velvet mantle Harrison 03 10 00; for 2 pair of
andirons, 2 pair of bellows, 2 pair of tongues & 2 fire pans 01 08 00; to
Mr Bracy for bands & boot hose tops my Lord 01 10 00; paid for Rose
and her husband & child coming up in the wagon & a maid from *Exon* &
the charges by the way as by bill appears £7 19s whereof John Hamlin rec.
of Mr Richard Pollard £2 & paid in earnest to the wagoner before 5s &
paid by Mr Tho: Pollard to the wagoner £2 1s & paid out by John Hamlin
which I paid him £3 13s so paid by me but 03 13 00; for an order of the
Lords that my Lord shall have the heads of his charge & liberty to answer
00 14 06; for a trunk with drawers for 00 15 00; 8 ounces of hair powder
for my Lady 00 02 08; for paper and ink 00 02 00; 9   a letter sent by post
to *Tawstocke* 00 00 06; 11   to my Lady at loadum 00 00 06; 12 to my
Lord & Lady at loadum 00 01 00; a letter from Mr Tarry 3d one
returned 2d 00 00 05; 13   to Mr Keene the joiner in full of his old bill
04 10 00; to my Lord & Lady at loadum 00 01 00; to my Lord & Lady at
loadum 00 01 00; for ticking for 2 folding stools 5s, for a yard of sack
cloth 1s, a pack thread nails & girt web 2s 00 08 00; to my Lord & Lady
at loadum 00 01 00; 16   for a sarsenet hood by Mrs Pollard 00 02 06;
14   to the porter at Sergeant's Inn 00 01 00   [page total] 18 14 09


[p. 32]   for a pack & half of mats £01 04s 00d; 6 yards of canvas to make
2 cradle beds 00 05 00; 2 yards ½ fine tick to piece a great bed 00 06 03;
10 yards ½ sackcloth to bottom the great bed 00 10 06; a thousand of lath
nails 00 01 08; 2 ounces brown thread 4d, 3 lines 9d to lace the great bed
00 01 01; to a porter to bring those things home 00 00 08; 2 ounces red
thread 6d, 4 caps for the cradle 6d 00 01 00; for a canopy frame & the
black cabinet frame 00 15 00; Feb. 19   to my Lord & Lady at loadum
00 01 06; 21   to the porter at Sergeant's Inn 00 02 00; 22   to my Lord &
Lady at loadum 00 01 0; 23   to my Lady at loadum 00 01 00; for your
Ladyship's slippers 00 02 06; 25   to your Ladyship & my Lord at loadum
00 01 00; to Mary Thorpe for a ducape hood 00 06 00; a letter from
Wantage 2d 00 00 02; to Tho: Connon to buy feathers for 2 cross stores
00 06 06; to Mr Bold to give to one brought stuff from Mr G.F. 00 10 00;
to George to buy tenter-hooks nails & pack thread 00 02 00; to your
Ladyship by my Lady Eliza: Cope 00 05 00; to Cammon to buy rings and
tape 00 01 00; for 2 letters sent to Wantage 00 00 04; for an Order of the
House of Commons 00 06 00; for 3 quire of paper 00 01 00; to my Lord
at loadum 00 00 06; for making a wool quilt & 2 cradle quilts 00 08 00;
Mar. 7   to the porter at Sergeant's Inn 00 02 00; for 1 lb & ½ blue figs
00 01 06; 9 to my Lord & Lady at loadum 00 01 00; to George to buy
hooks & pack thread 00 01 06; to Connon in part for his work 00 02 00;
for a tub for the little house by the stable 00 05 06; 11   for a load of hay
by Will: Booth 01 16 00; for 6 wooden chairs with mat bottoms 00 06 00
[page total] 08 16 10

**[p. 33]** 11 to Mr George Manby for the consideration of £300 due for
6 months the 12th January last £12 to him in part of the principal £100
whereof paid by my Lady 64 & by me £48 00s 00d; 14 to the porter at
Sergeant's Inn & the poor 00 02 06; to a porter brought things from
Mr Seale 00 00 06; to a glasier for work paid in January 00 06 00; to
Cannon to buy skins to make a carpet 00 02 06; for a pair of laced shoes
for your Ladyship 00 04 00; to Mr Seale the upholsterer in part of
£12 17s 6d by bill 06 10 00; to the furrier for the rich mantle 11 10 00; to
Mr Stone the upholsterer in full of his bill 11 18 00; to the plumber in full
of his bill 06 01 00; to Mr Brooks in part of £10 by bill 05 00 00; to
Mr Bowdler in full of his Christmas quarter bill 02 16 00; 22 for wine &
excise by bill 13 08 06; to the grocer in part of £10 15s 5d by bill 05 00 00;
19 to the woodmonger in part of £23 10s by bill 10 00 00; to
Mr Gildropp by bill 01 18 00; 19 to my Lady at loadum 00 00 06; a
letter sent to *Bruerne* another to Wantage 00 00 04; to the glasier
Mr Devaux by bill 02 08 00; to Tho: Cannon for 6 weeks about the bed
and other work in the house at 9s a week whereof paid him before 2s and
left in his hands of £4 he had of your Ladyship £1 so paid him in full
01 12 00; 20 to the porter at Sergeant's Inn 00 01 00; 23 to my Lord for
Doctor Gifford 01 00 00; to a man brought particulars from *Arrundel*
house 00 01 00; for removing the gravel & setting up 6 posts 00 02 00;
24 paid for plush & crimson taffeta by Mr Forard 08 07 00; to the keeper
of St James park by Mrs Sydn. 00 01 00; for 2 letters from Wantage
00 00 04; for a large wainscot box for the fard mantle 00 12 00
[page total] 137 02 02

**[p. 34]** to Mr Pollard upon his book £05 00s 00d; to Ann [blank] one of
the maids 00 05 00; for a broad trunk 00 09 00; 28 to the porter at
Sergeant's Inn 00 01 00 [total] 5 15 0

Sum total disbursed from the 14th of September 1646 until the 23th of
March 1646 £657 16s 1d
And rec. in the same time as appears 639 15 1
So, rem. due to this accountant this 24th of March 1646 £18 1s 0d
[signed] Will Lynn

## Expenses, 1647–1649

KENT ARCHIVES OFFICE, U269/A518/2

*The book measures 7½″ by 12″ and has a paper cover which records it is
'A book of all receipts and payments made by William Lynn for the
right Honorable the Earl of Bath since the 26th of March 1647'. At the
end of the account are five pages of estate receipts of mainly fines, greatly
damaged by worms, which have not been edited.*

**[p. 1]** March 27th 1647 Remaineth due to this accountant on the foot of
his last account ending the 26 of March 1647 £88 01s 00d; for 10 quire of
writing paper 00 03 10; 29 To my Lord and Lady at loadum 00 01 00;
for a table frame for the great box to put the rich mantle in 00 04 00;

30   for 2 China band pots 2 bottles & two beakers of china 05 10 00; for
a letter from John Mills of Harpen 00 00 04; 31   a letter from Wantage
00 00 02; April 1   To Mr Serjeant Glanvile for his advice upon the
2 grand conveyances of Wm Earl of Bath 02 00 00; To Robert Wood
which he gave your Ladyship by Mrs Pollard 00 05 00; 2   for a black box
and a letter from Tawstock 00 00 06; 6 a letter to Mr Hine 6d one to
Tawstock by post 1s 00 01 06; a yard and ½ of dowlas by Wilmot
00 03 09; a letter from Wantage and answer back 00 00 04; 9   To
Mr Hales for his advice upon Tawstock conveyance 01 00 00; for tortoise
shell frame for my Lord's spectacles 00 01 04; 10   for a load of hay by
Will Booth 01 16 00; To Mr Pollard to account for 02 00 00; 11   To the
Porter at Sergeant's Inn 00 01 00; 12   To Mrs Ann Howard due to her
last Christmas 04 00 00; To my Lord to give Mr Kirckan for dressing of
your Lordship for the toothache 01 00 00; for a copy of the Lords' Order
for my Lord to have a copy of his charge 00 14 06; To Mr Strong's clerk
brought his sermon 00 00 06; 17   To Wilmot to buy soap 00 18 00;
17   To Mr Pollard upon his week book 70 00 00; 19   24   for my journey
to Wantage with one horse hire spent in the same as by bill 02 10 11;
ferrying at *Winsor* 00 00 04; an oz of tobacco for my Lord 00 00 09;
porter Sergeant's Inn, Easter day and this, 2 clerks of Bartho: 1s 00 03 00;
To the poor there 00 01 10
[total] 92 06 07   [top total] 88 01 00

[p. 2]   1647 April 27th   To Mr Hill druggist in Lumbar Street in full of
his bill 04 05 00; To Mr Fitzwilliams the Mason in full p[er] bill 05 16 00;
To Mr Reade the mercer in part of £35 due to him by bill 10 00 00; To
Mr Jackson in full of his bill delivered the 23th of November 1646
10 15 00; To Mr Brookes in full for wares delivered 15 January 1646
05 00 00; To Mr Cooper the Hatter in full to this day 03 10 00; To
Mrs Pollard which was returned for her 01 02 00; To your Ladyship at
cards by Mrs Sydenham 00 10 00; for a book for my Lord, *Helmant
opusculum* 00 05 00; for a packet of letters sent by post 00 01 00; for
bringing home that money by a porter 00 01 00; for a month ended
15 April.   To Mr Varny Bourcher's wife for her boy's schooling 00 10 00;
28   To the porter at Sergeants Inn 00 01 00; To Mrs Sarah Pollard her half
year' wages 05 00 00; To Mrs Lovitt the like 05 00 00; To Wilmot the like
01 00 00; To Mr Cobb the like 07 00 00; To Mr Thomas Pollard the like
05 00 00; To Robert Wood the like 04 00 00; To Whimper the cook the
like 07 00 00; To John Burke the like 02 00 00; 28 To George Clevely the
like 01 00 00; To Will: Boothe the coachman the like 02 00 00; To Thomas
Armsbie the like 02 10 00; To Owins the like 01 00 00; To Rose Hamlin
for a year now due 03 00 00; To Mr Wild for ¼ due this Lady Day
05 00 00; To Eliza: Serle the like 00 15 00; To Ann Tassell the like
00 10 00; To Eliz: Thorne the like 00 10 00; To my Lord in money for
books &c 05 00 00   [page total] 99 01 00

[p. 3]   1647 April 28   To Mr Thomas Pollard in [illegible] on his week
book until the 24 of April £49 15s 09d; a letter from Wantage & one
returned 00 00 04; To the Chairmen that day to Sergeant's Inn 00 02 00;
30   To the Brewer in part of [blank] due in Decem. last 10 00 00; May 1
To the brick-layer in part of 12 3 3   05 00 00; To Mr Pollard in full upon

his week book to the 8th of May 32 08 06; To My Lady for a holland
quilt &c 15 00 00; paid the ale brewer by bill 02 11 00; To Goodwife
Redhead for last Lady Day 00 10 00; To Mary Thorpe for a fan 00 02 00;
May 12   To Colonel Cooke at cards 00 04 06; To the collectors for the
poor for half year ended at Lady Day last 01 00 00; 14   To Mrs Bourcher
in Chancery 00 10 00; for ½ lb of tobacco for my Lord 00 04 09; 15   To
Mr Rydor the carpenter in part of £17 19s 6d 10 09 00; for 4 oz of fine
silks at Mr Hornes 00 12 00; to the poor by the way in the streets
00 00 09; 16   to the porter at Sergeants Inn 00 01 00; 17   To Mr Bowdler
the coachmaker in part of his bill for Our Lady Day quarter being
10 10 2   05 00 00; To Mr Jarvis for half a year last Lady D. 05 00 00; for
8 oz hair powder for my Lady 00 02 08; 18   2 beds carried to Mr Seales
by a porter 00 01 00; To Mr Bold to lend Mr Roscaricke 02 00 00; To
Mr Keene the joiner in full of all due to him 05 00 00; 19   To the Beadle
for Lady Day quarter 00 02 06; a letter from Tho: Michell & one to
Wantage 00 00 04; 23 To the porter at Sergeants Inn 00 01 00; 25 To
Mr Perry in part of thirty pounds 10 00 00; 26 To the porter of Sergeant's
Inn the fast day 00 01 08; To the overseers for the highways 00 05 00; for
a letter sent by post 1s and to Wantage & answer 00 01 04; To a porter
brought [illegible] Mr Fuller 00 00 06   [page total] 151 16 11

[p. 4]   1647   To Mr Hales for his advice upon the reversion of the lease
of 21 years made in trust for the daughters of Edward earl of Bath
00 10 00; May 30   To the porter of Sergeant's Inn 00 02 00; To
Mrs Bourcher for her boy's diet & schooling for a month ending 15 May
00 10 00; To Mr Bold for Sir Morris Willyams for Rose 01 00 00; To
Mr Bold for [blank] 50 00 00; ['To Mr Pollard in full upon his book'
crossed through]; June 1   To the woodmonger in full of his bill 13 10 00;
To the smith in part of £7 19s 6d by bill 05 00 00; To the clerk of St Giles'
for Easter last 00 06 00; To Mr Pollard in full upon his week book until
the 29th of May last 41 08 11; 1   To the ['Wid' crossed through] post a
letter sent to Tawstock 00 00 06; 2   To Mr Kinge in part of his bills
20 00 00; To my Lady in money 02 00 00; To Mrs Deuox for a £100 due
last May 04 00 00; 3   To Mrs Hassett in part of £42 12s 3d due to
Mr Barro 26 17 00; 3   To Mrs Barrow in full of all due to him as we
believe 15 15 00; To 13 prisoners to their box 00 13 00; 4   To Mr Lynsy
the brewer in part of £37 10s 9d 10 00 00; 5   To Mr Bowdler the
coachmaker in full of his bill £10 10s 2d due at our Lady Day quarter
05 10 00; 6   To the porter at Sergeant's Inn 00 01 00; To Richard
Bradshawe 02 00 00; To a woman for a mantle 08 10 00; To Mrs Boarcher
for her boy's diet & schooling for a month ended 6 June 00 10 00; To
your Ladyship at cards with my Lady Wharton 00 10 00; for a side for
Mrs Lovitt's bed 00 02 00; to my Lady Newton's man brought fruit &
flowers 00 01 00; 13   To the porter at Sergeant's Inn 00 02 00; a letter
sent by post to Tawstock 00 01 00; a letter from Wantage &c 00 00 04; an
ounce of conserve of rosemary flowers 00 00 05; 12 pair of gloves 23s, a
pair silk stockings 22s Mr Fane 02 05 00   [page total] 211 05 02

[p. 5]   1647 June 22   To Mr Parr the tailor in part of £17 5s 3d 07 00 00;
2 letters sent by post 1s to the letter carrier 6d 00 01 06; to the poor at
Sergeant's Inn last Sunday 00 00 06; 24   to Mr Murry in part of £64 due

to him for rent this Midsummer 20 00 00; To the porter of Sergeant's Inn
00 01 00; To Mrs Jarvis for a qu[arter] now due 00 10 00; 26　To
Mr Tho: Pollard in part of £58 18s due to him upon his weeks book this
day 50 00 00; 29　To my Lady in money to give away 06 00 00; 30　To
the porter at Sergeant's Inn the fast 00 01 00; July 1　To your Ladyship to
pay for ribbon 02 00 00; To Mrs Lovitt a quarter's wages due last
midsummer 02 10 00; a letter from Wantage & an answer returned
00 00 04; 2　To Mary Thorpe for a ducape hood 00 05 00; To Sprite for
weeding the court 00 00 06; 3　To the porter at Sergeant's Inn 00 02 00;
To the poor there then 00 00 06; 4　To Mrs Bourcher for her boy for a
month 00 10 00; To the Beadle for midsummer quarter 00 02 06; 6　for
cleaning the houses of office 01 12 00; for letters by post this week 6d to
the porter 6d & 2 sent 18d 00 02 06; 11　To the porter at Sergeant's Inn
00 02 00; 13　2 letters sent by post 00 01 00; To the Collectors for the
poor for Midsummer quarter 00 10 00; for bringing home a £100 from
Mr White 00 00 06; 14　a letter from Wantage & answer 00 00 04; 15　To
Mr Wm Beare for £150 for a year the 20th of April last 12 00 00; 16　To
Mr Pollard in part of £52 due to him upon his week book this day
50 00 00; To Mr Robert Austen in part of [blank] 70 00 00; 17　To
Mrs Ann Howard due at Midsummer last for a boat to bring the £30 from
London bridge 00 00 03; 19　To Mr Kinge for calico for a suit for my
Lord and making it by bill in full 10 05 00　[page total] 237 18 05

[p. 6]　1647 July 20　To Mr Trussell the mercer in part of [blank] due to
him by bill £10 00s 00d; *at that time*　To Mr Manby the silkman in part
of £39 7s 11d due to him by bill 10 00 00; This £200 is paid to Mr Manby
and borrowed of Sr Ra: Sydenham　To Mr Manby that married
Mr Baldwin's daughter for £200 for six months 08 00 00; To Sir Morris
Willyams for Eliza: Thorne 01 00 00; *at that time*　To my Lord in money
02 00 00; a letter from Mr Hynes 6d a box with copies to him 1s 00 01 06;
a letter to Mr Wyatt all by post 00 00 06; 22　In single pence & half pence
by Mr Willoby 00 10 00; 23　To my Lady in gold 00 10 00; 24　to
Mr Henry Binion for Mr Dowtie in part of £50 14s 8d due to Mr Tull in
his lifetime 20 00 00; To an old man that keeps the new building at
*Greenewick* 1s for fruit there 8d 00 01 08; 25　To the porter at Sergeant's
Inn 00 01 00; 27　a letter from Mr Hyne 6d & one returned 6d 00 01 00;
a packet then to Mr Wyatt 1s to the porter 6d 00 01 06; 28　To Mr Fuller
came with a buck 5s to him the keeps fee 10s to the carrier 10s his
porter 1s 01 06 00; for a suit of clothes for Mrs Bourcher's son 00 15 00;
for a swan's skin 5s for ⅛ of sarsenet 4s 00 09 00; for carrying my Lady
Westmorland's hangings 00 01 06; for carrying my Ladyship's bed &
blankets 0 01 00; for a piece of scarlet [illegible crossed through] 00 09 00;
August 2　To Mrs Bourcher for her boy for a month 00 10 00; for half a
pound of tobacco for my Lord 00 05 00; 3　To Mr Bold to pay for horse
grass 02 00 00; Letters by post to Tawstock 1s Jo: Mills 6d Mr Hyne 6d
porter 4d 0 02 04; a dressing box & 3 pair of gloves &c to give to
Mrs Rachel Fane 00 19 00; a pair of plain scissors for your Ladyship
00 00 06; 4　sent my Lady Rainsford's daughter 00 02 06; To Richard
Willis a pair of drawers 00 03 10; For the rich coach standing at
Mrs Skitlewood's 3 years 07 00 00; for oiling & dressing it in that time
01 10 00　[page total] 68 01 10

[p. 7]   Augu. 10   To Mr Pollard in full upon his week books unto the
7th of August £47 12 2 ½; To the woodmonger in part of [blank] by bill
10 00 00; To the brewer in part of his bill ending in May last there being
then remaining of the bill £27 10 00 00; *at the same time*   To the
Frenchman for for [sic] the rich fringe &c in part of £23 12s 3d remaining
of his bill 12 00 00; for 16 yards of tomah[?] sent Mr Wm Fane 3s 2d
02 10 06; 11   To Mr Bowdler the coach-maker in full of his bill for
Midsummer quarter 06 07 00; 28   To the Collectors for the visited houses
in the parish 00 10 00; To a porter that carried hangings to St Bartholmes
00 01 02; 13   To my Lady in money 13 10 04; To Goodwife Redhed for
Midsummer quarter 00 05 00; To Rose Hamlin's father 00 05 00; To my
Lady in money £165 out of which her Ladyship paid to Mr Tansell in part
of £73 11s 6d £20 and to Mr Greene in part of £29 9s 3d £10 & to
Mr Pescod the grocer in full £6 4s & to Mr Bigg for ale £2 19s 0d
165 00 00; 31   a letter to Mr Bulworthy 6d one to Mr Wyatt 1s by post
00 01 06; a letter from Wantage & one returned 00 00 04; for carrying
Mr Wm Fane's gown stuff 00 00 06; To Mrs Hardwicke half a year's
wages for Michaelmas last £5 & to bear her charges £2 07 00 00;
Septem. 6   a letter from Mr Hyne by post & answer 00 01 00; for 8 oz of
rose powder for your Ladyship 00 03 04; a letter to Mr Wyatt by post
00 01 00; a long letter from old Mr Wyatt 00 00 03; 14   a letter from
Mr Hyne by post 00 00 06; a packet to Mr Wyatt by post 00 01 00; to the
Chair men carried your Honour to Lady Kents 00 04 00; a letter from
Wantage ['and one Mr Wm Fane' crossed through] 00 00 02; for green
cythorne [*citron*] 00 01 03; To the porter bro[ught] a basket of pears from
old Nicholas & the carrier 00 01 06; To the Chairmen brought your
Ladyship Charing Cross 00 02 06   [page total] 276 09 02 ½

[p. 8]   for half a pound of cythorne [*citron*] in syrup 00 01 00; to a poor
woman's boy 00 00 06; Septem. 20   for a letter for Sir Francis Fane by
post 00 00 06; for 4 letters sent by post & to the man 6d 00 03 00; for a
letter from *Hunspill* by a porter 00 00 03; for weeding the court 00 00 06;
23   To my lord widow Hopkinson's fine 02 00 00; 27   for 28 lbs of sugar
at 13d, a porter 2d 01 10 06; [illegible crossed through]; for bow-strings
for my Lord by Mr Forward 00 04 06; laid out by him at *totnam*
[Tottenham] court 00 01 00; To my Lady a model of Prince Charles in
gold 00 15 06; More in old gold of Edward 6 & Queen Elizabeth 03 13 06;
28   My Lord's journey to Wantage with 4 men & 5 horses & return again
in 5 days p[er] bills 06 13 08; To John Burke his charges going for
Mrs Tarry twice & for Mrs Dericke once by bill 00 10 06; for making
clean the clock & lines 00 04 00; a letter from Mr Hyne p[er] post
00 00 06; Octob. 5   a letter to Mr Wyatt Mr Hyne Mr Hunt & Mr Mills
p[er] post 00 02 06; for a barrel of soap by Wilmot 00 19 06; To the poor
at the door 00 00 03; 13   To Mrs Bourchers child for 2 months ending
28 September 01 00 00; To the widow Fayne in part of a bill of £6 15s
01 00 00; To my Lady an Eliza[beth] crown at 00 06 00; To Mr Maynard
his advice upon a case &c 00 11 00   [total] 19 18 08

Sum total disbursed from the 30th of March last upon this book until the
14th of October 1647 is £1244 13s 09d ½

And received the same time as appears at the other end of this book the
sum of £1214 08s 08d
So, Remaineth due to me this 14th day of October upon this book the
sum of £30 05s 01d ½

[p. 9] 1647 Octo. 14   To pay Mr Pollard's book as appears £07 00s 00d;
16   More to pay the same as appears 47 10 00; 18   Spent going to
*Tawstocke* with 4 men & 4 horses by bill 04 12 11; Novem. 4   paid to
Mr Martin at *Cortondinham* [Corton Denham] for six years Lord's rent at
10d per *year* 00 05 00; 5   Allowed the Tenths at *Netherhaven*
[Netheravon] which sheriff [dis]strained them for a Relief after the death
of Edward earl of Bath 01 07 02; 7   to the porter at Sergeant's Inn
00 01 00; 8   3 yards ½ qr of ['scarlet baise' crossed through] flannel to
make a petticoat for my Lady 00 08 09; 9   a book for my Lord called
*Fleta* 00 09 00; a letter from Mr Hyne ['& answer' crossed through]
00 01 00; a letter to Mr Wyott by post & 6d the poster 00 01 06; To
Tucker the carrier for bringing up 191 lbs at 3d the pound by Mr Bold
02 07 06; for a load of hay by him 01 14 00; To Wilmot by
Mr Bold 00 06 00; To Mr Bassett the apothecary in full p[er] bill 07 00 00;
To Mr Cavill the sadler in full by bill 09 06 00; To Mr Milborne
Bit-maker in full by bill 03 04 00; 10   To Mr Bowdler in full of Mich.
quarter bill 14 00 00; To Mr Allopp a cutler in full of a bill 02 15 00; paid
for a pair of shoes for my Lady 00 03 06; paid to Mr Dowty in part of
£30 4s 0d due to Mrs Tull 10 00 00; To Mr Bold which he paid to
Mr Perry the 2 of September in full of £100 20 00 00; To Mr Thomas
Pollard by your Ladyship's appointment 03 00 00; This was borrowed the
15 March 46 as by the former book.   To Mr Robert Austen which was
borrowed of him 100 00 00; To Mr Vincent for scarlet baise 3 yards ½
04 07 00; To the porter at Sergeant's Inn 00 02 00; Crossing the water &
setting a horse up at *Putny* 00 00 11; sending letters by the post 00 00 10;
To Mr David Murry in full of all rent due to him at Midsummer
60 00 00   [page total] 300 13 01

[p. 10] 1647   To Mrs Sarah Pollard her half year's wages due this Micha.
£05 00s 00d; To Mr Wylde the chaplin the like 10 00 00; To Mr Thomas
Pollard the like 05 00 00; To Mr Richard Cobb the like 07 00 00; To
Whimper the cook the like 07 00 00; To George Cheverly the like
01 00 00; To John Burke the like 02 00 00; To Thomas Armsby the like
02 10 00; To Owen Prince the like 01 00 00; To Wm Booth the coachman
the like 03 00 00; To Elizabeth Searle the like 01 10 00; To Rose Hamlin
the like 01 10 00; To Ann Tossell the like 01 00 00; To Elizabeth Thorne
the like 01 00 00; Novem. 11   To Mr Lyle the Brewer in full for beer
delivered to the 9th of May 1647 more to him in part for beer d[elivere]d
since 01 08 03; To Mr Gumbleton Old Exchange in full 09 05 00; To
Mr Orlibeare in part of £49 0s 8d 10 00 00; To Mr Reade in part of
£25 2s 9d 10 00 00; To Mr Trussell in part of [blank] 10 00 00; To
Mr Manby in part of £29 7s 11d 09 00 00; 15   To the wood-monger in
full 15 13 00; To Widow Frame in part of £5 15s remaining of a bill of
hand 02 00 00; To J.B. for suit of clothes &c 05 10 00; To the porter at
Sergeant's Inn 00 01 00; To the Bead for Micha's quarter 00 02 06; a letter
from Mr Hyne by post p[er] answer 00 01 00; 16   A packet to Mr Wyott

by post oo o1 oo; 17  To the brick-layer in full of 2 bills o7 o3 oo; To him
for your Honour's part pume and well new making o3 oo oo; To your
Ladyship in money by Mr Bold o5 oo oo; To my Lord by Mr Bold
o2 oo oo; for a load of hay by him o1 12 oo   [page total] 159 o8 o6

**[p. 11]**  Nov. 18   To Mr Pollard upon his week book 1oo oo oo; for a
letter from Wantage oo oo o2; To a gardener for dressing the trees·& nails
oo o2 oo; 23 2 loads of hay £3 7s, a load of straw 12s  o3 19 oo; a dozen of
filleting 18d, a bunch of tape 2s oo o3 o6; 23   To Mrs Bourcher for his
boy for two months now o1 oo oo; to the porter of Sergeant's Inn
oo o1 oo; a letter to Mr Wyott by post & one to Jo: Mills oo o1 o6;
Decem. 2   To Mr Orlibeare in part of £39 os 8d 2o oo oo; To Mr Trasell
in part 2o oo oo; To Mr Kinge in part 2o oo oo; To Mr Rydor the
carpenter in full of a bill o7 1o oo; To Mr Povie's groom for using his
stable oo o2 oo; for 2 standards 1 shelf a frame for a glass, a screen and a
little basket o1 1o oo; 3 beer glasses & 3 wine glasses oo o7 oo; to a porter
to bring them home oo oo o6; for linen gloves &c for J.B. o1 o2 o6; an oz.
of tobacco for my Lord oo oo o9; for half a pound more oo o6 o8; paid a
paver's bill for the stable & street o1 12 oo; to a mason for laying 2 half
paces oo 1o oo; To Mr Bales for gloves for your Ladyship o1 o9 oo; To
Doctor Chamberlain's boy by Wilmot oo 16 oo; a fan for your
Ladyship 3s, a large curl 5s oo o8 oo; a vade mecum for my Lord oo oo 1o;
2 pair of spectacle frames for my Lord oo oo o8; 6   To Mr Thomas
Pollard upon his book 4o oo oo; 7   a packet to Mr Wyott & a letter to
Mr Hyne by post oo o2 oo; for 5 yards of blue stuff to cover a trunk
o1 18 oo; for a piece of gold of Queen Marie's coin o2 oo oo; for 2 French
pistolets o1 11 oo; 12   To the porter at Sergeant's Inn oo o1 oo; a letter
from Mr Hyne & answer by post oo o1 oo; 14   a letter to Mr Wyatt by
post oo o1 oo; 16   paid Mr Evans my Lord's shoe-maker in full by bill
o1 15 oo; 19   To the porter at Sergeant's Inn oo o1 oo
[page total] 22 13 o1

**[p. 12]**   1647 Decem. 19   To your Ladyship in gold by Mr Bold
£o1 oos ood; 21   To Wilmot to pay for a glass of water oo o8 oo; 23   To
Mr Rushworth at *Winsor* [Windsor] o1 oo oo; spent going thither lying out
one night with 2 horses dinner 2s 8d sup[per] & cham. 4 horses 3s 3d
oo o9 o9; for your Ladyship's blue trunk making up & porter o1 1o 1o; To
Mr Dennelle the minister o1 oo oo; 28   A letter from Mr Hyne & answer
by post oo o1 oo; For a packet to Mr Wyott 1s the porter 6d oo o1 o6; To
my Lady a piece of gold oo o5 o6; To my Lord at cards oo o1 o6; To the
brewer's box oo o5 oo; To the wood-
monger's box oo o2 o6; To the waits at Christmas oo 1o oo; To the king's
Trumpeters oo 1o oo; 3o   for a ream of writing paper oo o6 o8; To my
Lady in money 1o oo oo; To the beadle for this quarter & 6d to his box
oo o3 oo; Janua. 2   To the porter of Sergeant's Inn oo o1 oo; To 13 prison
boxes oo 13 oo; 3 To Mrs Bourcher for his son for a month ending the 2o
of Decem. oo 1o oo; To the clerk of the parish for Christmas oo o6 oo; To
Mr Pollard a bill for coming to London o2 14 o6; a bundle from Tawstock
with leases & returned back oo o1 o6; 8   To the collector for the poor for
half a year o1 oo oo; To Robt Wood his half year's wages due at Michas.
last o4 oo oo; To myself the like 1o oo oo; 9   To the porter at Sergeant's

Inn oo oi oo; To a Mason for stopping the pavement where the water
came into the cellar oo o4 oo; To widow Faine in part of £3 15s remaining
a bill of hand oi 15 oo; A packet to Mr Wyott oo oi oo; a lease to
Mr Hyne & one to Sr Francis Fane oo oi o6; To Mr Deaux & due in
Novem. for £100 o4 oo oo; To Mrs Ann Howard the like due at
Christmas o4 oo oo   [page total] 46 o3 o3

[**p. 13**]   1647 January 17   To the frenchman in full for fringe &c
£11 12s ood; To the porter at Sergeant's Inn oo oi oo; 18   a packet from
Mr Hyne & answer oo oi o6; a packet to Mr Wyott & the porter
oo oi o6; *at that time*   To the Collectors of Sir Thomas Farfax tax for
3 months ending 25 June last it being the land rent which Mr Murry must
allow oi 13 o4; for half of pound of tobacco for my Lord oo o8 oo; Paid
for J.B. from 8 Octo. to 23th Jan. being 15 weeks at 8s o6 oo oo; paid for
boots spurs & boot-hose tops &c oo 17 oo; 19   To Mr Denells oi oo oo;
To Mrs Bourcher for her son for a month ending 17th this month
oo 10 oo; for silk trousers & waistcoat Mr G. Fane o7 15 oo; 24   To the
Collectors for Sir Tho: Farfax for 3 months ending with December for the
rent which Mr Murry must pay oi 13 o4; 21   To Mr Pollard upon his
week book in part of £111 13s 2d due to this day 40 oo oo; 25   To the
post a packet to Mr Wyott oo oi oo; 76 13 8.   To my Lord John Speare's
fine o5 oo oo; To Mr Bold in part of [blank] due to him o2 o2 oo; 26   To
Mr Pollard in full due on his book 71 13 o2; 27   half a firkin of soap sent
to *Bruen* [Bruern] oo 10 o6; To 2 porters to carry burdens to that carrier
oo oi o6; for cord for a trunk & the porter oo oo o8; for carrying home
my Lady Kent pallet bed oo oo o2; To Finch the coachman in part to
*Bruen* o3 oo oo; To the waterwoman for a years ¼ o2 oo oo; 26   To
Mr Richard Pollard by your honour's appointment 10 oo oo; To my Lady
when their honours went to *Bruen* 50 oo oo; for bringing home the £99
oo oo o4; Feb. 1   Allowed to Tho: Hart of *Netherhaven* for which he was
distrained for a relief o2 o4 o2; To one watched the stable when you went
to *Bruen* & made it clean oo oi oo   [page total] 218 5 o2

[**p. 14**]   1647 Feb. 3   To the carrier of *Bruen* by bill £o2 o1s o9d; 5   To
Widow Fayne part of £2 remaining a bill oi oo oo; a letter from *Bruen*
oo oo o2; 7   More to Mr Richard Pollard o2 oo oo; A letter from
Mr Hyne & answer last week oo oi oo; A packet then to Mr Wyott
oo oi oo; 7   A letter from Mr Hyne this day oo oo o6; 14   a packet to
Mr Wyott oo oi o6; To the coachman that went to *Bruen* oo o2 oo; a letter
from Mr Samuell & answer oo oo o6; for carrying bottles twice to the
carrier oo oo o4; To Mr Rydor the carpenter in part of o2 10 oo;
21   A letter to Mr Hyne & one to Mr Wyott oo oi oo; A taffety &
masque 4s 2 toys 16d to *Brewe* oo o5 o4; for a runlet of Canary sent to
*Tangly* [Tangley] o2 oi o8; To the carrier for carrying it &c oo o4 o6;
28   for a packet from Mr Hyne oo oi oo; a packet to Mr Wyott oo oi oo;
March 2   sent to Oxford by return of Mr Hampson 40 oo oo; To
Mr Bowdler in full of Christmas quarter bill o3 18 oo; To the Widow
Fayne in full of a bill oi oo oo; 7   a letter from Mr Hyne & a packet to
Mr Wy[ott] oo oi o6; a letter from Mr Hyne by post oo oo o6;
14   a packet to Mr Wyott oo oi oo; for books sent to *Bruen* oo o9 o6;
paid the week book from 22 of January to the 21 of March following as

app[ear]s 21 16 03½; paid for a coach to go to *Bruen* to fetch your
honours servants to London 05 06 06; 16   paid the carrier's bill for
carriage then 01 10 00; 17   To the brewer Mr Lyndsey in part of
£49 3s 3d due to him for ber d[eliver]d to this day 20 00 00; To my Lady
to buy lace, thread & ribbon &c 20 00 00; To the brewer for ale
d[elivere]d since last May 03 06 00; To Mr Pollard then to account for
20 00 00; a letter to Wantage 00 00 02; the Parliament's Declaration in
answer to the Scotch paps 00 00 10; for half a pound of tobacco sent to
*Bruen* 00 08 00; 2 silver frames for my Lord's spectacles 00 03 06
[page total] 148 15 00½

[p. 15]   1647 March 20   To Mrs Bourcher for 2 months this day
£01 00s 00d; for books for my Lord 00 00 06; a packet to Mr Wyott to
*Exon* by post 00 01 00; 21   a packet to Mr Pollard to Tawstock by post
00 01 00; a letter to Sir Francis Fane by post 00 00 06; 22   To the
Collectors for the visited poor in full 00 10 00; Paid for J.B. from the 23th
of January to the 18th of March being 8 weeks 03 04 00; to him to buy
stockings & bonds 00 10 00; for helping him to a place 00 05 00; for a pair
of breeches & point for him 01 10 00; for books & a hat for him 01 00 00;
a letter from Wantage 00 00 02; a pair of gloves 3s 6d combs 2s for my
Lord 00 05 00; for 3 razors 7s 6d, 2 pair of beard irons 2s 6d, 2 pair of
scissors 4s 6d for my Lord 00 14 06; 23   To your Ladyship by Rose
Hamlin 05 00 00; To Ro: Wood for claret wine a tearce 50s, excise 12s 6d,
carman 2s 6d, porter 6d 03 05 06; To Owen 01 00 00; for 3 dozen of
wash-balls my Lord 00 04 08; for half a pound of tobacco my Lord
00 08 00; a packet to Mr Wyott by post 00 01 00; 28   a letter to Mr Hyne
& one to *Hunspill* 00 01 00; a letter to Sir Francis Fane & to the post
00 01 00   [page total] 19 03 09

Sum total disbursed from the 14th of October 1647 upon this book until
the 28th of March 1648 is £1151 7s 0d
And Rec. in the same time as appear at the other end of this book the sum
of £1159 9s 0d.
So remaineth in this accounants hand £8 2s 0d.

[p. 16]   1648 March 29   for a letter from Wantage & answer £00 00s 02d;
for 6 dozen of bottles for wine 00 19 00; for a trumpet & camblet for
Mr Cope 00 00 10; To Mr Jackson the linen d[r]ap[er] in part of £22 2s 8d
12 00 00; To Mr Brookes in full of his bill 03 07 00; To Mr Dunsterfeild
in full due to him 06 04 00; for a coat for Rachel 00 15 00; To Mr Walker
for books for my Lord by bill 03 01 06; 31   To the Beadles for Lady Day
quarter 00 02 06; for new lines for the clock 00 02 00; for 2 dozen of
wash-balls 00 02 00; *at the same time*   To Mrs Seale in full of all due to
her 06 07 00; To Mr Olibeare in full of old 19 00 00; April 1   To
Mr Blake in full til [blank] 12 00 00; 3   To Mr Keene the joiner in full
02 14 00; More for J.B. &c 00 05 00; To a porter brought & returned
cushions 00 01 00; a letter from my Lady Sydenham by post 00 00 06; a
letter & answer Mr Hyne by post 00 01 00; a packet to Mr Wyott by post
00 01 00; a letter to Sir Francis by post 00 00 06; 4   To Mr King in part
of £188 11s 0d 18 00 00; To my Lady then in money 20 00 00; 14   To my
Lady in gold 05 00 00; To Mr Reade the mercer in full of his debt

15 02 00; To Mr Manby for gold lace by bill 03 02 06; To Mr Higinson mercer by bill 08 11 00; spent in my journey to Wantage and Bath by bill 03 18 03; paid Whitfield's fine to my Lord from Mr Wyott 02 10 00; 17    To Mr Trussell in part of £75 11s 0d 15 11 00; for a letter from Mr Hyne & answer by post 00 01 06; a letter to Bath and one to Tawstock by post 00 01 06; 18    To the post 6d & 3d which he paid for a letter 00 00 09; To Mrs Bourcher for 2 months for her boy ending the 18th of May next 01 00 00; 19    To the Collectors for the poor for Lady Day quarter 00 10 00; To Mr King's men box 00 05 00; a box with lock & key for my Lord's wash-balls 00 01 00    [page total] 160 18 06

[p. 17]    1648 To Mrs Pollard her half year's wages now due £05 00s 00d; To Mr Wyld the like 10 00 00; To Mr Lynn the like 10 00 00; To Mr Thomas Pollard the like 05 00 00; To Mr Richard Cobb the like 07 10 00; To George Chevelie the like 01 00 00; To Will: Booth the like 03 00 00; To Eliza: Searle the like 01 10 00; To Rose Hamlin the like 01 10 00; To Wilmot Toogood the like 01 00 00; To Anne Tossell the like 01 00 00; To Eliza: Thorne the like 01 00 00; To Philip the postillion the like 02 00 00; To Robert Wood the like 04 00 00; To Mr Forward the like 07 10 00; To John Burke the like 02 00 00; To Owen Prince the like 01 00 00; To Thomas Armsby the like 02 10 00; To the Porter at Sergeant's Inn 00 02 00; April 20    To my Lady when her Honour went into Kent 03 00 00; given in earnest to Mr Dance for lodgings at Bath 01 00 00; for a tortoise shell spectacle case for my Lord 00 05 06; for 2 pieces ferrit ribbon 6 dozen 00 15 00; for a coat for Mr Robert Fane's child 01 06 00; 25    To my Lady when her honour came out of Kent 05 00 00; To Mr Bowdler the coach-maker in part of his Lady Day bill £13 1s 6d 05 00 00; for changing my Lord's silver spectacles & putting the glasses in 00 00 08; a letter from Mr Hyne & answer 00 01 00; a packet to Mr Wyatt 00 01 00; 26    To Mr Pollard in part of £55 due on his book 40 00 00; for a subpoena & label to it &c 00 03 00; to the clerk of the parish till Easter 00 06 00; for glasses by my Lady 00 18 00; To Messenger brought a ticket 00 01 00; To Mr Murry in [part] of £84 for 3 quarters rent due last Lady Day & £3 10s paid for taxes 30 10 00 [page total] 154 19 02

[p. 18]    1648 April 28    To my Lady to pay for lace &c £08 00 00; for half a yard flowered tabby by Mr Bold 00 12 00; for glasses by him 00 08 00; May 2    To the Collecters for my Lord Farfax Army for 3 months ending with March last 01 13 04; a letter from Mr Hyne & answer 00 01 00; a packet to *Tawstocke* 00 01 06; a letter to Bath & the porter 00 01 00; a book for my Lord called *Groshes* 00 03 00; To the porter of Sergeant's Inn last week 00 02 00; 7    To him this day 00 02 00; a letter to Mr Hyne 00 00 06; a packet to Mr Wyott 00 01 00; 9    a letter from Mr Comb & one from Mr Sammell 00 00 04; a dryfat for my Lord's books 00 02 00; a car to carry goods to Bath wagon 00 01 06; spent in beer there 00 00 07; ['To Ro. Wood to account for to Bath' crossed through]; To the carriers porter 00 00 06; for weighing the goods went to Bath 00 01 00; To my Lord to give to a poor scholar 00 02 06; To my Lady at play with Mr Bradnell 00 01 06; 3 yards ½ of tabby for a child's coat La: Griffith 01 11 06; for trimming & making it up 00 12 00; for a

coat for Mr Wm Fane's child 01 06 00; for 18 yards silver ribbon 00 05 00;
14   To the porter of Sergeant's Inn 00 02 00; a letter from Mr Hyne &
answer 00 01 00; 16   a packet to Mr Wyott & a letter to Sir Fra: 00 01 06;
['To Bath given in part for ...' crossed through]; To my Lady in money
50 00 00; To Mr Pollard in full upon his week book ended the 12th of this
May 52 01 03; 17   To My Lady Mr Cloberye's fine for 3 lives in a term
in Dunterton 36 00 00; To My Lord [blank] Speres fine for [blank]
01 13 00   [page total] 155 9 5

[p. 19]   1648 May 17   Paid for grass for 2 carrier's horse that was hired
to Bath 00 05 6; To My lady when my Lord & her honour went to Bath
50 00 0; for 8 lbs of soap to wash up the linen 00 03 0; to Rose to bear her
charges & her child 00 16 0; June 3   for a basket to send bottles in 6d a
porter 6d 00 01 0; To the wagoner's porter carried 2 burdens to his Inn
00 01 0; To the post for letters for 2 weeks from Mr Hyne Sir Francis &
sent to *Tawstocke* & Bath 00 08 6; for 2 oz hair powder sent my Lady to
Bath 00 01 0; for half a pound of tobacco sent my Lo: thither 00 09 0; a
letter by post out of France 00 00 9; To 13 prison[er]s to their boxes
00 13 0; 14   a packet by post from Bath 00 02 0; 2 letters by the same to
Bath & 1 to Mr Hyne 00 02 0; To Mr Michell a fee for half a stag last year
00 10 0; 16   To a porter carried the hamper of bottles to the wagon
00 00 6; pack thread to pack them bottles 00 00 1; for mowing the garden
00 00 6; to Mrs Bourcher for her boy for a month now ending 00 10 0; a
letter from Bath & answer by post 00 01 0; 19   a letter to Mr Wyott &
1 to Bath & porter 00 01 6; for packing up the dryfat of books by a
cooper 00 02 6; for a louver for the box to put other books in & nails
00 00 9; 23   To a car man & porter to carry them down & to the
wagoners in 00 02 10; Paid for carrying them to *Bristoll* by wagon by one
Sparrow being £5 ¼ at 5s p[er] *hundred* 01 07 9; 27   a letter by post from
Bath & answer 00 02 0; a letter to Mr Hyne & one to Mr Wyott 00 01 0;
for viol strings virginal strings & rosen 00 17 0; 29   a letter from Bath by
the carrier 00 00 3; July 4   a letter from Bath & a packet to Tawstock &
porter 00 02 6; a letter from Lady Cope & one from Wantage 00 00 4;
6   To Mrs Joane Greene which your honours had at Bath 04 00 0; To
Mrs Anne Howard now due 04 00 0   [page total] 65 03 3

[p. 20]   July 1648 8   To a porter carried a bag of budles [*buddles*] & bits
& other things & 2 trunks & a box to Tucker the carrier £00 00s 08d;
11   for letters sent by post to *Tawstocke* 00 00 06; To Mrs Bourcher for
her boy for a month this day 00 10 00; To Goodwife Bradshaw for last
Michas. by Joseph 01 00 00; To Goodwife Reed by him for that time
00 10 00; To Rose Todd's father for 3 quarters at Lady Day last 00 15 00;
To Eliza: Fuller which she paid Mr Manby for letters for your sweet bag
which my Lady Westminster furnished 00 11 00; To Sparrow the wagoner
in full of his bill for carriages to Bath 02 12 00; 18   a letter sent by post
that day to Tawstock & porter 00 01 06; for half a pound of tobacco for
my Lord 00 12 00; for drugs for his Lordship's diet drink 00 16 00; for
2 boxes & packing the glasses 00 03 08; for a satin cap for my Lord
00 04 06; for carrying the box of plate 00 00 06; for carry[ing] the great
trunk 00 01 06; for carrying 14 pieces of han. 4 carpets & cabinet 00 01 00;
paid Mr Murry in further part of his rent to Tossell 20 00 00; To

Mr Evans for a pair of new boots [for] my Lord 01 08 00; 25   a packet
from *Tawstocke* & answer 00 02 00; a hat & box Mrs Bourcher which
Mr Bold paid my Lady 01 14 00; Mr Hooker's book for my Lord
00 02 00; To a brick-layer for mending the kitchen chimney 00 03 00; To
the beadle for Midsummer quarter 00 12 06; for carrying the box of glasses
to the carrier 00 00 06; for mending my Lady Ingram's hangings and
carrying them home 00 02 00; Au. 1   a packet to *Tawstocke* & porter
00 02 00; packets sent then & by Tho: Irish 00 00 08; the kitchen chimney
sweeping 00 00 08; for searching with Mr Bellamy for my Lord
Middlesex's order 00 03 00; 8   a packet to Tawstock & a letter to Lady
Eliz: Cope 00 01 08; for a new shoo for the pump 00 01 06; wax & tallow
to colour the rooms 00 00 10; 15   a broom & a packet to *Tawstok* &
porter 2s 00 02 03; paid the farrier's bill till 17 May 00 02 06; 17   To
Mrs Bourcher for 2 months then ending 01 00 00; To the coach-maker in
part of £10 8s 1d Midsummer quarter 05 00 00; 19   for a box to put my
Lord's clothes in 00 03 06; for 2 dozen of candles & a box 00 12 10; bronn
[*broom*] to pack them 3d, porter 10d 00 01 01   [page total] 41 16 04

[p. 21]   August 1648   a pair of garters my Lord 6s, a taffety & sarsenet
hoods 8s £00 14s 0d; 26   a packet from Tawstock & answer 00 02 0;
books sent the 3 last weeks 00 02 0; 28   To the collectors for the poor for
Midsummer 00 10 0; 29   To Mr Price by your Lord's Command 01 00 0;
Sep. 1   a packet to *Tawstok* & porter & a letter to your Ladyship 00 02 2;
a mop & a broom 00 01 1; mowing the garden & plashing the trees &
nails 00 03 0; for 4 dozen of roots of flowers to set there 00 04 0; for
6 sticks of the best hard wax 00 02 0; 4   To Mrs Edny in part of your
Ladyship's promise 03 00 0; pistachio comfits nuts & caramels 00 10 10;
tobacco then for my Lord ½ lb 00 12 0; 12 shuttlecocks 4 battle-doors &
box 00 01 10; Mr Murry to pay.   paid 3 months tax for the rent of the
house to Sir Tho: Farfax Army ending in June 01 13 4; a box to send the
pap[er], wax, shuttlecocks &c 00 00 10; 8   a packet of letters & books 6d
by Mrs Potts 00 01 6; 15   a packet to Tawstock & porter 00 01 6; a
packet to Tawstock & books Mrs Potts &c 0 01 6; a letter Lady Eliza:
Cope 00 00 2; To Mrs Deaux due at Midsummer last 04 00 0; To
Mrs Potts 01 00 0; for seeds by bill sent by the gardener 01 05 11; paid the
churchwarden parish duties for Easter last 00 06 8; To J.B. in part for
Michaelmas last 01 00 0; to the gardener to bear his charges 00 15 0; a
letter out of France 00 00 9; 28   for more drugs for my Lord 00 09 0; a
packet to Taw: & porter 00 01 6; a letter to *Corton dynham* & one
to *Netherhaven* 00 01 0; a mop & brooms to rub &c 00 01 5; To Mr Edny
more in part 02 00 0; for emptying the vault 01 01 6; a ream of writing
paper & 6 qr of meon 00 11 0; a box to pack the papers & drugs in
00 00 8; Octo. 2   given in earnest to Exet. Coach 00 10 0; a packet to
Tawstock by post 00 01 6; for 2 pamphlets sent in it 00 00 2; a box &
letter from my Lady North by post 00 01 0; for carrying boxes to
['Tucker' crossed through] Tiverton Car. 00 00 6   [page total] 24 10 4

[p. 22]   1648   To Mrs Potts to give to Sprite &c £00 01s 0d d; Octo. 9 a
packet to *Tawstocke* by post 00 01 00; a diurnal 1d, to the porter 6d
00 00 7; 2 rubbing mops 3s, sand 2d 00 03 02; a letter from *Tangly*
00 00 02; 11   3 letters from Wantage 00 00 06; To Mrs Bourcher for her

boy for 2 months ending the 14th instant 01 00 00; 17 a packet to *Tawstocke* 00 01 06; 3 pamphlets 3d, a letter to Mr Hinson 6d 00 00 09; a letter to Sir Francis Fane all by post 00 00 06; 18 a letter from *Tangly* & one from Wantage 00 00 04; 23 a letter from Tawstock by post 00 00 06; a packet to Tawstock then & porter 00 02 00; a letter from Mr Hinson 00 00 02; to the beadle for Michas. quarter 00 02 06; 29 More to Mrs Edny 01 00 00; a packet to *Tawstocke* & porter 00 01 06; a letter to Sir Francis Fane by post 00 00 06; 31 a letter out of France 00 00 08; Novemb. for a gardener's spade sent by Tucker's man 00 04 00; for carrying that & a footman's coat to him 00 00 04; 7 a packet to *Tawstocke* 00 00 06; a letter from *Tangly* 00 00 03; 10 a letter out of France 00 00 09; Paid the week book from the 13th of May last to the 17th of the same 09 03 05; for a yard of ticking to mend beds 00 02 04; 14 a packet from Tawstock answer & post 00 02 06; Mr Murry to pay. To the collectors for the Irish tax for 6 months from the first of February last for the Landlord to pay 01 05 03; 15 To Mr Boundler the coach-maker in full 05 08 00; for wax & tallow for the rooms 00 00 10; 21 To Mr Blake the tailor in part of £29 10s 3d 10 00 00; To the Collectors for the poor for Mich. 10s 00 10 00; To Mrs Edny more in part of your Honour's promise 02 00 00; a packet to Tawstock 00 01 06; a letter to Sir Fra: Fane by post 00 00 06; Flanders tile & whiting to scour 00 00 06 [page total] 31 18 00

[p. 23] 1648 Novem. 23 for bringing in 12 loads of seacoal and a load of Scoch-coal by the colliers-men £00 02s 0d; To a porter for piling up 8 loads of billets & 4 loads of faggots & the Scoch-coal 00 02 4; To the overseers of the highways 00 02 0; for a ream of writing paper 00 07 6; 25 To Mr Autin the bricklayer in full 06 10 0; 2 yards fustion to mend beds & 6d thread 00 03 6; a letter by post from Sir Francis Fane 00 00 6; a letter from Mr Hyne 00 00 6; a packet to *Tawstocke* & porter 00 01 6; To Mrs Bourcher for a month ending 14 00 10 0; To Mr Sadlor a book seller for a book which my Lady had of him 00 16 0; To a cooper for hooping several things 00 04 6; for sand & ashes to scour with 00 00 8; To the water woman to help 2 days 00 01 0; for 14 birch-brooms 00 01 0; for vinegar to scour with 00 00 3; a letter from my Lady Griffith 00 00 02; Decem. 5 To the brewer in part of £29 0s 3d 10 00 0; a packet to *Tawstocke* & a letter Jo: Mills 00 01 6; a pack of matt for your Ho: chamber 0 14 0; for thread & nails 1s, porter 6d 00 01 6; 3 pamphlets sent down & a letter Jo: Mills 00 00 6; 9 to Mr Rydor the carpenter in full of 2 bills & of all due to him 06 16 6; To Ann Tossell her half year's wage Mich. 01 00 0; 12 A packet to Tawstock and porter 00 02 0; Tax Mr Murry. To the Collectors for Sir Thom: Farfax to & for June last for the landrate 01 13 4; 13 14 To Mr Deuop due 20 Novem. last 04 00 0; 16 To Mr Richard Pollard 01 00 0; To Mr Deane the wood-monger in full till the 14th of May last 12 00 0; 2 wings to sweep with & 2 door-mats 00 00 6; Tax Mr Murry. To the Collectors for the Lord Farfax for May & April 1648 for the land rate 01 13 4 [page total] 48 16 9

[p. 24] 1648 December To the several Collectors for the Lord Farfax Army for taxes for goods as by acquittances appears £10 10s 0d; 19 a packet to *Tawstocke* 00 01 6; for weeding the court yard 00 01 0; To

the beadle for Christmas quarter oo o2 6; 26 a packet to Tawstock, a
letter Mr Hyne & porter oo o2 6; To Mrs Bourcher for her boy for a
month ending 12, sent by Hen: Gardner oo 10 o; for laying the mats in
your Ladyship's chamber oo o2 o6; for nails to nail the mats oo oo 2;
Jan. 5 To Doctor Gifford's Apothecary in full of his bill o2 o6 o; a
packet to Tawstock & one to Mr Hyne oo o2 o; To Mr Rich for his advice
about beginning at Goldsmyths Hall on the petition o1 oo o; To the
door-keeper there oo o1 o; a coach to carry Mr Stapleton thither oo o1 o6;
a certificate of the Covenant & of the General's letter from the clerk of the
Parliament oo 15 4; 8 a packet to Tawstock, a letter to Hainton & post
oo o1 6; a certificate out of the Chancery of the taking the Negative Oath
o o5 o; 16 a letter out of France oo oo 9; a letter & answer to
*Netherhaven* oo oo 6; for nails & tenter hooks oo oo 6; to Cormon for
hanging the parlour [?door] oo o1 o; for fruit & spice by bill o1 12 6; to
J.B. in full for Michas o1 oo o; To him for Christmas o1 oo o; 20 To my
lady in money that day 150 oo o; to Will Lynn his wages due Mich. last
10 oo o; To Mr Forward for £50 2 years due in Aug. o8 oo o; To Will
Lynn the like for the like sum o8 oo o; To him for Anne Tossell's diet
from the 17th of May to 18 Janu: 32 weeks o8 oo o    [page total] 204 17 9

[p. 25]   1648   To Mr Trussell in part of [blank] due to him £20 oos od;
To Mr Jackson in part of [blank] due to him 10 oo o; Janu. 27   To
Mr Orlibeare in part of £34 due to him 12 oo o; To Mr Kinge in part of
[blank] due to him 20 oo o; To Mr Blake in part of [blank] due to him
10 oo o; To Mr Allen in part of [blank] due to him 32 oo o; To the porter
at Sergeant's Inn oo o1 o; half a pound of tobacco for my Lord oo o5 o;
2 ells of holland by Wilmot oo 13 o; To Mrs Bourcher for a month
oo 10 o; To Mr Allen's man at twice oo o4 6; for entering that order at
Go[ldsmith's] Hall oo o1 o; To the Collectors for the poor for Xmas
quarter oo 10 o; for parchment & sand &c oo o1 6; A packet to Tawstock
last week oo o2 o; a letter then to John Mills by post oo oo 6; a letter out
of Holland then oo oo 9; Paid the week book in full from 17 Jan. 1648 to
the 27 of the same 29 18 5; and given Mr Forward then to account for
10 oo o; To Mr Vavasor which your honour gave him order to lay out for
Fra: Hawthorne's child o2 oo o; the declaration of the secluded members
oo oo 4; Mr Prin's speech for my Lord oo o1 o; for a diurnal & a moderate
oo oo 2; To the porter went to *Merreworth* oo o5 o; ostlers 2s horses at
Eltham 3s 9d oo o5 o9; To the prisoners of 13 prisons oo 13 o; Feb. 3   To
Mr Rich the lawyer his fee o2 oo o; To Mr Dowtyn in part of £20 14s od
due to him as marrying Mrs Just 10 oo o; To Mrs Anne Howard due to
her o4 oo o; To the porter at Sergeant's Inn oo o2 6; 4   To Mr Herne the
lawyer a fee o2 oo o; for 2 razors for my Lord by Jo: Barke oo o5 o; To
the Collectors for the Army for six months ending Lady Day next for the
landlord o3 o6 8; To Mr Bold to buy a load of hay o2 10 o; To
Mr Redinge a fee o2 oo o; 6   A packet to *Tawstocke* & porter oo o1 6
[page total] 175 18 7

[p. 26]   1648 Feb. 7   To the ['Collectors' crossed through] Clerk for
weekly bills £oo o6s od; for the order to have your honour's goods not
taxed oo o2 6; To Mr Wilkins for Mr Rushworthe oo o2 6; To Mr Phillips
for cordial waters o2 o4 o; To the Gardener for seeds & towards his losses

01 01 0; To Mr Watson to go to Goldsmyths Hall 01 00 0;
15 To Mr Rich the like 01 00 0; To Mr Gape solicitor then 00 10 0; To
Mr Vincent the door-keeper 00 02 6; for the King's book by Mr Wild
00 04 6; a pair stockings 2s 8d, pair shoes 7s 4d [*for*] Fra:[ncis] 00 10 0;
for ½ 16 of tobacco for my Lord 00 08 0; To Mr Evans my Lord's
shoemaker for a pair of boots & a pair of shoes [for] My Lo. 01 10 0;
19 To Mr Rich his fee when the business finished 01 00 0; To Mr Wilson
the like 01 00 0; To Mr Gape the like 00 10 0; To the door-keeper then
00 02 6; To the poor there then 00 00 8; To Mr Wild for another of the
King's Books 00 06 0; To the Chair-men to Goldsmith's Hall 00 04 0;
21 for a coach to carry money to Goldsmyth's Hall 00 02 0; To
Mrs Bourcher for her son for a month 00 10 0; To the clerk of
Goldsmyth's Hall for making the bond & counterbond for 2 payments
00 05 0; To Mr Leeche's man for writing the particulars 00 05 0; To
Mr Leech fo[r] the 2 letters & particulars 01 10 0; 26 for several sorts of
sweetmeats 01 04 6; for a packet to Taw: & letter to Mr Hyne 00 02 0; for
a psalm book for my Lord 00 02 0; 28 To Mr Forward to account for
10 00 0; To my Lady in money when Mr Beare paid 10 00 0; To J.B. for
Lady Day next 01 00 0; for books for Randall by bill 00 07 7; To
Mr Cobb to pay for viol strings 00 15 0; Mar. 3 To Mr Forward upon
his book 07 00 0; To the Collections for Do: Manaring's daughter 00 05 0;
A packet to Tawstock & a letter to Sir Francis & porter & one to Mr Row
to Exet[er] 00 02 6 [page total] 46 14 3

[p. 27] 1648 Mar. 13 Given away at *Merreworth* £05 00s 00d; To the
coachman brought your Ladyship back 01 00 0; To Mr Bold to lay out
there by the way 00 10 0; To Mr Mildmay for a poor purse 00 02 06; To
the poor going thither 00 00 02; To the prisoners' box coming back
00 02 00; 13 An acquit. to Tawstock & letter to Mr Row 00 01 06;
To Mr Leech his man for a copy of your letter about goods 00 02 06; my
Lady Standish mending & burnishing 00 04 00; To Randall for a book
called [blank] 00 00 06; 16 To him for his Master in part for his
schooling at 40s per *year* 00 05 00; To Mr Hales for his advice upon the
Great Deed of Entail 02 00 00; To the poor by the way 00 00 07; To
Mr Forard upon his book 30 00 00; To Mr Leech for the letter about the
goods 00 10 00; To your Lordship at Tables with Mr Bold 00 02 00; for
bringing home the great trunk 00 01 00; 19 To Owen Prince his wages
now due 01 00 00; To him a gratuity at going away 01 00 00; Tax
Mr Murry to pay. To the Collectors for an assessment upon the Rent for
the Lo: Fairfax army for 4 months ending the last of Septem: 1646. Tho:
Raynor, Edw: Feild Collectors 03 06 08; 20 A packet to Tawstock 1s, a
letter to *Andovor*, 6d one to Mr Hyne 6d, one to Sir Francis 6d 00 02 06;
21 To Mrs Bourcher for her son for a month 00 10 00; To Mr Forard
then to account for 10 00 00; To Mr Austen in part of £82 20 00 00; for
5½ pounds of sweet meats 00 12 09; 24 To the Brewer in part of [blank]
20 00 00; for 2 oz of hair powder 00 01 00; Ma: 26 1649 To Mr Forard
to account for 10 00 00 [page total] 106 19 08

[p. 28] Sum total of all disbursements upon this book from the 28th of
March 1648 until the 27th of March 1649 is £1218 02s 00d

And rec. in the same time as appears at the other end of this book the sum of £1224 15s 4d

So, Rem. in this accountant's hands £06 13s 4d

1649 To my Lady one Oxford piece of silver £01 01s 00d; To Mr Wilkins which he laid out by bill 02 10 06; March 28th To Mr Murry in part of £129 7s 5d for rent due to him last Lady Day 29 07 00; To the wood-monger in part of £15 due to him before 17th January last 10 00 00; 29 To the Armourer for mending a suit of arms & keeping 2 arms 5 years 1 11 0; band strings for Randall & Sam 00 01 00; 31 for a load of hay all but 5s 02 10 0; April 2 To my Lady in half-crowns 01 00 0; To a poor Midwife came out of Ireland 00 05 0; A pair of stockings Ed: Wingfield 00 04 0; A letter from Sir Francis & answer 00 01 0; 3 A packet to Tawstock, a letter Mr Hine & porter 00 02 0; To Phillip his wages by Mr Bold 02 00 0; To him for his livery coat 01 00 0; 4 To Mr Forard to account for 1 00 0; 7 To your honour by Elizabeth Serle 05 00 0; To Doctor Wild for the King's book in 24 00 02 6; A letter from Mr Fane 00 00 9; 2 more of the King's books in 24 00 04 8; for 5 several sorts of sweet meats 00 06 3; a letter from Mr Wyott by Mr Smyth with a bill 00 00 6; To Mrs Philpott came out of Ireland 00 05 0 [page total] 67 12 [blank]

[p. 29] 1649 April 9 A packet from *Tawstocke* & answer £00 02s 06d; a letter to Sir Fra: Fane & one to Jo: Mills 00 01 00; a letter from *Merreworth* by carrier 00 00 02; 2 oz of hair-powder my Lady 00 01 00; 11 To your honour by Mr Bold in money 10 00 00; Lilbornes book and the Act about Sequ. 00 01 00; half a pound of tobacco for my Lord 00 01 00; for drugs to make 2 quarts of ink 00 01 00; letters from *Merreworth* 00 00 02; to the Paver in part for paving 01 00 00; for clasping 2 of the King's Books with silver 00 07 06; 14 To the Collectors for 2 months tax for Sir Tho: Faierfax for Septem: & October 1645 for the Landlord to pay 01 13 04; 17 A packet from *Tawstocke* & porter 00 02 00; a letter from my Lady Ermyn to my Lady Darcy 00 00 06; 18 To Mr Foward to account for 20 00 00; To Mr Richard Pollard when he went to Tawstock 05 10 00; for a warrant for him to go post 00 02 06; going by water to Mr Vinor 00 01 00; to the poor at Lincoln's Inn Gate 00 00 06; for 3 half pounds of sweet-meats 00 07 00; 21 To Mr Vinor in full of all due to him 02 05 00; Tax Mr Murry. To the Collectors for the Militia 00 16 08; To Mrs Bourcher for her boy for a month 00 10 00; To a porter carried a trunk to Mr Vinors 00 00 08; 21 To Mr Forard to account for 10 00 00; To Wilmot for lace &c 05 16 06; 23 To Mr Forard to account for 30 00 00; To Oundle carrier brought a basket Mrs Dorman 00 00 04; 24 To my Lady in money 20 00 00; To Mr Hales & Mr Beare 02 00 00; 25 To the poor there 00 00 03; searching for a deed enrolled 00 01 00; A packet to Tawstock & porter 00 01 06; To the Chairmen to Lincoln' Inn 00 02 06; To the Collectors for the poor for the Lady Day quarter 00 10 00 [total] 112 02 07

[p. 30] 1649 April 28 for a load of hay & a load of dung carried £02 17s 06; To Mrs Wingfeild for mohair 02 09 00; for 2 oz of hair-powder for my Lady 00 01 00; To your Ladyship at Tables with

Mr Bold 00 02 06; A packet to *Tawstocke* Saturday last 00 01 00;
May 1   A packet to Tawstock & porter 00 01 06; To Mr Hales for advice
01 00 00; To the Beadle for Lady Day quarter 00 02 06; for a leaden
standige [*standish*] 00 00 08; To Mr Cobb for one tuned the organs
00 05 00; April 28   To Mr Forard to account for on his books 25 00 00;
['April' crossed through] for 3 yards of ribbon for my Lord's waistcoat
00 01 06; May 2   To Mr Hales with my Lady Westmorland 01 00 00;
A letter sent from Wantage & answer 00 00 04; To a scrivenor's man
writing Lady Fane's bond, a bill of sale for Mr Vinor & *Coomb* bond and
attending here 3 times 00 10 00; for *Esops fables* in English 00 01 00; To
one that painted Campden's *Brittania* for Mr Robert Fane in part of
£23 10s  13 10 00; 4   To My Lady in money in a pap[er] one night
02 00 00; To a foot-post brought a letter & 2 capons from Mr Hart of
*Netherhaven* 00 02 00; 8   To Mr Hale's when he went to Mr Brown
02 00 00; To My Lady to give Mr Jenkins 02 00 00; To My Lady to give
Mr Mildmay 01 00 00; To the Porter [at] Lincolns Inn 1s, poor 10d
00 01 10; for a great gray coach horse 32 05 00; a packet to Tawstock &
post 00 01 06; to my Lady a Scoch piece King James 00 00 06; for a load
of hay & a load straw 03 14 00; To my Lord to buy paper 01 00 00; To
the porter at Sergeant's Inn 00 01 00; 9   To my Lady in money 05 00 00;
To the clerk of St Gyleses for Easter 00 06 00; To the post for several
letters to several bailiffs of manors & 1 to Sir Francis Fane 00 03 00;
12   To the paver in part of £17 8s  08 0000; To Mr Forard upon his book
20 00 00   [page total] 124 18 04

[p. 31]   1649 May 12   To Mrs Norton her half year's wages due at our
Lady Day last £05 00s 0d; To Mr Wild for a qu. then due 05 00 0; To
Mr Lynn for ['a quarter' crossed through] half year then due 10 00 0; To
Mr Bold in part of wages due to him 09 00 0; To Mr Cobb his half year's
wages 07 00 0; to Mr Forard the like 07 10 0; To Ro: Wood the like
04 00 0; To Whimper for a month 01 00 0; To George Cleviely his half
year's wages 01 00 0; To John Burke the like 02 00 0; To Will Booth the
like 03 00 0; To Elizabeth Searle the like 01 10 0; To Wilmot the like
01 00 0; To Ann Tossell the like 01 00 0; 14   To Mr Forard to account
for 20 00 0; Tax Mr Murry   To the Collectors for the Lord General's
Army for 3 months from 25th of March to 25 June for the rent of the
house 02 10 0; To my Lady in money when my Lord paid his last
payment at Goldsmyth's Hall 150 00 0; for 2 oz of rose powder for my
Lady 00 01 0; To my Lady to give it at My Lord Moone's christening
02 00 0; 26   To Mr Forward to account for 20 00 0; for a feather bed &
bolster for the stable by Mr Bold 02 05 0; 27 To my Lady in money
20 00 0; to the poor at Lincolns Inn gate 00 00 6; 29 A packet to
*Tawstocke* & 4 other letters to the several manors & 1s to the porter
00 04 0; 31   To Mr Forard to account for 20 00 0; a letter by the Saturday
post to *Hunpill* 00 00 6; June 6   To Mr Grigg by bill in part for the
charges of the suit with Pasmore ['of searching the subpoenas upon the
witnesses' crossed through] 02 00 0; 8   To Mr Hales to move in
Pasmore's suit 01 00 0; To Connon to serve witnesses twice with tickets
being 9, 18s to him for his pains 1s 6d [page total] 299 11 0

[p. 32]  1649  9 June   To Mr Forard to account for £15 00s 00d; 11 more to him to account for 20 00 00; To Mr Mainard & Mr Hales in the suit with Mrs Pasmore to be at the Trial 02 00 00; To Mr Grigg the Attorney for fees then 03 00 00; searching for Pasmore's Inventory 00 01 06; spent upon the witnesses 00 02 06; 14   To Mr Forard to account for 40 00 00; to my Lady by Mr Cobb 02 00 00; To Mrs Bourcher for 2 months by my Lady 10s and by me 10s 00 10 00; 19   a packet to *Tawstocke* & porter 00 01 06; To Mr Cobb to give Mrs Potts for your Ladyship 01 00 00; To the Paver in full of his bill 08 04 00; To Mr Deuox & his partners my Lord apothecary 09 10 00; To my Lady in money 30 00 00; To Randall for his schooling for a quarter 00 10 00; for a pound of tobacco for my Lord 0 14 00; To J.B. for Midsummer 01 05 00; To the scrivenor writ the Lord's bonds 01 00 00; 25   To Mr Forard to account for 50 00 00; To Mrs Anne Howard in full of her diet 104 00 00; 30   for 2 pieces of gold of Hen: 8 & 1 Eliz. 11 13 03; To Mr Jackson linen-draper in full to this day 21 07 00; To Mr Orlibeare a woollen-draper the like 20 00 00; To Mr Manby a silk-man the like 13 10 00; To Mr Forard to account for 30 00 00; July 2   To the Brewer in part of his bill 25 00 00; To him then in full for ale 02 19 00; To my Lady in money 200 00 00; 2   To Mr Forard to account for 10 00 00; 3   To my Lady Newport 100 00 00; To Mr King in part of his old Bills 016 00 00; 3   To him in full of his new bills 24 00 00; To Mr Bassett apothecary in full 03 00 00; To the farrier in full 03 06 00; To a bit-maker in full 06 06 00; for horse grass to a butcher 01 03 06; To the wood-monger in full 26 07 01; 4   To my Lady in money at going away 19 17 6   [page total] 823 7 9

[p. 33]   Sum total disbursed upon this book from the 27th of March 1649 until the 4th of July foll. £1427 11s 10d

And rem. in the same time as appears at the other end of this book the sum of £1072 4 0

So, remaineth due to me this 4th day of July 1649 the sum of 355 7s 10d. Whereof, Wilts. Rec. out of *Notton Bewley* &c £351 3s 1d

So rem. due to me this 4th of July £4 4s 9d.

## Expenses, 1649–1652

KENT ARCHIVES OFFICE, U269/A518/3

*The book measures 8″ by 12″ and has a paper cover. It is headed 'A book of all receipts and payments made by William Lynn for the right honorable the Earl of Bath since the 4th of July 1649'. There are eight pages of fines which have not been edited.*

[enclosure, dorse. Mr Wilkin's account. To 1.b. the 22th of March 1650 £5]

Mr Wilkins account since July 1650 to 12 of Novem. following.

Recd of Sir He: Crook 4 0 0; Letters & pamphlets from June 20  1 10 4; To Randall Payton 0 12 6; To Sir Hen: Crooke 10 0 0; for lute strings 2 0 0; for paper 10[s] 6; to Mr Lynne 10 0 0; for drugs 7 0 0; for portage

o 1 o; for wine bottles & honey 1 7 10; to Margaret 1 o o  [total] 34 2 2
rest 5 17 10  recd. 10 o o
pd to Mr Cox 1 o o; to his clerk for the [faint] o 2 6; for letters &
pamphlets 17 6; laid out for Mr Heynes 10 6; for letters & pamphlets from
March to June 4[s] 10; to Mr Rushworth protection 1 o o; to his man
o 2 6  [total] 3 17 10

[p. 1]  1649 July the 9th  Rem. due to this accountant the 4th of July
1649 £04 04s 09d; *Hunspill*  to my Lady at *Hunspill* Edward Cooke's fine
160 00 00; to her Ladyship then Henry Woollcott's fine 09 00 00; to her
Ladyship then which Elizabeth Pope paid 01 00 00; to her Ladyship then
in part of Tho: Shalmer's fine of £45  020 00 00; to her Ladyship then
John Collins his fine 08 16 00; to her Ladyship then in part of James
Cames fine of £36  01 00 00; to her Ladyship then Frances Ventman's fine
36 00 00; to her Ladyship then William Verman's 2 fines 152 00 00; more
to her Ladyship for a heriot by him 02 10 00; to her Ladyship then in part
of William Blore's fine of £110  55 00 00; 11 Norton Fitz.  to her
Ladyship in part of Tho: Musgrave's fine of £63  03 00 00; to her
Ladyship then John Piller's fine 08 00 00; to her Ladyship then Wm
Shutt's fine 02 00 00; 13 Uffculme  to her Ladyship in part of Mr John
Langdew's fine of £54  04 00 00; to her Ladyship in part of Nich:
Hollawaie's fine of £435  05 00 00; to her Ladyship John Fowler's fine
01 06 08; 14 Hackpen  to her Ladyship Alice Brooke alias Batson's fine
01 06 08; 17 Bampton to her Ladyship George Hatswell's fine & heriot
05 00 00; 23 of Octo. *Noning*.  to her Ladyship in part of Tho: Langden's
fine of £70  30 00 00; to her Ladyship in part of Robert Parrat's fine
of £60  38 00 00; *Hunspill*  to her Ladyship in part of Francis Everatt's
fine of £60  10 00 00; to her Ladyship in part of Amis Pingellie's fine
of £22  06 00 00; Bampton  to my Lord Alice Prout's last fine 02 00 00;
Sheldon  to my Lady in part of Mr Farthing's fine of £340  20 00 00;
Taunton  to my Lady in part of Mr Berrie's fine of £50  10 00 00; to
Mrs Temporance Murry in full of rent due to her father at Lady Day last
for the house in the Fields paid by Mr Gatcombe returned from *Hunspll*
100 00 00; 10 September  To Mr Jackman in further part of my Lord
Denbye's part which was secured by one Allin of London by bond
100 00 00; paid the bricklayers bill in full 01 10 00; to Mr Austen in part
of £62 due to him 20 00 00; to the beadle for Midsummer quarter
00 02 06; a packet to Taw: by post & a letter to Sir Fra: Fane 00 01 06; to
the post porter for 10 weeks 00 05 00; a troll-madam & bowls sent to
*Tawstocke* 01 00 00; 2 hoods for my Lady & a pair of black bobs
00 11 06; 3 dozen black penny ribbons 00 04 06  [page total] 818 19 01

[p. 2]  1649  for 2 pair of battle doors and 12 shuttle cocks £00 02s 00d;
to a glasier mended my chamber window 00 01 00; a bible Sam Bold
00 04 00; a quarter of a pound the best hard wax 00 01 06; a box to put
the black & white in & cords 00 03 06; for four viol bows 00 08 00; to a
porter carried the 2 boxes 00 00 08; for a dozen of bow strings 00 01 04; a
lock & key & nails for my Lord's books 00 00 07; to a porter brought the
pie plate 00 00 10; to Mr Michell a fee for a stag 01 00 00; Au. 28  for my
journey to London going by Mr Thornhurst with my man and horses
02 05 05; my horses 8 nights in London 01 01 10; my horses shoeing

blooding & drenching there oo o6 oo; my own diet there that time
oo 12 oo; myself and my horses one night by the way into North[amp]ton
shire oo o9 oo; to goodwife Bradshaw for 2 years this Michas o2 oo oo; to
goodwife Redhead the like & a quarter more being sick o2 o5 oo; to Rose
Hamlin's father for a year & half then o1 10 oo; to Mrs Wildbore from
your Ladyship by appointment o1 oo oo; for a pot of honey and carrier
oo o3 o8; July 9 &c   to my Lady at *Hunspill* [Huntspill] in part of
Everatt's rent 10 oo oo, to my Lady at Hackpen Alexander Gudrige's fine
45 oo oo, to my Lady Lady [sic] at Sheldon part of Smythe's heriot of
£6 13s 4d o3 oo oo, Bampton   to my Lady at Bampton Mrs Allin's
3 heriots 10 o6 o8, to my Lady which Mr Culme gave o2 oo oo, to my
Lady which one Milton gave o1 oo oo   [total] 84 o3 o

2 Novem.   to my Lady in money at my going from Taw: to London
10 oo oo; to the cook in full of his wages due Michas. last o3 oo oo;
13   a packet from *Tawstocke* oo oo o6; a packet to *Tawstocke* oo o1 o6; a
letter to Sir Francis Fane oo oo o6; to the post then for 10 weeks oo o5 oo;
for 1 lb of hair powder for my Lady oo o7 oo; to J.B. for half a year with
Christmas next o2 10 oo; to the beadle for Michas quarter oo o2 o6; to
Mr Trussell in part of £48 [blank] due to him by Mr Fuller the 28 of July
40 oo oo; Novem. 18   to Mr Kinge in part of £172 19s 6d due to him
60 oo oo   [total] 116 7 o   [page total] 201 10 oo

[p. 3]   1649 Nov. 16   to Mr Austen in full of all due to him £49 oos ood;
to Mrs Bourcher for 6 months for her boy o3 oo oo; to Mr Wild by
Mr Beare as Mr Wild's note o5 oo oo; 17 a packet to *Tawstocke* oo o1 oo;
20 a packet to *Tawstocke* & a letter to Sr Francis oo o1 o6; a letter to
Mr Michell & the post porter oo o1 oo; a packet then from *Tawstocke*
oo oo o6; to Mr Benifeild for a ring 24 oo oo; for 2 quarts of luke olives
oo o5 oo; for 4½ lbs of cotton wick yarn at £20 oo o7 o6; for enrolling the
deed from Sir Fra: Fane & Sir E: Hal o1 17 oo; to the collectors for the
poor for Midsummer & Mich. o1 oo oo; to the painter for work by bill
o3 oo oo; 23   to Mr Write a druggist by bill o4 16 oo; a packet from
*Tawstocke* & answer oo o2 oo; for a lock for the trunk sent my Lord's
clothes in oo oo o8; to a porter carried that & other things to the carrier
oo oo o8; a letter from my Lady Eliz: Cope & one from *Apthorpe*
[Apethorpe] oo oo o4; a bible from *Tawstocke* by the carrier oo o1 oo;
27   a packet to Taw. & porter oo o1 oo; paid a Hosier's bill for your
honours Mr Bradford o4 10 oo; paid for a copy of Mr ['wish' crossed
through] Welch his answer oo 14 o4; for 2 ells of canvas for fine cheese
strainers oo o2 oo; a letter from Wantage & one from *Hunspill* oo oo o4;
for nails to mend the cover of the cellar door oo oo o2; 30   a packet by
post from *Tawstocke* oo o1 oo; a pound of powder for clothes oo o7 o6; to
myself my half year's wages due Michas last 10 oo oo; more to myself by
bond sent to my Lady 55 oo oo; Decem. 1   a letter from Taw. by post
oo oo o6; 2 quarts of sallet oil & a bottle oo o5 o6; 2 quarts of olives & a
barrel oo o2 o4; a barrel to put the green ginger in oo oo o8; 14 lbs green
ginger at 3s per pound o2 o2 oo; 4½ lbs wax candle my Lord and 1 lb my
Lady oo 12 o4; to a gardener for a tree & seeds o1 10 oo; to Mrs Worner
£8 being given her before o5 oo oo; 3   a packet from *Tawstocke* & porter

oo oi o6; a box to send the tree, seeds & tumblers in & cord oo oo io; a
letter from Wantage oo oo o2; 7 a packet to *Tawstocke* by post oo oo o6;
ii a packet to *Tawstocke* by post oo oi oo [page total] 166 o7 io

[p. 4] 1649 Decem. to the glasier for mending the windows at my Lo:
of Middlesex entering on the house £oo ios ood; to Margett's husband for
24 letters from *Bruen* [Bruern], Aston & Wantage & to them places in my
absence oo o4 oo; to him for a letter for Randall out of France oo oo o6; to
the wagoner carried my Lord's books to *Bristoll* oo 13 o5; for cords porter
and car man oo oi io; for water to wash the linen left fowl oo oi oo; for
my Lord's beaver & band o4 io oo; for seeds by Gribble which Mr Beare
laid out oo 14 oo; to Mr Beare his salary for this year o3 o6 o8; to
Mr Townsend, Mr Jackman & Mr Waterhouse by by [sic] paying it to
Mr Bruerton their assignee 355 o9 o9; to Mr Boardman upon a bond the
like 355 o9 o9; ii to Mr Baker by my Lord of Dorset's assignment the
like 355 o5 o9; spent at Westminster with Mr Cox & Mr Wilkins oo o7 oo;
to Mr Leech of Goldsmyth's Hall for his certificate that my Lord
compounded on *Barnstable* articles 2s his man oo o7 oo; for a copy of
*Barnstable* articles from the clerk oo o9 o2; ii a packet to *Tawstocke* and
porter oo oi o6; going by water with Mr Wilkins oo oi oo; a case for my
Lord's mathematical instruments oo 18 oo; to Mr Bales for gloves &
ribbon for your honour o3 12 o6; to Mr Gape for a copy of *Barstable*
articles oo oi oo; 17 to Sir Raph Sydenham in full of £2oo due to him by
bond all but the interest since the first £ioo was paid ioo oo oo; a letter
from my Lady Eliz: i from Wantage & answer oo oo o6; a packet to
*Tawstocke* by post oo oo o6; to the post porter for a week oo oo o6; to
Mr Rich to beat the Committee of Haberdashers Hall oi oo oo; a dinner at
Westminster with him Mr Ash, Mr Reding & Mr Leech oi o3 oo; a *latitat*
for Tho: Hobson oo o4 oi; a letter from my Lady Eliz: Cope oo oo o2;
for my Lord Herbert's *history of Henry the 8* oo o9 o6; 21 a packet to
*Tawstocke* oo o2 oo; to Mr Rushworth for the Generals certificate bast.
oi oo oo; to his man and one that brought it to Westminster oo o3 oo; to
Mr Cox the clerk for an order &c in that business oo io oo; spent that
morning with Mr Rushworth &c oo o4 o6 [page total] 1187 o2 o7

[p. 5] 1649 to Mr Murrey in full of his half year's rent for his house
£8 6s 4d being paid in taxes it being due at Michas last £47 13s o8d; 22 to
the brewer in full for beer o2 19 o6; to Randall Paytons school-master for
a quarter by bill o6 13 o4; to Mr Blake the tailor in full of a bill o9 16 oo;
to Mr Allen when he had made my Lord's mathematical instruments
oi oo oo; to the brick layer for mending the chimney in the room over the
arch o3 15 oo; to the carpenter for his work & timber there o3 oo oo;
25 a packet to *Tawstocke* and porter oo oi oo; to the clerk of
Haberdasher's Hall committee oo o2 o6; 28 Mr Wilkin's dinner & wine
& going by water that day oo o2 o6; to the stone cutter to lay the hearth
at 2½d per foot oo o4 o6; to the glasier to mend the windows oo oi o6;
January i a packet to *Tawstocke* & porter oo oi oo; for a case for the
great glass oo o6 oo; for 3 books sent my Lord from Mr Bee oo 14 oo;
8 a packet to *Tawstocke* and porter oo oi o6; to Alderman Vinor in full
for plate by bill 31 17 o3; to the smith by bill 9s 4d whereof in old iron
2s iod oo o6 o6; ii a packet to *Tawstocke* oo oi oo; 18 a packet from

Taw. answer post & a diurnal oo oi o6; 25 a packet to Taw. and a pamphlet oo oo o8; to Mr Smith the oat chandler of old for oats & beans delivered in Mr Slowlie's time o4 15 oo; Feb. 2   to Henry Bradshaw for J.B. & in part for next Lady Day for him oi 18 oo; 5   a letter to Taw. porter & 2 diurnals oo oi o6; a letter for *Tangly* or Oxford oo oo o6; to my Lady in money ioo oo oo; a copy of my Lord's note left with Serg. Browne oo oi oo; to Mr Serjeant Glanvile for advice & meeting o4 oo oo; to Mr Norbourne the like o3 oo oo; a packet to Taw. *Hunspill* & porter oo o2 oo; to the poor at Sergeant's Inn oo oo o6; i lb of damask powder for clothes oo o6 oo; a ream of good white paper oo o7 oo; 15   to old Saunders the porter your last appointment oi oo oo; to the beadle for Christmas quarter oo o2 o6; a porter brought the linen chest oo oo o6 [page total] 224 13 o5

[p. 6]   1649 Feb. 19   to Mr Hales for counsel £oi oos ood; 25   to Mrs Bourcher for her boy for 4 months due the 18 of March next o2 oo oo; for my own board wages from the ioth of Nov. 1649 to the 3 of February following 12 weeks o6 oo oo; my journey from *Tawstocke* to London with my man & 2 horses & sending them into North[amp]tonshire my Lord of Westmorland to bear the one half so for your Honour to allow oi o5 oo; 27   Lady [sic] out in expenses for my Lady being at London 25 14 o4½; to Mr Beare in full of all debts due to him 54o oo oo; to Mrs Pagett in part of £25o due to her ioo oo oo; to Mr Eastland in full for your Honours lodgings o2 oo oo; to his maid helped keep the rooms clean oo io oo; to Margett the like for helping then oo io oo; to the poor when your Honour went from London oi oo oo; for coals the night before oo oo io; for a box to send the glasses in oo oo io; to a porter to remove all the goods oo o6 oo; to the porter packed & fetched the goods in a car that was sent by Glowin oo o3 o4; a packet to *Tawstocke* & porter oo oi o6; March 5   for a diurnal & act against delinquents oo oo o4; for 5 gallons & 2 quarts of Rheinish wine at 18d & porter oi 13 o6; paid for 7 barrels of beer & the excise o2 o5 o6; paid for 4 dozen of candles by bill 8s being in my bill oi oo oo; 8   paid the woodmongers bill in full o4 13 oo; for a dozen of bottles & corks to send to Taw. oo o3 o3; paid the baker in full 9s being in my bill for bread oo o4 o6; paid him for ½ bushel & ½ a peck of flour oo o8 o6; to my Lord of Middlesex porter oo o2 oo; 9   a packet to *Tawstocke* oo oi o4; 12   a packet to Taw. a diurnal & porter oo oi o7; for mending the pump in the stable yard your Honour's part oo o4 oo; for carrying the dung from your own yard oo o5 oo; 2 letters from Tangley & i from Wantage & answer oo oo o8; to my Lord Primate's servant brought Bishop Davent's book oo o2 o6; 15   a packet to *Tawstocke* and porter oo oi o6; 23   2 dozen quart bottles & corks & 26 quarts ½ pint Rheinish is 6d o2 o5 io; 29   a packet to *Tawstocke* & porter carried the bottles oo o2 oo   ex[amined] [page total] 697 o6 io½

[p. 7]   1649 March   for a pair of bowls sent by Glowin £oo o6s ood; 23   a pair of boots & a pair of shoes for my Lord oi oi oo; 23   a hamper for the bottles for the first wine & porter o o2 oo; for toothpicks for my Lord oo o2 oo; a hamper for the last 2 dozen of bottles oo oi oo; to the usher of Westminster school for Randall oo io oo; a packet to Taw. a diurnal & porter oo oi o2; 165o March 27   to the post for a packet & a

letter to Mr Thornhurst 00 01 06; Tax Mr Murry to pay to the collectors
for the Army for 3 months ending at Christmas for the Landlord 02 01 00;
to them the like for my Lord for goods 01 05 00; a letter from Tangley &
one from Wantage 00 00 04; paid the Attorney's bill in the suit with
Deacon 01 06 06; to the collectors for the poor for Christmas quarter
00 10 00; a letter to Taw. by post & 1 to *Bristoll* for Mrs Norton 00 01 00;
a quire of writing paper 00 00 05; April 2   a packet to Taw. porter &
diurnal 00 01 08; a packet that day from *Tawstocke* 00 01 00; for the
history of the civil wars of France 01 04 00; to the collectors for 3 months
assessment for the Army set upon goods ending Midsummer last 03 00 00;
3 a packet to *Tawstocke* 00 01 00; 9   a packet from Taw. answer porter &
diurnal 00 02 08; a parcel of viol strings 01 00 00; a pair of green silk
stockings for my Lord 02 10 00; a satin cap for his Lordship 00 05 00; a
letter my Lady Eliz: Cope 2d, for a box to send paper in & *the history of
the Civil wars of France* 1s  00 01 02; to Randall Paytons Mr Gregory he
being put out to be kept sick of the small pox 01 00 00; more to the
Attorney in Decon's suit 01 10 00; 12   a packet from Taw. & answer
00 01 06; 16   a diurnal, a packet to Taw. & porter 00 01 08; 23   a packet
to Taw. & porter 00 01 00; a letter from my Lady Eliza: Cope 00 00 02;
to Mrs Bourcher for 2 months ending 5 May 01 00 00; to Randall when he
went abroad after the small pox 00 02 06; 27   a packet to Taw. 00 01 00;
30   a packet to Taw. & porter 00 01 00; to Randall Payton more
00 02 06   ex[amined] [page total] 19 16 09

[p. 8]   1650   a ream of paper sent to *Tawstocke* £00 07s 06d; a box and a
letter from my Lady Elizabeth Cope 00 00 02; 2 bushel of coles [coals]
1s 5d to wash with 00 01 05; May 4   a packet to *Tawstocke* 00 01 00; for
10 quire fine paper sent to *Tawstocke* 00 06 08; 7   a packet from Taw.,
answer, a diurnal and porter 00 02 02; more to Mr Busbie for Randall for
a quarter 07 15 00; more for his keeping lodging & diet in the small pox
being 5 weeks from the scolem'r by bill 03 10 00; 10   to Mr Trussell in
full of all due to him 23 02 00; for 2 child's coats my Lady Eliza: Cope
06 00 00; to Mr Kinge in part of £138 12s 2d 50 00 00; to Mr Bletchington
upon a bond 150 00 00; to Will: Deacon in full 12 00 00; a letter from
Mr Elston 00 00 06; 11   a packet to *Tawstocke* 00 01 10; to Armsbie's
wife 02 00 00; more to J.B. in full for our Lady Day 00 12 00;
14   a packet to Taw. diurnal & porter 00 01 02; a letter to Taunton to
Mr Berry 00 00 06; 17   a packet from *Tawstocke* 00 01 04; for 3 lbs of
cassia for my Lord 00 04 06; the dispensitor of Amsterdam 00 03 00; a
pound & quarter of white wax lights 00 03 08; a pair of shoes for my
Lady 00 06 00; to Randall Payton which he will account for 00 10 00;
18   a packet to *Tawstocke* 00 01 00; 20 to Mrs Wingfeild on your
Honour's letter 03 00 00; a chamber for Randall for a week 00 02 06; a
letter from Baunton about money returning 00 00 03; 22   a packet to
*Tawstocke* and porter 00 01 04; 25   to Mr Dunsterfeild for trimning for
Laidries by bill 03 00 00; a packet to Taw., a letter to Ashton & one to
Bath 00 02 00; to Mr Seager for Mr Fane for costs 04 10 00; to Mr Rolls
in the suit about the robbery 05 00 00; to Mr Beare for his advice about a
suit at *Hunspill* 00 10 00; 28   a packet to Taw. a letter to Uffculme & 1 to
Parratt 00 02 0 0; to Mr Murry in part of his half year's rent due Lady

Day last 54 10 00; to my Lady Fane upon a bond 522 10 00; to my Lord
of Dorset upon a bond 355 05 09; to Mr Robins for my Lord Denbigh
now due by bond 100 00 00   ex[amined] [page total] 1306 05 03

[p. 9]   31 May 1650   to Mr Dowdswell upon your Ladyship's
appointment £10 00s 00d; to him which Mr Pollard gave your Honour
01 00 00; for wax candles sent to *Tawstocke* 00 14 00; June 15   a packet
sent to *Tawstocke* 00 01 00; 18   a packet to Taw. 1s, a porter 2 weeks 1s,
a letter to Bath 6d 00 02 06; a diurnal sent then to *Tawstocke* 00 00 02; to
Mr Cropley for my Lord Denbigh now due by bond 55 09 09; to
Mr Potts which he spent in Mr William Fane's business 03 00 00;
21   2 letters from Bath 00 00 04; 22   a letter to Bath, another to Taw. by
post 00 01 00; 25   a packet to Taw., another to Bath & porter 00 01 06; a
diurnal 2d, 6 bands & ruffs, 1 shirt 6 handkerchiefs Randall 00 18 02; to
Mr Rydor the carpenter for your Honour's part of posts & rails before
your door in the fields being 60 foot 06 00 00; 27   to J.B. in part of his
bill for your Ladyship 05 00 00; a quire of writing paper 00 00 05; to
goodwife Redhead for Lady Day last 00 05 00; to Tho: Armsbie's wife
02 00 00; to Mrs Bourcher for months ending 10th July 01 00 00;
29 a letter to Taw. and one to Bath by post 00 01 00; a letter from Bath by
post 00 00 02; for 10 lbs of soap to wash the linen 00 05 00; bread and
beer for 2 wash women 00 00 05; to Mr Robert Fane by your Honour's
appointment 40 00 00; water to wash the linen 4s, 2 women helped
wash 3s 00 07 00; to Mr Parr the tailor in full by his administrators
10 00 00; to Mr King for a suit for Randall by bill 06 00 00; more to J.B.
in part of his bill 05 00 00; for blue starch to rench the cloth withall
00 00 04; July 6   a letter to *Tawstocke* by post 00 00 06; to Mrs Bourcher
for 3 months aforehand 01 10 00; to Mr Blake the tailor in full of a bill
10 06 00; 10   a packet to Taw. and porter 00 01 06; a diurnal &
declaration 6s, 2 letters from Tangley 1d 00 00 10; to my Lord Primate's
man brought a book 00 02 06; epittomy my Lord Cook's report 00 02 06;
to Mr Dowdswell in full of all claimed to be due from my Lord of
the £600 4s 4d charged upon Mr Pagett for the 3 Lady Bourchers
47 05 02   ex[amined] 306 16 09

[p. 10]   1650 July   for 3 yards of blue gartering for my Lady £0 05s 00d;
to Randall for his Master 10s & himself ['10s' crossed through] to buy
stockings and books & keep him in repair 15s 01 05 00; 13   a packet to
Bath by post with the silk raines 00 02 00; for the silk raines 01 08 06; for
4 razors for my Lord 00 10 00; for a preserving ladle of silver 02 03 00;
for 2 lbs of pistachios for my Lord 00 05 04; for 1 lb of hair powder for
my Lady 00 06 00; for my own half year's wages due last Lady Day
10 00 00; for my own board wages from the 26 of Feb. to the first of July
being 18 weeks 09 00 00; to my Lord of Denbigh his legacy 100 00 00; to
my Lord Gray the like 100 00 00; disbursed for Mrs Norton in her
sickness from the 26 of February 49 to the 15th of July 1650 as by
particular bills appears the sum of 39 13 02½; more to her physicians in
that time 11 00 00; more to her surgeons in that time 02 10 00; more to
her apothecaries by bills 16 15 06; more for a horse-litter to carry her to
*Tawstocke* 15 00 00; more spent in that journey finding the two litter men
their diet, Mrs Norton, myself and my man and two horses 06 08 02
ex[amined] 316 11 08¼

Sum total disbursed upon this book from the 4th of July 1649 until the
25th of July *in the year* 1650 is £5245 10s 2¾d
And received the same time as appears at the other end of this book the
sum of £4381 9s 9d
Rec. more land and timber sold in Wilts. and for rent there as by
particulars remaining with my Lady appears the sum of £920 7s 8d
Sum total 5301 17 0
So remains in my hands this 25th of July 1650 the sum of £56 6s 9d
ex[amined]

[p. 11] Michas 1650 paid for 3 years high rent at *Cortondinham*
[Corton Denham] £00 02s 06d; *Netherhaven* paid for receipts of homage
for 4 years due in February 1645 to Mr Collins guardian to the Duchy
Liberty as by his account 01 13 04, to the bailiff that distrained for it
00 02 04; to the clerk of the Committee in Wilts. for allowing the order
for the taking of the Sequestration 00 10 00; Novem. 12 for my journey
to London 2 nights 00 04 06; 13 their going down by the carrier
00 04 06; paid to the collectors for the poor for Mich. quarter 00 10 00; to
your Ladyship in part of a bill of exchange 10 00 00; to Mr Beare his fee
for the year 03 06 08; to one Parsons where Randall Payton lay sick by
bill 5 weeks 05 00 00; to the physician for him 02 10 00; to the apothecary
for him by bill 01 07 00; to his master for diet & schooling by bill
09 07 06; to Mr Foster a gift from my Lady 01 00 00; 16 a packet to
*Tawstocke* 00 01 00; to the maids at Mr Busbies 00 02 06; for fine Naples
silk for Mrs Cope 00 04 00; tax Mr Murrey paid 3 months tax to the
Army ending 29 Decem. 01 10 00; To Mr Beare for his advice & a draught
about Heale 00 10 00; 19 a packet to Taw. & post a letter to Taunton &
1 to Bampton 00 02 06; a porter fetched Randall's bedding &c 00 01 00; a
quire of paper and 2 diurnalls 00 00 08; to Mr Evans my Lord's shoemaker
by bill 02 00 00; for 12000 of pins of several sorts 00 15 00; for 2 lbs
pistachio kernals 16s & 1 lb pistachio comfits my Lord 01 01 00; for books
for Randall & one to teach him 00 11 00; 3 dozen of washballs for my
Lord 00 03 00; for 13 foot & ½ of wire at 7d for the back window
00 08 00; for 4 lbs & half white wax lights 00 13 06; for 6 lbs 3 ounces of
cotton wick at 18d 00 09 03; for 3 viol books & 3 quire of ruled paper
00 07 00; a packet from *Tawstocke* by post 00 01 00; 23 a packet to Taw.
by the same 00 01 06; to Mr Bee the book-seller in full for books by bill
07 10 00; to Mr Bales for gloves, hoods & ribbon by bill 04 01 00
[page total] 59 03 07

[p. 12] 1650 Novem. paid for leather covers 14 for chairs by bill
£03 10s 11d; paid for 2 lbs & half of thread 1 lb of 6d, 1 lb of 4d &
½ a pound of 8d 00 18 08; to the gardener for seeds &c by bill 02 02 08;
to my Lord of Dorsett in full of a bond due 20 No. 1651 329 00 00;
20 to his Lordship by bond now due 355 05 09; for a box to send things
in to *Tawstocke* 00 00 10; to a porter carried the things to the carrier
00 00 08; to Mr Vinor's man delivered me the plate & porter 00 02 00;
26 a packet to Taw. & porter 00 01 06; to Mrs Bourcher for 3 months
ending 25 Decem. 01 10 00; 27 more to Randall's master 00 01 00; to the
beadle for Michas quarter 00 02 06; to my Lord Gray by Mr Boardman
due by bond 355 05 09; for a box to send the voider & another for other

plate oo o2 o7; for 2 gilt sconces & 2 hour glasses oo 13 oo; 1 lb of hair
powder 6s, 1 lb black sand & a box 1s 2d oo o7 o2; to goodwife Bradshaw
for last Michas o1 oo oo; to goodwife Redhead the like oo 1o oo; to my
Lord Gray by Mr Boardman in full of a bond due 1o No. 51 329 oo oo;
30 a packet to *Tawstocke* oo o1 o6; for a little gold cup and fation
[*fashion*] o4 oo oo; Decem. 3 for a packet to Taw. and porter oo o2 oo;
for 6 diurnals sent thither oo oo o9; for 2 pair of shoes for my Lady
oo o8 oo; for 3 dozen of 4d ribbon for her honour of 3 colours oo 12 oo;
6 to Mr Wilkins for Mr Wingfeild o5 oo oo; for a pair of furred gloves
Mrs Cope & sables to mend oo o3 o8; 7 a packet to Taw. by post
oo o1 oo; 2 letters from *Apthorpe* [Apethorpe] oo oo o4; to Mr King in full
of his bill for my Lord's 2 last suits making 16 11 oo; to him in full of a
bill for Mr Cobb o5 1o oo; to John Pawlin for him oo 1o oo; to Mr King
for Edw: Wingfeild's suit making o5 1o oo; 1o a packet to Taw. & porter
& a letter to Bampton oo o2 oo; for Randall's diet for 7 weeks to this day
at 7s o2 o9 oo; to him for a barber & in in [sic] his purse when he went
out oo o3 oo; 11 for letters from *Apthorpe* and Tangley oo oo o4
[page total] 1420 18 o8

[p. 13]   1650 Decem. 14   for 2 pair fine large worsted stirrups my Lord
£o1 oos ood; for 6 pair of worsted socks for his Lordship oo 12 oo; 2 pair
of large grey jersey stockings his Lordship o1 13 oo; a runlet of Canary
12 gallons at 6s o3 12 oo; for the runlet carrier and porter oo o3 oo; a
porter carried things to Mr King & a cord for a box oo oo o4; for 6 quire
of cook's paper oo o1 o9; for 2 cart-horse gears and head stalls o1 o6 o9; a
letter by post from Mr Hyne oo oo o6; 14 a packet to Taw. and a letter
to *Hunspill* oo o1 o6; to Armsbie's wife in full of her husband's M. wages
o1 oo oo; for half a pint of orange flower water & bottle oo o2 o9; for a
dozen of 1d black ribbon for Mrs Pollard oo o1 o6; 17 a packet to Taw. a
letter to Bampton & one Mr Mich. & porter oo o2 o6; a letter from my
Lady Elizabeth Cope oo oo o2; for a rich sable muff 22 oo oo; to Mr Blake
in part of his bill of [blank] 2o oo oo; for 6 French pistols at 17s & a 2s 9d
Scott 3s o5 o5 oo; for 3 quire of writing paper oo o1 o4; for 18 *Venis*
[Venice] glasses & a box to pack them in oo 19 oo; 2o a packet to Taw.
& a letter from Mr Hyne oo o1 o6; 23 a packet to Taw. a letter to
Sir Fra: Fane & porter oo o1 o6; laid out by Margitt that morning
Mrs Norton left London for butter & eggs, bread and beer oo o1 o4; for
soap 6d, water 4d, a cobweb brush 4d oo o1 o2; laid out for letters rec. by
her oo o2 o8; for 6 diurnals sent to *Tawstocke* oo o1 oo; for my own wages
due at Michas. last 1o oo oo; a packet to Taw. & a letter to *Hunspill*
oo o1 o6; for John Taylor's works to Mr Bee oo o6 oo; to a smith for
work by bill oo o6 oo; to the beadle for Christmas quarter oo o2 o6;
27 a packet to *Tawstocke* &c oo o1 o6; 31 a packet to Taw. & 1 from
Sir Fra: & porter oo o2 o6; Jan. 4 a packet to Taw. oo o2 oo; two pair of
silk stockings for my Lady o2 oo oo; 1 lb of ordinary hair powder
oo o4 oo; 7 a packet to Taw. per porter oo o1 o6; to the collectors for the
poor for Christ. quarter oo 1o oo; to Mrs Edny £13 being given him before
o5 oo oo; a letter from Parrat about Jenkins for Grascroft oo oo o6;
11 a packet to Taw., a letter to Parratt & 1 to Mr Hyne oo o2 oo; a letter
from Mr Wm Fane then oo oo o6; for 3 lbs of preserved eringoes & 3d the
pot oo o8 o3 [page total] 78 oo 11

[p. 14]  1650 Janu. 14   to Mr John Loope of Westminster in full upon a
bond for my Lord Denbigh due 20 May next £292 00s 00d; a packet to
Taw. & porter & a letter to Mr Gatcomb & a letter to Captaine Pike to
*Crookborne* 00 02 00; a letter from my Lady Eliza: Cope & one from
Wantage 00 00 04; 18   a packet to Taw. with a copy in it 00 02 00;
20   for Randalls going to Exet. in a coach 02 00 00; to him to bear his
charges thither 01 00 00; a pair of shoes for him 3s 6d, gloves & love 2s 6d
00 06 00; his breakfast & a pint of burnt wine that morning 00 01 04;
21   a packet to Taw. and post 00 01 06; 23 to Mr Neale a bill of exchange
of my Lady's 14 15 00; a hat & band Edw: Wingfeild 00 16 00; a hat and
band for Randall Payton 01 00 00; a box to send hats in 00 00 10;
25   a packet to *Tawstocke* 00 01 06; for a shirt for Randall Payton
00 08 00; 27   to Mrs Bourcher for 3 months ending 17 Mar. 01 10 00;
28   a packet to Taw. a letter to Norton & porter 00 02 00; 31   for seeds
sent to Taw. by the carrier 00 19 06; for sealing wax sent then 00 02 08; to
Mr Eaton for fine laces by bill 20 15 00; to Mr Ham's man bought boxes
& packed the plate 00 02 0; for 2 lbs of powder for linen 00 08 00; to
Mr Rolls in the suit with the hundred 10 00 00; to Mr Bales for gloves,
ribbon & dressing 02 05 06; for your Honour's last shoes 00 16 00; a box
to send the fine Holland & other things 00 00 10; for 20 ells of holland
at 12s the ell 12 00 00; for 12 ells of holland at 20s the ell 12 00 00;
Feb. 1   a packet to Taw. & a letter to Mr Hyne 00 01 06; 4 a packet to
Taw. a letter to Mr Hyne & porter 00 02 00; for seaching for Mr Wolton's
office copy of pt 00 07 08; more seeds by bill sent down with them
01 02 10; paid Mr Milborne the bit-maker's bill 01 07 00; 8 a packet to
Taw. 00 01 00; a box from Taw. with a copy in it for the porter 00 00 02;
for 13 pamphlets sent to Taw. 00 02 02; paid to the collectors 4 months
tax for the Army from 25 Decem. 1650 03 06 08; tax Mr Murrey   paid
also for the militia 0 16 08   [page total] 381 04 08

[p. 15]  1650 Feb. 11   a letter from Mrs Tarry to your Ladyship
£00 00s 02d; a packet with subpoenas to Taw. & porter 00 02 00; a letter
then to Mr Gatcombe about Mr Everatt 00 00 06; to a gardener for
pruning & nailing up the trees 00 02 00; for 2 bs of tobacco for my Lord
00 18 00; for a cap 5s, for a pair of garters 4s my Lord 00 09 00; for
13 gallons of Canary at 7s runlet 2s 6d 04 13 06; for a dozen of arrows &
a quiver for my Lady 00 09 00; for a dozen of bow strings 00 02 00; for
2 gloves & 2 brasers for ladies 00 04 06; for 6 ordinary gloves & 6 brasers
for recruits 00 06 00; 15   paid Mr Cavill the sadler's bill 06 15 00; paid for half the
turn stile in the new rails 00 17 06; a letter from Wantage 00 00 03;
15   a packet to Taw. & a letter to Parratt by post 00 01 06; for a box to
send the sadler and bit makers things in 2s, a porter 8d, a cord 2d
00 02 10; a letter from my Lady Eliza: Cope 00 00 02; 18   a packet to
*Tawstocke* & porter 00 01 06; a letter from Wantage 00 00 02; paid for a
piece of tuffed holland for Mrs Cope 01 10 00; to your Ladyship by Tho:
Stowle paying it at Taw. 25 00 00; 21   to Christopher Bason's brother
which your Ladyship rec. 03 00 00; to my Lord of Denbigh in full of one
bond for £55 9s 9d due the 20th of May next and for another of £55 9s 9d
due the 20th of Novem. next 106 11 06; 21   a packet to Taw. with those

bonds in it oo o1 oo; tax Mr Murrey   paid the collectors for 3 months
assessment for the Lord Farefax army ending 25 of March 1650 which was
paid by my Lord of Middlesex 30 Janu. 1649 02 01 08, paid more by his
Lordship Feb. 20th 1649 for the militia oo 12 06, paid more by his
Lordship 24 July 50 for 3 months tax (*vidzt*) July, Augu. & September
02 01 08; a packet to Taw. a letter to Mr Hanaford & porter oo o1 oo; a
letter from Mr Gatcombe & 2 from Wantage oo oo 06; paid to Alderman
Viner for 6 trencher salts with 1 ounce at 5s 2d & 2od a piece the fation
[*fashion*] 03 12 00; March 2   a packet to Taw. by post oo o1 oo; to I.B.
the 15th of Febru. £5 & £2 in full 07 oo oo; a packet to Taw. & porter
oo o1 06; for 9 pamphlets sent to *Tawstocke* oo o1 06
[page total] 167 07 11

[p. 16]   1650 Mar. 8   a packet to *Tawstocke* by post £oo o1s ood; for a
ream of writing paper oo 07 06; for Doctor Haman's 2 books oo 14 00; a
letter from Mr Hanaford by post oo oo 06; 11   a packet to Taw. & porter
oo o1 06; a letter from my Lady Eliza: Cope & 1 from Mr Gatcome
oo oo 04; for a very good beaver for my Lord 04 10 00; for 2 quarts the
best oil & a bottle oo 04 06; for 8 pair of gloves for Mrs Cope oo 12 00;
14   a packet to Taw. a letter to Parrat & 1 to Nether. oo o1 06;
18   a letter to *Tawstocke* & porter oo o1 oo; to Mrs Barrow in full due to
her husband 09 09 00; to Mrs Violett by your Honour's appointment
24 oo oo; for Mrs Cope to make her a gown 7 yards ½ of tabby at 11s the
yard 03 19 06; for 5 yards half pink prunella at 8s 02 04 00; to I.B. at my
coming out of London in part by bill 05 oo oo; for my own board wages
for 18 weeks from the 16 of Novem. to 22 Mar. 50 09 oo oo; for my
journey to Taw. the 29 of Mar. 01 17 oo; to Mr Kinge for Mr Cobb. by
bill 05 oo oo; to Mr Draper by paying it to Mr Cheany for my Lady Eliza:
Cope 100 oo oo [total] 167 3 4   for 2 loads of wood to air the stuff
01 oo oo; for Jeremy Taylor's book oo 02 06; for 3 yards serge to make
Randall a suit oo 14 03; April 4   a letter to London & 2 to Taunton &
Bampton by post oo o1 02 [page total] 169 01 03

Sum total disbursed upon this book from the 25th of July 1650 until this
5th of April 1651 the sum of £2275 16s 1od
And received the same time as appears at the other end of this book the
sum of £2398 16s 1od
Rem. in this accountant's hands this 5th of April 1651 the sum of
£123 oos ood
ex[amined]

[p. 17]   17th of April 1651   left then with my Lady in gold £11 oos ood;
left more with her Ladyship in silver 04 oo oo; more then to her Ladyship
by Mr Bold and Mrs Norton 09 08 01; more by Mr Richard Pollard £2 &
by myself £2 04 oo oo; my journey to London with a man and 2 horses
01 01 06; May 3   to Tho: Armsby for 2 days in London oo 02 oo; to him
for half a year's wages due Lady Day last 02 10 00; to him to bear his
charges to account 01 oo oo; for 2 horses in London 2 nights hay & oats
oo 03 oo; 3   a packet to Taw. by post oo o1 oo; 6   a packet to Taw. and
porter oo o1 06; a pair of bodies for Mrs Cope oo 11 oo; a box to send a
pot in & a cord for my Lord oo oo 05; for 13 beer glasses & 6 wine glasses

& a box oo 17 oo; 10  a packet to *Tawstocke* oo o1 oo; 13  a letter to
Taw. & 1 to Jo: Mills & porter oo o1 o6; for tooth picks and case for my
Lord oo o1 o2; a letter to Bridgwater & one to Wantage oo oo o8; for
letters from Tangley & *Apthorpe* by Margitt oo oo 10; paid Mr Boardman
by bond for my Lord Gray's portion 355 o5 o9; for 5 ells & ½ fine lawn
at 15s o4 o2 o6; to Mr Clarkson in full by bond for Mrs Kempe 70 oo oo;
14  to I.B. then by bill in full 12 oo oo; for a pair of boots and 2 pair of
shoes my Lord o1 18 oo; 15  to Mrs Bourcher for 2 months ending
12 May o1 oo oo; for a white wax book for the box oo o1 o6; 17  to the
post for the packet oo o1 o6; 24  a packet to *Tawstocke* oo o1 oo;
June 2  a packet to *Tawstocke* & porter oo o1 o6; to Mr Fane's footman's
wife oo o5 oo; to the overseers of the high ways oo o6 oo; to Whimper's
daughter in part of her father's wages o5 oo oo; tax Mr Murrey 9  to the
collectors for 3 months tax for the army for Lady Day last o2 10 oo; for
mending & keeping the washing taken oo o2 o8; to Sergeant Barthe's
advice on the conveyance o1 oo oo; to his man writ out the opinion
oo o2 o6; for a case & 2 pair spectacles for Mrs Herle oo o3 o6; paid
Mr Cavill's the sadler's bill oo 16 oo   [page total] 489 11 o7

[p. 18]  1651 June   Item for paving the street by bill £o8 o7s o6d; Item a
coach to go to my Lord Campden about letters oo o3 oo; 17  a packet to
Taw. & porter & a letter to *Hunspill* oo o1 o6; 9  to Mrs Bourcher for a
month ending then o1 oo oo; paid Mr Write a druggist in full for my Lord
o6 oo oo; to Keepe which your Lordship had of Tho: Lovering o3 oo oo;
to Mr Murry in full of his rent till our Lady Day last £12 9s 8d being paid
in taxes 101 oo o4; to Mrs Bourcher for 4 months ending next Mich.
o2 oo oo; for a pair of garters & roses for my Lord oo 18 oo; for 6 dozen
of sweet meat glasses & 2 of pots & a box o1 oo oo; for 3 great
paperbooks o1 15 oo; for 3 lbs of preserved eringoes & a pot for my Lord
oo o8 o3; for 4 lbs preserved yellow citrons a pot & a box oo 10 o8; for
2 lbs of smooth carraway comfits oo o4 oo; for 4 lbs of pistachio nuts
oo 10 oo; a pair of silk stockings for my Lady o1 o3 o6; for 6000 & 3000
& 6 papers of long pins oo 15 oo; 20  for a letter by post oo o1 oo; for a
quire of brown paper for stools oo oo o4; for my half year's wages due last
Lady Day 10 oo oo; for a gray nag 10 10 oo; to Mr Orlibeare in full by
bill 15 17 oo; 24  a packet to Taw. & porter & a letter to Sir Fra: Fane
oo o2 oo; to Mr Kinge in part of £88 12s 2d 40 oo oo; to Mr Blake in part
of £83 6s 8d 40 oo oo; to old Joyce by Mr Lucas oo o5 oo; to Sprite then
oo o1 oo; a letter by carrier from *Tawstocke* oo oo o2; 27  a packet to
*Tawstocke* oo o1 oo; to Mrs Edny in full of your Ladyship's gift o2 oo oo;
for 6oo gilt & 6oo lesser nails at 5s 6d & 9d o1 18 oo; for 2 wax books
oo o3 oo; for a flag broom oo oo o4; to your Ladyship by return paid to
10 oo oo; for 6 French pistols at 17s a piece o5 o2 oo; to the beadle for
Midsummer quarter oo o2 o6; to the collections of the poor for
Midsummer quarter oo 10 oo   [page total] 265 10 o1

[p. 19]  June 30th 1651  a packet to *Tawstocke* and porter £oo o1s o6d;
July 1  for 18 diurnals sent to *Tawstocke* oo o3 oo; for my board wages
from 3 May to 1 July being 8 weeks & half whereof I was 10 days in
North. o3 10 oo; my journey from London as by bill o1 16 o4; to your
Ladyship by Mrs Pollard in silver lace o1 o2 oo; to goodwife Redhead in

full for a year till Michas next 01 00 00; to Mr Kinge for Mr Cobb in full
of his bill 00 03 00 [total] 7 15 10 for a dozen & half of washballs 6
being camphor 00 02 00; for searching the toll book & a certificate
00 03 00
Sum is 08 00 10

Sum total disbursed upon this book from the 5th of April 1651 to the 15th
of July following the same of £763 10s 06d
Received in the same time as appears at the other end of this book the sum
of £822 02s 10d
So, Rem. in this accountant's hands this 15th of July 1651 the sum of
£058 12s 04d
Whereof *Hunspill* in the widow Everatt's hands £27 9s 4d ex[amined]

[p. 20] Michas 1650 paid to Mr Loope in full due to my Lord Denbigh
£300 00s 00d; to my Lady in money then 020 00 00; for hair powder left
then 000 05 06; for 30 lbs of refined sugar at 22 for conserve of roses
02 10 00; for 3000 red roses bought towards making it 00 04 00; for
38 skins of parchment to write leases 01 06 00; for 2 lbs of soft wax
00 02 00; to my man for writing 02 00 00; to Bettie Fuller in holland for
cloth 01 10 00; *Corton Dinham* Item paid for one year's high rent there
00 00 10, Item paid there for suit of court to Popham 00 00 06; Item my
charges to London by bill 02 17 06; for shoeing my horses when I left
London 00 04 00; for 6 lbs cotton candle wick sent by Margitt 00 09 00;
for letters by post by Margitt & from my Lady Cope for 18 weeks &
diurnals 6 weeks 00 16 02; for viol strings sent by her 01 01 00; for 3 quire
ruled paper by her 00 02 00; for a ream of issue paper 00 03 08; for
3 lbs ½ of white & yellow wax lights 00 07 06; Aug. 14 tax
Mr Murry paid 3 months tax for the Army July, August and September
02 10 00; for 10 quire of fine paper at 8d 00 06 06; for a ream of the best
ordinary paper 00 07 00; for 8 reams of issue paper at 4s 01 12 00; for
3 hoods & a double & a single scarf my Lady 01 03 00; for 6 ounces the
best hard wax 00 02 06; tax Mr Murry No. 18 paid the collectors for the
Militia 00 10 10; paid the post porter for 20 weeks coming 00 10 00;
No. 11 I came to London for a packet to *Tawstocke* 00 00 06; a letter
from my Lady Eliza: Cope 00 00 02; a packet then to *Tawstocke* 00 00 06;
18 to your Ladyship then at Taw. 05 00 00; for several letters sent by
['Taw' crossed through] post from Taw. by myself when I was there
00 07 03; to Kitt the footman to go to *Woonham* 00 03 03; to Doctor Wild
I believe his half year's wages 10 00 00; to myself the like due at Michas
last 10 00 00; for 2 dozen of ferret ribbon of 4 colours 00 07 00; for 100 of
needles 00 01 04; for 4 lbs of thread of 6 several sorts 01 10 00; for a pair
of shoes for your Ladyship 00 03 06; for 2 lbs of wax candles & 4d for the
box 00 14 00 [page total] 370 06 04

[p. 21] 1651 for 10 yards of Turkey tomah [*tamin*] for Mrs Cope at 3s
£01 10s 00d; for a dozen of Ivy issue balls for my Lord 00 01 0; for a
dozen of washballs at *Tawstocke* & 12 camphor 00 02 00; to the beadle for
Michas quarter 00 02 06; for Plutarke's *Lives* & his *Moralls* in 2 books
03 04 00; for the Spanish rogue called Guzmond 00 11 00; 26 to
Mrs Bourcher for 2 months then ending 01 00 00; to J.B. his mother for a

year last Michas 01 00 00; to Tho: Armsbie's wife in part of his wages
02 00 00; for a box to send the third tomah [*tamin*] & waxlights in
00 00 08; a packet to *Tawstocke* and porter 00 01 00; Novem. 27 to the
collectors for the poor for Michas quarter 00 10 00; for 2 lbs of powder
for linen at 4s 00 08 00; for 4 pair of brown gloves for Mrs Cope
00 05 00; for 2 lbs of tobacco for my Lord 01 00 00; for a box to put plate
in 00 01 08; for a coard 3d, for porter 6d 00 00 09; for a gilt cup with
12 ounces at 7s 4d 04 10 03; for 2 silver extinguishers with 17d & fation
[*fashion*] 00 08 05; for one dozen wash & 1 dozen camphor balls 00 02 00;
Decem. 2 a letter to *Tawstocke* by post 00 00 06; for the book of the
psalms by Doctor Kinge 00 01 06; to Sprite when I came to London
00 01 00; for a box to send paper & other things when the viol strings
went down 00 01 00; for my horse 13 nights grass when I came to London
in May & returned in July at 7d 00 07 07; for my horse 2 nights when I
came to London & to a carrier to my brother 00 04 00; 6 a box to Taw.
by post 3s 6d, the box 6d 00 04 00; for 60 grains the best ambergris at 3d
00 15 00; for 20 grains the best musk at 3d 00 05 00; for 2 ounces of
cochineal at 3s 6d 00 07 00; for a book of leaf gold 2s & one of silver 6d
00 02 06; for 3 dozen ribbon for my Lady at 1s 01 16 00; for drawing
5 garden plots by a gardener 00 11 00; a packet to *Tawstocke* the 2 of July
last when I had sent my books to Taw. 00 01 06; a letter to Mr Thorning
by post 00 00 06; for my horses shoeing at London twice 00 04 04
[page total] 22 00 08

[p. 22] 1651 Decem. 8 to your Ladyship in part of a bill of
disbursement £10 00s 00d; tax Mr Murry to the collectors for 3 months
ending the 24 of December for the Army 02 10 00; for a dragon & ½ oil
of cinnamon at 40s per ounce 00 15 00; for a box 1d, sending it by post 1s,
post porter 6d 00 01 07; 11 for a pair of battle doors & 12 shuttlecocks
00 01 04; for 2 fine combs 3s 8d, 3 pair pendants 1s, box 3d 00 04 11; for
a keg of sturgeon 01 00 00; for 3 quarts of Luke olives & a barrel
00 03 04; 13 a porter to carry them to the carrier 00 00 06; for a cloak
for Sir Garrat Rainsford 01 15 00; for a pair of breeches for him 00 08 00;
*at the same time* a letter by post to *Tawstocke* 00 00 06; 16 a letter by
post and porter 00 01 00; to Mr Kinge by bill for your Honour's little
cloak 05 01 00; a pair of green silk stockings for your Ladyship 01 01 00;
23 a packet by post and porter 00 01 06; to Mr Cobb's brother for a
composing card 01 03 00; 29 to Mr Blake in part of [blank] 40 00 00; to
Mr Bassett in full for Mrs Norton 04 08 06; to him for my Lord in full
00 16 06; to the beadle for Christmas quarter 00 02 06; to the collectors
for the poor for that quarter 00 10 00; a packet by post with Sir Fra:
Fane's letter 00 01 00; Janu. 1 to Mr Robert Fane by appointment
50 00 00; a packet by post 00 00 06; 10 a packet by post & porter
00 01 06; to Mr Alexander Rolls in full by bill 01 10 00; 13 a letter by
post & one to John Mills 00 01 00; a letter from my Lady Cope & one
from *Apthorpe* 00 00 04; a pound of tobacco for my Lord in August
00 09 00; for a dozen of wash balls & 6 camphor balls 00 01 06; to
Mr Kinge for George Chevily by bill 03 02 06; for 4 quire of paper and
quills 00 01 09; for 4 yards ¼ ⅛ crimson velvet to make a child's cloak
Mr G.F. at 24s 05 00 00; 7 ounces ½ of gold & silver lace at 4s 10d in 8

01 16 00; 4 silver & gold parchment spangled lace at 5s 01 03 06; to
Mr Manbie for Randal Payton 01 00 00; for 14 *Venis* glasses 00 10 00; for
a case of knives 00 10 00   [page total] 135 13 09

**[p. 23]**   1651   to I.B. to go see a house and grounds £01 10s 00d; a letter
from John Mills about the livery cloth 00 00 04; Janu. 31   a letter to
*Hunspill* by post 00 00 06; a letter from my Lady Eliza: Cope 00 00 02;
for taffeta & making the velvet coat 00 10 00; for 5 smoothing irons
00 06 06; to your Ladyship in further part of a bill of parcels 02 10 00; to
Bowdler in part for the coaches 15 00 00; for a screen and 3 *venis* glasses
00 08 00; Feb. 4   spent and given at Mr Ro: Fane's christening 02 07 00;
to Mr Forard to account for on his book 20 00 00; to Glowin the carrier
in part of [blank] for carriages 12 06 03; 7   a letter to *Hunspill* and post
porter 00 01 00; for a pair of tables & porter 01 08 06; to the scavenger for
Christmas quarter 00 03 00; tax Mr Murry 10   to the collectors for
3 months tax to the Army ending 25 March next for the landlord 02 01 08;
to Mr Cobb for a harpsicon 10 00 00; for linen cloth by Wilmot 00 16 04;
to Mr Bee for Doctor Downe 30 00 00; for 1 lb of tobacco for my Lord
00 12 00; for a packet from Taw. by carrier 00 00 06; for a letter from my
Lady Eliza: Cope 00 00 02; 14   a letter to Taw. one to *Hunspill* & post
porter 00 01 06; to Mr Forard to account for on his book 20 00 00; for a
suit of rich hangings 5 pieces 147 ells 148 00 00; for a parcel of seeds sent
to Taw. 00 14 00; a porter carried hangings & a carpet 00 00 06; for my
own board wages 12 weeks from the 11 of Novem. to 3 February
06 00 00; for 3 dozen purple ribbon for the coach 00 12 00; for a set of
box table-men for the hall 00 02 06; for the K. of S. picture 03 00 00; for
2 bottles of Rheinish wine 00 02 11; 4 lbs of pistachios at 16d 00 05 04; for
a pot & 2 lbs 12 ounces of green ginger at 3s 6d 00 09 07; 16   to
Mr Forard to account for on his book 20 00 00; to Mr Cobb for your
Ladyship 05 00 00; to a poor minister near *Bristoll* 00 10 00; for
bricklayers work about mending the little chamber over the arch 01 03 06
[page total] 306 03 09

**[p. 24]**   1651 Feb. 18   to Spright in money £00 01s 00d; to Wilmot to
buy holland 02 10 00; for new laying the steps in the garden 00 04 00;
21   to Anne Stoane when she went away 01 00 00; for a new spring for
Mrs Cope's watch 10s, mending 3s   00 13 00; to Mr Cobb when my Lady
went to *Thensford* 10 00 00; to Sir Fra: Fane for Colonel Geo: Fane
01 00 00; to Doctor Wild by your Ladyship's appointment 00 01 06;
21   a packet to Taw. and porter 00 01 00; 24   a letter by post 00 00 06;
laid out for several things against your Honour's coming to town as by a
note appears 15 16 05; paid cinnamon and aniseed water 00 09 10; paid for
a book called *Horrace* for Ran: Paiton 00 01 06; sugar candy a pound for
my Lady 00 01 10; to Justice Barklett and Mr Palmer 04 00 00; to
Mr Forard on his book to account £3 & £17 20 00 00; for 6 wax books
for my Lord's box 00 06 10; to the three twins 2s 6d a piece 00 07 06; to
Mr Bowdler in part for the coach 20 00 00; to Mr Smyth for a violin for
your Ladyship 03 05 00; for a packet to Taw. and porter 00 01 06; a letter
from Mr Gatcombe 00 00 03 [page total] 80 01 08

Sum total disbursed upon this book from the 1 of Novem. 1651 to the 28
of February following 914 06 02

And rec. in the same time as appears at the other end of this book with
Captain Masons's fine 961 00 07
So, remaining in this accountant's hands this second of March 1651
46 14 05 ex[amined]

[p. 25] 2 March 1651 to Mr Forard to account for on his book
£20 00s 00d; for 2 pair of gloves sent Mr Cope 2s 6d, carrier 4d 00 02 10;
for the Act of Oblivion 8d, a letter from *Bruen* 2d 00 00 10; for a letter by
post to Taw. 00 00 06; for 2 pieces of ferret ribbon 00 15 00; for a tin
plate for my Lord's silver box 00 00 06; to the coach-maker for to buy
stuff for curtains 01 00 00; 6 a packet of letters to Taw. one to Bamp. &
porter 00 02 00; for cloth for 3 dozen of napkins 01 07 06; 4 to Robert
Norton the cook for a month then ended 01 00 00; for 2 new deal turns
00 07 00; 10 for 8 lbs of green ginger at 3s 6d & pot 1s 01 09 00; for a
letter from *Apthorpe* & one last week 00 00 04; 5 to Mr Seale the
upholsterer in part of [blank] 38 00 00; 12 to Mr Forard on his book to
account for 20 00 00; for pair of dogs with great brass heads 00 10 00;
13 a packet to Taw. & to Mr Hyne & porter 00 02 00; for 10 lbs of
Spanish honey & a pot 1s 00 09 04; 16 to Mr Forard to account for
20 00 00; for mending Mrs Cope's silver ink-horn 00 01 00; to J.B. in
farther part of a bill 01 15 00; 16 to Mr Cavill the sadler in full by bill
07 10 00; 15 to Mrs Bourcher for 4 months ended 02 00 00; for a letter
from *Apthorpe* 00 00 02; a letter to my Lady Eliz: Cope 00 00 02; for a
quire of paper & 1 lb of black sand 00 01 04; for stuff to make ink and a
pot 00 01 10; 20 to my Lady by Mr Cobb 03 10 00; for mending my
Lord's watch 00 04 00; for a glass for my Lord's tobacco & 1 for powder
00 01 02; *at the same time* a packet by post to Taw. & porter 00 01 06; a
packet to Aston & a letter from Sir Francis 00 01 00; a letter from John
Mills on Mrs Merson's death 00 00 03; to your Ladyship in farther part of
reckonings 04 00 00; for a ferkin the best soap & porter 01 02 04; to
Cannon for a feather bed & for work by bill 05 09 11; for 2 lbs of tobacco
for my Lord 01 04 00; 24 for 4 quarts of sack by John Burke 00 06 08;
paid for Mrs Norton which Mr Bold must pay your Ladyship 04 19 02
ex[amined] [page total] 137 16 04

[p. 26] 25 March 1652 to the collectors for the poor for that quarter
£00 10s 00d; to the coachmakers men made the new coach 00 05 00; for
spirit of carraways for my Lady 00 03 06; 27 to Mr Forard on his book
to account for 20 00 00; a letter from Mr Hyne 2d, one from Sir Fra: Fa:
post 6d 00 00 08; a letter from my Lady Darcy by post 00 00 06; a letter
to *Hunspill* & one to Mr Hyne by post 00 01 0; 27 a packet to
*Tawstocke* & porter 00 01 06; to Mr Gildocke for 14 ½ lbs prunellas at
14d a pound 00 06 06; to Elizabeth Searle her ½ year's wages 01 10 00; to
Wilmot Toogood the like 01 00 00; to Margaret Hooper the like 01 00 00;
to Dr Wild the like 10 00 00; to Mr Lynn the like 10 00 00; to Mr Cobb
the like 07 00 00; to Mr Sam: Bold the like 05 00 00; to Mr Forard the like
07 10 00; to John Burke the like 03 00 00; to Whimper the cook the like
07 00 00; to George the like 01 00 00; to Kitt the like 02 00 00; to Tho:
Armsby the like 02 10 00; to Mr Smyth the like 05 00 00; to Whimper a
gift 02 00 00; to John Burke the like being sick 00 10 00; to George the

like by a new hat oo 12 oo; to Will Boothe his wages o3 oo oo; to Tho:
Postillion the like o2 oo oo; 30   to my Lady by Mr Cobb o1 oo oo; to my
Lord then by him oo 10 oo; since received by me   to Eliza: Searle for my
Lady Chichester o2 o4 oo; to her more upon a bill of disbursements
o7 o7 o1; to my Lady to pay for a viol case a theorbo &c 10 oo oo;
April 2   to Mr Walter Mildmaye's son o5 10 oo; to Mr Bowdler the
coachmaker in part of his bill of £95 8s 10d, £35 being paid before hand
35 oo oo; 2   for 1 ounce of hair powder 6, a letter to Mr Gray 2d
oo oo o8; 3   to Mr Forard to account for on his book 10 oo oo
ex[amined] 165 o2 o5

[p. 27]   April 1652   for clasps for your Honour's *Issopp's fables*
£oo oos o6d; 3   to your Honour by Wilmot to lay out 10 oo oo; 3   to my
Lady to pay for ribbon by George o2 o2 oo; spent at Blackwall when I
went to get grass for the coach-horses & to see a tenant of Uffculme
oo o1 oo; 3   to the post porter for a packet to *Tawstocke* oo o1 o6; 5   to
Mr Eaton for bone lace by bill 23 o6 oo; 6   to 2 gate keepers going to
Hyde Park oo o1 o6; 6   a letter to Taw., one to *Hunspill*, one to Mr Hyne
& one to Mr Smyth of Ilchester by post oo o2 oo; to Dr Gillingham in
gold o1 oo oo; 7   a letter to my Lady from *Apthorpe* & one from
Mr Gray oo oo o4; for drawing a rent in the cloth of the coach boot
oo oo o6; for new covering mending the linen trunk oo o4 oo; for 4 yards
tawny serge for coach curtains oo 16 oo; for 3 dozen of tawny ribbon to
tie in the covers of the seats of the new coach oo o7 o6; 8   a quire of
paper for writing oo oo o5; to the beadle for Lady Day quarter oo o2 o6;
9   to Mr Forard to account for on his book 15 oo oo; a letter from
Mr Canworthy oo oo o3; 10   a porter brought 6 join stools from
Mr Darby oo oo o8; a letter by post to Taw., 1 to Bamton, 1 to Sir Fra: &
porter oo o2 oo; 13   a letter to Taw. by post & 1 to *Hunspill* oo o1 oo;
14   to Mr Forard to account for on his book 20 oo oo; to Mr Palmer for
his advice about *Hunspill* for the sea walls 10s, to his man writ the petition
oo 11 oo; to the secretary of the Great Seal for a letter about it oo 15 oo;
15   to Mr Castle to buy stuff of several sorts 50 oo oo; to Mr Smyth lent
him by your Honour's appointment o1 10 oo; to Mr Marwood a minister
of Ireland oo o5 oo; for a pair of stockings for Mr Payton oo o6 oo;
for 2 coats for 2 poor girls twins in part oo o5 oo; a new hat for
Mr Payton & dressing his old o1 o3 o4; 17   to Mr Castle more to buy
stuff 20 oo oo; for mending your Ladyship's silver clock & new crystal
oo 11 oo; to Mr Bourcher by your Honour's appointment oo o5 oo; 17   to
Mr Forard to account for on his book 30 oo oo; a letter by post to John
Mills & porter oo o1 oo   ex[amined] 179 2 o1

[p. 28]   May 1652 8   my journey to *Hackpenn* & back to London with a
man & Mr Bold & another man from *Hunspill* as by bill £o5 19s o3d; for
the hire of a horse that journey o1 o5 oo; for a coach to bring money out
of London oo o1 oo; 12   to Mr Forard upon his book to account for
40 oo oo; tax Mr Murry to the collectors for 3 months tax to the Army
ending at Midsummer next o2 o1 o8; 13   to them then for my Lord for
goods oo 12 oo; 14   to my Lady by Mr Cobb in money 20 oo oo; for a
quire of writing paper oo oo o5; 12   for a packet to Taw. & porter for

4 weeks 00 03 00; to Mr Rydor the carpenter in full of his bill 03 18 00; to
Mr Forrard to account for on his book 15 00 00; 15 a packet to Taw. & a
letter to *Exon* 00 01 06; to my Lady in money the week before Easter
60 00 00; for 12 black lead pencils, 3 pieces of glue & wax 00 04 00; to
Mr Robert Fane by your Ladyship's order for a satin band & cuffs for
myself 00 11 06; 20  to Mr Forard to account for on his book 20 00 00;
for 2 quire of writing paper 00 00 10; a letter from *Exon* to Mr Cobb by
post 00 00 06; to Mr Evans for 2 pair of shoes for my Lord 00 12 00;
2  a letter from Mr Hannaford & a packet to Taw. & porter 00 02 06; to
the collectors for the repairs of *Ivie* bridge 01 00 00; 24  a post letter from
Mr Hannaford and answer 00 01 00; to Mr Sergeant Glanvile for his advice
02 00 00; 26  to Mr Castle more for stuff 40 00 00; to the smith in full
upon 3 bills 06 10 00; for a horse to go to Sir Edw: Hales & 2 men
charges & clerk's pains 01 03 00; 3 letters from John Mill, Mr Gatcombe
& Thurston 00 00 07; to 2 porters brought hangings, a book & paper
00 01 00; 29  to Mr Forard upon his book to account for 20 00 00; a
packet to Taw. and porter 00 01 06; to one that writ out Sergeant
Glanvile's notes 00 02 00; for parchment to engross the new jointure
00 03 00; to the coachmaker in full of his bill 25 00 00; to the brick-layer
in full of his bill 03 00 00; to Mr Hassett in full for stockings for my Lord
06 00 00; to Mr Cowes by your Ladyship's appointment 04 00 00
ex[amined] 279 15 03

[p. 29]  1652 June  to the glasier in full of his bill £03 15s 00d; to
Mr Clarke laid out for your Ladyshp by bill 06 05 00; 1  to the overseers
of the highways 00 06 00; to Mr Bee for *the English Historions* 01 16 00;
to your Honour by Mr Cobb 09 00 00; ['to Mr Bee in part of his bill for
books 17 00 00' crossed through] to him in exchange for a great Bible
00 15 00; paid for canvas & holland & lockram by bill in full there being
£7 2s paid by Mr Wyott to Mr Lovitt 08 03 00; paid for 19 ells of holland
at 5s 2d 04 18 00; to Mr Keene the joiner in full 03 19 00; to the turner in
full 03 13 00; to Mr Bold due to him upon account from your Ladyship
07 00 00; for slating the blue turret stair-case 00 10 00; to John Burke in
part of his wages aforehand 02 00 00; paid for engrossing your Honour's
jointure 00 14 00; to Eliza: Searle upon a bill of parcels 10 01 06; paid my
Lady's shoemaker by bill 02 08 00; to Mr Stone for a carpet by Tho:
Cannon 01 15 00; paid for Mr Murrye's lease new making 00 12 00;
19  to Wilmot to bear charges to *Tawstocke* 03 00 00; for 2 fine ivory
combs for your Ladyship 00 03 00; a letter from Mr Hyne by post
00 01 08; *at the same time*  a letter to him & 1 to Mr Mills & porter for
3 weeks 00 02 06; 21  to your Ladyship at your going to Taw. from
London 20 00 00; to the poor when your Ladyship went away 01 00 00;
to the porter helped 3 days 00 03 06; to an old man helped in the stable
00 05 00; to my Lady Ingram's house-keeper using her stables 00 05 00; to
Mr Bold to account for then 02 00 00; a cap for my Lord 00 04 06; to a
porter waited & helped 3 days 00 03 00; for bullets & powder 4d,
coach-hire 1s  00 01 04; to the grocer in full 10 08 00; to Mr Foster by
your Honour's appointment 01 00 00; 23  to Mr Seale in part of
£55 18s 6d 25 00 00; to Mr Lindsey the brewer by Luke White in part of
his bill of £23 2s 3d 10 00 00  ex[amined] 149 05 04

[p. 30]   1652 June 26   to Cavell the sadler in full of his bill £23 oos ood;
to Mr Tennant the sadler in full by bill 16 oo 00; to Bowdler the
coachmaker in full by bill 04 19 00; to the farrier in full by bill 02 19 06;
to Millbourne the bit-maker in full by bill 10 08 00; a letter from Mr Mills
about Mr Wolron oo oo 03; for 12 wax books for my Lord's box 6 lbs
6 ounces weight oo 14 08; 26   a letter by post then oo oo 06; 30   a letter
from my Lady Eliza Cope oo oo 02; for the book of maps oo 18 00; for a
ream of paper 6s 6d, 12 red pencils 18d oo 08 00; to the collectors for the
poor at Midsummer quarter oo 10 00; paid the church duties for a year
oo 06 00; paid for my Lord's box to *Bristoll* sent by William Parker of
*Abson* [?Topsham] oo 06 00; for nails and cords for boxes oo oo 08; for
2 great boxes which Mr Bold sent things in oo 07 00; for a box to send my
Lord's books in oo 04 00; for a box to send my Lord's clothes in and
many other things E. Serle left behind her oo 04 00; paid for D.W. gown
making 01 oo 00; for a box to put it in & one for my Lord's pots
oo 08 00; for a box to send the trenchers waxbooks &c oo oo 04; to the
beadle for Midsummer quarter oo 02 06; July 3   a packet of letters & post
for 2 weeks oo 02 00; a letter then to *Hunspill* to Mr Jarvis oo oo 06; 5   to
Mrs Bourcher in full for his son till Mich. 03 10 00; to Margitt Grococke
for 2 years service 04 oo 00; for a great cypress chest for linen oo 13 00;
7   a letter from my Lady Eliz: Cope oo oo 02; 10   to Mr Seale the
upholsterer in full of his bill 30 15 00; a letter by post from Jo: Hannaford
but no bill oo oo 06; for a greater pair of fire irons for starching oo 04 06;
to Mr Murrey in part for levelling the fields 05 oo 00; to him my Lord's
part for the pump making 08 oo 00; 10   a letter to Taw. & porter & one
to *Exon* oo 01 06; to Mr Blake the tailor in part of £93 10s od 43 oo 00; to
Mr Kinge in full of his old bill 58 10 00; to Mr Murry in full of his rent
till Lady Day last 100 oo 00; to the woodmonger in full by bill 24 16 00;
for 13 lbs of soap 4s 9d, one to wash 3s, water 2s oo 09 09; 14   a letter to
Taw., one from *Exon* & answer to it oo 01 06 ex[amined]
[page total] 342 01 oo

[p. 31]   July 1652 15   to Mr Linsey the brewer in full of his bill
£13 02s ood; to Mr Orlibeare in full of his bill 21 15 00; to Mr Manbie the
like 28 oo 00; paid for a barber's case filled with instruments 01 19 00;
paid for clock & turner's tools by bill 02 10 00; a box for the voider, basin
& cord oo 02 06; 2 boxes for wax lights, barber's case &c oo 02 04; a box
for the 5 dishes and a cord oo 02 0; my horses to London by Glowin's
bill oo 18 03; for their meat 3 nights in London 1s, Smith oo 13 00; to the
scavenger in full for a year's wages oo 09 00; to Mr Ham's man helped
pack the plate oo 01 00; to the smith more by bill oo 09 00; to Whimper
for a quarter's gratuity 01 oo 00; 1 lb black sand, cap paper, nails & porter
oo 01 06; to the bricklayer for finishing the little house 01 14 06; to the
joiner for work done there 01 17 00; to Alderman Vinor in full by bill
13 12 06; to Mr King in part of his bill of £63 18s 9d 50 oo 00; to
Mr Blake in part of his bill of £50 10s 40 oo 00; to Mr Bassett the
apothecary in full of his 2 bills 08 11 00; to Margitt from your Honour 5s,
Sprite 1s oo 06 00; my journey from London by bill 01 18 06 ex[amined]
[page total] 189 04 01

Sum total disbursed upon this book from the 2 of March 1651 to the 29th
of July 1652 is £1442 06s 05d

And received in the same time as appears at the other end of this book
£1641 13s 06d

So rem. in this accountant's hand's this 29th of July 1652 £199 07s 01d
ex[amined]

And he is charged with Wm Jarvis his time for 2 small tenements in
*Hunspill* at his going to London 1652 £110 00 00; more with a debt from
John Jarvis the audit 075 18 00; more that he was to receive of one Freak
at *Corton Dinham* 015 00 00; now that he was to rec. of Bach at
*Netherhaven* 005 00 00; more that he was to receive of Herne at Wantage
006 00 00 besides the rents of those 3 manors for a year [total] 4511 5 01

of this money W. Lynn paid me when I went to London £56 1s to
Mr Cobb & £4 to the steward & £5 in gold of £9 being formerly entered.

[p. 32]    Also John Stand fasts 2 fines £45 0 0; widow Evarat 27 9 4;
Mr Kelsome 65 0 0; from Fluelline 30 0 0

# General Account Book of Rachel, Countess of Bath, 1639–1654

KENT ARCHIVES OFFICE, U269/A518/5

*The book measures 8½" by 13¾" and has an unmarked vellum wrapper. There are two sets of numbering, both of which were made by the record office in 1996: the second run, which was under-lined, has been used for this edition. It numbers only those pages which were used and not all sheets in the volume. The volume comprises twelve reams together with miscellaneous sheets of paper which, at some time after the paper was used, were bound together. To some extent this accounts for the haphazard order of material: it is divided into half by pages running from both ends of the volume with some pages running in reverse order. In some instances both ends of individual pages were used. This edition does not include estate fines noted at the bottom of occasional pages in reverse order on pages 18–21, 23–34 and 61–73. There are twenty-four lined blank sheets between pages 101 and 102, two between 205 and 206, and twenty-seven between 204 and 205. Two loose unmarked pages lie at the front and end of the volume. Since the transcription of this volume many of the enclosures have been removed and placed in a separate envelope. These are noted between the pages originally known to the editor. There are the remains of three red seals on page one with remnants of paper attached. A slip of paper on page one notes '... wool 95 lbs ... wool 24 [lbs]'.*

[p. 1] ... Grand Deed of the whole estate
Tho: Wyote hath that for Taws. this 23 of March 1639

Cloth made in the house for to give away coarse 20, of fine cloth for liveries 47 yards this April 1645.

Cloth made in 1646 3 several pieces 47 yards.

Spent before I came home for Tho: Cooman, Mary, Watt &c 16 yards.

Since I came home 8 yards: for 2 suits for old Mr Wiote Aug. 1648, for Sam: Bold & Randle Peayton 13 yards, made them each a suit & cloak. For Mary & Thom: 7 yards & half, for white stockings 2 yards & half.

1648 left wool to spin of the finest sort 50 lbs, of the coarser 17, whereof given Walt: Humble 7 lbs No. the 15th 1648, & the women in the kitchen 3 lbs, the 7 lbs of coarsest made up in 1649.

Fine wool to spin together with the 50 lbs more—45 lbs in all. coarse wool
this year—24 whereof give Cody, Richard ...

**[p. 2]**   *Abundanc cautesa non nocet*
Frances Everat bailiff of *Hunspile* [Huntspill], Rob: Southby dischargeth
the Bailiff's place at Wantage there being 2 lives on it, Edw: Randall Bailiff
of *Warkley* [Warkleigh], *Rowboro* [Roborough], Marwood, *Bearcharter*
[Beer Charter], Harford *with* Newland & *Wolrington* [Worlington], John
Milles Bailiff of *Hakpen* [Hackpen], Sheldon & Bolham.

**[p. 3]**   The Lady Margaret Mintts died the 8 day of March 1638.
Edw: Earl of Dorset died the 19th of July 1652.

1640 the 9th day of April departed this life Mary Myldmey Countess of
Westmorland my dear mother, being Thursday, the 59 year of her age.

1643 Decem. the 17th old William Bellamy the steward & faithful servant
to Sir Walter Mildmey, Sir Anthony Mildmey & Grace his wife, Francis
Earl of Westmorland & Mary his wife, & to Mildmey Earl of
Westmorland, departed this life at *Apthorp* [Apethorpe] in his sleep, having
been a servant there about 60 years.

**[p. 4]**   1639 [corrected to 1638] the 4th day of March received 19 13 6
Spent for a suit of damask 5 0 0; to the coach man 4 17 2; to the wash
woman 4 1 4; for the burnt groom 1 9 7; for suits for Will & Jack 1 12 6;
the 4th of April received £19 00;   for Baldwin to Mr Tomkins 2 0 0; lost
at cards 2 13 0; to Doctor Fryer 1 0 0; to Bolld for his journey 3 0 0; for
2 warrants 0 10 0; spent more 2 0 0; paid upon bill 1 15 0; spent 3 0 0;
more 1 6 0; received the 10th of April £10; to Besse 0 15 6; to a carpenter
0 8 0; to a mason 0 8 0; to my brother George 0 9 0; to marking irons
0 5 0; for weights 0 5 4; to a apothecary 0 13 4; to Desborow 0 2 6; to a
brief 0 2 6; to a work woman 0 9 6; for pence 0 5 0; to Darby 0 5 8;
received the 13th of April £10; to the coach man 0 4 0; several little bills
0 15 6; fruit dishes 14  0 14 0; a small bill for lace, tape, thread & tiffany
0 5 0; Jane's wages 1 10 0; for washing kitchen clothes 0 5 11; for biscuits
0 5 0; for hiring a cook 0 5 0; 4 other bills 6 4 6; spent more 2 0 0;
received the 17th April £20
[total] 51 12 10   [margin total of receipts and first line] 78 13 6

**[p. 5]**   Spent as appeareth by bills bearing date from the 8th of March to
the 11 of May

Received the 28th of April £10; 4 little bills 1 1 2; from the 12th to the 15
1 5 11; from the 15 to the 18  1 7 1; a bill of extraordinaries 0 7 7; from
the 18th to the 25th 2 2 3; extraordinaries 0 14 5; from the 25 to the 30
3 16 10; from the 30 to the 6 of April 3 8 9; extraordinary 1 3 11; received
the 4 of May £10; the butcher's bill from the 28 of March to the 20 of
April 11 0 11; the chandler's bill from the 6 of April to the 13  1 3 2; from
the 8th to the 16  3 9 5; extraordinaries 2 11 1; the chandler's bill 1 2 9;
received the 11 of May £10; the poulterer's bill date the 12 of April 1 5 2;
from the 16 to the 21  2 4 3; extraordinaries 2 0 8; chandler's bill 0 11 10;
from the 21 to the 28  3 10 5; extraordinaries 1 9 5; chandler's bill
0 13 4½; received the 13 of May £5; poulterer's bill 0 8 8; from the 28 to
the 4 of May 1 15 4; butcher 1 14 1; from the 4 to the 9  2 13 9; \

extraordinaries o 17 7; butcher 5 1 o; poultry o 7 6; received the 18 of May
£10; extraordinaries o 12 11; grocery o 16 o; a bill of o 5 8; a bill of
o 17 3; a bill of o 13 3; a bill of o 17 6; extraordinaries 1 13 o; chandler's
bill o 17 o; a little bill o 10 6; butcher's bill the 11 of May 4 18 11;
chandler's bill o 18 11½; a little bill o 8 4
[page total] 72 4 4   [margin total] 45 o o

[p. 6]   the 23 of May to Crosse o 10 o; the 25 of May to Crosse 1 o o;
the 27 to Crosse o 14 1; received the 26 of May £10; to the chandler
o 16 3; to the butcher 4 16 9; to Crosse 1 o o; for wine o 8 o; for peas
o 2 4; for herbs o 12 8; for artichokes o 1 o; for wine o 6 5; for
strawberries o 1 6; for a goose o 1 6; other things o 1 2; for two cakes
o 1 o; for sack & a letter o o 9; for gloves for Lynn o 1 6; to Crosse the
29 of May o 8 o; for the house the 31 of May o 14 6; to Crosse the 31
1 o 9; to one that brought a present o 1 o; to the wash-woman the 1 of
June o 17 o; to the butcher the 1 of June 4 11 1; received the 1 of June
£10; the chandler's bill the 1 of June o 15 6; herbs, artichokes, asparagus
o 8 5; for wine the 3 of June o 3 6; received the 3 of June £5; to the
butcher o 11 6; to the steward the 3 of June 4 o o; to the butcher the 10 of
June 4 14 6; to a wash-woman o 2 o; received the 8th of June £5; to the
steward 3 o o; the 18th of June to the butcher 4 12 2; for the chandler
2 weeks 2 7 o; received the 11th of June £5; to the poulterer o 12 6; to the
steward 1 6 o; to the steward 2 6 o; to the herb woman for 2 weeks 1 4 o;
received the 17 of June £5; to the chandler's bill dated the 13 to the
20th of June 1 4 10; to the poulterer o 13 3; the milk woman o 7 3;
received the 19th of June £5; paid the half of the butcher's last week's bill
2 15 o; received the 21 of June £5
[page total '49 4 8' crossed through]

received the 15 of June £5; to the steward the 25 of June 5 o o
£65   £178 1s 1od   re[ceipts] £178 13 6   [page] total 54 4 8

[p. 7]   Received at London 1639 the 27th of June £5; paid the other half
of the butcher's bill dated from the 15th to the 20th of June 2 15 o; the
chandler dated the 21th of June 1 8 6; the poultry the 23 of June to the 21
o 9 o; the herb woman o 11 7; the 3 day of July paid for washing 1 18 6;
received the 4th of July £20 1639; to the butcher 13 10 6; to the poulterer
2 6 6; to the chandler 1 15 6; to the herb woman o 12 o; to the vintner for
wine & vinegar o 19 4; for milk o 6 o; for grocery, soap & starch 1 19 o;
for half a year's baking in a cook's oven 1 10 o; for washing kitchen cloths
o 9 6; for the hire of a cook 3 days o 15 o; for flour o 18 3; for a woman
that helped in the kitchen o 10 o; for making Lynn some linen o 5 6; for
chickens o 1 o
total 32 18 8   [margin total] 25 o o

[p. 8]   Received the 4th of July 1639 £100 to my Lord £60 o o; to my
Lord 2 o o; to my Lord 16 o o; paid some bills for Walker 4 o o; to my
Lord 4 o o; Mr Pansford o 3 o; cherries 3 lbs o 1 o; to Besse Fuller for my
men lying 5 weeks o 6 o; to Slowly for the horses in our journey 5 o o;
spent at *Henly* [Henley] in meat & drink 2 7 7; in rewards at my sister
Eliz: Copes 2 14 o; in rewards at my Aunt Stapleton's 2 16 o; received also
the 4th of July £60 at *Bathe* the 11th of July dinner 2 5 o; spent at

*Glassonbery* [Glastonbury] 2 2 0; laid out by Coyse in the way 1 0 1; delivered more to Slowly for the horses 3 0 0; to Wilmot to buy things for the dairy 1 0 0; for Toe to stuff the blue chairs 0 14 8; for spurs for Lynn 0 1 2; for ribbon for him 0 0 9; to my Lord to give away 1 0 0; to my Lord for guns 3 0 0; 1639 to my Lord when he went to Exeter the 5th of August 1 0 0; make Coyse's reckoning even the 7th of August & paid him 3 13 0; for to [sic] presents 0 2 0; to the poor 0 10 0; to Rose for her wages which I paid at London 1 0 0; to 2 that brought some fruit 0 2 0; to Rainger that brought dogs 0 10 0; for biscuit 0 2 6; to fiddlers 0 5 0; to fiddlers from Hartland 0 5 0; for Tap. for the shirts 0 1 0; to one that brought grapes 0 1 0; for my Lord to give a *Loth-gere* man 0 2 6; to Mr Slowely's boy 0 1 0; to my Lord Chichester's man that brought a hawk 0 10 0; for making household linen as by bill appeareth 1 17 3 [margin total] 60 0 0

[p. 9] for 3 capes for the boy 0 3 0
[including previous page] total 123 16 6

1639 Lost at play to Mr Ames Pollard 0 17 0; paid to myself for my allowance £25 0 0; 63 0 6 I received for my Lord & my journey of him 63 0 6; disbursed as by bill appeareth 61 11 3

so my receipts of my Lord for these expenses amounts to 426 14 0

['So I find due to myself more than I have received 0 12 3. I stand yet indebted 4 8 3. Received in all 427 13 6. spent in all 397 5 3. remains 30 8 3.

Made a Holland table cloth 3 breaths 7 yards & half long at 4s 10d the ell about 5 10 0. So, now there rests due to me 1 1 9.' crossed through]

Received 426 14 0. Spent 421 8 9 Remains 5 5 3.
[margin total] 63 0 6

[p. 10] 1639 100 ['Received the 1 day of March £100 0 0' crossed through] which was part of that money Mr Smith is to pay for a parcel of wool bought of my Lord in *Ierland*

£10 delivered out for my Lord's journey to the south hams £13 15 0; delivered to Slowely for his journey to London 20 0 0; to my Lord for a reward to him that brought the Parliament Right 1 0 0; to Doctor Chiester 1 0 0; for the servants & wagon going to London the 19th M. 5 8 6; paid a bill for Jack Burke 0 2 0; paid a bill for Webber 0 16 6; for a large table-cloth of Holland 5 10 0; received of this money for the journey to London 30 0 0; received for my own use in part of my allowance this 1 of April 1640 15 11 6
Sum total £93 3 6 R.B.

[p. 11 'Received of Ball left of the journey to the *Southhames* £6 6s 0d 1639 Received of Mr Pagget at my going to London the 23 of March £60 0s 0d' crossed through]
[received £]100 disbursed in servants wages there 38 0 0; paid a smith's bill there 2 5 6; paid a sadler's bill there 2 14 4; paid a shoemaker for the page there 0 13 0; for washing 2 of the groom's linen there 0 6 0; for presents there 0 2 6

London 1640 for 12 drinking glasses, 2 water glasses & a screen 1 10 6; laid out for several things by Bold 0 17 8; to Polard 2 4 0; for 6 dozen of ribbons for the foot-men & Page 1 14 [0]; to Polard 10 0 6
60 8 0

['Received of the £6 the servants had that went in the wagon to London 0 11 6' crossed through]; for a desk shelf & table 0 19 6; for a little wooden cabinet for my Lord 0 14 0; for a glass charne [*charnel*] 0 2 0 received as appeareth ['60 0 0' crossed through] disbursed as appeareth ['62 13 6' crossed through] ['remains 5 3 0' crossed through] spent above the £60 in this ['2 3 6' crossed through] total disbursed 62 3 6

**[p. 12** 'Received the 3 day of April 1640 of Mr Sowden in London £100 0s 0d' crossed through]
1640 delivered to my Lord 1 0 0; for a barrel of 112 lbs of Crown soap 1 4 6; for 3 ells of coarse cloth for wipers 0 4 0; paid a bill of Voysine's 0 5 0; to my brother of Westmorlande's groom 0 5 0; delivered to Pollard the 18th of April 1640 12 15 6
100 for my own allowance 30 08 6; ['laid out for my sister of Westmorland' crossed through] received again ['4 17 0 lent my sister Kate 1 6 0' crossed through] [total '16 0 6' crossed through]; delivered to my Lord 2 0 0; to Mr Brace my Lord's band-maker for 6 plain bands & cuffs the 27 of April 1640 1 10 0; delivered to Polard the 27 of April 10 0 0; paid the gardener in part of his bill the 27 of April 2 0 0; to Sam: a little bill 0 6 9; to the carpenter for making a coach house the 28 of April 5 9 0; to Darby 0 10 0; to the maids 0 3 0; to Sam: 0 10 0; to Sam: to go to *Apthorp* the 10 of May 0 6 0; for 4 new Spanish tables 4 8 0 the total expense ['88 4 3 more than received 3 4 3' crossed through] to my cousin Kemp an old bill concerning *Armore* 2 1 6
Just: sum total 84 6 9

**[p. 13]** paid to Mr Read, mercer, the 21th of April 1640 12 12 0.

Paid to Mr King, my Lord's tailor, in part of his bill the 27 of April 1640 20 0 0.
Paid Mr King the 17th of June in part 1640 20 0 0.
To Mr Webber the 13th of June 10 0 0.
£100 Paid Mr Allen the 13th of June 164[0] in part 30 0 0
Just. sum total 92 12 0

**[p. 14** 'Received the 4th of May Doctor Tucker in part of rent for Wantage 1640 30 0 0
7 0 0
9 0 0' crossed through]

Delivered to my Lord the 6 of May 1640 2 0 0; paid the gardener more the 9th of May 1640 1 0 0; paid a cooper for tables & other things 1 11 0; to Mr Bouchier the 10th of May 5 0 0; to James the blackamore 2 0 0; to Rose & Alice 2 0 0; for a drinking glass 0 2 6; to my Lord the 14th of May 2 0 0; to my Lord the 15th of May 3 0 0; for nails for the crimson velvet 0 13 0; delivered to Slowely the 20th of May 1640 10 0 0; to John Ceaton the groom 23 May 1640 0 10 0 [total] 29 16 6

To Mr Bouchier the 15th of June 1640  5 0 0; for Edward Barry the same
time 5 0 0; wages to Ralph Booth also 5 0 0; to William Deacon then
6 0 0; Christian 0 10 0; paid a bill to William Deacon 0 5 6; paid for pence
2 0 0; in other things 0 10 0; to Pollard for wages the 24th of June 1640
10 0 0  [total] 34 5 6
Just: sum total 64 2 0

[p. 15  'Received of Mr Lambe of Mr James Smithe's money due to my
Lord for wool the 12th of April 1640 £100 os od' crossed through] 100
delivered to Pollard the 4th of May 1640  20 0 0; delivered to Pollard the
16th of May 1640  20 0 0; delivered to Pollard the 28 of May 1640  20 0 0;
delivered to Pollard the 6th of June 1640  20 0 0

100 delivered to Pollard the 15th of June 1640  40 0 0; delivered to Pollard
the 22 of June 1640  20 0 0  [total] 140 0 0; given to Clement Lynn at his
going away May 1640  2 0 0; to my Lord the 1 day of June 1640  23 0 0;
to my Lord the same day 2 0 0; to my Lord the 8th of June 1640  6 0 0;
to my Lord the 13th of June 1640  5 0 0; to my Lord the 23 of June 1640
10 0 0; to my Lord for Mr William Beare the 25th of June 1640  5 0 0
[total] 53 0 0

delivered to Slowely the 6th of June 1640  5 0 0; delivered to Slowely the
20th of June 1640  10 0 0; delivered to Slowely this 24th of June 1640
10 0 0; Mr Smith a chandler the 12th of June 1640  5 13 0

100 paid the cutler the 13th of June 1640  4 10 6; paid 2 apothecaries
3 7 0; paid the farrier the 24th of June 1640  5 8 0; paid the hatter for
6 hats & 12 bands the 24th of June 1640  3 3 0; paid Mr Gelthrope for the
Lady Peterborough's picture 12 0 0; for a fair looking glass 3 5 0; a little
bill of ['Willy Deacon's' crossed through] Bold's 0 5 6
[total] 62 12 0   Just: sum total 255 12 0

[p. 16]   paid Mr Tatt, mercer, the 18th of June 1640  40 0 0
paid Mr Grinder for nails the 19th of June 1640  6 9 0
sum total 46 9 0

[p. 17]   100 paid to Mr Austine, mercer, the 21 of April 1640  60 0 0.
paid Mr Austine the 22 of June 1640 in part 20 0 0.
paid Mr Parsons the 15th of June 1640 in full 12 10 0.
Sum total 92 10 0

[p. 18]   Due from the former accounts ['3 4 9' crossed through] 5 5 3

1639 received of Mr James Smith for wool 1th of March 100 0 0

received of Mr Paget the 23 of March 1639  60 0 0; received of Mr Sowden
the 3th of April 1640  100 0 0; received of Mr Lambe the 12th of April
1640 £100 os od; received the 20th of April of Mr Beare 1640  53 18 6.

[p. 19]   one of these bags fell short 20s
received of Mr Sowden the 17th day of April 1640 £300 os od; received of
Doctor Tucker in part of Wantage rent the 4th of May 30 0 0; received the
6 day of May 1640 of Mr [blank] 60 0 0; received of Tom: Wiott the 12th
of May 1640 for creation money of the sheriff of Wilt: fees discharged
19 3 4; received from Mr Hugh Sowden the 26 of May 1640  200 0 0
[total '1027 10 1' crossed through]

['1159 19 1 1319 19 1' crossed through] received from Irish men the 10th of June 1640 132 0 0; received from the earl of Westmorland in part the 17th of June 1640 160 0 0

1320 18 7 total receipts till the 13th of July 1640

[p. 21 'received of Mr Beare the 20th of April 1640 53 18 6' crossed through]

paid the baker for bread the 28 of April 1640 5 0 0

paid the brewer the 7 day of May 1640 for small beer [at] 6s 36 barrels £10 16 0.

at the same time for 9 barrels & one hogshead of strong beer [at] 10s beer 5 5 0.

to make up the next £100

for wool & coal 10 15 0

sum total 31 16 0

[p. 22] 100 to Pollard the 29th of June 1640 30 0 0; to Slowly then 6 0 0; to Wiote the same day 10 0 0; to Darby then 1 0 0; for shoes for footmen then 1 0 0; to Sam: 0 10 0; to Ceaton 0 8 0; for seiing [?sewing] John Dreke skins 1 4 0; for Waker's washing 0 6 0; other small gifts 1 0 0; for Walker's learning of the fiddle 0 7 6; for the fiddle & strings 0 16 0; a little bill of Bold's 0 5 6; for boots & shoes for my Lord this quarter 1 4 0; paid the wax chandler 0 17 6; for a black wrought sheet to Miriam 2 2 0; a little bill 0 7 6 want £10; for great lace 5 4 0; the expense in traveling 27 8 0

100 ['lent this 2 of July 1640' crossed through] 10 0 0; laid out for myself 80 14 10

just: sum total 180 14 10

[p. 23] paid the sadler's bill the 21 of April 1640 9 15 0; paid the coaler the 29th of June 1640 in part 5 0 0; also the same day paid the embroiderer 7 0 0; to the embroiderer 1 4 0; paid the same day to Mr Greene, mercer, 25 0 0; paid the full sum of all Mr Green's bills 20 0 0

just: sum total 67 19 0

[p. 25] 100 paid the coach-maker in part the 22 of April 1640 20 0 0; paid the painter for his work about the coach the 23 April 15 10 0; paid the coach-maker in part of his bill the 30th of April 20 0 0; paid the coach-maker in part of his bill the 4th of June 20 0 0

just: sum total 75 10 0

Thomas Pollard paid the coach-maker in part of his bills of £67 the 10th of October 1641 £10 0 0

[p. 35] Paid the furrier for my Lord's robes furring the 28 of April 1640 14 0 0; a bill of Bold's this journey in July 1640 2 10 10; paid by Slowley for 13 yards & half of scarlet at £2 5s the yard cost 30 7 6; also the tailor's bill for sarsnet gold lace, hooks & making up 13 11 3

the whole robes 58 9 7

The Great Coach

this cast up the 18 of May 1641 for wheels, woodwork & leather & harness & reins [and] making 109 0 0; the gilt & brass 57 10 0; the velvet 53 17 0; the fringe 33 7 3; the curtains & linings 9 0 0

the whole charge 262 14 3

the fine & furnishing the house with all necessaries 1000 0 0
the liveries for coach-man postilian 4 foot-men & a page 110 0 9
the foot-cloth 109 15 0

household stuff, plate & linen in the house at *Tawstok* since my coming
£1500 0 0
for horse meat & man's meat 40 weeks living in London a family of
between 30 & 40 & about 8 horse £1000 0s 0d
for servants' wages that I have paid out 261 0 0
Sum 4261 0 0

my accounts made even with Richard Slowely from the 1 of March 1639 to
the 26 of June 1641, whereby it appeareth he hath received in this time and
disbursed in the same time £468 12s 9d.
so, remained the 26 of June 1641 in his hands £8 17s 3d

[enclosure 35a]   a note of fringes and lace & nails which came from
London the 6 of November 1639

57 ounces of deep fringe containing 69 yards, 50 ounces & half of framing
fringe cont. 72 yards, 29 ounces of top fringe containing 59 yards & half,
43 ounces of lace containing 72 yards, eleven hundred & seventy great
bullen nails [and] eleven hundred of small burnished nails 5 score to the
hundred

[p. 36]   £100 paid to Mr Gosse the silk man in part of his bill the 27 of
April 1640  20 0 0; paid Mr Gosse in June 1640  30 0 0
these 2 sides makes £133

[p. 37]   £13 paid to Mr Nitingale the fringe maker the 18th of April 1640
in part of his bill £10 0s 0d; paid to Mr Nitingale the 27 of April 1640
30 0 0; paid to Mr Nightingale the 4th of June 1640  30 0 0;
Mr Nightingalle received of Mr Beare in August 20 0 0; paid
Mr Nightingale in Novem. 1640  20 0 0; paid Mr Nightingale the 12 of
Decem. 1640  20 0 0; paid Mr Richard Cuttberd in part 13 0 0
just total 83 0 0
sum total 133 0 0

['moneys received from the 1 day of March 1639 to the 17th of June 1640
being in London 1319 10 7.
Disbursed as here appeareth by the bills & dates 1295 3 5
so remains, this present 12th of July 1640  24 6 8
to Dick Burton that stayed with the coach horse at the *Bathe* 1 0 0; to the
porter brought my Lady Peterborow's picture 0 1 0; to my Lord in
London the 4th of May 1640  1 0 0; to my Lord the 15th of July 1640
1 0 0
now remains 21 7 8
disbursed 1327 17 5' crossed through]
received 1320 7 1
disbursed 1296 14 5
['remains 023 9 6' crossed through]
just remains 23 12 8

**[p. 37a]** Spent £1300
1640 remaining of the account formerly July the 13th 023 12 8

**[p. 38]** received the last payment of Mrs Smith's money for wool the
13th of July 1640 54 19 6; received the 24th of August of Mr James
Smithe 50 0 0; received the 7th of September 1640 of Mr James Smithe
50 0 0; wanting 6d received the 9th of October 1640 of Jefferys an
apothecary 50 0 0; received from one King of *Warkley* in part the 13th of
Octob. 1640 10 0 0

£200 by R. Poll. received of Pollard the 22 of ['August' crossed through]
October 1640 160 0 0; by him returned to London to me this time
100 0 0; received of him then 10 0 0; received the 23 of Oct. 1640 30 0 0;
received of Raphe Booth at my Lord's coming to London 6 0 3; ['received
of Thom: Pollard the 4th of Novem. 1640' crossed through] from
Mr Thom: Finiks 100 0 0; received from my brother of Westmorland the
10th of No. 1640 in gold 100 0 0; received more of him a week after
60 0 0; received of Thomas Pollard the 20th of Novem. 1640 Gamon
100 0 0; received by Pollard of Mr Sowden the 1 of Decem. 1640 in gold
100 0 0; received by Pollard of Mr Sweete the 1 of Decem. 1640 100 0 0;
[total '1081 0 0' crossed through]

received of Doctor Tucker of Wantage rents ['the' crossed through] in
Novem. 1640 45 0 0; received of Marchant's wanting £9 for the change
300 0 0; received of Willy: Fuller from the Earl of Westmorland 100 0 0;
received from Wantage for the sealing of a copy Decem. 20 1640 35 0 0
[total] 1664 9 3 the 17th of Decem. 1640
The true receipts above mentioned ['1475 12 5' crossed through]
1475 12 8   1200 the above 1452

**[p. 38a]**
100 transferred   transferred 100

**[p. 39]** £100 to Jack-paine his whole year's wages the 15th of July 1640
3 0 0; ['for 20 bushels of oats 2 10 0' crossed through; to Pollard for my
Lord's journey to Exeter the 1 of August 1640 15 18 10; more to my
Lord that day 1 0 0; to the Irish man that brought the cattle 1 0 0, of
money left at London 1 20; to my Lord the 19th of August 1640 1 0 0; to
my Lord the 6 of Sept. 1640 1 0 0; to Slowely for my Lord's journey to
*Plimoth* in August 1640 10 0 0; to my Lord 1 0 0; to the fiddlers at
Hallorod 1640 1 0 0; to Webber 0 2 6; to my Lord—1640 1 0 0; £100 to
Mrs Downe the 15th of Sept. 1640 100 0 0; for a watch with cloke [clock]
& larum bought of Philip Norcould the 24th of Sept. 1640 17 10 0; for
2 Irish men the 28th of Sept. 1640 0 15 0; paid Moor a bill the 29th of
Sept. 1640 0 4 0; laid out to fetch Wright out of prison the 25th of Sept.
5 0 0; to Doctor Chiester the 10th of October 1640 7 0 0; to Doctor
Villven at the same time 5 0 0; to Mr Bidgood his apothecary then 2 0 0;
to Pollard who went for the Doctor 1 0 0; to Mr Hart-man of ['Bastab'
crossed through] *Barnestable*, physician 1 0 0; paid a tailor's bill for my
Lord 0 4 6; to Besse Seairl for half year's wages the 15th of Octo. 1640
1 10 0; to Joan Elis at the same time for a year's wages 2 0 0; to Wilmot
for her half year's wages then 1 0 0; to Alice Tearil her half year's wages

1 o o; to Besse Randle the like 1 o o; to Besse Humbile at the same time
1 o o; to Christian also 1 o o; to Hardwick half a year's wages this 15th of
Octo. 1640  5 o o; want. 5s 2d for cloth bought of Voysin this 15th of
Octo. 1640  9 2 o; for my Lord's Parliament rite the 18th of Octo. 1640
1 o o

to Mr Bouchier the 18th of Octo. 1640  8 o o; to Barry the 18th of Octo.
1640  10 o o; to Jack-paine the 20th of Octo. 1640  1 o o; to James the
Blackmore the 22 of Octo. 1640  2 o o; the hop-man then 1 15 o; a bill of
his o 1 6; Zachary 1 o o; Willy: Geare 1 o o; Thomas Armesbey 1 o o;
Darby 1 o o; Dick Cooke o 15 o; to the brewer & baker in gift o 10 o

[p. 40]  100 for the maids journey to London the 22 of October 1640
2 o o; to a shoe-maker for Dick Burton's boots o 10 o; to the apothecary
4 13 o; to Barry given 2 o o; paid a bill for Dick Burton's 2 2 o; for shoes
for foot-men o 10 o; laid out for Wright to Mr Punchard the 22 of
October 5 o o; for frieze coats for the foot-men then 1 17 6; for Joan
Widdon o 1 6; spent in my journey to London in Octob. 1640  29 10 o
[total] 275 12 10; want 7 17 6 to William Fuller for keeping the plate Octo.
1640  o 5 o; to 2 porters that brought bedding of my sister Betty o 2 6; for
a sable for my neck 8 10 o; to my Lord the 8th of Novem. 1640  1 o o

100 for a green velvet bed & other things as by the bill 78 oo o; my cousin
Jarvis paid her half year's benevolence for Michaelmas last 1 o o; to
Mr Nightingale in Novem. 1640  20 o o; lent my Lady Eliz. Boucheir for a
guitar & book & strings 2 5 o

100 for a smith as by bill o 18 o; for sweet powder 2 lbs & one pint of
Orange Flower water o 19 o; for [?]babys o 6 o; to a apothecary o 13 6;
for a perfumed cabinet 2 15 o; to Sam: to carry letters & a poor man
o 1 6; to Slowely in Novem. 1640  10 o o; to a carpenter about that time
as by bill 7 10 o; for bottles & knives o 10 o; to go to a play o 4 o; for a
hat for Sir Ralph Sidnam 3 o o; laid out in odd things o 10 o; for a
chaldron of seacoal 2 o o; a small bill of o 8 4; to my Lord the 19th of
Novem. 1640  1 o o; to the coachmaker the 21 of Novem. 1640  o o 6

[p. 41]  to Thom: Pollard 5 o o; to Pollard the 9th of Novem. 1640
25 o o; more 3 15 10 to Pollard the 20th of Nove. 1640  20 o o; laid up in
gold o13 o 6

100 for a rich sweet bag the 1 of Decem. 1640  14 10 o; to Miss Bethell in
full payment of her year's rent 40 o o; to the gilder of the buckles for the
coach 12 o o; to Willy: Deacon 6 o o; to Doctor Moore 2 fees 2 o o; for
hay bought by Willy: Deacon 1 o o; for Scotch coal a tun 1 14 6; Robert
Wood for wine & casks 1 6 o; to Canname o 10 o; over 9 o 6 to Pollard
the 30th of November 1640  30 o o

100 to Pollard the 5th of December 1640  20 o o; to Mr Olibear the 3 of
Decem. 1640  20 o o; to Mr Rider, scrivener, & his man the 1 of Decem.
1640  22 10 o; ['to Mr Parrett the 3 of Decem. 1640  12 o o' crossed
through] just. 373 18 4; want. 3 18 o  to Slowely the 5th of Decem. 1640
15 o o; to the coach-maker the 10th of Decem. 1640  15 o o; to the wax
chandler in Decem. 1640  3 12 o

100 over 37 2 0 to Sir Antony Wellon's man the 10 of Decem. 30 0 0; to
Mr Nightingale in Decem. 1640 20 0 0; to Mr Gosse the 16th of Decem.
13 0 0; to Mr King the 16th of Decem. 10 0 0; for music 1 2 6; to my
Lord Newbuck's cook & butler 0 15 0; Madam Le Mote 1 14 0; to
Mr Lawley for hangings the 12 of Decem. 1640 60 10 6

for ribbon 0 01 0; to Mr Webber for stockings 11 13 6; to a porter 0 1 6;
to a French man of Queen Mothers 10 0 0; to my Lord sent by Barry to
the Parliament House 2 0 0
just 195 0 0
total 1207 17 7 the 17th of Decem. 1640 384 19 6

**[p. 42]**   100 to Pollard the 24th of Decem. 1640 20 0 0; this with the
former over-pluses which amounts 51 13 4; given 0 1 6; the sum wanting
being £12 0s 8d; So that this last £100 is but 84 0 8

to this place spent £860 wanting 0 7 4

**[p. 43]**   Received from Willy: Fuller the 26 of Decem. 1640 60 0 0;
received from Mr Ferris by Pollard the 29th of Decem. 1640 100 0 0;
received from Mr Smith in part of this year's wool the 12th day of January
1640 165 0 0; received of Mr Sowden the 25 of Jan. 1640 100 0 0
425 0 0
taking the 23 12 8 left in the former the whole receipt is just. 1900 12 5
From the 13th of July 1640 to the 25 of Jan. 1640 1900 12 5

**[p. 44]**   £100 of one hundred pound had of Willy: Fuller

to Pollard the 6th of Jan. 1640 12 16 0; transferred 10 0 0; Puluy the 7 of
Jan. 1640 1 0 0; for making 8 smocks 1 0 0; the boy's periwig 0 15 0; for
ribbon & Mr Major 0 11 0; for hanging of Mr Pasmore 3 pieces 7s the
stick 30 0 0; to my Lord the 6 of Jan. 1640 1 0 0; to Pollard the 19 of
Decem. 1640 20 0 0; lent to Bold the 23th of Jan. 1640 5 0 0; light gold
0 3 0; to Slowely the 2 of Jan. 1640 14 0 0; ['remains yet this 25th of Jan.
1640 1 17 0' crossed through] to the Queen's footmen at 1 Jan. 1 0 0; to
my cousin Mildmey's son 0 10 0; for needles 0 2 0; the corn cutter 0 6 0;
now remains this 25th of Jan. 1 17 0
just. 88 3 0

['to Pollard the 19th of December 1640' crossed through] 0 0 0

**[p. 45]**   to Pollard the 24 of Decem. 1640 20 0 0

60 to Pollard the 26 of Decem. 1640 10 0 0; from Willy Fuller transferred
8 10 0; to my Lord 1 0 0; to myself 4 0 0; Darby 0 10 0; Slowley the 2 of
Jan. 1640 18 16 0; Pollard the 6 of Jan. 1640 7 4 0
just. 69 10 0   want £10

to the King at New Year's Stead the 1 of January 1640 20 0 0; in fees
2 3 0; in Christmas to my Lord [blank]; to my brother Robin the 1 of
January 1640 1 0 0; to my Lord's shoemaker the 18th of Decem. 1640
2 4 0; paid an old herb woman's bill 2 13 4; paid the sadler an old bill
Decem. the 12 1640 6 5 0; a smith's bill the 17th of Decem. 1640 1 4 6; a
bill of Caton's in travelling 0 4 0; for 5 pair of fringed gloves for men the
13 of Decem. 3 2 0; to my Lord Paulet's harper 0 15 0; ['to the Queen's
footmen' crossed through] 0 0 0; to a poor tailor 0 10 0; to Miss Speket's

maid brought apples 0 2 0; for pheasants 1 2 0; shoes for footmen the 24th of Decem. 1640 1 2 6; To ['Darby to' crossed through] Sam for ['their' crossed through] wages the 1 of January 1640 0 10 0; ['lost at play' crossed through] to Mr Beare the 24th of Decem. 1640 30 0 0; to Mr Prise the 24 of Decem. 1640 10 0 0; for a doe sent 0 6 8; to the prisons in London 1 12 6; to Mr Tomkins 3 0 0; to boxes at Christmas 0 16 0; to Slowely in Decem. 1640 & the beginning of Jan. 7 4 0; to Miss Gritty 2 0 6; to my Lord of Arundell's man 0 10 0; at St Bartlemus church 0 10 0; to my cousin Mildemey's son 0 6 0; ['to Besse Searle for needles' crossed through] 0 0 0; to Breame the corn cutter 0 0 6; given 0 0 6; to Voysin for to buy ribbon 0 12 0; ['more' crossed through] 0 0 0; to my Lord Willoby's man that brought venison 0 10 0

of the money charged upon weeks £100 just. £100 [total] 115 19 6

[p. 46] for band strings [blank]; given 0 0 0; lost at play 0 0 0

the 25th of Jan. £100 to Miss Taylore the 8th of January 1640 1 0 0; to Pollard the 12th of Jan. 1640 20 0 0; to Mr Beare the 14th of Jan. 1640 10 0 0; to Slowley for hay the 14th 2 0 0; for Rushey red leather chairs 1 dozen 4 0 0; to the coach-maker the 18th of Jan. 1640 10 0 0; to Pollard the 19th of Jan. 1640 24 0 0; to Mr Barrow the 19th of Jan. 1640 20 0 0; ['to Mr Harper an old bill 0 0 0 to my brother Robert lent the 19th of Jan.' crossed through] 0 0 0; a bill of Bold's 4 0 0
just. £100

165 transferred the 14th of Jan. 1640 39 0 0; for a sweet bag the 23 of Jan. 6 10 0; for a suit of hangings 8 pieces 9s 6d the stick 106 0 0; to Mr Pasmore that made the bargain the same 23 of Jan. 5 0 0; to the brick-layer for 7 chimneys the 23 of Jan. 2 3 0; light gold 0 1 0; for the iron monger the 30th of Jan. 1640 in part 5 0 0; to the Chancellor's man of *Exetor* 0 6 0; given to Robin's man that went in to *Ierland* 1 0 0
Just. 126

[p. 47] £100 to Slowelly the 26 of Jan. 1640 10 0 0; to Pollard the same day 20 0 0; for silver & gold lace for my best sweet bag 1 8 6; to my Lord the 2 of Feb. 1640 10 0 0; lent Miss Taylore then 3 0 0; for a cabinet, table & 2 standers of China work 8 3 0; to Pollard the 7th of Feb. 1640 30 0 0; in small parcels 3 5 6; transferred in gold 2 0 0; a bill of Bold's 6 0 0; to Mr Bouchier the 12th of Feb. 1640 ['just 852 17' crossed through] 3 0 0; to Rose Tod then 0 10 0

The total receipts in this book from the 4th of March 1638 to the 25 of Jan. 1640 3737 14 7

disbursed as may appear 3470 18 4
so this 12th of Feb. 1640 remains 266 16 3
from the last to this £615 0 0

Mr Hind St. of my Lord's courts about *Exetor* rece. from Michal. 1642 to the like 1643 John Martin's *Combintinhead* [Combeinteignhead] last payment being £19 & of Will: Lee for Agnes Bickford's fine *Kingcarswell* [Kingskerswell] in part £14, Thomas Benit *Kingscarswall* 15 the [illegible] 039 0 0; also for rents from these manors then 046 19 10 [total] 085 19 10

whereof returned to London to Will: Lynn in that time 080 0 0 & now
paid to Rich: Polla. this Audit 1643  005 19 10

**[p. 48]**  266 16 3
Willy: Lynn received for me May the 25th 1642 of the High Sheriff £20 &
of Mr Vaveser 30  50 0 0; his account cometh to of [sic] disbursed 49 7 0
so remains 00 13 0

Will: Lynn's receipts from the 25 of May 1642 to the 5th of August 1643
was 1855 15 6½
Thom: Pollard in London in May 1642 received for me of several men
whereof £10 was from Willy: Lynn he disbursed for my occasions as by
bill appeareth 360 0 10
so remained 000 19 2

Thom: Wiote's account from 1642 the Audit until the same time 1643
580 12 8
His receipts in that time as appears
His disbursed in the same time is 574 7 5
so remains in his hand 6 5 3, which I gave him with £13 14s 9d, for
2 years wages

Hardwick hath rec. this year 1644 for hops 32 16 10, whereof she hath laid
out several ways 27 7 0, & due to her at Michaelmas 1644 for wages 5 0 0,
so now rec. the remainder this present 1644 21 of March 0 9 10

Hardwick's accounts since the Audit 1641 to the 8th of August 1642 her
receipts 205 9 0.

I have received by returns to London & other ways 191 10 0
Rests due 013 19 0

Hardwick's receipts since 1642 until 1643 the Audit 541 5 6, whereof
disbursed by her in that time 393 12 0, so received now of her 147 13 6,
received of her this 23 of Nov. 1643 whereof I gave her for wages £10
which was due the last Audit she being 2 years before the steward paid her
behind, I say rec. 012 0 0

**[p. 49]**  Taken out of the Red bag nothing.
Received of Mr [blank] 100 0 0; received of Mr Whatsonne in part of £200
due 80 0 0; wants 1s received from Mr Sowden the 6 of March 1640
200 0 0; received for a watch my own money again ['4' crossed through];
received of an Irish man the 16th of March 1640  194 3 0; received of
Mr Sweete my own money the 30th of Mar. 1640 ['20' crossed through]
0 0; received from Mr James Smith in part for wool 100 0 0; received from
Mr Dimond the 11th of April 1641  50 0 0; received from Wantage the
13th of April 1641  30 0 0
[total] from the 25 of Jan. 1640 to the 23 of April 1641 ['778 3 6' crossed
through] 654 3 0

received the 8th of May 1641 of Mr Sweete ['29' crossed through] 14 6;
received from Mr Perrin, merchant, in London 100 0 0; then received from
Mr Perkins in *Ierland* 100 0 0; received also from Mr Dimond the 50 0 0
[total] 279 14 6

took out of the Red Bag in April 1641 150 0 0; received from Hardwick the 23th of May 1641 ['20' crossed through] 0 0; received by Mr King ['4' crossed through] 0 0

leaving out them that are crossed 904 3 0
them that be crossed 77 14 6
these monies received 981 17 6

['Mr Paggett's total receipts for 5 years from 1637 until 1641 5164 12 0
his disbursements were in that time 6331 16 1
whereof of the young Ladies moneys 0373 15 1
the interest of the money he was out of purse for each year came to
0181 0 0' crossed through]

October the 27th 1643 the rents & profits of the 6 manors for the young Ladies as is now supposed to be right cast up for those 6 years, after the Countess Anne's death. In my Lord's hand as is thought now 908 15 4 qr.

And in Mr Pagett's hands 624 5 2 qr.
And at this time there is certainly in the bailiff's hands unpaid 153 7 5
['77 14 6' crossed through] total 1686 7 11½

Lyon had unpaid for the year 1642 73 18 10, Tho: Polla. rece. for the year 1643 24 15 8 & 0 11 6 unpaid for work done.

[enclosure 49a] John Lyon hath paid in part of his debt for the last year the sum of £59 15s so rest 73 18 10d. this year's estreats for 1644 35 8 9 & the debit 107 16. a heriot mare. Lyon's mare & colt. a stray colt

[p. 50] 1644 Oct. & £5 Bongler the coachmaker had.

Thom: Polla: receipts of *Hunspill* [Huntspill] debet for the year 1643, paid 11s 6d for work done there, 25 7 2; he also then rec. from *Woonham* [Wonham] 10 0 0, & from *Banton* [Bampton] 6 0 0
Thom: Pollard received from the 15th of Jan. 1640 until the 20th of April 1644 in all 129 19 5; Disbursed by him in that time as by his account 122 2 2, & £5 to him for wages, So I received from him 002 17 0

[p. 51] My steward Richard Pollard's receipts in the year 1641 after the Audit in 1642 is 2210 4 9½.

First, he delivered me in October 1641 830 0 0; his disburs[ements] the first quarter 234 3 2; the second quarter 272 13 8; in the third 290 16 7; in the fourth quarter 681 11 3 [total] 2309 4 8
So, rested then due to Polla: 0098 19 10½

The same steward's receipts from 1642 until 1643 is 1220 6 9½
His disbursements in that year 1171 12 7½
So, rests due to my Lord 1643 this 25th of Octo. 0048 14 2
at this time I have rec. from him which he newly received at 0500 0 0
Also of Drak's fine 0090 0 0
The said Rich: Polla: hath disbursed other ways from the time above mentioned to the 25th of March 1644 0517 11 4½
also for his then half year's wages at our Lady Day 1644 0000 0 0
In all from the Audit to our Lady Day 1117 11 4
Received by him in the same time 1137 02 0
So this 30th of March 1644 remains due to my Lord 0019 11 4

His whole year's receipts from the 22 of Octo. 1643 until the same time in the year 1644 is 1435 0 8½  His disbursements in the same time is 1426 8 2  so remained then in his hands 8 12 6½

[p. 52]  October the 25 1640 to 1641
The Steward Richard Pollard's accounts for one year
His receipts appears 1177 8 4 ¾
his disbursements 1232 13 9
so due to him 0055 5 4¼
Also due to him for one whole year's wages 0020 00 0
whereof there was due from him to me by a former bill 0004 11 4
So, rests due to him 0070 41 0½

He received this Audit 1641 for which he is to account for fines ['775' crossed through] 765 ex[amined] 5 0
And the debit 223 1 3¼.  44 10 9

Cattle which are left upon the barton at my coming away for London milk kine 17 whereof one is gone to feeding.
bulls 2, oxen to plough 8, oxen to feed 10, steers to feed 6, steers to plough 2, heifers to feed 3, calves 12, yearlings 11, sheep 180, lambs 5

I came up with 17 & 7 coach horses & Armsby had one
horses [blank], Mares [blank], colts [blank]
Since my coming way from from *Tawstok* there is come from *Louthgar* 2 stone horses, 2 mares, 2 geldings

Richard Atherton sent his accounts in to England by Mr Willy: Beare for 4 years & half from ma. from 1637 to 1641

The rent being £579 18s 9½d for 4 years & half cometh to 2609 14 6 ¾, his disbursements being in this time 1734 19 6, remains due in May 1641 0874 15 0 ¾, whereof as appears by a note he sent in the tenants hands of this 874 15 0 ¾  0427 19 7

[p. 53]  To Pollard the 18th of Febr. 1640  100 0 0; for a looking glass 5 0 0; for glass for the lantern at Comb. the 6 of Mar. 1640 4 10 0; to the smith at that time in part of his bill 5 0 0; to Pulluy then 2 5 0; given him by Bold before 0 5 0; for hay the 7th of March 1640 2 0 0 ['to Mr Bouchier the 12 of Feb. 1640 3 0 0 to Rose then 0 10 0' crossed through]; to my brother Robin 2 0 0  [total £]21

To Mr Pasmore the 16th of Feb. 1640 20 0 0; for a looking glass then 21 0 0; paid Mr Goldsmith at that time 25 0 0; for hay the 19th of Feb. 1640  2 0 0; to a nurse 10 0 0  [total] 68 10 00

he came in July 1639 £20 per. Mathew Coyse the steward of my Lord's house in one year & quarter which was the time he served him, but remained in the house 3 quarters of a year after & then made up his accounts.

his disbursements the whole time amounted to 799 6 11
his first receipts as appeareth in his book 736 4 2

and delivered him by Mr Paget the 24 of July 1641 at his going away
063 2 9
which made his reckoning even, £25 of the money being wages for one
year & quarter service   total receipts 862 9 10
Miss Searle hath in her hands of the money for the woods £128 3s 8d

[p. 54]   My Lord's steward William Weekes made his accounts to me
from the year 1637, in March, unto the 25th of March 1641 full 4 years his
receipts as appears by his book was £3945 2s 0d

wool sent into England for which my Lord had the money in
1637—479 10 0, in 1638  505 0 0, in 1639  515 1 0, in 1640  437 18 0.   In
all 1937 0 0

Also six score wethers sold to James Dyer for which my Lord received in
England of him 0060 0 0
Also sent to my Lord to *Tawstok* 600 wethers, 100 ewes & 4 rams in
all 704
owing yet in *Ierland* by several persons for corn until the time above
mentioned 0290 10 0
Also Philip Sexton oweth for 200 ewes 0100 0 0
owing more for sheep's skins 0008 0 0
There is also owing for grassing of cattle for this year & the last years
Justice Gernon oweth by bill 0022 0 0   [total] 6342 2 0

these behind with rent The Lady Southwell, per £30 Sir William Poore, per
£9 18s Mr Steevenson & the La. Castle Conill, 10s Meaugh, per £7 0 0
David Roach

William Weekes his disbursements in these four years 3943 13 11
whereof returned into England by several men of this money here
mentioned 1437
& in cattle bought for *Tawstok* £45
At *Glenogar* being 4 plowland cattle there now of 3y:2:1 58
at *Lough-garr* milk cows 17
there is dry cows 19
there is oxen 16
calves of this year weaned 14
there is wethers 1087
ewes 0500
lambs wethers 0260
at *Lough garr* 1065

[p. 55]   ['delivered to Pollard the 100 0 0' crossed through] to Slowely the
8th of March 1640  20 0 0; to the coach-maker that day 5 0 0; to a silk
man for fringe the 9th of March 1640 [£]16; to Sir Humphrey Payton's
servant at the same time 30 0 0; for the painter as by bill 10 0 0; for
2 chimney hearths of marble 4 0 0   [total] £85

for 1 dozen & 2 great chair frames 2 4 0; to the joiner the the [sic] 9th of
March 1640  30 0 0; to the carpenter the 10th of March 1640  18 0 0; to
Pollard the 9th of March 1640   [total] 61 4 0

a bill of Wiote's then 1 0 0; Darby the joiner the 11th of March 1640
13 3 0; his son for andirons &c 8 3 0; for buggle [?buckle] lace 1 10 0;
more to the joiner the 18th of March 1640 13 0 0; more to the smith then
5 0 0; for tape & thread 0 11 0; to Slowely the 18th of March 1640
30 0 0; for bands for Jack Burke 0 8 0; for a sword & trimming one other
of the footmen 1 10 0; for gilt nails for the wrought velvet 6 5 0; for
turning the boys old clothes 0 7 0; for drinking glasses & 2 standers a bill
due in Nov. 1 19 10; 2 little bills of Jack Burk 0 9 0; to Mr Pasmore the
12th of March 1640 37 19 0   [total] 120 4 10

to Pollard the 19th of March 1640  6 0 0; to my Lord for Nan Howard
the same day 4 0 0; paid the shoe-maker 0 15 6; for a tiffany gorget
0 10 0; for comfits 2 lbs 0 14 0; to Mr Major in part of his wages the 8th
of March 1640 2 10 0; to the brick-layer 0 9 0; for faggots & wormwood
beer 0 4 6; to my Lord in March 1 0 0; lent to E. Bold March 1640
2 0 0   [total] 22 1 0

At *Bally Regan* 0040
At *Glenogre* rotten ewes presently to be sold 0600
old rams at the Lough island 0160
of rams, lambs & [?]rigills at *Rahan* Island 0107
of all sheep 4619
other cattle 0124

[p. 56]   to my sister Fane's, Anthony Fanes, nurse & midwife by my
Lord 4 0 0 ['to Pollard the 19th of March 1640  6 0 0' crossed through] to
Pollard the 30th of March 1641  20 0 0; the 2 of April 1640 I laid out for
bone lace 12 0 0; for the King's subsidies the 5 day of April 1641  32 0 0
[total] 68 0 0

Miriam Tarry in full paid the 11th of April 1641  4 0 0; paid the smith in
full this 16th of April 1641  9 18 0; to Mr Bouchier the 13th of April 1641
2 0 0; to Mr Tomkins the 17th of April 1641  3 0 0; to Rose Todd 1 0 0;
to Alice Tearle her half year's wages April 1641  1 0 0   [total] 20 18 0

[p. 57]   to Mr David Murrey the half of the fine the 15th of April 1641
£100 0 0; to Pollard the 12th of April 1641  50 0 0; to Pollard the 6th of
April 1641  50 0 0; to Slowely to go to the fair the 23th of April 1641
40 0 0   [total] 240 0 0

From the 24th of Decem. 1640 to the 23th of April 1641  1331 18 0
So from the 13th of July 1640 to the 23 of April 1641 is totally disbursed
2191 18 0
The receipt in this time 2678 15 0
so this present 23th of April remains £500 0 0

To Mr King the 14th of April 1641  10 0 0, to Mr Beare 10 0 0, to my
Lord 1 0 0, to Bold [blank], to Bold [blank], to Bold the 6th of April
[blank], to my Lord 1 0 0, for filling of lace 1 4 0 for making 2 gorgets &
tiffany to one of them Miss Antony 1 0 0, for the fur of my Lord's coat
8 0 0, for the pied nag bought of my sister Eliza. Cope 8 0 0
[total] £40 4s 0d

**[p. 58]** The 20th of April 1641

Paid Mr Lawles in full for the 14s stick hangings 104 0 0

To Pollard the 5th of May 1641 30 0 0; to Mr Pasmore the 5th of May 1641 20 0 0; to Mr Nightingale the same day 20 0 0; to my Lord the 24th of April 1641 4 0 0; to Mr Baincroft the 6th of May 1641 26 0 0; the painter in full payment then 7 10 0; to Ned Barry the same day 10 0 0; to the painter in full of £42 this 6th of May 1641 10 0 0; for linen for Sam. Starling 2 0 0; spent in my journey to *Brewern* [Bruern] 12 11 8; paid my glover the 6th of May 1641 4 10 0; to a clerk the 6th of May 1641 1 0 0; 2 little bills 1 13 6 [total] 252 13 2

for 8 bands for my Lord 2 0 0; 1641 to Mr Major the 10th of April in part of his wages 2 10 0; to Mr Prises my tailor's brother in full of his bill of 37 0 0 the 12th of May 1641 26 0 0; to Goody Hall the 12th of May 1641 1 10 0; to Goody Redhead then 0 10 0; taken out by Bold 2 0 0 [total] 34 10 0

to Mr Smith for oats the 11th of May 1641 10 0 0; to Slowely the 18th of May 1641 5 0 0; to Jesper Micheall 1 0 0; to Mr King the 11th of May 1641 4 0 0; to my Lord 0 8 0; to Chriestian part of her wages 0 10 0 [total] 20 18 0

**[p. 59]** £100 Paid Mr David Murry in full of £200 for the fine of our house in Lincon's Ine Fielldes the 6th of May 1641 £100 0s 0d

Rec. from the 4th of March 1638 until the 29th of May 1641 as appears by the particulars before in this book wherein I am satisfied the sum of ['£4709 12s 7d' crossed through] 4731 18 1
and disbursed in the same time as by the particulars in this book also appears 4547 12 1
So, rem. in my hands this 29th of May 1641 £184 6s 0d
[signed] R. Bathe

Remains in my hands this 29 of May 1641 184 6 0; rece. short 10s received from the Earl of Westmorland the last day of May 1641 for the £2000 due the 1 of Nove. 1640 £80 0s 0d; received the 4th of May 1641 of Mr Ric: Dimond £100 0s 0d; received of the Sheriff of Somerset for my Lord's creation money due at Michaelmas the 5th of June 1641 19 3 4; received the 23 day of June 1641 of Willy: Beare 200 0 0; received from the Earl of Westmorland the 24th of June 1641 for the last half year for the sum of £4000 160 0 0; received of Mr Boolworthy the 16th of July 1641 050 0 0; ['R' crossed through] Received of Richard Mills for a lease sealed the 27 of July 1641 as the one half of a fine 74 0 0; received at the hands of Susan Baldwin the 4th day of August 1641 200 0 0; August the 16th 1641 received of Willy: Lynn & Thom: Wiote for 11 year's rent of the 4th part of the manor of *Coren-Dinam* ending in February last at £1 0 7½ by the year 11 6 10½; Received also by them for the 4th part of Joan Norman's heriot 2s & of Thomas Boolen the like 2s of Leonard Breane the like 5s 0 9 0
ex[amined] 1078 15 2½ [total] 1078 15 2½

[p. 60]   Received at *Tawstok* the 22th of August 1641 of a servant of Sir William Poors that brought over cattle to sell in money £42 0s 0d; & then bought of him cattle, 12 cows, to the value of £28; rece. of Alice Teirle remaining of £4 which she had of Thomas Pollard at London for her journey & 4 more & a dog 0 10s 0; Sept. the 2 1641 received Mr James Smith's last payment of the wool of 1640 the whole sum being 437 18 0 37 0 0; received the 13th of June 1641 of Susan Baldwin 20 0 0; and of Samuel Starlings then 5 0 0

Ex[amined] 104 10 0

Received since the 29th of May until the 2 of September following 1183 05 2½

and disbursed in the same time as appears 1343 10 0 Ex. 1342 0 1

So due to me this 2 of Sept. 181 14 10½ ex. 158 14 10½ this 23 of June 1643 R. Bath ex.

**[enclosure slip 74a]**
those sums following I have received since my Lady went for London
received for hops £18 1 0
received for apples 4 14 0
rec. for rotten trees 3 1 0
the two beefs were killed, 3 sheep died rec. for hides and three sheep skins that died 1 13 0
rec. of Mr Wyott 10 0 0
received of the butchers 50 0 0
received for pigeons 0 10 8
received for lampreys 0 3 0
sum £88 2 11
Rec. more for several small commodities 0 18 0
I paid the Sunday after my Lady went for London from [illegible] to Sunday the 9th of April is 16 weeks.
I have sent your Honour these several sums to give all the satisfaction I can unto your Honour but I do humbly desire Mr Steward and Mr Wiott may receive the particulars and that your honour would speedily if not already procure the pass.

Paid out. Those sums following [illegible crossed through] since my Lady went for London.
the first week 1 9 2, second week 1 9 5, 3 week 1 13 6, 4 week 2 11 1, 5 week 1 12 10, 6 week 2 9 11, 7 week 8 1 5, 8 week 3 2 9, 9 week 3 10 9, 10 week 5 15 9, 11 week 9 16 10, 12 week 6 7 2, 13 week 3 0 3, 14 week 3 19 6, 15 week 2 4 3, in the 16 week at *Corington* Fair and since 16 12 3
sum is 73 12 10
I have in money 15 10 0   [total] 89 2 10

[p. 73]   ...
paid where it was due the 28th of Octo. 1645 502 12 0
So remains this day of Octo. of this account 29 18 5
& 20 angels my Lord hath for counters which is 10 0 0
& 18 French pieces of 15s that I have for the like 13 10 0
& £20 I had of the steward which he hath write in my book that he paid me on the other leaf following.
so in all I have this day 73 8 5

**[p. 74]** [*written upside-down*]   What stock is in the house the 8th of Aug. 1648
oxen for the plough 8, steers to feed 2, heifers to feed 3, yearlings 6 calves 3, cows to milk 7

William Weekes bought at *Kilkington* Fair the 15th of August 1648 cost £26 3s 4d
oxen whereof 2 of them for the plough 4
steers 1, cows to feed 3   £21 cost
cost in all 47 3 4

He bought in Hartland of Jo: Bragg sheep 40   cost £14 10s the score
also then the 28 of Aug. 1648 at *Bradeworthy* fair one steer £5
black 9s   killed.
oxen for the plough 2   cost £12 10s
and of John Bragg at Hartland bought 5 steers & one cow 6   £30

the same 8th of Aug. 1648 above written in the house
greace [*grease*] hogs 7, middle hogs 8, young pigs 8.
fat sheep 28, rams 3, ewes 2, lambs 2
bought of the widow Cunibeare [blank]
horses of all sorts 23 & of the servants horses 6, 2 heriots 1 black mare
her[iot] from *Beare* [Beer] charter

William Weekes bought at *Torington* Fair 1648 in the spring
sheep wethers 21   cost £13 21
both killed   steers cost 9 14 8   2
this killed   one cow motley 1   4 6 8
Weekes paid for 40 bushels of barley to sow £16   April the 21 1648

Bought at *Torington* Fair the 29 of Sept. 1648
oxen for the plough cost £12 5s 0   2
for a gale cost £5   1
oxen to feed one & 2 steers cost £16 2 3

baskets made 19 in the store cha[mber], 4 the gardener hath, 2 the catorer, 2 in the kitchen, one the hop-man hath & one in my Lady's closet
brooms bought [blank]
there is 30 fleeces of wool this 4th of Nove. 1648 weighted 67 lbs

**[p. 75]** ['25 October 1645 paid my Lady in money £20 00s 00d' in a different hand]; rece. of Rich: Britton by allowing the residue of the rent for the 2 closes for which he gave £40, £20 formerly allowed upon the old account & now in full of that money 20 0 0; rece. of him likewise for pasturing cattle & horses 2 10 0; rece. from Edw: Symons of Instow in full of his fine 27 0 0; rece. from the port reeve of Bow by Mr Varney Bouch: the 27 of Nove. 1645 in part 2 14 6; rece. from Widow Cunibear the 5 of Decem. in part of £80   10 0 0   [total] 112 2 11 this 17th of Decem. 1645

Rece. from Geo: Thorn in part of James Bond's money the 7th of Jan. 1645 9 0 0; rece. from Will: Ellis in full for the adding of Margaret N [blank] in a town tenement in *Tawstok* after the lives of old Miss Stribling & Joan his wife 35 0 0; rece. the 15th of Jan. 1645 of Geo: Cheivley in part of £9 due to me, now rece. 3 0 0; rece. in 2 gr. oxen £13, one lesser £3 & 60 bu. of barley, 4s 6d at 4s 8d, & one bushel over, these things rece.

from the widow Cunibear in part of £70 due the 5 of Decem. & now this
paid the 15th of Jan. 1645 £30 0 0; Tho: Wiote & Tho: Polla: brought out
of Cornwall 32 14 10 of which delivered the stew. [£]30 0 & spent in their
journey about 3 weeks 3 4 10 so due to ['him' crossed through] Tho:
Wiote 0 13 9  32 14 10; rece. the 22 of Jan. of Will: Fairchild in part of
£15 12s & for the profits of 3 years of widow Amner's ten. £3 more being
due for a heriot rece. now 4 6 0; this the st. receiving is not included the
steward rece. in part of Chris. qu[arter] of Taws. 5 16 2 and of Ned Randl
of *Warkly* as part of £23 4 13 4; rece. for 6 dozen [seams] of wood sold
the 22 of Jan. 1645 5 8 0; rece. of Ned Randall the 24 of Jan. in part of
the former sum 3 0 0; rece. in part then of £30 of the young Widow Squier
6 0 0  [total] 239 13 4

[p. 76]  Rece. by Ann Steevens the 23th of Jan. 1645 in full (of Leonard
Bond of Kerton the butcher) of his fine 90 0 0; rece. for wood 2 dozen &
ten seams sold at Bar. 2 11 0; rec. for hops at £5 8s 0 per hundred 7 10 4
238 1 8 to the 12 of Feb. 1645

rece. for wood sold at Barnstap. 5 4 6; rece. for the great rent due from
Jonathan's nurse's husband at Candlemas this 14th of Feb. 1645 0 6 8;
rece. for 3 bush. & half of beans out of my new orchard 1 4 6; rece. of
Jona[than']s father for a qr rent due at Candlemas 0 1 0; rece. the 21 of
March 1645 of Ed: Randall in part of £15 6 8½ due the last Audit 3 0 0;
Hardwick rece. for beans sold 0 18 0 & for kitch. st[uff] then 0 2 0; rece.
of the reeve of *Tawstok* in part of Christmas qr. 0 18 3

Paid again rece. the 24th of March 1645 from RC of Bar. to pay again
upon demand 230 0 0, paid £30 of this the 26 of May 1646 in the same
gold it was d[elivere]d me in & paid presently after the other 200

Rece. for one qr rent due at our Lady Day now from Anto: Brother at
*Colibear* 0 5 0; rece. from the South *Hames* out of several manors by the
stew. as by his bill appears 84 7 11  [total] 96 7 10

So rece. as appears here from the 25 of Octo. 1645 to the 25 of March
after being 1646 677 0 5, and £17 10s which I borrowed in all
£694 10s 5d. Disbursed in the same time 609 19 6, so remains this 30 of
March 1646 084 10 11

1646 Will: Lynn hath rece. this June of my bro. West 291; for a fine in
Wantage 20; of Mr Hames to be paid at *Tawstok* at twice 100; rece. by
myself the 17th of October from Tho: Mich: 150 0 0; rece. from my bro.
Fran: in part of what Oct. 14 I have laid out for my b[rother] Ge. Will:
Lynn rece. soon after the other £80 so in all £100 from Franck 20 0 0

[p. 77]  Rece. from the widow Cunibear in 252 lbs of cheese 1 11 6; more
in 400 faggots to mend the hutch 0 16 0 ['more in br. B' crossed through];
rece. now in money this 3d of April 1646 7 12 6 in all £10 in part of £40
due; rece. of Jo: Scott in full of his fine for exchange of 2 lives, Will: Elis
& his wife, in *Linscott* the 8th of April 7 0 0; rece. of Tho: Wiote of part
of Hartland rents 12 0 0; more of him in part of the Widow Squier's fine
of *Warkely* there now remaining to pay £19 5 0 0; rece. from the stew. of
*Tawstok* rents this present 10th of April 6 0 0; rece. of Thom: Polla. which
he left of his journey to London begun the 23th of Jan. 1645 himself, Tho:

Armsby & 2 horses until the beginning of March spent £9 6 2, rece. of the
stew. £2 10s & of Will: Lynn 8 3 2, so I rece. of him 1 7 0; rece. for
Yorke which was sold to Col. Fortescue £20 0 0; rece. from Geo: Cheively
in part of £6 remained due for his fine this 14th of April 1646 1 0 0; rece.
the 15th of April of David Hill in part of 175 & a bill to rece. the other
£42 4s 0 of Jo: Clark in London 132 16 0; rece. from the stew. in part of
*Tawstok* rents Lady Day qr the 15th of April 1646 4 16 0; rece. of the
stew. for one fat ox the 17 of April 12 0 0, there is another sold for £10
the next week; rece. of the stew. in part of our Lady Day rent for
Hartland then 5 0 0; rece. more from Miss Horwood of Barnst. being in
all £21, for which she hath a note of my hand for 3 15 0, Grace Shapely
widow whose money it is, this 19th of April; rece. from the stew. the 20th
of April 5 0 0; the stew. rece. from the reeve of *Tawstok* for Lady Day qr
9 2 1; also he rece. from Rich: Best the widow Pittego's heriot 3 0 0; rece.
from Jo: Terry the farrier the 22 of April in part of his fine for changing
of lives being £10 now 5 0 0; rece. from Hardwick [blank]; rece. from
Mr Elston the stew. of *Hunspill* Court for the common fines due for one
year & half this 24th of April 1646 2 16 0; rece. at *Hunspill* for one
widow Duniecon heriot the 25 of April 4 10 0; rece. at *Nether-Haven* for
one Henry Bauche's heriot 1 10 0; rece. there in part of one year's rent
due at Mich. 1644 7 10 1; rece. for old Spinollo which Bold sold at
*Mamesbery* the 29th of April 4 0 0; rece. of Hardwick before my coming
from *Tawstok* 1 1 9 the sum total of my receipts since the 30th of March
1646 with that 84 10 11 then remaining is this 6 of May 338 12 9

[enclosure 77a   Lewis the painter is to have £8 for 2 pieces & 18s for one
frame & £5 for a copy drawn by him of my picture. 13 18.

dorse. my own 271 10 10½, by my Lord 4731 18 1, since 0941 0 2½ rec.
total 5944 9 2.
4547 12 1   1314 10 1]

[p. 78]   Rece. of Will: Lynn the 14th of May 1646 41 18 6; rece. for a
coach horse sold June the 23 1646 4 9 6; rece. from Will: Lynn the 13th
of August then in gold in part of Arthur Webb 3 0 0; Gr. West[minster]
nurse & midwife & one 20s more bor. of Bo: rece. more in part of Arthur
Webb's rent £2 6s 8d 2 6 8; rece. the 28th of Sept. 1646 from Mr Hames
to be paid Mr Lamb by Rich: Polla: at Taws. 50 0 0

Rec. in the whole year 789 19 0 & disb. in that time 704 6 11, ['rem. the
17th of Octo. 1646 from Tho: Michell' illegible crossed through] So,
remained in my hands the 16th of Octo. 085 12 1 which is part of the go.
the Lady Boules brought me from *Kurton*

Will: Lynn rece. from my bro. Frank for £100—£80, £20 of it I rece.
before of him, he also rece. of Mr Hames £100, from *Wantng* £60 my
brother Frank 20 rece. the 17th of Octo. 1646 from Tho: Mich. 150 0 0
rece. the 12th of Decem. 1646 from my sister Elizabeth Cope by the
assignment of my brother Frank, for the same use the £100 was I last had
from him £20 0 0; rece. the 24th of Jan. 1646 in part of 2. by Doc.
Chichester who hath my bill to rece. of the steward at *Tawstok* 30 0 0;
Jan. the 28th 1646 225 rece. from Tho: Wiote for Hobsons & [blank]
5 0 0 .

Will: Lynn rece. from Wantage the 11th of March 50 0 0, this paid to Sir Ralph by Bold from Lynn the 3d of Jun., I borrowed with promise to pay it again the 1 of April of Sir Ralph Syd. the 9th of March ['50' crossed through] 0 0; rece. from my bro. Frank in part for Geo. the 11th of Mar. which I presently paid to Tho: Polla: 30 0 0; Taw. R:W: brought 200 0 0; ['Will: Lynn borrowed of Mr Austin which I have promised to pay in April 1647 100 0 0' crossed through]; Will: Lynn had from Tho: Wiote of mine in April 200 0 0; also the stew. returned more of mine 100 0 0; Hardwick brought me from Tho: Wiote in Gold 008 4 0

[p. 79] I rece. of my brother Frank the 3d of Aug. for the use of the former £150 was £50; £100 Tuker had & the other Palmer had rec. from Will: Lynn part of the last £100 which he had of Mr Hames this Aug. 13 10 4; rece. of one Tuker of Sou. Molton which he is to be paid again by Tho: Wiote the 13th of Aug. 60 0 0; rece. from Josi: Hames by a bill from Mr Lambe the 24th of Aug. 1647 60 0 0; rece. returned from Mr Hyne this August 23th 1647 45 0 0; Sept. 29th rece. in part of £7 6s 8d due from Wilmot Toogood for a rever[sion] of a kitchen at *Ilfordcomb* 5 0 0 Disb. 233 10 4

Rec. from Tho: Michell the last of Sept. 1647 whereof £10 Will: Lynn is to be accountable as also the rest, for I had but 5 from Bold of it, the other he hath already given account for 250 0 0; rece. the 2d of Nove. 1647 of Mr Hames returned by Mr Lamb 100 0 0; Will: Lynn rece. this 9th of No. of Mr Hames 100 0 0; rece. of the carrier Tucker the 6 of No. 020 0 0; Will: Lynn rec. the rent of Cort. *Dynha*: for 6 years £6 6s, also £10 of Cosene's fine of *Neth. Heaven* & rent in all about 030 0 0; rece. from Bold part of the £250 in Nove. 5 0 0; rece. from Will: Lynn on Christmas Eve 1 0 0; also from him on New Year's Eve 10 0 0; rece. by Rich: Forrad from my bro. Frank for to be returned to Geo. the 4th of Jan. 1647 which was immediately returned to him into Fran. £1 0 0

[p. 80] Rece. from Will: Lynn the 27th of Jan. 1647 for my Lord's journey & mine to *Brewern* [Bruern] then 50; rece. from Mr Robert Southby the 29th of Feb. 1647 by the hands of Rich: Forrard of rent but £15 10 0, & for Rich: Symon's first payment of his fine of £24, £8 10s so in all rece. at *Brewen* £24; rece. from Will: Lynn by the hands of [blank] Potter, mercer in Oxford, the 6 of March 1647, that Rich: Forward fetched there £40 0 0; Recd. borrowed of Rich: Forrard in gold 5 0 0; rece. from Will: Lynn the 23 of March 1647 5 0 0; rece. from Will: Lynn the day before 20 0 0; rece. from Will: Lynn the 4th of April 1648 20 0 0; rece. from Will: Lynn in gold the 14th of April 5 0 0; rece. from Will: Lynn the 20th of April to go into Kent 3 0 0; rece. of the same hand the 25 of April for what I spent in the journey into Kent more 5 0 0

1648 rece. the 10th of May from Will: Lynn 50 0 0; rece. of Will: Lynn the 17th of May Mr Clowbery fine 36 0 0; £3 he had again rece. of P. Bolld the 22 of May in gold 05 0 0; I rece. of Will: Lynn £50 the day I went from London Rece. from Thom: Wiote the 6th of June by Bold 12 11 0; rece. from Thom: Wiote that he returned by *Bristole* to *Bathe* the 26 of June 1648 60 0 0; rece. from Mr Tho: Michell the 29 of June 21 3 0

Rece. from Tho: Wiote the 6 of July in go. 37 10 9; rece. from Tho: Wiote
the 13th of July of Will: Cunibeare of Harford his fine 18 0 0; rece. of
Tho: Wiote the full fine of [blank] of *Illford-comb* £15 to my Lord & 20s
to me in all 16 0 0; received of Walter Sowley of *Illford-Comb* in part of
£2 fine the 25 of July 1648  0 10 0; rece. of Tho: Wiote being the last of
£40 fine from Lawrence Gibson of *Illfordcomb* the 28 of July 10 0 0; rece.
of the stew. the 21 of July in part of Mr John Downe's £100 fine 40 0 0;
rece. from Ned Randale in part for rent by Tho: Wiote paid me 8 0 0;
rece. by Tho: Wiote delivered me a fine of Mr John Watsonne parson of
*Rowborow* for changing a life to put in his child at Kingston 20 0 0; rece.
at Hartland the 17th of Aug. of a smith in part of £11 10s 0  0 10 0
[page total] 150 10 9

[p. 81]   Borrowed of Joseph Ley the 18 of Aug. 1648  20 0 0; borrowed
the 21 of Aug. of John Heirle 20 0 0; rece. of the widow Skicth for
Loggerhead sold the 21 of Aug. 02 5 0; ['borrowed of Ralph Booth the
16th of August at Killkington Fair {blank}, borrowed of {blank}
Marchant then {blank}' crossed through]; taken up upon bond of Hugh
Horsom of Barnstaple which Sir John Greenwise ought to pay the 22 of
Aug. 1648 £200 0 0; rece. of Widow Skicth the 23 of August 1648 in full
of all reckonings between us to this time 4 8 6; 1648 Aug. rece. from
Mr John Downe in full of £100, whereof £50 Doctor Downe had for corn
due in 1645 but paid reckoned in No. 1648  10 0 0; rece. from Tho:
Hobson the 28 of Aug. 1648 in part of £255 due for the tenement at
*Hollonk* [?] late widow Burgeses 100 0 0; rece. of Tho: Wiote for 3 heriots
due from *Dunterton* in 1644  2 10 0; rece. more this 1 of Sept. 1648 for
rent due there, there is yet unaccounted the years 45 46 & 47, 1643  0 7 0;
rece. from him more for half a heriot at *Beare-charter* the other part which
is 50s more Ned Randale is to get 2 10 0; remained in Tho: Wiote's hands
when he made his account this Aug. 1648 which I now rece. 2 2 4; rece. of
Nick: Marchant for ['hay' crossed through] 1 acre of grass 1 4 0; rece. of
the same man for 2 oxen grassing one month 0 12 0; rece. for a hide sold
by Wilmot the first of Sept. 1648  0 15 0; rece. from Tho: Wiote the other
part of the £5 due for a heriot on John Harris death of *Bear-Charter* the
3d of Sept. 1648  2 10 0

rece. 126 18 10, 242 5 [0], from the 18th of Aug. 1648 to in all 369 3 10
rece. from John Hamline the 5 of Sept. for a reversion at *Upacot* for Susan
Drew 5 0 0, the whole receipt 374 3 10
the disbur. in this time from the 18th of Aug. 1648 to the 6 of Sept. is
356 4 2, so should remain 017 19 8, but doth remain but 017 13 2, 7s 6d
being lost.

[p. 82]   Remained in my hands £17 13s 2. Rece. the 7th of Sept. of Miss
Skicth for 23 lbs of hops £7 10 0; rece. for a field at *Holhok* that was
sowed with barley after the Widow Burges' death, re. this 27 of Sep. 2 0 0.
also I had 11 horse loads of oats from that tenement. rec. for 5 lbs of hops
at 22d the lb the 28 of Sept. 0 9 2; rece. from Thom: Wiote at his coming
out of Corn. [blank]; rece. of Goody White for her fine of 60 foot length
& 24 in breadth of ground upon the Strand at *Illfordcomb* to build upon

paying 20s rent yearly & for fine 3 o o; rece. from Thom: Wiote that he brought out of *Cornwell* this Audit 1648 56 2 3; rece. in part for 100 Q. & 16 lbs of hops at £6 the hundred 6 4 o; borrowed of John Lovering the 29th of Sept. for Toring[ton] Fair 30 o o; rece. of [blank] Bradford of *Illfordcomb* for his fine of 60 foot in length & 24 in breadth upon the Strand to build, he paying 10s rent & this 17th of Octo. 1648 3 o o; rece. of Mr Cooke of Hartland his first payment 20 o o; rece. also of John Vine in part of £21 his first of 11 o o; rece. of Will: Copper for his half years rent due the 29 of Sept. 1648 2 16 8; rece. for 9 pecks of apples o 6 o; rece. then the 17th of Octo. for 9 lbs ¼ of old hops o 9 9; rece. of Walter Sowley in full of his fine of 40s for a place upon the quay upon the Hill of *Illford-comb* to build of 30 foot in length & 30 in breadth rent 5s a year paid now 1 10 o; for 1 quart of oil to Dick: Britt: o 1 6; for 6 lbs of old hops sold o 7 o; rece. the 21 of Octo. as part of Jonas Haris fine 40 o o; rece. of Rich: Beale of Dunterton his whole fine of 41 o o; rece. of John LitleJhon of that place then for his first payment of his fine of £80 30 o o; also then from Daniel Cornish the half of his fine 12 o o; also Rich: LitleJhon for the first payment of £12 4 o o; and Tristram Gendle his first payment of 16 5 6 8; rece. for the rents of Dunterton for 4 years from 1645 & 1648 9 12 o; rece. for Mr Squier of Hartland his 2 fines then 13 o o; rece. of Joseph Ley for pasturing 7 calves 5 weeks o 11 8; rece. for 2 bushels of apples the 21 of Octo. o 5 7; rece. for 11 lbs of hops then o 11 o; rece. Roger Whitefeild's fine of Taws. 2 10 o; Taw. John Lake his last payment 30 o o, William Ley his second payment 20 o o; Octo. the 23 *Upex* rece. from Rich: Richards in part of £9 for his fine 7 o o; also from Robert Drake his old fine of 2 o o; Nicholas Kingdon in part of the debit of £13 17s 4d 13 o o [total] 369 13 3

[p. 83] Rece. for the benefit of the quay at *Illford-Comb* this 24th of Octo. 1648 9 10 5; rece. from William Britten for his debit of *Illford*. 16 9 o; also from James Marchant, reeve of *Tawstok* [blank]; Mr Lawrence Izake's rent not being rece. but set of for Randale Payton's boarding with him 38 6 1½; likewise of John Mills for *Shelldon* then 12 11 5½; 6 14 6½ more due from him also of the same for *Bollham* whereof 6 14 6 he hath given a note under his hand to pay it by Jan. next, & now paid 2 6 2½; rece. for 2 bush. of apples o 6 o; for 10 lbs of hops then the 2 of Octo. o 8 4; rece. of the reeve of Bow in part of 9 3 3; rece. for the borough of Bow in part 4 o o; likewise of Ned Randle in part of [blank] from *Warkly* 17 o o; from Hartland Thomas Penherwood's part of his fine of 36 16 o o; also John Baytes in part of £32 16 o o; Mr Prust in part of his debit 29 o o; John Kinthorne in full of his fine 2 o o; Mr Tho; Prust the steward in part of £100 for his fine for the moiety of Thorn his first payment 30 o o; rece. from Miss Skicth in full for the 100 qr & 16 lbs of hops 2 3 o; likewise for cider & 4d the quart the whole was 12 quarts but set of for bread & sack so rece. o 2 o; rece. for 3 lbs of hops o 3 6; rece. of Miss Dorothy Carry of *Clevella* [Clovelly] for her fine of the Lords Mead then 3 10 o; rece. of Nick: Prust for rent formerly due at har. 3 o o; rece. of one Cooke of Hartland in full of his fine 9 o o; *Warkly* rece. from Edw: Randale as formerly due he oweth 24 3 3 more of his former debt 4 o o [total] 225 10 8½ 595 3 6½

Rece. since the 5 of July 1648 992 19 3½ until the 30th of Octob. 1648, disb. in the same time 992 19 3½

The widow Dodridge had a tree given her to repair the mills at *Chappleton* in *Tawstok* the 16 of No. 1648 & one more in Decemb. after.

[p. 84]   In my hands in gold then 0 0 0;.rece. for 31 lbs of hops the 1 of Nov. 1648   1 13 7; also then for 1 bu[shel] & half of apples 0 4 8; rece. from Miss Pagget for a heriot due at *Corfe* 3 6 8; likewise more upon the death of her husband also, Nov. the 13th 1648, for one ten[eme]nt at Harford the cheese house 2 0 0; rece. then for one hogshead of cider sold to Alice Dellbridge & the hogshead is to be returned again 1 0 0; rece. of Mr What-sonn, parson of *Rowborow* for his 2 sons James & John after the widow at Kingston 20 0 0; rece. from Lawrence Gibsonn of *Illford-Comb* in part of £21 his first payment 11 0 0; rece. from Nicholas Marchant of *Tawstok* for changing his cousin James Marchant to put in his own life 23 0 0; rece. of John Brage in sheep & cattle bought of him as part of his fine of £110, at Bradworthy Fair 40 0 0; rece. for 2 b[ushels] of apples at *Bidiford* the 14th of No. 0 5 4; also then for 3 lbs of hops 0 3 6; rece. of Mr John Downe by turning it up in a reckoning for corn from Doct. Down the full sum in full of £100 fine the 16th of Nov. 1648 50 0 0; rece. from William Pavey of *Tawstok* for exchange of Rich: Hamlin's life for Philip[a] Lange, widow, whom he now marrieth the 17th of No. 1648 rece. 20 0 0   [total] 174 13 9

Rece. since the 6 of Sept. 1648 787 10 10½, disb. in the same time to the 20th of Nov. 771 9 1, so should remain 016 1 9½, but doth remain this present 20th of No. 011 0 0

Rece. the 21 of Nov. 1648 of John Lithibridge of *Dioport* in *Hatherly*, parcel of Hartland Manor in part of 47 & £5 more if within this 2 year he change either life rece. now 35 0 0; borrowed of John Ley of *Taws.* the 25 of Nov. 1648 upon bond 100, the bond is to pay the £100 the 20th day of June 1649; rece. for a heriot upon the death of Dorothy Berry widow paid by her son Thomas the 27th of No. 2 0 0; Rec. of Walter Thomas for adding a 3d life in a tenement in *Tawstok* town the 28 of Nov. 1648 50 0 0; borrowed upon bond of John Brother of *Tawstok* the 29th 40 0 0; rece. for 5 lbs of hops at 14d the lb 0 5 10; £1 more Mr Carry promised me rece. from one Sandders a smith at *Clevella* in part of £21 for a re. of [a] tenement in Hartland the 1 of Decem. 11 0 0   [total] 238 5 10

[p. 85]   Borrowed of Mr John Chamney the 2d of Dece. 1648 towards the £250 paid the Committee for my Lord's Personal Estate 20 0 0; rece. the 2d of Decem. for 2 b[ushels] of apples 5s 9, also for 10 lbs of hops 10s 10d in all 0 16 7; rece. of Edward Randal in part of [blank] for rent due this 4th of Decem. 1648   6 0 0; rece. of Bold for hay & straw 2 0 0; rece. from the 17th of Nov. 48 to the first of Decem. 1648 for 2 hides 30s & for 5 sheep skins then 12s in all 2 2 0; rece. of James Bond the 9th of Decem. 1648 in part of £5 then due of the £125 which he gave for his life upon [h]is mother's tenement after her 2 10 0; rece. the 11th of Dece. for 2 sheep's skins 0 4 6; rece. then from Susan Drew for her life after Tho: Moore & his wife of which I gave Tho: Wyote 10s 6 0 0; borrowed of Mr Welch the 25 of Nov. 1648 toward the £250 I paid the Sequestrators

20 0 0; rece. of Charles in part of £35 which he is to pay for changing of Hester Hall's life for his own & adding his wife's upon £10 a year in Taws. town now 10 0 0; borrowed of John Heirle for the payment 20 0 0; rece. of John Holne of Bow in part of £120 the 14th of dece. 20 0 0 [total] 109 13 1

rece. more then of John Hole 5 0 0, [total] £114 13s 1 rece. in all since the 20th of Nov. to the 14th of Dece. 357 18 11, remained then in my hands 11 0 0 [total] 368 18 11 disbu. since to this time 357 6 7, so should remain 11 12 4, but doth remain 10 13 10

Rece. of John Hole the 14th of Dece. in gold 1 0 0; rece. of Charles Allen more in part of £35 5 0 0; rece. for one hide the 15th of Dece. 0 13 6; also then for 2 sheep's skins 0 4 6; rece. the 25 of Decem. in full of Humphrey Thorn of *Warkly* his fine 20 0 0; rece. from Tho: Wyote of several fines from Hartland 29th of Dece. as by this note of particulars appeared 1648 137 0 0; rece. from Tho: Wyote in part of £12 due from Jasper Bonde of Hartland the 5th of Jan. 1648 6 0 0; rece. from Mr William Bouchier by the hands of Bold for so much laid out by Will: Lynn in London for a hat for him 1 14 0; rece. of the cateror for 3 hides & 4 sheep skins the 22 Dec. 2 6 0; rece. of him the 5 of Jan. 1648 for 3 skins & 18d for reed 0 7 6; rece. of Hobson in part of £155 the 9th of Jan. 55 0 0; rece. of Joseph Ley for 2 trees sold out of Shorley Wood 05 0 0 [total] 234 5 6

[p. 86] for 3 lbs of hops 0 3 6; sold to Miss Baker 126 lbs of hops for which she paid now for the 100 5 0 0; from Lewice £2 rece. from Jo. Scott reeve of *Tawstok* in part of Christmas qr the 9th of Jan. 1648 10 0 0; one £3 piece spent

1648 Carried with me this 11th of Jan. for my journey to London with 20 persons & 18 horse—£49; also rece. at Bow of the reeve 0 4 0; rece. the 20th of Jan. 1648 of Wi: Lynn 150 0 0; taken up of Wilmot's brother to pay it at *Tawstok* the 19th of Feb. 10 0 0; borrowed of my aunt the Lady Fane at 61 the 100 500 0; to pay Mr Will: Beare &c with Will: Lynn lent me the 1 of March 010 0 0; for k[itchen] stuff since my coming to London to the 5th of March 1648 0 6 6; bo[ught] a little basin & ewer cost £10 5s 0d then the 3d of March 1648 rece. for 2 double gilt tankards, 31 oz ¼, at 5s 6d the ounce & one Great Silver Tankard, 29 oz ¼, at 5s the ounce [£]16; rece. of Rich: Polla: for which I sent a note of my hand to have it paid by Tho: Wyote at Taws. rece. this 21 of March 1648 50 0 0; also the 2d of April in half crowns 1; rece. of Will: Lynn the 7th of April 1649 5 0 0 ; also the 11 of April Bold had of him which he laid out for me 10 0 0; rece. from the same hand the 24th of April 1649 20 0 0; rece. the 9th of May 1649 of him 5 0 0; rece. from Thomas Micheall the 18th of May 1649 250 0 0; also from Will: Lynn the 25 of April 150 0 0; ['£150 bor. of Will: Lynn May the 16 1649, and £35 of M: Brewdna: to pay for my horse' crossed through] rece. from John Milles part for a fine the 19th of May 1649 10 0 0; rece. from Will: Lynn the 28th of May 20 0 0; rece. of Will: Lynn the 13th of June 2 0 0; Will: Lynn had them both ['rece. from Notton in part of £300 the 16th of June 100 0 0 rece. from James Parrett then bailiff of Norton Fitz 100 0 0' crossed through]; rece. from Will: Lynn the 22 of June, Bold had £10

30 0 0; £100 from Mr Diamond rece. from Will: Lynn of Mr Hames &
Mr Diamond 200 0 0; rece. from Will: Lynn at coming from London the
4th of July 49 19 17 6; rece. in my journey from London began the 4th of
July 1649 upon the surveying the manors formerly set out for the
3 daughters of the late Earl of Bathe's, rec. in all 444 06 0; rece. at
*Hunspill* more the full of one Cooke's fine the 9th of July 100 0 0, in all
544 6 0

[p. 87] Rece. the 5 of August from Thom: Wyot 5 11 10

Rece. from Thom: Wyote the 25 of August 1649 after his being & Will:
Lynn in the South *Hames* to keep court, of Robert Morrell's fine of £102
of *Combintynhead* in part £20, & of John Goard's fine of 64 there £10
30 0 0; rece. then more whereof he spent in the journey 2 19 6 part of
2 year's rent of South-brook for 45 & 48  2 16 3 & £2 from Shepard for
myself & 17s 8d from Nick: Kingdon of *Upex* in all 5 13 11; rece. from
Thom: Wyote from Mr Hyne for rents due from the South-*Hames* then
20 0 0; ['borrowed the 27 of August 1649 of Will: Lynn 65 0 0' crossed
through]; rece. of [blank] Prust at *Killkington* Fair 5 0 0; rece. that I laid
out for Miss Slowely 1 11 0; paid borrowed of John Heirle the 7th of Sept.
1649 ['20' crossed through] 0 0; ['also borrowed then of Tho: Wyote
which he paid himself again 10' crossed through] 0 0; borrowed of Forrard
toward paying for 5 weigh of coal 1 10 0; also of the seals 0 10 0;
borrowed of ['Balch' crossed through] & Miss Skicth the 21 of Sept. 1649
to pay for a suit of damask ['18 9 0' crossed through]; rece. for hops sold
at *Bidiford* the 25 of Sept. 1649  1 8 6; of the widow Cooper for the close
the 2 of Octo. 2 16 8; rece. from Anice for apples sold at *Bidiford* Octo.
0 6 6; rece. from the stew. the 10th of Octo. 1649  20 0 0; also from Tho:
Wyote then 0 0 0 [sic]; rece. the 18th of the stew. in gol. 1 0 0; rece. the
19th of Mr Black-downe, Mayor of ['Bidiford' crossed through] Tiverton
in part of £83 due for his fine for a tenement in Sheldon 43 0 0; rece. from
Tho: Wyote of fines from Dunterton 37 6 8; rece. in go. from Miss Berry
of Taunton in part of £50 for the changing 12 years certain & putting her
life 55 & her husband's 60 in the House in Taunton valued in £20 a year
received 10 0 0; rece. one Vittery's fine of *Combintynhead* then in go.
12 0 0; also from Sheaperd of Kingston in silver 1 0 0; £2 go. rece. of
Francis Everat, bailiff of *Hunspile* in part of £60 for a fine for himself then
10 0 0; a bond rece. from Ames Pengise in part of £22 for his fine at
*Banton* then 06 0 0; rece. of Thom: Wyote from Southwood of *Banton* for
rent in part 25 0 0; rece. of Thom: Prust of Hartland 40 0 0; rece. from
Mr Hyne 37 10 0; more from Mr Hyne 16 0 0; rece. from Will: Lynn the
2d of Nov. 1649 at his going for London 10 0 0; *Noning* rece. of W: Lynn
in part of 70 of Tho: Langdon 30 0 0; likewise from Robert Prate in part
of £60 38 0 0; *Hunspill* and from Francis Everite in part of £60 fine 0 0 0

[p. 88] The Steward received of which he gave me account at the Audit
1649 in debits 231 7 10½; Holne also then for fines of Edw: Beare 12 0 0,
Joan Pemroy widow 29 0 0; Kingston James Watson 28 0 0, also of
Shepheard 10 0 0, of Tho: Browning 02 6 8; Hartland of Peter Walden in
full 36 0 0; more £14 in full turned over in 20 sheep. also of Mr Cooke
40 0 0; South-*Hames* likewise of Mr Thomas Hyne as by his account
which is with the bonds 19 6 0

Ed: Ran: £2 is mentioned in the 231 7 10    176 12 8    231 7 10 total 408 o 6

The steward rece. before this from the 19th of April 1649 until the 26 of Octo. 49 in all 268 10 11, he disbursed in the same time as by his book 259 9 4, so remained of that due to my Lord then 009 1 7 which with 2 2 2 makes in all 11 3 9. Which he immediately laid out in this manner—in servants wages 99 5 o, Octo. the 25 1649 to Mr Lambe then to return to W: Lynn to London 100 o o, for a coach horse 023 10 o, in part for a suit of damask cost 16 9 paid to Wilmot 012 9 o, at the christening of Mr Jo: Basset's son Francis at Barnstaple which Cob laid out 05 o o, paid the plumber in part 06 o o, paid Rich: Lake for 100 of sugar 03 19 4, also to Dick Britton by bond 100 o o, also to Miss Hartley for H[illegible] [blank], and to Mr Chamnus 020 o o, and so in all laid out by him 405 18 4. Rich: Pollard Remains this 4th of Nov. in his hands 1649 011 3 9

Thom: Wyote rece. since the 19th of Jan. 1648 until the 4th of No. 1649 1398 6 0½, disbursed by him in the same time as by his book 1365 10 5, so remained due to my Lord 032 15 7, whereof to Will: Lynn at his going towards London the 2 of Nov. 1649  5 o o, and to me 27 15 7

in Wilts. also Will: Lynn rece. from the 4th of July 1649 to this ['4th' crossed through] first of Nove. after in all 3162 6 o; laid out & appointed by me to be laid out that term 2335 19 o, so remained in his hands & to rece. then 0826 7 o.

[p. 89]   Rece. the 8th of Nov. 1649 then of Charles Allen in full of his fine & given up his bond 15 o o; borrowed more of the seals 04 10 6; also from the seals 02 6 6; rece. the 14th of Nov. 1649 of Roger Jeffrys, apothecary of Barnstaple, in part of £25 due for a fine now 12 10 o.

I have at present in the House by me £20 besides gold 1649 Nov. the 15th.

Rece. of Miss Skicth for hops at £16 the 100  9 17 o; rece. of John Holne of *Nimit Tracy* in full of his fine this present 17th of Decem. 1649 60 o o; rece. the 26 of Dece. of Ed: Fleming 50 o o; rece. then of John Sheapard of Kingston 50 o o; rece. then of [blank] Warde of Kingston 40 o o; rece. of Tho: Wyote in part of £18 William Heard of *Tawstok* 9 o o; rece. then of Rich: Denys in part of £14 of Hartland 8 o o; & £1 in go. rece. then of Mr Squire 18 o o; & 11s in go. rece. from Daniel Carre a minister for an estate in Harford the 10th of Jan. 1649  20 o o; rece. in part of Chr[istmas] Quar[ter']s rent for *Tawstok* the 21 of Jan. 1649  10 o o  [total] 258 5 8

3199 7 3 now due to the M. this 21 of Jan. 1649

Tho: Wyote rece. in his journey to *Exetor* in the 8th Jan. 24 3 4; whereof he paid to Rob: Drak & Jo: Hanafor for Rober. Drake of *Upex* in part of £108 due to him at this present Jan. 19 3 4; also to my Lord Nich: Mallie's fine 2 o o; spent in his journey to *Exetor* & to *Banton* & for letters &c 1 19 5; also formerly he did owe me upon his last account 2 o o; so now this 21 of Jan. due to me from him 3 o 7

[p. 90]   Rece. from the reeve. of *Tawstok* the 25 of Jan. 1649 in part
7 0 0; rece. the £3 0 7 from Tho: Wyote & of my Lord Roberts rent due
for 5 years from *Bedardale* [Bodardle] in all 23 0 7; rece. in full of James
Bond of *Tawstok* 2 10 0; rece. of Tho: Hobsonn in full 30 0 0; likewise
then from Lawrence Britton in full 61 0 0

Jan. the 26 1649 Bold made of wood in the Park in all £8 15s whereof the
stew. had formerly 20s & now 4 10s whereof he paid 28s for lime ashes so
he hath now £3 2s. there is to receive by him 3 5s 0

Rece. returned to London by Mr Jam: Smith by bill 100; I gave Rich:
Forrad 15 3 6 in silver for so much in gold, which I have now in silver &
20s over for the change is to pay him at *Tawstok*; rece. from my brother
Francis Fane by my br[other] George Fane's appointment to pay Hugh
Horsom rece. the 13th of Feb. 1649 £200 0 0; gol. £11 13 0 changed in to
silver for my journey in to Devon; the 23 of March 1649 rece. of David
Hill in part of £300 in go. he hath given his own bond for the other £100
to pay next Audit, for 3 lives in a tenement in Upcott valued £20 per'
Tawst. £200 0 0; rece. now of Arthur King of *Warkley* for changing &
adding a life in £6 per' 24 0 0; in go. this 25 of March 1650 246 9 0; rece.
in full of Roger Jefry's fine the 25 of Ma. 12 10 0; rece. in full of the
widow Rowe then likewise of Taw. 45 0 0; rece. likewise of Ralph Booth
9 0 0; also then more 1 0 0   [total] 291 10 0

in go. £8 1s rece. for one stall-fed ox sold the 10th of April 17 0 0; in
go. £1 rece. of John Lovering of *Tawstok* for the exchange of his brother
Thom: life for his wife 30 0 0; and in go. 1 0 0; rece. for this Lady Day's
rent of *Huntscourt* 3 13 4; rece. in full of John Brage's fine of £35 whereof
£31 was in cattle, & 6s 8d in corn, so now in full 3 13 4; rece. for one
other ox sold 14 10 0   [total] 69 16 8

[p. 91]   Bant. rece. of Ed: Mellton, Jo: Chamberlain & Tho: Comes in
part of £830 the 23 of April 1650 276 13 4; for the tenement called
*Cudmer* in *Banton* in hand worth £60 per' 276 13 4; likewise for that
tenement from Christmas to our Lady Day set for 8 10s 0 whereof in taxes
2 6 11 so rece. now in money 6 3 0; gold £1 more in gold to myself 1 0 0;
Nov. rece. then from Mr Tho: Morce due in part of £250 the 3d of May
100 0 0; Taunt. rece. then of Mr David Berry of Taunton in full of £50
040 0 0; Norton also rece. then of John Poole in part of £40 020 0 0;
go. £2 2s 0 Thom: Wyote made his accounts even the 27th of April 1650
wherein I allowed him £3 for his Lady Day wages & he delivered me in
gold in full 2 2 0; £30 rece. the 9th of May of [blank] Warine of Bow
30 0 0; rece. for La[dy] Day Quarter's Rent of the reeve of *Tawstok* in
part 19 10 0; rece. from Mr Hyne as by his note appeareth in all 204 4 0;
go. £1 rece. of Tho: Wyote for La[dy] Day Quarter rent of Hartland 16s
being abated of the £10 for rates 9 4 0; rece. more of him for the rent of
*Harfort Cum.* 4 12 8; rece. in part of £500 of Miss Palmer's fine of
Kingston for her ten. & the wood 100 0 0; rece. from the steward that he
should have lent Mr Dowdswell's officer & had it again 1 0 0; rece. of
Mr Hyne in part of his fine likewise 25 0 0; rece. from James Parat of
Norton Fitz. in part of £60 due for arrearages last Audit 30 0 0; likewise

more of him then being the 6th of June in part of the Chri. Quarter rents 20 0 0; rece. of Tho: Wyote in full of the rent of *Hartfo. with. New.* the 12 of June 2 0 10   [total] 891 14 10

carried with me £20 besides Rece. at Bath of Rich: Cripps in part of £150 of *Hunspill* the [blank] of June 1650   50 0 0; likewise of Eliza: Pope of *Hunspill* 20 0 0; likewise of James Came of *Hunspill* 15 0 0; borrowed of John Johnsonne there, paid 30 0 0; borrowed of my sister Eliza: Cope 10 0 0   [total] [£]125

[p. 92]   Rece. the 21 of July 1650 out of *Cornwaill* from [blank] by Randal 46 13 8, so now in my hands in silver this 23 of July 104 16 0, also 046 13 8.

Thom: Wyote rece. in my absence at Bath these sums began the 14th of June 1650, *Warkly* of Ed: Randall for 2 heriots from Jonas Pinsent upon the death of John Pearse £5, *Killyneck* the last payment of £99 due from one John Easticke £50, Hartland from William Squier the last of £37 being £18, *Nonington* from Robert Parrot the last of £60 being 22, *Hartford with* Newland Hugh Gibbonse's fine of £14 in all 109 0 0. 05 50 18 22 14   [total] 109

Rece. from Ralp: Booth by Bold who hath accounted it to me in part of £10 he oweth me 5 0 0; rece. of James Lake of *Warkly* in part of £30 for the exchange of his own life for his son John 14 0 0; £61. £41 more is by him to be ret. to Lond. for Will: Lynn to account for rece. from Jo: Hanaford at *Exetor* returned by Will: Lynn's order to Rich: Briton of Tawst. who paid it to the stew. 40 0 0

Rece. in gold the 3d of Octo. 1650 for the tenement at Harford for myself 1 10 0

1650 remained in silver in my hands this 17th of Sept. £10 0 0.

[p. 93]   Rece. in full of Mr Farthing's fine of the 19th of Sept 1650 160 0 0; rece. from David Hill in part of £100 this 29th of Sept. 080 0 0; Taws.   rece. the 3d of Octo. in full of old Hearder's fine 009 0 0.

Octo. the 21 1650   rece. of Jo: Prayer of *Hunspill* in part of £66 in go. 001 0 0; rece. of Robt Clark of Hunsp. in part of £29   001 0 0; likewise from George Vawles in part of £70 5s 0   000 5 0.

*Banton*   rece. from Alexa: Bidgood for the rent of *Whoonham* for the year 1649 the whole being £55 whereof formerly rec. by Will: Lynn & accounted to me £30 the weekly taxes amounts to £9 9s 10d he hath stopped for Quartering £4 1s 6d, & so now paid 011 8 8; *Tawstok* £1 of this in gold   rece. of Will: Bud for a life by copy after the whole fines being £11 now in part 006 0 0; Harford   rece. from John Weastcoat the 22 of Octo. in part of £140 being his fine for 3 lives by copy re. now 050 0 0; rece. for the profits of the quay & lanthorn at *Illfordcomb* now 003 12 8; Hartland   rece. of John Buse then in part of £28 014 0 0; rece. of John Blagdon then in part of £15   005 0 0; rece. of William Hooper for 2 tenements one is £56 the other £7, so rece. his first payment 031 0 0; *Nonington*   rece. of Thomas Langdon in full of his fine of £70 040 0 0; *Kingston*   rece. of Miss Pallmer in part of £400 this 25th of Oct. 100 0 0;

*Banton* rece. from Amice Pengelly in part of £16 then 006 0 0; Hackpen £2 of it in gold rece. of John Rawlins in part of £68 008 0 0; rece. of the stew. in part of the debits 100 0 0

Rece. this Audit as here appeareth here 626 6 4, I had remaining which was designed for Sir Ra: Syd. 010 0 0, so, returned to Will: Lynn by Mr Lambe the 23 of Octo. 300 0 0, whereof £100 I had of the stew. which was part of the debit, so ['remains now in my hands in silver 226 12 4 226 12 4' crossed through] remained then in my hands the 26 of Octo. in ['silver' crossed through] 115 5 0.

*Killyneck* rece. of Hugh Thomas in part of £35 this 30th of Oct. 17 10 0, also more out of *Cornwell* by him 02 0 0; rece. of my Lady Button for the setting up the pale by her ground, which she is not now tied to repair & for her felling timber without licence, & for the end of all differences 02 10 0; rece. of [blank] in part of £8 for change of her estate for [blank] the 11 of Nov. 4 0 0 [total] 26 0 0

**[p. 94]** 1650 Remains in my hands this 12th of Nov. 1650 in silver 120 0 0; Decem. the 2d rece. from David Hill in full 020 0 0; rece. then of Ed: Randale of *Warkly* in part of £40 05 0 0; Hartland rece. more in part of £32 of William Hooper's fine [blank] 10[s] 0; in go. of that man 11s & 2s 9[illegible] which makes of Tho: Wyote part of the 10 in gold £5 2 6 rece. from the stew. which was part of the £20 in part of £33 given by Digory Ponstow of Taws. so remained due £12 5 0 0; rece. from Tho: Wyote for the exchange of his life 10 0 0; rece. from George Moore in part of £57 10s 0 for the [blank] 17 10 0; rece. from the stew. of tithe money 8 0 0; rece. of Tho: Penhorwood of Hartland in part of his last payment & in full of the second of this 10th of Jan. 1650 10 0 0; £10 of it lent Geo: Fane & £13 10s in go. counters rece. of [blank] Warine of Bow in full 30 0 0; rece. of Thom: Stowell of *Hunspill* in full 25 0 0; rece. of [blank] of Hartland in p: 35 0 0; rece. from George Balch reeve of *Tawstok* for Chris: Quar this [blank] of Jan. 1650 20 0 0; rece. from [blank] returned from *Exetor* by Jo: Hanaford who rece. [blank] £100 & other moneys 90 0 0; rece. from Mr Hugh Prust, bailiff of Hartland by Geo: Palmer in part of Christmas Quar. rent the 7th of Jan. 6 0 0; rece. from Christop: the footman to return to London for him this 11th of Feb. 1650 3 0 0; rece. of the widow Ann Booth, 7s, in full of £250 for the adding Ralph Booths life, 38 more, after her own upon her tenement in *Tawstok* this 19 of Feb. 5 0 0; rece. the 22 of Feb. 1650 of Tho: Wyote for the Chris. Quarter's rent of Wid. Cunibear reeve of *Hartford* Cum. whereof Tho: Horwood rent for a tenement in *Rowborow* is 4s 6d part of the sum 3 6 8 [total] 293 6 8

Remains in my hands this 22 of Feb. 55 7 0; rece. from Martha Violet to return for her to London to Will: Lynn the 26 of Feb. 12 0 0

**[p. 95]** 1650 Rece. borrowed of Tho: Wyote the 3rd of March 40 0 0; rece. of Edw: Randale the 5th of March in part of *Warkly* rent 2 0 0; rece. of Dick Britton for which he had a bill from *Extor* to be paid presently which the stew. had toward the butt of sack bought of Mr Short which he hath since rece. from Jo: Salsbury charged from Jo: Haniford 20 0 0 [total] 74 0 0

Remained in my hands the 12th of No. 1650  120 0 0; rece. since that time
to this present 24th of Mar. 267 6 8   [total] 487 6 8
Disb. in this time 429 5 6
and to my brother Geo: Fane who had of the steward £2 & in gold
counters £13 10s 0 & of me 050 0 0 all in part of £100 Will: Lynn hath
rece. from him at London by his wife's mother. In gold left £5.
[total] 479 5 6
So remains this 25 of March 1651  3 2 3

Rece. borrowed of Joseph Ley the 26 of March which is to be paid again
the 20th of May next 50 0 0; April 1651 rece. of James Lak of *Warkly* for
the full of his fine for dividing one half of his tenements to his son 16 0 0;
rece. of Geo: Balch reeve of *Tawstok* for Lady Day Qua. 20 0 0; rece. of
Robert Trikes of Hartland the 11th of April in part of £22  10 0 0
[total] 99 2 3

Remained in my hands now this 11th of April 1651  15 13 11

more I am to rec. of Bold, Norton & the stew. £11 8s 0 for him, which I
have Rece. from Will: Lynn in silver the 17th of April at his going to
*Warkly*, & so toward London 6 0 0; more rec. in gold of him then 11 0 0;
also in part of £15 which is for my part of two fines at Bolham now rece.
in gold 1 2 0; Holne   rece. of Will: Hewite in part of £48 the 23 of April
15 0 0; *Warkly*   rece. of Edw: Randale in part of [blank] Quart. rent
3 0 0; *Cardynham*   rece. in part of £20 from Nick: Row now 6 13 4;
*Bodardall*   rece. of my Lord Roberts now 4 0 0; *Tawstok*   rece. of Will:
Budd in full of his fine the 3d of May 5 0 0; also of the widow Fairchild in
full of hers 4 0 0; bor. of Bold the 1 of May £5  rece. in part for 100 qr.
of hops & 21 lbs at £5 12s per 100  5 0 0   [total] 60 13 4

[enclosure 95a]   [dorse. £367 256 050 wages M. 100 Austin Up. 900 Bond
212 other ways 009 sadler [total] 1894 debit the 16th of Octo. 1647]

*Corke* 18th 8ber 1645

paid for 7 gallons & one pottle usquebaugh at 7s per gallon £02 12s 06d,
paid for cask & the bark's company 00 03 00   [total] 2 15 06

[p. 96]   1651 May   Hartland   rece. of Will: Quart in part of £9 the 5 of
May 4 10 0; & in go. to me £1 2s 0d rece. of Will: Browne by paying it
for sheep to Jo: Bragge his first payment in part of £35  11 13 4; paid to
T: Prust likewise of Barnabas Hatherly in part of £30  10 0 0;
Harford   rece. of Jo: Westicoat his second payment 45 0 0; May the 10th
Holne   rece. in part of £100 due from the widow Webber 50 0 0; rece. in
part of £35 that Jo: Haneford of Exto. charged upon [blank] Salsbury of
Barnstaple 5 0 0; Holne   rece. in full of the widow Webber's fine both
[?]fifetyes [illegible crossed through] from Jo: Haniford from Barnstaple
the 16th of May 1651  50 0 0; Harford *cumb.*  rece. of Will: Cunibear the
17th of May for Lady Day 03 2 2   [total] 179 5 6

Rece. since the 11th of April 1651 to this 17th of May 255 12 9, disbursed
since that time 196 1 6, so, remains at present in my hands silver 51 12 9 &
in gold of these last leaf 8 0 0

May the 23, 1651   rece. of John Poole of Norton Fitz. in full 45 10 0;
rece. then of James Parret, bailiff there, in part for rent 20 0 0; rece.
borrowed of Robert Drake of *Upex* now 60 0 0; likewise the stew. rece.
from Jo: Hana: of Exet. 13 0 0; rece. the 26 of May 1651 of Mr Hugh
Prust in part of Lady Day rent for Hartland 6 0 0; the two £5s the stew.
rece. both & set them down together in his book.   rece. more of Jo:
Salsbury 5 0 0; rece. from Mr Seldon of Barnstaple that he rece. from
Cardinham of Rob: Billing 5 10 0; rece. from Tho: Wyote which Will:
Lynn must pay in London for keep this 3d of June 3 0 0; *Tawstok*   rece.
for the change of [blank] Burche's life for [blank] Marchant 20 0 0; rece. of
Geo: Moore in part of £40 the 19th of June 1651  20 0 0; *Banton* · rece.
by Will: Lynn for Whille-Hames the 10th of July 18 0 0; Norton F:   rece.
of Mr Morse then in part of £50  30 0 0; the 2d of May   rece. by
Mr Seldon out of *Cornwale* which the st. had 2 2 0; the 28 of
[May]   rece. which the steward had of Miss Baker retur. from Jo: Hana:
6 10 0, also which he had from Damarice Jones by return. of Hana. 3 14 0,
likewise of Mary Frace by the same the 9th of June 2 18 0, also of Jo:
Willyame's returned by Hanaford 10 0 0, also of Jo: Salsbury in part of 25
the 22 of June from Hana. 10 0 0, also the 25 of June from Tho: Edmonds
Mr Elston's servant by retur. of Jo: Hanafoord in part of £66 18s  55 0 0;
Cardinham the 4th of July being 1 16 0 went for taxes   Thom: Wyote
rece. of Mr Celdon which the ste. had which was in part re. 2 payment of
Nich: Rowe's fine the rest 4 17 0, also more of Salsbury in part of £15
which the ste. had 10 0 0

[p. 97]   Borro. of Thom: Wyote in June 1651  50 0 0; likewise 4 bonds of
Hartland excepted by Jo: Bragge for cattle bought abought [*about*]
Torrington Fair of him 13 beasts & 20 sheep, one bond from Tho: Prust
31 10 0, from Jo: Blagdon £5, Jo: Buse £14, Tho: Penhorwood £10
60 10 0; remains in my hands this 11th of July 1651  10 0 0

So.   Rece. of the widow Nash of *Tawstok* for the exchange of 2 lives in
the two Pott House in go. the 14th of July 9 0 0; go. Miss Baker bought
two bags containing 200 gr. & 26 lbs at £3 10s, comes to 8 13 9   rece. the
23 of July by Wilmote for £1 1 7 gr. pound of hops 4 11 0; 40 in go. of
the £50 Bold brought me rece. of Peter Bold in part of £200 which is part
of the £242 which my Lord should rece. of Mr Gardner for the robbery
whereof paid Mr Alexander Rolls in the charges following the suit
formerly paid by Will: Lynn in London £15 & now by me £21 & by
return from *Salsbury* to *Exetore* so in all rece. this 2 of August 1651
200 0 0; rece. from Thom: Wyote which he had of 3 bailiffs Tho:
Ballyman, John Mills, Charles Salter of *Upex* 22 0 0; rece. of Will: Lynn in
part of a fine of £10 in go. at his coming from Ex. 1 0 0; allowed 3s 9d for
rates   rece. of W: Par: reeve from *Wollrington* 1 13 0; rece. of Edw:
Randale in part of Warkly qr. rents 02 0 0; rece. of Geo. Balch in part of
Midsummer Quar. rent 20 0 0

259 4 0 & 1 0 0 in my hands 310 7 0 disb. & in go. 268 14 6 & 20s so
remains in my hands 0 16 6

Rece. of Will: Cunibear in part of *Hartland with* New. rent & Thom:
Horwood's rent 3 11 4; rece. from John Hanaford by Will: Lynn who
charged this £5 paid to my Lady Harice, so now Will: Lynn allowed it me

5 0 0; rece. of John Haiford of *Exeto*. the week in Sept. 1651 that my Lord & I was there 21 0 0; borrowed likewise then of Robert Drak of *Upex* 40 0 0; Sept. 22 rece. of one that went from a bargain in Hartland 02 0 0; borrowed of Miss Heirle the 1 of Octo. 1651 20 0 0; Hartland rece. of Robert Tricke upon his bond the 14 of Octo. in full 12 0 0; also of John Stanburie by bond then in full 15 0 0; more likewise then of Will: Browne in part of 23 6 8 11 13 4; 8 yards & ½ of go. & silver lace rece. since the 3d of Sept. 1651 to this 21 of Octo. in all 125 4 8, disbursed in the same time whereof in gold £53 2 0 1[smudged]1 5 4, so, remains in my hands 0 17 6

£1 in Banton gold formerly but given away rece. of John Glasse in part of £33 1 0 0, also of Mich: Choleman in part of 36 1 0 0

[p. 98] Octo. 1651
Hartland rece. of Peter Hatherly of his fine 10 0 0; rece. likewise by delivering the bonds to Tho: Prust of two £5 & one 4 10 0 the 25 of Octo. 1651 14 0 0; *Hackpan* rece. of John Myles in full of his old fine 06 0 0; also of him from Geo: Welsh 06 10 0; *Uffculm* rece. this present 24th of Octo. 1651 from John Donn in part of £90 30 0 0; Kingst. from Miss Palmer in part of £300 100 0 0; from Geo: Moore of Taws. in full 020 0 0; also of Digory Ponston then in full 012 0 0; St Just of Mr Thomas in part of £17 10s 012 10 0; Holne of Will: Hewit in part of £23 010 0 0; from Daniel Jones 002 0 0; *Uffcullm* of John Rawllinges in part of £40 020 0 0; *Hunspill* of Geo: Cook alias Towless 040 0 0; Rob: Cane in full 010 0 0; rece. of Mr Thomas Hine in part of 62 4 4 050 0 0; he gave a bill for 13 9 4 more due Norton Fitz. of James Parret in part of 60 11 6 for rent & the arrears of Mr Henly's rent which came to £22 3s 4d paid me which this present year 058 3 4; more Ja: Parrat 002 8 [0]; *Banton* rece. likewise from Hart & Bunida in part of £20 by Thurstan 010 0 0; there is yet to pay for some yearlings also more of him for stake that went up Whoo: 014 6 8; rece. of Grace Allen in part of 125 100 0 0; Bolham rece. of Tho: Bromfielld in part of £400 130 0 0; W:L: re. £24 as appears besides rece. of Hen: Croker in part of 180 030 0 0; Norto. rece. of Eman. Slape in part of £100 050 0 0; Taunton rece. of Antho. Michell for grass Croft part of 50 025 0 0; of Rich: Leaker in part of £16 010 0 0; *Banton* more of Hart & Bunida in part of £15 005 0 0; Uffc. of John Fowler in part of 7 10 03 15 0; *Hunsp.* of John Crips in full of £9 04 10 0; *Banton* rece. of Chr: Southwood in part of 14 13 4 09 0 0 [total] 795 3 0

Rece. from my Lady Button for a heriot upon the death of Miss Elizabeth Roscarick who died in July 1651 1 0 0; rece. of Will: Lynn the 3d of Nov. 1651 at his going towards London of his own money 20 0 0; Hartland rece. from Mr Hugh Prust in part of £20 due 10 0 0; *Tawstok* rece. from [blank] in full his whole fine for my Lord 3 0 0; likewise of Thomas Baliman the 2d of Sept. 4 0 0; Bolham also of Thomas Bronfielld in gold 1 0 0 [total] 60 0 0

in go. of this £60 10s & for Will: Lynn £300 so in my hands in silver this 6 of Nov. 1651 £105

**[p. 99]**  Harford *with*: the 18th   Rece. the 10th of Nov. of Dick Britt: in
part of £137  82 0 0; rece. of John Westicoat in part of £45  22 10 0; rece.
of Arthur Pollard for woods sold at *Warkly* last year due upon one bond
7 14 0; borrowed of Tho: Wyote the 4th of Decem. 1651  10 0 0; rece. of
Mr Hugh Prust in full of the Audit 10 0 0; rece. of Tho: Prust in part
of £55  18 6 8; also by him in part of £5 due from John Blag. 3 19 6; of
my brother George that I gave him his gold for 55 0 0; one sealed
bag  part of the money Will: Lynn should have had 50 0 0; rece. of Tho:
Prust that he laid out more for sheep 3 13 0; so these receipts since the 6th
of Nov. with the amount to in all at this present 24th of Decem. 364 10 2,
or 368 3 2 if so then should rec. 8 3 2

Hartford   rece. of John Westicoat in full of his fine 22 10 0; rece. of
Mr Celdon out of Cornwall in full of his fine 6 13 4 & more in rent all
which the ste. had 8 3 4; *Banton*   rece. of Mr Tristram of *Banton* for
woods sold in part of £102 ['& £1 for myself' crossed through] 52 0 0;
Cardinha.   rece. from [blank] Opia his first payment for woods sold at
Cardinham the 13th of Jan. 1651  40 0 0; rece. from Cobb £7 & Wimper
£4 to pay them in London 11 0 0; rece. from Thom: Wyote as by this note
appears 66 18 8; also by him in full from Mr Morce 20 0 0; and from Ed:
Pearce of Holne in part of 70  20 0 0; rece. from Mr Elston due formerly
04 16 0; Taws.   rece. from Rich: Hamlin upon changing 3 lives 05 0 0;
*Warkly*   rece. from Robert Edbrook in part of £65 due 35 0 0;
Kingston   rece. for the arrears due from Kingston of Mr John Ford's
debit 65 10 0; more for Quarter Rent there 2 13 4

one Bag sealed £50   rece. of Will: Lynn when I went to Tetsworth 10 0 0;
g[old] 2 co[unters] 3 & 17s more then   rece. of him likewise by Cobb
5 0 0; of him by Cobb £3 10s & 20s  4 10 0; rece. from Will: Lynn the
14th of May 1652  20 0 0; also I had before part of my sis. Betty Money
out of the red trunk 60 0 0; more of him for the theorbo, my viol case &c
10 0 0; from him the first of June it came from Wantage 9 0 0; likewise of
my brother George which the stew. paid Miss Baker 3 8 0
[total] 121 18 0

Rece. from Miss Palmers in part of £200 in April by Farrard 150 0 0; Will:
Lynn had from John Hanaford more in part 42 14s 0. so there yet wants
from her this August 1652  7 6 0

**[p. 100]**  June the 21 1652   Rece. from Will: Lynn at my coming from
London £20 0 0; rece. of John Miles in part of £100  10 0 0; also of
Mr Hyne for rent 2 0 0, this with the £9 from Wantage I had of W:L: &
the £150 which Forrard rece. by Lynn's appointment comes in all to the
sum of £191, & my disbursements in the same time appeareth to be
191 10s 0. £20 the ste. had the [blank] of July,  so, this present 30th of
June I have no silver & but 30 10s in gold. I have laid out since I went to
London being there 20 weeks in silver 304 8 10, out of my own purse
besides the journeys in gold 112 10 0.

Rece. in part of £50 from [blank] Pearce of *Warkly* 25 0 0; July the 22.
go.  rece. of Mr David Berry of Taunton in part of £62  8 0 0;
*Banton*   rece. from Mr Tristram £2 & from John Glasse £10  12 0 0; paid
John Bragg in part of £52 for 10 steers   rece. of Mr Tho: Prust his

2d payment the 29th of July 18 6 8; more of him in full of a reckoning as by his bill o 17 6; rece. from Will: Lynn the ste. had towards the rates 4 o o; he is to have £10 more of Hatherly of *Hunsl.* rece. borrowed of John Heirle August 2d for rates 10 o o; likewise of Joan Elise then 15 o o; more of her in gold then 55 o o; rece. of Will: Lynn in gold o5 o o; [blank] 90 o o; [blank] 14 o o; of my own go. £20, ordinary 30 10 o so in all 307 14 2. Borrowed more go. 9 18 o & 80 o o which I [?]pawn with my old go. being 16 o2s count. [illegible] Bold all goes for £200 this Augus. 1652

Disb. in the same time from the 30th of June to this 7th of August 307 13 8, so remains o o 6.

Rece. by Richard Hanaford in part of £35 due from Elis Foord of Holne this 13th of Aug. 10 o o; rec. from my Lady Chichester that W:L: laid out in Lond. 2 4 o; Sept. the 22 1652 rece. in full of Mr David Berry of Taunton 54 o o; rece. from Geo: Mules of *Tawstok* his 2d payment 20 o o; rece. from John Sergant of Dunterton in full 65 o o; the hops this year 1110:22 lbs

rece. since the 7th of August 1652 151 4 o, disbursed since by me 31 16 6, so remains this 4 of Octo. 1652 119 14 o

**[enclosure 100a]**
Love's Diet

To What A cumbersome unwildynes
and burdenous corpulence my love had ['gra' crossed through] growne
But that I did to make it less
and keepe it in proportion
Give it adiet made it feed upon
that wch love worst indures discretion
Above one sighe a day, I alowed him not
of wch my fortun & my faults had part
And if sometimes by chance he got
ashe [?sic] sighe from my mistres harte
And thought to fatt on that, I let him see
twas neither very sownd nor meant to me

**[enclosure 234a]**   [dorse. for his right honorable Lord the Earl of *Bathon* at the Court]

Right Honourable, I received yesterday two letters from you dated the 24th and 27th of February last. That of the 25th by Sir William Bos[torn]ell I have some times since answered. Lest that should miscarry, this is to advertise you that the ten ordinary armours will be ready against the end of May, as also your own armour, with all the pistols. Your Honour's own arms will cost £25, your pistols £3 4s. The ten curasses £4 2s a piece. The ordinary pistols £2 4s a pair. The eleven cases (here called holsters) about 10s a pair. This your Honour seeth nigh about what these particulars will amount unto. When the things are ready I will send them to London to your Lady, whom the Almighty give you joy, and a blessed child of that your name and posterity may abide in our Israel. When your Honour's convenience will permit, you may please to send me a bill of

exchange. If any thing for the service of my King and country or your
Honour should happen in your troubles, whereby I might better subsist
then here I beseech your Honour to be mindful of me. Who to the
uttermost of my ability shall ever express myself to be, Your Honour's
most humble and obedient servant, Hum. Pliftor

quarter at Terhey [?Tilburg] by Breda the 8th of May still now 1639
£25 00s 00d, 3 4 00, 41 00 00, 22 00 00, 5 10 00   [total] 96 14 00

[p. 234]   Mr William Bouchier, chaplain, preferred to Bowe in Devon the
   10 of May 1640  5 0 0, the 15th of June 5 0 0   5 of Coyse 20 0 0
Mr Edmond Snow died 1644
1639 the 2 of June gone Mathew Coyse, steward £20 0 0
Peter Bold gentl. Usher 10 0 0
1639 the 25th of March dead Richard Slowly, Gentl. of the Horse 10 0 0
Thomas Wiott, secretary 10 0 0
gone Edward Barry, the 15th of June 1640  5 0 0,   killed in *Ierland* 1645
   10 0 0
the same gone Steward Walker at Michaelmas 1639  5 0 0   10 0 0
25 of Mar. Rich. Pollard the [blank] of July 1640  10 0 0   1639  10 0 0
the 25 of December Raphe Booth the 17th of June 1640  5 0 0   8 0 0
Robert Wood in June 1639  4 0 0   1638  8 0 0
gone Samuel Starling 10s died in Aug. 1644  4—
gone Darby at our Lady Day 1640 & after £1 1s 0   1640  4—
In August { Zachary Chevlly 1640 Marc. 25  1 10 0   2 0 0
            { Willy: Gever 1640 Mar. 25  1 10 0 died Tuesday the
              [blank] May 1652  2 0 0
January 1638 } Willy: Elis, died the 14th of March 1647, Usher of the
              Hall 4 0 0
            { married Hugh Combe the bailiff, the 25 of March
              1640 £3  6 0 0
In June gone   John Underlian, gardener, 1640 25 Mar. £3  6 0 0
gone   Willy: Deacon, coachman 1640 25 March 1 10 0   8 0 0
gone 25 of Mar.   John Ceaton 1640 25 Mar. 20s, the 23 of May 10s
   4 0 0
dead   Thom: Sweet 1640 25 Mar. 0 10 0   3 0 0
gone   John Come-last 1640 25 of Marc. 2 0 0   2 10 0
Hunnicot the porter, he died about 11 of the clock the 9th of Feb. 1645 it
   being Shrove Monday 1 0 0
gone   Francis Watts the keeper 1640 25 of Marc. 2 0 0   4 0 0
Baldwyn Stephen the Brewer & fisher. 1640 25 Marc. 3 man. £5
January 1638   James the Blackamoor 25 of March 1640 £5   4 0 0
Jack Burk, And. Webber gone }
December Richard Burton      } this April 1650 now £6 a year
Febr. 1639   Ned Heall kitchen boy maintained died 1645 in March
dead   Willy: Gibbons hop-man 1640 25 March £2 0 0
Willy: Rumson cateror 1640 25 Marc. 3 0 0   £5 0 0
gone   Robert Crosse received 25 of March 1640  5 0 0
died   Jack-Paine £3  £4 0 0
['Lylle came the 20 of May 1640  10 0 0' crossed through]
at Michaelmas 1639   James Berry firemaker

came the 1 of July Dick Cooke married 3 0 0
4 4 0 came then to Thomas Armesby 5 0 0 Chris: Winge old Turnspit
    died ... Sept. 16 ...

[p. 233]    Sara: Voysin married the [blank] day of April 1646   10 0 0
married    Susan Baldwin married Mr Peck in April 1643   10 0 0
Cordelia Hardwick 1640 25 March 5 0 0    10 0 0
Rose Tode 1640 25 March £1 os od, married in Jan. 1644 John Hamlin £3
    per.   2 0 0
Besse Ceairll 2 0 0 she went to Hall to serve the Lord Chichester in 1642
    & came to me again in the 17th of Octo. 1646 £3
gone    Joan Elis 2 0 0
Wilmot Toogood 2 0 0 paid at our Lady Day 1640 by St:
married    Alice Teairle 2 0 0, 1640 25 of March 1 0 0
Besse Randall 2 0 0, paid at our Lady Day 1640 by St., married Geo:
    Brother Sept. 1645
the 25 of March 1640    Christian [blank] gone ['2' crossed through] 0 0 the
    15th of June 0 10s 0
Besse Hambile gone 2 0 0 paid at our Lady Day 1640 by St.
Thomas Pollard came the 22 of Octob. 1640   10 0 0
gone    Harry Howard came in January 1640   10 0 0    £5 in Nove. 1641
gone    Jonas Pulluye came in Jan. 1640 ['8' crossed through] 0 0 had £4 0 0
    went away in March
gone    Thom: Cannam came in January 1640   10 0 0
gone    Cobley 2 0 0
Cobb the Organist came the beginning of Sept. 1641 is to have by the year
    14 0 0
Thom: Wimper a cook hath been from 6 weeks after midsummer to
    Christmas day with me for £5 & now serves me by the year for 16 0 0
    went away in Octo. 1644
gone    ['Thom' crossed through] Bold came in the summer 1641 run away
    Michaelmas 1643
Irish Thom: clothes came in 1641 ran away in Aug. 1644
Edward Lewin my boy came in July 1642 I bound apprentice 1643. I took
    him at 12 weeks old before I, from *Apthorp* [Apethorpe], was married
    many years
Randall Payton being 8 years of age came in the beginning of August 1643
gone    Richard Wickett the barber came a little before Michaelmas 1642 is
    to have £4 a year & some old clothes
Thom: Coman a boy came in Octo. 1643 stayed one year & quarter had
    £6 one suit & cloak new, & one old suit of my Lord's. he went away
    the 17 of Jan. 1643.
Edward Fostor a ward fallen to my Lord from his manor of Holne came
    with us from *Exetor* assizes before Christmas 1643 since which time I
    have rece. in money £6 & his mother is to pay for suit & cloak & she
    left a mare with him about the 1 of Mar.
Agnes Tearle came at the Audit 1643
Rawling Thorn came the 21 of Decem. 1643 married Ja. Bond 1644
[blank] a fowler & to look at the warren & park he came this 27th day of
    Jan. 1643 is to have £4

Rich: Rook, postillian, came the 25 of March 1644 is to have £2 10s & one suit

Owin came [blank]

Will: Booth came the last of April 1644 £4 in 1646 6

[p. 232]   Rob: Amery came the 22 of Decem. 1644 no wages

Anne Steevens came 2 weeks before Michaelmas 1645, was married to Sir Charles Boles of Louth in Lincolnshire the 23 of March after

Edw: Wingefielld came in Jan. 1644 being about 5 years old died in 1648 Mary Raymore came about the same time being 8 years old

Jonathan Pikard I took being 2 weeks old in Sept. 1645. I put him to Barnstaple school the 21 of Jan. 1651. I pay 5s a quarter schooling & 2s a week tabling.

Ro: Whimper, cook, came the 16th of May again 1646 is to have 12 or £14

Rebecca Lovett came in January 1643 Sir Robert's daug[hter]

Ann Killygrey came in March 1646 Sir William's daug[hter]

Elizabeth Fiztsmorice came 1646 in May the Lord Kerry's daughter

Mr Wilde a minister came in August 1646

Geo: Chievly came in Novem. 1643 £2

Dick Willis in Decem. 1644

Elizabeth Sydenham came in Jan. 1646 Sir Ralph's d[aughter]

Decima Norton came in July 1648 £10

Francis Gottier a French boy came in July 1648

Walter Balch not 6 years old till Easter came then

Ann Tossell came Sept. 1646 2

Besse Thorn came Jan. 1646 2

John Jordan, a gardener came the 29th of Sept. 1648 £10

Edward Wingfielld 8 years old came then

Joane Gifford came in Jan. 1648

[blank] Violet came in July 1649 10

John Smith came in June 1649 8

[blank] Mihils came the Lady Day before him 4

Thom: [blank] postillion came June 1649 4

gone   Rich: [blank] a cook came in May 1649 12

Samuel Bold came in May 1648

Christopher [blank] foot-man came June 1649 £4

Octo. 1649   Margrite Cooper dairy-maid 2

Ann Ston came in June 1649 1651 2

Thomas Wimper came again in Jan. 1649 14 or £16

Thurstan Ha: came the 26 of March 1650 is to have £12 a year the lodge at *Woonham* [Wonham] going for 2 cows & one horse

Nicholas Balch 1 years 3 quarters old brother to Watt. taken this 25 of Sept. 1650, put with Jonathan to nurse

a fowler came Will: Feather-ston 4 10 0

Jo: Limbery the 7th of March 1650 about 8 years old

July 1652 gone   Simon Colline cook in July 1650 £6

**[p. 231]**   The names with the yearly rent of all my Lord's Manors
These set out for the 3 young Ladys' portions to raise £4000 a piece

| | | |
|---|---|---|
| Somer[set] | 1. Huntspill | 107 18 4 |
| | 2. Norton-Fitzwaren | 074 19 9 |
| | 36. *Nonington* [Nunnington] | 012 13 8 |
| | 3. Taunton | 009 3 6 |
| Devon | 35. *Banton borough* [Bampton] | 007 4 8 |
| | 4. *Banton* | 036 1 4 |
| | 5. Uffculme | 053 18 10 |
| | 6. Hackpen | 035 4 9 |
| | | total 337 5 10 |

These in my Lord's hands
| | |
|---|---|
| 7. *Tawstok* | £108 1s 10d   or 5s |
| 8. *Warleigh* [Warkleigh] | 018 0 6 £1 *cumin* |
| 9. *Bear* [Beer] Charter *with* [Church] Marwood | 011 10 5½ |
| 10. *Wolrington* [Worlington] | 002 10 11 |
| Muscott only a barton, Combe *Martaine* | |
| [Martin] tenem. & *Berry Narber* [Berrynabor] | |
| tenement | 004 4 0 |
| 11. Harford *with* Newland | 014 0 2 |
| 12. *Roborow* [Roborough] *Cliston* & staple-park | 004 10 8 & a red rose |
| 13. Sheldon | 017 13 2½ |
| 14. *Upex* | 015 8 2 |
| 15. *Nimett Tracy* [Nymet Tracey] & *Borough* | 022 7 0 |
| 16. Holne | 026 0 3½ |
| 17. Spitchwich | 017 6 0 |
| 18. *Combintynhead* [Combeinteignhead] | 020 7 9 |
| 19. *Ilford Combe* [Ilfracombe] *borough* | 017 7 2 |
| 20. Hartland manor & hundred & *borough* | 064 18 6½ |
| 21. Bolham *with* buckland | 013 0 9½ |
| 22. Dunterton | 002 17 10½ |
| 23. 4 part *Kings Carswell* [Kingskerswell] | 014 12 8 |
| 24. Kingston | 049 9 6½ |
| 25. Harpford | 005 11 6¼ |
| 26. *South brooke* [Southbrook] | 001 15 1¼ |
| Som. 27. 4 part Corton *Dynham* [Denham] | 001 0 7½ Langford |
| | Leister £4 |

Cornwall:
| | |
|---|---|
| 28. *Killynack* [Kelynack alias Colinack] | 014 5 9 £1 pep. or 4s |
| 29. 4 part *Cardinam* [Cardinham] | 017 8 9½ £1 of pep. |
| | value 4s |
| 30. *Doneckney* [Downeckney] | 001 19 7 |
| 31. *Boberdell* [Bodardle] | 004 0 0 |

| | |
|---|---|
| Berks[hire] | |
| 32. Wantage | 090 14 10½ |
| Wilts[hire] | |
| 33. *Nether Haven* [Netheravon] | 013 4 4 |

*Glostor* [Gloucester]

34. Hunts court                                    007 13 4

36 in all

Somers. 3, Berks. 1, Wilts. 1, *Glost.* 1, Cornw. 4, Devon 24

A note of the allowances which are in my Lord's gift
  1. *Killenacke* not clear
  2. the 4th part of *Cardinham*
  3. *Nimitt Tracye*
  4. Marwood
  5. *Rowborow*
  6. *Warkley*
  7. *Saterley* [Satterleigh]
  8. Little Torington
  9. the 4th part of Dunterton
  10. *Tawstoke*
  11. Alphington
  12. *Combyntinhead*
  13. the 4th part of *Cortoundynham* [Corton Denham]
  14. ¼ Maptan
  15. Huntspill
  16. Norton *Fitzwarin.*
*Roch* in dispute

[total] 932 18 2

[p. 230]   Linen bought the first year I was married before I was married my mother gave it me. For making these 4 board cloths which be 3 yards wide o 2 8.
Marked Cost

| | |
|---|---|
| B<br>HR  £14 | One suit of damask containing 4 board cloths which be 3 yards wide<br>o 2 8<br>One long cloth 5 yards & half, side board cloths 3, napkins 3 dozen & one for making  7 6 |
| B<br>HR  £5 | one other suit of damask containing one lond [?long] cloth, one side<br>board cloth  at London 1648, one dozen of napkins  at Lond. [16]48, one towel. |

Bought 4 table cloths of 4 yards long at yard [sic] & half broad & 41 yards of napkining made 3 dozen of napkins & 1 towel  cost £9 the 23 of May 1649.  the finest diaper may serve for side board cloths to it.

| | |
|---|---|
| Marked HB | X of fine diaper short square cloths 4  at Lond. 1 dozen & 3 in 1648.  napkins of the same 2 dozen & 9. |
| B<br>HR  £9 | goose-eyed diaper table cloths at Lond. [16]48 3 yards & half long—6.  o 4 2  side board cloths the same at Lond. [16]48 2 yards half half quarter—6.  40 yards 2s 2d cost  napkins of the same, 4 of these nap. are lost 1648 August, 5 doz. & |

|     |      |     |
|-----|------|-----|

11 at London,  8 dozen & 6   Ma.Mr   18 6, towels 4 yards long 3 at Lond.  6,   towels 3 yards long 3 at Lond.   6, one little table cloth yard & half long 0 0 4.

HB  2  ordinary diaper little square cloths   6, napkins to them 2 doz. & 11, one of another sort which is lost 1648

B  one narrow Holland table cloth

HR  hall table cloths 7 yards long 1 yard broad   7
short table cloths breadth & half 8 at Lond. [16]48   12
table cloths for the maids 3 lost at Lond. [16]48   4
long hall cloths   2

B  cupboard cloths for the hall 2 yards & half   6

HR  £52  long cloths for my own table 4   making in all 2 7 0
napkins to them—10 doz. & 3 at Lond. the rest lost this [16]48 20 doz
short towels 6 at Lond. & rest lost [16]48   20
3 breadth sheets 2 yards & half long 2 pair & half long 2 pair & one at Lond. [16]48   5 pairs
2 breadth & half   11 pair old broad & gone 1648 & 4 pair at Lond.   17 pair
2 breadth sheets   4 pair
long table cloths above 7 yards & 3 breadth   2
towels to them   2
pillow beres 11 pair & one.

**[p. 229]**

HBR  One table cloth for the hall waiters

HBR  ordinary table cloths 6
of a coarser sort 3
napkins 14 dozen
and 6

HBR  £20  short towels for the men, gone 48   12
whippers, worn out 48   16
of brown broad cloth long clothes, 4 of them at Lond. in 48   6
of shorter the same cloth   3

HB  Holland sheets, 2 pair broke up & one lost   6 pair

HBR  Holland sheets 11 pair
small Holland pillow beres, one pair at Lond. 48   3 pair
of a coarser sort pillow beres, one lost at Lond.   4 pair

HB  of Holland more   3 pillow beres

HB  10  ordinary sheets   5 pair

HBR  10  other ordinary sheets   14 pair
['pillow beres' crossed through]
one long Holland Table cloth 3 breadths

old little table cloths 3
old hall cloth marked HB, 2 of them in Lond. 48   4

French cloth bought of Voysin cost 9 12 0, made, 2 pair at Lond. one pair lost,   10

Made the 14 of Octo. 1645 out of one piece of canvas containing sheets
    6 pair
napkins, 2 dozen & 4 lost this 48,  6 dozen
hall clothes   3
dresser cloths   2
more napkins then, at London in 48   6 dozen
the 3 pieces of broad canvas containing 242 ells cost £10 14s 0

Cut out this 14th of April 36 ells of canvas to make 6 dozen of napkins
    6 dozen
8 ells of the coarse canvas made the 22 of July 1648 4 pair of sheets, also
    2 dresser clothes 3 yards & half—which made the whole piece 49 & half
['one pair at London 48
    5 pair of 2 breadth yard & half broad for my Lord's bed made' crossed
    through] one lost 48   9 pair
Narrow cloth—240 yards, 15 pair of 2 breadth & half one pair of them at
    London 1648,   pillow beres to them 15 pair
napkins made 1644 in all, whereof 10 dozen at Lond. 1648 & 7 lost,
    39 dozen & 7

Broad cloth 220 yards
sheets of 2 breadth large Irish cloth, one pair at Lond.   5 pair
long board cloths   2
side board cloths   12
and short cupboard cloths all of the same fine broad Irish   2

1643 Nov.   bought at Barnstap. 10 dozen & 7 napkins, the 7 lost in 48, of
    coarse napkins of dowlas cost £5 14s 3d
also one dozen of browner cloth cost 0 11 0

August 1648   There is 35 pieces of broad Irish cloth 29 containing
    20 yards apiece & one more of 14 yards, the other 5 pieces contain
    20 yards
2 yards for Drayes for Wat. in my wardrope
3 pieces of small canvas—one 35 yards, one other 43, the other 39, in all
    117 yards cost £5

[p. 228]   An Inventory of plate 1638 the 13th of February
One Great Voider & plate

| basins | 3} | 1 stolen | |
|---|---|---|---|
| ewers | 3} | £70 | 1 stolen |
| dishes | 12 | £200 | 3 stolen |
| 12 £42 plates | 30 | £50 | 6 stolen |
| spoons | 2 dozen | £10 | 2 lost |
| forks | 12 | 3 | |
| Great Salts | 2 | 10 | one melted |
| Trencher Salts | 12 | 5 | |
| One Chaffen dish | 1 | 10 | stolen |
| Saucers | 6 | 8 | ['4 stolen' crossed through] |
| Candlesticks | 8 | 90 | 4 stolen |

flagon pots       2      20
crewets for oil      2      7      melted
sugar boxes one of these changed    3    20    & one little sugar spoon
one bowl       1      5      stolen
tunes       3   }
other drinking cups    3   }    12      stolen
porengers      4      10      left one with 2 ears with
                                 Mr Viner

one pot & coffer      1      2
a perfuming pan      1      8
a ladle        1      2      left at Mr Viner 1642
one warming pan      1      £18 9s 8d
one hand basin      1      3
tankards       3      20      one melted or stolen
pestle & mortar      8
a Bell        7      left at Mr Viner 1643 returned again
a Scummer ladle      2
a colander      3
a chamber pot      12      one stolen
a sotto [*sotter*] pot      7
my own spoons      0      12s
a hot water cup with a tunnel
a Great Silver Standish      £28
a silver spoon with a whistle      0 12s 0
a silver pie-plate      £7      one stolen
a silver tunnel      £2
a Great pair of snuffers      £2
A Box for a wax book with 2 sockets    £12    left with Mr Viner 1643
Gilt tankards      2      £10
One gilt sugar box      10
Left with the Spai. ambassador one soto[*sotter*]-pot, porringer, spoon
     & fork all of gold £142
One silver toasting fork      £2    left in my closet at London 1643
                                 robbed

One great silver kettle & ladle      £42
A Posset Pot      £7 0 3
one fruit dish      4 3 7   }
one basin & ewer      15 19 8   }   robbed stolen
one great perfuming pot      £4
one roaster for eggs or apples      £7 robbed
one old Gilt Salt given
2 Fair Gilt Drinking Cups
one little pocket box
one little ladle bought 1646
also then a child's porringer & little spoon
and a little hand candlestick    robbed
a lesser pair of snuffers 2 larding needs
bought the 3d of March 1648 a maudlin pot & cover cost    5    robbed
['a skillet bought Aug. 1646 cost' crossed through]

[p. 227]   2 pieces of Irish cloth cut out the 9th of August 1649 made of
   long 2 breadths clothes for the parlour   4
side board clothes one breadth   2
cut out then out of a piece of brown cloth napkins   4 dozen & 3
1649 bought the 26 of August 8 yards & half of damask 7s a yard, made of
   it London table cloths   2
£16 5s 4d   bought the 22 of Sept. 1649 of very fine damask 2 yards &
   quarter, broad   12 yards & of napkining 40 yards at 13s the
   yard.   made one cloth 8 yards long one other 4 yards & half &
   napkins   3 dozen
My Lord began to plant an orchard in Novem: 1644 of above two acres of
   Forbery Close wherein is set in perfect order apples, pears, quince trees
   & damson in all 268, besides which is on the walls.
With a fair wall about it slated & tiled against which hath been set in the
   year 1645 apricots, peaches, cherries & nectarines.


Long table cloths of 3 breadths   2
long towels to them   2
long hall cloths one breadth 7 yards long each   7
short cloths for the hall   2
of 57 yards of dowlas cost £2 17s 6d made 4 towels 2 yards & half long,
   the rest made shirts & linings & aprons for everybody
1639   narrow canvas sheets, 5 pair gone, 17 pair
Irish table cloths of breadth & half 2 yards & half   6
the same cloth one breadth   6
square table cloths   4
brown broad table cloths, 4 is [sic] at London 1648,   9,
little old table cloths   3
old hall cloths, marked with HB   2
short cupboard cloths   6
coarse canvas hall cloths   6
coarse canvas for the maid's table   4
dresser cloths 2 old & 2 new   4
the whole piece cost £5 12s   coarse canvas almost yard broad   1s a yard,
   110 yards made the 14th of Sept. 1648   sheets 10 pair

Sep. 1648   for hop bags 14 yards, 1649 made hop   1
for a winnowing sheet 8 yards
for 5 corn bags then made 8 yards, 1649 made 13
Bought of coarse cloth at 20d the yard   2 13 8,   it made 4 beds &
   bolsters chaff beds 1649
1649   narrow canvas bought at Barnstap. cost [blank] it made hall
   clothes   3
another piece of yard broad canvas cost 1s the yard made sheets   3 pair

112 yards made 1650 Sept.   coarse sheets 12d the yard   7 pair, and
napkins of the same   7 pair, also Dick Rook a coat & a little loft
4 dozen, a little left one other piece of 50 yards coarse sheets 14d the
yard   4 pair, 5 yards left   one fine canvas 25 yards & half made 2 breadth
& half sheets   1 pair

[p. 226]   A note of all the moveables that were in the house & yard at Tawstock when the Lady Anne, Countess of Bath, died which was the 6th of Ja. *in the year* 1638.

In the Parlour
1 drawing table, 2 side tables, 1 court cupboard, 1 billiard board, 25 green stools, 1 chair & cushion, 1 pair of organs with virginals, 1 pair of brass andirons, 1 pair of dogs, 3 large maps, 15 small pictures, 3 green carpets, 1 green cupboard cloth, 1 goose board, 1 pair of bellows with fire shovel and tongs, 4 low stools & 1 chair all of green velvet with red baize cases.

In the Drawing Room next the Parlour
6 pieces of Arras Hangings, 1 drawing table, 1 side table, 1 livery cupboard, 1 couch, 12 chairs all suitable with their cases, 2 murry carpets and a cupboard cloth, 2 window red curtains, 1 pair of dogs with tongs, firepan & bellows, 1 landskipp

In my Lady's Bed Chamber
1 bedstead, 1 mat, 2 feather beds, 1 mattress, 2 bolsters, 2 pillows, 3 blankets, 1 red covering, 5 curtains with canopy of the same, 1 black cover, 1 red chair, 4 red stools, 1 livery cupboard, 3 red cupboard cloths, 1 red window cushion, 1 foot cloth, 1 wought [?sic] bench, 1 sweet meat case, 4 pieces of red hangings, 1 fire shovel, tongs & bellows

In my Lady's Closet
1 cupboard table, 1 pair of tongs & bellows, 5 dozen of banqueting glasses, 3 dozen of small *Vennis* glasses with other vials, 1 red stool

In the Maids Chamber
2 bedsteads, 1 mattress, 1 old chair, 5 stools, 1 livery cupboard, 1 warming pan, 1 cupboard table, 3 curtains with with [sic] tester suitable, 1 canopy with 2 curtains

In the Folding House
2 old chests, 1 old form, 1 folding table

In the Stair Case
1 little table, 2 broken stools, 1 map, 1 picture, 1 screen, 1 oyster table

In the Buttery Chamber
1 bedstead, 1 featherbed, 1 bolster, 2 pillows, 3 blankets, 1 mattress, 1 mat, 1 quilt of silk with curtains & valance & tester of the same, 1 table, 1 livery cupboard with their clothes, 6 pieces of Arras hangings, 3 chairs, 2 stools, 1 pair of andirons with tongs, firepan & bellows, 1 pair of dogs, 1 landskipp, 6 red curtains and a red tester cover

In the Inner Chamber
1 bedstead, 1 bolster, 1 featherbed, 1 mat, 1 yellow rug, 2 blankets, 1 canopy, dornick curtains, 1 joined stool

In another Chamber over the Buttery
1 landscipp, 1 close stool case

In the Nursery Chambers
2 landscipps, 1 close stool case, 1 long screen

**[p. 225]** In the Chamber up the North Tower
1 livery bedstead, 2 pair trussel

In the Draw Room next the Great Chamber
1 landscippe

In the Great Chamber
1 bedstead, 1 canopy with a green say curtain, 4 small maps, 3 pictures, 2 great window curtains, Speed's *Scripture Genealogie*, 1 small window curtain, 1 pair of dogs

In the Chamber up the Turret by the Library
1 livery bedstead, 1 close stool case

In the Library
1 little table with a green carpet, 1 chair, 3 stepping stools, 5 printed pictures, 1 old desk, some mathematical instruments, 1 pair of dogs, 1 green window curtain

In the Closet by the Parlour Door
1 little table, 1 joined stool, 1 pair of dogs

In the Cellar
1 table, 6 stools, 8 hogsheads with cider, 2 beer hogsheads, 1 water tub, 1 brass candlestick, 3 keeve or kellers [*kiver*], 2 press cupboards, 2 bushels of bay salt

In the Buttery
1 little press, 5 hogsheads, 5 tubs, 2 dozen of trenchers, 4 flaskets, 8 jugs, 1 stool, 1 form, 1 iron hanging candlestick, 1 candle chest

In the Hall
2 brass hanging candle sticks, 1 fire fork, 1 little table

In the Still House
1 cupboard, 1 chest, 2 little tables, 3 pewter stills, 2 glass stills, 3 brass pans, 1 limbeck head, 1 little scummer, 1 alabaster mortar & pestle, 1 green stool, vials, 2 glasses of May Butter

In the Dairy & Chambers
4 bedsteads, 4 stools, 7 washing tubs, 1 brass frying pan, 1 churn, 3 cheese presses, 4 great cheese vats, 1 tub to dry tiffany, 1 sutor [?sic], 1 great knife, 1 old tub, 2 pot hangers, 1 trivet, 14 milk pans, 1 old chest, 3 boards on trussels, 1 trussel, 1 pair of bellows

In the Outer Folding house
1 long table on trussels, 1 table frame, 1 form, 1 old tub, 1 old flasket

In the Cheese Chamber over the folding house
4 cheese racks, 1 brass pan, 1 pair of great scales & beams, 2 candle chests, 2 cheese boards on trussels, 2 old tubs, 1 old hamper

In the Dairy Court
3 old tubs

In the Gardener's Chamber
1 livery bedstead

In the 2 bed Chamber
1 old form, 1 old table, 1 pair of trussels, 1 anchor

In the Audit Chamber
1 bedstead with curtains, valance & tester, 1 livery cupboard, 1 feather bed, 1 bolster, 1 pillow, 2 blankets, 1 rug, 1 long table, 2 green stools

In the Lady Elizabeth Chamber
1 stool, 1 truckle bed, 1 clasping table, 1 close stool case

In the Lady Dorothy's Chamber
1 bedstead with curtains, valance and tester, 1 chair, 1 stool, 1 livery cupboard, 1 little table, 1 red cupboard cloth, 1 red window curtain, 4 pieces of red hangings, 1 pair of dogs with tongs & bellows

In the Inner Chamber
1 livery bedstead, 1 old stool, 1 close stool case

[p. 224]   In the Wardrope
3 presses, 1 bedstead, 1 table, 1 chest, 2 sets of green curtains with valance & tester, 7 featherbeds, 7 bolsters, 2 pillows, 9 blankets, 11 rugs & coverlets

In the Chamber by Mr Mannarings
1 bedstead, 1 canopy, 2 darnix curtains

In Mr Manawaring's Chamber
13 pieces of coarse hangings, 1 window curtain, 1 little table, 1 livery cupboard, 1 bedstead with blue curtains, valance & tester, 1 blue chair, 4 stools, 1 pair of andirons, 1 landskipp

In the Inner Chamber
1 livery bedstead, 1 mat

In the Porter's Lodge
1 bedstead, 1 featherbed, 1 bolster, 3 coverlets, 1 blanket, 1 table, 1 livery cupboard, 2 joined stools, 1 green carpet, 1 brass candlestick, 1 window curtain & a curtain rod

In the Old Lodge
1 bedstead, 1 feather bed, 1 bolster, 1 pillow, 2 rugs, 2 blankets, 1 table, 2 joined stools, 1 chair

In the Cider House
15 hogsheads of cider

In the Chamber up the stairs by the Closets
1 livery bedstead, 1 table, 1 chest of vials, 1 livery cupboard

In the Store Chamber & Kitchen Chambers
3 bedsteads, 1 suit of curtains, valance & tester, 2 little tables, 2 livery cupboards, 1 green carpet, 1 cupboard cloth, 2 pair of snuffers, 1 low stool, 2 low back chairs, 2 window curtains, 9 pieces of coarse hangings, 1 green coverlet, 2 looking glasses, 6 green stools, 25 saucers, 24 trencher plates, 3 basins & ewers, 6 Great Dishes & voiders, 16 candlesticks, 16 Chamber Pots, 2 bed stools, 7 close stool pans, 7 dozen & 5 dishes great & small, 1 dozen dish plates, 3 basins, 2 flagons, 1 cistern, 1 chest, 2 iron trunks, 1 cloth press, 1 cupboard table, 1 sweet meat press, 2 salts, 1 great brass candlestick, 2 foot cloths, 2 voider knives, 1 case with 6 oyster knives, 1 case with 7 long knives, 2 tallow choppers, 2 warming

pans, 2 pair of tongs, 2 fire shovels, 3 dozen of trenchers, 5 window
cushions, 1 little cushion, 1 pair of brass scales, 3 flaskets, 1 pair of hair
cloth, the hangings belonging to the nursery chamber, 1 rod net, 2 pair of
dogs, 1 little table, 2 close stool cases

In the Pasteries
1 sieve, 1 table on trussels, 1 grater, 1 low bell, 1 mortar of bell metal,
1 iron pestle, 1 wooden pestle, 1 table, 2 forms, 4 pastry presses, 1 rolling
pin, 1 child's chair

In the kitchen, scullery & wet larder
1 form, 2 stools, 2 brass ladles, 2 scummers, 1 fire shovel, tongs & fire
fork, 1 frying pan, 3 pair of racks, 2 irons to lay before the fire, 1 iron
grate for coal, 2 beef forks, 8 spits, 4 pair of pot hooks, 3 pair [blank],
6 pothangers 7, 2 iron dripping pans, 2 cleavers, 1 mincing knife, 2 buttery
knives, 1 pair of dogs, 1 salt box, 2 skillets, 4 brass crocks or pots,
4 kettles, 1 copper, 2 chests, 1 old chair, 2 salmon tubs, 4 salting tubs,
1 stool to dry pewter, 2 trays

In the Chamber over the wet Larder
1 feather bed, 2 bolsters, 3 old rugs, 1 old stool


[p. 223]   In the workmens Hall
6 black jacks, 1 old chest, 1 iron pitch pot, 15 hogsheads & pipes

In the Boulting Chamber
2 old tubs, 1 keller 1 bolster

In the Chamber over it
[blank]

In the Bakehouse
1 old kettle, 1 pair of great scales & beam, 1 iron peel, 1 kneading trough,
1 great hutch, 1 barrel hutch, 1 keller, 1 greater keller

In the Brewhouse
7 kellers, 2 tubs, 2 mashing tubs, 1 great keller, 1 barrel, 3 hogsheads,
1 brewing copper

In the slaughter house
1 butcher's axe, 1 chopping stool, ropes to draw up oxen

In the stables
4 old chests, 3 pails, 1 horse litter, 1 wheel barrow with other lumber

In the Groom's Chamber
2 bedsteads

In the Apple house & Pounding house
1 old chest, 1 old frame of a stool, 3 pipes of cider, 1 spade, 2 iron shovels,
1 gardener's line with an iron turn, 1 great tub, 1 tunnel

In the Yards
50 loads of oaken wood, 20 load of faggots, 10 load of block, 2 loads of
furse, 1 water cart

Hops and gunpowder: *necioquare* [*I do not know why*]

Bought at Bampton the 22 of Oct. 1648 trenchers round 11 dozen & half,
Bought at Barnst. then 2 dozen of square trenchers cost [blank]
Bought at Banton the 6 of Sept. 1650 trenchers 15 dozen cost 17s

June the 21th 1651 bought 6 dozen of preserving glasses & pots 2 dozen,
beer glasses about that time 13, wine glasses then 6

[p. 221]  York   bought 1642 August   £22 10s 0d   sold April 1645
Backer   stole by the rebels of Barnst.   9 10 0   bought a nag for my own
    saddle, also soon after bought one for my Lord cost £25 10s
May 1649   cost £35 & 20s
bred   Turk [?]   cave
Chest-Nutt   cave
Wiote   cave   Trust: Pollard 10 0 0
Baye Sumptor   dead

           Gundemoor
           Spindeloe
coach      White Flank
           Parson   4 cost £52
           Conneway   £18
           White gelding   19
           Rennolls   rebel Hazillrige both given

bred   Pudding   Barnst. rebels
bred   Light-foot   cave.
My Lord's roan sold
Whiy:   £18 10s lent my Lord Stafford in 1644 & one more with saddles
    &c never returned
bred   Sorrell Irish   cave.
Fiddle fadle   given
bred   Rickett
Tomkin's Mare   8
Mr Mare's mare
Graye Wiote's
Swillivant   Roger hath 6
Gray Salsbery
bred   Made Robin   sold
Gray Smithfield   sold
Gray Lynn   £14
           dead Keepe   13 5s
           Kaet   £11 10s geilt
Coach:     Butler 8   a black stone horse astray from *Hunspile*
           Buggalla haye 8         Sept. 1648, a black
mare then a heriot from *Beare* charter then.   An iron gray gelding bought
for my Lord's saddle cost £16 10s
                        bought the 25 of Oct. 1649 of
Mr Harice from Heyn's brother one gray coach horse cost 23 10s
           Logerhead Lambe
in May      a stray from *Norton-Fitzwarin* value £3
& June     a stray from *Warkley*
           one ['other stray' crossed through] heriot from *Warkley*

one heriot from *Killyneck* upon the death of Mr Benit
one gray gelding bought at Croan cost    £7 13s 6d the colt
one bay crape-eared mare Bold's cost 1 13 0
one gray gelding cost the Irish mare & 39s, Mr Hallet had one
gray horse for the coach    cost in June 1646 £14 10s 0

March the  one gray coach horse bought at *Brewern* of one Crafts in
11 1647    *Gloster-shire* cost 15 10 0
one bay gelding a felon's goods taken at Wantage brought to
London in April 1648 one gray coach-horse bought in May
1649 cost 32 10 0

[p. 220]   Made the 13th of Octo. 1650 of 99 yards of canvas
napkins then 8 doz, sheets 2 breadth & half 2 pair, sheets 2 breadth 9 pair,
sheets of fine canvas 2 breadth & half 1 pair, dowlas napkins then made
7 dozen, coarse napkins 4 dozen.

1650 Jan.   2 pieces of broad fine Irish made table cloths for the
3 withdrawing room of 2 breadths
1651 also the other made pillow beres 6 pair, and table clothes of breadth
& ½ 2 & one breadth

Aug. 9th 1651   Taken out of the Great Chest where was 26 broad pieces
& 5 narrow of Irish cloth & two pieces of canvas
of the broad cloth 4 pieces & 2 pieces, of narrow 1 piece, of canvas
2 pieces
the narrow—which made sheets 2 breadth & ½ 1 pair, & one table cloth
2 breadths
2 pieces of the broad made 2 breadths sheets   3 pair
one piece of canvas made napkins   2 dozen & 6
in all 6 doz: one other piece of canvas made napkins   3 dozen & 6
one piece more made 2 breadth sheets 1 pair & one, & one breadth for the
table cloths for the withdrawing room
one table cloth more for the withdrawing room 2 breadths & half   2
one of but one breadth   1
in all 7   table cloths 4 yards quarter 2 breadth 2, in all 9 pair   also more
sheets of 2 breadth   3 pairs & one
1651   the rest made shirts   cost 7 5 8,   8 yards of coarse canvas at
12d the yard made sheets 66 yards of it   6 pair, 48 yards at 13d made
6 dozen of napkin 41 yards   6 dozen
Sept. the 1 1651

Octo. the 14th 1651 cut out of one large pair of fine woollen blankets of
my own spinning—3 yards long & better, 12 qr. there is remaining of the
blanketing stuff 2 yards qr.

March 1652 the 29th bought 154 ells of canvas 16½d a yard to line & face
the two best suits of hangings in London.
bought for napkins then

[p. 219]   An Inventory taken the 9th of March 1639 of all the household
goods and furniture which is in every room & office in the House as
followeth:

In the Great Chamber
8 pieces of Arras of forest work £106, 1 long foot carpet Turkey work £6,
4 Spanish tables, 2 great chairs of red wrought velvet, 2 dozen of back
chairs suitable, 1 great looking glass £15, 4 curtains of red baize, 2 curtain
rods, 1 pair of brass andirons £2, 1 pair of creepers with brass heads, 1 pair
of tongs & firepan of brass, 1 pair bellows which is in my Lord's closet,
1 fair organ £100

In the withdrawing room within the Great Chamber
£38 besides the canopy  5 pieces of Arras of forest work, 1 Spanish table,
1 couch of red velvet, 1 canopy of state of red velvet, 1 Great Chair of red
velvet, 1 long cushion of red velvet, 6 high chairs, 2 low chairs, 4 low
stools all suitable, coverings of red baize for all the chairs, stools, cushion,
couch & canopy. 1 long foot carpet Turkey work £4, 2 curtains of red
baize, 2 curtain rods, 1 pair of brass andirons with cases of baize, 1 pair of
creepers with brass heads, 1 pair of tongs & fireshovel of brass, 1 pair of
bellows. the room matted.

In the best bed chamber within the withdrawing room
4 pieces of Arras of forest work, 1 great bedstead, mat & cord,
1 featherbed, 1 bolster, 1 quilt, 1 pair of blankets, 3 little pillows, 1 red
rug, 4 curtains lined with yellow sarsnet, 3 curtain rods, double valance,
2 tester & train, 1 counterpain, 2 great elbow chairs, 4 high stools, 2 low
stairs, all of scallet with yellow & white lace suitable, 1 window curtain of
red baize, 1 curtain rod, 1 pair of andirons, firepan, tongs & billows,
1 chimney piece

In the Inner Room
1 half headed bedstead, mat & cord, 1 bed, 1 bolster, 1 pillow, 1 pair of
blankets, 1 green rug, 1 green say curtain, 2 green stools

In the Chamber over the Steward's Table
4 pieces of red stammel hangings with green lace, 1 bedstead, mat & cord,
1 feather bed, 1 bolster, 2 pillows, 1 pair of blankets, 5 curtains lined with
sarcenet, tester valance & train & counterpain all suitable to the hangings,
3 curtain rods, 1 great chair, 1 high stool, 3 low stools, 1 cupboard cloth
suitable, 1 pair of creepers, 1 firepan, 1 pair of tongs. there wants a pair of
bellows.

The Stair Case
4 maps, 2 great pictures, 16 other small pictures, my Lord's cabinet,
1 organ with virginal, 1 chest of viols, 1 dozen of blue cushions, one dozen
more, one very great double base viole, one Irish harp, one little viol, one
violin.

[p. 218]   The Inner Nursery Chamber
7 pieces of Imagery cost 28 16 0   5 pieces of hangings of Forest work,
1 bedstead, mat & cord, 1 feather bed, 1 bolster, 1 quilt, 1 pair of blankets,
1 counter paine, double valance tester & frame, 4 curtains, 3 curtain rods,
2 window curtains, 2 curtain rods
the red cloth cost 10s the yard 32 yards £16 1638 April 2   the re. [blank]
1 little carpet, 1 great chair, 2 high chairs, 2 low chairs, 2 high stools,

2 lower stools, all suitable to the bed which is red with yellow & red lace with cases to the same of red baize, 2 pillows, 1 red rug, fire pan & tongues, 1 landskip.   there wants 1 pair of andirons & a pair of bellows.

The Inner Room
1 half headed bedstead, mat & cord, 1 feather bed, 1 bolster, 1 rug, 2 blankets, 1 stool case

The Entry Chamber
5 pieces of old arras hangings, 1 couch, 1 great chair, 6 high chairs, 4 low chairs, 1 foot carpet, 3 window clothes all which is covered with baize suitable to the same colour which is murry. 1 landskipt. there wants andirons, fire pan, tongs & bellows & 5 cases for chairs.

My Lady's wardrobe
1 table, 1 press, 1 trunk, 2 red leather chairs

The Chamber next to the wardrobe
4 pairs of Arras hangings, 1 bedstead, mat & cord, 1 feather bed, 1 bolster, 1 pair of blankets, 1 green rug, 1 pillow, 5 curtains, 3 curtain rods, 1 tester train, single valance of Norwich stuff £4 with 1 low stool of the same stuff, 1 livery table, 1 great chair, 2 high stools, 2 low chairs all of Turkey work, 1 landscape.   there is wanting andirons, tongs, fire pan & bellows.

The inner chamber within
1 half-headed bedstead, mat & cord, 1 feather bed, 1 pair of blankets, 1 bolster, 1 yellow rug, 1 green stool

The chamber over the buttery
6 pairs of Arras hangings, 1 bedstead, mat & cord, 1 feather bed, 1 bolster, 1 quilt, 1 pair of blankets, 2 pillows, 1 green rug, 5 curtains, tester, valance & train, 1 counterpain, all of changeable taffety, 1 great chair, 2 high stools, 2 low stools, all of green velvet with cases of red baize, 1 table, 1 green carpet with a border, 2 window curtains of red baize, 2 curtain rods, 1 landskipt, 2 andirons with brass heads, 2 creepers, 1 pair of bellows.   there wants firepan & tongs.

The Inner Room
1 half headed bedstead, mat & cord, 1 darmix canopy with 2 curtains, 1 joined stool.   there wants 1 bed, 1 bolster, 1 pair of blankets, 1 rug. now all here.

In the Parlour
1 long tableboard, 2 side tables, 1 Spanish table, 1 billiard board, 2 sticks, 3 boles, 1 pin, one bridge, 4 gilded sconces, 2 great chairs, 1 dozen & half of high chairs, 2 low chairs all of blue cloth suitable—£13 13s 0d, 5 curtains of blue baize, 5 curtain rods, 4 turkey work carpets, 1 pair of andirons of brass, 1 pair of creepers brassen heads, 1 pair of tongs, firepans & bellows, 1 pair of silver snuffers, 1 great sconce, 1 pair of tables, 2 chess boards with set of men, 7 books of Common Prayer, a clock, a goose board & one Great Bible.

[p. 217]   The withdrawing room within the Parlour
5 pieces of Arras hangings forest work, 1 gilded sconce, 1 couch, 1 dozen of high chairs, 2 low chairs all of blue cloth suitable, 2 curtains of blue

baize, 2 curtain rods, 1 table, 1 Spanish table, 2 carpets of Turkey work,
1 little screen, 2 globes, 1 pair of brassen andirons, 1 pair tongs, fire pans
& bellows, 2 standers for candle sticks, 1 pair of creepers.

In my Lord's Chamber
5 pieces of Arras hangings of forest work, 1 bedstead, mat & cord,
1 feather bed, 1 quilt, 1 pair fustian blankets, 1 pair of woollen blankets,
1 yellow rug, 4 curtains, double valance, tester & train counterpain of
green cloth with yellow lace, 3 curtain rods, 1 foot carpet of Turkey work,
1 great chair, 2 high stools, 2 low stools all suitable, 1 little table, 1 green
carpet, 1 great cabinet, 1 little cabinet of red velvet with gold lace with a
red leather cover, 1 silver standish, 1 warming pan of silver, 1 perfuming
pan of silver, 1 silver bell, 2 looking glasses, 1 pair of andirons with tongs,
firepan & bellows, 1 screen.

In my Lady's Closet
1 table, 1 cross stitch carpet, 1 chair, 1 long cushion of the same, 1 high
red leather chair, 1 great cabinet with drawers, 1 carpet of green damask,
1 pair of andirons, tongs, firepan & bellows, 1 screen.

The room without the Gentlewomen Chamber
5 trunks, 1 viol with a case, 1 gittern with a case, 1 joined stool, 2 close
stools

In the Gentlewomen's Chamber
5 pieces of stripped stuff hangings with a carpet of the same, 1 bedstead
with single valance & tester, 4 curtains, mat & cord, 1 feather bed,
1 bolster, 2 pillows, 2 blankets, 1 red rug, 1 half headed bedstead, 1 feather
bed, 1 bolster, 1 pair of blankets, 1 red rug, mat & cord, 1 square table,
1 livery cupboard, 1 high stools, 1 low stool, 2 low chairs of turkey work,
1 low red leather chairs, My Lady's trunk & cabinet, 1 pair of creepers,
tongs & firepan.   there wants a pair of bellows.

In the Gentleman Ushers Chamber
1 field bedstead, 5 curtains with single valance, tester & train of red cloth,
1 bed, 1 bolster, 2 pillows, mat & cord, 2 blankets, 1 blue rug, 1 livery
cupboard, 2 high red leather chairs, 1 little back chair, 1 little stool, 1 great
high green stool, 1 pair of bellows, firepan & tongs.   there wants creepers.

In Mr Bourchier's chamber, chaplain
1 little field bedstead, mat & cord, 5 curtains, tester, valance & train,
1 bed, 1 bolster, 1 pillow, 2 blankets, 1 yellow rug, 4 pieces of hangings of
red cloth with valance, 1 red cupboard cloth, 1 livery table, 1 little table,
1 high red leather chair, 1 little back chair of needlework, 2 old lined
stools, 1 pair of bellows, 1 firepan.   there wants tongs & creepers.

In the Pantler's Chamber
1 half headed bedstead, mat & cord, 1 feather bed, 1 bolster, 1 pair of
blankets, 1 ['yellow' crossed through] green rug, 1 little table, 2 joined
stools

In the Chamber over the Gent. Usher
1 half headed bedstead, mat & cord, 1 feather bed & bolster, 1 pair of
blankets, 1 green rug, 1 little table.

[p. 216]   In the Chamber over the Audit Chamber
1 high bedstead, 1 feather bed, 1 bolster, 4 curtains with tester, double
valance & train, 1 counter pain of blue cloth, the cloth cost 10s the yard
29 yards £14 10s, with crimson, blue & white lace, all suitable, 2 pillows,
2 blankets, 1 great high chair, 2 high chairs, 2 low chairs, 2 high stools,
2 low stools suitable covered with red baize, 2 window curtains of blue
baize, 4 curtain rods, 7 pieces of blue leather hangings gilded, mat & cord,
1 pair andirons, 1 pair of tongs, fire pan & bellows

In the Chamber next to it
1 half headed bedstead, mat & cord.   there wants 1 bed, 1 bolster,
2 blankets, 1 rug.

In Jo: Boothe's chamber
13 pieces of coarse hangings, 1 bedstead, mat & cord, 5 curtains with
tester, valance & train of blue saye, 1 great chair, 2 low stools suitable,
1 lined stool, 1 little table, 1 livery cupboard, 1 bed, 1 bolster, 1 pillows,
2 blankets, 1 blue rug, 1 window curtain, 1 landskip.   there wants
creepers, firepan, tongs & bellows.

In Will: Ellis chamber
1 half heade bedstead, 1 feather bed, 1 bolster, 2 blankets, 2 coverlets,
1 canopy with 2 curtains of darnix, 1 square tableboard, 1 joined stool,
1 green stool, mat & cord.

In the wardrobe
1 half headed bedstead, 1 featherbed, 1 bolster, 1 pair of blankets, 1 yellow
& green rug, mat & cord, 1 great tableboard, 1 great chest, 5 great presses
no bedding here.

In the Audit Chamber
1 high standing bedstead with tester, valance & 5 curtains of green say,
1 bed, 1 bolster, 1 pillow, 2 blankets, 1 green rug, mat & cord, 1 long
tableboard, 1 livery cupboard, 2 red leather chairs, 2 green stools, 1 joined
stool, 1 pair of creepers, tongs & bellows.   there wants a firepan
1 warming pan.

In the Gent: of the Horses Chamber
1 half headed bedstead, 1 feather bed, 1 bolster, 2 pillows, 2 blankets,
1 green rug, 1 green canopy with 1 curtain, 1 livery cupboard, 1 little
Turkey carpet, 2 high red leather chairs, 2 green stools, mat & cord.
there wants firepan, tongs, bellows & creepers.

In the Gent: Sewers Chamber
1 half headed bedstead, 1 feather bed, 1 bolster, 2 blankets, 1 red rug,
1 green canopy with 2 curtains of stuff, 1 livery cupboard, 1 red carpet,
2 high red leather chairs, mat & cord.   there wants firepan, tongs, bellows
& creepers.

In Mr Snowe's Chamber, curate of Tawst.
1 great standing bedstead, tester & valance, 5 green curtains, 3 curtain
rods, 1 bed, 1 bolster, 1 pillow, 2 blankets, 2 coverlets, 1 white rug, mat &
cord, 1 livery table, 2 square tables, 1 great chair, 2 joined stools, 1 green
carpet, 1 pair of tongs, firepan & bellows, 1 pair of creepers.

[p. 215]   The Porter's Chamber
1 half headed bedstead, 1 feather bed, 1 bolster, 2 coverlets, 1 blanket, mat
& cord, 1 livery cupboard, 1 square table, 1 great chair, 2 joined stools,
1 form, 1 green carpet, 1 latten sconce, 1 window curtain, 1 curtain rod

In the stable chamber
2 half headed bedsteads, 2 feather beds, 2 bolsters, 1 rug, 2 blankets,
2 rugs, 1 blanket in the grooms bed, mats & cords.

The lower chamber in the Old Lodge
1 standing bedstead, 1 old tester, 1 little table, 2 joined stools, 1 feather
bed & bolster, 1 dust bed & bolster, 2 blankets, 2 coverlets

In Mr Wright's Chamber
1 half headed bedstead, 1 feather bed, 1 bolster, 1 mattress, 2 blankets,
1 coverlet, mat & cord, 1 table, 1 green stool

In the Paistery Chamber
5 pieces of Arras hangings, 16 17s 0, 1 bedstead, mat & cord, 4 curtains
with tester, double valance & train of green cloth, the cloth 28 yards cost
13 6 0 9s 6d the yard, with green & yellow lace & counterpain all suitable
2 blankets, 1 yellow rugs, 2 pillows, 1 great chair, 2 high chairs, 2 high
stools, 2 low chairs, 2 low stools suitable to the bed.   there is wanting
1 bed, 1 bolster, 1 table, tongs, firepan, creepers & bellows & andirons.
all the bed is now lopside.

In the Musicians Chamber
2 bedsteads, 2 dust beds, 2 dust bolsters, 4 coverlets, 2 high red leather
chairs

In the Chamber over the Bakehouse
1 half headed bedstead, 1 featherbed, 1 bolster, 2 blankets, 1 rug, map &
cord, 1 red leather chair, 1 joined stool, 1 brass chafer, 1 pair of fire
screens to trammel

In the Chamber over the Wet Larder
2 half headed bedsteads, 2 feather beds, 2 bolsters, 3 blankets, 4 rugs, mats
& cords, 1 great chair painted white & black, 1 red leather stool, 1 shelf

In the Chamber over the scullery
2 bedsteads, 1 featherbed, 1 bolster, 2 coverlets, 1 dust bed, 1 old bolster,
1 coverlet, 1 blanket, mats & cords

In the Pantry
1 press cupboard, 2 table boards, 4 high red leather chairs, 1 latin sconce,
2 shelves

In the Cellar
1 table, 2 joined stools, 1 cupboard

In the Hall
3 long tableboards, 4 long forms, 2 little side boards, 1 steward tables,
2 shortforms, 2 green stools, 2 joined stools, 2 brass sconces, 1 great brass
hanging candlestick, 1 pair of tables, 1 fire pick

1642   A trumpet I bought cost 45s for Will: Elis to sound when I went
upon the water.

**[p. 214]  In the Buttery**
1 long binger, 1 little press, 1 candle chest, 2 great flasks, 2 little flasks,
1 trencher table

**In the kitchen**
14 spits, 4 pair of racks, 6 kettles, 1 great brass pot, 2 little brass pots,
1 pair of tongs, 1 fire fork, 2 fire shovels, 4 brass ladles, 5 skillets little &
great, 2 brass scummers, 9 pothangers, 4 pot hooks, 3 dripping pans,
1 grate for the coal fire, 2 irons for the coal fire, 2 cleavers, 1 mincing
knife, 1 scraping knife, 2 tubs, 1 bucket, 1 pestle & mortar of bell metal,
1 beef fork, 1 grater, 1 girt box, 1 salt box, 2 frying pans, 1 shelf,
2 gridirons, 1 coal rake, 3 iron bars in the 2 chimneys

**In the Outer Paistery**
4 peels, 2 trays

**In the Inner Paistery**
1 safe [*seive*], 1 board, 2 tressels, 4 shelfs

**In the Wet Larder**
5 cor tables to salt meat in, 1 great tub to water fish in, 2 great brass pots,
2 old brass kettles, 1 chafer, 1 mustard mill, 1 iron grate & 2 spits which
came from London, 1 trindle, 1 chopping stock

**In the Dairy chamber**
2 bedsteads

**In the Outer Foulding Chamber**
1 long tableboard upon trestle, 1 little table, 3 flaskets

**In the Inner Foulding Chamber**
4 trunks, 2 great chests, 2 table boards, 1 form, 1 high red leather [chair],
1 pair of tongs, 1 pair of bellows.  there wants a firepan.

**In the Cheese Chamber**
1 brass pan, 2 cheese racks, 2 candle chests, 2 girt barrels, 1 pair of scales,
2 boards & 2 trestles

**In the Candle House**
1 candle mold, 1 tub, 1 pan, 2 tallow choppers

**In the Scullery**
1 great chest, 1 old Iron chest, 1 old chair, 1 shelf, 3 tubs

**In the Brewhouse**
1 copper, 1 cooler, 1 working tun, 1 mashing vat, 1 tunner, 3 buts, 2 small
cools, 7 keelers, 2 stillings, 1 jet, 1 bucket, 2 roers, 1 plump, 1 underback,
16 iron bars or grates, 1 coal rake, 1 trundle, 2 carriage troes, 1 clensen
sieve

**In the Bakehouse**
1 moulding board for bread, 1 brake, 1 pair of scales & beam, 1 great
hutch, 1 hogshead, 1 kneading trough, 2 sarges, 1 straining sieve, 1 peck,
1 half peck, 1 bucket, 1 bowl dish, 2 bunters, 1 boulting hutch, 1 trivet,
1 iron peel.   there wants a kettle.

[p. 213]   In the Workmens Hall
3 table boards, 3 forms, 1 coffer, 4 black jacks

In the Chamber Over the Dresser or the Maids Chamber
1 half headed bedstead, gone to the Lodge, 1 truckle bed, 2 beds,
2 bolsters, 3 blankets, 2 rugs shelves about the chamber, mats & cords one
high bedstead with valance and 4 curtains of stripped stuff

In Mrs Hardwick's Chamber
1 bedstead, 5 curtains tester, valance & train of stripped stuff, 1 bed,
1 bolster, 1 pillow, 2 blankets, 1 yellow rug, mat & cord, 1 livery
cupboard, 1 table, 1 great chair, 1 low red leather chair, 1 child's chair,
1 low cupboard, 3 green stools, 1 old cushion, 2 window curtains of
darnix, 2 curtain rods, 1 old carpet, 9 pieces of coarse hangings, firepan,
tongs, & bellows, 1 warming pan.

In the Store Chamber
2 iron bound trunks, 1 great press, 2 tables, 1 cupboard, 1 chest, 1 jack
which came from London, 2 pair of scales & weights, 1 brass pestle &
mortar, 3 hair sieves [?sic], 1 tiffany crace curtains of green say with tester
& valance—are in the chamber over the ['backhouse' crossed through]
workman hall, piece of hair cloth for the malt house, 2 pressering skillets,
1 brass ladle

In the Still House
4 stills, 1 old table, 1 old kimbeck

The Chamber over the Workmens Hall
1 feild bedstead, mat and cords, 1 bolster, one featherbed, 1 pillow,
2 blankets, 1 green rug, 5 green sea [say] curtains & valance and tester,
1 table, 1 green carpet, 1 red leather chair, 1 stool

[enclosure 214a]
A note of what horses are left
Yorke: grey coach horse
Weke: tow black
Irish mares: Rickard
Bay smith field mare
Salsbury, White gelding
the gray mare

[enclosure 214b]
1.  My wife went from Oxford into Devon on Tuesday the 26th of Sept.
1643.  My Lord Digby was sworn a Privy Councillor & Secretary of State
on Thursday the 28th of Sept.   The Lord Grandyson died on Friday the
29th of September in Jesus College in Oxford, & was buried at Christ
Church on Monday the 2nd of October.   The Lord Cottington was made
Lord Treasurer of England on Sunday the 1 of October at Christ Church
in *Oxon*.   I sent letters to my wife by Mr Amias Pollard the 7th of
October.   I sent letters to my wife the 9th of October.   James came to
Oxford the 9th of October.   I received letters from my wife by D.
Downe's man the 11th of October.   I sent letters by D. Hunckwill the

12th. Raph Booth came to Oxf. the 12. I went to *Brewerne* the 14th. I returned the 15th. I sent letters by the carrier the 17th. I sent letters by Mr Ward the 18. The French Amb. came to Oxford the 19th.

2. I agreed with Robert Keate for 2 lives his wife & his son in a cottage in Wantage & his son exchanged for one sadler who had his lease by copy. the fine £4  20 Oct.

Sir Jo: Bonaugh died at Ox. the 21 of October, I sent letters to my wife by a foot post of Barnstaple the 26th of October. I came from Oxford to Faringdon 2 Nov., From Faringdon to Malmesbury 3 Nov., from Malmsbury to *Bathe* 4 Nov., from *Bathe* to Pilton 6 Nov., from Pilton to Bridgwater 7 Nov., from Bridgwater to Exford 8 Nov., from Exford to *Tawstocke* 9 Nov.

3. On Monday the 11th of December 1643 I went from *Tawstocke* to Bow, From Bow to Exeter the 12th, At Exeter the 13 & 14, From Exeter to Bow the 15th, From Bow to Tawstock the 16th

[enclosure 212a]
The New Orchard
About the wall there is 73 trees, in the easter quarter on the higher side 80 trees, in the easter quarter on the lower side 80 trees, in the west quarter on the higher side 87 trees, in the west quarter on the lower side 39 trees.

The trees in the orchard besides these on the wall are in all 268

[p. 212] in Gr. St Bartholomews  My Lord & I was married the 15th day of Decem. 1638  [signed] R. Bathe  by Doct. Westfeild

The 4th day of March following 1638 my Lord went to *Tawstok*, he returned to London in April  1639

1  My Lord & I began my first journey into Devon the 5 day of July 1639 to *Henlly*, the 6 day to *Brewern*, the 9th to *Laycok*, the 11 we dined at the *Bathe* & went to Glastonbury, the 13th at Exford & the 14th of July to *Tawstok*.

The 5th day of August 1639 my Lord went to *Exetor*.

2  My Lord & I went toward London in [blank] 1639, he lay at Mr Clark's & I stayed at *Brewern* [blank] days & [blank] day went to Northampton, the next day to *Apthorp* where I christened the Lady Mary Fane, my niece, & on the [blank] day my Lord came & stayed [blank] days & [blank] day we began our journey for the west: to Northa[m]p[ton] next day to *Brewern* & the 13th & the 13th day of Decem. 1639 from *Brewern* we went to *Cisichster*.

3  In March following my Lord went to the South *Hames*. My Lord & I began our journey to London to the Little Parliament 1640 to St Giles in the Fields.

We went out of London the [blank] of June 1640.

4  1640 We went up to London  first I began my journey on a Friday about the 20 of October & in a litter having had a dangerous sickness. My Lord began his the Monday after.

1641 we came down in [blank]
1641 we went up the 25 of Octo. in 6 days 24 horse & men
1642 we went to *Meyworth* Castle on Friday the 27 of April to a house of
 by bro: Westmorland
being 19 in all & sta.
1642 we came up to my Lord Breudnall's house in London on Saturday
1642 we went towards York on Wednesday the 25 of [illegible crossed
 through] to Baldock to *Apthorp* [illegible crossed through]
Friday to Fulbeck where my Lord left me & went on Saturday to
 Doncaster & on Sunday being Whitsun day to York, I followed him.
We went from York to *Beverlly* & so to York the next day being Saturday
The Monday after we set from York homewards
We came home [blank]
We went to *Exetor*
My Lord went into Cornwall
1642 my Lord was carried prisoner at 11 a clock in the night by the rebels
 to Barnstaple & so for London on the 28 of Sept.
1643 we got from them the 4th of August 1643 & so came to Oxford.

[p. 211]  An inventory of the armour in my Lord's house in London
 taken the 4th of June 1641
my Lord's own armour for himself
then 10 head pieces, 10 pieces for the breast, 10 back pieces, 20 thigh
 pieces, 20 arm pieces, 10 pieces to come over the saddle, 11 pair of
 pistols, 11 pair of bullet moulds, 10 keys
The armourer my Lord had £6 for keeping them 2 years & now I have
 agreed with the same man for £1 a year to cleanse them, in my house.
My Lord & I with 23 or 24 went towards *Exetor* to Bow the 11th of
 Decem. 1643 to the [A]sizes on Monday
on Tuesday the 12 to *Exetor*
there stayed Wednesday & Thursday &
on Friday the 15th to Bow &
on Saturday the 16th of Decc. home to *Tawstoke*

My Lord is gone this present Monday being the 15th of Jan. 1643 towards
 Oxford to Mr Ashfords &c with him Will: Weekes, Thom: Polla., John
 Burk, James, Wilmot a sumptor, Mr Mare & Thurston to bring down
 the horses & money £41, 3 case of pistols & dragons, the horses came
 back the 29th of Jan. all but my Lord's own, the little black mare &
 Oxford.
My Lord was made Lord Privy Seal the [blank] of Jan. 1643.
My Lord went to *Exetor* with 27 persons & as many horse is come back.

the 23 of June 1644   Tho: Polla. went to London & came home the
 [blank]  My Lord & I went into Cornwall the 29th of June 1644 to
 Stow, from thence to Croan in the parish of *Egglshell* the 1 of July,
 from thence to *Treveneiy* the 25 of July, from thence to the Mount the
 27th of July
We went on the 10th of August to the Armed Knight by *Burien* & so
 came back by St Just.
We came to *Exetor* out of Cornw. the 19t of Sept. 1644
We came home to *Tawstok* the 25 of Sept. 1644

[p. 210]   An Inventory of the goods in my house at London taken the 16th of April 1641 [blank]

We came out of London the 17th of May 1648 & to the Bath the 20th, 18 servants, 10 horses besides Hyered [hired].

I went to London without my Lord the 29th of Jan. 1649 to Exford &c.

came home to *Tawstok* the 8th of March following

I went to Bath & so to *Tayngle*

[p. 209]   Taken here the 17th of Feb. 1643   *Tawstok* the Customary 20 Elizab.

The presentment of all the Homage of the manor of *Tawstok*, concerning points of their customs here after mentioned presented & delivered upon their oaths at a court holden there the 6 day of August in the 20th year of the reign of our sovereign Lady Elizabeth the Queen's Majesty that now is 1578 [blank]

121½ yards in all   cloth made 1651 for blanketting 20 yards, made into blankets 1652 in August Cloth made 1651 for blanketting 20 yards of coarse broad cloth 2 pair, 21 yards of broad fine blanketting made 2 pair.

Cloth coarse for the kitchen boy, gardener's boy, Croyde's boy, Jonathan, Nick, &c

made 1652 Sept.   of the fine for Mr Wyote 3 yards & half, for Randale & Ned 6 yards, for Tho: Hathorn suit & cloak 8 yards, for blue stockings 12 yards, for the livery 12 yards 3 quarters, one piece more for liveries

Bought of Wilmote the 13th of Octo. 1652

cost 31s 6d coarse white Irish cloth at 18d a yard—21 yards. 53s 4d somewhat narrower at 16—40 yards.   [total] £4 4s 10d

blankets made of the narrow 3 breadth—3 pair, of the broader cloth 2 breadth cloth 2 breadth & half—1 pair, & of 2 breadth—1 pair.

1652 Octo.   21 yards of grass green serge, £2 12s 6d, at 2s 6d made a bed for the Audit Chamber with buckeram, 10s, 17 yards ½ & crewel fringe, 2s 9, cost about £3 10 0, 65 yards of dowlas cost 13d the yard made then 5 dozen ½ of napkins—5 doz. & ½.

11 yards in a pair   60 yards of fine canvas 15d the yard made 44 yards sheets 4 pair, one yard in a napkin   napkins of the same then 2 doz. & 4, 39 yards & half of coarse canvas at 13d made sheets 3 pair, napkins of the same 1 dozen.

8 doz. & 10 napkins, 7 pair of sheets this Octo. 1652

4 yr. 3 qr left   Nove. the 15th 1652 made of 60 yards of dowlas 12 yards & half in a dozen of napkins so 56¼ makes at 13 the yard   4 doz. & 6; made an apron   canvas 31 yr. ¼ at 13d made napkins   4 doz.; a fowling bag   coarse canvas 33 yr. at 11d made sheets 3 pair, 34 yards faced 6 pieces of hangings over the doors & the brewer had 2 ells.

[p. 208]   Cloth made this Sept. 1650

whereof made 2 pair of blankets, one pair of them 2 breadth ½   2 pair given to Mr Wyote for 2 suits   8 yards

to Anice for a coat   2 yards ½

to the caterer

to Dick Rook
for Thom: Wathorn
1650   for ['William Balch' crossed through] John Burk 4 yards ½

given of coarse cloth to the poor for waistcoats now Margaret Herder,
   Eliza: Marchant, Dorothy Sweete, Ann Holland, Katherine Richards,
   Eliza: Symons, Susan Peace, Mary Tossell, Eliza: Hokines, Mary Grigry
also Watt: Jonathan, Nicholas

one other piece bought
made Will: Balch 4½
Tho: Comman
Nan Ston a petticoat

Made March the 16th 1650   Ned, Lewine, Banton's girl & Jo: Limbery
   the gardener's boy.
the kitchen boy
Sept. 1651 made Will: Balch one suit of clothes & 2 shirts 12d a yard
   8 yards.   also Jonathan's clothes
cloth my own making   and the dyer hath for Mr Wyote for a suit of
   cloth   4 yards ½
also he hath for the liveries to dye   8 yards
Mr Wyote had a red baise waistcoat then

given John Burk the 26 of April 1653 cloth of my own making 4 yards ½
more of the same to make him a cloak
cut out of the same piece Octo. the 6 1653 for a coat for Ned Wingfield,
   also more then for a pillion cloth 2 yards ½

[p. 207]   1652 June the 21 left in the trunk with drawers one piece of the
livery of serge & a bunch of the lace.

In the great long trunk the best bed the canopy.

[p. 206]   1652 Decem. the 4th Decem. taken out of the chest where was
20 pieces of broad Irish cloth, cut up one piece of 14 yards & of one other
piece 3 yards & quarter.   And of narrow—4 pieces cut out of one them
being 20 yards 11 yards 3 quarters.

One of the 20 pieces had but 14 yards quarter left which made
draw room, table clothes breadth & half 3 yards long   2
side board of one breadth 2 yards & half   2
one other broad piece begun to be cut 3 yards & quarter made
   pillow-beres   3 pair
one of the narrow pieces 20 yards made large pillow beres 7 yards
   3 quarters   3 pair
also one breadth side board 2 yards long of fine broad canvas X   2
Cut out then out of a remnant of 9 yards & half
* table cloths for the gentle women long ones 2
shorter 1

October 1653 taken out two pieces of the Irish cloth to carry to London
   there to cut out for sheets, one of them was but 17 yards
cut out then out of a remnant of 9 yards & half

[p. 205]   servants came 1652 the 24th of June
Eliz: Loveden is to have by the year £20
Peter Raymond 12
the cook came the Lady Day before 16
Hern. Howard came again 10

[p. 189]   April the 26 1639   Received of my Lord towards my allowance
for maintenance 20; for taffety ribbon 24 yards 0 9 0; for 2 yards of lawn
0 16 0; for 6000 and 6 papers of pins 0 10 0; for 2 pair of penants 0 3 6;
for 2 woodbine flowers 0 2 6; for 14 yards of silver lace for the peach
coloured tabby 3 8 9; for mending my watch 0 8 6; received more £10 the
3 of May   for thread of several sorts 1 8 4; to Bold 5 0 6; to Rose 1 0 0;
to Besse 1 4 6; given to the burnt groom 0 5 0; for a fan 0 14 0; for broad
ribbon & gartering 0 19 0; for a black hood 0 3 0; for 1 lb of powder for
my hair 0 6 0; for 2 lbs [of powder] for linen 0 6 0; for a comb & brush
0 3 0; given at *Tarte* [?] Hall & to a porter 0 3 0; to my Lady Litleton's
nurse 0 10 0; for tape 3 bunches & 6 yards of filleting 0 6 6; spent 0 3 6;
for velvet 2 yards 2 quarters 1 15 0; received £10 the 18th of May   for
3 pair of silk stockings 3 15 0; for a poor minister 0 5 0; for paper; pens &
sand 0 3 04; other small ways 0 4 2; spent 2 5 0; in pence 0 5 0; to Lynn
0 1 0; for making up my velvet cabinet 1 17 4; for the case to my standish
0 5 6; for a razor 0 1 0; to Besse 1 10 0; to the guitar man 0 2 6; to my
cousin Guger 0 1 0; received the 30th of May £10   for canvas 0 14 0; to
the shoemaker 1 12 0; for gloves 4 4 6; to Mosier [?Monsieur] Masonet's
child 1 0 0; to a poor woman 0 0 6; to Mr Jumperd 1 5 0; to my Lady
Katherine Wentworth's man 0 1 0; to Sam: 0 2 0; to Mr Jumperd 0 7 0
sum ['44 0 0' crossed through] 46 13 9

[p. 190]   for a silver seal 0 4 6; [blank] 3 0 0; spent [illegible crossed
through] 0 12 0; for 7 lbs 5 ounces of crewels 2 0 0; for a present 0 1 0;
received this 27 of June £25   paid to Mr Hearn for silk 4 0 0; given away
4 10 6; for gold parchment lace 0 16 0; Besse Fuller's bill 0 8 4; paid my
cousin Lynn 12 0 0; to Susan Bellamy 1 0 0; for starching a night-stuff
cover 0 10 0; for making a band 0 5 0; a bill of Bolde's for ringers & other
gifts 1 6 10; to the coach-man's boy 0 1 0
[total] 77 10 3

Bought of a pedler 8 papers of Horne Flowers 0 4 6; for 7 yards ½ of
lawn at 8s the yard 2 18 0; for a yard & half of cobweb lawn at 4s the
yard 0 6 0; lost at play 0 6 6; lost at play 0 1 ['6' crossed through]
[total] 3 16 0

received from St: Walker's uncle at Exeter the 11th of August £6
1639   given of that money to Walker there at Exeter 0 10 0; paid to Bold
a debt of his of 1 15 0; ['so there remains to me but' crossed through] paid
Bills at London for him 3 15 0; given at *Bastaple* fair to Waker 0 5 0;
given to Walker when he went to his uncle 0 5 0; bought for Walker linen
1 13 0; received of my Lord £5 for Walker's wages the 27th of
October   so I have paid £2 8s 0 more than received paid for the making of
it 0 8 4; paid for a quarter's washing 0 6 0; paid a tailor's bill 1 1 8; paid
for Walker for a gold ring 0 5 0; received from St Walkers uncle at Exeter
the 9th day of March 1639 £5   paid a tailor for him 1 0 0; paid for linen

bought & made the 16th of March 3 2 6; paid for boots in London o 10 o; paid for washing at *Tawstok* o 8 o; to Walker o 5 o; paid his glover o 9 o; for his journey away & to redeem a coat 1 10 o; to Lak a debt & for his journey 1 3 o

[p. 191]   spent o 5 o; to Raingner o 10 o; to another o 2 o; for making 3 smocks o 4 o; to a passenger for *Iarland* o 2 6; to poor o 2 o; lost at play o 2 o; to my Lady Button's maid o 1 o; to a Loth-gear man o 2 6; to a poor man o 5 o; to ringers & poor at Fremington o 7 o; to a groom that brought me a horse 1 o o; lost at play o 16 6; to the fisher-men o 2 o; to a traveller o 5 o; to threshers o 1 o; to the poor the 13th of October o 10 o [total] 4 17 6

for a psalm book at London o 5 o; to bind Zachary's son 3 10 o; lost at play o 10 o; for needles o 10 o; received as due to myself £25 of that £160 which I received the 4th day of July 1639 4 8 o

received here in all 100 o o
paid also for Walker to Miss Eliza: Potts a debt of £6 o o
& to his linen draper Mr Barrow 1 10 o
so that his expenses by me amount to 26 2 o

[p. 192]   received the 26 day of October 1639 £45 os od; to Rose Tode o 5 o; to Baldwin for 3 quarter's wages 7 10 o; a debt to her 1 5 o; to Voysin her year's wages 10 o o; in gift more 5 o o; for pines [pins] o 15 o; for black & white ribbon o 4 o; for black twist o 1 o; given away o 1 6; to a tailor o 2 o; to a nurse o 5 o; to Bold a quarter's wages 2 10 o; to Bold given 2 o o; also to Bold at Christmas 1 o o; for 2 pair of worsted stockings o 13 o
spent in my journey to *Brewen* [Bruen] & *Apthorp* [Apethorpe] 30 11 6 at *Brewen* as by Bolde's bill 4 17 6; at *Northamton* 3 6 2; at *Apthorp* to my sister's nurse & midwife 4 o o; to Mrs Brograve for work 1 o o; spent more 14 o o; to Goody Hall 1 3 o; to blind John o 5 o; to Allby o 2 o; to the coach-man & Darby o 5 o; to Sam: o 9 o; to fiddlers at *Bridge-water* o 2 o; to poor o 7 o; in gifts o 15 6   [total] 30 12 2

at my Lady of Petterborow 2 15 o
received 145 o o
spent 154 13 9
['more than rec. 6 6 3' crossed through]
a bill of Bolde's o 12 o
more than received 6 6 3   [total] 33 19 2

[p. 193]   this I took out of moneys I received of Mr Smith & Mr Sowden 1640

received for my allowance 55 o o; to Bold for his wages the 25 of March 1640 5 o o; lent to Tom Wiotte the 16th of Feb. 1639 10 o o; for bone lace 3 11 6; at Christmas when I received o 11 o; to old William Timewell o 10 o; for 3 bands o 6 11; spent 4 8 9; sent to my old cousin Kemp 1 o o; for a tiffany hood laced o 12 o; for a tiffany hood o 4 6; for ribbon o 18 o; for thread & needles o 10 o; for 2 gorgets 1 6 o; for a wooden cabinet 1 12 o; for a mask & pendants o 10 o; for 2 flowers o 5 o; for pines [pins] o 5 o; for gloves & a fan 1 o 6; for 2 ells of Holland o 10 o; for a basket

0 2 6; spent 0 17 0; spent 1 9 2; for silk the 23 of April 1640 1 6 9; 1640 to Mr Clark for letting me blood 27 of April 0 5 0; to the poor at Easter & the minister 1 10 0; lost at play 0 6 0;—2 5 6; to Mary Thorpe an old bill 0 16 0; to Clemt. to buy a bible 0 4 0; for books 1 9 6

the total of all these receipts is 200 0 0

the total of all the expenses is 233 8 10

[p. 194] to Bold of his wages 2 0 0; in going to take the Air 0 3 0; for silk 1 6 6; for 6 yards of canvas 0 6 6; to Miss Gritty the Queen's dresser 1 10 0; for gelding a lock & key & hingells 0 5 0; the 22 of May 1640 5 0 0

for 10 yards 3 quarter of blue taffeta at 5s the yard 2 13 0; the 5th of June 1640 20 1 0; to Miriam for silk for my sheet ['1 2 0' crossed through.] to her for working ['1' crossed through.] 0 0; given to Harry the [blank] 2 0 0; for Mr Binnion 0 12 0; to Bold his wages before hand the 18th of June 1640 3 0 0; for Goody Hall the 20th of June 1640 4 0 0; Goody Homes 0 2 0; to Mr Griffeth for black stuff for gown & petticoat 4 5 6; given Bold 1 2 0 [total] 48 6 0 more than received 80 14 10

lost at play 0 9 0 this out of Mrs Smith's rent money; Bold the 23 of July 1640 3 0 0; to my old cousin Kemp the 1 of August 3 0 0; to Sam: at *Bastable* fair 1640 0 2 0; lost at play 0 2 0; to Tom: Armesby the baker 1640 given 1 0 0 to Baldwin a bill paid the 15th of Sept: 1640 1 3 0; to Voysin lost at play to her 0 4 0; a bill of Bold's 1 7 0; Bold 0 8 0 ['10 15 0' crossed through.]

[p. 195] to the town of *Tanton* the 20th of Sept. 1640 2 0 0; ['to my cousin Kemp in part of my sister Ka: watch the 23 of Sept. 1640 4 0 0' crossed through.]; to Mr Hazard the dancer the 8th of October 1640 4 0 0; to Mr Hazard's boy 0 5 0; for a baize petticoat & waistcoat the 10th of Octo. 1640 0 14 6; to Voysin the 15th of Octo. 1640 her year's wages 10 0 0; to Baldwin for ['a quarter of' crossed through.] a whole years then 10 0 0; paid a little bill of Voysin's 0 10 0; to Rose for half a year's wages the 15th of Octo. 1640 1 10 0; to Mr Blanchard of Fremington 1640 1 0 0; to 2 maid's charges at market 0 1 2; for dyes 0 6 0; to my cousin Kemp 2 0 0; to Bold the 22 of Octo. 1640 onward of his wages 2 0 0 [total] 49 1 8

to Miriam Terry in Novem. 1640 4 0 0; to Nurse Moys 0 5 0; to Barbery Tomkins 0 10 0; to Bold 4 0 0; to Mary Thorpe 1 1 0; to Harnybye's wife 0 5 0 [total] 10 1 0

in these accounts I received from my Lord £120 & after out of monies received for him £25 after that again £55 in all £200 spent 340 17 6 spent more than received 140 17 6 [signed] R. Bathe

the total receipts from the 4th of March 1638 till the 17th of Decem. 1640 3531 10 4

disbursed 3021 1 8
remains 510 8 8
disbursed from the 4th of March 1638 until the 29th of May 1641
4547 12 1 Ex.

[p. 196]  Slowely came about the 25 of March 1639 [£]5, he hath received of me the 18 of March 1640  30 0 0, also by the misreckoning of his account 1641  5 0 0, he died in London at my Lord's house on Tuesday the 2 of May 1642, also the 5 day being Friday there died Tho: Sweet the coachman. Slowely had more £5
I made Slow. accounts straight since his coming to the first of October 1641 & there remained in his hands £0 16s 1d. Besides this which I account to be his wages.

he came at Midsummer 1642   To Keepe the coach-man the 17th of April 1643  4 0 0, also this Audit 1643  4 0 0, and now this 2 of May 1644 4 0 0. the 17th of August Will: Lynn paid Keepe's wife for him 2 0 0, 1645 the stew. paid him for our Lady Day last this May 4 0 0.

to the cook came at Midsummer 1641 had the first half year 5 0 0, from St Thomas to the same time 1642  16 0 0, & the April [sic] 1643  4 0 0, & in August 1643  4 0 0, & the Audit after the like 4 0 0. James had also his quarter due now   ['& the 15th of Jan. by the steward in 1643 for his quarter 4 0 0' crossed through] to the cook the 30th of March 1644  8 0 0, Will: Linne paid his wife at Mich. 1643 in London also 4 0 0, also to his wife at Christmas 1643  1 0 0, so at the Audit 1644 there will be due to the cook £3.

Thomas Pollard came in October 1640. paid in Octo. 1641  10 0 0, paid by Will: Lynn in Decem. 1642  10 0 0, paid to Thom: Polla. the 13th of Nove. 1643  10 0 0, paid him this 2 of May 1644 for our Lady Day 5 0 0

[p. 197]  I paid his bills & £2 gift & £3   Edward Barry which came to my Lord when Edward earl of Bath died was to have £10 a year received of me the 15th of June 1640  5 0 0, also the 18th of October 1640  10 0 0, also the 6th day of May 1641  10 0 0, also the 23th of Jan. 1641  5 0 0, also the 31 of Feb. 1641  5 0 0, the 1 of Novem. 1642  5 0 0, to Ned Barry the 17th of April 1643  5 0 0, to Ned Barry at his going away at Oxford in Oct. 1645 in full 15 0 0

he came a little before Michaelmas   Dick the barber the 17th of April 1643  2 0 0, also for Michael. 1643  2 0 0

to John Burd now began this 26 of Octo. 1644  2 0 0, the steward paid him the Lady Day wages 2 0 0

Wiote came a little before Barry or at the same time is to have the like in the beginning of 1637 he received of me the 28th of Octo. 1643 for 2 years (leaving yet unpaid 4 years £45 wages & a half) the sum of 20 0 0, to Tho: Wiote the 26th of Octo. 1644 in part of £55  5 0 0, to him due at our Lady Day 3 0 0, to Tho: Wiote a copy for his life in Davie's tenement in *Warkly* in hand for 46 0 0, & paying for a licence to dwell from it

so now due to him £4 since paid him

**[p. 198]**   Ralph Booth came [blank]
hath received of me the 15th of June 1640   5 0 0, also the 8th of March
1640   2 10 0, also the 10th of April 1641   2 10 0, my Lord gave him at
Oxford in Nov. 1643   1 0 0

William Booth came the later end of April 1644

Howard came in January 1640, went away in August 1643, had his full
wages of £10 a year 25

Audit 1643   Richard Polla. steward these last 3 years hath had 60 0 0, &
now this 30th of March 1644 allowed him he having moneys in his hands,
for his half year wages 10 0 0

**[p. 199]**   Mr ['Bouing' crossed through] William Bouchier came in
January 1638 rec. of my Lord 10 0 0, of Coyse 5 0 0, also 2 0 0, received
of me the 10th of May 1640   5 0 0, also the 15th of June 1640   5 0 0
also the 12th of February 1640   3 0 0, also the 13th of April 1641   2 0 0,
and the 18th of October also in 1640   8 0 0, also the 5th of August 1641
2 0 0   [total] £12.   by Hardwick in Octo. 1641   1 10 0, paid him in full
to Michaelmas 1641 [to] the 4th of Nov. 11 10 0, paid the 1 of Novem.
1642   10 0 0, to Mr Bouchier the 17th of April 1643   10 0 0, to
Mr Bouchier the 13th of Octo. 1643 £10 so at next Jan. will be due to him
£15, to Mr Bouchier the 30th of March 1644   05 0 0, to Mr Bouchier the
30th of August 1644 at *Trevenege* 1 0 0. 24 now due this Audit whereof
paid by Mr Butler of *Exetor* to him now 5 0 0, & also this 21 of Octo. at
Bowe he rece. more 5 0 0, £14 now due to Mr Bouchier in full of all dues
to the 26 of Octo. 1644   14 0 0
[total] £115

Rusell came in Octo. 1641

Pollard gave him by my command at *Tawstok* the 25 of Octo. 1 0 0.

The Postillian came the 25th of March 1644 is to have 50s a year & one
suit of clothes

**[p. 200]**   Robert Woode came in January 1638
['R. Wood in my hands £0 this 14th of Dece. besides his quarter from
Michaelmas' crossed through] received of my Lord the first year 4 0 0, also
the 5th of August 1641   6 0 0, & now this 18th of May 1642   5 0 0, paid
the 1 of Novem. 1642   5 0 0, also the 17th of April 1643   4 0 0, also in
Octo. after then 4 0 0, also paid him by the steward at *Exetor* the 14th of
Dece. 1643   5 0 0, to Robin Wood the 3rd of March 1643 in full until our
Lady Day 5 0 0, to Robin Wood the 2d of May 1644 due at our Lady Day
4 0 0, the steward paid him the 26 of August 1643   2 0 0.

Thomas Cannam came again in January 1640

the 5 of August 1641   5 0 0

Jonas Pulvey came in Jan. 1640 & stayed till the next March after received
4 0 0.

Walker came in March 1639 & stayed one whole year & half received for
that time 15 0 0

**[p. 201]**   he died of the small pox in Lent 1642 at Taw.   Jack Paine came in August 1639 hath had 4 0 0, in full discharge this 29th of June 1641 3 0 0, he had of Richard Pollard the 25 of Octo. 1641 in full 1 0 0, his father had after his death of R. Polla. 2 0 0

Samuel Starling came [blank]. he died in August 1644

**[p. 202]**   Rich: Cob came the beginning of Sept. 1641

due £04   paid by R. Pollard at several times 4 0 0, & the 24th of Octo. 1643 in full of one year's wages 10 0 0, paid the 5th of Feb. 1643 in part of £14 due to him 10 0 0, paid Rich: Cob the 26 of Octo. in part of £18 then due 14 0 0, to Cob the 28 of April 1645 in part of £11 7 0 0, to Cob the 22 of Octo. 1645 in part of £11 7 0 0

Robert Whitfield came [blank]

**[enclosure 202a]**   A note of all my Lord's arms at *Tawstok* in the armoury 1 Feb. 1643

*First*, of musket 10, Item of calivers 7, Item of harquebuses 7, Item of halberds 6, Item of black bills 10, Item cuirasses 17, Item coats of mail 10, Item of horse-men's arms 3, Item carbines 1, Item arms for pike men 10, Item armour of proof 1, Item swords 3, Item brass base 1, Item of head pieces 32, Item old pistols 1

My Lord's own arms & some pieces more left with a armourer in London cost £25

the 2nd of April 1648

**[enclosure 202b]**   [legal paper regarding estate matters, n.d.]

**[p. 203]**   Voysin came in Decem. 1638 had the first year 15 0 0 & ever since fully paid to this present Audit 1643. This 30th of March 1644 paid as her half years wages 5 0 0, the like the 26 of Octo. 1644 5 0 0, the 28th of April 1645 to her 5 0 0, to Voysin the 22 of Octo. 1645 5 0 0

And to Rebecca Lovett then in Octo. 1644 5 0 0 & to her at Lady Day 5. To Lovet the 22 of Octo. 1645 5 0 0

Eliza: Seirle came in Feb. 1639

the 15th of Octo. 1640 1 10 0, the 5th of August 1641 2 0 0, she went from me in August 1643. And to Hardwick in part of £10 then due in Octo. 1644 5 0 0

Alice came in Jan. 1638 had 40s a year, she married from me the 20th of Nov. 1643

the 5 of August 1641 0 10 0

**[p. 204]**   Due to my Lord from the King.

For his Majesty's first journey against the Scots in March 1638 500 0 0. for subsidies £64   delivered to Sir Tho: Mints in Devon at the time Sir Ralph Hopton passed in to Cornwall in the year 1642 100 0 0. for the Gr. ride £80   To Captain Slingsby about that time 020 0 0. Also then to the Earl of *Bristowe* son John Digbey 040 0 0 Creation money & Impost money for the year 1642 when my Lord both gave his New Year's Gift & paid the fees for that which he never had.

For 5 good horses
for arms & ammunition
for the 100 thousand pound ordered to be lent the King at their first great
meeting at Oxford in Jan. 1643 Lent towards it by my Lord at *Exetor* to
the Mayor the 18th of March 1643  200 0 0
The fee due for his diet from Jan. 1643 [blank]

[p. 188]  Provision bought at *Bristole* [Bristol] by Rich: Pollard for
Christmas 1643

sack 2 hogsheads £12 per hogshead 24 0 0, soap 2 barrels 212 lbs at 23 per
hundred 2 8 6, currants 3 9 9, sugar 7 3 4, raisins of the sun 1 17 6, prunes
1 19 0, aniseed 0 5 0, licorice 0 3 0, sanders [alexanders] 0 1 4, candy 0 6 0,
nuts 0 12 0, cloves 0 3 6, ginger 0 2 6, cinnamon 0 7 0, small white starch
24 lbs at 5d per lb 0 10 0, p: blue 0 2 4, brimstone 1 pound 0 0 6,
carraway seeds 3 lbs 0 3 0, almonds jar 6 lbs 0 12 0, pepper 12 lbs at
2s 4d per lb 1 8 0, capers 9 lbs & vinegar to them 6d 0 5 0, large mace 1 lb
0 16 0, 4 quire of paper 0 1 4, 2 barrels 0 5 0, one barrel with capers is
0 2 6, 4 bags 0 2 0, 2 barrels more 0 2 0, 4 quarts & one pint of olives at
1s 10d per quart 0 8 3, the barrel for them 0 0 6, 2 gallons of red wine &
the barrel 0 5 0, given to the cooper &c 0 2 6, 15 ounces of syrup of
mulberries 0 5 0, for the bottle for it 0 0 4
the steward's charges 48 11 1
Spent in a journey to *Exetor* with 27 horse 26 men in 5 days 17 7 11
besides laid out by myself in extraordinaries 8 7 6
Spent in a journey to *Ilford Combe* [Ilfracombe] the 16th day of May
1644  2 8 7

[p. 187]  Disbursed from the 29th of May 1641
To Pollard the 1 day of June 1641 £74 14s 0d; to Mr Norburn for his
advice about my jointure 3 0 0; to his men for drawing it by bill 3 17 0; to
Mr King in part of his bill 7 13 0; to Mr Tutt in part of his bill 20 0 0; to
Mr Cutburd in part of his bill 20 0 0; to the coach-maker the full of
another bill 13 0 0; to Mr Austin in part of his bill 20 0 0; to Mr Pasmore
in part of his bill 10 0 0; to Sir Antony Vandick in part for my picture
20 0 0; to Goody Hall by Willy: Lynn in May 0 10 0; by Wi: Lynn to
another 2 0 0; to a poor woman by my Lord 1 0 0; the brick-layers bill
1 11 0; for ribbon 0 8 6; for a cistern which cost 44s  2 0 0; to Darby in
full discharge 2 10 0; to my Lord 0 10 0; to Bold the 2 of June 2 0 0
this 4 of June sum total 204 13 6 Ex.

to Mr Allen in full of a bond of £62 14s 0d & also towards the payment of
another bill of the 4th day of June 1641 paid him £80 0s 0d; delivered to
Wiote the 4th of June 19 3 4; to Slowely to buy hay the 4th of June 2 0 0;
for crewel, silks & canvas the 8th of June 6 13 0; the same day for the
subsidies 32 0 0; to Sir Antony Vandick for my picture 10 0 0; for the
frame 4 0 0; to his man 1 0 0; for bone lace 11 3 6; for gloves & ribbon to
Mr Bradburn 2 15 0; to Doctor Moore for Pollard 1 0 0; to my Lord the
13th of June 1641  1 0 0; to Bold for the kitchen the 14th of June 1641
5 0 0
this 14th of June 1641 sum total 175 14 10 ex.

[p. 186]   Lost at play 0 5s 0; to Doctor Moore for Pollard 1 0 0; delivered
to Slowely the 24th of June 1641  2 10 0; delivered to Bold the 24th of
June 1641 for the kitchen 5 0 0; to Mr Ridder sri: & his man the later end
of May 1641  22 10 0; 20 20. paid the chandler by Slowely as charged
upon him for oats the 25 of June 1641  20 0 0; to Dawson the brick-layer
in part toward the building the 26th of June 1641  50 0 0; to Mr William
Beare in full of all his bills June 28th 8 9 6; to my Lord the 28th of June
1641  1 0 0; to the Farriour his last quarter as by bill 5 6 0; to Mr Mason
in part of his bill the 28 of June 1641 being 33 14 6 paid 10 0 0; paid the
coach-maker then the full of the quarter betwixt Michaelmas & Christmas
20 0 0; paid the butcher in full discharge of 6 bills beginning the [blank] of
[blank] to the 25 of June 1641  43 5 0; Jack-Paine in full of his wages the
29th of June 3 0 0; to Robert Woode to pay 3 bills for wine 6 0 0; to
Mr Goffe in full of his bill of £83 the last of June 20 0 0; to Mr Nitingall
in part of [blank] the same day 10 0 0; also in full more to Mr Goffe 3 0 0;
['for the iron chest 4 0 0' crossed through] paid Mr Webber's bill in full
the 1 of July 1641  9 10 0; for hats 2 several bills 12 0 0; paid the
fringe-maker in full of his bill 17 12 0; paid the shoe-maker for the
foot-man 2 6 6; Mr Bellamy for books 1 8 0; for washing Dick Burton's
linen 0 10 0; to Bold for the House the 1 of July 5 0 0; paid the wax
chandler in full 10 0 0; to Mr Beare & Hackwell for fees 2 0 0; for a
11 yards [sic] & half of French tabby 5 3 6; paid for a small iron chest
4 0 0; to Doctor Gibbes 0 10 0; paid a butter-woman's bill the 3 of July
7 0 0; my Lord's shoe-maker paid 0 10 0; to the carpenter for work to be
done about my building in Lincon's Ine Fieldes the 8th of July 1641
40 0 0; for my Lord's poll-money the 10th of July 1641  40 0 0; to
Sargeant Powell in full for his stables the 10th of July 1641  12 0 0
441 15 6   sum 445 15 6 ex.

[p. 185]   To the woman that kept Pollard when he was sick 1 0 0; to Bold
for the kitchen the 6th of July 1641  4 16 6

To one Pallam an organist for work to be done 7 0 0; to the nurse &
midwife when my Lord christened Harry Fane my brother France's son
4 0 0; to the over-seers for the poor for Midsummer quarter 0 10 0; to my
Lord the 8th of July 0 10 0; to lawyers in Midsummer term 8 10 0; Willy:
Lynn 2 journeys to London 2 10 0; for 5 brass cokes for *Tawstok* 0 14 6;
delivered to Slowely the 17th of July 1641  5 0 0; to Doctor Moore the
19th of July 1 0 0; to Bold the 19th of July 1 0 0; to Doctor Moore 1 0 0;
to my Lord the 23 of July 1 0 0; to Mr David Murrey his quarter's rent
Midsummer 25 0 6; to the mason in part for work to be done 10 0 0; to
the armourer in full of his bill the 22 of July 4 0 0; to Christian her full
wages 1 0 0; to the clerk for his whole year's allowances 0 6 0; to Bold the
26 of July 1641 for himself 1 0 0; to a Spaniard's servant brought a present
& the maid 0 12 6; to men that brought a little pair of organs the 27 July
0 5 0; pollard paid to Choyze 0 10 0; to a man in the Turks hands 2 0 0;
paid Pollard in full of all to the 24th of July the 27 91 17 10
[total] 189 02 10

to Nan Howard due at Midsummer last the 29th of July 4 0 0; paid a
grocer that Mr Willy: Beare bought of the 30th July 10 0 0

paid a mercer in *Patternostre* Row for 2 suits, taffety & stuff my brother
Robin & H. Howard the 5 of August 11 12 0; paid the smith for the iron
grates over the vault 2 12 6; one other smith for work done 0 5 6; Irish
Tom for a hat the 4th of August 0 5 6; a carpenter at 2s the day for
making & setting up shelfs 0 7 0; to Mr Bouchier the 5th of August 1641
2 0 0; to Robin Woode the same day 6 0 0; to Besse Seirle then 2 0 0; to
Alice Teirle also 0 10 0; to Thomas Cannam 5 0 0; to Cobley 0 10 0; to
*Brewern* Carrier for bring up a horse 0 4 0
ex. 220 0 4 sum 289 19 4

[p. 184]   paid a grocer's bill the 5th day of August 1641 £14 10s 0d; paid
the brick-layer more the 5 day of August 1641 40 0 0; delivered to
Slowely the same day 1641 3 0 0; paid the Chandler for oats the 6 day of
August 10 0 0; paid Mr Pasmore the same day 1641 20 0 0; for wine at
St Giles 0 17 6; to Mr Tomkines in full of £9 given for a viol 3 0 0; given
Alice 1 0 0; to a poor Minister 0 5 0; for going by water 0 5 0; put in my
purse for poor 0 10 0; to Wiott the 8th of August 1641 being to go to
Want. 5 0 0; for diverse wooden & tin ware 1 10 0; to Pollard in full
payment to the 7th of August 30 2 5; paid my Lord's shoemaker's bill the
10th of August 1 13 0; to Willy: Lynn the 9th of August when he went to
Wantage 3 0 0; to Old Pott given 3 0 0; to the water woman for work
done 0 15 0; for ferrying my coach & 6 horses to *Lambath* 0 5 6; for
casting of waters 0 3 0; paid my shoemaker his bill the 10th of August
1 13 0; to Bold then 1 0 0; for powder 0 2 0; paid 2 bills for wine 5 9 0;
paid the chandler Mr Smith for oats in full of 91 16 0 for the time of being
in London 19 14 0; paid the apothecary Mr Hyckes in part of £9 1 3
5 0 0; the whole bills for the bear [beer] this time comes to £68 4s 0d,
whereof before paid 44 12 0 & now 16 5 6, so remains unspent & unpaid
£7 0 0; a bill of a dripping pan 1 10 0; given the boy 0 2 6; gloves for my
Lord the 11th of August 0 17 0; for fees as by bill to Clarke & officers of
the Council Board the 9th day of August 1641 25 0 0; paid by Willy:
Lynn & Thom: Wiote to Baronet Portman for 11 years High rents at
10d by the year for my Lord's 4th part of the manor of *Corten-Dinan*
[Corton Denham] 0 9 2; more at that time for suit of court 0 8 0; for my
Lord of Arundell's man brought me a cabinet 2 0 0; spent in our journey
to *Tawstok* in August 1641 30 5 4
248 11 11 ex.   [total] 248 11 11

[p. 183]   for oysters £0 5s 0d; to my Lord the 2 of Sept. 1641 0 10 0; the
2 of Sept. 1641 paid Mrs Mary Downe in full of £100 due at Christmas
last £50 0s 0d; disbursed from the 29th of May until this 2 of Sept.
1365 10 1 ex.

E.   Upon my own occasion the 8th of Sept. 1641 £11 0 0; paid to Doctor
Downe the 10th of Sept. 1641 10 0 0; to Richard Pollard steward the
21 day of Sept. 1641 07 0 0; Willy: Lynn paid it to Miss Mary Downe
paid the 8th of October 1641 in full of last year's £100 whereof Mr Pagget
paid by my appointment then £50 & by myself I paid £2 for allowance
£050 0 0; Mr Scikner had of me the 18th of Octo. 1641 to return which I
received ['200' crossed through] 0 0; S:R:S:   Mr Nottell's servant had of
me the 22 of Octo: to return this is received also ['200' crossed
through] 0 0; taken a full account of Mr Paget the 23th of October 1641

from 1637 so paid him this present day 618 18 7 & assigned him from
Wattsonn £100, from Langdon £70, from Perin out of *Ierland* £100, &
from John Scitch £30, being £300 which is in full of 918 18 7; paid
Hardwick for her whole year's wages £10 0 0; delivered to Pollard the
25 of Octo. the other Mr Slowely had £200 of this Mr Scikner returned
['300' crossed through] 0 0 the 2 whereof is to be returned to me presently
the other to pay Mr Slowely 100 0 0; to my Lord the 25 of Octo: being
the day we begin our journey for London 001 0 0; to Pollard to pay the
Organist 0['33' crossed through] but rec. the £10 back again 23 0 0; paid
Mr Tomkins for his being at *Tawstok* 3 mon. 005 0 0, he had also of
Richard Pollard £1 10s 0, & kept his girl & gave her clothes; lost at cards
0 1 0; spend in our journey 6 days travelling with 24 horse & men
025 12 0; paid Mr King the 4 of Novem. 1641 in part 010 0 0; given
Voysin the same day for her wages due at Michaelmas 1641 010 0 0; given
Mr Bouchier in full of his allowance to the same time 011 10 0; for a little
psalm book 0 5 0; laid out by Howard 0 3 0; to Harry Howard due at
Michalemas also 5 0 0; to Thomas Pollard besides £100 which he received
before I came £10 0 0; also due to him for his year's wages now due
10 0 0; lost at cards 0 7 8
1058 17 3    958 17 3

[p. 182]    paid Mr Austin the 6th of Nove: 1641  21 2 6; paid the cook
what he laid out by the way to London 0 4 6; delivered to Thomas Pollard
the 6th of Novem. 40 0 0; paid a bill of Bold's 0 5 6; paid Lewis the 6th of
Novem. for a copy of my own Dick to the [illegible] 18s & also for the
chimney pieces of Moyses & now there is £3 due for Luere 10 0 0; paid
Mr Nightingal in full of a sum of 18 7 9 the 8th of Novem. 1641  18 7 6;
paid Mr Parris bills the same day 11 0 0; paid Mr Pasmore the same day
20 0 0; to Susan Baldwin the 9th of Nove: her whole year's wages 10 0 0;
paid Mr Murrey's quarter rent due at Michaelmas 1641  25 0 0; to my
Lord the 8th of Nove. 01 0 0; paid a tailor for myself his bill 5 10 0; paid
Mr King in full of his old bill the 10th of Novem. 20 0 0; paid the
coach-maker in part of a bill of £43 14s 8d whereof Pollard paid him £10
before I came to town & I the 10th of Novem. 10 0 0; paid the sadler in
full of his bill 10 9 0; paid Mr Dunsterfielld the 15th of Nove. in part
20 0 0; paid Bold a little bill then 0 6 6  [total] 1121 2 8

sent a token to Miss Young the 13th of Novem. 4 0 0; paid Mr Mason in
part of £23 due to him upon his bill 10 0 0; paid for a pair of ebony tables
& men 01 15 0; paid Mr Read the 16th of Nov. in part of 39  19 0 0; paid
Mr Bellamy for the woman of which I bought my best looking glass
20 0 0; also for 1 dozen of gloves for myself 0 15 0; paid at the Green
Dragon for an ebony perfumed box 3 0 0; there for mending my sables
0 2 0; to my Lord the 21 of Novem. 1 0 0; for my lord's last 2 subsidies
the 23th of Novem. 1640  32 0 0; paid Mr Pasmor the 23 of Novem. 1641
29 0 0; paid the scrivenor Ridger the 24th of Novem. 1641 in full of one
bond 312 0 0; also interest for £200  08 0 0; & to the man & to the porter
01 4 0; for ribbons for myself & garters & roses for 6 men 02 6 0; paid the
apothecary Hyx in full the 27th of Nov. 1641  4 0 0; paid the coach-maker
more in part of his bill 5 0 0; a bill of Bold's 0 15 6; to my cousin Jarvis

due at Michaelmas 1641  1 0 0; paid Alexander the porter in full of his
wages to this Christmas 2 0 0; paid Willy: Lynn in part of his bill for a
horse & other layings out which comes to 26 15 2 paid the 29th of
Novem. 6 15 0  [total] 686 15 0

[p. 181]  paid the cook in part of his wages where I received before from
Pollard £1 & now the 27 of Novem. by me 1 0 0; for pins for myself
0 10 0; paid Pollard in full to this 29th of Novem. 1641  37 8 8; paid the
brick-layer Willy: Dodson the 24th of Novem. in part 30 0 0; paid the
mason then Richard Veze in part 20 0 0; paid the plumber for his work in
full 8 10 0; given my Lord Mantraversse's chair men 0 5 0; 106 7 4 paid to
Thom: Wiote the 2 of Decem. 1641  14 0 0 there remains due to him
£2 10s 2d; paid Willy: Lynn in full of his bill the 2 of Decem. 1641
20 0 0; delivered Pollard the last of Novem. 1641  20 0 0; paid for
15 chaldron of sea coal & billet & faggot & scotch coal [blank] the 7 of
Decem. 1641  40 0 0; paid for grocery the same day 12 0 0; given my
cousin Fitzwilliamese's nurse & midwife 2 0 0; taken out for my spending
by Bold the 3 of Dece. 1 10 0; paid a bill for swords of one John Allsupp
the 14th of Dec. 2 10 0; paid Pollard in full for the week book to the 11th
of Decem. 27 7 7; delivered him the same day being the 14th of Dece. for
the hay 20 0 0; paid Willy: Lynn a bill then 04 19 6; given Mr Willy:
Tomkins at the same day 02 0 0; paid Mr Pasmor in full of £120 14s 0 &
7s 10 17 0; paid Mr Mason the upholsterer in full of his bill of 63 14 6
paid 13 13 6; takend out by Bold 1 10 0; paid the coach-maker in full of
his bill of £43 ending in March 1641, paid him this 17th of Dece. 1641
18 14 0; ['lent my brother George the same day £22' crossed through] paid
Mr Tutt in part of his bill of £130 this 18th of Dece. 1641  20 0 0; paid
Mr Olibear in part of his bill of [blank] the same day 20 0 0; given
Mr Hathorn 01 0 0; paid for my Lord's sword the 20th of Decem.
03 12 6; paid Mr Parsons in full his bill of 2 4 0; paid in full to the farrier
for 2 qrs shoeing this 22 of Dec. 6 0 0; paid in full the ostler's bill at the
Maiden-head 3 11 4; delivered to Pollard the 23 of Decem. 1641  30 0 0;
given at the church the 25 of Decem. 0 10 0; put in my purse then 0 6 0;
to Bold the 24 of Decem. 1641  1 0 0; to my Lord the 25 of Decem. 1 0 0;
for ribbon the 27 of De. 1 14 0
£399 13s 1d  [total] 399 13 0

[p. 180]  given the ['Kings' crossed through] Prince's drummers at
Christmas 0 10 0; to the Queen's foot-men then 1 0 0; to the King his
New Year's Gift 20 0 0; in fees more 2 0 0; paid for the plate more than
the allowance 2 14 0; given to the porters at White Hall 0 10 0; given in
the presence Cham. then 0 10 0; given Rose then 0 5 0; to Alice & Wilmot
0 5 0; to the cook 0 5 0; & to his children 0 5 0; to the coach-man 0 5 0;
to Dick & Cobley 0 5 0; to the page & footmen 0 8 0; 1641 paid Tom:
Cannam in full of his wages the 31 of Dec. 5 0 0; given the King's
drummers 1 0 0  [total] 35 2 0

Sum total from the 2 of Sept. 1641 disbursed till the 1 of January following
is 2080 2 1
And due to me as appears the 2 of Sept. last 0181 4 10  [total] 2261 7 2

to Nan Howard due this Jan. 1641  4 0 0; to my Lord of Arundell's
lodging keepers 0 15 0; paid Mis Bethell in full of all payments the 8th of
Jan. 1641  48 0 0; delivered Pollard the 10th of Jan. 1641 for the House
Keeping 68 5 5½; paid the shoemaker for Sam: Starling by bill 0 19 6; also
paid him for Bold then 1 0 0; paid my cook in full of his wages till
Christmas 3 0 0; delivered Pollard the 17th of Jan. 1641  28 14 6; paid the
Doctor for Robert Woode then 02 0 0; given the 14th of Jan. 1641 to be
sent 2 0 0; to Mr Hazard the 17th of Jan. who came but 5 times 1 0 0; to
the mason in full of 29 9 0 for paving the great court the 18th of Jan.
9 5 0; to Slowely the 18th of Jan. 1641 in full 5 0 0; paid for gloves &
ribbons 1 19 0; paid the shoemaker for the page & footmen 1 19 6; to Ned
Barry the 23 of Jan. 1641  5 0 0; to my Lord the 18th of Jan. 1 0 0; to the
King's footmen at New Year's Tide 1 0 0; to the King's gardener 1 0 0; to
my Lord 1 0 0; ['to the Queen's jeweller' crossed through] 0 0 0
186 17 14 ex.   [total] 186 18 0

[p. 179]   to the King's ['garde' crossed through] porters 0 10 0; to my
Lord Mantraversse chairmen 0 7 6; given 0 5 0; also to poor 0 4 8; for
pens, sand & paper 0 4 0; for pamphlets 0 1 0; to Robin Wood's physician
2 0 0; to the glover his bill 3 5 0; to my Lord 1 0 0; paid Mr Cutburd in
full of [blank] the 25 of Jan. 1641  29 9 0; paid Mr Barrow in part of
54 8 5 the 27 of Jan. 1641  20 0 0; paid the bite maker in full 2 5 0; paid
Mr Austin in full the 27 of Jan. 1641  20 0 0; paid Mr Goldsmith in part
then 20 0 0; paid Mary Thrope in full 04 6 6; paid Mr Olibear in part the
28 of Jan. 1641  20 0 0; spent in one journey to *Windzor* [Windsor] my
Lord & I one night 2 7 6; my Lord went & came in a day his horses lieing
1 16 9; given a fee to Mr Bishe the 4th of Feb. 1641  1 0 0; spent one
other journey to *Windzore* the 8th of Feb. 2 4 2; paid Mr Murrey his
Christmas rent the 9th of Feb. 1641  25 0 0; delivered to Pollard then
33 9 6; delivered to Pollard the 13th of Feb. 1641  35 13 8; paid
Mr Webber in part of his bill of £11 9s 0d the same day 5 0 0; paid Ned
Barry for wages the 13th of Feb. 1641  5 0 0; paid the brewer a little
before 8 2 0; ['paid Mary Thorpe in full 4 60' crossed through] to my
Lord 6 0 0; paid in a little bill [blank]; in 2d 5 0 0; in ½ pence 0 10 0; by
bills 2 6 8; paid Susan Baldwin for £200 due the 10th of Jan. 1641  8 0 0;
paid the coach-maker in full till my last coming to town 17 6 0; paid the
free mason in part of £26 in Feb. 1641  10 0 0; T.P. he had £1 15s
before   paid Dick the cook the 4th of March 1641 for wages now due
3 5 0; paid Mr Dunsterfielld in part of 29 14 7 paid the 5 of March 1641
9 14 0; paid Pollard the 5 of March 1641  43 10 41; to the doctor the 15 of
March 1641  1 0 0   [total] 355 3 3

[p. 178, page cut approximately 2½" down]   for ribbon & gloves [cut
away]; for 2 long bowes for my Lord 1 10 [cut away]; to Mr Tomkins
from B: 0 10 0; paid my cousin Jervis her anuity due this La. day 1 0 0;
band strings for my Lord & the foot-men 0 8 0; paid for 2 red velvet night
boxes & a cymbal 3 4 0; delivered Thom: Pollard the 28 of March 1642
17 0 0; delivered to Thom: Pollard the 5th of April 1642  20 0 0; delivered
to Thom: Pollard the 14th of April 1642  20 0 0; paid Coneway for a
coach-horse bought in April 1642  18 0 0; delivered my Lord the 21 of
April 01 0 0; paid the 26 of April to Mr Pasmor in part of £56 & 26

16 0 0; delivered to Pollard the 28th of April 30 0 0; paid T. Pollard a bill the 29 of April 22 10 6; taken to carry in my journey to *Merryworth* [Mereworth] then 5 0 0; spent more in my journey in to Kent at that time being 19, we stayed there a fortnight [blank]; paid Dick the cook at his going away the 20th of May 1642 in full 2 0 0; paid Robert Wood in part of £13 due to him for wages then 5 0 0; for my Lord the 18th of May 1642 2 0 0; taken for my journey to York this 25 of May 1642 62 0 0 & spent £100 & £40 & 22 all in my Lord's journey to York 162 0 0; the 5th of August 1642 paid Mr Smith the £100 that week should have paid 100 0 0; taken with me to *Exetor* £8 of Hardwick's money I last received & £11 of that I had to York 019 0 0; delivered to R: Pollard when my Lord went into *Cornwell* 06 0 0; in August paid Mr Skiner for so much received by Thom: Pollard of Sowden 50 0 0; paid then Mr Lamb for my Lord's black cloth 021 0 0; to my Lord 000 13 6; lost at play 0 5 6; paid the carrier at twice in August & Sept. 1642 015 0 0; to Willy: Elis the bailiff 020 0 0; to the steward a little after 028 0 0; to a porter 1 2 0; to Rose part of her wages the 17th of Sept. 1642 0 10 0

**[p. 177, reverse of cut page]** spent at Torrington the 22 of Sept. 2 0 0; to Wiote the 21 of March 1641 for himself 3 0 0; also for his journey then into Devon 3 0 0; to Mary Thorp 1 1 0; paid a bill of Willy: Lynn's 3 19 7; paid for bone lace the 27 of March 1642 10 10 0; for emerod pendants 1 5 0; paid the carrier the 19th of Sept. 1642 10 0 0; paid Doctor Downe in part of £100 which is since wholly paid but then the 20th of Sept. 1642 paid 40 0 0; SJM MH 100 0 0; KD 40 0 0; 60 KPS 20 0 0; paid to the cook at the Tower the later end of Octo. & other ways 5 7 6; £52 brought up for my journey & then spent £32 & 8 11 6 to Thomas Pollard the 15th of Octo. 1642 14 12 6; 1642 paid to Mr Bouchier due at Midsummer but paid this present 1 of Nove. 10 0 0; paid then to Voysin for her year's wages 10 0 0; also to Baldwin then 10 0 0; delivered to Thom: Pollard for the House 5 10 6; to Tho: Pollard to pay the butcher being due in August 08 9 6; also to Pollard to pay a debt borrowed before I came to town 10 0 0; paid to Ned Barry then 5 0 0; to Nan: Howard the 1 of Nove. but due a Midsummer 4 0 0; to Roger his whole year's wages now due 4 0 0; ['to Robin Wood that I borrowed' crossed through] 0 0 0; ['more to' crossed through] To Robin Wood for wages the 1 of Nove. 1642 5 0 0; 100 to Mr Murrey for his Michaelmas quarter 28 0 0; to the coach-maker in part of his bills the 9th of Nov. 10 0 0, & paid about Bartholomew tide by Thom: Pollard £20 10 0 0; paid to Mr Dunsterfielld in Novem. 1642 30 0 0; paid to Mr King in part of his bill the 21 of No. 20 0 0; paid for 7 years of my livery cloth for 3 suits at 12s the yard 4 4 0; paid to Pollard in full ending the 12 of Nove. 24 19 9½; received of Willy: Lynn the 22 of Nov. for my Lord's provisions of the Tower 10 16 2½

**[p. 176]** at St Bartholomew's church in Novem. 1642 £0 10 6; spent in my journey last in Octo: 1642 32 12 0; given Miss Swanstead's boy at *Salsbury* 1 0 0; also laid out by bill in the journey by Bold 8 11 6; delivered to Pollard the 19th of Nove. 3 0 0; given Miss Sherburn in part for her lodgings this Nove. 4 0 0, ['more to her for beer & sea coal for 4 weeks out of the £10 16 2½ 2 8 0, also out of the same 10 16 2½ paid to the cook on the other side 6 18 0, more to the cook in Decem. 1 10 0' crossed through]; to the cook in Nov. at the Tower 7 18 0; delivered to Pollard the 28 of Nove. 7 17 6; brought to the Tower £20 the [blank] of Dece. 1642 [blank]. to the cook then 7 12 4; to the cook the 24th of Dece. 2 0 0; £20 to Miss Sherburn then 7 0 0; for the baker then there 1 1 0; for coals & beer to Miss Sherburn at the same time 1 10 8; ['to the warders on Christmas day 1 0 0' crossed through] to the cook the 26 of Dece. 0 18 0; to the warders sold at the Tower on Christmas day 1 0 0; at St Bartholomew's church on New Year's day 1642 0 10 0; I had of Willy: Lynn £1 & £7. To B: the 28 of Jan. 1642 6 0 0; also more 0 15 0; for pins 0 7 0; to old Miss Taylore 0 5 0; to B: 0 10 0; at Mr Sheuit's church on Ash Wednesday 1642 0 1 0; to B: in W: account in April 1643 2 0 0; so in April 2 0 0; [blank] 5 0 0; to the man that came out of London with us 0 10 0; at *Breweren* the 28th of August 1643 1 0 0; to Mr Langham the phi. [physician] the 4th of Sept. 1643 1 0 0; also to him the 6th of Sept. 1 0 0

For a set of 6 harnesses, postillian, saddle & bits & all belonging which comes to £4 15s 0 paid out of my purse 30 0 0, & received of my sister Keat to give Will: Lynn for so much laid out upon blind John £20 which I now lay out upon the harness & £20 more out of the first £100, £5 in all The first £100 in gold. to Mr Jackman the 22 of August to account for 7 0 0; to Pollard 32 0 0; given away at *Brewern* 01 0 0; lent N: 2 5 0; to Mr Jackman the 11th of Sept. 5 0 0; paid for the lodgings for 2 weeks the 12 of Sept. 6 0 0; to Pollard the 14th of Sept. 14 0 0; for 2 coach-horses then 24 15 0; to Mr Langham the 15th & 16th of Sept. 02 0 0; to Wardes the buying of the set of harness 1 0 0; to Mr Langhorn 1 0 0; £100 for a Great Coach Horse which cost £8 paid out of this £100 4 0 0

**[p. 175]** [delivered to Thom: Pollard the 22 of Sept. 1643 which I rec. from Mr Southby £20 0 0.

Jonathan [blank] Born the [blank] day of Sept. 1645 his mother died of him so I took him & paid for his nursing 1s a week, he is this 23 of Nove. six weeks old. I gave her 4s 6d now & in Octo. 4s 6d & the 22 of Jan. 4s 6d & the steward gave her in Decem. 1645 £5

Brought from Oxford for my journey being 13 persons & 16 horse to *Tawstok* the 26 of Sept. 1643 15 0 0; spent at *Malmsbury* [Malmesbury] Tuesday night 2 16 10; at *Bristole* 2 17 10; given to the convoy to *Bristole* 2 0 0; spent in the other part of the journey to *Hunspile* [Huntspill], *Bagborow* &c 4 15 10 [total] 12 10 6
Bold received of Polla: £2 18s 6d & 12s, so of the £15 brought there was spent 10 0 0. So remains in my purse £5.
Given to Mr Jackman who came down with me & stayed employed by me until the 30th of Octo. out of the 28 11 4 of Cornwall 10 0 0

100 the other £100 which I brought from London in August 1643 spent of that gold in my journey to *Tawstok* £10, paid for the Great Coach Horse that cost £8 4, to Mr Launghum 1, to Bold then his wages 5, paid for the lodgings for 2 weeks more 6, to Tho: Polla. then 9, my Lord gave him at Exford 1, also he gave Mr Major at Oxford 1 Spent £37, remains 63

[p. 174]   My Lord's expenses in his journey to Tawstock after me being but 5 horse & 6 men of his own, lay 7 nights & had 3 ['horse &' crossed through] men in his company more 12 17 3; he spent also in 6 weeks staying there after me, whereof Ned Barry had £15 68 14 1 & 0 2 6; by the same hand laid out in 5 weeks my journey down from London with 3 coaches beign part of the time 76 5 4; he received from the 17th of August until the 7th of Nov. 159 11 6

Received out of Cornwall £28 11s 4d whereof laid out as before mentioned to Jackman £10.

1637 to Moor the tailor when I took George [illegible crossed through] Chevly the 2 of No. 2 0 0; paid the carrier in part for bringing down my Lord's goods & in gold 9 2 6 put in to the net purse 6 0 0

£18   Paid for 28 sheep for the house the 9th of No. 10 0 0 & in part of £30 which I paid the carrier for so much borrowed in Oxford by my Lord of him 8 0 0

29 12 6   Paid the Oxford carrier in full of the £30 for which I have his aquitance 22 0 0 & £7 changed into gold in the Net Purse. to P:B & 1s 6 left in the purse 0 10 0.

Rec. of her £12 the £1 left put in to gold.   Paid Hardwick one year's wages the 23th of No. 1643 £10 0 0; Paid Miss Down for corn the same day in part of £63 30 0 0 & whereof £29 was out of Hardwick's 100 & the £1 out of the 12. Paid Sir Ralph Sidnam the 24th of Nov. 1643 with 2 year's interest 500 0 0 paid by the steward; Paid the 5 day of Decem. 1643 to Mr Delworthy for Mr Will: Beare 029 6 0; of the £5 borrowed of Hardwick to my Lord the 11th of Dece. 001 0 0; to Thom: Pollard then 002 0 0; to Bold at Bow for the horses the 12 day spent about the horses but £1 2s 0d 001 5 0; to the steward the 15th of Decem. at Bow 000 15 0; also to him money I rece. from Miss Foster the 14th day when I took her some 001 0 0; more laid out by Rich: Polla in the journey being out from Monday to Saturday 19 horse, 3 or 24 horse & about 25 persons, also then bone lace bought & a sword & 13s in books & £5 to Robin Wood & other extraordinaries 023 17 11 [total] 30 7 2

also laid out for paper &c by Tho: Wiote more then 0 9 3; to B: the 24th of Dece. 1643 0 15 0; to the music[ians] the 1 of Jan. 0 5 0; to the King's messenger the 2 of Jan. 1643 0 10 0; lost at cards the 3 of Jan. 0 15 0; taken out for my Lord & I to play with this 4th of Jan. 0 10 0.

[p. 173]   Delivered to the steward the 10th of Jan. 1643  00 15 0; to my Lord this 15th of Jan. 1643 when he began his journey to Oxford in gold £20 in silver 20s  21 0 0; also then to Tho: Polla: for my Lord's journey with 9 horse & 8 persons 20 0 0; to Bold that cooper gave me in the hall 01 0 0; to Dick Wilet the 17th of Jan. at his going away 1643  2 0 0

[p. 172]   In my hands this present 23 of Jan. 1643  311 16 6  0 2 0

Paid the 27th of Jan. 1643 to Rich: Cooper shoemaker of Barnstaple to bind apprentice Edward Lewin until he be 24 £4 0 0; lost to Miss Down at play 0 17 0; and the like 0 3 0; to B: to pay Punchard the 5th of Feb.

o 17 o; to Jhonson the 8th of Feb. 1643 in part of £23 my Lord had of him 06 13 o, the other £3 7s o I cut off in granting him a copy of license to live from *Prestycoat* [?Prestacott] paying besides 1s a year 06 13 o

Paid to Rich: Cobb the 5th of Feb. 1643 in part of £14 due to him £10 o o; paid to Jhonsone for so much my Lord received in Wanta: in part of £20 the 8th day of Feb. 1643  10 o o; to K:N: the 27th of Feb. 1643 whereof by him laid out 10s 6d 1 o o; to Mr Geo: Bear as by a fee the 2 of March 1643  1 o o; to Ro: Woode which I had of Miss Fostor the 3d of March 1643  5 o o; lost at play o o 6; to the steward the 10th of March 1643 at his going to Ext. 02 o o, & in gold which he brought back to me again ['40' crossed through] o o; one bag wanted £10  to the steward the 17th of March 1643 at his again going to *Exetor* a bond of Robert Drak's of *Uppex* [Up Exe] for the payment of £50, also in money then £150 both which sums he is to pay to the Mayor of *Exetor* as my Lord's loan to the King at this present 200 o o; to Mr Beare as a fee the 17th of March then 001 o o; to the catorer when Polla. was gone to *Exeto.* the 23th of March 001 o o, Polla: had of me £17 & gave me in gold again £14 13 o so due £2 7s o; ['to the steward the 26th of March 1644 to buy coal with 000 o o' crossed through] laid out as appeareth since the 30th of Octo. 1643 until the 25th of March 1644 by me the bond being £50 in part  925 3 6; and received in the same time as appeareth in this book 1252 6 2.  So should remain 0327 2 8.  But, this present 25th of march I have remaining but 0325 16 o.

[signed] R: Bathe  to remem. the La: Grinvell & speedily to answer Estate & Religion.

[p. 171]  lost at play o o 6; to the steward the 26th of March 1644 to buy coal with 2 o o; to the steward the 29th day of March then 4 5 o; given to John Terry the farrier for work done to the horses as a reward—4 good fair timber trees valued £6; to Voysin her half year's wages due the 25 of March paid the 30th day 5 o o; also then to Mr Bouchier having due to him [blank] then 5 o o; also at the same time to Bold 5 o o; the like to the cook in all due now this 30th day 8 o o; and to Rose Todd then 1 10 o; to Besse Randall then 1 o o; to Agnes Tearle then 1 o o; to Honour then 1 o o; to Rawling then o 10 o; to Ro: Whitfielld then 1 5 o, & 15s left which I gave toward the £5 for the sadler £30; to Hardwick for 2 handkerchiefs for John Burk £0 1s 4d; to the steward to pay Mr Atley for sheep the 1 day of April 1644  10 o o, Mr Prust is ordered to pay him £10 more out of our Lady Day rents at Hartland; delivered to Ralph Booth the 9th of April 1644 for his & Thurstan's journey to Oxford with 6 horses to fetch my Lord down 02 o o; to the steward the 10th of April to pay the ['farrier' crossed through] sadler in part of his bill of £7 16s 05 o o; to the steward the same day of April £20 os od; to the steward the 19th of April 05 o o; to the steward the 22 of April 30 o o

To Bold the remainder of the £50 for the mare sold to Will: Elis 01 6 o, & he had the other part paid for a bill of his 01 4 o; to Rich: Britton for cattle bought in the winter in part the 1 day of May 1644  024 o o; to Keepe the coachman for his wages due at our Lady Day last this 2 of May 1644  004 o o; to Thurstan at the same time then 002 o o; to Robin Wood

then due at our Lady Day 004 0 0; to Wilmot the like time due then
000 10 0; to Tho: Polla. due at our Lady Day paid now 005 0 0; also to
James the blackamoor then for the like 001 0 0

[p. 170]   to the sadler in full of his bill the 4th of May 1644 of £7 16 11
2 13 0; to Mr Gifford's nurse & midwife the 6th of May 1644 when I
christened his son Henry 2 0 0; to my Lord at *Exetor* the 9th of May
1644   1 0 0; for bone lace there 3 2 0; for a French beaver for my Lord
there 3 5 0; to the steward then there 4 0 0; to Bold there also 1 0 0;
lost 0 0 6

£20   remaining of the £20 ['whereof that to the nurse & midwife in non'
crossed through] one £3 piece in gold & 1 19 6 which with 6d more makes
the 40s up which was given at *Brightly* [Brightley] to the nurse &
midwife   [total] 17 0 6

To Miss Downe the 20th of May 1644 in full of what was then due 54 0 0;
Also the 21 day of the same month lent to my brother George 20 0 0; to
Bold for his horse bought the 22 of May 1644 07 10 0; to Mr Beare the
1 of June 1644   1 0 0; to the steward the 7th of June 1644 whereof for
30 fat sheep he paid to Mr Atkey's man of Hartland 19 10s 0   20 0 0; also
to him the 9th of June then 02 15 0; to the steward the 17th of June 1644
10 10 0; to Bold the 20th of June then 0 10 0; to the steward the 22 of
May 1644 at my Lord's going to Ext: 10 0 0; to my Lord then 0 5 0; to
the stew: the 27th of June 1644   9 0 0; to the steward the 24th of June
1644   5 0 0; to the steward that day we went to Stow being the 29th of
June 4 0 0; to Will: Weekes whereof £5 he intended to lend Mr Grady &
is to give me account of the whole delivered him the 29th of June 20 0 0

Disbursed since the 25 of March 1644 until the 24 of June 1644   332 1 10,
should remain [blank] but doth remain now 289 17 6

[p. 169]   The 2 of July 1644 in gift to the Lady Grinvell's servants 2 4 0;
spent at Camelford that night in all 3 2 0; at Mr Roscarick's in oats at first
0 8 0; to the ringers at *Cardinam* [Cardinham] the 5 of July 0 5 0; paid
Tho: Polla: bills the 6 of July in full as appears whereof 4s is formerly
accounted in rewards at Stow 3 13 0; delivered Polla: the 6 of July to
account 1 0 0   [total] 10 12 0

To music. the 11th of July 0 2 6; to a sadler at Mr Roscaricks 0 5 6; to the
coachman to buy oats the 11th of July 0 5 0; to Mr Prust's boy the 12th of
July 1644   0 2 0; delivered Polla. the same day 2 0 0; to Tho: Armsby the
13th of July when he went to Taws. 0 2 6; for oats then 0 5 0; for the
young coach horse for drenches &c 0 5 0; to hay then 0 7 6; to Tho:
Polla: the 18th of July 1644   10 2 6; to the carriers man then in part, this
was not paid him by Poll. but he put it to his account 01 0 0; to Bold to
lay out for me 01 0 0; to Tho: Polla. the 19th of July 02 0 0; to him, Bold,
that he laid out for sack 0 2 0; to Bold for hay & oats the 19th of July
1 3 6; to the cook to go to market then 1 0 0; to the poor at my Lord
Mohun's 0 2 0; [blank] 0 4 6; to Bold then to lay out 2 5 8
[total] 22 14 8
given at my Lord Moune's the 16th of July besides what Polla. & Bold
paid 1 15 0   [total] 33 6 8

to Polla. 2 4 0; to Tho: Polla. the 29th of July 1644  8 2 0; spent by water
& to 2 soldiers 0 3 6; to Miss Fransis for sheep 1 2 0; to her in gift when I
came away 1 2 0; for shoeing & gift 0 5 6; in gift at *Trerize* [Trerice]
0 13 0; paid Bold what he laid out more in full the 29th of July 1 3 4; to
the smith at *Bodman* [Bodmin] 0 9 0; to the servants at *Crone* [Croan]
1 4 6; to the 3 houses my servants lay at there 0 4 0; [blank] 0 7 2
[total] £18 19s 0d

[p. 168]  To my brother for his man Robinsonn in the Mount 0 11 0; to
Polla. when he went eastward 0 11 0; to Polla: the 3rd of August 1 2 0; to
Bold the 5th of August 1 2 0; to the carriers man in part 0 11 0; lost at
play 0 7 0; to Polla: at *Treven* [?] 5 3 0; to Bold for oats & hay 2 4 0; to
Pollard at 3 several times the last the 13th of August 3 6 0
[total] £14 17s 0d

To Polla. the 14th of Aug. [illegible sum crossed through] 1 2 0; G: to
Bold for 6 bushels of oats the 15th of Aug. 0 15 6; to the cook the 16th of
the same 1 2 0; to Ned: Foster to buy shoes then 0 3 0; to a woman
brought me fruit that day 0 1 0

To Thurstan for the smith for shoeing the horses the 22d of Aug. 0 15 0;
to Bold for the bone-setter then 0 2 6; for oats the 22 of Aug. 0 05 0; to
the Lady Basset's man brought honey the 23  0 1 0; to Bold for hay the
24th 0 12 0; to Wilmot laid out at market the 24th 1 9 0; to Bold for the
farrier to cure the L: black mare 0 5 0; for mending the harness 0 0 6; to
Mr Godolphin's groom 0 1 0; to Polla: in full of his book 0 19 0; more to
him the 27th day 0 10 0; to the bone-setter 0 5 0; to Miss Godolphin's
foot-man 0 1 0  [total] £8 9s 6d

To Polla: the 29th 1 0 0; to Mr Bouchier then 0 3 6; for mending of the
harness 0 3 6; for shoeing of horses the 1 of Sept. 0 10 0; to Hugh Thomas
man brought 2 bushels of oats 0 0 6; to Voysin for the house in my
absence, £4 but of Wales £20  1 16 0; to Polla: to account for the 2 of
Sept. 5 0 0; in to my own purse then 0 18 6; to Polla: then in full of his
book at *Treveneg* 2 1 0; taken to supply part of the 15s 6  0 14 6; Rob:
Walles 20 0 0; to Voysin in gold then 2 4 0; of the £4 Voysin had laid out
there £3 5s 9d & brought me again 0 14 3

Bold had to lay out at Croan of Tho: P: £2 & of me £20 17s 6d my purse
money, he laid out £11 18s 6d whereof £9 6 6 was for a great gelding
6 15 6 & a mare 2 13 0, so remained due to me 10 19 0, I rec. but 0 17 0

Given by myself away 0 1 0; to Jo: Burk to lay out for candles, soap &c
0 5 0; to the cook at Croan 00 17 6; for oats then 1 7 6  [total] 2 4 6

to Bold the 14th of Sept. 1644  1 3 6

[p. 167]  £10 Mr P.  To Thurstan his bill the 14th of Sept. 0 3 6; taken
then to go to *Tawstok* 0 5 0; for oats the 16th of Sept. 0 7 6; to John Burk
3s for to mend his boots & 1s laid out more 0 4 0; to the cook at Croan
then 0 13 0; to Mr Roscarick for expenses there in all 6 16 6 but of this
money 3 10 6; to Polla: then to go to *Treveneg* in all £5 of this money
1 14 0; given in the house at Croan the 17th day when we went east 1 1 0;

for stockings for Fostor then o 3 o; to the smith then 1 3 o; for John
Burk's washing o 1 o; to a poor women there o 2 o; to poor soldiers by
the way to Ext: o 12 6   total 10 0 0
The other money paid to Mr Roscarick at Croan the 16th of Sept. was
3 6 0; to Polla: the last remainder of the £8 1s 3 for Treven. 1 2 0
3 13 0 & 4 8 0   [total] 8 1 3
In gold to Polla: for Treven. the 16th of Sept. 2 4 0; Polla. had then more
o 2 o; spent at *Lanscon* [Launceston] by the horses 1 10 0; spent in bread
& beer there o 11 0; spent then by the cook there o 10 8
Spent at Bow the 18th of Sept. 1644   2 0 0; to the cook at Exet: the 19th
of Sept. the day we came there o 10 o; to the music. there o 5 o; G: Bold
there at Ex. o 10 o; to Miss Francis at ['*Treveneg*' crossed through] Croan
1 2 o; more given o 1 o   [total] 9 10 8
Now remains of 34 11 11 £7 the 20th of Sept. 1644

To the cook the 21th of Sept. o 8 4; Lent my brother Geo: the 23th of
Sept. 1644  6 10 o; ['to the cook the 24th of Sept. when we were going
towards *Tawstok* 2 16 o; [blank] o 1 8
8 1 3   Pr: 10 0 0   Go: 10 0 0   06 10 8   [total] 34 11 11
The 26 of Decem. 1648 the homage of *Tawstok* presented their customs
under their hands

[p. 166]  £24 10s 6d   For a black satin cap 6s, for a hood 6, for gartering
ribbon 7s  o 19 o; to a boy at church o 1 o; for powder o 4 o; for gloves
for my Lord at Ext. o 5 o; to Tho: Wiote the 24th of Sept. 1 0 o; to the
cook then at our going to *Tawstok* 2 16 o; for 6 yards of serge at 3s 8d per
yard 1 2 o; for 6 yards 3 quarters more of the like 1 4 9; for wine & bread
candles &c there 1 7 o; to Thurstan for shoeing o 1 o; given at Mr Alldans
o 5 6; a bill for wine [blank]; a bill of Wiotes o 9 3; books for my Lord
o 8 6; fruit brought o 1 o; to the sexton o 2 6; Bold's lodging o 4 o;
shoeing horses o 10 6; horse meat 6 18 o; ostlers & drinking o 5 6; in my
pocket o 8 6; in part for 28 ells of Holland 5 0 o; for beer o 16 6; in one
of the Grand Deeds there is the lawyer's opinion upon the 21 years
afterlives let by Ed: Earl of Bathe, given by Jo: Hailes 1647  o 1 o

Tho: Wiote for paper 3s
Remained the 24th of June 1644 in my hands 289 17 6
Received from that time until the 28th of Sept: following 077 4 11
In all 367 2 5
Disbursed by me in the same time taking 1 £7 14s 0 of the next side in to
this account 71 4 5
So, should remain but 195 18 o, but doth remain now 198 18 o.

these £500 satisfy this present 22 of August 1648   My Lord becomes
bound the 29 of Jan. 1645 for my brother Geo: for £200 to Tho:
Horwood & for £100 to Alexander Horwood & the 30th day he was
likewise bound to Walter Tucker for £100 paid & taken in & to Mr Palmer
the old man paid & taken in my Lord & James Heirle are bound for £100
in all £500

for which my Lord hath George bound & a deed to bind £1000 now in
Frank's hands for the remaining my Lord. R:B:

my brother Geo: delivered his counter part to me to keep for him, my Lord is paid all but the £200 borrowed of Thom: Horwood of which my Lord hath neither principal nor interest which is due from [blank] paid all since.

[reversed]   From the 25 of March 1640 to the 24 of June 1640 received by Mr Paget 580 0 0; from the said 24th of June to the Audit 131 8 10½; at the Audit to come in 691 8 10

this 17th of August 1640 cast up 1402 16 11½

[p. 165]   £10   For holland the whole coming to £11 11s 0 6 11 0; to Miss Lynn's woman 0 10 0; to the other 3d & to help cleanse the house 0 05 0; to the house at Bow the 25 of Sept. 0 5 0; to the cook laid out at Exet. 0 3 0   [total] £7 14s 0

To Tho: Armsby to go to Oxford the 30th of Sept. 0 10 0; to Doctor Chichester the 3rd of Octo. 1 0 0; for setting up the organ then 0 16 0 [total] 10 0 0

£20   For 20 sheep bought at *Bannton* by the steward the 4th of Octo: paid by me in full 10 0 0; G:  to Bold the 4th of Octo. 1 0 0; in go. 5 12s 0  to the poor at Taw. church the 13th of Octo. when we rece. the communion 0 10 0; for the clock maker for the 2 clocks 4s & for my Lord's watch 2s the 14th Octo. 0 6 0; to play at cards 0 5 0; G: to Bold then the 15th of Octo. 0 5 0; paid for Tho: Wright to Punchard the mercer the 15th of Octo. 5 0 0, whereof £3 was John Skitches last payment on his lease; to play at cards 0 2 0; This with the £5 12s 0 Ch: Gol: makes 23 0 0

£2 skit: in go. £1 10s   to Mr Rowles' man that brought a doe the 15th of Octo. 0 10 0

In my hands at my coming from Oxford in Sept. 1643  63 0 0
Rece. from that time until the 20th of Octo. 1644  1592 9 9
Disbursed in the same time by me 1429 17 11
So remains in my hands 0225 11 10
This present 18th of Octo: 1644   It is but 0204 8 0

Moneys from the earl of Westmorland since Midsummer 1643 there being that day due 280 0 0, by Will: Lynn from the said Earl in London & £5 more by Mr Warde the 14th of Sept. 1643   060 0 0, Tho: Michell hath paid to Will: Lynn for my Lord's use the 8th of August 1644 £50

Also the said Tho: Mich: hath paid to Mr Halowell near Christ Church in Oxford for my Lord's lodgings there £34.
the 22th of March My Lord rece. in Oxford the Spring before of him £50
More due from my brother of West: at Christmas 1645 £280
the 8th of August Will: Lynn 50, the 10th of Feb.  50, more now to Will: Lynn 300   [total] 534 & 060
So due from him the 24th of June 1645   £806 0 0

[p. 164]   Rich: Polla: made an account from Octo. 1645 until the ['sam' crossed through] next Octo. 1646 in which time rece. 872 10 ½, disbursed in the same time 805 13 8, So due then from him to my Lord 066 16 11. Likewise from the last of Octo. 1646 until the 25 of Octo. 1647 of which the 66 6 11 is part is 904 2 2, disbursed in the same time 891 13 10. So, Due then from him 012 8 4.

There was due from the steward at the end of his year's account in Octo. 1644 the sum of 8 12 6 ¼. & when that was allowed & how the account stood in 1645 Oct.

8 yards & 3 quarters of red taffety the saddle cloth

Lent Bold the 26 of Octo. 1644 which was part of the ¼ I had from Miss Fostor £3 o o.

Lost [blank]; paid for Ed: Fostor to *Banton* the tailor o 5 o; to my Lord in Sept. o 5 o.

**[enclosure 164b]**  Re: due to the steward in Octo. 1647 7 11 8, & for bringing their trunks from London 1 10 o, & for his wages 24 o o [total] 33 1 8

There is due to me 23 13 11, so due to him 9 7 9, there is also charged by Tho: Wiote on him 2 15s, paid him 9 10 o.

[dorse. oo3 12 4, o18 oo 11, o16 o7 6, o19 19 7, o26 19 3, o19 12 10, o18 15 5, o21 12 8, o17 17 7, o29 4 5   [total] 192 o2 6 paid]

**[p. 163]** To Tho: Wiote in part of £3 14s 7d then due to him the 24th of Octo. 1 10 o, so remains 2 4 7, which was paid the 26 of Octo. 1644

To Voysin the 26 of Octo. 1644 due then £5 o o; to Lovett then 5 o o; to Hardwick in part of £10 then 5 o o; to Mr Bouchier in full 14 o o; also paid a bill o 5 6; to Rich: Cob in part of £18 then 14 o o; to Tho: Wiote then in part of £55 then due 5 o o; to John Burk then 2 o o; also a bill of his o 6 o; to Tho: Polla: his wages then due the 29th of Octo. 1644 5 o o; to the plumber by him for half a year then due & 7s of it for other work as by his bill doth appear 3 7 o; to Robin Wood then in full 4 o o; to Keepe in part of £4 then due 2 o o; to James then in full 2 o o; to the cook for one month above the quarter then 1 5 o; to Thurstan then due 2 o o; to Will: Booth the like due 2 o o; to Rich: Rook then due 1 5 o; to Will: Geare then due 1 o o; to Baldwin Better then Bold paid his daughter £4 in Octo. 1649 which I have since allowed him & the steward paid for him 2 2 8, 3 o o; lost at play to Sir Tho: Ashton in Octo. o 7[s] [total] 79 15 6

To Bold in full of his wages the 30th of Octo. 1644 where of the £3 lent him is part & now more £7 o o; to the steward for Mr Shorte of *Bidiford* [Bideford] in part of the 12 10 o of this money in odd money 3 17 o laid by 5 o o

To John Heirle in full of all dues the 2 of Nove. 1644  30 o o; o5o for Sir Ralp:  to Mr Issack in full the 4th of Nove. 1644  12 10 o; to the steward for Mr Shorte of *Bidiford* in all £12 10s o but of this bag but o7 10 o

To Rich: Britton the 9th of Nov. 1644 in part of £41 then due 11 18 6, the whole debt to him was 62 18 6 whereof £10 set off for the 2 closes due at Midsummer & £6 for *Shorely* [Shoreleigh] park due at Michaelmas & £5 for *Shorely* wood due for the same time, in all £21, so remains due to him £30

To Bold by bill then o 10 o; to him likewise then 1 o o; to Tho: Armsby due from our Lady Day to Michaelmas 1644 2 10 o; Cha: £1 7 o which makes the 17 5 4 rece. from *Banton*. Cha: more 14s out of odd money. In all the 10th of Nov. £2 1s od.

[p. 162]   £2 widow Mortimor's heriot   to Doctor Chichester the 19th of
Nov. 1644  1 0 0; to him the like the 22th of Nov. 1 0 0; to the saddler in
full of all bills due this present 23 of Nov. 3 16 9; £13 Barnes   delivered
the steward the 23th of Nov. then 5 0 0; to Edw: Fostor the 26 of Nove.
then 0 10 0, & £4 he had of Bold then; delivered to the steward the 29th
of Nov. 6 0 0; to Bold in g. 0 13 3
5 12s hops   Sent then by him to Alice Delbridge 1 0 0   [total] 178 4 6
On the other side & to this place this present 2 of Dece. 1644, disbursed
by me 179 14 0
In my hands at the Audit 204 8 0, rece. since to this time 301 13 0, so
remains now in my hands 326 7 0.

14 17 Delivered to the steward for Jo: Hamlin in full of his bills to the
4 day of Decem. 1644  6 5 6; to Ralph Booth for his sorrel horse died in
my service 2 2 0; to Abell my brother's man for necessaries 0 8 0;
delivered the steward the 5 of Decem. 6 0 0

£50 R:S:   to Mr Lambe for 16 yards & half of good black cloth at
£1 6s 6d 21 17 0; to Bold the £4 which he gave the steward above
mentioned then 4 0 0; to Bold likewise then which he laid out for young
trees 3 10 0; to Whitefielld for 6 bushels of barley 0 19 0; to Joan Ellis for
work done for Fostor & others 0 5 0; to Roger Thorne in part of £20 paid
the 13th of Decem. in full of all demands to that time 17 7 0
2 yoke of oxen rece. the 5 of April 1645 from Squiel of *Warkley* 2 of them
heriots the other 2 I pay £6 for. 2 cows from the same place for the young
man's heriots
When I cast up Hardwick's accounts she appeared in debt to me £5 9s 10d,
so she had the £5 for wages due to her at Michaelmas last & I rec. the
9s 1d, whereof paid a bill of Bold's being 6s 6d.

Sir Henry Spiler oweth for several Knight's fees, for the manor of Colquite
held of Cardinham fee

[p. 161]   Also to Ralp: Booth, in all £5, more for his sorrel horse 2 18 0;
more spent 0 1 6.
£5 Squier   To the steward the 11th of Decem. 1644 £5 0s 0d; to Roger
Thorn in full of the 20 then due for carriages the 13th of Decem. 1644
2 13 0; paid an old grocery bill from *Exetor* the 17th of Decem. £2 15 0;
to Rich: Britton ['in part of' crossed through] this £4 he paid to widow
Sumers for one steer & so remains yet £30 due the 18th of Dece. 4 0 0; to
the poor at the communion the 22 of Decem. 1644 0 10 0; lost at play
0 2 0

£25  to the steward the 21 of Dece. 1644 5 0 0; to the stew. the 2 of
Janu. 1644 8 0 0; ch. in go. £12

From the 20th of Jan. followeth laid out
100  to Dick Britton in part of 36 3 4 due to him this 5th of Feb. 1644
6 3 9; to Polla. for 2 oxen then 8 10 0; to Rob. the gardener for 2 oxen
more then 6 0 0; to Mr Ja: Welsh for corn then 18 6 0; to Bold for 2 oxen
then 11 0 0; to the steward to pay Miss Down & others then 30 0 3; to the
steward the 6 of Feb. when he paid Miss Downe 80 0 0. In full of 66 5 all
to this day delivered him for her 20 0 0

To the steward the 22 of Feb. 1644 4 13 10; misreckoned 2s 3d & 7½d; X lent my brother Geo: the 23th of Feb. 1644 13 10 0; added to my counters 0 0 6; lost at play 0 1 0; delivered to the steward the 23 of March 1644 7 9 0

50 Paid Dick: Britton a bill the 27 of March 1645 12 0 0; X Lent Mr Will: Bouchier the 27 of March 1645 to be paid in Octo. following next 10 0 0

To the steward for 10 sheep the 1 of April bought at *Yarnscom* [Yarnscombe] 3 15 0; to the steward the 2d of April for 20 sheep bought at Buckland 7 10 0; to Dick Rooke in part of Lady Day wages 0 10 0; to Bold for his journey to *Stowe* 0 5 0; delivered the steward the 5 of April 1645 for the masons 3 0 0 [total] 37 0 0

[p. 160] To Doctor Chichester 2 fees the later end of April £2 0 0; lent Miss Downe for which I am to have corn for it 6 0 0; lent her in *Exetor* by Mr Butler £12 for which I had but £7 yet of her 45 0 0

280 10 0

My brother George had of me the 17th of April 1645 which I then rece. from the steward £5 0 0

[p. 159] to Rich: Britton upon 2 bills the 12 of April 1645 £46 6s 8d; to the stew[ard] the 18th of April for servant's wages 29 18 10 whereof he paid £14 1 2; to Voysin then 05 0 0; to Hardwick then 05 0 0; to Tho: Polla: the like 05 0 0; to Cob: whereof 10s was laid out for me to the 2 midwives 07 10 0; for dyeing some cloth 01 4 6 [total] 100 0 0

To Bold that I borrowed for my gold counters 2 15 0; lost at play 0 3 0; To Bold in part of £10 due at our Lady day this 30th of April 4 0 0; more laid out by him 0 2 0 [total] 7 0 0

£10 To my brother Geo: the 31 of April 1645, in all £50, 5 0 0; to Lovett then her wages due at our Lady Day last 5 0 0; paid for 3 young beefs to widow Cunibear 9 5 0, & to Tho: Wiote as part of the £3 below paid him 0 4 0

£50 Paid the masons the warreners the 3d of May 1645 3 0 0; to the steward for 12 servants wages more then 24 5 0; to Rose Hamline due at our Lady Day last now 1 10 0; to Bold in full of his wages then due at our Lady day last 06 0 0; to the steward for Dick Britton the 6 of May 12 9 0; to Tho: Wiote his wages due at our Lady Day in all £6 but of this 2 16 0 Bought of Archilles Ackland 10 sheep which he is allowed for out of money which I receive of him for Rawling Thorn 50 0 0, 4; paid R: Bou: the coach maker the 12th of May 1645 in part which was money I rece. for Rawling Thorn of her brother 13 0 0

£50 Paid the shoemaker as by bill the 17th of May 1645 £1 0s 0d; paid the steward the 23 of May 1645 28 19 6; to Bold that the steward borrowed of him for me then 8 0 0; paid the steward the 24th of May to pay the masons then & paid more Bold laid out 0 8 6; at play lost 1 11 0 [total] 50 0 0

May the 21th Paid to Dick Britton in part of 25 19. by Tho: Polla. of the money which he rec. from Hartland for our Lady Day quarter 8 4 8; Lost at play the 30th of May 1645 0 5 0 [total] 251 18 8

[p. 158]   Paid Tho: Wiote this 28 of May 1645 in full of £50 due to him,
he having a copy in *Warkly* for his use for £40 of the money 4 0 0
Laid out at *Bristow* [Bristol] by Mr Farwod for silk stockings & soap &c
5 2 6; paid John Hamlin for black lace, buttons & silk for my Lord's cloth
5 13 0; for making clean 2 houses &c 0 7 0; to Sir Jo: Chichester for
100 bushels of oats at 22d 9 3 0; to the sadler in part of his bill of 8 3 3
3 0 0; paid Miss Baker in part of her bill of 26 2s this 4th of June 6 0 0;
paid to Dick Britton *Bodardale* money by T: Wiote in part of his bill the
10th of June 8 0 0; lost at play & laid out other ways 1 0 0; lost at play
0 10 0; to the steward the 17th of June 1645   10 0 0; to Dick Britton paid
by Tho: Wiote of Dunterton rent 7 7 0; to the steward for the masons
3 10 0 & in all d[elivere]d him 5 10 6; to the steward the 21 of June 1645
5 0 0; to the steward the 24 of June 5 0 0; to the steward the 29th of June
2 0 0; the steward had of Parker's money of Instow for coal 6 0 0; he had
also for the last payment of the land rate out of Rawling's money 5 0 0;
Also he had more then for the cateror's 2 bills 12 0 0; & for Mr Smith of
Torr for 100 bushels of barley 16 13 4; paid to Rich: Britton the 5 of July
4 5 7; paid more then to him 1 18 6
1645   ['paid Mr Bolworthy for Mr Will: Beare the 14th of July 20 0 0'
crossed through] received this again; to the stew. for the masons the
[blank] of July 04 0 0; lost at play 01 0 0; to the stew. the 2th of August
for the cateror 5 0 0; to the stew. the 11 of August which Tho: Wiote paid
him besides widow Squier's money 12 0 0; to the stew. the 14th of August
10 0 0; to Doctor's Chichestor of my Lord's angels 1 0 0; to the sadler
1 10 0; to Bold laid out for several things the 25 of August 1 13 6; to the
stew. the 21 of August 6 0 0; to Bold in part of his next half year's wages
this 22 of August 6 10 0; Aug. 23 1645   to John Swayne shoemaker of
Barnstaple to take Simon Underden for his apprentice until the age of 24
£4 0 0

[p. 157]   To Miss Downe the 23 of August 1645 in full of all £4 6 0; to
old Mr Liverland after his sermon preached the 24 of August 0 10 0.

100   To Will: Weekes to go to Bradworthy fair the 27 of August £20 0 0;
for cloth bought woollen then 3 12 5; more cloth bought 15 y[a]r[ds] cost
2 3 4 other money 1 6 6; to the steward the 2 of Sept. 1645   5 0 0
[total] £17 [sic] 5s
To Bold that he gave with the Irish mare in exchange for a gray gelding
1 19 0   1 19 0 Ho: money; to the steward the 5 of Sept. 5 0 0; to the
steward the 9th of Sept. to pay Widow Peard for one of the 2 fat oxen he
bought of her, he paid the like for the other 4 0 0; to the steward the 11 of
Sept. that Tho: Wiote rece. in part of £52 from widow Squier 10 0 0; to
the steward the 14th of Sept. 5 0 0; to Doctor Chichestor the 11th of Sept.
my Lord's gold 1 0 0   [total] 253 14 2
To the steward to pay for one but of sack containing 124 gallons 24 0 0; to
Bold in part of his wages 01 0 0; to Doctor Chichestor the 19th of Sept.
01 0 0; to the steward the 21 of Sept. 18 0 0; paid the sadler the 22 of Sept.
in full of £8 3s 3d & all demands 03 10 0; to Bold which he paid for a gray
nag for my own saddle 05 15 0; Ch. go. 6 4 0; lost at play 0 10 0; 100 lbs
all for 100 weight of tallow at 5d the lb, the 24 of Sept. of this 1 1 9 & of

other money to make this up 1 0 0; to the Steward which I had of Widow Cunibear the 26 of Sept. 10 0 0; to the nurse & midwife of Miss Wingfielld then 02 0 0
100 To the steward the 28th of Sept. 6 8 0; to the steward for 17 truss of hay 2 0 0; to John Skitch the 1 of Oct. paid his bill for wine 6 0 0; to Voysin for a pair of silk stockings 1 4 0; for 8 bushels of sowing wheat for the park at 6s 6d the bushel 2 12 0; Ch. Go. 9 19 0; to my b[rother] Geo: 1 0 0; to play 0 10 0; to the stew[ard] for 2 fat cows of Chamber's the 5 of Octo. 6 0 0; to the steward for sugar being 116 lbs, barrel & 1s besides in all 5 0 0; paid a bill of Bold's 0 18 6; for 12 bush[els] of sowing wheat for the park in all 20 bushels 3 18 0; for Mr Shorte of *Bidiford* in full of his bill the 9th of Octo. 11 0 0

[p. 156]   To the stew. the 28 of Sept. 1645 Dick Britain had this 6 8 0; to Doctor Chichester 1 0 0; to the stew. the 9th of Octo. for 4 weigh of coal 7 0 0; to the stew. more then 3 0 0; sent to Miss Steevens the 10th of Octo. 1 0 0; for 30000 of *Tindagle* [Tintagel] slate cost 6s 8d per 1000 paid the 14th of Octo. 10 0 0; to the stew. then for his journey to Exet. 1 0 0; to Will: Geare then 0 5 0; to Besse Brother for 20 bush[els] of oats at 22d 1 16 8; to Bold in full of his wages this 23 of Octo. 1645 2 10 0; to Rose Hamlin the like 1 10 0; to the stew. the 16th of Octo. 2 10 0

X   To my bro. Geo: the 7th of Octo. in all £10, but of this money which I had of Geo: Thorn in part of Rawling Bond's money but 9 0 0

To Voysin for her wages due this Audit 1645   5 0 0; to Lovet then 5 0 0; to Hardwick [blank]; to Cob then in part of £11   7 0 0; to Tho: Wiote his wages due this Audit 1645   3 0 0; paid him then a bill of 0 12 0; to Tho: Polla. the 23 of Octo: 1645 to pay servants wages as by the bill appears the 1 10s 0 to Rose being before written which is in the bill 36 6 8; to Tho: Polla: b[ill] that he laid out 0 13 3; to him likewise for his wages now due 5 0 0; to Hardwick the £5 which she had of Geo: Cheivly's money for her wages now due 5 0 0; paid Miss Nashe an old bill for cheese &c 1 3 0

Roche Southwell Sir Will: Power   disbursed since the 24th of Octo. 1644 1199 5 0; and the 28th of Octo. 1645 0502 12 0; Rece. & borrowed in that time 1240 2 5
So remains 29 18 5, besides my Lord's counters £10 & mine 13 10 0 & the £20 the stew. wrote paid me in this book

Sir Francis Cooke bound in a bond to make a perfect conveyance of Claire which he hath done this summer 1646

[p. 155]   Due to Rich: Britton one old bill of 1644 20 0 0; due upon borrowing the 13th of July 1645   30 0 0; due to him upon one bill dated the 19th of June 1645   50 0 0; due to him upon one other bill 41 7 10; turned up of this debt for the 2 closes he hath of my Lord £20 & allowed me for pasturing some of his goods £2 10s 0; paid remains due to him this 29 of Octo. 1645 £100 0 0 for which he hath my Lord's bond

Borrowed upon bond of Miss Baker the 30th of Octo. 1648 £100   Also Jo: Hei: hath my Lord's hand for £20 borowed of him & he hath my hand for corn bought at £18 4s 0 38 4 0; ['Miss Ba: of Barnst. hath my hand for

£10 borrowed of her my Lord is bound in a bond of about the 18th of Octo. 1645 for £200 I borrowed of [blank] & I am to pay interest for it, from that time & £30 uponbills besides due to her 210 0 0    30 0 0

due to her the 18th of Octo. 1648 for interest paid £48 other ways 15 12 2 in all 263 12 2' crossed through]

paid the 1 of March 1648 the bond of £100 is made in Mr Daye's name My Lord is bound to Mr William Beare for £200 borrowed of him in London the 23 of June 1644 which monies he should have rece. of Rich: Atherton my Lord's steward in the north of Ireland of which he rece. in Decemb. following from him there £42 & I paid Mr William bolworthy the 5 day of Decem. 1643 for Mr Will: Beare £20 6s & the 20th of April 1646 paid himself then 40 12 4 which was the full of the interest & £8 of principal so remains now due to him. there is now but [illegible] due for which he hath my [illegible]' crossed through]

['Paid My Lord is bound to James Baldwin or his daughter Mary for £300, & pays interest for it. paid to Mr Manby, Ma. Baldwin's husband the 11th of March £100 also the interest due until the 12 of Jan. last £12.' crossed through]

Paid My Lord hath £100 from the Countess of Petteborow of Nan Howard's money for which he pays interest. Memorandum that the note my Lord gave under his hand for the receipt of this £100 is not yet given up because it could not be found, but my Lady of Peterborrow gave a note under her hand for the receipt of it from my L. £100   £200   £150

My L. is bound for £500 for Geo. to 4 merchants of Barnst., £100 of this paid & discharged by my brother Fr., £100 more discharged by the same hand. £400  £400. one £100 not paid but the bond is to be called for by W: L:.

1 Rich. £100 Britton Jo. [illegible crossed through] Hairle  Miss 040 Baker Will. 100 Beare  2 Sir Ralph 200 Manby  Nan 100 Howard Miss 100 Devon  3 W.L. 100 R.F.

Tho: Haywoades 200 & £32 interest the 22 of Aug. 1648 my Lord paid but borrowed the £200 of Hugh Horsom then.

Mr Geo. Beard the lawyer hath my Lord's bond & Mr Will: Pagets for 200 dated on the 7th of June 1639 witness to this bond is Mrs Coyse & Tho: Wyote. to be paid the 8th of Decem., after which money (by the deliverers confession Mr Butler) was paid to Mr Paggett he being my Lord's receiver, who craves my Lord's allowance for it, without discharging himself of it, this paid likewise there is the very same case concerning £120 witness to this bond is Peter Bold & Tho: Wiote borrowed by the same Will: Pagget on the first of Novem. 1639, to be paid the 3rd day of May after of geo. Bear & is paid himself, & as Will: Lynn can witness with me about the 23th of Octo. 1641 when Mr Paggett had dell. in his full account of receipts, & disbursements which amounted more than recovered to £918 18s 7d, in £828 in all, besides monies due to the young Ladies about ['£500' crossed through] more when he set his hand to the book & his perfect & full account. I asked him if my Lord were not bound to Mr Geo. Bear & what

**[p. 154]** ['he had done' crossed through] was become of the bond he answered me that that money was paid & the bond taken up. Which answer Will. Lynn & I immediately carried to my Lord, who was satisfied with it. Since this Mr Paggett's memory failing him altogether, the money is demanded of my Lord by Mr Beare. My Lord must & doth require the money or some account of it from Mr Paggett who by good proof, even by them which paid it to him is found to be the receiver of it.

Mr Paget pays the last of Octo. 1639 to Mr Feris of Barnstap. which is said to be borrowed upon bond in March or April before the sum of 102. he never charges himself with the receipt of it & yet craves to be allowed it in his disbursements.

due to Grace Shapely of Barnstaple ['£21 0 0' crossed through] paid by the stew.

1648 April the 19th William Lynn hath the custody of my jointure made in two deeds, he being one of my feoffees in trust.

My brothers of Westmorland, Sir Francis Fane, Sir Henry Vaine, Sir William Earmine & William Lynn.

My Lo. was bound the [blank] of Sept. 1646 his sindle bond to Will: Lynn for ['50 0 0' crossed through]

['Also at the same time to Rich: Forward for 50' crossed through] 0 0

Upon casting up Will: Lynn's account there remained due to him the 23 of March 1646 the sum of £18 also the 26 of the same month 1647 there was due to him for 3 years & half wages then £70. paid all & made even the 28th of April ['88' crossed through] 0 0

This present 30th of March I owe in '['old bills in London 514' crossed through] 10 10

May the 1 £837 in new bills since May 1646 ['371' crossed through] 7 10

['Besides borrowed of Sir Ralph Syd: £50 & Mr Austin £100 £150 0 0'] crossed through Will: Lynn hath Mr Maynard's judgement upon Jackman's business to paid together with the old custom of *Tawstok* found in 15 [blank], with the survey of the manor.

£828   £1223 18s 8d   0153 10 10

['Due to Doctor Down upon bill in 1646 for corn paid by Mr John Downs in April 1648 053 10 10   100 0 0' crossed through]

['the 23 of Feb. 1648 all my servants wages for this half year except Mr Wilde who had £5 at Christmas & due to the week book this 30th of March 60 odd £' crossed through]

April the 29th 1647 all my servants every one except P: Bold to whom there is due from Michaelmas last wages. But all the rest were this day fully paid & the week book to the 24th day fully satisfied.

Borrowed upon bond of Sir Ralph Sydhenham the 17th of July 1647 £200 for which my bro. Frank & Will: Lynn stand bond, & my Lo. hath then given them a bond for £400 for counter security. ['£200' crossed through] 0 0

£100 paid Sir Ralph of the £200 the 24 of Octo. 1648. £100 more paid by Will: Lynn to Sir Ralph the 17th of Dece. 1649 in full of his bond which he promiseth to give up so soon as he comes in to Devon.

My Lo. this 22 of August 1648 borrowed of Hugh Horsome of Barnst. for which Thom. Hobson & Rich: Britten each stand bound with him for £100 a piece, for to pay Thom. Horwood the principal of what my Lord became bond for my brother George Fane who lent the bill to Sir John Greenvile £200.

Borrowed of Joseph Ley the 29 of Novem. 1648 to be paid the 20th of June 1649 ['100 0 0' crossed through]

Borrowed likewise of John Brother the 1 of Decem. 1648 upon bond ['40' crossed through]

Borrowed upon bond of Robert Drake of *Upex* the 12 of Jan. 1648 upon my Lord's single bond paid Feb. 5 1649 ['100' crossed through]

£500 Borrowed of my Aunt Fane upon my jewels for which my Lo. hathgiven a bill of sale under his hand & seal the 25 of Feb. for which he is to pay the 25 of Feb. 1649  515 0 0

The jewels taken up & Tho: Viner Ald. & citizen is bond & Will: Lynn with my Lord to pay £505 in Nov. 1649

[p. 153]   Paid Rich: Britton in part of £119 due to him the 28 of Octo. 1645 £19 0s 0d; also then paid him by turning over the rent remain. for the 2 closes 20 0 0; to the stew. the 2 of Nov. 1645 for 2 hogs 4 6 8 & for 16 sheep bought of Arch: Ackland 5 6 8 & for workmens wages &c 2 6 8 in all £12 0 0; paid for 7 gallons & one pottle of usquebaugh the 4th of Nov. 1645  2 15 6; paid the 6 of Novem. 1645 for 24 yards & 3 quarters, 20d the yard, of green kersey & 2 yards half of red baize at 22d 2 5 10; to my brother Geo: when Mr Farrard went to London in Novem. 1645 1 0 0; to the stew. in Novem. for Fairchild the constable for 30 b. of barley & 18 b. of oats in all 7 14 0 now paid in full £4 11 0; paid the sadler in part of [blank] 1 0 0; to the stew. the 22 of Novem. to pay the workmen & for peas 3 10 0; to my Nurse Hayne for nursing Jonathan the 22 of Nov. 0 4 6; paid for 3 pieces of broad ['cloth' crossed through] canvas at 12d per ell, 242 ells £11 14s & for 3 pieces of narrow canvas at 9½d per ell, 117 ells £5 & one piece of dowlas at 12d per yard, 57 yards 2 17s, all cost £19 11s 6, deducted for hops I sold £7 3s 0 so paid Mr John Slowely the 28 of Nove. 1645 £12 8s 0; paid then likewise to the stew. for 70 lbs of sugar at 10d p[er pound] 3 0 0; lost at play the 27 of Nov. 0 5 6; ['Cha. Go. £4' crossed through]; to Doctor Chichestor in Nov. 1645 2 3 0; to the stew. the 7th of Decem. 2 10 0; to Hardwick to pay for apples then 0 10 0; to Mr Basset in part of £12 10s for ['corn' crossed through] wheat the 7th of Decem. 10 0 0; to old Mr Liverland the 15th of Decem. 1645 0 5 0; to Dick: Willis then 0 2 6; to Bold the 16 of Decem. more in part of his wages 4 0 0   [total] 105 0 10 this 17th of Decem. 1645

To Ann Steevens the 24th of Dece. 1645 0 17 0

To John Heirle that the stew. borrowed for so much had of him for the go. I had of Sir Dudley Wiote which he paid to Mr Palmers son-in-law at Barnstaple the whole being £20 but of John Heirle borrowed £10 which was paid him of Will: Elis money

[p. 152]   To Bold in full of his wages to this 7th of Jan. 1645 0 10 0; to Bold then 1 0 0; to the stew. the 15th of Jan. to pay 8 several reckonings which came to 34 0 10  33 10 0; to Humphrey Lake in part of £4 3s for

one oxe 2 o o; to Jonathan's nurse the 20th of Jan. 1645 o 4 6; she had the
23 of Octo. o 4 6; to the stew. the 22 of Jan. to pay the plumber &c
4 10 o; to Mr John Steevens for 18 ells of Holland at 4d ell 3 12 o; to
Mr Clappaham the apothecary of Barnst. in full to the 25th of Jan. 1645
6 o o; to Ann Steevens then in gift 2 o o; the stew. had of Tho: Wiote that
he brought out of Corn. 30 o o; to Thurstan for 2 journeys 5s & that he
laid out to Jo: Terry for Christmas quarter 10s o 15 o; to Bold in part of
4 6 8 for 2 fat oxen the 31 of Jan. 4 o o; to Miss Skitch for a great wicker
chair o 11 6; to the stew. the 10th of Feb. 1645 for 10 fat sheep 4 o o; to
Bold then in part of 5 6 8 then due for his oxen 3 o o [total] £96 14s 6d
to the 12 of Feb. 1645

Bought of the widow Cunibear 2 fat oxen & one lesser & 60 bushels of
barley all which I take for 29 10s in part of £70 then due from her 29 10 o;
to Tho: Wiote as part of his & Tho: Polla: expenses in their journey in to
Cornwall then allowed him 2 14 10; the stew. received of the reeve of
*Tawstok* & the bailiff of *Warkley* 10 9 6 [total] 42 14 4 the aforesaid
12 of Feb. 1645 and 10 o o paid where it was due 90 o o.

To Jonathan's nurse the 14th of Feb. 1645 o 4 6; to Antony Rooke in part
for 4 ewes & 4 lambs 1 o o; lost at play o 2 o; paid for 2 barrels of
herrings 3 o o; for tobacco for my Lord d[elivere]d o 6 o; to Mr John
Copston the physician the 16th of Feb. 1645 for coming to Nurse Bannton
& the girl Rachel Wingfield o 10 o; to the stew. the 2 of March 1645
2 18 10; lost at play o 4 o; paid for 6 bush. of ['oat' crossed through]
wheat at 8s 6d to Jefferys 2 11 o; to the stew. the 13th of March 1645 for
peas &c 3 o o; to him towards the pork & the veal which cost 31s o 10 o;
to Wilmot Kimpflit in full of her wages this 24th of March 1645 1 o o

[p. 151] to the stew. for the caterer to buy fish the 19th of March 1645
2 o o; to the stew. then for his journey o 10 o; to Jonathan's nurse the
20th of March 1645 o 4 o; lost at play o 6 o; paid the paver in part for his
work o 8 o; paid Bold in part of £10 15s 6d now o 15 6; to the caterer the
25 of March 1646 5 o o; paid to the tucker I delivered it to Hardwick one
of my Lord's co. o 10 o; paid the stew. which I borrowed of Bold in the
beginning of March 7 10 o; paid the stew. the 30th of March 1646 2 o o;
paid about this time where it was due 230 o o

Rece. since the 25 of Octo. 1645 until the 25 of March 1646 in all
694 10 5, disbursed in the same time 609 19 6, so remains in my hands this
30 of March 084 10 11

[p. 150] Paid the stew. the 31 of March 1646 in full of his books to this
time 61 14 2; And lost in abatement by the pieces of 8 o 8 4; to John
Heirle that I borrowed of him this present March 10 o o; to the plumber
by bill o 18 o; to the stew. the 3 of April 1646 5 o o; to Thurstan & Will:
Booth for ['6' crossed through] 7 bushels of oats o 17 o; to the clock
maker for his quarter & mending my clock o 5 10; to Sir Thom: Farfaix
secretary the 6 of April 1 o o; to Bold in part of £10 I owe him 5 o o; to
old Miss Steevens due for her daughter Anne (now La[dy] Boles) 2 3 o; to
Jonathan's nurse the 11th of April o 5 o; paid for cheese to the stew. the
13 of April 1646 4 7 6; also to him for 3 bills of caterors ending the 11th
of Apr. 10 o o; to Geo: Cheively the 14th of April 1646 in full of his

wages due the last Lady Day now 1 0 0; paid to Dick Britton the 14th of
April 1646 in full of all (except the £100 for which he hath my Lord's
bond) 13 19 0; to Sarah Pollard, Lovett & Hardwick due this last Lady
Day 15 0 0; to Thom: Polla: then for the like 05 0 0; to Cob for the like
7 2 0; to Wiote the little man of *Instowe*'s bond for the like 3 0 0; to Rose
Hamline 1 10 0; to Robin Woode 4 0 0; to James Bla: 2 0 0; to Thurstan
2 0 0; to Will: Booth 2 0 0; to Dick Willis 1 0 0; to Tho: Armsby then
2 10 0; to Owyne 1 0 0; to Jo: Burk 2 0 0; for hay for the horses 1 1 0;
paid the stew. for Geo: Balch & Tho: Sumner in full of all demands for
corn, straw & one oxe the 17th of April 1646  30 8 0; given to Mr Varney
Bouchier & his wife the 20th of April 5 0 0; paid to the stew. for an old
bill of Mr Tucker of Barnstap. for one hogshead & one tearce & more of
claret wine 10 0 0; for schooling of a boy to Lady quarter 0 2 0; to the
stew. the 20th of April 1646 to pay in full to this time, to the cateror
7 4 11, to the smith 7 3 10, to Baldwin Steevens 4 19 1, to [?Bishop's]
Tawton Miller 14 6 8 for 2 hogs, to Ro: Whitfielld £3 for oats, to Eales
2 12 0 for barley this Eales hath had of the stew. 12s more, to Humfrey
Lake 1 19 0, to Besse Humble 9 10 9 in all 31 16 4; to the stew. for a case
I bought of him 0 4 0; paid Mr Will: Beare in full for interest & £8 of
principal to the 20th of April 1646, so that now from this time the debt
will be but £150, paid him now 40 12 4.

1646 taken with me for my journey & my Lord's to London the 22 of
April 20 0 0

**[p. 149]** ['rece. the 24th of April 1646 of Mr Elston at the court held at
*Hunspill* then for common fines there for one year & half to this time
£2 16s 0d; rece. from Hardwick the 22 of April the day we came from
*Tawstok*; rece. from Jo: Terry the farrier the 22 of April then in part
of £10  5 0 0' crossed through]

To Bold in full of all ['wages &' crossed through] other demands the 22 of
April then, there remains £5 due to him yet for wages 5 0 0; to Tho: Polla:
to account for this 27 of April in my journey to London ['6 10 2' crossed
through]; to Bold at *Hamersmith* the 2 of May for horse meat there
['1 10 0' crossed through]; to Bold at *Baysingstoke* or Egham 1 12 0

Disbursed by Bold upon the way toward London of which I have full paid
him the 5 of May 1646 13 6 8; disbursed by Tho: Polla: upon the like
occasions in the same journey at that time & now fully paid him 17 0 11;
laid out by myself by the way except 8s 4d for pins &c & for combs 9s in
all 12 12 10; paid the 5th of May 1646 to Mr Perin in part of £55  5 0 0
[total] 48 0 5

Taken with me expressed in the last side £20, also in gold 10 10s, received
upon the way where of 1 1 9 from Hard. 21 7 10  [total] 51 17 10
Disb. 48 0 5, re. 03 17 5
Rece. since the 30th of March 1646 with that 84 10 11 remaining in my
hands 338 12 9
Disb. in the same time to this present 6 of May 1646 338 3 5, so remains
0 9 4

I took Will: Lynn's account the 16th of March 1646 & found due to him
for wages at Michaelmas 1646 60 0 0, his receipts from the 14th of Sept.
1646 until the 12th of March following 534 15 1, his disburs. in the same
time came to 562 18 11, so, remains due to him more laid out then rece.
besides wages 028 3 10. The old bills comes to at this time the sum of
514 10 10, the new ones then 449. Whereof £100 of this is immediately to
be paid out of the go. which at present until it come out of Devon

[p. 148]   1646   To Mr Trussell for 5 yards of 2 coloured tabby at 9s the
yard 2 5 0; likewise to him for 3 yards & quarter of wrought satin at
12s the yard 1 19 0; to Mr Dunsterdield for 4 yards of black lace 0 16 0;
to him likewise in part of his bill then being the 20th of May 10 0 0; for
2 law books for my Lord the 26 of May 1646 0 12 6; to Thom: Pollard in
full of his book to the 23 of May paid the 26th of the £41 rece. of him
17 14 6; to Will: Lynn when he went to Wantage 0 19 6; paid the
upholsterer for 4 piece of hangings & green chairs &c for one month
1 10 0; to the farrier the 29th of May 1646 1 15 0; paid a bill of Bold's
2 3 0; laid out for bone lace when I bought Holland & more lace the 26 of
June 2 0 6   [total] 41 15

delivered to Will: Lynn the 7 of July 1646  2 0 0; paid in part of 6 15s 0 to
Mr Trussel the 13th of July 3 0 0   [total] £5

£7 July 27 1646 L: [total] 6 11 6 Paid the coach-maker a bill due for work
done since I came to town, paid in full of that bill the 27th of July 3 3 6,
there is of the old bills yet due to him about £13 & for mending the old
each about £5; paid for the recovery of the silver cup then 1 10 0; also for
hay then 1 16 0; given to the workmen the masons 0 2 0

[sideways in margin. the 15th of Sept. 1646 was the first fillip]   to my
sister of Westmorland's nurse & midwife the 20th of August at my Lord
being godfather to her son Harry 1646  4 0 0

to Jouce the 18th of Sept. 1646  0 5 0; to Miriam the 21 of Sept. 0 10 0;
lost to Sir Charles B: at cards 0 3 6; to John Burk in part of his
Michaelmas wages the 3rd of Octob. 1646  1 8 2

Paid the dyer for dyeing 31 yards of cloth of my own making for liveries
paid by Bold of the £50 rece. the 26 of Sept. 1646 of Mr Hames 4 10 0; to
Tho: Pollard in part of 40 [blank] then due the of [sic] October 30 0 0;
Bold paid him a bill then due to him 5 9 0; also to Bold for my Lord's
journey to *Tawstoke* the 6 day of October 1646 whereof given Will:
Deacon then by Bold 20s 10 1 0   Total £50

Nov. 1646 I had from Will: Lynn £9, £7 I paid Cob wages which due last
audit & £2 I gave him

disbursed from Octo: 1645 until the 16th of Octo. 1646  704 6 11, rece. in
the same time 789 19 0, so remains then 85 12 1

[p. 147]   £150 Westmorland   To Tho: Polla: the 19th of Octo. 1646 in
full of his book to the 17th £47 18s 5; also to him then for the brewer in
part of 10 0 0; also to him for the wood monger in part of 10 0 0; paid my
cousin Newport then in part of £50 30 0 0; paid the organist then in part
of £20 05 0 0; paid then to Seal the Upholsterer for my own hangings &

green cloth chairs & stools in part of £22 10s paid before by Will: Lynn
for the same £30 12 10 0; paid for ordinary mat 16s, for thread & nails 4s
in all 1 0 0; paid for ribbon & 2 white hoods 2 13 0; paid for 5 yards &
half of fine bone lace [blank]; given to Tho: Wimper for the binding his
son apprentice to a cook the 28th of Octo. 1646 2 0 0; given Robin
Woode when he brought my goods the 31 of Octo. 1646 1 0 0; given my
cousin Wat: Fitzwilliams that day 2 0 0; to Tho: Cammam to buy green
serge & fringe for a canopy for my chamber 2 3 0; given my tailor's man
0 2 6; paid Mr Lamb's carrier brought up my hangings Robin Wood &c
7 15 0; paid Mr Dunsterfield for lace for 2 flowered tabby petticoat & one
figured satin petticoat & waistcoat 6 5 0; paid to Mr Barrow for one piece
of fine fustian, for blank. & one piece of shag 5; to Tho. Pollard the 6 of
Nove. 5 0 0 [total] 150 6 0

Paid my cousin Newport in full of the £50 20 0 0, which I had from
Frank in part of &c; Bold given to the nurse & midwife at my sister of
Kent's daughter the La: Elizabeth Graye's baptising 2 0 0

Cob 0 5 0; nurse Briton 1 10 0; [blank] 2 2 6 3 0 0; to the Sp. Embas.
servant the 24th of Decem. 1 10 0; Miss Taylor 0 10 0

£27 36 7 6 Given my cousin Watt: Fitzwilliams the 31 of Oct. 1646
besides the 40s above mentioned this out of the £97 go. £1 0 0; to Miss
Tarry the 9th of Nov. 1646 for being with me six weeks, besides the cloths
4 0 0; to Varney Bouchier the 23 of Decem. 1646 0 10 0

[p. 146] To Sir Theodore Miarn the 27th of No. 1646 2 0 0

£20 Betty to Mary Thorp an old bill 1 17 0; to Tho: Polla: the rest of the
£20 I had from Betty 18 3 0

To my Lo. for his purse 9 15s pieces the 21 of Jan. 1646 6 15 0; delivered
Tho: Polla: in part of 34 14 9½ due the 16th of Jan. 1646 now this 22 of
Jan. given him 15 8 0; to a poor kinswoman 0 10 0; to a poor gentleman
1 0 0; for a cabinet the 26 of Jan. 1 2 0; Jan. the 29th paid for 6 yards
quarter of crimson velvet for the cradle & he had 2s 6d more by Forward
5 10 6; delivered to Tho: Polla: in part of 31 [blank] due the 23 of Jan. &
now paid him this 1 day of Feb. 30 0 0; delivered to Will: Lynn in Feb.
the 2 of which he paid £3 10s 0 to the embroiderer for my best mantle
setting the lace on 5 15 0; delivered to Will: Lynn the 8th of Feb. 5 0 0; to
Miss Scott for sending letters &c 1 0 0; 26 9 of Feb. to the organist in
part of £10 remained due to him 5 0 0; to Tho: Polla: the 10th of Feb. in
part of 27 0 9 due the 6th of Feb. 20 0 0; to Mr Wilde due at Christmas
now paid 5 0 0; lost at cards 0 5 0 [total] 160 13 0 the 11th of Feb. 1646

To Tho: Polla: the 22 of Feb. in part of [blank] 25 0 0; for my gr.
bible 24s, the clasps &c & for a curral 10s in all taken out then 02 0 0; to
Miss Bouchier for to pay for diet & schooling of her son Thom: for
2 months begun the 18th of Jan. 1646 which is all due until the 15th of
March £1 0 0; paid Mr Vinner the 1 day of March in part of [blank]
15 0 0; to him then for a child's porrenger & spoon 32s, for a small ladle
17s 6, for pence 5s, for exchange of the gold 5 in all 2 19 6; to a mercer in
Paternoster row at the Wheat Sheaf for 6 yards of flowered tabby
hearcouller [hair colour] 4 14 0; [sum crossed through] for an ell of lace at

Mr Eattens 0 7 0; [total] £24 3s 6d for handkerchief band & cuffs welted in the old exchange 0 12 0; to the poor then 0 0 6; for 10 glasses & 2 porrengers 0 10 6

To the fringe maker in part of £52 due the 2 of March for my bed cradle &c 30 0 0; at cards 0 1 6; Tho: Connam to buy things in Feb. 4 0 0

[p. 145] £100 5s 0d March the 11th paid to Mr Manby the silk man for the interest due at Jan. last to his kinsman for £300 12 0 0; likewise for a load of hay then £2 0s 0d; paid Tho: Polla: then in part of his book 30 0 0; Mr Manby rec. likewise then £100 which is endorsed upon the bond in part of the £300 then due, £50 of it came from Wantage & £50 I borrowed of Sir Ra: Sydanham which comes in this account repaid again 50 0 0 [total] £100 0 0

Will: Lynn Will: Lynn left with me the 29th of April 1647 15 3 8; also of his money [blank]; to the brewer the 2 of May 10 0 0; to the bricklayer then 05 0 0

£15 I had from Will: Lynn the 12th of May 1647 To Thurstan when he went away the 5th of May a bill 0 13 0; for the holland quilt for my bed 2 10 0; laid out for the taffety & lace for my coat & divers things else 11 13 0; & to play at Loadum 0 4 0 [total] £15

there was this year 21000 lbs of hops tried 1646
I took W: Lynn's account from Octo. the 24, 1647 until the 25 of March 1648 & in that time received by him 1159, disbursed in the same time by him 1151 7, so rests due this 29th of March 1648 from him 0008 2

[p. 144] an account of the £50 I had the 3rd of Aug. 1647
50 B. Fr. To Cob then in part of £4 due to him for wages before the 30th of March last £2 0 0; to Tho: Polla: to buy hay &c the 7th of Aug. 2 0 0; to Miss Murey's gardener 0 5 0; August to Will: Lynn to fetch home the gr. coach 10 0 0; to Mr Ridle the 15 of Aug. 5 0 0; to Cob in full of £4 due to him for wages heretofore 2 0 0; for 12 gallons & 3 quarters of sack & 6 quarters of sack & a vessel 3 5 6; to Mr Green the mercer in part of [blank] the 26 of March 10 0 0; to an old pot brought to me 0 5 0; to the grocer in full to the beginning of Sept. 6 4 0; W:L: 13 10 4 to Bold in part of a bill 3 10 0; one morning in July borrowed of Forward but paid for cham. £1 3 0 0; to Bold in full of that bill the 17th of Aug. £2 was odd money 5 7 0; to Will: Booth then 0 15 0; to Miss Dir:K: for Eliz: Sydenham the 30th of Aug. 0 0 0; [illegible crossed through] paid to Bold his wages in full of what was due to him at our Lady Day last, this 18th of August 1647 14 0 0; to my Lord the 20th of Aug. for Speede's Maps & *Chroni.* 3 0 0; to my cousin Francis Myldmay then in gift 3 0 0; for [Francis Mildmay] the 1 of Sept. 3 0 0; to my Lord the 3d of Sept. 1647 2 0 0; for a fair laced scarf & hood & 2 pair of pearl pendants & a screen fan 3 0 0; paid the farrier's bill for shoeing 1 4 0; to Betty Fuller & lost at cards 0 3 0; Aug. the 24th to Mr Trussell then in part of [blank] 20 0 0; to a brewer then 02 19 0; Mr 60 Hams: to Tho: Polla: in full of his book to the 28 of Aug. also for 30 dozen of candles 9 3 6 in all 44 3 6; paid a bill then of B: 1 8 6; to Miss Bouchier the 3d of Sept. 0 10 0
[totals] sp[ent] 150 10 0 rec[eived] 77 19 10

To Doctor Fryer the 30th of Sept. 1647 1 o o; Mr Hayne £45 paid a bill
of Bold's whereof 30s of it was for Mathematical instruments for my Lord
2 o o; paid William Booth for a horse for my Lord the 16 of Sept. 25 10 o;
paid a bill of Bold's whereof 4 yards of frieze for a coat for my Lord cost
£1 10s o, the bill in all paid the 4th of Octo. 3 o o; to Will: Lynn for one
of my gold counters o 15 6; to Sir Morice Willyams 2 o o; to Tho: Polla:
in gift this Sept. 3 o o; to Willy: Lynn for Tho: Polla:s book the 15th of
Octo. 5 o o; for ['himself then' crossed through] the same book then 2 o o;
to Miss Lovett the mid. o 10 o; to Bold his wages due this Octo. 1647
12 o o; to Miss D. the 19th of Octo. 2 o o; to Dr: Cham: then & to him
next day 1 o o; for a syrup then o 16 o [total] £212 11s od

[p. 143] £5 to Wilmote for her wages due this 29th of Sept. 1 o o; also
that she laid out to a French Doct. o 7 o; to Sir Harry Ley the 1 of Octo.
1 10 o; to ['Sir Morice Willyams' crossed through] Ralph Booth in part of
£3 10s 6d spent in his journey from Taws. with Dick Rook & 4 horses,
Rich: Polla: gave him 50s & I now 1 o 6; to Do. Cham: the 25th of Octo.
1 o o; to Miss Lovett then o 10 o; to Sir Morice Willyams then 1 o o; to
his surgeon then for Le: for my Lord o 10 o; to Do. Cha: the 27th of
Octo. o 10 o; to Do. Cha: the 29 of Octo. 1 o o; to Mr Heyne 1 o o; laid
out o 6 6; for hay one load 1 13 o; to the chair men the 28th o 5 o; to the
postillion in part of his wages 1 o o; for letters by the post o 2 o; to
Doctor Cham: the 3d of Nov. 1 o o; ['to Will: Booth the 2 of Nove. for
his wages due at Michaelmas last 1647 1 o o o 10 o' crossed through] to
Mr Symones the divine 1 o o; to Doct. Cham: the 16 of Nove. o 5 10;
spent o 5 10; lost [sic] to the organist in full 5 o o; rece. since the 3rd of
Aug. 1647 until the 2d of Nove. after 233 10 o; disbursed in the same time
as appeareth 233 10 o; of the £5 I had from Bold to one man the 16th of
Nov. 1 10 o; to Doct. Cham: the 17th day 1 o o; of Bo: to Doct. Cham:
the 22 of Nove. 1 o o; to Wilmot that she laid out o 4 6; to Wilmot the
1 of Decem. o 2 6; lost at play this Christmas o 5 o; to P:B: the 1 of Jan.
1 o o; 10 of W:L: to Doct. Cham. the 10th of ['Dece' crossed through]
Jan. 1647 2 o o; £1 of W:L: to Doct. Hynton the 12 of Jan. 1 o o; to Sir
Theod. Myarn the 25 of Jan. 5 o o; to Do. Cham. then 2 o o; to Doct.
Cham: the 27th of Jan. 1 o o
[total] 16 2 o

Returned to my bro. Geo: in to France so soon as it was received the 4th
of Jan. 1647 From my bro. Frank 50 o o

There was writing sealed of articles of agreement between my Lord Rich:
Harris & one Mr White & his wife & my Lord's tenants the denices
[*demises*] for the dividing of *Mulcott* [Mullacott] the 1 of Nov. 1648

[p. 142] Brought out of London the 27th of Jan. 1647 £50
Delivered then to Tho. Polla: for the journey &c £10 o o; delivered him
the first & 2d of Feb. to buy malt &c 04 o o; paid Rich: Forrwad that he
laid out for oats, straw, candles, bread, trenchers, butter, eggs &c 3 4 o; to
the fiddlers at Oxford o 5 o; to Sir William Walter's man brought
6 partridges, 6 carps o 2 6; for 2 bushels of beans o 12 6; to Tho: Polla:
the 3d of Jan. whereof 14s for the cooper 1 o o; to Tho: Polla: the 7th of
Feb. 10 16 o; to Tho: Polla: the 11th of Feb. 5 o o; given to Little Betty

Cope's nurse the 21 of Feb. 1647 o 10 o; lost at play o 10 o; to Tho: Polla: in full of his book to the 18th of Feb. £11 3s 2½d 14 o o & also to account for then 2 16 9½ in all [total] 50 o o [total] 50 o o

24 to Tho: Polla: the 29th of Feb. 1647 that came from Want. 24 o o

£40 to Bold to pay for hay at *Brewern* the 7th of Mar. 7 5 o; to Bold the 11th of March 1647 for a coach horse bought of one Mr Craffts in *Gloster-shire* 15 10 o, & to the man that brought him o 2 6; given in gift at Tangley & *Brewern* the 12 of Mar. 3 12 6; for oats then o 19 6; to the vicar of *Sarsdin* [Sarsden] that read prayers then o 5 o; to Tho: Polla: in full of his book to this day 4 15 o; to Bold for oats more o 6 6; to. Tho: Polla: in full for the journey from *Brewern* to Lond. & to Bold for the horse &c where of 32s was for a hind wheel bought of the Lady Horwood by Wheatley [?]Town Bridge 5 17 6

Laid out since the 27th of Jan. until the 15th of March in [blank] 112 13 6, so now remains 1 6 6

A satin cap for my Lord the 16th of March o 6 o; at *Paules* & to the poor the 16th o 2 o; for thread in part of 2 3 6 o 3 6; for 4 rolls of tape & one of filleting 5 laces 3 yards &c o 14 o; needles 18d o 1 o [total] 1 6 6 [total] 114 o o

£20 laid out then for ribbon 1 o o; also the 17th for bone lace 15 5 o; for thread then 2 o o; for 3 combs o 11 o; for 1200 of pins & 2 black papers of pins o 11 6; the horses coming from *Aylesburey* the 28th of March 1648 o 3 10; Bold must account for [o] 8 8 [total] 20 o o

[p. 141] Bor. of Ri: Forard £5 the 28th of March 1647 in gold o; whereof to Sir Theodore Miarn the 25 by me 2 o o; to Doct. Cham: the next day 2 o o; given by my Lord to Doct. Miarn the 23 day where of one was my own before 2 o o

£5 from Will: Lynn the 23 of March to the surgeon let me blood the 24th of March o 5 o; to Doct. Cham: the 25 [March] 1648 2 o o; to the nurse & midwife that day in the Strand at the christening of Rachel ['Gri' crossed through] Griffeth 2 o o; for silver & gridelin penny broad 6d a yard ribbon o 8 o [total] 10 13 o

Disbursed since the 2 of Nove. 1647 until the 28 of March 1648 210 15 o, rece. in the same time 211 o o, so remains this 29th of March 1648 o 5 o

£20 W:L: the 4th of April 1648
To Mr Jakson for 7 ells of holland at 7s the ell 2 9 o; to Doct. Cham: the 6 of April the 8th day 2 o o; to Miss Der: the 7th of Ap. o 10 o; also that day to Sir Theo. Myarn 2 o o; paid Bold the 8th of April in full of a bill for a hat for my Lord & the snuffer & little candlestick & in gold whereof William Lynn paid the 26 of Jan. 1647 £2, in all 6 4 10, & I now 4 5 o; to Thom: Polla: for candles & soap the 8th day 3 o o; paid for herbs the 12th of Apr. 5s, lost at play 3s & in part of 6s 6d for my comb case 2s in all o 10 o; to Tho: Polla: for the cooper &c the 15th of April 2 o o; to my tailor's man o 2 o; the 20th of April 1648 the day I went to Mereworth put in my purse ['2 1 o' crossed through] & in gold then ['2 o o' crossed through]; for 2 hoods & a tiffany 15s & for ribbon 7s 1 2 o; [blank] o 2 6;

£5 go.   To Doct. Cham: the 14th of April 1648 £1 0 0; to Sergeant
Glanvill the 16th of April when he gave his advice under his hand for the
sueing Miss Pa: Mr Geo: Bear & Mr Balta: Bea: in the Chancery 2 0 0,
also the like under his hand against Jackman's copy; for mending my
clock 4s & mending my own stool 2s 0 6 0; £3   Laid out in a journey
which my Lord & I went the 20th of April & came back the 24th to
Mereworth castle only in gifts 8 12 6; more 0 5 0; May the 15th 1648   to
buy toys for the 3 boys at Mereworth then 0 6 0; to Doctor Cham: the
5 of May at Cholley [?Chawleigh] 1 0 0; X 15 17s 0   to Sir Theo: Miarn
then the remain. of the £5 in gold 2 0 0; to the 3 children the 8th of May
0 7 0   [total] 22 17 6

[p. 140]   £50   The 10th of May 1648 paid John Webb in full to the 28 of
Decem. 1646 his bill 10 17 6; also then gave 01 10 0; paid the 15th of May ·
to Mr Will: Beare due the 23th day of April 1648   08 0 0; for making a
pair of satin bodies & for a plain pair 01 10 0; for a dressing box 22s &
pendants & ribbon powder 02 11 0; for the wagoner the 12 of May when
6 servants & 1200 & odd £ went toward the *Bathe* 05 0 0; to Robin Wood
for their diet then 03 0 0; 1648 the bit-maker £1 9s, the shoemaker 13s 6, a
French dressing 8s, binding the *Faire Queen* 2s 0d &c 03 0 0; for the
coach-maker then the 17th of May in full of one bill of £13 his last at
present being not paid 10 8 11   08 0 0; to the sadler in full then 06 4 0; to
the band woman Miss Watson for making 2 crabets [*cravats*] 6, for one
plain handkerchief & cuffs 1s 6, for one plain one 1s, for one laced
han[dkerchief]. & cuff 00 10 6   [total] 50 3 0

Clowb: £36 17th May   to my apothecary, in full of mine & 11s for
physick for Cob, Samuel Scutt the 17th of May 09 0 0; for a horse bought
the 18th of May the morn. we began our journey toward the Bath 06 10 0;
given Rachel Griffeth's nurse the 16th day 00 10 0; to Bold for horse meat
being 12 horses at Reading 01 18 0; to Thom: Polla: for our diet there
02 10 0; to my purse for the poor 01 10 0; at *Malborow* deliv. to Bold for
the horses £2 & to Polla. then £2 04 0 0; the 25 day of May we began to
use the *Bathe*   to Tho: Polla: the 24 of May 05 10 0; to one & one other
Minister the 26 of May 01 0 0; to Mary at 12 a clock at night the 29th of
May 0 2 6; to Tho: Polla: the 30th 3 10 0

£5 go.   to Doct: Brewer the 23 of May at *Bathe* 01 0 0; to the same
Docto. the 29th 01 0 0; the other £3 Bold had again 3 0 0
£50   to Tho: Polla: the 7th of June 1648   20 0 0; lost at play 01 0 0; lost
at play the 6th of June [blank]; to Tho: Polla: the 9th of June for the
butcher 5 0 0; to Tho: Polla: due upon his book to the 9th day 4 5 4½,
more given him then to account for 5 14 7½ in all the 12 of June 1648
10 0 0; to Thom: Polla: the 20th of June 12 0 0; lost at play 02 0 0
[total] 141 3 0

[p. 139]   £12 11d in gold   lost at play 0 10 0; given to Christopher
Ashley's wife 0 10 0; lost at play the 22 of June 3 0 0; lost at play 9 10 0;
to a goldsmith in Bath 0 9 0; to Mary Warder the guide 1 0 0; £60 to Miss
Dancy for 7 weeks lodging in Bath 24 15 0; to Tho: Polla: for his book
1 2 0; to the brewer [blank]

£21 3s 0   paid at *Lacoke* [Lacock] the 29th of June for the going & curing in part of a horse 1 3 0; to the 5 guides & the young woman 6 10 0

Bor. in gold of Bold 3   to Doctor Brewer the 1 of July at *Bathe* 3 0 0; to the brewer for 12 hogsheads of beer in six weeks 8 0 0; to the sergeant at the *Crosse* Bath 1 2 0; to the 2 chair men 11s a piece 1 2 0; to the pumper & his wife 1 7 6; to Tho: Polla: the 1 of July 6 8 6; to the old woman at the slip 0 5 0; to the pumper for my Lord 0 11 0

2 3s   to the apothecary the 2d of July at Bath 4s in 3 of my Lord's counters & 4s & 2s more Bold laid out for me so in all 2 9 0
To Tho: Polla: the 4th of July where of 8 counters of my Lord's at 15s a piece & one 22s in all 7 17s 0; to Tho: Polla: at Bath in his hands of the £60 25 5 0; also more due to him paid then 0 11 0; he had ['of' crossed through] from Mr Wilde for Will: Lynn to pay a book binder in London £4 4 0 0
whereof my Lord's 12 counters are 8 18 0 so then it is £102 11s 0 [total] 111 9 0

£37 10s 9   to Bold that I borrowed of him at Bath 3 0 0; to Rich: Forrard that I borrowed likewise 5 0 0; to Bold more borrowed & laid out in his journey from Bath to *Tawstok* & at *Bristole* in part of £11 1s 1 1 0; £17 to Jonathan's nurse due the 30th of July 4s but given 0 6 0; £40 to Rich: Britten in part of what he laid out at Bristo[l] fair paid the 5 of August 1648 20 0 0; also sent to Mr Lambe by the stew. for so much taken up by Will: Lynn in London of Mr Haines 34 0 0; to the stew. the 5 of August to pay a carrier in part of £5 5s he formerly paid him 17s so now 4 8 0; to a carrier Geo: Tucker the 21 of July 1648 1 5 0   [total] 60 0 0

[p. 138]   Paid for 2 month's rate for the Barton this 8th of Aug. 1648 2 10 0; towards the 2 weigh of coal cost 3 16 6 paid here 2 3 10; to the stew. then for hay-makers 3 0 0; ['to Tho: Polla: in full of the expenses at Bath 1 11 0' crossed through] to Robin Woode that he laid out coming from *Bristole* 4 persons to Tawstock in all 3 11 4 3 1 4; £16 to Ralph Booth in part of £2 6 0, for his bring[ing] 6 horses to Bath & Dick Rook, whereof the stew. gave him 15s & now by me 1 11 0; £1 to the plumber in part of £10 7s 6d the 29th of July £2 the stew. left unpaid the 27th of Octo. 1646 5 0 0; to Docto. Chichestor the 7th of August 1 0 0; to the ['sadler' crossed through] stew. the residue for the coal & whole being 3 16 6 1 12 8; sum is £19 18s 10d [total] 19 18 10

£10   my Lord hath delivered by me 11 angels that is £5 10s 0 which I had again; £20 to Tho: Polla: a bill 0 9 4; for making Randale & Frank 6 p[air] of stockings 0 1 8; for petticoat apron & waistcoat for Maule 16d the yard 0 10 0; Aug. the 10th   to the carrier whereof Rich: Forrard is to give me 17s back 3 9 0; to the stew. then for Tho: Armsb. to buy corn 2 10 0; 10s to the constables for 10 weeks behind of the new rate at 15s a month more than former the 12 of Aug. paid 7 10 0; to Tho: Polla: when I paid the bill above 0 5 0; to the stew. the 13th of Aug. to pay the workmen 2 weeks ['laid out by Tho: Pola: £1 of the £3 of his own' crossed through] 2 0 0; given at *Clevelley* [Clovelly] the 18th of August 1648 3 0 0; to the stew. the 20th of August for workmen & hay-makers 1 15 0   [total] 21 10 0   [in margin crossed through 'due to John Heirle this 18 of August for 6 bushels of wheat £3 18s. Borrowed of Joseph Ley this 18th of August £20. also of John Heirle the 21th of August. 1648, £20 in all due to John Heirle at present 62 12s 0. & £2 more for cheese. 10s'] Laid out by William Weekes & Rumson at *Kilkington* fair the 15 of August 1648 for 4 oxen, 3 cows dry & one steer in all 47 3 4 & for their charges 11s 5d in all 47 14 9 of which is borrowed of Ralph Booth £4 & of Nick: Marchant £3 & of money I gave them, of which they brought back 5s 3d, 40 14 9; paid for 100 lbs weight of sugar of 2 sorts bought the 18th of August 1648 by Rich: Britton 7 0 0; paid for the interest of 2 years of £200 borrowed of Thomas Horwood of Barnstaple for which my Lord was bound for my brother, who lent Mr Horwood's bill of £200 to Sir John Greenvile, who ought to pay both principal & interest, but paid by my Lord to them the 22 of August 1648 in full of which the £200 is taken up of Hugh Horsom of Barn. 232 0 0; to Thom: Poll: that he laid out more at *Clovela* [Clovelly] 0 10 6; in all 5 bush. to Thom: Armsby to buy wheat the 23 of Aug. 1 5 0, to Tho: Armsby to buy wheat at 14s & 3d the bush. 2 6 6; to the fiddlers then the 24th of August 1648 0 2 6; to Honour then 0 1 0 [total] 284 0 3

laid out by Bold out of Joseph Ley's £20 001 00
Aug. the 23 1648 rece. & borrowed since my coming home in July 1648 397 4 3, disb. since my coming home in July 1648 395 9 1,so remains in my hands £1 15s 2d
since the 18 of August 294 5 6

**[p. 137]** Bold laid out at *Ilfacombe* the 25 of August 1648 0 19 0; to Doctor Wilde then 3 0 0; to the stew. the 27 of Aug. to pay for a b[ushel] of new wheat at 12s & workmen's wages 2 0 0; to Jonathan's nurse then who henceforth is to have 18d a week 0 5 0; Bold laid out more 0 9 0; to Rich: Britton the 29th of Aug. 1648 in full of what he laid out at *Bristole* fair now 12 2 7; also his charges at *Appledor* 0 2 0; and also for 9 bush. of oats at 4s 6d being 2 0 6; ['to Thom: Lovering for 37 bush. of barley malt at 9s the bushel' crossed through]; their charges in April 1648 at St George's fair at Torrington was 1s 2d where they bought 21 sheep & 3 beasts William Weekes laid out at Hartl[obscured by ink] & Bradworthy Fair the 30th of Aug. 1648 for 5 steers £30 & one cow & 40 wethers at £14 10s the score at John Braggs in Hartland at the fair one yoke of draught oxen cost £12 10s & one black steer cost £5 9s & his charges 10s 6d, laid out in the whole £77 9s 6d whereof £4 is to be turned up at the audit in a bargain for Wellsford to John Bragg, the rest he had in money of me £37 9s 6d; to Mr Pagge by Wilmot Toogood the 1 of Sept. 1648 an old bill for wine 7 6 6; to Tho: Wiote that he laid out at Dunterton in Aug. 1648 0 4 0; paid the widow Nashe for butter at 6d p[er] lb & cheese at 2d the lb bought Jan. 1647 paid the 1 of Sept. 1648 2 9 0; paid Tho: Polla: a little bill for a horn book for Watt &c 0 4 9; paid Ralph Booth for so much borrowed of Will: Weekes at *Killkington* fair August 1648 4 0 0; paid Nick: Marchant by turning up for 1 acre of grass £1 4s & for feeding 2 oxen one month 12s, the rest of the £3 paid which is 1 4 0, the other allowed 1 16 0; paid for a hat for the French boy 6d & for a peck of oatmeal 3s 3d & white wine 6d & rec. in all 0 10 7; delivered the stew. the 2 of Sept. 1648 to pay 2 bills of Uxtable of May & June [blank]

and the workmen's last weeks bill which came to £1 11s 3, gave him
3 10 0; to Rich: Cobb in part of his wages this 3d of Sept. 1648 2 10 0;
13 yards of cloth sent to the dyer the 4th of Sept. brought home the 13th
of Octo. 1648 paid the dyer in full of all bills, £6 4s 0, to this 3d of Sept.
paid 6 2 0; to Tho: Lovering for 37 bu[shels] of barley malt then at 9s the
bushel 16 13 0; paid 2 women for cleansing 2 houses &c the 5 of Sept.
0 7 0; paid John Hamline in full to the 5 of Sept. his bills then coming to
£6 14s 4d whereof £1 5s 0 was borrowed of his wife by me paid now all
£5 he allowed me for Susan Drew's life in a tenement & all I paid 6 14 0
[total] 111 18 8

From the 18th of Aug. 1648 to the 25 laid out 244 5 6, these 2 sums makes
356 4 2, rece. & borrowed in the same time 374 3 10, so should remain
this 6 of Sept. 1648 017 19 8, but doth remain but 017 13 2, 7s 6d
misreckoned. The 6 of Sept. 1648

[p. 136] Paid the 9th of Sept. 1648 in full for all wine except the white
wine 12 bottled new fetched 6 12 5; paid for 112 yards of canvas cloth for
[blank] sheets the 9th of Sept. 5 12 0; paid a carrier then for bringing a
little trunk with my clothes 0 5 0; to the tailor Lewice 0 3 6; given Sir
Will: Essex his widow the 14th of Sept. 1648 0 10 0; bought a bucking
sheet for Wilmot 4 yards of coarse canvas at 10d the yard the 15th of Sept.
0 3 4; also then 6 sieves & a cream dish 0 3 6; to the stew. for
2 haymakers 0 10 0; for 6 lbs & ½ of pepper at 20d the lb 0 10 10; for
4 tunn at 11s the tunn bought at Barnstaple 2 6 0; for a pair of shoes for
Randle at Barnstap. fair 0 2 8; Sept. the 19th for 2 pigs bought of James
Crowder one is ['nea' crossed through] to be reared with the black spot
upon his back 16s a piece 0 2 8; given to him for a pig he brought me
0 1 0; paid the hop gatherers for this year's gathering at 5d the day for
90 days Sept. the 23 1 17 6; lost at play the 28 of Sept. 1648 0 6 3; paid
for 2 months of the highest rate for the barton this 4th of Octo. 1648
4 0 0; paid an old bill for butter & cheese to Tho: Ley's wife that was
spent when I was at London 5 12 1; to Besse Seirle for brown thread, 1 lb,
2s 6d, for shoes for the woman in the kitchn 3 0 9 0; to William Weeks
which he laid out at *Toring-ton* fair the 29th of Sept. for 6 beasts in all
33 8 6; to Wilmot for one brought lobsters 1s, for samphire 2s 0 3 0; lost
at tables 0 10 0; lost at tables 0 10 0; Anice laid out at *Torington* Fair the
29th of Sept. 1648 [blank]; To Bour. Steevens to pay for 10 bus[hels] of
oaten malt the steward paid £5 for the other 20 b. which he had of the
reeve of *Tawstok* & I now this 12 of Octo. 2 10 0; to Charles the
carpenter in part of £6 which he is to have by agreement for building my
threshing floor £1 0 0; paid 2 bills of workmens wages one 22s the other
is £1 9 10 2 11 10; for brooms 0 2 6; for 12 bus[hels] of barley malt at
7s the b[ushel] & 10 bus[hels] of oaten malt at 4s the bus[hel] the 12 of
Octo. 1648 6 4 0; for 2 great flaskets for cloth then 0 5 0; for 4 weigh of
coal at £2 the weigh then 8 0 0; to Sir Ralph Sydenham due the 20th of
July last for £200 16 0 0; to Wiote that he spent & Tho: Pollard in their
journey to Cornwall 2 17 3; and for his expences in following the courts
with Mr Bolworthy 0 7 8; to Tho: Wright when he went to survey
*Spicthwick* [Spitchwick] 0 10 0; laid out by Bold 0 7 6; also by the same
0 7 0 [total] 105 2 0

**[p. 135]** Sept. the 29 1648 paid the carrier for John Jourdans the
gardener coming down & his box 5s 4d, he had in money of him 6s & 20s
for riding 1 16 0; lost at play 0 10 0; paid Cob that I borrowed of him
0 10 0; to the stew. to pay the last week's workmans wages 1 1 6; Anice
laid out at *Bidiford* market the 17th of Octo. 0 0 5; to Charles Allen the
carpenter for work done since the 27th of May to the 16th of Sept. 1648
by him & his men paid in full of all demands the 18 of Oct. 5 0 3; to the
smith Rich: Huxtable paid 2 bills due the 5th of Aug. 1648 6 2 0; to
Bourn Steevens to buy a net to fish with the 20th of Octo. 1648 0 16 0; to
a tinker for mending kettles at ½ a nail 0 6 4; repaid John Lovering that I
borrowed of him the 29 of September 1648 this 2 of Octo. 30 0 0; repaid
Joseph Ley the £20 borrowed of him by Bold against Molton fair & for
5 bush. of malt at 7s the bush. 1 15s & 2 bus. of barley at 9s 4d, 18s 8d in
all 22 13 8; laid out by Besse at *Torington* market the 21 of Octo. 0 0 7;
given to Roger Jeffreys the apothecary the 22 of Octo. when he came to
my Lord in the night 0 10 0; to Jonathan's nurse for 2 months the 23 of
Octo. 1648 0 12 0; to Tho: Polla: a bill for post letters & gifts then 0 9 6;
to the poor the 22 of Octo. when we rece. the comunion 1648 0 10 0; to
the cateror the 24 of Octo. to buy butter & cheese 1 0 0; charges laid out
upon the key & lantern, the whole year post at *Illford Comb* & allowed
this 24 of Oct. 5 13 5; Thom: Wright when he went to survey *Spicthweek*
[Spitchwick] *Parke* laid out for himself & man & horses 6 days 12s 2
whereof ['Tho:' crossed through] paid formerly 10s & now 0 2 2; paid Sir
Ralph Sydenham part of his bond of £200 100 0 0, & for the interest of
that £100 then the 25 of Octo. 1648 2 0 0; laid out by Anice at *Bidiford*
market the 24 of Octo. 0 1 1; to the cateror for Barnst. market the 27th of
Octo. 1 0 0; Octo. the 27th 1648 to Mr Lambe in full of all between him
& me for 2 yards of scarlet baize at 17s the yard & for all other reckonings
9 19 0; paid to John Heirle in full of all demands for £40 borrowed & for
corn 22 12s 0 & for cheese £2 in all 64 12 0; ['paid Widow Cunibear in full
for sheep & cattle 20 0 0' crossed through] left in the closet in the store
chamber this 10th of Jan. 12 sugar loaves & a piece, powdered sugar of
2 sorts, much cinnamon &c [total] ['255 12 3 255 12 5' crossed through]
255 6 10

**[p. 134]** To Doctor Wilde in full of what's due to him this Octo. the
28th 1648 7 0 0; to Voysin the like then 5 0 0; to Tho: Pollard then in full
5 0 0; to him for Owine also 1 0 0; to Cob the like in full 5 0 0; to Rich:
Forrad the like 7 10 0; to Tho: Polla: for 2 post letters 0 2 6; to Tho:
Wiote in full then 6 0 0; to Besse Searle then 1 10 0; to Norton in full
2 10 0; to Will: Booth then 3 0 0; to Philipe the like 2 0 0; to Wilmote for
her wages due now £1; ['due to Forrard that he laid out to Doctor Ch:
Octo. 21 1648, £2 that is note here accounted paid the 8 of Jan. 1648'
crossed through] to Doctor Chichestor the 24 of Octo: 1648 1; to the
plumber in full of all demands to this day 7 18 0; to Dick Rooke in full
2 5 0; to Rose Hamline the like 1 10 0; to 2 weeders for a week 0 5 6; to
Besse Thorn her wages due now 1 0 0; to Agnes Tearle the like 2 0 0; to
Honor also then 2 0 0; to the stew. then for the like 9 10 0; to the stew.
then to pay John Johnson for 3 b. of wheat at 14s & 10d the b. & the
widow Sumner for one b. at 14s & 2 b. of barley malt at 10s 3 18 6; to

Will: Rumson in full of all due to him 5 0 0; to Baldwin Steevens the like 4 0 0; to the miller for one year & half 4 10 0; to Rob: Whittfielld the like 3 0 0; to Welsh John in full 0 10 0; to John Burk the like 2 0 0; to Tho: Armsby then 2 10 0; to Will: Geare 2 0 0; to George Chevily 1 0 0; to Robin Wood in full 4 0 0 [total] 106 09 6

['John Milles note of his debt at 6 14 6 Octo. the 30th 1648' crossed through] Edw: Randall of *Warkley* in Devon made his accounts even with me the 24th of April 1650 for his debits for the years 1647 48 & 49 in 1647 rested due 24 3 3, in 48 34 9 5, in 49 32 0 11 [total] 90 13 7 Whereof he paid as by the acquitance appeareth to Tho: Pollard £17 to myself, £6 to Rich: Polla: £24 & £2 in all £49 0 0 [leaving] 41 13 7 also he is to pay by promise 144 days hence £5 for Mr Pincent's heriot & £6 13 4 for 2 quarters rent due from *Warkly* now.

he hath this day given bond to my Lord to pay £40 in two years & half.

[enclosure 134a] A bill for the right Honourable the Count. of Bath this 25th of March 1641

*First*, for the gold of the pendants £2 19s 00d, for the fashion of them set with 150 dia. £18 00 00, for the 9 dia. added 3 great and 6 small at 17 0 0 ['for the case' crossed through] the sum is 38 9 00

rec. in the pendants 040 dia., rec. in the tags 132 dia. rec. all 172 delivered in the pendants 150 dia., delivered back loose dia. which could not be used 031 dia.

181 172 the 9 dia. not added 009.

due upon a bond £62 14s, the interest for 8 months comes to 03 06 [total] 66 00

besides the bond due upon this bill 38 09, the whole sum 104 09

Rec. in part of this bill the sum of four score pounds I say rec. per me Fra: Allein

[p. 133] £10 of this borrowed of Tho: Polla: & £20 payned old gold to J: Heirle & £5 10s Ro: Wood hath go. for & £4 borrowed of Tho: Wiot all paid given to Robin Meare brought pears 0 1 0; paid Miss Baker the 30th of Octo. in full of all demands to this day when my Lord entered into a new bond to her of £100, now I say paid 166 18 6; to Avice Starlling for washing [?sic] the French boy for one quarter & half the 30th of Octo. 1648 0 5 0; for knitting a pair of stockings for Randall Payton 0 1 0 [total] 167 5 6

Ja. the 10th left provision in my house at *Tawstok*
beer 14 hogsheads, cider 4 hogs., bread 54 cast, soap half a barrel the whole cost cost [sic] 16s, butter 10 pots & one tub, cheeses 77, candles one box of London candles—12 lbs of middle lights more gr. candles, 3 tubs of salt salmon containing 50 salmons, bacon 10 flitches 4 of them in salt & 6 dry, ling 14, wet fish 1 hogshead, salt 7, poor John 9 couple, the offal of 2 hogs, pork 3 pieces, one mutton, one beef there is one cow more fit to kill, also apples, some fruit and spice, 7 cows, turkeys 7, hens 5, cocks 3, ducks 5, capons 7, geese 2

[p. 132] paid the 1 of Nove. 1648 for 1 bushel of salt 0 5 10; for the market maids horse standing 3d & her dinner 4d 0 0 7; for 24 lbs of *Chedder* cheese bought by Miss Heyne the 2d of Nov. 0 12 0; no more

bought in part for 60 yards of coarse dowlas at 12d the yard, gave Owine
12 yards of this 1 o o; given at Ex. 3 6 o; given at home the 8th of Nov.
1648  1 o o; paid Robert Whitfielld at his going away 1 2 8; paid John
Terry for 14 bush. of the best lime at 8d the b[ushel] & 270 bush. at
4d the bush. in all paid 4 19 o; paid workmens wages o 19 o; for threshing
9 bus. of wheat o 7 6; for threshing 7 bus. of wheat o 5 10; paid workmens
wages the 12 of Nov. o 18 5; 24 b[ushels] of barley malt made but
13 hogsheads more then to Pikett for work done in the Park & 1d a yard
in part o 4 o; paid for 8 yards of dowlas for Sam: Bold at 13d the yard
o 8 8; for a pair of wool cards 1s 4d & for spiles 1d o 1 5; 20 to John
Heirle that I had of him toward the payment of Miss Baker [blank]; to
Will: Weekes his son William the 14th day of No. o 10 o; 10 to Tho:
Polla: that I borrowed of him ['for' crossed through] toward the payment
of Miss Baker's £166; to Peter Bold to buy a horse for my Lord the 10th
of Nov. 16 o o; more to him that he laid out then & [illegible] I borrowed
& £3 8s towards his wages 4 o o; William Weeks had cattle at Hartland of
John Brage at 40 o o; Besse Thorne spent & laid out at *Bidiford* market the
14th of No. o o 10; to Miss Downe in full for corn & straw formerly due
in 1645 & 46 to the 16th of No. 1648  55 19 o; paid the tucker for work
done to the liveries made now o 12 o; to William Weeks to pay the
workmen the stew. paid 10s for [blank] & now this 19th of No. o 19 o; to
Jonathan's nurse then o 5 o; short 3d to the stew. in full to the 20th day of
Nov. 1648  3 10 o  [total] 137 5 3

Disbursed the 6 of Sept. 1648 to the 20th of No. 1648 in all 771 9 1, rece.
in the same time 787 10 10, so should remain 016 1 9½ but doth remain
this present 20th of Nov. 1648  011 o o

This is sold for 16 16s being 6 ac[res] at 56 the acres this 12 of No. 1650
There is between 5 & 6 ac[res] of wood at *Warkly* ready to be sold this
present 28th of Nov. 1648, if Dorothy Jermain will give £3 a acre & fence
it to keep cattle from spoiling the growth of the wood she shall have it.
She giveth £56. Other woods there will be ready in 2 years called
Shortlidge Com. 50 acres more of greater quantity in 4 years, Ashrenton
woods 140 acres.

[p. 131]  to John Terrey the farrier due at the audit 1648 in full for
2 years wages £4 os od; Nov. the 21 1648 to Charles the carpenter in full
for building the threshing floor 20s being formerly paid & now 5 o o; to
May for 11 quire of paper at 3½d the quire, 3s 2½d & for several other
things fetched them 21d in all o 5 o; to widow Cunibeare in full for sheep
& the 23 of Nove. 1648  20 o o; to the glasier in full of all demands then
2 8 o; paid for 10 bushels of salt at 4s the bushel 2 o o; paid for 8 yards of
canvas 13d the yard for 2 shirts for Tho: Comman & 3d for a letter paid
to May the 24 Nove. o 9 o; to Robin Wood in full payment of Mr Pike at
Barnst. for wine then 4 o o, Bold had then also o o o; to Mr Row at Tor.
the 25 of No. 1648  1 2 o; then to the committee there in part for my
Lord's personal estate 100 o o; laid out for Frank Gotier for a pair of
shoes 4s, for stockings 2s 6d & a belt 2s 6d o 9 o; paid William Weekes for
the last week's workmen's wages the 28 of Nov. 1648  1 11 6; to the
Committee the 1 of Decem. 1648 one other part of pay 150 o o; to
Mr Rowe at Barnstaple the 2 of Decem. o1 2 o; lost at play o 1 o; Anice

laid out at *Torington* market the 2d of Decem. 1648  o o 5; paid the
workmens wages & for threshing 9 bu. of wheat the 3d of Decem. 1648
1 16 8; to the stew. for his journey the 3d of Decem. 1648  5 o o; Bold
had £3 toward his wages & other debts the 10th of Nov. 1648 & £2 in hay
& straw & more that is £6 there was then due to him, £24 for his wages,
£10 he lent me & £4 for a cow to kill so this 4 of Decem. remains due to
him £33, the hay is 2 o o; 6 beasts to be fed for Easter paid the cateror his
3 bills from the 17th of Nov. to the first of Decem. 48  4 4 9; paid for a
pair of spurs for Randale the 5 of Decem. o 2 o; paid the smith in full of
3 bills from the 5 of Aug. to the 30 of Decem. 1648  9 3 3; for hair & lime
to plaster the gallery o 5 o; paid 2 month's weekly rate from the 30th of
Sept. to the 30th of Nove. 1648  2 10 o; to Doctor Chichester the 7th of
Decem. when he came to my Lord first about his arm £1 o o; to the sadler
for work done for our journey to London 2 1 6; 30 bushels & 2 pecks of
wheat sowed in the Park now. to Miss Paget's plowman & widow Somers
wrought 2 days £5 Dece. the 9th & to my own servants the day the[y]
ended sowing the wheat o 7 o   [total] 326 18 1

[p. 130]  to the workmen for wages & threshing the 10th of Decem. 1648
2 10 o; give for fish & 2 pullets presents o 2 o; paid the cateror the 11 of
Decem. 1648 for Poor John, eggs & 34 lbs of butter at 4d the lb 1 o 6; to
Tho: Wyote for Susan Drew's lease o 10 o; for 2 bushels of culm the 11 of
Decem. o o2 6; for the chimney sweeper for the kitchen & backhouse 1s &
for 3 other 6d o 1 6; to an apothecary for the horses o 7 o; for 2 pair of
stockings 3 6d for Tho: Com: & Mary &c o 4 6; Dec. 13th to Roger
Jefferys the Apothecary for giving my Lord a Gl. o 5 o; to Lewice the
tailor for himself & boy 23 days o 13 o; to the old cobbler the 14th of
Decem. for the boys o 10 2; for an lantern & *Calise* sand &c o 4 4; to
Besse brought canvas for the girl o 1 o; to Bold then in part £43 now
10 o o; paid a bill for diverse things then to Bold 2 o o; for Booth mending
for Sam. o 2 o; paid in full to Will: Weekes for Humphrey Lake & John
Terrey for about 700 lb b[ushels] of lime for the Park 15 15 o; Bold had
when he paid the Widow Cunibear 1 o o   [total] 35 8 6

For mending the coach harness o 3 4; for culm 5 bushels o 6 o; for
2 b[ushels] & half of rye & 6d for the man & horse o 19 6; to the
apothecary Geytton of Barnstaple in full 2 o o; paid the workmens wages
the 17th of Decem. 1 8 9; to the Cateror his bill Dece. the 15th 1 16 2; to
the Brewer & Baker their night o 5 o; to Jonathan's nurse the 17th of
Dece. o 6 o; lost a[t] play o 1 o; in all 12 bu[shels] since the 10th of Dece.
1648 for more culm the 19th of Dece. 1648 5 bushels o 6 o; to Will:
Weekes the 22 of Dece. for threshers o 10 o; for letters by 2 posts o 2 o; to
William Weekes in full for the workmen's wages o 13 o; to Doctor Wilde
due this Christmas the 26 of Dece. 5 o o; to Will: Weekes in full of Welch
[sic] John's wages o 10 o; paid a bill of May's for shirts for Phillip & other
things o 6 o; for lines to hang the clothes on o 2 8; to Miss Slowely's man
brought oranges, Mr Isazaks brought brawn at Christmas o 2 o; to the
post the 29th of Dece. o 1 o; to Robin Wood for wine that he laid out
o 5 o; to Tho: Wyote for 2 journeys to *Exetor* & for 24s & 6d that he paid
Mungwell the bookseller there & for a pair of gray stockings 7 6 in all
2 19 2; paid him then the 29th of Dece. that I borrowed of him toward the
paying of Rich: Briton for 2 fat cows £10 10s  5 o o   [total] 58 5 7

[p. 129]   Also paid the 29 of Decem. 1648 to John Heirle for £20 borrowed of him toward the payment to the Committee 26 1 0 & 6 1s 0 for cheese & butter bought at 4½ & 2d the lb 0 5 0; to Miss Baker for raisins & currants at Christmas 0 18 0; for 2 bu[shels] of wheat at *Bidiford* the 3d of Jan. 1 3 0; & Thom: spent there 0 0 6; more then for 10 bu[shels] of wheat 5 3 6; paid Bold by turning up 34s for a hat bought for Mr Bouchier in London that Will: Lynn paid for there & now this 8 of Jan. paid 6s more in all £2 2 0 0; lost at play 0 10 0; to Tuker the carrier at £2 & 25s a horse for a man & he is to give me the over-plus the 20th day of Jan. 10 0 0; in a £3 piece given the 1 of Jan. 1648 3 0 0; paid Dick: Britton in full for 2 fat cows bought 5 10 0; there is 16 left paid Dick Britten then the 8th of Jan. 1648 for lings bought 2 11 0; paid Rich: Forrard that I borrowed in Octo. last to give Doct. Chichestor 2 0 0; paid the Cateror his bill of the 22 of Decem. 1648  2 6 8; paid the Cateror his bill of the 5 of Jan. 0 16 2; to Robin Meare then 0 2 6; for bringing a spade from London 0 1 3; for one quarter's washing of the French boy to Avice 0 4 0; to old Heard for mending 0 0 6; to Will: Weekes for lime & lime ashes 0 10 9; to Will: Weekes for workmens wages the 7th of Jan. 1648 0 11 2; paid the Widow Somer, Thom: Ley, John Johnsonn for about 300 lbs of butter & about 400 lbs of cheese at 4½d & 5d & 2 the che. 8 14 6; paid Miss Baker in full to this day the 19th of Jan. 1648 0 10 0; to the shoemaker Swain in full of all 1 17 0; for oaten malt to Tho: Hobsan 12 bu[shels] 2 16 0; Mr Carry hath undertaken the smith Sanders of Hartland shall send me 20s 1648 Jan. 5 for William Mayn for work done at task at 10d the day from the 1 of Nove. 1647 to the 24 of Decem. following 1 12 6; for wet fish 1 hogshead of Born. Steevens 2 11 0; paid Miss Baker for a pair of harpsical virginals 4 0 0; paid Huxtable the smith in full from the 3d of Decem. to the 10th of Jan. 1648 when we went toward London 3 0 0; paid for wine then tent. 5 quart. for the communion 8s 4d & other wine 11s 8d paid in all 1 0 0; paid the cobler 0 3 0; paid Rich: Forrard that he laid out 0 5 0; George laid out paid 0 1 0; paid a bill of Tho: Armsbys for barm for 32 weeks 16s at 6s the week & other things 1 0 6; lost at tables 0 5 0; for 6 mops bought in Decem. 1648 0 3 0; delivered Tho: Wyote to return with speed to me now 100 0 0 [total] 191 13 6

taken of Lewice 40s to give him in London. paid him 25s for him to the carrier & 15s given in money.

Given to Edw: May for his pains with 3 or 4 horses in money & one tree for fireing worth better then as much more 1 0 0; paid a bill for sugar candy paper &c 0 3 6; paid the carrier at *Tawstok* in part for bringing up my Lord's carriages ['20' crossed through] 0 0; & now the 20th of Jan. 1648 in full for carriages & bringing up 2 servants 0 12s 0 & since paid Lewice 1s besides paid for Lewice coming up 1 5 0 of the 40s I had of him.

[p. 128]   Jan. 1648 Spent in my Lord's journey & mine from *Tawstok* to London 23 persons 21 horses being 8 days 38 0 0; more then 01 18; & to Lewice to the Lawyer Mr Whatsonne in gold £2 then not yet paid the 15s the 7th of Feb. 1648  2 0 0; ['un paid ex. for 6 gallons of muscadine 16d the qu. 1 13 6' crossed through] for 3 hats for Randale, Sam: & Nedd

& bands 1 14 0; to Bold in part of £31 or £41 due to him formerly 3 0 0; for Cob he laid out 0 1 6; to Mr Symons the 25 of Jan. 1648 1 0 0; to the stew. who had £5 of me & £1 of W: Lynn before for his journey post from Taw. to Lon. which cost £4 18s 7 & for 6 weeks board wages in Lond. & 6s for the carrier at 10s a week £3 so he rece. £6 before & now of me 2 4 6; to the tailor's man 0 2 6; for 3 ells 3 qrs at 6s 6d the ell 1 4 0; to 3 children 0 3 0; for 2 p[air] of stockings & trimming the 2 boys 11s 6d, lost at cards 2s 6d, a black jack, a pail & a sieve 5 6, a comb, brush 6d 1 0 0; for hay & straw this week 3 12 0; spent more in the journey to London X 3 12 0; the 6th of Feb. 1648 paid Mr Manby in part of £23 due to him 10 0 0; to Mr Willkines then 02 0 0; X paid Robin Woode for his expenses & Wilmote's up to Lon. 01 6 0; given to Miriam's man the 7 of Feb. 1648 00 1 0; delivered to Rich: Forrard to account for this 7th of Feb. 10 0 0; lost 0 1 0; paid Will: Lynn out of this £40 I had of him in part of £31 2s 9d then due to him the 7th of Feb. 1648 6 0 0; given to two poor came out of *Ierland* 0 10 0; bor. of Bold in gold given Mr Reading 5 0 0; my gold given formerly 3 6 0; to Mr Wilkins the 19th of Feb. upon the finishing our composition 3 0 0; to him for Rush. &c then 5 0 0; Feb. the 21 to Will: Lynn in part for Goldsmith Hall 45 10 0; to him the 15th of Feb. 10 0 0; to Rich: Forrard then for the book 10 0 0; to Will: Lynn the 21 of Feb. 03 10 0; to Goldsmith Hall in full of the first payment this 21 of Feb. 1648 300 0 0; paid Mr William Bear & taken up his bond 106 13 6; paid Miss D'evo. & taken up her bond 101 10 0 Borrowed at 6 the 100 of my Aunt Fane this 21 of Feb. 1648 £500

For powder for clothes £1 0 4 0; one quart. of lb of fennel comfits 0 0 8; 2 pair of gloves for Ned Wingf. 0 1 8; to Myldmey Fane 0 2 6; for oil 0 1 8; spent in a journey to Amerse [?Amersham] 0 5 6 my Lord entered into bond with Mr King to pay 3 months after the 22 of Feb. 1648 to Goldsmith Hall 346 10 0 & Mr King hath a counter bond taken up

[p. 127] Robin Wood had for to buy Muscadine 10th for my Lord £1 9 6; Feb. 25th 1648 Rich: Forrard had for the book & to account for 20 0 0; Will: Lynn had the 27th of Feb. to buy sweet meats 2 0 0; to Mr Willkins the 27th of beb. [sic] 5 0 0; to my Lord then 1 0 0; X for 13 glasses 9 for beer & 4 for wine 0 13 0; to the Oxfordshire carrier & & [sic] for oil 2 6 lost at cards which makes up the £2 Bold laid out 0 11 0; Will: Lynn had [blank]; paid for a little basin & ewer sent to my niece the Lady Mary Fane the 3d of March 1648 0 5 0; for a Great Maudling Cup & Coffer the 3d of March 5 17 6; 2 years ago for cloth & making 2 bands laced for my Lord 0 6 0; for a pair of purple silk stockings for my Lord 1 15 0; for hay the 8th of March 1648 2 14 6; to two poor bills the 21 of March 1648 2 0 0; sent Mr Ridley then by Wilmot 3 0 0; 12 yards & ½ of fine black cloth cost 28s the yard bought of Mr Lamb the 21 of March 1648. Mr Lambe is to be paid at Tawst. for it ['£17' crossed through] 10s 0 to Mr King for my Lord's mo[u]rning suit came to £16 10s, 8 yards of black cloth at 29s the yard & for making Wingfeld a suit the cloth his mother gave him, this paid the 21 of March 1648, his old bills came to 19 1 0 18 0 0; to Mr Rob: Austin then in part of 82 paid by W: Lynn ['20' crossed through] 0 0; to the coach-maker in full to the 3d of March 1648 paid the 22 of March 1648 for all done since I came 21 10 0; to a

Bishop the 24 of March 1648  1 0 0; to a poor old Minister then of
*Tansover* in North. 0 10 0; to Miss Coney then for her sister 0 10 0; to
Mr Rich: Bouchier the 26 of March 1649  0 10 0; to the glasier the bill due
in Jan. 1648  2 15 0; to a poor man 0 5 0; to Trumpeters 0 10 0; I had of
R: For. £5 which I lent the 7th of April to my brother Robin 1649 £5 for
bringing up two pictures to a coachman & other things laid out by Bold in
all 1 10 6 paid now 1 7 6; to Mr Gettett the Apothecary the 8 of April
1 15 0; to Bold a bill for ribbon & given & other ways 2 0 6; to a poor
minister 0 2 6; Will: Lynn had to have given Mr Hales but he took it not
then, the 9th of April Lynn gave it him the 19th day 1 0 0; £10 to my
Lord delivered by Bold out of the £10 he had from W:L: the 11th of April
1649  2 0 0; lost at play then by myself 2 0 0; to the fire woman that day
1 0 0; to the farrier in full to that day 3 11 0; remains in Bold's hands now
£1 9s 0 which he hath since laid out for sweet meats, Hyde Park, combs &
give to poor 1 9 0; given by me to young Bartle Burton & my Lord gave
0 15 0; to Webber for stockings in full of all demands the 24th of April
1649 paid by Bold but my money 13 0 0; also to Bold then in part of £31
due to him in full of all demands to this 24th of April 1649  5 0 0

**[p. 126]**  to Mr George Beare the 24 of April £1 0 0; for mending the
guitar 0 4 0; for viol strings then 0 7 6

these Will: Lynn paid to Mr Jenkins the 8th of May 2 0 0; to my cousin
Walter Fitzwillyams then 2 0 0; to young Mildmay 1 0 0 [blank] 2 0 0
to Mr [blank] for teaching Cob on the guitar one month 1 0 0; £2 I had of
W: Lynn & £2 of it from Forrard also then to the nurse & midwife at the
baptising of my Lord Moune eldest son called Charles the 15th of May
1649 ['4' crossed through] 0 0; to Mr Beare the 17th of May 4 0 0; to John
Pawlin his clerk then 2 0 0; to Rich: Forrard the money I had from Joh:
Mills the 19th of May 1649  10 0 0; to Cob that he laid out for a churn 3s
& 1 dozen of good Maple trenchers 2 6, 4 music books 6s, combs 3 6 &
other things 1 2 0; to Goldsmith Hall in full of all payments for my Lord's
fine the 21 of May 1649  346 10 0; made even Rich: Forrard's week book
to the 19th of May 08 14 0; delivered him then to account for 11 6 0; paid
for 12 yards & half of 2 yards broad fine damask about 8s 8d the yard &
41 yards of napkining at 2s  09 0 0; for 1 lb of biskets & jumbles 0 2 0; for
4 ounces of thread 8d the ounce & black silk to make & mark the new
damask 0 4 0; paid for a lawn suit & a fine Holland handkerchief & cuffs
& mending other plain linen & making a band & cuffs to Miss Watsonne
the 23 of May 1649  2 0 0; 9 ells of lockeram for 2 shirts for same Bold &
2 for Ned: Wingfielld then 0 13 6; for the full discharge at Goldsmith Hall
the 21 of May 01 3 6; also then to Mr Wilkins 01 0 0; also lost in the
telling of the £346  01 0 0; laid out by Bold when I bought my horse 15s
& several other ways, *Hyd* Park & poor &c 04 12 6; to my Lord the 24th
of May 3 0 0; *Hyd* Park & given away 0 2 6; paid Will: Lynn to give for
Mr Murrey for weekly pay the 25 of May 1649  2 10 0; to the poor at
*Sargeants* Inn 0 5 0

**[p. 125]**  20 paid the Glovers bill the 29th of May 1649 £7 8s 0; for 3 ells
of Holland then 3 0 0; for 3 great pearls 2 5 0; to John Smith in part of his
wages then 2 0 0; to Mr King for Edw: Wingfielld's serge suit 4 1 0; to the
barge men 4 owers [*oars*] for one day from 10 in the morning to 6 the next

day being the 6 of May 1 14 0; lost at play to Mr Vouell that day & given
a poor la[dy] [blank]; W: £2 L: for Tho: Hathorn's nurse that kept him
2 weeks when he had the small pox in June 1649 0 10 0; to Thom:
Bouchier for schooling in part Wil: Lynn paid the rest 10s & I 0 10 0;
charged on W: Ly: book paid by him to Miss Anne Howard James
Parrett's money one hundred pound for so much borrowed of the
Countess of Petterborough Decem. 1638 which was money the Duchess of
Richemond gave Nan Howard & my Lord gave a note under his hand for
the receipt of it, which they cannot find at present but the Lady of
Peterbor: hath given acknowledgment of the receipt of it this 16 of June
100 0 0; Farrard paid £52 of it to the picture drawer for a copy of my
mother's picture 50s & for the frame 12s in all & now paid by me 00 10 0;
to Bolld in part of what's due to him the 22 of June 10 0 0; to Sergeant
Glanville for his advice 2 0 0; to Cobb the 22 of June 2 0 0; to the
3 children born at a birth 0 15 0; to the Earl of Middlesexe's maid brought
his daughter 0 [blank] 0; to John Smith 2 0 0; to the fire woman 0 10 0;
for a wooden standish for my Lord 2 0 0; to one smith brought my Lord
a book 0 10 0; to Randall Payton the 30th of June 1649 0 10 0; to Doctor
Willde then 5 0 0; for one ell of Holland for soaks [*socks*] 7d & for one
pair of nets 0 9 0; towards the buying a gelding for my Lord then 2 0 0; to
Cob for to buy strings with 1 0 6; to Barbery Tomkins 5s & for 2 books
of the Articles of the Ch. 0 9 0; for two books of the Articles of the
Church of England 0 4 0; in groats for strings £1, to soldiers £1, for
teaching Ned to write 30s, Bett's lodgings &c & to poor 6 0 0; £100 to
Bold the 30th of June 1649 10 0 0; in part of 25 10s for a gelding for my
Lord then 9 10 0; to Mr Beare £10 & to John Pawline his man £5 15 0 0;
to Mr Buzby by the schoolmaster of Westminster for one quarter for
Randale Payton beginning the 2 of July 1649 his age being 14 & for
entering 6 10 0; to the scholars there that day 1 0 0; to Mr Brewdnale that
he lent me to buy me new nag with all 35 0 0; given groats to John Burk
in part of his wages the 2 of July 1649 1 10 0 & £14 more was for the
*Harbeatten* sumpter horse that was sold the next day after he was bought

[p. 124]   £100 the coachmaker in full the first of July 21 0 0; to my
shoemaker then 03 10 0; for a leather sumpter male 02 15 0; for the sadler
in full to this day 22 10 0; to Mr Blake my tailor then 18 0 0; to Sir
Morice Willyams for visiting George Cheevlly the 2 of July 1 0 0; for hay
the 3d 1 10 0; for ribbon 20s & 3 combs 7s 1 7 0; for John Hamline
0 10 0; for a sumptor horse 12 0 0; my Lord for to pay Mr Bee for books
10 0 0; £100 repaid to the Lady Newport the 4th of July 1649 £100 rece.
from Mr Lamb whereof paid Mr King £40; paid the wood monger [blank];
spent in 3 days journey, at *Harford Brid. Andever Amsbery Brutton*
19 19 0; laid out at *Banton* by me 8 15 0; & also by me 1 5 0; to Rich:
Polla: the 20th of July 1649 05 14 0; Bold had of me the day before I
came from London whereof he paid the farrier 3 6 10 the bit ma. 6 6 6,
grass 23s 10d in all 13 17 10   20 0 0; £23 9s re. by the way paid the carrier
the 19th of July 1649 in full 27 16 0; £100 of Hunsp. paid Mr Lambe for
so much taken up the 3d of July of Josia: Haines paid the 20th of July
1649 100 0 0; £10 to Robin Wood £3 when I came from London to pay
their charges of 7 coming down with the carrier & he & Wilmot laid out
more X1 13 6 in all they had 04 13 6; & given George Chevelly then 01 0 0

£100 of Hunsp. paid Miss Baker of Barnstaple in full the 23 of July
105 0 0; for tuning & stringing the organ & harpsequall [harpsichord]
0 12 0; to Smith the 25 of July 0 10 0; to the steward the 26  2 5 0; £40 to
John Brother due upon bond in full the 27 of July 40 0 0; paid Mr Lambe
for black cloth for my Lord 12 yards at 28s  17 5 0; to Rich: Farrard paid
a bill of his laying out coming from London where remained in his hands
£2 1s 2d & he gave the cateror £2 to go to *Bidiford* market with the of
[sic] July his whole laying out was 5 1 2, so now paid him in full as also
for Amerys going to *Apledor* to fetch the sack 2s  3 2 0; to Lewice to buy
cloth & serge & necessaries to make up 4 suits, 2 for the grooms of cloth
& one of serge for Thom: Hathorn & one old suit for Watt. [blank]
Hugh Thomas will undertake for the payment of £35 that his brother John
oweth. he is new bond to the water woman of London 1 0 0; paid Prise
the shoemaker for Harry Howard an old debt 1 9 0; for a dictionary for
Randle then 0 3 0; to Ned Wingfielld 0 3 0
& more £100 re. Laid out since the middle of Feb. 1648 in all by me
1811 4 6; Rece. several ways since since that time to this 3d of August
1649  1942 3 4
Rece. in total 2042 3 4

[p. 123]   In my hands this 3d of August 1649 in gold 43 10 0;
in silver 20 12 6

paid Will: Lynn the 9th of July to pay Mr Murrey's rent in full until
Midsummer last 1649 100 0 0; for apricots 0 1 0; to John Grible when he
went to Bow the 3d of August 0 2 0; given Lewis to buy cloth to piece the
red bed with 2 0 0; to John Grible when he went to Kingston the 10th
of Au. 0 2 6; to my Lord then 0 12 0; for holland for bands for Sam.
6s 4d, for dowlas for shirts for Thom: Hathorn & Jonathan 9s & for alum
& brimstone to R: May 0 16 6; for white woollen cloth at 4s the yard for
4 pair of stockings 0 10 0; to John Smith then 0 10 0; to Cob 1 0 0; 1649
paid Joseph Ley, borrowed formerly, in part of £100 due to him the 21 of
August 92 0 0; paid for 8 yards & ½ of damask the 24th of August 1649 at
7s the yard 02 19 6; also then bought 14 ells of fine holland at 10s the ell
07 0 0; and more 7 yards & quar[ter] of sleazy fine cloth called Rostin [?]
0 18 6; to Lewice who had of Will: Lynn £5 & formerly of me £2 & now
in full of all reckonings to the 25 of August for work done & monies laid
out 3 13 0; also then to buy the kitchen boy clothes & shirts 1 0 0; laid
out by Thom: Wyote & Will: Lynn when they went to the South *Hames*
to keep courts of survey the [blank] in August 1649 spent in all 5 15 6, laid
out by Wyote but 2 19 6; paid Will: Lynn in full of all reckonings in these
journeys in to Devon & at the South *Hames* & £5 of it Lewice had to buy
clothes for the 2 grooms Tho: Hathorn &c & 6s more 9 15 10  0 6 0;
Ri: 20 Fard: paid the gardener who had before 20s paid by Bold & £4 by
Thom: Wyote & now this August by ['me' crossed through] Rich: Farrd
[blank]; to William Roson who laid out at *Kilkington* Fair £50 13 4 he
bought 9 beasts 10 13 0; to the steward the 28th to buy 5 weigh of coal
with, given £7 the other £1 10s 0 borrowed of Forrard 7 0 0; paid for 1500
of nails & other things to May 0 8 9; given to two men brought a buck
from *filla* [Filleigh] 0 2 0; for 18 yards 3 quarters of red baize for window
curtains at 17d a yard to Rich: May 1 6 6; re. again the gold paid for a

very large fair Per[?s]ia carpet in gold ['25 6 0' crossed through] also to the
stew. likewise to go to the fair which I borrowed of John Heirle ['20'
crossed through] o o; more borrowed of Thom: Wyote which the stew.
had for the fair 8 o o; also Bold had of Tho: Wyote for the smith then
2 o o; to Smith then that I borrowed from the seales o 10 o; to my Lady
Chichester's man brought quinces o 2 o; £2 13 8 bought coarse cloth for
sheets 2 yards broad at 20d, bought 12 yards of very fine damask at
13s the yard & 40 yards of napkining cost in all the 21 of Sept. 1649
['16 9' crossed through] o

£12 9 0 paid by the stew., the other £4 paid by me the 27 of Nov. 1649

[**p. 122**]  1649 to the cateror for 12 bush. of oats of Will: Larrimer the
3d of Octo. 1 10 0; to Mr Gifford's gardener that brought Barberys o 2 o;
lost at play then to Mr Wingfielld & his wife 1 16 o; also then given
o 10 o; for post letters the 5th of Octo. 1649  o 1 o; lost at cards & tables
1 o o

paid to Thomas Prust of Hartland the 25 of Octo. 1649 for 20 sheep
12 o o; paid Rich: Forrard in full for £50 formerly borrowed of him this
3d of Nov. 1649 paid 55 o o; the cook rec. by Forrard in Lond. £3 & now
Will: Lynn is to pay for him £3 more this Nov. 1649 as his half year's
wages. to Bold in part of a bill of £8 13s o wherein he paid for Bourn
Bater's wages £4 & the gardeners 20s & for other things now paid this 4th
of Nov. 1649 in part 05 o o; so there remains due to him for the remainder
of this bill & for wages 41 13 o; to Jo: Smith who had formerly 5 10s o
now this 8th of Nov. 1649  5 o o; ['Miss Downe oweth 40s' crossed
through] also to Christop. [blank] footman then 1 o o; to John Heirle that
I borrowed of him the 7th of Sept. paid now the 14th of Nov. 1649 ['20'
crossed through] o o; to my brother William Fane [blank]

[**p. 121**]  to Will: Lavercomb for 30 bu. of oaten malt paid the 10th of
Nov. 1649 6 10 o; to Tho: Ley for wheat 4 o o; to Lewice the tailor in
part of 2 bills of 12 18 4 this 10th of Nov. 10 o o; ['Tho: Wyote paid this
out of the money that I was to have of him' crossed through] to Tho:
Wiote his wages then due 06 o o; to Thom: Somer for 20 bushels of oaten
malt 03 16 8; to William Larrimer for 100 bush. of oats in all 12 10s o at
2s 6d the bushel, but formerly paid £1 10s & now 11 o o; to Rich: Berry
for 20 bush. of oaten malt 04 3 4; to Rich: Britton for 3 months rate in
2 5 11 a month paid this 14th of Nov. 1649 in full to his time 06 17 9; for
Hugh Wyote's man brought 2 trees & for post letters o 4 6

Nov. the 15th 1649 given George Chievly to buy him a coat with now
o 12 o; paid Will: Geare for sheep bought last year 2 14 o; paid for letters
& lost at play o 10 o; given away at Sir Hugh Pollards the 22 of Nov.
5 2 6; lost at cards & loadum & tables & 2s 6d to Will: Maine 1 16 6; paid
in full for the damask I bought in Sept. 4 o o; also then the 27 of Nov. for
wine o 17 8; paid Cob for letters & play &c 1 9 o; to Jo: Smith then the
27 of No. [blank]; to my brother Will: Fane the 4th of Dece. 5 o o; paid
for 32 gallons of sack 5 5 o; to the stew. the 7th of Decem. 1649 5 o o;
also the 9th day 2 o o; also—to buy capers, almonds, stockings, &c 3 o o;
paid 2 bills of Mays 1 9 o; to William Ramson the cateror 2 o o; more to
him in full of a bill of the 7th of Decem. 2 8 o; to the stew. the 16th of
Dece. 5 o o; also to him the 18th 3 o o; to the stew. the 20th of Decem. to

pay divers bills for corn, one oxe £7 & other thinds & wine 35 0 0; to
Lewice the tailor in full for all work done & cloth & kersey &c to the
24th of Decem. 1649 12 16 0; to John Terry in full till Oct. last this 20s
being in augmentation of his wages which is now to be £3 a year the 24th
of Decem. 1 0 0; paid Huxtable the smith in full for 8 months bills due
this 1 of Decem. whereof paid formerly by Bold from Tho: Wyote £2 &
now by me the 24th of Decem. 16 10 8 [total] 116 14 4

[p. 120] to my Lord 0 10 0; to Norton the 1 of Jan. 0 10 0; to Jo: Smith
then 0 5 0; to Mullins then 0 2 6; paid Glowine the carrier in full to the
last of Dece. 2 13 0; £22 in all to my brother William Fane the 2 of Jan.
6 0 0 he had £5 of the stew. formerly & £5 of myself & £6 of Mr Hayn;
lost at dice 3 17 0; to the baker & brewer 0 10 0; to the fewellers [*fuelers*]
0 5 0; to Doctor Wilde for some poor 1 0 0; to Cob for several things he
laid out made even this 7th of Jan. 1 0 6; lost at tables & dice the 7th, lost
at tables 0 7 0; [total] 17 0 0

the excise is to pay for which is £2 10s to the stew. delivered by Tho:
Wyote the 5th of Jan. 1649 for a but of sack bought then 18 0 0; to the
steward for butter, cheese &c the 8th of Jan. 10 0 0; Mr Squier's money
paid to Mr Atkin by the cateror for 20 sheep 15 0 0; for weekly pay for
Hartland due 4 13 0; to Mr Attkins of Hartland for 20 sheep the 17th of
Jan. 1649 21 10 0; to the 4 Sequestrators then 8 0 0; to Doctor Wilde then
5 0 0; lost at play 0 5 0; for [blank] barrels of *Clavelly* herrings then 2 4 0;
to the stew. the 19th of Jan. 1649 10 0 0; to him likewise part of
Christmas Quarter rent of *Tawstok* the 21 of Jan. 10 0 0; to the stew. to
Mr James Welsh that I formerly bor[rowed] 20 0 0; for Sl. & St. for Smith
0 8 6; 11s 8d due to [illegible] to my Lord 0 7 0; to pay Joseph Ley in full
of £100 he lent me last year now 15 0 0; to Hugh Horsham of Barnstaple
for one year's interest for £200 bor. for my brother George due the 22 of
August 1649 16 0 0; Jan. 23 to the stew. to pay Tho: Hobson, John
Johnsonn & Tho: Lovering for 62 b[ushels] of oaten malt in all £10 18s 0
& for 32 brewings &c 11 18 8, also more to him for the smith now due
03 3 0, and for John Heirle for 100 b[ushels] of oats £11 13s 0 to him for a
gale £6 & for 6 ewes £3 12 0 21 5 0; Jan. the 23 delivered the stew. more
to account for then 08 13 4; to Bold in part of 42 5 6 now due 09 0 0 the
whole side is 216 17 6

returned to London by Mr Lamb in Nov. 1649 £200

[p. 119] Returned to London by Abraham Denis the 25 of Jan. 1649 to
Will: Lynn for me 100 0 0

To the stew. the 25 of Jan. part of ['*Tawstok* Quarter' possibly crossed
through] 7 0 0; to Miss Hartley for stock bought last year 35 15 0; spent
by Charles & Thom: Wyote going to Cardinham the 26 of Jan. 32 0 0; to
the stew. the 26 of Jan. 2 10 0; left with Thom: Wyote to return up to
London 60 0 0; Jan. the 28 paid Farrard due to him upon bill & 20s 6d for
Ralph Booth in all 12 6 0; Brought to London with me 24 4 4 more laid
out of the £100 I returned £8. also Farrards gold since ch. in silver
£15 3s 6d & 20s the profit which he is only to have. which is paid out of
the £30 for my journey at my coming home the 9th of March laid out in
my journey to London 13 persons, 12 horses begun the 29th of Jan. 1649
& came to London the 7th of Feb. 32 1 6; to Jo: Smith the 23 of Feb.

1649  1 10 0; delivered to Rich: Cob to account for the expenses of the
house at twice 10 0 0; paid Bold in part of £33 3s 0 due to him the 23 of
Jan. 1649  13 3 6; also to him then that I borrowed at *Tawstok* when I
came from thence last 2 0 0; also more he laid out by the way coming up
1 0 0; delivered to Cob now 10 10 0; delivered Cob for the cook 05 0 0;
more to him for the cook 10 0 0; also to him for the lodgings for one
week ended the 16th of Feb. 1649  4 0 0; delivered Cob the 19th of Feb.
6 0 0; to Wimper the cook in full of his wages until our Lady Day next
2 0 0; for 30 ells of Holland 9 0 0; for 2 handkerchiefs, cuffs & a gorget of
plain Holland 2 0 0; to Sergeant Glanvill 1 0 0; to George given 1 0 0; to
Cob then for his wages 2 0 0; for lozengers 1 0 0; for shoes & boots 2 4 0;
for my self 2 0 0; ['delivered to Will: Lynn that I had from Frank for
George to pay Horsom the 21 of Feb. 1649  200 0 0' crossed through]
delivered to Cob 2 6 0; paid the 23 of Feb. 1649 to Josp: Jackman in full
120 0 0; £11 13 0 delivered Cob the 27th of Feb. 2 0 0; £100 paid the
sadler in full to this 25 of Feb. 014 10 0; likewise then the oat chandler for
11 5 0; also then to the coach-maker in full 9 0 0; the stable hire & coach
house then 1 8 0; to the farrier 3 6 0; spent in all 21 4 0 for my journey
the 26 of Feb. 1649 from London into Devon 30 0 0; paid for 2 pair of
silk stockings 46s & socks &c 3 0 0; paid for one week & 2 days for the
lodgings now 6 0 0   [totals] 379 15 0 & 160 0 0

[p. 118]   In full of the cook's bills paid to Cob 8 10 0; for a sword & belt
for Ned Wingfielld 1 10 0; to Sir Morice Willyames 3 10 0; to Mr Clark
the 25 of Feb. for letting Norton blood twice 0 10 0; to replevy my coach
horses 1 4 8; to the bit maker 4 9 0   [total] 19 13 8
£340 to Cob [blank]
rece. 17 9s 0 part of the 41 13 which I had for my journey to Taw. the
28 of Feb. 1649 Whereof to the cook that went away at Taws. the 12 of
March then in wages due £4 8s in all 6 0 0; to the carrier at 2½d the lb in
full to the 14th of March 7 14 0; to Mr Ble: the 14th of March with a
bond for £150 disb. thus 5 0 0
['£5' illegible crossed through] to the stew. the 18th of March 1649  5 0 0;
to David Hill's boy the 23 of March go. 0 11 0; to himself then 3 0 0; at
Blackford £3 in go. to Miss Wingfielld's boy & girl Warick & Rachel
2 0 0; delivered Rich: Polla: in full of his account this present 23d of
March 1649  18 10 0; besides the 246 9 0 left delivered the stew. in go. the
24th of March 1649 with which he got clear of the £350 he stood engaged
for, & I am to have letters up 10 0 0   [total] 39 1 6

116 14 4; 216 17 6; 379 15 0; 019 13 8; 039 1 0   [total] disb. 772 1 6
[total] Rec. 1080 17 3
So remains 308 15 9 March the 26 1650
Whereof in gold 246 9 0, and in silver 068 1 0, whereof laid out on the
other leaf 29 8 11, also 25 0 0 And in the House this 4th of April 1650
[blank]

[p. 117]   12 10s 0 to the steward the 1 of April 1649  5 0 0; paid a bill
2 3 0; for a weekly pay then 2 6 0; spent 0 5 0
£10
to the stew. 5 0 0; to Cob by bill for post letters &c 1 2 6; to the stew. the
7th of April 5 0 0; £45 to the stew. the 3d of April 1650  10 0 0; also then

to him for the gardener's wages now due 5 0 0; to Besse Seirle for Jo.
Smith to pay for cloth for shirts, bands &c 3 4 0; 22 10 delivered the stew.
the 10th of April 1640 8 0 0, delivered the stew. the money for the last ox
that was sold 14 10 0; £30 delivered the stew. the 23 of April 1650 to buy
cattle at Torrington Fair whereof he bought there one cow cost £5 10s 6d,
one other cow £5 & 2 steers cost £13 0, so in his hands 6 7 6  30 0 0; go.
£4 2 to Doctor Chichester the 22 & 24th of April in Gold 3 0 0; also in
gold to Robin Goldsom now at his going into France 1 2 0; 7 6 8 paid a
bill for cattle 25 0 0; 6 3 0 to [blank] Violet in full of her wages to the
26 of March 1650 7 10 0; paid Tho: Wyote then in full the 27th of April
as appears upon his account
Rec. 138 2 8   Disb. 128 2 6   Rem. 010 0 0 [sic] this 29th of April

£60 Paid Rich: Forrard his wages due the 27 of Ma[rch] 1650 now this
29th of April following in full 7 10 0; to Cob for the like now 5 0 0; to
Smith then 0 10 0; to Sam: Bold 1 0 0; to Bold in part of £46 now due
6 0 0; to him then to pay John Terry in full to our Lady Day 1 10 0; to
Will Booth the like 3 0 0; to Mylls for the like 2 0 0; to Thom: the
postillian 2 0 0; to Dick Rook also 1 10 0; to the stew. for himself & his
wife for the like 15 0 0; to him to pay Ro: Wood, Jo: Burk, the maids &
others 23 0 0; to the stew. to pay for 20 bu. of oats 2 0 0 in all £70
So now 76 13 4 in silver

Paid Hugh Horsham of Barnstaple & taken up the bonds of £200 which
was my brother Geo. Fane's money he lent Sir John Greenvile paid in full
now this 4th of May 1650 £210 0 0

**[p. 116]**  to the steward the Lady Day Quarter Rent of *Tawstok* 19 10 0;
to the stew. the 9th of May 05 0 0; to my brother Will: then 01 0 0; to the
stew. the 11th of May 1650 25 0 0; to Thurstan to pay for 40 wethers to
go upon *Woonham* this 14th of May 31 0 0; Mr Hyne paid Mr Hanaford
for Robert Drake of *Upex* [Up Exe] at two times 58 0 0; also to the said
Jo: Hanaford to buy fish at Exet. 8 0 0; Also to the stew. at *Exetor*
Assizes in Lent &c, to my brother Will: for the like occasions in all
27 0 0; paid Tho: Wyote for pease, holm & straw 2 8 0; paid to Bold for a
dry cow to feed 4 3 4; also the 20th of May 1650 to Miss Skicth for
10 0 0; 2s 6d T: Wy: gave him before  for 30000 of *Tindagle* [Tintagel]
slates at 8s 6d 12 12 6; to the stew. for Romson to go to *Killkinton* fair the
22 of May 1650 30 0 0; to the stew. 5 0 0; to Thurstan in part of £16 for
20 fat sheep then 14 0 0; which I have yet forgot what I did with it 1 10 0;
300  paid to Mr Robert Vigores for the use of Miss Pagget in full of £250
in full of all demands to this 23 of May 1650 150 0 0; paid for a but of
sack the 23 of May when it was pierced 019 0 0; to the stew. the 24th of
May 015 0 0; to Jo: Burk then 01 0 0; to my Brother William Fane at his
going to North[?ampton] the 27 of May 1650 then 06 0 0; to Chri: the
footman in part of Lady Day last wages 1 0 0; to the stew. the 31 of May
6 0 0; to Thurstan in full of £16 for 20 fat sheep 2 0 0; to the stew. for
*Baunton* fair 10 0 0; to the stew. the 3d of June for *Baunton* likewise
10 0 0; to Tho: Wyote in full being even this 12 of June 1650 0 0 6; to the
woman for 20 weeks spinning 120 lbs of wool 0 13 4; to Besse for the
stocking maker 0 2 0; to Smith for shoes, stocking 0 15 0; to Moulines for

teaching Tho: Hathorn to sing 10 weeks 0 5 0; paid Cob in full to the 12th of June whereof 30s was for Lewice & 30s to two men &c in all 7 4 0 [total] 483 3 8

[p. 115]   spent in a journey to the Bath as by the bills may appear, for bone lace 13 9 6, for stockings 1 0 0, spent at *Tayngle* & other ways in all, whereof Bold laid out for the horses homewards 7 10 0 of it 91 14 0; given also in go. 1 0 0; returned by Tho: Micheall to Will: Lynn then 50 0 0; brought home with me 3 6 0; more laid out by Bold who came with the coach & 6 horses to *Tayngley* 7 8 3; Bold delivered the steward in my absences 1 0 0

So I have now this 23 of July 1650 0 3 6; in silver 104 16 0, also from *Killyneck* [Kelynack] a fine of 46 13 8, from James Lake 14 0 0

Delivered the stew. the 2d of August 40 0 0; to Mr Ley of Northam for the infected people of *Aple-doore* the 24 of July 1650 05 0 0; to the carrier then 2 12 6; to Doctor Downe the Physician for Mr Heyn 1 0 0; to Bold the 20th of Augus. in part of £40 1 0 0; to Lusmore of *Exetor* for tuning the organ &c 3 0 0; to Betty Cope 0 10 0; to the gardener in part of his half year wages 1 0 0; to a poor man 0 5 0; laid out by Cob whereof to Doct. Wilde the 2d of August £5 in all then 6 13 4; August the 2d to Smith for a hat, gloves, boots &c 1 5 0; to Miss Skicth for things she put in to the glass of strong water for my Lord 0 12 6; to the midwife at Miss Downes 0 10 0

my Lord's Canding oweth me for Qu. rents £82

to Doctor Chichester the 24th of Sept. 1652 1 0 0; gold 3 also the 26 then 1 0 0; more the 1 of Octo. 1 0 0; more in gold spent 1 0 0; the stew. had from Ric: Britton that Will: Lynn returned from *Exetor* this 23d of August 40 0 0

[enclosure 115a]   my brother Will: in money £22, more 28, more 6, more Mr Pots had 3, more for costs 4

[p. 114]   £100 paid in part of £62 10s 0 for a fat oxen & for the plow bought at *Killkington* fair by Rumson who had £30 with him & now in full this 28th of Aug. £32 10s 0; paid the stew. the 8th of Sept. for Barnst. Fair 20 0 0; paid Rich: Forrard for a carrier's bill £1 12s 0d & other things laid out by him this 12 of Sept. 02 7 0; to Bold then in part the 10th of Sept. of £39 then 02 0 0; to Bold more the 26 of Sept. 1650 05 0 0; to Robin Wood his half year's wages now 04 0 0; to Jo: Johnsonne in full of £30 I borrowed at Bath 15 0 0; paid Cob whereof he laid out to the stew. the 18th of August £5 & to the physician Doct. Down for Wimper 50s 4d and for post letters & gifts in all to this present 2 of Oct. 8 12 0

Octo. 1650 here the account must begin

£80 to the stew. for Miss Downe who had £20 formerly & now this 27th of Sept. 1650 20 0 0; to the stew. to buy pigs &c then 10 0 0; to the stew. the 30th of Sept. for Torrington fair 50 0 0

£160

£9 to the stew. for Miss Downe the 15 of Octo. 1650 10 0 0

1650 Octo. to Mr Lambe to be returned to Will: Lynn in London by the 10th of Nove. d[elivere]d this 25th of Octo. 300 0 0; Jo: Rawlins of Hackpen 006 0 0; Octo. the 29th to Doct. Willde in full 010 0 0; to Norton her whole year's wages 010 0 0

£446 disbursed   £4 gold   216 rem. in silver   & 017 10s

To the stew. the 30th of Octo. 1650 that had been rec. by Cob of the debits that with the £100 sent to *Londd.* is 02 10 2; to Bold in part of £31 & £12 now due to him for wages this 4th of No. paid him 05 0 0

1650   £33 10s 0 & 2 10 0 L4: But: go.

Rece. this Audit 1650 October since the 19th of Sept. 1648 [blank], disbursed since to this present 6th of Nov. 423 10 0, so in silver remains in my hands this 6 of Nov. 224 0 0

[p. 113]   No. 1650 the 8th delivered to Mr Lambe to be returned to Will: Lynn in Lond. £100 0 0; to Bold the 11th of No. in part of £38 now due to him 004 0 0; to Sir Ralp: Sydenham then in full of all demands now due 010 0 0

Rece. since the 19th of Sept. Audit & all in silver 648 6 4; also then remained in my hands besides 010 0 0; disbursed since to this present 12 of No. 537 10 0, so now there remains 120 0 0

Delivered the stew. this present for *sarv*: [servant's] wages & rates 12th of No. 032 10 0; paid a bill of Bold's whereof 4s 6d for stockings for Sam: the rest in gifts to grooms at *Steeven-sonne Rawly* &c 00 15 0; to the stew. for sheep &c the 16th of No. 12 10 0; to the stew. to pay Miss Baker in full this 19th of No. 32 5 0; to the stew. the 25 of No. for Rumson to carry to Hartland to pay Jo: Bragge for 20 sheep & 9 beasts which cost in all 66 6 8d but paid now 30 0 0; to Lewice the tailor the 26 of No. in full to this day 07 5 0; delivered the stew. the 2d of Dece. Davi: Hills money 20 0 0; given a poor minister of *Clovella* 1 0 0; to Mr Jo: Beare for teaching Betty Cope to make hair rings the 10th of Dece. 0 5 0; to my Lord then 0 5 0; to Sam: Bold then 0 10 0; to Mr Pollard's man the 24 of Dece. brought turkeys capons 0 2 6; lost at play besides what I had from Cob 0 13 6; to Betty Cope to give the servants at New Years Tide Jan. the 1 1650 besides 7 pa[ir] of gloves, 6 ells of Holland & ribbon—in money 2 3 0; to Thom: Wyote for 6 fat sheep bought & eat in Octo. paid 5 0 0; to Moulins the 1 of Jan. 0 5 0; lost at play more & laid out for post letters & ['other' crossed through] one fee to Doctor Chichestor & other ways laid out by Cob & now paid him in full to the 10th of Jan. 1650 9 1 2; lost at tables to Mr Ed: Wingfielld paid him before Christmas 1 2 0; and to Ned: Wingfield the son 0 2 6; lost more at dice now 3 0 0; to the 3 fiddlers 0 15 0

Given in gold to Betty Cope 20s & to Cob then 10s the 15th of No. 1 10 0; to Betty Pagget the 1 of Feb. 1650 1 2 0; to Cob also then 1 2 0; and to Jo: Smith then all in gold 0 11 0

[p. 112]   to Forrard that I laid out for ribbon & holland 7 0 0; to Jo: Smith the 10th of Jan. 1650 5 0 0   [total] 175 3 2

also in go. from Th:Wyo: £5 2 6 In silver this present 10th of Jan. 015 1 6 to the stew. the 11th of Jan. 010 0 0; to the stew. his wages due the last Audit 010 0 0; to the stew. the 18th of Jan. 1650  10 0 0; X lent Geo: Fane £10 then to him this 24th of Jan. 1650 to pay Peter Sumer & the full of the servants wages & the Cateror's bill in full 20 0 0; to Voysin her wages due last Audit 05 0 0; to the stew. the 28th of Jan. for the cater. to go to Hartland 20 0 0; to Docto. Willde due this Christmas 05 0 0; to Docto. Chichestor 1 0 0; to Cob for post letters &c made even this 7th 1 2 0; lost at play now 1 1 0; to Betty Cope 0 5 0; to the stew. he had of Miss Baker 10 0 0; to the stew. to pay the smith the 10th of Feb. Huxtable 10 0 0; X lent Geo: Fane £10 the 11th of Feb. to the stew. the 15th of Feb. 10 0 0; to the stew. the 21 of Feb. to pay for [blank] of brown sugar to Rich: Lake 10 0 0; more the stew. rece. of Hanaford's bills the [blank] 10 0 0; paid the stew. the 13th of Decem. which I bor[rowed] of Jo: Heirle & paid him back again 7 0 0    [total] 140 8 0

There is in silver in my hands this 22 of Feb. 55 7 0

old Hugh Prust had a bill of my hand for £14 15s due to him for 30 sheep which Will: Lynn hath since paid him in London to Cob for post letters & given Doc. Wilde for a poor minister &c 01 9 0; to the stew. the 2d of March 1650  10 0 0; to Robin Wood & Tucker the 25 of Feb. 2 0 0; to Bold that went the next day after them toward *Salsbury* [Salisbury] with Violet, Will: Booth, George Cheev:, Nan about the trial concerning the robbery 8 0 0; to Cob then 3 0 0; lent Geo: £5 the 25 of Feb. X to Christian for making my gorget 0 5 0; lost at play 0 6 0; to the stew. the 9th of March 5 0 0; to Tucker the carrier to whom I lent by the stew. 30s before & 18s also at *Salsbury* & now this 8th of March 1 0 0; to the stew. the 13th of March 5 0 0; to the stew. the 14th 5 0 0    [total] 41 0 0

[p. 111]   For my Lord & myself lost at play 1 0 0; for stockings for Betty Cope; for cloth for Banton's girl 0 7 4; paid the carrier in full to the 19th of March 3 5 0; paid the stew. the 8th of March it was part of the £90 returned by Jo: Hanaford whereof he pair Miss Baker 11 13 2   20 0 0 [total] 25 4 4

To the stew. to pay Thurstan the plumber & for the 20th of Ma[rch] 1650 a cow & calf from Austin at Chaple-ton in all 15 0 0; to the stew. the 23d of March in part of £37 0 0 then due to him 1650  5 0 0; to Geo: Fane the 24 of March 1650 £5 X to Lewice in part of £13 4s 8d 5 0 0; to Docto. Downe the phys. 1 0 0; to the stew. which he took up of Dick Britton for which he gave him a bill from *Exeto*. to pay in part for the last but of sack 20 0 0; to Sam: Bold 1 0 0; to Betty likewise this 24th of March 1650 0 10 0

Alexander Rolls hath disbu. in the cause about the robbery £25 besides £6 he lent then to Bold he Mr Rolls hath had already from Will: Lynn £15 April the 7th 1651 Disbu. since the 12 of No. 1650  429 5 6; likewise to my brother Geo. in part of £100  050 0 0, he had also in money from the stew. £2 & in gold counters £13 10s   in all 479 5 8

So remains in gold £5, in silver this 25 of Ma. 3 2 3

lent Geo. Fane more to his wife this 31 of March £5 To the stew. the 26 of March 1651 in full of his book to this time besides the £5 which he rece.

the 13th of this month but entered it since 32 o o; to the stew. the 31 of March o5 o o; to bind a girl of Banton's of Taws. called Elizabeth Brinstcome apprentice to one Ley of Barnstaple the first day of April for 7 years 1651 o4 o o; to Mr George Beare for his advice about the 5 ac. in Taunton claimed for 21 years from the year 1647 o1 o o; to the stew. for Doctor Downe the 20th of April *Tawstok* quarter rent 20 o o; to the stew. for herrings the 9th of April 3 15 o; to him the 7th o6 o o; to Besse Sairle for shoes, shirts &c o 13 4; to my sister Fane in part of £29 10s o rem. of the £100 5 o o; to the poor o 10 o; lost at play o 10 o; to the stew. the 4th of April for the town of Torrington 2 10 o; to Cob that he laid out 1 10 o; to Doctor Down the physician the 6 of April 1 o o [total] 83 8 4

remains in my hands the 11th of April 15 13 1

['Sir Edw: Hales hath the last encrease of my jointure made of *Hunspile*, Norton Fits. &c also the lease for one year & the trust transferred by Samuel Brown & the rest to him & my brother Frank. & the release of the manors by the Lord & the 3 Ladies' crossed through] I have them Will: Lynn hath the *Wiltishire* deeds for that land.

[p. 110]   April the 11th 1651 To Doctor Chichester by Cob for Betty Pagget, Norton &c also more laid out by Cob 14s, for stocking cloth & for post letters &c & in full of his wages at the audit last 20s, Will: Lynn having laid out of my money at London for him in the Winter £6, now in all 2 10 6; to the stew. the 10 of April 10 o o; given a counterfeit young man whose name was Turneyr but called himself Butler o 10 o; for letters & Will: Lynn's expence at Hartland the 9th of April o 5 9; for a saw to graft with for the stew. & for leather 2s 6d arrows, gloves &c o 15 8; for Thom: Ierish given o 5 o; for 4 old silver pieces 1 o o; to my sister Fane in part of £24 os od the 24th 5 o o; to the stew. then for 10 sheep that Dick Britton caught 5 10 o; £10 the 23 of April to the carrier then in full from the 31 of March to this 23 of April 1650 being 2 5 o and to the rest to the stew. in all now 4 10 o; lost at play o 18 6; to the steward the 27 of April 4 o o; paid to Mr Seldon the clothier for 114 yards of blue also red baise at 18d the yard 8 11 o; to the stew. the 2 of May 2 2 o; for making one chimney in the lodge now 3 8 o; given Betty Pagget 2 o o; bought of a pedler 18 ells of Holland at 7s &c 15 8 9; to my sister Fane then in part of 24 10s o o 12 o [total] 67 7 o

Rece. in silver since the 11th of April 1651 64 7 3, disbursed to this present 4th of May 67 7 o, so disbu. more then rece. o3 o 6

Bo: £5 of Bold the 1 of May for the pedler which sum Will: Lynn laid out in Lond. for Bold 1651 in go[ld], to Doct. Chichestor when my Lord took physick in April 1651 3 o o; also Norton had then to hold in her mouth 1 o o; * to my sister Fane in part of £10 10s o the 6 of May 5 o o; to Christopher the foot-man then to go to *Tayngle* 1 o o; paid to Jo: Bragg for sheep at Hartland Will: Browne's first payment 11 13 4; also then to Tho: Prust Barnaba Hatherly's first payment 10 o o; to Mr Squier in part of £27 10s o for six steers £20 & to Mr Shorte £6 fell due to him & to Tuker the excise man for beer, given the stew. to pay these this 9th of May 1651 4o o o [total] 71 13 4

**[p. 109]** £5 of this he rece. of Jo: Salsbury & £5 more near the same time
& so set then down together in his book To the stew. the 10th of May to
pay Thom: Postillian & other servants wages £57 0 0; give 2 of Charles
men 0 1 0; lent to Geo: Tucker £4 formerly & this 22 of May 02 0 0; paid
to Forrard that I formerly borrowed of him to pay the carrier 05 0 0; to
Bold in part of £35 due this 23 of May 1651 10 0 0; X to my sister Fane
in part of £14 10s 0d then 10 0 0; to Major Pellham the best grey gelding,
the bay mare, the black mare, Kitt, Ashelly's mare & in money 55 0 0; £73
to the stew. part whereof he had of Jo: Hanaf. £13 8s other £5 is part of
Rob: Drake's money of *Upex* in all 18 0 0; to Bold paid the 24th of May
1651 a bill of £1 10s lent to Tucker the carrier, £1 for leather, 10s at play,
15s 6d for stuff for Sam: Bold, more 10s 6d, in all 4 6 0; to Norton her
wages due at Lady Day last laid out by Will: Lynn £4 7 7 now given her
by me 0 14 0; to Voysin the like 5 0 0; to Tho: Wyote the like 3 0 0; to
Cob: for his wages then due 7 0 0; to Betty Cope the 24th of May 1 0 0;
to Jo: Smith then 5 0 0; to Rich: Forrard the like 15 0 0; to the stew. the
26 of May 1651 5 0 0; to Doctor Wilde due at our Lady [day] last 5 0 0;
to the stew. for the like he having had £2 that Will: Lynn laid out in
London for him & reckoned it to me so now his wages due at our Lady
Day last 8 0 0; paid a bill for post letters &c & for a hat for
Mr Wingfield's man to Cobb the 28th of May 1651 2 4 0; the stew. had
¼ bonds of Hartland came to £60 10s 0 the 19th of June 1651 toward
paying for cattle in Hartland to Mr Atkins &c to the stew. now his book
& the full of all the servants wages excepting Tho: Armsby's for Lady Day
last which all now comes to 42 3 11 paid him this 28 of May 40 0 0; to the
stew. the 30th of May which was money Mr Seldon rece. in *Cornwell*
5 10 0; to my sister Fane in full of £100 0s 0d paid her by the steward
when Miss Trott went away, & 16s over, £5; to Doctor Chichestor the
14th of June 1651 for myself 2 0 0; to my Lord the 20th of June that he
had for a pedler 0 10 0; to the stew. the 21 of June Cobb paid him 10 0 0;
likewise by Cobb to him the 22 of June 1651 5 0 0; to the stew. to pay
Thurstan for 20 sheep the 25 of June 12 15 0; laid out about setting of
Whilde hames [wild haulms] 1 0 0; to Bold the George for his journey to
*Salsbury* the 10th of July 3 0 0; to the stew. to pay for stuff for millstones
then 15 0 0 [total] Ex. 313 0 0

**[p. 108]** A bill of Besse Sairle 1 11 0 & Jo: Burk for taps 6 6 1 17 6; to
Cobb the 11 of July in full of his book 5 10 6; spent in my journey to
*Hunspile* with my sister 8 8 0, besides the bill to pay at *Hunspile* 12 12 1;
lent my sister then 10 0 0

I think this is in the 57 on the other side the stew. had in May 1651 of me
to pay Myles 2 0 0

Paid Jo: Heirle which was for Docto. Downe for the tithe in part of £263
now paid this June 100 0 0; the stew. had besides which he rece. of several
at several times in Barnstaple besides the £50 which is part of the £100 that
Jo: Heirle had to this 10th of June 52 19 4; to the stew. in 4 Hartland
bonds for cattle due there in part at Torrington Fair 60 10 0

In my hands this present 11th of June 1651 10 7 0

to the stew. the 12th of July for excise & other things 5 0 0; July the 17th
to the shoemaker Rich: Row of Barnst. in full to this 2 2 0; Bold spent in
his journey & Geo: to *Salsbury* in all 4 0 1 more he laid out for a cloak
bag, a male pillion, 2 lines & furniture for hunting, 2 money bags all cost
£1 12s 0, so he had £3 before & now 2 12 0; also in part of his wages this
24th of July 5 0 0; more to Bolld in part of £30 due for wages this 28th
10 0 0; also to Mr Alexander Rolls his disbursements about the robbery,
he had formerly of Will: Lynn £15 of this £36, £6 was to Bold for their
charges at *Salsbury* besides £10 they had of me 21 0 0; paid Robert Drake
that the stew. borrowed of him the 21 of May toward the horse for Major
Pelham who had 4 horses my Lord's gray gelding, Christo: Ashley's mare,
the bright bay mare, the black mare & £55 in money 60 0 0; paid the
carrier in full to this 2 of August 02 0 0; paid Lewice this time in part of
£22 16s 2d now due to him, the whole bills came to 27 16 2 but he had £5
of me formerly & now 12 16 0; to the stew. the 19th of July 1651 02 0 0;
to the stew. the 3d of August 10 0 0; to Randall Payton given him 1 0 0;
to Cob in go. 1 0 0; disbursed by Tho: Wyote & Will: Lynn in going to
*Exetor* 2 2 6; to the stew. by Wyote's delivery the 2 of Augu. 2 0 0; for
4 weigh & 3 qu. of coal at 48s the weigh now paid 10 9 0   [total] 148 1 6

[p. 107]   *Wolrington* [Worlington] To the stew. the 1 of August the rent
of *Wolrington* 1 13 0; to the stew. the 9th to pay for things bought at
*Bristole* Fair fruits, spices, starch, soap 112 lbs, butter 2[?oo] qr—£13,
11 doz. 2 lbs cost £6 14s 0, nails £7 7s 0, sturgeon, cheeses 38 weighing
308 lbs, anchovies, capers & olives & sugar 1 qr of a hundred & other
things & his charges came in all to £44 11s 0d so now given him to pay
these & other things 50 0 0; to the stew. Midsummer Q[uarte]r rent of
*Tawstok* by G. Balche 20 0 0   [total] 71 13 0

148 1 6   71 13 0   go. 49 0 0

rece. in this time 259 4s 0, & in my hands 00 7 0, disb. go. £268 14s 6d, So
rema. 0 16s 6d this 9th of August 1651

To Mr Beare for his counsel 1 0 0; to Mr Squier in full of 27 10 0 for
6 steers this 9th 7 0 0

in go. To the stew. the 12 of August in part for Jo: Bragg 28 so due yet to
Bragg £40 to the st. to pay his book to the full to this time & somewhat
over reckoning near £30 which he hath rece. for tithe besides £105
formerly before Lady day last now 100 0 0; in go. the 20 of Sept. 1651 to
Jo: Smith £2; Tho: Wyote had for the two Bolham men the lemons in
go. £2 sm. £2; paid Mr John Butler of *Exetor* the 12 of Sept. 1651 for
which I have his general acquittance with sufficient interest in full
discharge of all demands now paid 23 2 6; one of the pots of conserve of
Red Roses made by Will: Lynn 1650 it weighs, pot & all, 34 lbs this Sept.
1651. more pots at London weigh 8 lbs qr bought cloth in Exet. for a
gown for myself & a suit for Ned, a cloak for Cobb in all cost 10 6 0; my
brother Geo: had £5 in silver of me for 5 pieces in gold which I keep for
him, in gold 11s; due at Bow on Wednesday night the 30 of Sept. 3 0 0; So
spent besides these sums above mentioned in our journey to *Exetor* the
3d of Sept. being 19 horse & as many persons, the horses went back the
next day & came the 12 & we came home the 13th, spent in this time the

lodging cost 2 5 0, the other expenses came to 19 15 6, so in all laid out
£64; to Cobb in part of [blank] the 22 of Sept. 2 0 0; to the stew. to pay
the smith in full to the 9th of Oct. 12 0 0; £4 5s to the stew. to pay for
10000 of slates at 8s 6d a hundred and for other things in all then 5 10 0;
to Cobb more 02 10 0; to the stew. in gold for Torrington Fair &c 50 0 0;
to Doctor Chichester in gold in Octo. 1651 03 02 0; to John Bragge of
Hartland in part of £40 formerly due 26 13 4; paid for one green rug 30s
& 2 more 30s in all 3 0 0; to Cobb to account for the 16th of Octo. 3 0 0;
to my brother George who formerly owed me £60 & £24 & now this
20 of Sept. 1651 lent him 6 0 0, so my brother gave me thena bond to pay
me £90 the first of Nove. 1653 to which my sister is witness Will: Lynn &
Cobb.

Disbursed since the 3d of Sept. 1651 to this 21 of Octo. in all 178 5 4.

[p. 106]   Octo. 1651 To Tho: Bragge of Hartland in further part of
the £40 10 0 0; more sent him by Thom: Prust in 3 bonds for 20 fat sheep
bought of him this Octo. 14 10 0; to Thurstan Hamer for his wages £6 &
a bill 15s 6 06 15 6; also in part of £22 for 46 sheep 05 0 0; to Chr:
Southwood due upon his debit this year 1 11 1; to Phillips at Bow that we
spent going to Exe. 3 8 1; to Mr George Beare his fee for this year 3 6 8;
to the stew. in two £5s by Cobb & W: Ly: the Audit week 10 0 0; to
Thom Wyote in full of a bill for the business of the two Lemons [?Loman]
£17 of Bolham; & £6 12s 6 the Troopers had when they brought the
horses home & 6 3 2 for the tenth of Bolham, *Shelldon* & Hackpen in all
29 17 1; more to him for his wages now due 03 0 0; to the stew. to pay
several servant's wages as by the note appeareth this 3 of Nove. 50 0 0;
No. the 5 to the ste. who paid Miss Down 13 11 1 in full of all accounts
for the last year & £60 for this year, he is to give from my Lord to the
town of Torrington £10 & to Mr Tuker for Irish beef £10, in all to him
100 0 0; to Lewice in full for all work & £4 to put Rumson's boy to him
at Easter last 16 5 0; to Bold due this Audit 12 0 0; to Doct. Whilde then
in part 5 0 0; to Voysin now due 5 0 0; to Sam: Bold 5 0 0; to Smith the
like 5 0 0; to Forrard then due 7 10 0; to Cobb. for the like 6 19 0; for a
blue rug bought of Wilmot 1 15 0; to Betty 0 10 0; to John Heirle in full
of all demands now 87 7 6   [total] 389 14 11

In go. laid by 050 0 0, more 010 10 0, for Will: Lynn 300 0 0
[total] 750 4 11

1651 so in my hands silver this 6 of Nove. £105

To Dick: Britto: the 10th of Nov. in part of his bill of 105 0 6 £100 0 0; to
Joseph Ley that I borrowed of him the 6 of March 50 0 0; May the 10th
to Bold in full for wages & all other demands 23 16 6; to the apothecary
for Norton [blank]; to Mylls the groom for two [blank]; to him for wages
due Octo. 1651 [blank]; to the stew. upon his book the 12 of Nov. 14 0 0;
to the stew. the 18th which was one of [illegible] Polla: bonds 7 4 0

[enclosure 106a]   [dorse. Accounted with my Honorable Lady the 28th
of October 1651 for one whole year then ended as followeth.

Sum total of my disbursements as by my book doth appear £1715 2s 9d
Sum total of my receipts as by my Book doth appear £1622 10s 5d

So remain due to me upon my book £92 12s 4d
Received upon several debits at the audit 1651 as by the particulars doth
   appear £256 7s 7d
Out of which sum I paid for six fat oxen £43
More to be deducted for Mr Hearle's tithe which is charged upon my
   book of receipts and must be allowed me £6 10s 0d
So there remains due from me to account to my Honorable lady in cash
   the sum of £114 5s 2d

Richard Pollard]

August 1652
4 barrels of brown sugar, 2 barrels of wheat, a piece of a loaf, all spices,
seeds, almonds, soap, starch, rice, barley, wick yarn, great nails, trenchers,
glasses, candlesticks, wax & great candles.

raisins, tobbaco pipes
knives
Great Home Candles
cloth, white woollen
china dishes
sweet meats
raspale [raspberries]
gooseberry
apricots
plums
Quince abundance 50 lbs

[written sideways]
To sell apples, cider, hops,

to buy fresh fish, butter, cheese, salt fish, vinegar, salt, wine, capers, coal,
culm,

to pay weekly rates, nursings, workmens wages

we have without buying hay, straw, corn, cattle, sheep, hops, apples, cider,
wood, herbs, roots, milk, hogs, pigs, geese, does, rabbits, pigeons,
woodcocks, salmons

[p. 105]   Nov. the 19th 1651 Paid John Hamlin for making 3 gowns & a
pa[ir] of bodys for Betty Cope 4 13 8; also for making my cloth morning
petticoat & waistcoat 0 12 9; paid a bill of Besse Seirle of stocking cloth
for Anice, Jonathan's master, 2 books of *Issope's Fables*, wine &c in all
1 14 0; to Harry Fane's nurse & his mother's midwife the 20th of Novem.
1651 at his christening 4 0 0; to Wimper the cook in part of £3 2 0 0; to
Rowe the shoemaker in full 1 11 0; for ribbon & bandstring to a pedler
1 6 0; to the stew. the 31 of Nov. 1651 2 0 0

I had of T:W: to Norton at her going away the 4th of Dece. 7 0 0;
to Robin Woode then toward the money he is to have about the robbery
3 0 0

£50 go. £25 to the stew. the 8th of Decem. 5 0 0; to Cobb the 10th of
Decem. 10 0 0; to the stew. the 14th 8 0 0; to Rich: Farrard to buy sack &
raisins at *Bidiford* 03 0 0; to the ste. the 19th of Dece. 1651 10 0 0; to

Kitt: Ashelly then for this crope mare o8 o o; to the stew. the 21 of
Decem. 1651  45 o o; to Bold for a fat cow bought last summer 4 10 o;
more paid Geatton the apothecary for Norton in full 6 10 o; to Doctor
Chichester for Betty Cope then 1 o o

Paid for 20 ewes of Tho: Prust Rumson bought 2 10 o; also then to John
Bagihole for 13 sheep 4 2 6; paid the other Thom: Prust for 30 ewes
13 6 8; to Will: Booth his wages due at the Audit last 3 o o; to Wilmot for
[blank] of wool spinning o 9 o; for stockings for Wat o 1 6; to Randale
Payton o 10 o; remains of the £50 5s to Cob due upon his book full the
24th of Decem. 2 14 6; in go[ld] also disbu. since the 6th of Nov. 1651 to
this present 24th of Decem. 360 17 4

to Mr Getty the 29th of Decem. 1 o o; to the stew. money Mr Seldon rece.
in *Cornwell* one bond was 6 13 4 the rest was rent in all 8 3 4; to Thom:
Somers for 2 fat oxen 4 o o; for a music card o 19 o; to Betty Cope now
2 10 o; to Betty Pagett 2 o o; go. to Cobb 2 o o; go. to Smith o 11 o; to
Moullins o 5 o; go. to Voysin then the first of Jan. 1651  1 o o; go. to
Randale Payton 1 o o   [total] 33 8 4

[p. 104] Jan. the 3d 1651 to Thurstan at *Whoonham* in full for £46 which
was to have been but £22 but he had formerly £5 now 18 o o; to Mr Tho:
Moore of *Exetor* the 8th o1 o o; to the stew. the 6 of Jan. 30 o o; to the
school-master gift & teaching o 10 6; to the steward the 13th of Feb. 1651
40 o o; Jan. 17 paid Besse Sairle for part of the lace of an apron 1 5 o; to
my brother George which Will: Lynn received of him in London paid this
19th of Jan. 1651  40 o o; also to him for bringing down the K: of Spain's
bible o1 6 6; to the stew. the 20th day to pay for butter 5 14s 10 o o; Jan.
1651 paid Robert Drak by Tho: Wyote at Exet. 40 o o; Wyote spent in his
journey to *exeto.* 1 4 2; he made even with John Hanaford who had rece.
from [blank] to the 16 of Jan. 1651  413 o 1od & disbu. in the same time
416 10 7 so Wyote appointed him £3 to be paid by the reeve of *Upex* & he
paid him in full to that day o 9 9; to the stew. the 23 of Jan. £5 for the
carrier in part of £17 16 1od that will be due to him for carriages 12 6 1od
& 5 servants 5 10 o, also £3 he gave Wilmot for their diet, he had £2 more
in all 10 o o; paid for 36 French half pistols 7s 6d a piece & a box of gold
£4 in all 17 10 o

more due to him this 23 of Jan. in go. 38 11 9 to Thom: Wyote that I
borrowed of him pa. in go. 100 o o; whereof this 25 is part the stew. had
from Thom: Wyote to pay for part of £27 due to Geo: Shorte for a butt of
sack £20 & for other disbursements £5 in all the 2 of Jan.   25 o o

For sweet butter to Geo: Balch o 7 6; to old Hearder for making sto.
o 2 6; I paid for Geo: Cheavlly to King the tailor £3 that he said I had of
& lost it at play to George Cheevly for twine o 1 6; to Kitt: for an old hat
for Watt: o 2 o; to John Hamlin for Betty Cope's tammy gown making
o 18 o; to Thom: Berry for 2 pieces of cloth 2 7 o; to Betty Cope at Ash
o 7 6; for 3 yards of stockings cloth to Annice o 13 o; to the stew. this
24th of Jan. 1651  11 o o

I had this of Cobb £7 & Wimper £4 to Robin Wood who had £3 before of
me in part of his money due upon the robbery now o5 o o; to the steward
his wages due at Michaelmas last 10 o o; to Robin Wood more in part of

his money 02 0 0; to Lewice the tailor in full of all 10 14 0; paid Wimper
& Cobb that I had to bring up for them 11 0 0; to the man that mended
the organ then the 10th of Octob. 1 0 0; paid Cobb in full of his book to
this day 6 13 2

[enclosure 102a]   The right honorable the Lady Bath bill
for a pair of shoes for your Ladyship 4s
for a pair of shoes for his worshipful 3 6
for a pair of shoes for your footmen 3 6
Sum is 11s

[p. 103]   To Farrad as by his bill in the journey up to London 1 11 4; for
gloves, cauls & ribbon 1 7 0; to Cobb to lay out in the journey up
3 12 10; more to him in part to account for 1 0 0; to him for a looking
glass cost 38s to him then 2 0 0; spent in a journey to London being about
20 horse & 28 or 30 persons above £50 but part is set down before so now
44 13 7

£5 from Will: Ly: to smith the 19th of Feb. 1651 2 0 0; to Cobb then
3 17 0; the 5 pieces of rich hangings cost £148, the K. picture £3 to Will:
Lynn 2 bags that he had sealed to him the 3 or 4th of Feb. 1651 200 0 0;
paid Cobb's book & made all even to the first of March 5 14 6
[total] 11 11 6

£10 I had of Will: Ly: to my Lord the 3d of March 1 0 0; to Cobb then to
account for 3 5 6

£10 I had of him the 31 of March 1652 this Cobb had he was to pay £6 for
a theorbo & 20s for the case of my viol, the other 3 to him 4 5 0
[total] 10 0 0; 20s I had of Will: Lynn, to Miriam for Myldmay 0 10 0

£60 my sis: Bettys to my Lord 1 0 0; to my Lord the 27 of April 1 0 0; in
go. to Sir Mo: Willyams £3, to Mr Cardwarthen's son £1 to Miss Blackall
0 5 0; to Cobb in full of his book to the 16 of April, to Mr King *Iaesop's
Fables* &c 4 0 6; to Randal & Ned 0 7 6; to Cobb given 2 0 0; for one fair
dia[mond] 40, Carwarthen's da[ughter] 2, Sir Morgan's woman 1, Miss
Kirby 20, Mr Polweel 10s, cousin Brand £5, in all 112 10s   to Doct.
Cholman & his son for one month a piece 4 0 0; to the 3 children the boy
had a suit of Ned's & for coats for the two girls Will: Lynn & given 5s
now 1 5 0; for 3 dozen of melon glasses 30s & 3 dozen & half of
preserving glasses 3s a dozen the barrels 5s 6 in all 2 6 0; for a pair of
trimmed gloves 0 14 0; paid Cobb's book to the 26 of April 1652,
Mr Bing. Hampton Court 2 0 6; paid for viol strings the 27 1 3 6; to
Mr Trussell for 6 yards of cloth of silver 18 0 0; to Rachel Burton 01 0 0;
more the 4th of May 1652 Cob 08 0 0; for a viol for Miss Edney 01 10 0;
to Mr Binge for one month's teaching of smith 01 0 0; for crimson taffety
to line the great Mantle [£]3; to Mr Perin for a coral for Harry 1 6 6 for
two lockets 4 1 6, paid him in part 0 8 0; to Cobb 1 0 0; for one pair of
waistcoat silk stockings for my sis. Betty 2 combs & a brush the 13th of
May 1 4 0; paid Cobb's book 3 14 4 & 3 5 6 in all 6 14 10; to Cobb in
part of his book for young Cholman 10s, powder 10s 1 0 0
[total] 73 13 10

the 13th of May Will: Lynn had a bill for my bro. Geo: to pay of Miss Baker's ['3 8 0' crossed through], also order to rece. from Will: for sis. Betty 4 10 0

£20 to Cobb in full of all reckonings to this 14th of May 1 9 6; to Mr Binge for books & one month's teaching 3 0 0; for Mr King by Cobb 7 0 0; to my Lord 20s for a lace hook 30s, to Mr Perin in full £5 7 10 0; to Cobb in part £1 0 6 & £3 8 0 to account for 4 8 6 [total] 23 8 0 [total] 112 18 10

[p. 102] to June the 3d to Mr King in full for the steward 6 0 0; bor. of Besse 11s to Mr Carwarthen for a copy of my picture 50s & frame 3 10 0 Kitt: had £2 & the cook £4 for wages of Farrard to Farrard the 10th of June 1652 50 0 00; to him the 14th 20 0 0

£30 To Mr Gumbleton for 4 diamonds & making two pair of lockets the one 18 diamonds the other 25 & 17 & a little ring 5s with 5 diamonds. He had old gold the weight of them diamonds & all, also in burnt silver at 5s the ounce 17s 6 & old gold 20s in all, paid now in money in full 8 10 0; with porter & boxes one pursline [porcelain] basin 30s, 5 other dishes, great water glasses two, 5 drinking glasses, two cruets, 2 flow.[*flower*] pots 4 4 0; to Cobb to account for powder, strings &c 3 0 0; to the body maker for my own 22s & for my sister Bet. 20s 2 2 0; to Smith for a viol for Randale 1 10 0; June the 21th 1652 to Mr Eaton for the lace for my Quoite & in full 4 15 0; to Mr Lawes for teaching Betty Pagget one month 2 0 0; Forrard laid out upon his book more then he received at London the 21 of June 14 6 3, also upon the way he had but 23 10 & laid out 28 17 11 so more due 5 7 11 this 30th of June 1652 in all 19 14 2, paid to Forrard at *Huniton* [Honiton] the 25 of June 3 19 0; & more there 1 1 0; to Cobb the 29th of June to account for 0 19 0; to Mr Hyne the younger to return to Will: Lynn to London whereof £10 was from Jo: Miles in part of £100 of a new bargain & £2 Mr Hyne pays for rent so in all returned this 25 of June 21 0 0; to Farrard at Bow 3 0 0; more at *Tawstok* now to make even 2 0 0

For a great coach gelding to Jonathan Cope 20 10 0; left with Dick Rook at *Salsbury* with 2 coach horses 05 0 0; to Bold then there 01 0 0; £50 to my Lord who made even with Mr Bee: the 21 of June 10 0 0; to Farrard at *Salsbury* 10 0 0; at *Dochester* [Dorchester] to him 3 10 0; in all 191 10 0

to a kinswoman in gold my cousin Bra. 5 0 0; for jewels & gifts more in gold 107 10 0 so now remains no silver & but 30 10s in gold June the 30th 1652

To the stew. the 1 of July go. 20 0 0; more then of Pearce of *Warkly* in part of £50 25 0 0; more from *Banton* to him [blank]; paid John Bragge of Hartland in part for 10 steers cost £52 paid this 29th of July 1652 18 6 8; more to the steward from *Banton* £2 from Mr Tristra: & £10 John Glass 12 0 0; to the stew. in go. Frank Bassett my godson 2 0 0; to the tucker at 6d the yard & some in 4d & washing 4 coverlets for 121 yards & half of my own making this year 2 11 6; to the stew. to pay the carrier & the 3 months rate this 30th of July 1652 7 8 6; he had of Will: Lynn then £4 4 0 0; for bringing the harpsicord & virginals from *Exeto.* 1 7 0

[p. 101]   to the ste. that I borrowed of Joan Elice the 3d of August 1652
£15 0 0; to the stew. the 4 & 5 of August that I borrowed & Paw'd go.
200 0 0; so disb. since the 30th of June 1652 307 13 8; rece. in the same
time & borrowed 257 4 2; in go. in my hands that 30th of June 030 10 0;
in old go. laid out besides 20 0 0; so this 7th of August I am out of purse
in old gold £20 ordinary £38 10s in borrowing £193 in all 251 10s
307 14 2
So remains in my hands 0 0 6

Paid a bill for one month for Harry's nurse & for other things glove[s] &
shoes &c for him & others, to Besse Searle the 27 of August 1652   1 8 0;
to Cobb then in full of all reckonings made even this day, 16s he had
before which made even the 2 4 0 I had from my Lady Chichester that
W:L: laid out & now in full to Cobb in all 1 2 6

£20 to young Miss Cempe the 30th of Sept. 1652   2 0 0; to the stew. the
2d of Octo. 18 0 0; to Voysin in gift in Sept. 3 0 0; to Mr Selly 0 10 0; to
Irish Tom 0 10 0; to Cobb in full of all reckonings 0 6 6; to Cobb the 4th
of Sept. 1 0 0; to Ned Wingfielld 0 5 0; to Randale Payton 0 10 0; to
Cobb then 0 5 0; to Betty Cope when she went to Ash 0 5 0; to Bold at
twice 1 10 0; to Smith 0 10 0; for post letters 0 3 0; to Cobb for his book
0 9 0; given away 0 2 6

Disbursed since the 7th of August 1652 by me 31 16 6, rece. in the same
time 151 4 0, so remains this 4th of Octo. 1652   119 14 0

The stew. had for rates the 20th of Octo. 08 0 6, he had for Miss Downe
the 21 of Octo. £5 & more £5   in all 10 0 0

Mr Simon Grey the 4th of August 1652 had a copy of my Lord's lands in
the county of Armagh & a note of all rent unpaid with the tenants names
due in 1641. he hath also in London left for him of a letter of attorney to
let set receive &c. And one other letter of attorney dated the 22 of Feb.
1652 to set & let for 7 years to any.

[enclosure 101a]   ... may be gotten, by ... next he will return. The great
present without the outer case cost 26 5s & the outer £8 5s the other I
hope will be rec. at some little loss to the book-seller.

# Appendices

## APPENDIX 1

*Estimate by Richard Pollard of the weekly expenses for a noble household of eighty persons, n.d.*

KENT ARCHIVES OFFICE, U269/A525/11

An Imaginary proportion for the weekly expences of a noble family consisting of 80 persons.

| | | | |
|---|---|---|---|
| Beef 1 per week value at | £7 | os | od |
| Mutton 5 per week value at | 3 | o | o |
| Veal and lamb at | 1 | o | o |
| Butter and Cheese at | 2 | o | o |
| Bread corn at | 3 | 10 | o |
| Poultry at | 1 | o | o |
| fish of all sorts at | 1 | o | o |
| Beer 6 hogsheads per week | 2 | 8 | o |
| Wine | o | 10 | o |
| Horse corn and hay at | 1 | 10 | o |
| Sum is | 22 | 18 | o |

which is £1190 16s od per *year*
Or thus £20 per week is £1040 p[er] *year* which is 5s per week for each person.

But I believe a family consisting of so many persons and of such quality will hardly be provided for with less than £25 per week, accounting all provision, which is £100 per month and so £1200 per *year*: a great sum and requires a great estate to maintain this and all other necessary expenses proportionable.

[initialled] R[ichard]P[ollard]

## APPENDIX 2

*List of Tawstock servants, c.1645*

KENT ARCHIVES OFFICE, U269/E314/1

[There is a tear on the left-hand side.]

A note of the Servants at Tawstock
        Mr Pollard
        Mr Wyott
        Mr Wyott
        William Geare porter
... £ 10s p *year*  Robert Whitfeild gardener
... p *year*      James Blackmoore  cook  £2
... *year*       Baldwin Steevens  brewer

... per *year*     Rich: Rooke  groom  £1 5s
...               John Martyn miller  £1 10s
...               Baldwin Bater  keep[er]
...               William Rumson  }
... *year*        Simon Lake     }  for husbandry
...               John Cowman    }
...               Tho: Cowman    }

... Women servants
...               Mrs Hardwick  and Rose Hamlyn
... per *year*    Anne Rowe
... £2 per *year* Avis Tearle
£2 per *year*     Honor Wood
                  Mary Reymor

Besides Mr Weeks his family consisting of seven persons.

# APPENDIX 3

*Estimate of Tawstock Room Sizes for curtains, n.d.*

KENT ARCHIVES OFFICE, U269/E314/1

These are to certify your honour concerning the rooms in *Tawstocke* house and for their private necessaries.

Item Lord's bed chamber it containeth in length about 17 yards, in depth 3 yards, the chimney piece to the same room 2 yards in length and 1 yard and 1 quarter in depth, for 2 windows to the same room for their curtains 2 yards in depth and 2 in breadth.

The higher drawing chamber.
It contains in length about 21 yards and in depth 3 yards 3 quarters the 2 windows belonging to the same 2 yards broad and 3 yards deep for curtains.

Another room adjoining to the dining room
It containeth about in yards 11 yards and half and in depth 3 yards and half of a quarter for one window to the same for curtains 2 yards deep and a yard of breadth.

The Inner Nursery
It contains in yards about 19 yards and in depth 3 yards 1 quarter, 2 windows to the same room 2 yards and half in length and 2 yards and half in broad for the same room for curtains one little window to the same room 1 yard and half for curtains.

The other nursery
It contains about in yards 17 yards and half about, and in depth 3 yards and 1 quarter for 3 windows in the same room 2 yards and half in depth and to 2 yards and half in breadth to each window of the same room for curtains.

The Green Bed Chamber
It contains about in length 20 yards and in depth 3 yards the curtains to the same 2 windows 2 yards deep and 2 yards in breadth.

The Oaken Leaf chamber
It contains in length about 17 yards and in depth 3 yards and quarter for one window in the same room ie in length 2 yards and half and in breadth 2 yards for the curtains.

The Chamber in the New Building
It contains in length about 20 yards in depth a yard 3 quarters the curtains to
the same window & 5 yards broad and one yard and half deep which rooms
aforesaid are most necessary for the place and as for some other rooms they are
indifferently furnished.

# APPENDIX 4

KENT ARCHIVES OFFICE, U269/E314/2

An inventory of linen taken at London in May 1648.

1 pair old & costItem. flaxen, Irish & canvas sheets of all sorts—27 pair, 1 odd
    flaxen pillow-beres—6 pair, 1 odd
    Square table cloths flaxen, 4 come to Tawstock in 47—12
    Long coarse brown flaxen table cloths—6
    Little flaxen table cloths for the maids—2
    Great table cloths 3 breadths—2
    fine Irish napkins, 2 dozen brought to Tawsto. 1648—12 dozen
1 dozen, 7 costold plain napkins—11 dozen 10
    Canvas napkins allowed   1 dozen & 11 lost in 48—4 dozen
    Coarse towels—1
    Towels for my Lord—6

    fine linen from Tawstock 11 Septem. 1647
    damask napkins marked H.B.R. one dozen brought to Tawstock 1648
        —2 dozen
    drinking napkins—2
    damask table cloths—1
    damask cupboard cloths  brought down to Tawstock 1648—2
    damask towels—1
                Holland
2 pair of these made new        fine holland sheets 3 breadths  2 pair
                       brought to Tawstock 1648—6 pair
                       large holland pillow-beres—3 pair & 1
2 pair of these very little ones  lesser holland pillow-beres—5 pair

6 pair of sheets was brought from *Tawstok* to London the 18th of Decem. 1646
whereof 3 were old.

[new page]              coarse diaper
                    table cloths—12
                    napkins—5 dozen 11
                    large towels—6
                      finer diaper napkins—1 dozen 3

There came from *Tawstocke* the 26 of Decem. 1646 canvas sheets 8 pair which
Wilmot hath, & must be put out of Rose's inventory in the country—6 dozen
of coarse napkins, 4 dresser cloths & 2 rubbers from *Tawstocke* since April
1646.

Also at the same time came 3 pair of sheets 2 breadths & half which Wilmot
hath and 3 pair of the same which was given to Eliz. Searle to break, these
6 pair must also be put out of Rose's inventory in the country & 3 holland
pillow-beres which came in ['December' crossed through] Septem. 1647 &
1 long holland table cloth 3 breadths which is made into a pair of sheets being
one of the 6 pair on the other side. there was 3 pair & an odd sheet given away
& used to be broken.

There was 2 pair of flaxen pillow-beres came from *Tawstocke* since ['May' crossed through] April 1646 & must be put out of Rose's Inventory in the country, of which one was given away of the 6 pair of fine Holland sheets on the other side 3 pair of them are in Rose's Inventory at *Tawstocke*, 2 pair of them having 3 breadths & 1 pair 2 breadths & half.

There was also left formerly in London 2 pair of holland sheets marked H.B. which are broken & charged upon Rose at *Tawstocke*.

The 6 long brown table cloths on the other side 4 of them are in Rose's charge at Tawstock & 2 other in Wilmot's there.

[new page] There was 7 old sheets cut & given away before this Inventory was taken.

And 3 dozen of old napkins broken & torn for rubbers & 2 dozen wanting whereof Ro: Wood had & Owen a dozen & Lady Westmoreland had 3.

[new page]   3 pair of odd old Irish sheets 3 breadths
4 pair of 2 bedclothes & half old Irish sheets
1 pair of Irish cloth, 2 breadths of yard & half broad cloth
4 pair are little 2 breadths Irish sheets
1 pair of new Irish sheets & 2 breadths & ½
2 pair of dowlas sheets
2 pair of large canvas sheets
6 pair of narrow canvas sheets

[new page]   Goods sent to London Jan. 24th

|  | weight |
|---|---|
| Mr Peyton's and Thomas Whimp's trunks | 142 pounds |
| Mr Forward's & William Boothe's trunks | 159 |
| Mr Cob's & Elizab: Searle's trunks | 153 |
| Two boxes of my Lords | 140 |
| Wilmot's box, Mr Cob's little trunk & Doctor Wild's two boxes | 116 |
| One great fardel of my Lord's and one of William Boothe's | 132 |
| Two bundles of linen of my Lord's | 132 |
| Doctor Wild's, Wilmot & Christoper Bason, Meg Cooper, Ann Stone and with my Lord's hatcase | 94 |
| One box of my Lady's, two pair of boots & other things | 35 |
| One box more of my Lord's | 20 |
| A great cheese and a barrel | 46 |
| One box more | 16 |
| Sum is | 1185 |

At 2d ½ the pound comes to ['£19 6s 10d ½' crossed through] 12 6 10 ½ more for five fardel [?]riders £5 10s 0d

Will: Lynn paid him 12 6 3
& the ste[ward] at Tawstock  5 0 0

[new page]

|  | pounds |
|---|---|
| Two Sumpter trunks weight | 212 |
| one great Box of my Lords | 82 |
| another box of my Lord's with a little trunk & a bundle & a trunk of Mrs Norton's | 92 |
| Three bundles & a little box of my Lord's | 146 |
| another great box of my Lord's | 38 |
| Doctor Wild's trunk | 117 |
| Mr Bold's trunk | 74 |
| Mrs Jefford's & Mr Wingfeild trunk | 140 |

Mr Cob's & Mr Forward's trunk                              76
George Chevelye's box & Owen's with Frank's portmanteau
   & Will Booth's and Phillip's bundle       60
The Keeper's skins                                         28
[total]                                                  1060
At two pence the pound comes to £8 16s 8d


# APPENDIX 5

*Linen inventory, 1652*

KENT ARCHIVES OFFICE, U269/E314/1

February 2 51 [1652]
Irish sheets   12 pair & 1 odd sheet        some old
2 Irish table cloths   3 breadth
canvas sheets   6 pair & 2 pair             some old
Irish cloth pillow-beres   4 pair ['& 4 old one' crossed through]
fine Irish napkins good   8 dozen 3 ['& 2 dozen old ones' crossed through]
Irish Table cloths 1 breadth & ½, 7 for my Lord's table, whole table cloths 6.
   [illegible crossed through] 2 canvas napkins.

| | |
|---|---|
| brought up now | *Barstable* canvas sheets   6 pair |
| sent down again | 3 new Irish cloth pillow-beres |
| | New Irish table cloths   6 breadth & ½  4 |
| sent down again | 2 canvas & 3 dowlas napkins old from Tawstock |
| | New Canvas napkins 6 dozen 5 dozen & 1 |
| carry down | New dresser cloths 3 ['5 one being old' crossed through] |
| | & 4 new made |
| My Lady hath them | 4 little towels of old |

Of old Irish napkins there was 2 dozen of which remain
   1 dozen & 6 and the other six Wilmot tore up.
New Dowlas napkins bought in London in March 52
   3 dozen. of the 12 pair & 1 odd Irish sheet Phillip had
   one sheet & one pair past wearing.
Mrs Cope hath a pillow-bere
['2 pair of old canvas sheets' crossed through]


# APPENDIX 6

*List of Coins, 1651*

KENT ARCHIVES OFFICE, U269/A529

100
100
055
020  Geo.
19 6 6

| | [number] | [value] |
|---|---|---|
| gold pistoles 15s a piece | 36  27 | |
| £3 pieces one Eng[lish], one Spa[nish] | | |
| He: the 8 one gr[eat] piece, one less | 10 | 10 |

Ed: the 6                            202
Qu: Mary                              1        2
Qu: Eliza:                            7        6
K: James                             2        1 7s
K: Charles one little piece           1        0 2 6d
Prince Charles                        1        0 15 0
the new stamp                        1        1
Ferdinand & Isabella                  1        0 11
a sheep [?sic] angel                  1        0 11
one French pistole                    1        0 15
strange pieces                       2        1 10
one 10s Kin. Charles

                                     62              32 11 6
                                     the counters 27 0 0
['the counters' crossed through]     22
                                     294 16 6
                                     358 16 6  July the 23 1651


more of Go. 020
plain go.314 16 6

plain 314 16 6
counters 27 0 0
odd gold 32 11 6
[total] 374

odd silver about 6 0 0
mille [*milreis*] 6d & some plain 1 0 0
& in silver to spend [blank]
so in all this 30th of July 1651 above £400
£100 changed for silver
2 given Smith


50 changed for silver the 23d of Sept. brought home again.

£250
055 George had again
009 16 6


Decem. the 24th 1651
gold                                 75
                                     55
                                     50
                                     44
                                     9 10
                                     8 14 6
I am now to have from the steward    14 0 0
[total]                              256 4 6
                                     25 I am to cha. when I have silver to
                                        add to this  256 4 6
taken out                            £40

gold T:W:                            100
to London                            100
&                                    048 oweth one
This is all remains this 23 of Jan. 1651
£2

150 if this brought up then wants £7
40 Ri:
40 Ric:
03 Carw:
1 Marg:
Wi: Lynn 3 10s
[total] 87 10
63

| [new page] | Jan: 1650 the 11th | Gold | | |
|---|---|---|---|---|
| | in one purse | 050 | | |
| | one other | 050 | | |
| | one other | 100 | | |
| | in another | 050 | | |
| | in the other side of that purse | 015 | 10 | 6d |
| | [total] | 265 | 10 | 6 |
| rece. from Will: Brown of Hartland | | 22s | | |
| In counters | 31 15s pieces | 023 | 5 | 0 |
| my bro. Geo. | also 36 7s 6d pieces | 013 | 10 | 0 |
| | one half crown of K: Cha: the first | 000 | 2 | 6 |
| I gave Geo. | 3 £3 pieces | 009 | 0 | 0 |
| Fane's wife | 6 several pieces of Q. Eliza: | 005 | 12 | 0 |
| | one more 22s of hers given me by my sis. | | | |
| | Q. Mary | 001 | 18 | 0 |
| | 2 pieces of Ed: the 6 | 001 | 14 | 0 |
| | Hen. the 8 one piece | 008 | 0 | 0 |
| | K. James 2 pieces | 001 | 7 | 6 |
| | 2 strange pieces | 002 | 0 | 0 |
| | Prince Charles | 000 | 10 | 0 |
| | [total] | 67 | 0 | 0 |

a 20s of the new coin; one sheep angel
    one of Ferdinanda & Isabell of Spain
    May the 10th in old gold    52    0    0
£265 in odd gold 10s 6  in ordinary go. 266 12 6
067 in counters & old coin
Left with me by Will: Lynn this 17th of April 1651    £11    0    0
given me by two men of Sheldon    1    2    0
to Docto. Chichestor & Norton    4
This 10th of May    266    12    6
&    052    1    0
in all    318    13    6

# APPENDIX 7

*List of disbursements, c.1646*

KENT ARCHIVES OFFICE, U269/A528

What there hath been disbursed since the 8th of October 1646 for expense of Court & other disbursements

*First* for sending of a letter to Mr Pagett £0 2s 6d
for sending of a letter to Mr Canworthy 0 1 0

given by Mr Doweswell order to one which did light him to his lodging o 1 o
for one quarter of beef 1 6 o
for 3 pieces of ribs, a tail piece & rand o 13 2
for a quarter of veal & a ledge o 7 6
for half a mutton o 6 o
for one whole mutton o 8 o
for a line [*loin*] of veal o 3 o
for half a veal more o 6 o
for one whole mutton more o 13 4
for two roasting pidges o 4 4
for two turkeys o 4 o
for three geese o [torn]
for seventeen other poultry o 8 6
for fruit & spice o 10 3
for sugar o 13 1
for 21 quarts & half of sack 1 5 8
for six pecks of beans o 5 2
paid Elizabeth Bishopp for 24 pecks of oats o 12 o
paid for two sacks of oats more 1 2 o
hay for 15 horses for 6 days at 4d day & night 1 10 o
[total] 11 10 3

for bread, beer, fire & candle light [torn]

# APPENDIX 8

*Sequestrators' Inventory of Tawstock, 8 November 1648*

KENT ARCHIVES OFFICE, U269/O262

[dorse. Thomas Ley constable of the hundred   William Larrymed constable of the parish   George Berry   John Johson   sign PS   Peter Somers]

Devon   An Inventory of the goods & chattles of the Right Honorable Henry Earl of Bath taken and appraised by Anthony Moore, John Pike and Timothy Weymouth agents and collectors for Sequestration by and with the assistance of George Berry, Peter Somer & John Johnson in the presence of Robert Spry, Gentleman Solicitor for Sequestration and Thomas Ley, constable of the hundred & William Laramy, constable, this eighth day of November *in the year* 1648.

1   *First* in the hall one brass candle stick & other timber stuff £03 oos ood
2   in the parlour & the with drawing room the furniture therein valued at 20 oo oo
3   in the Countess' lower chamber things valued at 35 oo oo
4   the gentlewoman's chamber things at 05 oo oo
5   in the gentlemens dining room things 09 oo oo
6   three chambers over the buttery things 09 oo oo
7   in the outer nursery things valued at 06 oo oo ·
8   in the inner nursery things valued at 06 oo oo
9   in the upper with drawing room things at 35 oo oo
10   in the upper parlour the things valued at 60 oo oo
11   the plate in the cellar valued at 05 oo oo
12   the audit chamber things valued at 04 10 oo
13   in the blue bed chamber things valued 10 oo oo
14   next the blue bed chamber things at 03 oo oo
15   in the chamber called Ellis chamber 02 oo oo

16 in the room over the pastry 05 00 00
17 in a chamber adjoining 03 00 00
18 in the maidens chambers things at 10 00 00
19 in the chamber over the diary 02 10 00
20 linen in the pastry chamber 03 00 00
21 a feather bed in the dairy chamber 02 00 00
22 in the gate house chamber 02 00 00
23 in the chaplain's chamber 02 13 04
24 in the wardrobe a featherbed & bolster &c 05 00 00
25 in the two upper chambers things valued at 06 00 00
26 brass and pewter in the kitchen & scullery 06 10 00
27 linen in the starching room 26 00 00
28 the room adjoining divers chambers 02 00 00
29 the brewing vessel & the furnace 20 00 00
30 divers things in the buttery & cellars 10 00 00
31 malt in the floor 06 00 00
32 in the hop chamber, a quantity of hops 15 00 000
33 in the stable 6 coach horses & a coach 50 00 00
34 in the horsemans chamber saddles & other furniture belonging to horses with a bed 06 00 00
35 three other horses valued at ['20' crossed through] 00 00
goods without doors
36 six horses valued at 24 00 00
37 twelve oxen valued at 60 00 00
38 seven cows valued at 21 00 00
39 twenty four sheep valued at 09 00 00
40 twelve young bullocks valued at 36 00 00
41 three young bullocks more at 07 00 000
42 six labour horses valued at 16 00 00
43 ten fat sheep 05 00 00
44 divers hogs at the doors at 08 00 00
45 the plow stuff with the wheels 10 00 00
46 five mowes of corn valued 200 00 00
47 wood valued at 005 00 00
48 two ricks of hay 006 00 00
sum total 801 03 04
All the residue of the standing goods belonging to the former Earl's heirs
The barton of *Tawstocke* per *year* 100 00 00
[signed] Timothy Weamouth   Anthony Moore
Rob: Spry Solicitor Sequestra.
John Pyke agent

# APPENDIX 9

*List of husbandry items at Tawstock, 20 January 1642*

KENT ARCHIVES OFFICE, U269/E314/1

*Tawstocke* An inventory of all the implements of husbandry under the bailiff's charge taken the 20th day of January *in the year* 1641

*First* 2 scythes, item 3 bill hooks, item 3 axes, item 1 hatchet, item 5 mattocks, item 6 shovels, item 1 hay knife, item 2 dung forks, item 12 ox bows, item 7 ox yokes, item 2 drays, item 1 cart, item 1 wain, item 3 soles, item 2 sheers and 2 coulters, item 6 iron strings, item 11 pack saddles, item 11 pack girts, item

9 pair of dung pads, item 7 pair of sand pads, item 6 pair of trusses, item 11 pair of truss ropes, item 8 halters, item 3 pair of panniers, item 6 pair of wood crooks, item 1 pair of corn crooks, item 1 seed lip, item 2 long corn pikes, item ladders, item 2 bar irons, item 3 wheel barrows 2 buts and wheels, item 1 slide car, item 1 pair of horse draughts, item 2 taw pins, item 3 iron crooks, item 2 pair of harrows, item 1 thwart saw

Capt. per Richard Pollard

# APPENDIX 10

*List of stock at Tawstock, 5 November 1653*

KENT ARCHIVES OFFICE, U269/E314/1

Tawstock   An Abstract of my Lord's stock of cattle, sheep and hogs taken the 5th of November 1653

| | |
|---|---|
| Cows to milk | 14 |
| Bulls | 3 |
| Oxen to plough | 12 |
| Oxen to feed | 6 |
| steers to feed | 0 |
| Steers to graze | 2 |
| Cows to feed | 3 |
| Calves | 7 |
| wethers, ewes and rams | 32 |
| great hogs | 11 |
| middle hogs | 8 |
| rearers | 31 |
| boars | 2 |

Provision of Store in the Store Chamber the day abovesaid

| | |
|---|---|
| Raisins *of the sun* | ½ barrel |
| currants | ½ barrel |
| prunes | ½ barrel |
| candle-wick | 1 doz. & 3 rolls |
| plutch for bags | 2 pieces |
| nutmegs | ½ lb |
| cloves | ½ lb |
| mace | ½ lb |
| cinnamon | ½ lb |
| ginger | ½ lb |
| aniseed | ½ lb |
| rice | 6 lbs |
| French barley | 12 lbs |
| sugar loafs | 7 |
| cap paper | 2 reams |
| New trenchers | 20 dozen |
| nails | 3 bags |
| porcelain dishes of all sorts | 21 pieces |
| soap | 1 barrel and half |

| | |
|---|---|
| Corn of all sorts | |
| wheat | 32 bushels |
| barley | none |
| oats | 2 bushels |

| peas | none |
|---|---|
| beans | 22 bushels |
| vetches | 5 bushels |
| barley malt old | 44 bushels |
| barley new | 23 bushels |
| old hops | 5[oo] 28 lbs |
| new hops | 8[oo] 2 quarters 19 lbs |

p[er] R[ichard] P[ollard]

# APPENDIX 11

## *List of medicine, 1639*

KENT ARCHIVE OFFICE, U269/A530

for the Right Honorable Henry Earl of Bath since 8ber the 17th 1639

| | | |
|---|---|---|
| First | a preparative syrup | oo oo o6 |
| 18th | a laxative potion | oo o3 o4 |
| 19th | a preparative | oo o1 oo |
| 2oth | a laxative potion | oo o3 o4 |
| March | for 2 days fees | oo 1o oo |
| 2oth | a clister | oo o3 o4 |
| | a fomentation | oo o3 o6 |
| | fees for one day | oo o5 oo |
| | troches Alhandal {1 | oo o2 o6 |
| 7ber | diagrydium {ounce | oo o2 oo |
| 3th | mastic {2 | 2oo oo o3 |
| 1640 | syrup of *stacodos* {2 | oo oo o8 |
| | oil of cloves | oo oo o6 |
| 25th | materials for a bear [*bier*] | oo o5 oo |
| for my | a clister | oo o3 oo |
| Lady | a cordial electuary | oo o5 oo |
| | *Hordis Mundat* lb | oo oo o8 |
| 8ber 2th | a clister | oo o3 o4 |
| | a julep | oo o2 o6 |
| | vng stomach | oo o2 oo |
| | a fomentation | oo o2 o6 |
| | for the use of 2 sponges | oo oo [blank] |
| | a syrup | oo oo o6 |
| | theriac Venetia | oo oo o6 |
| | the clister again | oo o3 o4 |
| | the fomentation again | oo o2 o6 |
| | suppositories no.:3 | oo o1 o6 |
| 3th | a plaster | oo o1 o |
| | a syrup | oo o1 oo |
| | manus Christi plate {1 | oo o1 oo |
| | *Sem. foeniculi dulci* {1 | oo oo o3 |
| 4th | *rosar. rub. siccacu'* {3 | oo oo o4 |
| | *Sem. foeniculi dulci* {1 | oo oo o3 |
| | *anisi carvi ana* {1 | oo oo o2 |
| 5th | a vial | oo o2 oo |
| | the clister again | oo o3 o4 |
| | syr[up] of Papapare [*poppy*] {3 | oo o1 oo |

| 6 | a drink ex. lb 5 | oo o4 oo |
| | the clister again | oo o3 oo |
| | Rad[ix] China  {1 | oo o2 oo |
| | *Cor. Cerv. Raspt*  {6 | oo o3 oo |
| | *olea' Chamomelim*  {3 | oo oo 10 |
| | *olea' Laurimi*  {3 | oo oo 10 |
| | *Sem.* Cumim  {3 | oo oo 10 |
| | ... *tt Laurii*  {2 | oo oo o4 |
| ... *lelota et Chamomel: Spii* | | oo oo o4 |
| Sum is | | o4 13 o2 |

[torn] ... Servant Culpepper Clapham

# APPENDIX 12

## List of medicine for the Countess, *1654*

KENT ARCHIVES OFFICE, U269/A537

[dorse. Received in full of this account the sum of £4 13s of say [sic] received by me Arthur Clapham for the use of my father Culpepper Clapham.]

1653 for the Right Honorable the Countess of Bath
February

| 23 | for a compounded glister anodin [*anodyne*] | o 3 6 |
| | for a compounded mixture with cassia 12 ounces | o 12 o |
| 25 | for a glister as before | o 3 6 |
| | for liniment with cassia | o 5 6 |
| 26 | for 2 doses of compounded aposennes [?sic] | o 5 6 |
| | for a glister as before | o 3 6 |
| 27 | for 2 doses of aposeines | o 5 6 |
| 28 | for a purging potion clarified | o 4 6 |
| | for a box of pectoral tablets | o 5 6 |
| March 1 | for 2 doses of aposeines | o 5 6 |
| | for the maid 2 doses of purging aposeines | o 4 o |
| 2 | for my Lady 2 doses of aposeines | o 5 6 |
| | for mixture with cassia | o 6 o |
| 3 | for 2 doses of poseines | o 5 6 |
| | for a glister as before | o 3 6 |
| 4 | for 2 doses of aposeines | o 5 6 |
| 5 | for 2 doses of aposeines | o 5 6 |
| 6 | for 2 doses of aposeines | o 5 6 |
| 7 | for 2 doses of aposeines | o 5 6 |
| | for mixture with cassia | o 6 o |
| 8 | for 2 doses of aposeines | o 5 6 |
| 12 | for mixture with cassia | o 6 o |
| 17 | for mixture with cassia | o 8 o |
| 19 | for a purging potion | o 4 6 |
| 20 | for a young gentlewoman a purging potion | o 3 o |
| 21 | for a glister as before | o 3 6 |
| 25 | for a mixture with cassia 8 ounces | o 8 o |
| | for liniment | o 4 6 |
| 29 | for a bottle of fomenting liquor with sponges | o 14 6 |
| | for a runlet of diet drink | £1 10 o |

| | | |
|---|---|---|
| 30 | for a dose of emulsion with cassia | 0 3 0 |
| | for 2 doses of aposeines | 0 5 6 |
| | for liniment as before | 0 4 6 |
| 31 | for a dose of emulsion with cassia | 0 3 6 |
| | for 2 doses of aposeines | 0 5 6 |
| April 1 | for a dose of emulsion with cassia | 0 3 0 |
| | for 2 doses of aposeine | 0 5 6 |
| 2 | for a dose of emulsion with cassia | 0 3 0 |
| | for 2 doses of aposeines | 0 5 6 |
| 3 | for a dose of emulsion with cassia | 0 3 0 |
| | for 2 doses of aposeine | 0 5 6 |
| | for fomenting liquor as before | 0 14 6 |
| | for a bottle of oils of Juniper | 0 10 0 |
| | for liniment | 0 4 6 |
| | for a glister | 0 3 6 |
| 4 | for a dose of emulsion | 0 3 0 |
| | for 2 doses of aposeine | 0 5 6 |
| | for a pot of mixture to apply | 0 10 0 |
| 5 | for a dose of emulsion with cassia | 0 3 0 |
| | for 2 doses of aposeine | 0 5 6 |
| 6 | for 2 doses of aposeine | 0 5 6 |
| | for 2 doses of aposeine | 0 5 6 |
| | for mixture as before | 0 10 0 |
| 7 | for 2 doses of aposeine | 0 5 6 |
| | for a young man purging potion | 0 3 0 |
| 8 | for 2 doses of aposeine | 0 5 6 |
| | for mixture | 0 10 6 |
| 9 | for 2 doses of aposeine | 0 5 6 |
| 10 | for 2 doses of aposeine | 0 5 6 |
| 15 | for a runlet of diet drink as before | £1 10 0 |
| 23 | for a glister as before | 0 3 6 |
| | [total] | 19 5 0 |

Received May 26 1654 of the right Honorable the Countess of Bathe by the hands of Mr Richard Forrand the sum of nineteen pound five shilling in full payment of this bill by me. £19 5s 0d [signed] Fouraud

apothecary
£19 5s 0d paid

# APPENDIX 13

*List of mourners at the funeral of Henry, fifth Earl of Bath, 1654*

KENT ARCHIVES OFFICE, U269/F39

Mourners at the funeral of the Right Honorable Henry Earl of Bath

The Right Honorable Countess of Bath
The Honorable Lady Eliz. Cope
The Honorable Sir Francis Fane
Mr Francis Fane
1. Mrs Rachel Fane 5:00
Mrs Pagett
2. Mrs Loveden
Mrs Abigail Cope
3. Mr Henry Fane 200 *each year* land or lease

4. Mr Deane
Mr Ridley
5. Mr Lynn
6. Mr Pollard
7. Mr Bold
Mr Peyton
Mr Howard
8. Mr Wyatt sen.
9. Mr Wyatt jun.
10. Mr Cobb
11. Mr Smyth
Mr Wingfeild
12. Mr Forard
Mr Wood
John Burke
13. George Chiveley in Ireland a lease
14. Thom Hathorne £6 a lease
15. Kitt Bason £6 a lease
16. Will Booth a lease £6
17. Will Fetherstone £20
Mr Norton £20
18. Thom: Moore £10
19. Rich Rooke a lease
20. Thom Cooman a lease £4 10s
21. Steeven Pinckome £5
Zachary Chiveley
22. Thurstyn Haymor a lease £4 10s
23. Will Rumson £20
24. Baldwin Steevens £20
25. Thom Ambsby £5 £20 [sic]
26. Thom. Penrose £5
27. Nedd Lyddon
28. Will Meave
29. Sym. Lake
30. Peter Hearder
31. Old Cooman gown & suit

32. John Ridley £6
33. John Ashley £6
34. John Terry
35. Will Balch
36. George Pitts
37. John Gribble
38. Will Croydon
39. Cobley
40. Welsh Dicke
John Warren
Will Morrice a coat
Rich: May coat 12
Thom: Pollard cloaks
Rob: Crosse
Dick Britton
Huxtable a coat 13 coats 24
['Peter Terry cloak' crossed through]
Charleife
Will: Weekes

41. Bes Searle £200 [sic]
42. Wilmot Booth £10
43. Rose Randle £5
44. Doll Cooman
45. Avis Cooman
46. Honor Wood £10

48. Watt lease
49. Kate
50. Tym £2
51. Lymbary leases

13. Mr Hugh Prust stewards of courts
14. Mr Tho: Prust
15. Mr Thom: Hyne
16. Mr Elston
17. 18. Mr Hugh Thomas, young Mr Hyne

Francis Leakar   bailiffs
James Parrett
Thom: Ballyman
John Mylls
Will Britton

19. My lady Cope's grant
20. Sir Francis Fane's woman
47. Mr Deane's man

['Earl of Westmoreland, the Countess, Mr George Fane, his wife, Mr William &
Mr Bourchier 2 gowns, Will: his wife, Mr Robert, his wife, Mr Cope, the Lady
Darcy' crossed through]

John Hamlin, Lewice 17 if these have cloaks
['Mr Hell' crossed through]
Pow John Mules

£4500   0500 1000 0100 0500 0170 0250   [total] 7020
£1000 the gentl. 0100 3000 [total] 1400

24 poor people in gowns

133 3 4 wages

in all 108 [in ?total]

# APPENDIX 14

*Legacies to servants and others, c.1654*

KENT ARCHIVES OFFICE, U269/A528

| Years | Wages | [legacy] |
|---|---|---|
| 14 William Lynn | £20 | £40 |
| 15 Richard Pollard | £20 | £40 |
| 21 Peter Bold | £24 | £40 |
| 17 Thomas Wyote | £06 | £40 |
| 12 Randall Peyton | £10 | £20 |
| 5 Hen: Howard | £10 | £20 |
| 13 Richard Cobb | £20 | £40 |
| 5 John Smith | £12 | £20 |

| | | |
|---|---|---|
| 9 Edw: Wingfielld | came at 5 | £10 |
| 6 Richard Farrard | £15 | £20 |
| in all 10 | | |
| | | |
| 16 Robert Wood | £8 | £30 |
| 16 John Burgh | £6 | £20 |
| 11 Geo: Cheevlly | £2 | £10 |
| 2 Thom: Hathorn | £3 | £3 |
| 10 William Booth | £6 | to him then £10 |
| 14 Thom: Armsby | £5 | £10 |
| 16 Baldwin Steevens | £4 | £10 |
| 2 the cook | £18 | £5 |
| 2 Thom: Moore | £2 | £2 |
| 5 Kitt: Bason | £4 | £5 |
| 4 William Fether-ston | £4 10s | £2 |
| 10 Richard Rook | £3 | £5 |
| Thom: Cooman | 2 | £2 |
| Steven Pinckome | 3 | £2 |
| Thurstan Haymor | £12 | 10 |
| 15 William Rumsom | £5 | £10 |
| Thom: Penroses | £2 | |
| Ned Lyddon | £2 | |
| John Rydle [blank] | | |
| I would give as [blank] | | |
| | | |
| years | | |
| 2 Loveden | £20 | |
| 15 Besse Seirle | £3 | |
| 16 Wilmot | £2 | £20 |
| Rose Randall | £2 | |
| Dole Cooman | £2 | |
| Avis Cooman | £2 | |
| John | £2 | |

£10 Honor: married
Rachel Fane
The Dean
Old Mr Wyote
The Dean's man
Jack Ashley
Rich: May

William Maine £2
George Pitts £2
Welsh Dick £2
Will: Balch £2
Old Croyder £2
young Croyder
John Gribble £2
Jack
Simon Lake £2
Peter Hearder £2
old Cooman
Will: Morice
Watt: Balch
Nick:
Jonathan
Simon

Keat
Harry
a year ago Thom: Bouchier £6
two Miss Kemps £5
a year during my life, a year out of Bow

# APPENDIX 15

*Inventory of Tawstock, c.1655*

KENT ARCHIVES OFFICE, U269/T96/4

A Schedule of all such goods, chattles, hangings, household stuff and implements of household and other things of the late Right Honorable Henry Earl of Bath deceased at his house at *Tawstocke* in the county of Devon as are sold and granted away by the Right Honorable Lionel Earl of Middlesex and the right Honorable Rachel Countess of Middlesex his wife, executrix, of the last will and testament of the said Earl of Bath deceased unto Sir Francis Fane, George Fane and William Lynn in the deed hereunto annexed & pressed as followeth

In the Parlour   *First* four table boards and a Turkey carpet with two and twenty [illegible] chairs, one chest, four gilded sconces and five blue baize window curtains, one green cloth carpet & a pair of brass andirons, a pair of creepers, a shovel, tongs & bellows.

In the Drawing Room   Item the black baize hangings and two black baize carpets, one couch and nine blue cloth chairs covered with black baize, one gilded sconce and a child's chair, one table and cupboard, a turkey work carpet, one screen, two standards, one pair of andirons, fire shovel and tongs, bellows and snuffers.

In my Lady's Chamber below   Item one standing bed and quilt with the hangings, curtain, valance, counterpane and carpet black baize, one velvet cushion and three blue chairs covered with black, one little table, curtain rods, creepers, tongs and bellows.

In the Closet within   Item one great Ebony looking-glass, one close stool, a little screen, a chessboard and men, one child's chair, one little old chair and one creeper.

In the Dining Room   Item eight pieces of forest work hangings, one fair organ, sixteen stools of red wrought velvet, one little table with a Turkey carpet, ten chairs only covered with baize, two gilt standards, one pair of virginals & frame, one feather bed & bolster, two blankets and a coverlet, one pair of brass andirons, one pair of creepers, brass fire shovel and tongs, bellows and snuffers

In the Upper Drawing Room   Item one standing bedstead and trundle bed with feather bed and bolsters, blankets and coverlets and other furniture belonging [illegible] pieces of old hangings, two window curtains, one little table, four old stools, one pair of brass andirons, fire shovel and tongs, one pair of bellows, a pair of creepers & a close stool

In my Lady's Upper Chamber   Item one bedstead, one [illegible] wrought bed with a counter valance, one great chair and couch, six high chairs, two low chairs and four low stools of red velvet & covered with baize, one pair of creepers with brass heads, one fire shovel and little table witth a chimney piece.

In the Little Chamber within   Item one half-headed bedstead mat and cord, one leather chair, one little chair frame, one little painted screen with a desk.

In my Lady's closet    Item one little table with wrought carpet, one cushion suitable to the carpet, two join stools, one red baize window curtain, one trundle bed, feather bed and bolster, one pillow, two blankets & coverlet, two creepers with brass heads, five shovel tongs, bellows and snuffers.

In my Lord's closet    Item one table board & a great chair, one green carpet, one pair of creepers, one pair of bellows, one Jacob's staff, one mathematical jewel with many other mathematical instruments and two fair globes.

In the Chamber over the starching house    Item one bedstead, feather bed & bolster, four pillows with curtains, valance & counerpain of red cloth lined with sarsnet & fringed with tester and head, six pieces of hangings, four chairs & five stools suitable to the bed, one Turkey work stool, two creepers, fire shovel, tongs & table.

In my Lady's Wardrobe    Item one standing bedstead, feather bed & bolster, one blanket, one rug with the furniture, two old pieces of hangings, one chair, one cupboard, one pair of bellows.

In the Buttery Bedchamber    Item one standing bedstead, feather bed & bolster, a pillow, two blankets & one rug with its furniture, six pieces of hangings, three chairs, one cupboard & carpet, one window curtain, creepers, fire shovel & tongs

In the Chamber within    Item one bedstead, feather bed & bolster, blanket and coverlet

In the Chamber next the Music room    Item one bedstead with feather bed and bolster & three coverlets, four chairs of several sorts, one Turkey carpet & folding screen of striped stuff.

In the Great Stairs    Item seven Spanish tables, one little one [?sic] one cupboard, one old cushion, three old maps, one picture, one dozen & half of cushions, one old stool & screen.

In the Audit Chamber    Item one standing bedstead, feather bed & bolster, two pillows, three blankets, one rug with green serge furniture, one long table, two leather chairs, one green stool, one pair of bellows, creepers and a pair of tongs.

In the Through Bed Chamber    Item three bedsteads, one feather bed, two feather bolsters, two dust beds, two dust bolsters, one mattress, four blankets & four coverlets, one great cradle and pedestal, one old stool & one old Organ.

In the Chamber next the Blue Bed Chamber    Item one half-headed bedstead, feather bed, bolster & pillow, one blanket, one rug, one leather chair, one close stool, one old window curtain and four oaken boards.

In the Blue Bed Chamber    Item one standing bedstead, feather bed & bolster, two pillows, two blankets, one blue rug with counterpane, curtains & valance head and tester of blue cloth raced, five chairs & four stools suitable to the bed, two window curtains of blue baize, one table board with a baize carpet, one fair looking-glass covered with cloth of silver, the hangings of gilded leather, a piece of blue baize, one pair of creepers, fire pan, tongs and bellows.

In the Wardrobe    Item three great wainscot presses, two table boards, one bedstead, mat & cord with a piece of old striped stuff upon it, three pieces of striped stuff, one blue rug, two baize window curtains and three to be cushions.

Seventeen pieces of forest work hangings coarse and fine, one fair Persia carpet and seven Turkey carpets, two green velvet carpets and three green velvet cushions, one green cloth seat for a chair, one green & blue chair, & several other pieces of lumber with a great chest.

In the Chaplain's Chamber   Item one standing bedstead, featherbed & bolser, one pillow, two blankets with a coverlet & furniture thereunto belonging, one piece of Arras hangings with the chairs and stools, one table & cupboard with fire shovel, tongs, creepers & bellows with other lumber

In the Porter's Lodge and room within   Item one bedstead & featherbed & bolster, one blanket, three coverlets, one table and three old stools and one firepan, seventeen pair of bowls, one pair of stocks & some other old lumber

In the Saddle Chamber   Item one fair foot cloth and trappings

In the Cook's Chamber   Item two bedsteads, two feather beds, two bolsters, four blankets, four coverlets & one old green stool

In the Feather Bed Chamber   Item two great brass pots, one brass chaffer, two pair of racks, one great kettle, three old dripping pans, two rack pothangings, one pair of creepers for coal fire, one jack spit, one iron bar and five pack saddles

In the Chamber over the Larder   Item three bedsteads & their beds & furniture of bed clothes with one old trunk & Chest & a folding trundle bedstead.

In the Chamber over the Scullery   Item one bedstead, feather bed and bolster, three blankets & coverlet, ten latten candlesticks & other old lumber

In the Maid's Chamber   Item two bedsteads & two feather beds, two bolsters, three pillows, two blankets and a coverlet, one great trunk, one chair frame and one old cupboard

In the Preserving Room   Item one table board & cupboard, a preserving pan & one warming pan, one pair of bellows, fire shovel, tongs & creepers

In the Store Chamber   Item two great iron-bound chests & one wooden chest, one great press & a little one, one table, one iron jack, one brass pestle & mortar and one of alabaster, two pair of brass scales & two sets of weights, four trunks, one cupboard with aras, one frying pan, one piece of plutch for bags & two bags of nails, one press for oils and seventeen dozen of trenchers with other lumber.

In the Kitchen   Item fifteen spits, two brass kettles, one large boiler, two pair of racks, one iron pot, one brass pot, four skillets, three frying pans, two dripping pans, two great iron bars and a great range of iron grates with other utensils for the kitchen.

In the Scullery   Item pewter of all sorts, one old chest, one chair, two shelves & 1 dozen of candlesticks

In the Cellar   Item three & twenty hogsheads, five pipes, six runlets, one tableboard, two chests, one great salt tub with other necessary utensils

In the Malt House   Item fourteen plutch bags, one winnowing sheet, one peck, one half peck, one bushel, one shovel, a pair of scales & two lead weights, one hair cloth with other necessaries, one iron grate, fire shovel & tongs with a cistern. Item corn of all sorts in the house and ricks, hogs of all sorts, timber in the park, welgars, fourteen cows and one [illegible] at parsonage, implements for husbandry, twenty horses, mares and colts, oxen at Wonham, [illegible] steers, heifers, twelve yearlings, apples, a copper bottom. [illegible] and bed linen of all sorts.

# Glossary

| | |
|---|---|
| *Alhandal* | Arabic name for *Citrullus colcoynthis*, the bitter cucumber |
| *anisi* | *Pimpinella anisum*, anise, a plant cultivated for its aromatic and carminative seeds |
| Arras | a rich tapestry fabric |
| battledore | an instrument used in playing with a shuttlecock |
| Bay salt | salt imported from the shores of the Bay of Biscay |
| browse | young shoots and twigs of shrubs, trees, etc. |
| bugle lace | lace used for the tube-shaped glass bead |
| bullen nail | var. spelling of bullion nail, a rounded nail |
| cap-paper | a type of wrapping paper or writing paper |
| *cassia* | a kind of cinnamon |
| cate | provisions or victuals |
| clister | var. spelling of clyster, a medicine injected into the rectum |
| coral | a toy made of polished coral or other material given to infants |
| cornelian ring | a ring made of chalcedony, a semi-transparent quartz of a reddish colour used primarily for seals |
| counters | an imitation coin or token used to represent real coin |
| creepers | small iron dogs, of which a pair were placed on a hearth between the andirons |
| crewel | a thin worsted yarn used for tapestry, embroidery, etc. |
| curral | obs. form of coral |
| dareny | dornick, several types of cloth named after the Flemish town |
| Diagrudium | a preparation of scammony |
| diurnal | daily news-sheet |
| drench | a draught or dose of medicine administered to an animal |
| dresser clothes | a table cloth |
| dryfat | a large container or vessel used to hold dry goods |
| ducape | a silk fabric |
| electuary | a medicinal conserve or paste |
| emerod | hemorrhoids |
| eryngo | candied root of *Eryngium maritinum*, the sea holly |
| farcin | obs. form of farcy, a disease of animals, particularly horses |
| ferret | a narrow tape or ribbon originally woven from silk |
| flitch | side of an animal, generally a hog, which was salted and cured |
| forest work | a decorative representation of sylvan scenery |
| furze | popular name of *Ulex europaeus* also known as gorse, a spiny evergreen shrub with yellow flowers, which was used for fuel |
| gale | a castrated bull |
| girth web | woven material; a strong tape |
| glister | see clister |
| gridelin | a pale purple or red colour |
| hobby | a small or middle-sized horse; a pony |
| hone | a whetstone |
| horse meat | food or provender for horses, generally oats |

| | |
|---|---|
| hutch | a coop or enclosure of wickerwork, spars or iron as a trap for taking salmon |
| imagery | pictoral elements of a natural scene or landscape |
| Jacob's staff | an instrument used for measuring the altitude of the sun or measuring heights and distances |
| kiddle | a barrier across a river, often partly made of nets, for the purpose of catching fish |
| landskip | var. spelling of landscape |
| larum | an apparatus attached to a clock or watch |
| latitat | a writ of the King's Bench |
| latten | a mixed metal of a yellowish colour |
| livery cupboard | in which liveries of food were served out, in later times apparently an ornamental buffet or sideboard |
| loadum | a card game |
| lough | to stack |
| love | borde of thin silk stuff |
| *Manus Christi* | rose sugar |
| marchpane | marzipan |
| mastic | oil from *Thymus mastichina*, Spanish Wood Marjoram |
| meon | spignel |
| mettle | var. spelling of metal |
| *olea' Laurimi* | possibly *Oleum Laurinum*, oil of bay laurel berries |
| ostler | a man who attends to horses at an inn |
| oyster table | a table inlaid with mother-of-pearl |
| periwig | an artificial imitation of a head of hair |
| pettitoes | pig's trotters |
| plutch | a thick hempen material |
| pompion | the plant *Curcurbita pepo*, pumpkin |
| posnet | a small metal pot used for cooking |
| postillion | a horse-rider either for a carriage, coach or for the post |
| *radix China* | China root |
| raines | a kind of linen or lawn cloth from Rennes |
| rode | a rope particularly used for boats |
| rose | rosette, used on shoes |
| rotten | in regards to sheep, affected with the disease sheep-rot |
| rubbers | a cloth used for cleaning |
| sarsnet | a fine silk material |
| scammony | the plant *Convolvulus scammonia*, bindweed |
| sconce | a lantern or candlestick with a handle and protected from the wind |
| *sem. cumim* | seeds from *Cumino aigro*, cumin |
| *sem. foeniculi dulci* | seeds from *Foeniculum dulce*, Finnochio or Florence fennel |
| sempster | a seamster |
| slay | an instrument used in weaving |
| spar | a pole or piece of timber of considerable length and some thickness |
| *stacodos* | *stechados* or *Lavandula stoechas*, French lavender |
| stammell | a coarse woollen cloth |
| standish | a stand for writing instruments including pens and ink |
| strike | a bundle or bunch |
| sucket | obs. form of sucade, fruit preserved in sugar, either candied or in syrup |
| tabby | a general term for silk taffeta |
| table-men | pieces played on a board game especially backgammon |
| taffety | obs. form of taffeta |
| tenter-hook | hooks set in a close row on a bar for holding cloth |

| | |
|---|---|
| tester | framework or canopy over a bed |
| theorbo | a musical instrument similar to a lute |
| *theriac* | treacle |
| troches | var. spelling of trochisk, a medicated tablet or disk |
| troll-madam | game played by ladies |
| turnsole | a colouring matter of a purple or violet-blue hue |
| usquebaugh | whiskey |
| valance | drapery attached to canopy; border or edging |
| verdor | obs. form of verdure, ? |
| viola | musical instrument |
| virginal | a keyed musical instrument resembling a spinet |
| welgars | a name given to various species of willows especially *Salix viminalis*, the common osier |
| wethers | a male sheep, generally castrated |

# Index of Personal and Place Names

Abingdon, Oxon, 116, 119
Acklands, Archilles, 254, 259
  Mr, 23
Adams, Giles, 72
Ager, Mr, 116
Aldersgate Street, London, xxviii
Alldans, Mr, 250
Allen (Allein, Allin), of London, 149
  Charles, 5–6, 36, 195, 197, 270, 271, 273
  Fra., 272
  Grace, 203
  Mr, 144, 151
  Mrs, 150
Allopp, Mr, 136
Allsupp, John, 242
Alphington, xxv, 210
Amersham, Bucks, 276, 278
Amery, Robert, 208, 279
Amner, widow, 189
Amsby (Ambsby, Armsby, Arnisby), Thomas,
  38, 40, 42, 48, 53, 78, 102, 113, 117, 119,
  120, 121, 122, 123, 125, 128, 132, 136, 140,
  153–4, 156, 158, 161, 163, 178, 183, 189–90,
  207, 234, 248, 251, 252, 261, 268, 269, 272,
  275, 288, 310, 312
Amsterdam, 153
Anderton, Mr, 115
Andover, Hants, 145, 278
Antony, Miss, 185
Apethorpe, Northamptonshire, xxi, xxiii, 150,
  156, 159, 161, 163, 164, 170, 173, 207, 228,
  229, 233
Appledore, xxxiii, xliii, 9, 12, 16, 33, 38, 52, 55,
  59, 63, 64, 65, 67, 78, 87, 93, 95, 103, 269,
  279, 284
Apsley, Sir Allen, 47, 61
Armagh, county, Ireland, xxv, 126, 173
Arundell, House, 131
  Lord, 180, 240, 243
Ash, Anthony, 51, 60, 102
  Mr, 151
Ashford, Mr, 229
Ashley, 288
  Christopher (Kitt), 267, 289, 291–2
  John, 310
  Jack, 312
Ashrenton wood, 273
Ashton, Mrs, 52
  Sir Thomas, 252
Aston, 151, 153, 163
Atherton, Richard, xxx, 183, 257
Atkey (Atkins, Atley), Mr, 36, 39, 247, 248,
  281, 288
Austin (Austen, Austyn), John, 88
  Mr, 145, 149, 174, 191, 201, 238, 243, 258,
  286
  Robert, 134, 136, 276

Autin, Mr, 143
Axminster, 57
Aylesbury, Bucks, 266

Backer, 219
Bagborow, 245
Bagshot, Surrey, 123
Baincroft, Mr, 186
Baker, 13
  Mr George, 3, 6
  John, 96
  Miss, 202, 204, 255, 257, 272, 273, 275, 279,
    285, 286, 294
  Mr, 12, 97, 151
  Mrs, 23, 74, 80, 82, 84, 87, 92, 96, 97, 99,
    102, 109, 110
  Mr William, 1
Balch (Balche), 95, 100, 101, 102, 104, 105, 106,
  107, 108, 109
  George, 35, 36, 58, 83, 99, 200, 201, 202, 261,
    289, 292
  Cilly (Silly), 72, 90, 108
  Nicholas, 208
  Walter (Watt), 208, 212, 231, 312
  William, 36, 37, 59, 76, 102, 231, 310, 312
Baldock, Herts, 229
Baldwin, James, 257
  Mr, 114, 134
  Mrs, 115, 117
  Mrs Mary, 121, 122, 257
  Susan, 186, 187, 207, 241, 243
Bale (Bales), Mr, 120, 137, 151, 155, 157
Ball, 172
Baller, John, 48, 50, 102
Ballyman (Baliman), Thomas, 202, 203, 311
Bampton, xxv, 2, 5, 6, 8, 11, 12, 21, 32, 36, 42,
  53, 64, 89, 90, 91, 93, 100, 103, 106, 107,
  109, 149, 150, 153, 155, 156, 158, 163, 164,
  182, 196, 197, 198, 200, 202, 203, 204, 209,
  219, 251, 252, 278, 283, 294
Banton (Bainton, Bauton), Edward, 22, 26, 34,
  35, 39, 90, 93, 231, 286, 287
  nurse, 260
Barbican, London, 125
Barklett, Justice, 162
Barnes, 81, 253
  John, 82
Barnstaple, xx, xxi, xxxiv, xl, xliii, xlix, 2–3,
  5–6, 9, 12–17, 19, 34, 37, 39, 46–9, 54–5,
  58–60, 61, 64, 68–9, 71, 78, 79, 80, 82, 83,
  85, 90, 93, 95, 97, 99, 101, 103, 104, 105,
  107, 109, 110, 111, 112, 151, 177, 189, 190,
  192, 197, 201, 202, 212, 214, 228, 229, 232,
  234, 246, 255, 257–8, 259, 260, 261, 269–71,
  273, 274, 279, 281, 283, 284, 287, 288, 289,
  301
Barons, Mr, 4

Barre, Mr, 119
Barrow, Mr, 115, 119, 133, 158, 180, 233, 243, 263
Barry, Edward (Ned), 114, 174, 178, 186, 206, 235, 243, 244, 246
Mr, 114, 117
Barthe, Sergeant, 159
Barwood, Mr, 128
Basingstoke, 124, 261
Basly (Balsy), David, 71, 74, 91
Bason, Christopher (Kitt), 157, 300, 310, 312
Bassett, Francis (Frank), 197, 294
Mr John, 197
Lady, 249
Mr, 48, 128, 136, 148, 161, 166, 259
Bath, Somerset, 119, 140, 141, 154, 171, 176, 191, 199, 228, 230, 267–8, 284
Batson, Lady Alice, 149
Batten (Baten, Bater, Better), Baldwin, 39, 63, 68, 252, 298
Bourn, 280
Bauche, Henry, 190
Baughton, Thomas, 123
Baytes, John, 193
Bealbury, Mr, 5
Beale, Richard, 193
Beaple, Mr, 116
Beare (Beard, Beere), Edward, 196
Mr George, 257–8, 267, 277, 287, 290
Mr John, 285
Lewis, 5
Mr, 127, 128, 145, 146, 150, 151, 152, 155, 175, 180, 185, 248, 278, 289
Mr William, 49, 134, 174, 183, 186, 195, 239, 246, 255, 257, 261, 267, 276
Beck (Becke), Mr, 115, 116, 119, 122
Beckett, Mr, xxiii, 48, 51, 65
Bee, Mr Cornelius, xxxviii, 155, 156, 162, 165, 278, 294
Beer Charter, 4, 170, 188, 192, 209
Bell, Mr, 53
Bell, the, at Barnstaple, 107
Bellamy (Bellamye), Mr, xxiii, 124, 142, 239, 241
Susan, 232
William, 170
Benifeild, Mr, 150
Mr, 220
Thomas, 180
Berkshire, xxv, 209, 210 *see* Maidenhead, Reading
Berry (Berney, Berrie, Berrye), Mr David, 198, 204, 205
Dorothy, 194
George, 304
James, 206
Lawrence, 32, 33, 37, 51, 65, 72, 90, 110
Martha, 91, 93
Miss, 196
Mr, 12, 33, 34, 38, 56, 149, 153
Richard, 43, 44, 280
Thomas, xiv, 34, 79, 93, 103, 194, 292
Berrynarbor, xiv, 209
Best, Richard, 190
Bethell, Miss, 178, 243
Bethem, Roger, 44
Beverley, Yorkshire, 229
Bickford, Agnes, 180

Bideford, xxxiv, 4, 6, 8, 10, 11, 12, 15, 22, 34, 39, 47, 53, 54, 56, 69, 70, 76, 79, 80, 82, 83–4, 85, 87, 88, 90, 91, 92, 93, 95, 97, 99, 104, 109, 111, 194, 196, 252, 256, 271, 273, 275, 279, 291
Bidgood, Alexander, 199
Mr, 177
Bigg, Mr, 135
Billing, Robert
Bing (Binge), Mr, 293–4
Binion, Mr Henry, 134, 234
Bishe, Mr, 243
Bishop's Tawton, xliii, 9, 36, 261
Bishopp, Elizabeth, 304
Blackall, Miss, 293
Blackdown, Mayor, 196
Blackmoore (the Blackamoor), James, xxxi, 33, 52, 65, 117, 173, 178, 206, 248, 297
Black Wyott, 44
Blagdon, John, 199, 202, 204
Blake, Mr, 139, 143, 144, 151, 154, 156, 159, 161, 166, 278
Blanchard, Mr, 17, 234
Bletchington, Mr, 153
Blore, William, 149
Boardman, Mr, 151, 155, 156, 159
Boconnoc, Cornwall, xl
Bodardle, Cornwall, 198, 201, 209, 255
Bodmin, Cornwall, 249
Bold (Bolde), Mr, 4, 30, 31, 37, 45, 49, 51, 52–3, 55, 65, 109, 115, 124, 125, 126, 129, 130, 133, 136, 137, 138, 140, 142, 144–7, 158, 170, 173, 175, 179, 183, 185, 190, 194, 195, 201, 207, 220, 232, 238, 239, 241, 246, 247, 249, 253, 260, 269, 276, 277, 281, 282, 283, 285, 310
Peter, xxxiii, 191, 202, 206, 257, 258, 273
Samuel, 149, 163, 169, 208, 273, 283, 285, 286, 288, 290
Thomas, l, 21, 117, 119
Boles (Boules), Sir Charles, xxxii, 208, 262
Lady, 190, 260
Bolham, 43, 170, 193, 201, 203, 209, 289, 290
Bonaugh, Sir John, 228
Bond (Bonde), Agnes, 61
Ja., 207
James, 188, 194, 198
Jaspar, 195
Leonard, 59, 189
Boole, Mr, 91, 95
Booth (Boothe), 274
Ann, 200
Mr John, 15, 224
Mr, 12, 30, 40, 43, 60
Mr Ralph, 4, 5, 14, 30, 41, 73, 174, 177, 192, 198, 199, 200, 204, 228, 236, 247, 253, 265, 268, 269, 281
William, 55, 90, 100, 128–9, 130, 132, 136, 140, 147, 164, 208, 236, 252, 260, 261, 264, 265, 271, 283, 286, 292, 300, 301, 310, 312
Wilmot, 311
Bourchier (Bouchier, Bourcher, Bourgchier, Bowrcher), Anne, countess of Bath, xli, 182, 215
Lady Dorothy, xxv, 217
Edward, fourth earl of Bath, xix, xxv, 133, 136, 196, 235, 250
Lady Elizabeth, xxv, 178, 217
family, xix, 154

Sir George,   xix
John, first earl of Bath,   xi
John, second earl of Bath,   xi
Lady Martha,   xix
Miss,   263, 264
Mr,   51, 54, 55, 64, 114, 117, 173–4, 178, 180,
   183, 185, 240, 241, 244, 247, 249, 252, 275,
   311
Mrs,   126, 133–5, 137–46, 148, 150, 152–4,
   157, 159, 163–4, 166
Mr Richard,   277
Thomas,   278, 313
Varney,   132, 188, 261, 263
William, third earl of Bath,   xi, 132
Mr William,   xxii–iii, 195, 206, 223, 236, 254
Bowdler (Boundler, Bongler), Mr,   xliii, 4, 119,
   121, 123, 127, 129, 131, 133, 135, 136, 140,
   162, 164, 166, 182
Mrs,   120, 122, 143
Bow,   xiv, xxiii, 4, 6, 17, 35, 39, 49, 50, 51, 58,
   188, 193, 195, 198, 200, 206, 228, 229, 246,
   250, 251, 279, 289–90, 294, 313
Bowen, Mr,   101
Box, Mr,   44
Brace, Mr,   173
Bracy, Mr,   115, 130
Bradborne (Bradbourne, Bradburn), Mr,   116,
   117, 120, 121, 238
Bradford, Mr,   150, 193
Mr,   129, 140
Bradshaw, goodwife,   115, 129, 141, 150, 156
Henry,   124, 152
Richard,   133
Bradworthy,   188, 194, 255, 269
Bragg (Bagge, Brage, Brogge), John,   85, 86, 93,
   95, 188, 194, 198, 201, 202, 204, 269, 273,
   285, 287, 289, 290, 294
Braunton,   xxv
Braunton Burrows,   xxxiii, 22
Brawne, Edward,   5, 6
Breame,   corn cutter,   180
Breane, Leonard,   186
Breda, Flanders,   206
Brewer, Dr,   xliv, 267–8
Bridgwater, Somerset,   5, 159, 228, 233
Brightley,   xl, 248
Brinstcome, Elizabeth,   287
Bristol,   xxxiv, xli, 15, 32, 33, 38, 71, 84, 85–6,
   88, 89, 93, 99, 103, 141, 151, 153, 162, 166,
   191, 238, 245, 254, 268, 289
Bristol, earl of,   237
Britton (Britain, Briton),   96
George,   8, 9, 12, 15, 17
John,   101, 102, 257
Lawrence,   198
Mr,   83, 90
Richard (Dick),   45, 47, 49, 51, 56, 57, 58, 60,
   63, 71, 80, 83, 89, 95, 96, 97, 112, 188, 193,
   197, 199, 200, 204, 247, 252, 253, 254, 255,
   256, 259, 261, 268, 269, 274, 275, 280, 284,
   286, 287, 290, 310
William,   50, 63, 110, 193, 311
Brograve, Mrs,   233
Bromfielld (Bronfielld), Thomas,   203
Brookes, Lady Aice alias Batson,   149
Mr,   132, 139
Brother (Brothers), Anthony,   189
Elizabeth (Besse),   74, 207, 256   (*see* Randall)
John,   194, 259, 279

Browne, Humphrey,   43
Mr,   114, 118, 119, 121, 122, 125, 126, 147
Samuel,   287
Sergeant,   152
Will,   201, 203, 287
Browning, Thomas,   196
Bruder (Brewdnale, Breudnall), Lord,   113, 229
Mr,   278
Bruern, Oxon,   xli, 121, 131, 138, 151, 163, 186,
   191, 220, 228, 230, 240, 245, 266
Bruerton, Mr,   151
*Bruton*,   278
Brutton, William,   43
Buckingham,   *see* Amersham, Aylesbury
Buckland,   254
Bud (Budd), Paul,   101
Will,   199, 201
Buggalla,   219
Bullen (Boolen), Thomas,   186
Bulworthie (Bolworthy, Boolworthy, Bul-
   worthy), Mr,   4, 23, 58, 135, 186, 255, 257,
   270
Burche,   202
Burges,   192
Burgh, John,   312
Burk (Barke, Buck, Burke), Jack,   118, 172, 185,
   206
John,   6, 33, 34, 38, 39, 41, 42, 58, 62, 114,
   118, 120, 125, 128, 132, 135, 136, 140, 144,
   147, 163, 165, 229, 231, 235, 247, 249–50,
   261, 262, 272, 278, 283, 310
Burman, Balthazar,   xxv
Burrowe, ship carpenter,   74
Burton, Bartle,   277
Rachel,   293
Richard (Dick),   176, 178, 206, 239
Busbie (Buzby), Mr,   153, 155, 278
Buse, John,   199
Butler (Buttler),   287
Mr,   59, 69, 236, 254, 257
Mr John,   289
Butler,   219
Button, Lady Martha,   xxx, 200, 203, 233
Sir William,   xxx

Cambridge,   xi, xxv
Camden, William,   xxxviii, 118, 147
Camelford, Cornwall,   248
Cames, James,   149, 199
Campden, Lord,   159
Canada xxxiii, 1,   *see* Newfoundland
Canding, Lord,   284
Cane, Robert,   203
Cannon (Cannam, Cammmam, Comon Coman,
   Common, Connon), Thomas,   124–7, 129–
   31, 147, 163, 165, 207, 231, 236, 240, 263,
   264, 273
Canworthy, Mr,   164, 303
Carder, Nich.,   96
Cardinham, Cornwall,   43, 201, 202, 204, 209,
   210, 248, 281
Cardinham Fee, Cornwall,   253
Care, William,   77
Carpenter, Mr,   125
Carre, Daniel,   197
Carwarthen (Cardwarthen), Mr,   xxxix, 293–4
Cary (Carie, Carry), Miss Dorothy,   193
Mr,   36, 194, 275

Castle, Lady, 184
  Mr, 164, 165
Caule, Digory, 112
Cavell (Cavill), Mr, 120, 129, 136, 157, 159,
  163, 166
Ceaton (Seaton), John, 118, 173, 175, 206
Challacom, 6
Chamberlyn (Chamberlain), Dr, 137, 265, 266,
  267
  John, 79, 198
  Lawrence, 31, 37, 39, 51, 53, 56, 60, 63, 80,
  101
Chamney, Mr John, 194
Chamnus, Mr, 197
Chandler, 240
Chapleton, 194
Charing Cross, London, xxx, 135
Charles I, King of England and Wales, xix–xx,
  xxviii, xxxi, xxxviii, xli, xlviii–l, 179, 238,
  242, 243, 247
Charles, Prince of Wales, later Charles II, xxx,
  xli, xlix, 60, 135, 242
Cheany, Mr, 158
Cheeveley (Chevely, Cheevlly, Cheively, Clev-
  ely, Chevlly, Chimeley Chiveley), George,
  20, 128, 132, 136, 140, 147, 161, 188, 190,
  206, 246, 256, 260, 272, 278, 280, 286, 292,
  310, 312
  Zachary, 36, 47, 56, 58, 63, 178, 233, 310
Chestnut, 219
Chichester, Dr, xliv, 33, 71, 104, 177, 190, 251,
  253, 254, 255, 256, 259, 268, 271, 274, 283,
  285, 286, 288, 290, 292, 295, 303
  Mr Henry, 14
  Sir John, 14, 31, 36, 37, 39, 54, 58, 91, 255
  Lady, 54, 164, 205, 280
  Lord, xxxi, xlii, 33, 51, 172, 207
  Mr, 31, 57, 89
Chilcott, John, 51, 59
Chillington, 104
Chittlehamholt, 101
Chollish, Henry, 44
Chulmleigh, 13, 14, 36, 123
Church Marwood, 209
Clapham (Clappaham), Arthur, 308
  Culpepper, 308
  Mr, xliv, 56, 260
Clarendon, Edward Hyde, xix–xx, xlviii
Clargis, farrier, 116, 120, 129
Clark (Clarke), 240, 282
  Jo., 190
  Mr, 116, 124, 165, 228, 234
  Robert, 199
Clarkson, Mr, 159
Clovelly, 193, 194, 268, 269, 281, 285
Clowberry (Cloberye), Lady, 141
  Mr, 191
Cobb (Cobbe), Mr, 24, 26, 29, 35, 55, 56, 61,
  83, 85, 96–9, 110, 111, 125, 128, 132, 140,
  145, 147–8, 156, 158, 160–5, 197, 204, 247,
  252, 254, 261, 262, 264, 267, 270, 271, 276,
  277, 280, 281, 284–6, 288, 290–5, 300, 301,
  310
  Mr Richard, 136, 237, 282, 311
Cobleye (Cobley), organist, 8, 18, 100, 207,
  240, 242, 310
Cocke, James, 27

Coleman (Choleman, Cholman), Michael, 203
  Mr, 119, 120, 121, 127, 293
Collamoor, Mr, 32
Collibear, 47, 189
Collins (Colline, Collyns), John, 149
  Mr, 155
  Simon, 60, 86, 101, 108, 208
Colquite, 253
Combeinteignhead, xxv, 43, 82, 180, 196, 209,
  210
Combe Martyn, xiv, 209
Come-last, John, 206
Comer, fuller, 11
Comes, Thomas, 198
Coney, Miss, 277
Coniber, 5, 36
Connell, Simon, 85
Conneway (Coneway), 219, 243
Conniber (Cunibear), John, xxvi, 59
  widow, 26, 35, 188–9, 200, 254, 256, 260,
  271, 273
  William, 6, 192, 201, 202
Conyer, Sir John, 119
  Lady, 113
Cooke, 193
  Colonel, 133
  Dick, 178, 207
  Edward, 149
  Sir Francis, 126, 256
  George, 203
  Lord, 154
  Mr, 110, 120, 196
Cooman, Avis, 311, 312
  Doll, 73, 79, 311, 312
  old, 310, 312
  Thomas, 52, 104, 109, 169, 310, 312
Coombe (Comb, Combe), Hugh, xxx, 1–112,
  206
  Mr, 140
Cooner, Rebecca, 40
Coop, John, 52
  Mr, 51
  Mrs, 20, 23, 36, 58, 59
  Robert, 40, 86, 87, 88, 89, 91, 101
  William, 37, 38, 48, 49, 50, 58, 80
Cooper, Margaret (Meg), 208, 300
  Mr, 48, 123, 132
  Richard, 106, 246
  Robert, 90
  widow, 196
  William, 72
Cope, Mrs Abigail, 309
  Betty, 265–6, 284, 285, 286, 288, 290, 292,
  295
  Lady Elizabeth, xli, 120, 130, 142, 150, 151,
  153, 155–8, 160–3, 166, 171, 185, 190, 199,
  309, 311
  Lady, 141, 311
  Mr, 139, 311
Coplestone (Copston), Dr, 52
  Jonathan, 294
  Mr John, 260
  Mr, 83
  Mrs, 301
Copper, William, 193
Corffe, 194
Cork, Ireland, 201

Cornish, Arthur, 43
Daniel, 193
Cornwall, xxv, xxvi, xlix, 22, 39, 40, 45, 57, 99,
189, 193, 199, 200, 202, 204, 209, 229, 237,
244, 245, 246, 260, 270, 288 *see* Boconnoc,
Bodardle, Bodmin, Camelford, Cardinham,
Cardinham Fee, Croan, Downeckney, Eglo-
shayle, Hall, Kelynack, Launceston, Roche,
St Buryan, St Erme, St Just in Penwith, St
Michael's Mount, Stow, Tintagel, Trerice,
*Trevenege, Treveneiy*
Corton Denham, Somerset, 136, 142, 155, 160,
167, 186, 191, 210, 240
Cote, Mrs Alston, 66
Cottingham, Lord, 227
Covent Garden, London, 125
Cowes, Mr, 115, 117, 119, 165
Cowman, John, 298
Thomas, 298
Cox, Mr, 44, 149, 151
Coyse (Coyce, Coys), Mathew xxx, 2, 3, 6, 7,
9, 10, 14, 19, 172, 183, 206, 257
Crafts, 220, 266
Cranfield, Anne countess of Middlesex, xxiv
James, second earl of Middlesex, xxiv, xxix,
142, 151, 158, 278
Lionel, third earl of Middlesex, xi, xxiv–v
Crediton alias Kerton, 189, 190
Crewkerne, 123
Cripps (Crips), John, 203
Richard, 199
Croan, Cornwall, 5, 220, 229, 249–50
Croker, Henry, 203
Crooke, Sir Henry, 148
Lady, 118
Mr, 193
Crookhorne, Ireland, 157
Cross (Crosse), 170
Robert, 4, 60, 206, 310
Crowder, James, 270
Croyde, 230
Honor, 109
Croyder, 107
old, 312
James, 93
young, 80, 312
Croydon, Will, 310
Cudmore, 198
Culme, Mr, 150
Cure, Humphrey, 96
Cuttberd (Cutburd), Mr Richard, 176, 238, 243

Dance, Mr, 140
Dancy, Miss, 267
Darby, joiner, 115, 164, 170, 173, 175, 178, 180,
185, 206, 233, 238
Darcy, Lady, 163, 311
Davent, Bishop John, xxxviii, 152
Davis, John, 128
Davy, 235
Alexander, 6
Henry, 17, 18
William, 9, 47, 62, 91
Daw, Mr, 9, 22
Mrs, 25
Dawson, brick-layer, 239, 240
Day, Mr, 257
Deacon (Decon), William, 120, 121, 129, 153,
174, 178, 206, 262

Deane, Mr, 84, 85, 143, 310, 311
Mrs, 103
Deckport, Hatherleigh, 194
Delbridge (Dellbridge), Alice, 104, 108, 194,
253
Joseph, 48
Mr, 101, 102, 108, 110, 111
Mrs, 102
Dell, Mrs, 118
Delworthy, Mr, 246
Denbigh, (Dennby, Denbye), Lord, 118, 149,
154, 157, 160
Dennelle, Mr, 137
Dennis (Denys), Abraham, 281
Mr, 71, 84
Mrs, 90
Richard, 197
Dericke, Mrs, 135
Desborow, 170
Desbury, Mathew, 41
Devaux (Deaux, Deuox), Mr, 130, 138, 143, 148
Mrs, 129, 133, 142
Diamond (Dimond), 181, 195
Mr Richard, 186
Digby, Colonel, 29, 30
John, 237
Lord, 227
Diggorie, Lady, 85
Dobb, 108
Dodderidge (Dodridge), Mr, 9
widow, 194
Dodson, William, 242
Dolham (Dallam), Mr, xlii, 15, 16, 18, 44
Doncaster, Yorkshire, 229
Donne, John, 203
Dorchester, Dorset, 119, 294
Dorman, Mrs, 146
Dorset, Edward earl of, xi, 170
Dorset, Lord, 151, 154
Dorset, *see* Dorchester
Doweswell (Dowdswell), Mr, 154, 304
Downe (Down), Dr, 5, 11, 15, 18, 43, 44, 55,
92, 162, 192, 194, 227, 240, 244, 258, 284,
286, 287, 288, 290
Mr John, 37, 102, 192, 194, 258
Mrs Mary, 240
Miss, 246, 248, 253, 254, 255, 273, 280
Mr, 51, 88, 96
Mrs, 54, 56, 83, 98, 101, 177
Downeckney, Cornwall, 209
Downman (Downeman), Richard, 9, 22
Dowrish, Mr, 5
Dowtie (Dowty), Mr, 134, 136
Dowtyn, Mr, 144
Drake (Drak, Dreke), 182
John, 175
Mr, 112
Robert, 99, 193, 197, 202, 203, 247, 259, 283,
288, 289, 292
Draper, Mr, 158
Drew, Susan, 192, 194, 270, 274
Dublin, Ireland, xix
Dulverton, Somerset, 30
Duniecon, widow, 190
Dunterfield (Dunsterdield, Dunsterfield), Mr,
117, 121, 122, 124, 126, 139, 153, 241, 243,
244, 262, 263
Dunterton, 141, 192, 193, 196, 205, 209, 210, 255,
269

Dunterue, 5
Dyer, James, 184
Dyman, Mr, 4

Earmine, Sir William, 258
Easticke, John, 199
Eastland, Mr, 152
Eaton (Eattens), Mr, 157, 164, 264, 294
Edbrook, Robert, 204
Edmonds, Thomas, 99, 202
Edny (Edney), Mrs, 142, 143, 156, 159, 293
Edwards, Hugh, 92
Eeles, Phil, 48
Effingham, Essex, xix
Egham, Surrey, 261
Egloshayle, Cornwall, 229
Ellis (Elice, Elis), Johan, 21, 36, 38, 59, 81, 177, 188, 205, 207, 295
  William, xxx, 6, 14, 19, 44, 188, 189, 206, 224, 225, 244, 259
Elston, Mr, 96, 99, 153, 190, 202, 204, 261, 311
  Philip, 3
Eltham, London, 144
Ermyn, Mr, 146
Essex, Sir William, 270 *see* Effingham
Eure, Humphrey, 48
Evans, Mr, 117, 119, 120, 121, 137, 145, 155, 165
Everat (Everatt, Everite), Francis, 149, 170, 196
  Mr, 157
  Mrs, 128
  widow, 160, 167
Exeter, xlix, 2, 3, 4, 5, 10, 12, 16, 20, 31, 33, 36, 38, 41, 48, 50, 51, 52, 53, 55, 57, 63, 65, 70, 82, 88, 90, 92, 94, 95, 99, 101, 104, 109, 129, 139, 142, 145, 157, 172, 177, 180, 197, 199, 200, 202, 203, 228–9, 236, 238, 244, 247, 248, 250, 251, 253, 256, 274, 283, 284, 286, 289, 292, 294
Exford, Somerset, 228, 230

Fairchild (Fairechild, Fairechild), constable, 259
  Edward, 26
  Mr, 15, 19, 57
  widow, 201
  William, 189
Fairfax (Faiorfax, Farfax), Sir Thomas, 123, 125, 128, 138, 140, 142, 143, 145–6, 158, 260
Fane (Faine, Fayne), Anthony, 185
  aunt, 259
  Dorothy, xlvii
  Elizabeth (Betty), 178, 204, 294
  family, xi
  Francis, first earl of Westmorland, xix, xxi, xxiii, 170, 311
  Mr Francis (Frank), 126, 309, 313
  Sir Francis, 135, 138, 139, 142, 143, 145–50, 156, 159, 161, 163–4, 189, 190, 191, 198, 239, 250, 258, 309
  Colonel George, 162
  Mr George, 123, 130, 161, 170, 191, 198, 200, 201, 204, 248, 250–1, 253, 254, 256, 259, 281, 283, 286, 289, 292, 294, 303, 311, 313
  Harry, 239, 262, 291
  Mr Henry, 309
  Lady Katherine, 121, 173, 245
  Lady, 134, 147, 154, 195

Lady Mary, 228, 276
Mary, countess of Westmorland, xxi, xxiii, 170
Mildmay, second earl of Westmorland, xxiii, xxiv, xlii, 170, 229, 258, 276
  Mr, 3, 48, 86, 88, 102, 153, 159
  Mrs, 102
  Mrs Rachel, 111, 134, 309, 312
  Mr Robert, 127, 140, 147, 154, 161, 162, 165, 180
  Robin, 47, 179, 183, 240, 277
  sister, 287, 288, 293
  widow, 135, 137, 138
  Mr William, 79, 116, 124, 135, 141, 156, 280, 281, 283, 284
Faringdon, Oxon, 228
Faringe, Mr, 127
Farthing, Mr, 149, 199
Featherstone (Fether-ston), Will, 95, 208, 310, 312
Feild, Edward, 145
Fenchurch Street, London, 119
Ferris, Mr, 43, 179, 258
  Mr Richard, 3
Fetter Lane, London, xxviii
Fiddle Faddle, xliii, 219
Filleigh, 279
Finch, coachman, 138
Finiks, Mr Thomas, 177
Fitzmaurice (Fiztsmorice), Lady Elizabeth, xxxii, 208
Fitzwilliams, cousin, 242
  Lord, 125,
  Mr, 127–8, 132
  cousin Walter (Wat), 263, 277
Flanders, xxxix
Flaye, Peter, 2
Fleming, Edward, 197
  Mr, 79, 103
Forberry, 68
Forde, xi, 44
Forde (Foorde), Elis, 205
  John, 204
Forrard (Farrard, Forard, Forrand, Forward), Mr, 89, 90, 91, 101, 123, 124, 126, 127, 130, 135, 140, 144–8, 162–5, 191, 196, 198, 204, 254, 259, 263, 264, 275, 277, 278, 279, 280, 281, 283, 285, 290, 291, 294, 300, 301, 310, 312
  Richard, 266, 268, 275, 276, 284, 288, 309
Fortescue, Colonel, 190
Foster (Forster, Fostor), 250
  Edward (Ned), 41, 55, 57, 59, 207, 246, 249, 252, 253
  Miss, 247, 252
  Mr, 155, 165
Fowelscombe, 4
Fowler, John, 149, 203
Fox, Mr, 124, 126
Frace, Mary, 99, 202
France, 71, 120, 141, 143, 144, 151, 265, 283
  ambassador of, 228
Francis (Fransis), Miss, 249, 250
Freak, 167
Fremington, xliii, 37, 38, 62, 91, 233, 234
Friday Street, London, 114
Fryer, Dr, 170, 265
Fulbeck, Lincolnshire, 229

Fuller, Elizabeth (Besse, Bettie), 141, 160, 171, 232, 264
Mr, 125, 127, 133, 150
William, 177, 178, 179

Gammon (Gamon), Mr, 101
Mr Ja., 14, 43
Ganfield hundred, xxv
Gape, Mr, 145, 151
Gardner, Henry, 144
Mr, 202
Garfield, John, xiv
Garnseye, Edward, 3
Gatcombe, Mr, 149, 157, 158, 162, 165
Geare (Gever), William, 20, 22, 24, 53, 72, 178, 206, 252, 256, 272, 297
Geaton (Gettet, Geytton), Mr, 101, 274, 277, 292
Geldorp (Gelthrope, Gildropp), Mr George, xxxix, 131, 174
Gendle, Tristram, 193
Gernon, Justice, 184
Gibbes, Dr, 239
Gibbons (Gibons), a smith, 129
Hugh, 199
John, 45, 47
William, 1, 10, 206
Gibson (Gibsonn), Lawrence, 192, 194
Richard, xxiv
Giffard (Gifford), Colonel, 29
Dr, 128, 131, 144
family, xl
Henry, 248
Joan, 208
Mr, 248, 280
Giffery, Mr, 108
Gildocke, Mr, 163
Gillingham, Dr, 164
Glanvile, Sergeant, 132, 152, 165, 267, 278, 282
Glasse, John, 203, 204, 294
Glaston, John, 104
Glastonbury, Somerset, 171–2, 228
Gloucester, xxv, xlii, 15, 16, 210, 220, 266 *see* Huntscourt
Glover, Mr, 127, 129
Glowin, 152, 162, 166, 281
Gloyne, James, 107, 108
Jane, 85
Goard, John, 196
Godolphin, Miss, 249
Mr, 249
Goldsmith (Goldsmyth), Mr, 124, 125, 183, 243
Goldsmiths' Hall, London, 144–5, 147, 151, 276, 277
Goldsom, Robin, 283
Gooscott (Goolcott), Avis, 103, 107, 108
Edith, 109
Gosse, Mr, 176, 179, 239
Gottier (Gotier), Francis (Frank), 208, 273
Grady, Mr, 248
Grandison, Lord, 227
Grant, John, 43
Grantham, Colonel, 122, 123, 125
Grascroft, 156
Gray (Grey), Lady Elizabeth, 263
Lord, 154, 155, 156, 159
Mr, 164
Mr Simon, 295
Gray Lynn, 219

Gray Salsbery, 219, 227
Gray Smithfield, 219
Gray Wiote, 219
Gread, John, 110, 111
Great Torrington, xxxiv, xl, 4, 7, 10, 12, 13, 16, 18, 29, 37, 43, 50, 51, 56, 58, 67, 68, 78, 79, 83, 88, 89, 91, 95, 188, 193, 202, 244, 255, 269, 270, 271, 273–4, 283, 284, 287, 288, 290
Green (Greene), Mrs Joan, 141
Mr, 134, 175, 264
Greenwich, xxx, 118, 126, 134
Greenwise, Sir John, 192
Grenville (Granville, Grenevile, Grinvell), family, xi
Sir Bevil, xlii, 22
Sir John, 259, 269, 283
Lady, 247, 248
Gribble (Grible), 31, 51, 151
Edward, 106
Humphrey 2, 3, 22, 24
John, 14, 15, 20, 29, 40, 41, 48, 52, 65, 69, 77, 78, 79, 80, 84, 86, 88, 90, 93, 95, 279, 310, 312
Griffith (Griffeth), Lady, 140, 143
Mr, 234
Rachel, 266, 267
Grigg, Mr, 124, 147, 148
Grigry, Mary, 231
Grinder, Mr, 174
Gritty, Miss, 234
Grococke, Margaret, 166
Grone, John, 44
Gudrige, Alexander, 150
Gumbleton, Mr, xxiv, 116, 136, 294
Gundemoor, xliii, 219
Guzmond, 160

Hackpen, xxv, 149, 150, 164, 170, 200, 203, 209, 285, 290
Hackwell, 239
Haiford, John, 203
Haines, (Hayne, Haynes, Heynes), Josia., 278
Miss, 272
Mr, 2, 15, 149, 219, 265, 268, 281, 284
nurse, 259
Hales (Hailes), Sir Edward, 165, 287
John, 250
Mr, 132, 133, 145, 146, 147, 148, 150, 152, 277
Hall, Cornwall, xxxi, 207
Hall, goodwife (Goody), 186, 233, 234, 238
Hester, 195
Richard, 96
Hallet, Mr, 220
Halowell, Mr, 251
Ham, Mr, 157, 166
Haman, Dr, 158
Hames, Mr, xxiii, 190, 191, 262
Hamlyn (Hambile, Hambling, Hamblyn, Hamblyon, Hamlin), Besse, 207
John, 31, 35, 36, 47, 48, 52, 66, 101, 102, 110, 130, 192, 207, 253, 255, 270, 291, 311
Rich, 55, 83, 85, 194, 204
Rose, 33, 39, 67, 132, 134, 139, 140, 150, 254, 256, 261, 271, 298
William, 57, 92
Hammersmith, 261
Hampshire, *see* Andover, Romsey, Tangley

Hampson, Mr, 138
Hampton Court, 293
Hanaford (Haniford, Hannaford), Edward, 43
John, 82, 99, 166, 197, 199, 200, 201, 202, 204, 283, 286, 288, 292
Mr, 97, 99, 158, 165, 283
Richard, 205
William, 43
Hardwick, Mrs Cornelia, xxxvi, 3, 10, 12, 22, 31, 39, 42, 44, 45, 61, 62, 64, 65, 70, 135, 178, 181, 182, 189, 190, 191, 207, 227, 236, 237, 241, 244, 246, 247, 252, 253, 254, 256, 259, 260, 261, 298
Harford with Newland, xii, 170, 192, 194, 197, 198, 199, 201, 202, 204, 209
Harford bridge, 278
Harle, Mr, 38
Harper, Mr, 180
Harpford, 4, 209
Harnybye, 234
Harpen, 132
Harris (Harice), John, 55, 61, 91, 192
Jonas, 70, 95
Mr, 102, 219
Philip, 96
Lord Richard, 265
Mr Richard, 94
Harrison, 130
Hart, Thomas, 138, 147
Hartford, 47
Hartland, xxxiv, 30, 31, 42, 43, 51, 57, 75, 84, 91, 93, 123, 172, 188, 189, 190, 193, 194, 196, 198, 199, 200, 201, 202, 203, 209, 247, 254, 269, 280, 281, 285, 286-8
Hartley (Hartly), Miss, 197, 281
Mrs, 34
Hartman, Mr, 177
Hartnoll (Hartnall, Hartnell), James, 27, 29, 55, 60
Harvy, Richard, 43
Hasebrigg, Sir Arthur, 118
Hassett, Mr, 121, 123, 133, 165
Hatherleigh, 194
Hatherly, 205
Barnabas, 201, 287
Peter, 203
Hathorne (Hathor, Hathorn, Hawthorne), Francis, 144, 242
Thomas, 100, 230, 231, 278, 279, 284, 310, 312
Hatswell, George, 149
Haymor (Hamer, Heymer), Thurstyn, 25, 36, 92, 208, 290, 310, 312
Haywoades, Thomas, 257
Hazard, Mr, xlii, 234
Heale (Heal, Heall), 83, 85, 155
Ned, 20, 27, 206
Heanton Punchardon, xliii, 22
Heard, 107, 275
Mr Walter, 18
William, 33, 60, 78, 197
Hearder (Harder, Herder), 48
Henry, 21-2
Margaret (Magg), 105, 231
Mr, 109, 112
old, 199, 292
Peter, 79, 93, 310, 312
Thomas, 19, 40
Ursula, 100, 103

Hearding, Rich, 85, 96
Heare, Will, 34
Hearle (Heirle), James, 250
Mr John, 92, 192, 194, 196, 204, 252, 259, 260, 268-9, 271, 273, 275, 280, 281, 288, 290
Miss, 203
Mr, 44, 45, 291
Mrs, 73
Hearn, Mr, 232
Hearson, John, 63
Hearte, Mr, 77
Henley, West Sussex, 171, 228
Henly, Mr, 203
Henrietta Maria, Queen, xli, xlviii, 242, 243
Herbert, Lord, 151
Herle, Mrs, 159
Herne, Mr, 144, 167
Hertfordshire, see Baldock
Herwill, El., 79
Hewit, Will, 201, 203
Higison, Mr, 140
Hill (Hyll), David (Davy), 87, 101, 112, 190, 198, 199, 200, 282, 285
John, 57, 59, 60
Mr, 110, 132
Hilldown, east and west, xiv
Hinson, Mr, 143
Thomas, xxx
Hinton (Hynton), Dr, 265
Hix (Hyx), Mr, 241
Mrs, 120
Hoare, Mr, 116
Hobby, John, 88
Hobbs, John, 50, 66, 84, 90, 93, 108
Mr, 78
Roger, 86
Hobson (Hobsan), 96, 190, 195
Thomas, 44, 67, 151, 192, 198, 259, 275, 281
Hodge, 124
Hokines, Elizabeth, 231
Hole, John, 194
Holgood, John, 49
Holland, 88, 144
Ann, 231
Joseph, 20, 50, 71-2, 77
Hollawaie, Nicholas, 149
Holman, Mary, 91, 93, 95, 100
Holmes (Homes), Goody, 234
Mr, 2
Holne, 4, 43, 196, 201, 203, 204, 205, 207, 209
Holne, John, 195, 197
Honiton, 294
Hooker, John, xxvii, xlv
Mr, 142
Hooper, Margaret, 163
William, 199, 200
Hopton, Sir Ralph, 60, 237
Horne, Mr, 133
Horsom (Horsham), Hugh, 192, 198, 257, 259, 269, 281, 282, 283
Mary, 46
Horwood, Alexander, 250
Lady, 266
Miss, 190
Mr, 51, 92
Mr Richard, 6
Mr Thomas, 14, 200, 202, 250-1, 259, 269

Hosegood (Hosgood), 106
  Ann, 107
  Gregory, 7, 15, 23, 30, 51, 52, 62, 65, 106
Howard, Harry, 207, 241, 279
  Henry, 232, 240, 311
  Lady Martha, xix
  Mr, 23, 26, 28, 120, 129, 310
  Mrs Ann (Nan), 117, 121, 122, 123, 128, 132,
    134, 138, 141, 144, 148, 185, 239, 243, 244,
    257, 278
  William, first Baron Howard of Effingham,
    xix
Humble (Humbles, Umbles, Elizabeth (Besse),
  46, 47, 48, 49, 50, 63, 73, 75, 178, 261
  Walter, 169
Hunckwill, D., 227–8
Hunnicot, porter, xxxi, 206
Hunt, Mr, 135
Huntscourt, Glos., 198
Huntspill, Somerset, xxv, 15, 77, 95, 135, 139,
  147, 149, 150, 152–3, 156, 159, 160, 162, 163,
  164, 166, 167, 170, 182, 190, 196, 197, 199,
  200, 203, 205, 209, 210, 245, 278–9, 287, 288
Huxtable (Huxtabell, Uxtable), 269, 275
  Richard, 1, 2, 6, 7, 8, 10, 14, 18, 23, 31, 48,
    52, 86, 95, 99, 101, 105, 109, 271, 281, 310
Hyckes, Mr, 240
Hyde Park, 164, 277
Hyne (Hind, Hine, Hynes), Mr, 49, 80, 82, 134,
  135, 136, 137, 139, 140, 141, 144–6, 156, 157,
  163, 164, 165, 180, 196, 198, 283, 294
  Thomas, 196, 203, 311
  young, 311

Ilfracombe, xxv, 3, 4, 6, 7, 10, 11, 15, 34, 38, 43,
  51, 62, 67, 69, 95, 183, 191, 192, 193, 194,
  209, 238, 269, 271
Ilminster, Somerset, 20, 164
Incledon, Mr, 32
Ingram, Lady, 142, 165
Instow, xiv, 44, 188, 255, 261
Ireland, xix, xxv, xxvii, xxx, xl, 8, 122, 126, 146,
  164, 172, 173, 180, 181, 183, 184, 185, 201,
  233, 241, 257, 276
Isaac (Isacke, Izake), Mr, 15, 53, 55, 74, 252,
  274
  Mr Lawrence, 193
Isbell, Mr, 113

Jackman, Joseph, xxx, 24, 31
  Mr, 149, 151, 245, 258, 267
Jackson (Jakson), Mr, 128, 132, 139, 144, 148,
  266
Jammon, Mr, 13
Jarvis (Jervis), cousin, 178, 241–2, 243
  John, 167
  Mr, 133, 166
  Mrs, 118, 122, 123, 125, 129, 134
  William, 167
Jaye, Mr, 12
Jeakin, Mathew, 59
Jeffery (Jefferys), Mr, 109, 177, 197, 271
  Roger, 274
Jefford, Mrs, 300
Jeffrys, Roger, 198
Jenkins (Jenkyn), 156
  Mathew, 5
  Mr, 147, 277

Jermyn (Jermain), Dorothy, 273
  Mr John, 25
Jerom (Jerron), Nicholas, 59, 60
Jewell, Barnard, 59, 60
Johnson, Cornelius, xxiv
  John, 44, 51, 62, 65, 199, 247, 271, 275, 281,
    284, 304
Jones (Joanes), Damarice, 99, 202
  Daniel, 203
Jordan (Jourdans), John, 208, 271
Jose, William, 96
Jumperd, Mr, 232
Just, Mrs, 144

Keat (Kaet), 219
  Robert, 228
Keene, Mr, 114, 127, 130, 133, 139
  the joiner, 115, 165
Keepe, coachman, 117, 159, 235, 247, 252
  Mrs, 122
Keepe, 219
Kelynack, Cornwall, 200, 209, 210, 220, 284
Kelsome, Mr, 167
Kempe (Cempe), Mrs, 159, 173, 234, 295, 313
Kent, xi, xii, l, 140, 191, 229, 244
Kent, Lady, 135, 138, 263
Kerry, Lord, xxxii, 208
Kerton, see Crediton
Kilkampton, 188, 192, 196, 269, 279, 283, 284
Killegrew (Killygrey), Anne, xxxii, 208
  Lady, 125
  Mrs, 124
  Sir William, xxxii, 208
Kimpflit, Wilmot, 260
Kimpthorne, Jo., 88
King (Kinge), Arthur, 198
  Dr, xxxviii, 161
  Miles, 110
  Mr, 115, 116, 118, 122, 124, 126, 127, 133,
    134, 136, 139, 140, 144, 150, 153, 154, 156,
    158, 159–60, 161, 166, 173, 177, 179, 185,
    186, 238, 241, 244, 276, 278, 294
  taylor, 292
Kingdon, Nicholas, 193, 196
Kingskerswell, 180, 209
Kingston, 43, 192, 194, 196, 197, 198, 199, 203,
  204, 209, 279
Kinthorne, John, 193
Kirby, Miss, 293
Kirckam, Mr, 132
Kneebone, Thomasin, 73
Knight, Mr, 121
Knowle Park, Kent, xii

Lacock, Wiltshire, 228, 268
Lake (Lak), 233
  Humphrey, 48, 51, 74, 91, 95, 259, 261, 274
  James, 199, 200, 284
  John, 193
  Richard (Dick), 31, 36, 49, 51, 87, 88, 90, 97,
    197, 286
  Simon, 26, 29, 51, 64, 298, 310, 312
  Thomasin, 53
Lambe (Lam), Mr, 12, 22, 50, 51, 65, 68, 123,
  126, 174, 190, 191, 197, 200, 244, 253, 263,
  268, 271, 276, 278, 281, 285
  Mr James, 52
Lambeth, 240

Landkey, xiv
Langdew, Mr John, 149
Langdon (Langden), 241
  David, 44
  Thomas, 96, 149, 196, 199
Lange, Emmanuel, 82
  Phillipa, 194
Langford Barton, xxv
Langham, Mr, 245
Langwoorthy, Mr, 20
Laramy (Larrimer), William, 90, 92, 94, 280
Larkbeare, 2
Larrence, Mr, 91
Larrymed, William, 304
Launceston, Cornwall, 5, 250
Lavercomb, William, 280
Lawes, Mr, 294
Lawles, Mr, 186
Lawley, Mr, 179
Leakar, Francis, 311
  Richard, 203
Leaydon, miller, 105
Leech, Mr, 145, 151
Leg, Thomas, 108
Leicester, earl of, xx
Le Mote, Madam, 179
Lerrawill, John, 17, 18
Lesland, fowler, 6, 207
Lethbridge (Lithbridg), Mr, 44, 54
  John, 194
  Wilmot, 44
Leuton, Mr, 5
Levie (Lewie, Lewis), Mr, painter, xxxix, 116, 190, 241
Lewins (Lowens, Lowins), Edward (Ned), xxiii, 39, 113, 207, 231, 246
Lewis (Lewes), Amias, 21
Ley (Lee), 101, 284, 287
  constable, 58, 60
  Sir Henry (Harry), 126, 265
  John, 194
  Joseph, 27, 44, 84, 110, 112, 192, 193, 195, 201, 259, 269, 271, 279, 281, 290
  Thomas, 48, 86, 95, 112, 270, 275, 304
  William, 36, 50, 52, 55, 59, 60, 66, 68, 76, 78, 84, 86, 95, 103, 180, 193
Leyhill, xi
Lightfoot, 219
Limbery (Lymbury), 105, 311
  Jo., 77, 208, 231
  William, 96
Lincoln, xi
Lincolnshire, xxxii, 208, *see* Louth
Lincoln's Inn Fields, London, xxviii–xxx, 113–40
Lindsey (Linsey, Lyndsey, Lynsy), Mr, 122, 133, 139, 165, 166
Linscott, 189
Linton, Mr, 114
Littlejohn, Richard, 193
Littleton, Lady, 232
Little Torrington, xiv, xxv, 210
Liverland, Mr, 255, 259
Loggerhead, xliii, 192, 219
London, 2, 4, 5, 7, 8, 12, 15, 16, 18, 19, 20, 22, 23, 27, 28, 43, 44, 48, 50, 51, 65, 69, 75, 76, 106, 113–40, *et seq.* see Aldersgate Street, Barbican, Charing Cross, Covent Garden,

Eltham, Fenchurch Street, Fetter Lane, Friday Street, Goldsmith's Hall, Hyde Park, Lincoln's Inn Fields, Lumbar Street, Paternostre Row, St Giles, St James Park, Tottenham, Westmorland House
Loope, Mr John, 157, 160
Loosemore (Lesamoore, Losamoore), Goodman, 2, 3, 21, 35
  Mr, 110, 284
Loring, wagoner, 2
Lorrimer, William, 93
Louth, Lincolnshire, xxxii, 208
Loveden, 312
  Elizabeth, 232
  Mrs, 309
Loven, Edward, 54
Lovering, John, 193, 198, 271
  Mr, 69, 83
  Mrs, 59, 133
  Thomas, 33, 36, 51, 95, 159, 269, 270, 281
Lovett (Lovitt), 256, 261
  Miss, 265
  Mr, 112, 165, 252
  Mrs, 55, 127, 128, 132, 133, 134
  Rebecca, xxxii, 208, 237
  Sir Robert, xxxii, 208
Lucas, Mr, 159
Lugg, Mr, xlii
Lumbar Street, London, 132
Lyddon, Ned, 108, 310, 312
Lyle (Lylle), Mr, 136, 206
Lynn, 170, 172
  Clement, 174
  Henry, 117
  Mr William, xxix, xxx, 27, 65, 81, 100, 111, 113–40, 144, 147, 163, 167, 181, 186, 189, 190, 195, 196, 197, 199, 200, 201, 202, 203, 204, 205, 235, 238, 240, 242, 244 *et seq.*
Lyon, John, 182

Mad Robin, 219
Maidenhead, Berks, 119, 124, 242
Maidstone, Kent, xi, xii
Major, Mr, 62, 179, 185, 186, 245
Malaga, Spain, 101
Malborough, 267
Mallie, Lord Nicholas, 197
Malmesbury, Wilts., 228, 245
Manby (Manbie), Mr George, 123, 125, 131, 134, 136, 140, 148, 162, 166
  Mr, 257, 264, 276
  Sir Ralph, 257
Mannaring (Manaring, Manawaring), Dr, 145
  Mr, 217
Manning, Connett, 58
Mantraversse, Lord, 242, 243
Marchant, Elizabeth, 231
  James, 44, 193, 194
  John, 37, 50, 76, 77
  Mr, 42, 75, 177, 192, 202
  Nicholas, 192, 194, 269
  Thomas, 63
Mare, Mr, 229
Markham, Gervase, xvii
Martin (Martyn), Francis, 47
  John, 50, 180, 298
  Mr, 136
Marwood, xiv, xxiii, xxv, 170, 210

Marwood, Mr, 164
Mason, Mr, 9, 25, 63, 163, 239, 241, 242
Masonet, Mons., 232
May (Maye), Edward (Ned), 107, 275
  Richard, 15, 30, 37–8, 42, 57, 69, 84, 86, 91,
    95, 103, 310, 312
Mayn (Maine), William, 275, 280, 312
Maynard (Mainard), Mr, 49, 148, 258
Meane (Maine, Meave, Meline), Pauline, 49, 73,
    79, 91, 109
  William, 13, 16, 18, 19, 23, 33, 48, 49, 50, 63,
    77, 79, 93, 310
Meare, Robin, 272, 275
Mellton, Edward, 198
Mereworth, Kent, xxi, xl, 144, 145, 146, 229,
    244, 266, 267
Merrick, Nathaniel, 27
Merson, Mrs, 163
Merwood, 126
Miarn (Myarn), Sir Theodore, 263, 265, 266
Micheall (Michell), Anthony, 203
  Jesper, 186
  Mr, 125, 141, 149, 150, 156
  Thomas, 133, 189, 190, 191, 195, 251, 284
Midway (Medway, Midday), John, 18, 19, 20,
    24, 33, 34, 35, 52, 65, 66, 68
Mildmay, Sir Anthony, xxi, xxiii, 170
  cousin, 179, 180
  Francis, 264
  Lady Grace, xxiii, 170
  Lady Mary, xxi, 170
  Mr, 145, 147
  Sir Walter, xxiii, 164, 170
  young, 277
Millbourne (Milborne), Mr, 136, 157, 166
Mills (Males, Miles, Milles, Mylls, Myles), 107,
    290
  John, 43, 54, 100, 132, 134, 137, 143, 144,
    159, 161, 162, 163, 165, 166, 170, 193, 195,
    202, 203, 204, 272, 311
  Mr, 135
  Richard, 186
Milton, 150
Mints (Mintts), Lady Margaret, 170
  Sir Thomas, 237
Modbury, 4
Mohun, Charles, 277
  Lord, xl, 147, 248, 277
Moore (Moor), 177
  Anthony, 304–5
  Dr, 178, 238, 239
  George, 200, 202, 203
  Mathew, 52–3
  Mr, 120, 310
  Mr Thomas, 6, 9, 11, 20, 21, 22, 23, 29, 69,
    194, 292, 312
  the tailor, 13, 246
Morce, Mr, 203
Morcombe (Morcham, Morckham, Morcome,
    Morkam, Morkham), Philip 8, 13, 16, 21,
    23, 55, 63, 69, 80, 83, 95, 109
Mordant, countess Peterborough, xxxix, 174,
    233, 257, 278
Morgan, Sir, 293
Morrell, Robert, 196
Morrice (Morce, Morice), Thomas, 198
  Will, 310, 312
Mortimer (Mortimor), John, 43

Moulins, singer, xlii, 283–5, 292
Moys, nurse, 234
Moyse, 241
Mules, George, 205
Mullacott, 265
Mullins (Mullyns), 281
  Ann, xxiii, 25, 49, 51, 65, 67, 84, 100, 102,
    105, 107, 108
  Will, 97
Mungwell, bookseller, 274
Murray (Marrie, Murrey, Murrie), Mr David,
    xxix, 114, 116, 121, 122–3, 125–6, 128, 133,
    136, 140–3, 145–7, 151, 153, 155, 157–62,
    164–6, 185, 186, 239, 243, 244, 277, 279
  Miss, 264
  Mrs Temporance, 149
Muscott, 209
Musgrave, Thomas, 149
Myles, 99

Nash, Miss, 256
  Mr, 47
  Mrs, 84
  widow, 202, 269
Neal, Mr, 157
Nedd, Mr, 112
Netheravon, Wiltshire, 124, 136, 138, 142, 144,
    147, 154, 158, 167, 190, 191, 209
Newbuck, Lord, 179
Newfoundland, xxxiii, 1, 6
Newport, Lady, 148, 262, 263, 278
Newton, Lady, 133
  Mr, 1
Nicholls, Mr, 12, 13, 89
Nicks, James, 8, 9, 10, 14, 17, 19, 22, 23
Nightingale (Nitingale), Mr, 176, 178, 179, 186,
    239, 241
Norbourne (Norburn), Mr, 152, 238
Norcott, Mr, 89, 91
  Robert, 47
Norcould, Philip, 177
Norman, Joan, 186
North, Lady, 142
Northam, 284
Northamptonshire, xxi, xxiii, xl, l, 150, 152,
    228, 283 see Apethorpe, Tansor
Northcott, Mr, 85
North Tawton, 84–5
Norton, 271, 281, 285, 288, 290, 291, 291, 303
  Decima, 208
  Mr, 310
  Mrs, xliii, 147, 154, 156, 158, 161, 163, 201,
    282, 300
  Robert, 163
Norton Fitzwarren, Somerset, xxv, 39, 149, 157,
    198, 202, 203, 209, 210, 219, 287
Nottle (Notles, Nottell), Mr, 4, 19, 50–1, 240
  Mr William, 85
Nunnington, Somerset, xxv, 149, 199, 209
Nymet Tracey, xiv, xxv, 4, 43, 44, 197, 209, 210
Nympton, 85

Orlibeare (Olibear), Mr, 124, 136, 139, 144,
    148, 159, 166, 178, 242, 243
Osberstone, Mr, 127
Outne, Mr, 123
Owins, 126

Oxford, xviii, xl, xlviii–ix, 30, 33, 39, 42, 53, 119, 120, 138, 152, 227–8, 236, 238, 245, 246, 247, 251

Oxfordshire, xxiii, xli, 276, see Abingdon, Bruern, Faringdon, Oxford, Sarsden, Tetsworth, Wantage

Page, Mr, 25, 56, 269
  Mrs, 91
  Mr Robert, 17
Paget (Pagett, Pagget), Andrew, 44
  Betty, 285, 287, 292, 294
  Miss, 194, 274, 283
  Mr, 28, 34, 41, 42, 44, 52, 65, 154, 172, 173, 174, 182, 184, 240, 251, 258, 303
  Mrs, 77, 92, 152, 309
  William, xxv, xxx, 3, 257
Paine (Pain), Jack, 177, 178, 206, 237, 239
Pallam, xlii, 239
Palmer (Pallmer), George, 200
  Miss, 198, 199, 203, 204
  Mr, 71, 162, 164, 191, 250, 259
Pangbourne, 124
Pansford, Mr, 171
Parker, 255
  Joan, 121
  William, 99, 166, 202
Park Gate, xxx
Parr, Mr, 117, 123, 133, 154
Parrett (Parat, Parot, Parrat), 153, 156, 157, 158
  James, 35, 195, 198, 202, 203, 278, 311
  Mr, 178
  Robert, 149, 199
Parris, Mr, 241
Parson, 219
Parson (Parsons), John, 9, 13–14, 18, 22, 39, 40, 78, 91
  Mr, 174, 242
Pasmore, Mr, 115, 116, 119, 147, 148, 179, 180, 183, 185, 186, 238, 240, 241, 242, 243–4
  Mrs, 124, 125, 127
Paternostre Row, London, 116, 140, 263
Paulet, Lord, 179
Pavey, William, 194
Pawlin, John, 156, 277
Payn, John, 26
Payton (Paiton, Peyton), Mr, 104, 110, 111, 151, 164 310
  Sir Humphrey, xxxix, 184, 206
  Randall, xliii, 48, 148, 153–7, 162, 169, 193, 207, 278, 289, 292, 295, 300, 311
Peace, Susan, 231
Peane, John, 32
Peard, widow, 62, 255
Pearse (Pearce), 204, 294
  Ed., 204
  John, 199
Pecke, Mr, 121
  Mrs, 119
Pelham (Pellham), Major, 288–9
Pemroy, Joan, 196
Pengelly (Pingellie), Amice, 149, 200
Pengise, Ames, 196
Penherwood (Penhorwood), Thomas, 193, 200, 202
Penrose, Thomas, 83, 91, 109, 112, 310, 312
Percy, Algernon, fourth earl of Northumberland, xxviii–ix
Perkins, Mr, 181

Perrin (Perin), Mr, 181, 241, 261, 293–4
Perry, Mr, 124, 133, 136
Pescod, Mr, 135
Philips (Phillips), Mr, 2, 119, 120, 144
Philpott, Mrs, 146
Pikard (Peckard, Pickard), 78
  Henry, 75, 80
  Jonathan, xxiii, 49, 52, 65, 75, 76, 79, 102, 109, 189, 208, 230, 231, 245, 259, 260, 268, 269, 274, 290, 312
Pike (Pyke), Captain, 157
  John, 304–5
  Mr, 110, 273
Pikett, 273
Piller, John, 149
Pilton, 2, 7, 27
Pilton, Somerset, 228
Pinckome, Steven, 310, 312
Pinsent (Pincent), Jonas, 199
  Mr, 272
Pittego, widow, 190
Pitts (Pitt), George, 34, 35, 36, 37, 38, 48, 49, 69, 70, 77, 310, 312
Plymouth, 177
Pole, Sir Courtenay, xlvi
Pollard (Polard), 173, 174, 175, 178, 179, 238, 239, 240, 242, 297
  Mr Ames, 32, 172, 227
  Arthur, 204
  Sir Hugh, 21, 22, 280
  Lady, 31, 32
  Sir Lewis, 12, 13, 15
  Mrs, 125, 132, 156, 159
  Richard, xxx, xxxii, xxxv–vi, xlviii, l, et seq.
  Sarah, xxxii–iii, 132, 136, 140, 261
  Thomas, xxx, xliv–v, 27, 28, 41, 54–5, 113–40, et seq.
Polweel, Mr, 293
Ponston (Ponstow), Digory, 200, 203
Poole, John, 198, 202
Poore (Poors), Sir William, 184, 187
Pope, Elizabeth, 149, 199
  John, 96
Popham, 160
Porter, Mrs, xliv, 119, 121
Portman, Baronet, 240
Potter, mercer, 191
Potts (Pott), Mr, 284
  Mrs, 125, 142, 148, 233, 240
Pounstock, Digory, 96
Povie, Mr, 137
Powell, Sergeant, 239
Power, Sir William, 15, 256
Prate, Robert, 196
Prayer, John, 199
Preston, Richard, 35, 44
Price (Prise), shoemaker, 113, 115, 142, 180, 186
Pridham, Gilbert, 96
Pridis, Mr, 50
Prince, Owen, 136, 140, 145
Prout, Alice, 149
Prust, Mr, 6, 7, 16, 22, 23, 26, 31, 36, 42, 61, 69, 70, 116, 193, 196, 247, 248
  Hugh, xxx, 3, 5, 24, 43, 200, 202, 204, 286, 311
  Nicholas, 82, 193
  Thomas, 111, 193, 201, 202, 203, 204, 280, 287, 290, 292, 311

Prynn (Prin), 144
Pudding, xliii, 219
Pulluy (Pulvey, Puly), 179, 183, 207
Jonas, 236
Punchard, Mr, 10, 16, 178, 246–7, 251
Putney, 136
Pyle, Captain, 118
Pyne, Captain, 21, 50, 77

Quart, Will, 201
Quick, Christopher, 30

Radwaye, Sir Edward, 5
Rainger, 172, 233
Rainsford, Lady, 134, 161
Raleigh, 61, 285
Ramson (Roson, Rumson), 284, 285, 290, 292, 312
John, 20
Mary, 79
William, xxxv, 3–112, 206, 269, 272, 279, 298, 310
Randall (Randale, Randell, Randle), Edward (Ned), 36, 42, 43, 45, 59, 64, 170, 189, 192, 193, 194, 199, 200, 201, 202, 272
Elizabeth (Bess), 28, 30, 33, 62, 178, 207, 247
Jaspar, 43
John, 50, 111
Robert, 4
Rose, 311, 312
Rawlins, John, 200, 203, 285
Raymond, Peter, 232
Raynor, Thomas, 145
Read (Reade, Reed), Goodwife, 141
Mr, 124, 132, 139, 173
Reading, Berks, 124, 267
Reading, Mr, 276
Redhead, goodwife (Goody), 117, 122, 124, 125, 129, 133, 134, 150, 154, 156, 159–60, 186
Reding, Mr, 151
Reeve, May, 51
Rennolls, 219
Reymor (Raymor, Raymore), Mary, 51, 76, 77, 78, 80, 208, 298
Reynell, family, xvii
Rich, Mr, 144, 145, 151
Richards (Richard), Elias, 61, 70, 71, 72
Katherine (Kate), 41, 93, 231
Richard, 193
William, 47, 57, 87, 97, 102
Richmond, Duchess of, 278
Rickett, 219
Ricks, James, 7
Ridger, Mr, 118, 241
Ridler (Ridley, Rydle), John, 59, 264, 312
Mr, 276, 310
Ridor (Ridder, Rider, Rydor), Mr, 128, 133, 137, 143, 154, 165, 178, 239
Risdon, Tristram, xxvii
Roach, David, 184
Robartes (Roberts), Lord, 198
Robins, Mr, 154
Robinsonn, 249
Roborough, xxv, 170, 192, 194, 200, 209, 210
Roche, Cornwall, 4, 210, 256

Rolle (Rolls, Roole, Rools), Mr Alexander, 161, 202, 286, 289
Mr, 25, 35, 38, 94, 153, 157
Sergeant, 121
Sir Samuel, 49
Rolleston, 40, 72, 77, 108
Romsey, Hants, 123
Rooke, Anthony, 260
George, 47
Richard (Dick), 48, 50, 70, 73, 89, 92, 93, 94–5, 208, 214, 231, 252, 265, 268, 271, 283, 294, 298, 310, 312
Roscarick (Rascarrocke, Roscarrock), Miss Elizabeth, 203
Mr, 43, 60, 133, 248–50
Rose, shoemaker, 101
Rosier, Mr, 120
Rowclife, George, 44
Rowe (Row), Agnes, 66, 70
Anne, 298
Mr, 110, 145, 273
Nicholas, 201, 202
Richard, 289
the shoemaker, 23, 291
widow, 198
Rowles, Mr, 251
Rushey, 180
Rushworth, Mr, 137, 144, 149, 151
Russell, Mr, 14

Sackville, Richard, xii
Sadler (Sadlor), Thomas, 48, 143
St Buryan, Cornwall, 229
St Erme, Cornwall, xxvi
St Giles, London, 113–40
St James Park, London, 131
St Just in Penwith, Cornwall, 229
St Michael's Mount, Cornwall, 229, 249
Salisbury (Salsbury), 201, 202, 244, 286, 288, 294
John, 99, 200, 202, 288
Mr, 97
Salter, Charles, 202
Saltram, 4
Sammely, Peter, 88
Samuel (Sammell), Mr, 138, 140
Sanders (Sannders, Saunders), Joan, 105
Mr, 112
old, 121
the porter, 116, 152
a smith, 194, 275
Sarsden, Oxon, 266
Satterleigh, xxv, 210
Scott (Scutt), John, 78, 81–2, 189, 195
Miss, 263
Mrs, 113
Samuel, 267
Seager, Mr, 153
Seale, Mr, 128, 129, 131, 133, 163, 165, 166, 262
Searle (Ceairll, Sarle, Seairl, Seirle, Serle, Teairle, Tearil, Tearle, Teirle), Agnes, 207, 247, 271
Alice, 28, 177–8, 185, 187, 207
Avis, 298
Elizabeth (Bess), 19, 28, 29, 51, 84, 85, 100, 102, 128, 132, 136, 140, 147, 163, 164, 165, 177, 207, 237, 240, 270, 271, 283, 287, 288, 290, 292, 295, 299, 300, 311, 312
Miss, 184

Sebastian, 11
Selden (Celdon, Seldon), Mr John, 99
 Mr, 98, 101, 110, 202, 204, 287, 288, 292
Selly, Mr, 295
Sergant, John, 205
Sexton, Philip, 184
Shaftesbury, 123
Shaites, Mr, 118
Shalmer, Thomas, 149
Shapley (Shapely), Grace, 190, 258
 Mr, 69
Sheapard (Shepard), 196
 John, 197
Shelbury, Mr, 120
Sheldon, 43, 44, 149, 150, 170, 193, 209, 290, 303
Sherbourne (Serborne), Miss, 244–5
 Mr, 115
 Mrs, 116–19
Sherland, Henry, 64
Shile (Skiles), Mr, 89, 98, 103
Shorleigh, 90, 195, 252
Shorne (Sherne), Abraham, 5, 6
Shortlidge, 273
Shurt (Short, Shorte, Shurte), George, 11, 12, 52, 53, 88, 110, 292
 Mr, 63, 65, 68, 90, 92, 97, 200, 252, 256, 287
Shute, xlvi
Shutt, William, 149
Singe, Lewis, 101
Skinner (Skynner), Bartholomew, 7, 12
 Mr, 4, 244
 Mr Roger, 3, 4
Skitches (Skiches, Skich, Stitch), Mr John 1, 8, 12, 29, 36, 50, 52, 65, 86, 240–1, 251, 256
 Miss, 193, 196, 197, 260, 283, 284
 Mrs, 79, 84
 widow, 192
Skitlewood, Mrs, 134
Slape, Eman., 203
Slingsby, Captain, 237
Slowley (Slolye, Slowly), Mr John, 42, 259
 Miss, 274
 Mr, 5, 13, 18, 58, 152, 171–5, 178, 179, 184–6, 235, 238, 239, 240, 241, 243
 Mrs, 79, 94
 Richard, 176, 206
Smith (Smithe, Smyth), 150, 174, 255
 Mr James, 5, 174, 176, 187, 198
 John, 208, 277, 278, 279, 280, 281, 283, 285, 288, 289, 311
 Mr, 33, 56, 60, 146, 152, 163, 164, 172, 179, 186, 240, 244, 310
 Mrs, 177, 234
Snow (Snowe), Mr, 33, 224
 Mr Edmond, 206
Somerset, xxv, 113, 186, 209, 210 *see* Bath, Bridgwater, Corton Denham, Exford, Dulverton, Glastonbury, Huntspill, Ilminster, Norton Fitzwarren, Pilton, Nunnington, Taunton, Wellington
Sorrell, 219
Southbrook, 4, 196, 209
Southby, Robert, 125, 126, 170, 191, 245
Southcott, Mr, 54
South Hams, 23, 79, 80, 172, 196, 228, 279
South Molton, xxxiv, xlviii, xlix, 19, 22, 23, 109, 112, 191, 271

Southwell, 256
 Lady, 184
Southwood, Christopher, 2, 196, 203, 290
Sowdon (Sowden), Mr Hugh, 174
 Mr, 4, 173, 177, 179, 181, 244
Sowely, Walter, 192, 193
Sparrow, Mr, 2, 141
Speket, Miss, 179–80
Spiler, Sir Henry, 253
Spinollo, 190, 219
Spitchwick, 43, 209, 270, 271
Sprite, 142, 159, 161
Spry, Robert, 304–5
Squire (Squier), Mr, 193, 197, 253, 281, 287, 289
 widow, 189, 255
 William, 199
Stafford, Lord, 219
Staines, Surrey, 118
Stanbury (Stanburie), John, 203
 Richard, 32, 36, 49
Stand, John, 167
Standish, Lady, 145
Staple Park, 209
Stapleton, Aunt, 171
 Mr, 144
Starling (Starlling, Sterling), Avis, 6, 15, 23, 34, 38, 49–50, 54, 55, 57, 60, 63, 73, 90, 106, 107, 108, 272
 Doll, 73, 79
 Sam, 4, 13, 16, 186, 187, 206, 237, 243
Steevenson, Mr, 184
Stephens (Steevens, Stephen, Stevens) Ann, xxxii, 189, 208, 259, 260
 Baldwin, 20, 21, 22, 23, 27, 33, 37, 48, 54, 60, 74, 94, 95, 206, 261, 272, 297, 310, 312
 Bourn, 270, 271, 275
 Mr John, 260
 Miss, 256, 260
 Mr, 4
 Mr Nathan, 5
 Thomas, 12, 13, 40, 47, 48, 59, 60, 84, 93
 William, 38, 49, 50
Stevenstone, xl, 285
Stirril, Mr, 120
Stone (Stoane, Ston), Ann (Nan), 162, 208, 231, 300
 Mr, 131, 165
Story, Mr, 123
Stow, Cornwall xi, 5, 52, 248
Stowell (Stowle), Thomas, 157, 200
Strand, 266
Stribling (Striblings), Edward, 96
 Miss, 188
Strong, Mr, 132
Sumner (Simner, Somer, Somers, Suminer, Summers), George, 9
 John, 52, 58, 65, 96
 Peter, 63, 77, 86, 87, 89, 286, 304
 Thomas, 37, 48, 63, 74, 93, 261, 280, 292
 widow, 62, 253, 271, 274, 275
Surrey, *see* Egham, Bagshot, Staines
Swanstead, Miss, 244
Swayne (Swain), John, 255, 275
Sweet (Sweete), Dorothy, 231
 George, 17–18, 19
 Mr, 177, 181
 Thomas, 44, 206, 235
Swillivant, 219

Swyne, John, 52, 65
Sydenham, xi
Sydenham (Sidnam), Elizabeth, 208, 264
 Lady, 37, 55, 97, 139
 Mrs, 131, 132
 Sir Ralph (Raph), 32, 54, 79, 134, 151, 178, 191, 200, 208, 246, 258, 264, 270, 271, 285
Symons (Simons), divine, 265
 Edward, 188
 Elizabeth, 231
 John, 49
 Mr, 276
 Richard, 191
 widow, 61

Tangley, Hants, 138, 142, 143, 152, 156, 159, 230, 266, 284, 287
Tansor, Northamptonshire, 277
Tarry, Miriam, 185, 234, 262, 276, 293
 Miss, 263
 Mr, 124, 130
 Mrs, 115, 157
Tatt, Mr, 116, 174
Taunton, Somerset, xxv, 149, 153, 155, 158, 196, 198, 203, 204, 205, 209, 234, 287
Taw, river, xxvii, 4
Taylor (Taylore), Jeremy, 158
 John, xxxviii, 156
 Miss, 180
Temple, Sir Peter, 117
Tenby, 127
Tennant, Mr, 166
Terry (Terrey), Besse, 110
 John, 31, 48, 51, 61, 65, 74, 76, 91, 100, 102, 190, 247, 260, 273, 274, 281, 283, 310
 Mrs, 135
 Peter, 84
Tetsworth, Oxon, 204
Thomas, Mr, 203
 Mr Hugh, 200, 249, 279
 Mr John, 15
 Walter, 194
Thoring, Robert, 82
Thorne (Thorn), 193
 Elizabeth (Besse), 132, 134, 136, 208, 271, 273
 George, 23, 188, 256
 Humphrey, 194
 Philip, 4
 Rawling, 207, 254
 Roger, 3, 4, 7, 18, 21, 24, 26, 28, 29, 32, 51, 65, 68, 140, 253
Thornhurst, Mr, 149, 153
Thorning, Mr, 161
Thorpe, Mary, 126, 128, 130, 133, 134, 234, 243, 244, 263
Throgmorton, Mr, 119
Thurstin, Mr, 26
Tilburg, Flanders, 206
Timewell, William, 233
Tinker, Dorothy, 44
Tintagel, Cornwall, 256, 283
Tiverton, xxvi, 2, 29, 30, 142, 196
Todd (Tode), Rose, xxxii, 115, 117, 141, 180, 185, 207, 247
Tolsell (Tassel, Tossell), Ann, 88, 132, 136, 144, 147, 208
 Mary, 49, 68, 231
 Simon, 40, 46–7, 48, 56, 57, 59, 60, 62, 63, 68, 70, 71, 80, 108

Tomkins, Barbery, 234, 278
 Mr, 170, 180, 185, 240, 241, 243
 Mr William, 242
Tomson, Mr, 7
 old, embroiderer, 26, 33
Tonkins, Mr, 14
Toogood, Wilmot, xxxi, 34, 63, 117, 140, 163, 191, 207, 269
Tooker, Mr, 4, 48, 86, 90
 Humphrey, 20
 Walter, 21
Topsham, 166
Totnes, 16, 20, 44
Tottenham, London, xxx
Towill, James, 54
Towless, George, 203
Townsend, Mr, 151
Tozer, John, 44
Tradescant, John, xlvi
Trassell (Trussell), Mr, 116, 117, 127, 134, 136, 137, 144, 150, 153, 262, 264, 293
Travis, Austin, 44
Trerice, Cornwall, 249
*Trevenege*, Cornwall, 236, 249–50
*Treveneiy*, Cornwall, 229
Trick (Trikes), Robert, 201, 203
Tristram, Mr, 204
Trott, Mrs, 91, 288
Tucker (Tucker), 136, 141, 191, 275, 286, 288
 Dr, 174, 177
 George, 268, 288
 Mr, 261, 290
 Walter, 250
Tull, Mr, 134
 Mrs, 136
Turk, xliii, 219
Turneyr, 287
Tutt, Mr, 238, 242
Two Pot House, Tawstock, 202
Tyson, 38

Uffculme, xxv, 4, 77, 149, 150, 153, 164, 203, 209
Underdon (Underlian), John, 47, 48, 50, 51, 55, 92, 206
 Simon, 255
Upcott, 198
Up Exe, 4, 43, 99, 193, 196, 197, 202, 203, 209, 247, 259, 283, 288, 292
Upton, Chester, xxxiii
Ursley, Mr, 113

Vaghan (Vaughon), Mr, 4, 86
Vaine, Sir Henry, 258
van Dyck, Sir Anthony, xxiv, xxxix, 238
Vaules (Vawles), George, 199
Vavasor, Mr, 144, 181
Veare, Lady, 118
Venice, 156
Ventman, Frances, 149
Verckill, Mr William, 2
Verman, William, 2, 149
Veze, Richard, 242
Vigires (Vigores), Mr Robert, 283
Villven, Dr, 177
Vimbles (Vumbles), Walter, 1, 48
Vincent, Mr, 136, 145
Vinor (Viner, Vinner), Mr, 146, 147, 151, 155, 158, 166, 213, 259, 263

Violet, Martha, 158, 200, 208, 283
Vittery (Vitrye), 196
  John, 4
Vouell, Mr, 278
Voysin (Voyceene, Voyceine, Voysyn), Mrs, 23,
  114, 115, 116, 117, 118, 173, 178, 180, 211,
  233, 234, 237, 241, 244, 247, 249, 252, 254,
  256, 271, 286, 288, 290, 292, 295
  Monsieur, xxxiii
  Sarah, 207
Vyne, John, 43
Vyner, Mr Thomas, 4

Walden, Peter, 196
Walker (Waker), Mr, 139, 171, 175, 206, 232–3,
  236
Walrond (Wolron), Mr, 166
Walter, Sir William, 265
Wantage, Oxon, xxv, 119, 124–34, 135–43,
  150–2, 157, 159, 167, 170, 174, 177, 182, 189,
  190, 191, 204, 209, 220, 228, 240, 247, 262,
  264
Ward (Warde), Mr, 118, 197, 228, 251
Warder, Mary, 267
Warkleigh, xxv, 3, 42, 43, 104, 170, 177, 189,
  193, 195, 198, 199, 200, 201, 204, 209, 210,
  219, 235, 253, 254, 260, 272, 273, 294
Warner (Worner), Mr, 150
Warren (Warine), Mr, 42, 198, 200
  John, 40, 44, 50, 57, 58, 59, 60, 62, 69, 310
Waterhouse, Mr, 151
Watson (Watsonne, Whatsonne), James, 194, 196
  Mr John, 192, 194
  Miss, 267, 277
  Mr, 145, 181, 194, 241, 275
Watter, William, 38
Watts, Francis, 206
Webb, Arthur, 190
  John, 267
Webber, 277
  Andrew, 206
  Mr, 124, 172, 173, 177, 179, 239, 243
  widow, 201
Weekes (Weeks), Mr, 62, 66, 67, 298
  William, xxx, 184, 188, 229, 248, 255, 269,
  270, 273, 274, 275, 310
Weely, Mr, 128
Welch, Mr, 150, 194
Wellington, Somerset, 5
Wellon, Sir Anthony, 179
Wellsford, 269
Welshe (Walshe), George, 43, 203
  Mr James, 253, 281
  Mr, 22, 38, 57, 81, 129
Wentworth, Lady Katherine, 232
Westcote (Weastcoat, Westicoat), John, 199, 201,
  204
  Thomas, xxvii, xlviii
Westcott barton, xiv
Westfeild, Dr, 228
Westminster, xxx, xl, xlii, 117, 118, 151, 152,
  157
Westmorland, 173, 177
  earl of, 175, 186, 189, 229, 251
  Francis earl of, xix, xxi, xxxii, 170 (*see* Fane)
  Lady, 117, 147, 262, 300
  Lord, 118, 121, 128, 152
  Mary countess of, xxi, 170
  Mildmay earl of, xxiii, xxiv, 170

Westmorland House, London 5
Weymouth (Weamouth), Timothy, 304–5
Wharton, Lady, 133
*Wheatley*, 266
Wheler, George, 52
Whiddon (Widdon), Joan, 178
  John, 6, 15
Whimper (Whimp, Wimper), 282, 291, 292–3
  Ro., 208
  Thomas, 120, 121, 122, 128, 132, 136, 147,
  163, 207, 208, 263, 300
White, goody, 192
  John, 3, 7
  Luke, 165
  Mary, 38, 110
  Mr, 134, 265
  widow, 39
White Flank, xliv, 28, 219
Whitfield (Whitefeild, Whitfeild, Whitfild), 140,
  253
  James, 34, 52, 65, 66, 69, 70, 96
  Johan, 53–4, 71
  John, 40, 44, 68
  Robert, 42, 48, 52, 237, 247, 261, 272, 273,
  297
  Roger, 44, 193
Wichalls (Wichehalse), Mr, 4, 29, 112
Wickett, Richard, 207
Wild (Whilde, Wilde, Wyld, Wylde), Dr, 110,
  132, 136, 140, 145, 147, 150, 160, 162, 163,
  269, 271, 274, 281, 284, 285, 286, 288, 290,
  300
  Mr, a minister, xxiii, 208, 258, 263, 268
Wildbore, Mrs, 150
Wilkey (Wilby), 101
  John, 93
  Roger, 85, 86, 87, 93, 94, 95
Wilkins (Willkines), Mr, 144, 146, 148, 151,
  156, 276, 277
Williams (Willm, Willms, Willyames), John 1, 7,
  8, 10, 12, 16, 19, 21, 23, 25, 27, 29, 31, 34,
  38, 46, 51, 54, 55, 57, 64, 73, 88, 93, 99, 100,
  103, 109, 112, 202
  Sir Morris, 120, 134, 265, 278, 282, 293
  Richard, 4, 6
Willis (Willes, Willet), Richard (Dick), 74, 128,
  134, 208, 246, 259, 261
Willoughby (Willoby, Wiloby), family, xvii
  Lord, 180
  Mr, 134 .
Wills, Richard, 125, 127
Wilson, Mr, 145
Wiltshire, xxv, 148, 155, 174, 197, 209, 210,
  287 *see* Lacock, Malmesbury, Netheravon
Windsor, xxx, 132, 137, 243
Wingfield, Chris., 207
  Mr Edward (Ned), 156, 157, 208, 231, 276,
  277, 279, 282, 285, 295, 312
  Miss, 256, 282
  Mr, 156, 280, 288, 300
  Mrs, 146, 153
  Rachel, 260
Wise, Sir Edward, xvii
Withebrook, John, 43
Wonham, 54, 96, 160, 182, 199, 208, 283, 292,
  315
Wood (Woode), Alice, 110
  Honor, 298, 311

John, 85, 101
Mr, 12, 30, 31, 51, 81, 310
Robert (Robin), 30, 35, 114, 117, 128, 132, 137, 140, 147, 206, 236, 239, 240, 243, 244, 246, 247–8, 252, 261, 263, 267, 268, 272, 273, 276, 278, 283, 284, 286, 291–3, 300, 312
Woollcott, Henry, 149
Worlington, xiv, 3, 94, 99, 170, 202, 209, 289
Wraxall, Sir Nathaniel William, xiii
Wright (Write), 177, 178
Mr, 2, 4, 6, 12, 13, 28, 150, 225
Thomas, 251, 271
Wynn, Eleanor, 44
Wyott (Wiote, Wiott, Wyatt, Wyote), Sir Dudley, 259
Edward, xxvi, xxxiii, xlvi
Mrs Edward, 4

Mr, 4, 14, 35, 39, 44, 52, 57, 65, 81–2, 84, 102, 111, 114, 125, 134, 135, 136–7, 138, 139, 140, 141, 169, 174, 175, 185, 187, 189, 200, 230, 231, 235, 238, 240, 244, 310
Hugh, 280
Thomas, xxx, l, 99, 169, 181, 186, 193, 195, 196, 198, 199, 200, 202, 204, 206, 235, 242, 280, 281

Yarnscombe, 254
Yearder, Thomas, 8
Yolland, Philip, 6
York, xxix, xlix, 114, 190, 229, 244
Yorkshire, *see* Beverley, Doncaster, York
York, 219, 227
Youlston, 36
Young, Miss, 241
Mr, 17

# THE DEVON AND CORNWALL RECORD SOCIETY

(Founded 1904)

*President:*
Sir Richard Carew Pole, Bt., DL

*Hon. Secretary:*
J.D. Brunton, LLB, BA, c/o Devon and Exeter Institution,
7 Cathedral Close, Exeter EX1 1EZ

*Hon. Treasurer:*
D.M. Hay, c/o Devon and Exeter Institution,
7 Cathedral Close, Exeter EX1 1EZ

*Hon. Editors:*
Professor N.I. Orme, MA, DPhil, DLitt, FSA, FRHistS
Mrs Margery M. Rowe, BA, DAA

The Devon and Cornwall Record Society (founded 1904) promotes the study of history in the South West of England through publishing and transcribing original records. In return for the annual subscription members receive the volumes as published (normally annually) and the use of the Society's library, housed in the Westcountry Studies Library, Exeter. The library includes transcripts of parish registers relating to Devon and Cornwall as well as useful genealogical works.

Applications to join the Society or to purchase volumes should be sent to the Assistant Secretary, Devon and Cornwall Record Society, c/o Devon and Exeter Institution, 7 Cathedral Close, Exeter EX1 1EZ. New series volumes 7, 10, 13, 16 and 18, however, should normally be obtained from the Treasurer of the Canterbury and York Society, St Anthony's Hall, York YO1 2PW.

## PUBLISHED VOLUMES, NEW SERIES
(Volumes starred are only available in complete sets)

1. *Devon Monastic Lands: Calendar of Particulars for Grants, 1536–1558*, edited by Joyce Youings (1955).
2. *Exeter in the Seventeenth Century: Tax and Rate Assessments, 1602–1699*, edited by W.G. Hoskins (1957, reprinted in 1973).
*3. *The Diocese of Exeter in 1821: Bishop Carey's Replies to Queries before Visitation*, edited by Michael Cook. Volume I, Cornwall (1958).

*4. The Diocese of Exeter in 1821: Bishop Carey's Replies to Queries before Visitation, edited by Michael Cook. Volume II, Devon (1960).

*5. Cartulary of St. Michael's Mount, Cornwall, edited by P.L. Hull (1962).

6. The Exeter Assembly: The Minutes of the Assemblies of the United Brethren of Devon and Cornwall, 1691–1717, as Transcribed by the Reverend Isaac Gilling, edited by Allan Brockett (1963).

7. The Register of Edmund Lacy, Bishop of Exeter, 1420–1455: Registrum Commune, Volume I, edited by G.R. Dunstan (1963).

*8. The Cartulary of Canonsleigh Abbey, calendared and edited by Vera C.M. London (1965).

*9. Benjamin Donn's Map of Devon, 1765, with an introduction by W.L.D. Ravenhill (1965).

10. The Register of Edmund Lacy, Bishop of Exeter, 1420–1455: Registrum Commune, Volume II, edited by G.R. Dunstan (1966).

*11. Devon Inventories of the Sixteenth and Seventeenth Centuries, edited by Margaret Cash (1966).

*12. Plymouth Building Accounts of the Sixteenth and Seventeenth Centuries, edited by Edwin Welch (1967).

13. The Register of Edmund Lacy, Bishop of Exeter, 1420–1455: Registrum Commune, Volume III, edited by G.R. Dunstan (1968).

14. The Devonshire Lay Subsidy of 1332, edited by Audrey M. Erskine (1969).

15. Churchwardens' Accounts of Ashburton, 1479–1580, edited by Alison Hanham (1970).

16. The Register of Edmund Lacy, Bishop of Exeter, 1420–1455: Registrum Commune, Volume IV, edited by G.R. Dunstan (1971).

17. The Caption of Seisin of the Duchy of Cornwall (1337), edited by P.L. Hull (1971).

18. The Register of Edmund Lacy, Bishop of Exeter, 1420–1455: Registrum Commune, Volume V, edited by G.R. Dunstan (1972).

19. Cornish Glebe Terriers, 1673–1735, a calendar, edited by Richard Potts (1974).

20. John Lydford's Book, edited by Dorothy M. Owen (1975).

21. A Calendar of Early Chancery Proceedings Relating to West Country Shipping, 1388–1493, edited by Dorothy A. Gardiner (1976).

22. Tudor Exeter: Tax Assessments 1489–1595, including the Military Survey, 1522, edited by Margery M. Rowe (1977).

23. The Devon Cloth Industry in the Eighteenth Century: Sun Fire Office Inventories, 1726–1770, edited by Stanley D. Chapman (1978).

24. The Accounts of the Fabric of Exeter Cathedral, 1279–1353, Part I: 1279–1326, edited by Audrey M. Erskine (1981).

25. The Parliamentary Survey of the Duchy of Cornwall, Part I: (Austell Prior-Saltash), edited by Norman J.G. Pounds (1982).

26. *The Accounts of the Fabric of Exeter Cathedral, 1279–1363, Part II: 1328–53*, edited by Audrey M. Erskine (1983).

27. *The Parliamentary Survey of the Duchy of Cornwall, Part II: (Isles of Scilly-West Antony and Manors in Devon)*, edited by Norman J.G. Pounds (1984).

28. *Crown Pleas of the Devon Eyre of 1238*, edited by Henry Summerson (1985).

29. *Georgian Tiverton: the Political Memoranda of Beavis Wood, 1768–98*, edited by John Bourne (1986).

30. *The Cartulary of Launceston Priory*, edited by P.L. Hull (1987).

31. *Shipbuilding on the Exe: the Memoranda Book of Daniel Bishop Davy (1799–1874)*, edited by Clive N. Ponsford (1988).

32. *The Receivers' Accounts of the City of Exeter, 1304–53*, edited by Margery M. Rowe and John M. Draisey (1989).

33. *Early-Stuart Mariners and Shipping: the Maritime Surveys of Devon and Cornwall 1619–1635*, edited by Todd Gray (1990).

34. *Joel Gascoyne's Map of Cornwall, 1699*, with an introduction by W.L.D. Ravenhill and Oliver Padel (1991).

35. *Nicholas Roscarrock's Lives of the Saints: Cornwall and Devon*, edited by Nicholas Orme (1992).

36. *The Local Customs Accounts of the Port of Exeter, 1266–1321*, edited by Maryanne Kowaleski (1993).

37. *Charters of the Redvers Family and the Earldom of Devon, 1090–1217*, edited by Robert Bearman (1994).

38. *Devon Household Accounts, 1627–1659, Part I*, edited by Todd Gray (1995).

39. *Devon Household Accounts, 1627–1659, Part II*, edited by Todd Gray (1996).

## FORTHCOMING VOLUME

40. *The Uffculme Wills and Inventories*, edited by Peter Wyatt, with an introduction by Robin Stanes (1997).

## EXTRA SERIES

I. *Exeter Freemen, 1266–1967*, edited by Margery M. Rowe and Andrew M. Jackson (1973).

II. *Guide to the Parish and Non-Parochial Registers of Devon and Cornwall, 1538–1837*, compiled by Hugh Peskett (1979).